Real World Instrumentation with Python

T0385552

Real World Instrumentation
with Python

J. M. Hughes

O'REILLY®

Beijing · Boston · Farnham · Sebastopol · Tokyo

Real World Instrumentation with Python

by J. M. Hughes

Copyright © 2011 John M. Hughes. All rights reserved.
Printed in the United States of America.

Published by O'Reilly Media, Inc., 1005 Gravenstein Highway North, Sebastopol, CA 95472.

O'Reilly books may be purchased for educational, business, or sales promotional use. Online editions are also available for most titles (*http://safaribooksonline.com*). For more information, contact our corporate/institutional sales department: 800-998-9938 or *corporate@oreilly.com*.

Editor: Julie Steele	**Indexer:** John Bickelhaupt
Production Editor: Adam Zaremba	**Cover Designer:** Karen Montgomery
Copyeditor: Rachel Head	**Interior Designer:** David Futato
Proofreader: Sada Preisch	**Illustrator:** J. M. Hughes and Robert Romano

Printing History:

November 2010:   First Edition.

Nutshell Handbook, the Nutshell Handbook logo, and the O'Reilly logo are registered trademarks of O'Reilly Media, Inc. *Real World Instrumentation with Python*, the image of a hooded crow, and related trade dress are trademarks of O'Reilly Media, Inc.

Many of the designations used by manufacturers and sellers to distinguish their products are claimed as trademarks. Where those designations appear in this book, and O'Reilly Media, Inc., was aware of a trademark claim, the designations have been printed in caps or initial caps.

While every precaution has been taken in the preparation of this book, the publisher and author assume no responsibility for errors or omissions, or for damages resulting from the use of the information contained herein.

ISBN: 978-0-596-80956-0

[LSI]

[6/2016]

1289498386

Table of Contents

Preface

This is a book about *automated instrumentation*, and the automated control systems used with automated instrumentation. We will look at how to use the Python programming language to quickly and easily implement automated instrumentation and control systems.

Automated instrumentation can be found in a wide variety of settings, ranging from research laboratories to industrial plants. As soon as people realized that collecting data over time was a useful endeavor, they also realized that they needed some way to capture and record the data. Of course, one could sit with a clock and a pad of paper, staring at thermometers, dials, and gauges, and write down numbers or other information every few minutes or so, but that gets tedious rather quickly. It's much easier—and more reliable—if the process can be automated. Fortunately, technology has advanced significantly since the days of handwritten logbooks and clockwork-driven strip chart recorders.

Nowadays, one can purchase inexpensive instrumentation for a wide variety of physical phenomena and use a computer to capture the data. Once a computer is connected to instrumentation, the possibilities for data collection, analysis, and control begin to expand in all directions, with the only real limitations being the ability to implement the necessary software and the implementer's creativity.

The primary objective of this book is to show you how to create software that you can use to get a capable and user-friendly instrumentation or control application up and running with a minimum of hassle. To this end, we will work through the steps necessary to create applications that incorporate low-level interfaces to the real world via various types of input/output hardware. We will also examine some proven methods for creating programs that are robust and reliable. Special attention will be paid to designing the algorithms necessary to acquire and process the data. Finally, we will see how to display the results to a user and accept command inputs. It is my desire that you will find ideas here that you might take away and creatively apply to meet your own needs in a wide variety of settings.

Who Is This Book For?

This is a hands-on text intended for people who want or need to implement instrumentation systems, also known as *data acquisition and control systems*. You might be a researcher, a software developer, a student, a project lead, an engineer, or a hobbyist. The application might be an automated electronics test system, an analysis process in a laboratory, or some other type of automated instrumentation.

One of the objectives with the software in this book is that it be as platform-independent as possible. I am going to assume that you are comfortable with at least the Windows platform, and Windows XP in particular. With Linux I'll be referring to the Ubuntu distribution, but the discussion should apply to any recent Linux distribution and I will assume that you know how to use either the *csh* or *bash* command-line shells.

Since this is a book about interfacing to the real world via physical hardware, some electronics are involved, but I am not going to assume that you have an extensive background in electrical engineering. Chapter 2 contains an overview of the basics of electronics theory as it relates to instrumentation, for those who might benefit from it. It turns out that it really doesn't take a deep level of electronics knowledge to successfully interface a computer with the physical world. But, as with anything else involving technology, it never hurts to know as much as possible, just on the off chance that things don't quite work out as expected the first time.

Regardless of the type of work you do, or where you do it, the main thing I am assuming that we have in common is a need to capture some data, and perhaps to generate control signals, and to do so through some kind of computer interface. Most importantly, we need the instrumentation and control software we create to be accurate, reliable, and relatively painless to implement.

The Programming Languages

The primary programming language we will use is Python, with a bit of C thrown in. Throughout the book, I will assume that you have some programming experience and are familiar with either Python or C (ideally, both). If that is not the case, experience with Perl or Tcl/Tk or analysis tools such as MatLab or IDL is also a reasonable starting point.

This book explicitly avoids the more esoteric aspects of the Python language, and the examples are profusely documented with comments in the code, diagrams, and screen captures where appropriate. The amount of C involved is minimal; it is used only to illustrate how to create and use low-level extensions for Python applications. Chapter 3 covers the basics of Python, and Chapter 4 provides a summary of the essentials of the C language. Some suggestions for further reading are also provided for those who wish to go deeper into either (or both) of these languages.

Why Python?

Python is an interpreted language developed by Guido van Rossum in the late 1980s. Because of its interpreted nature, there is no compilation step to deal with, and the user can create and execute programs directly from Python's command line. The language itself is also easy to learn and comprehend, so long as one initially avoids the more advanced features (generators, introspection, list comprehension, and such). Thus, Python offers the dual benefits of rapid prototyping and ease of comprehension, which in turn allows for the quick creation of sophisticated tools for a diverse range of instrumentation applications, without the development burdens and learning curve normally associated with conventional compiled languages or a vendor-specific programming environment.

Python is highly portable, and it is available for almost every modern computing platform. So long as a project sticks to using commonly available interface methods, an application written initially on a PC running Windows will most likely work without change on a machine running Linux. The odds are good that the application will also run on a Sun Solaris machine or an Apple OS X system, although these systems are not specifically covered in this text. It is only when Python is used in conjunction with platform-specific extensions or drivers that it loses its portability, so in these cases I will offer alternatives for both Windows and Linux wherever feasible.

The text includes example code snippets, block diagrams and flow charts to illustrate key points, and some complete examples utilizing readily available and low-cost interface hardware.

The Systems

The types of instrumentation systems we will examine might be utilized for laboratory research, or they might be used in industrial settings. An instrumentation system might be used in an electronics lab, in a wind tunnel, or to collect meteorological data. The systems may be as simple as a temperature data logger or as complex as a thermal vacuum chamber control system.

Generally, just about anything that can be interfaced to a PC is a potential candidate for the techniques described in this book. There are, of course, some devices with closed proprietary interfaces, but I will not address those, nor will I delve into complex data collection and process control scenarios such as oil refineries, nuclear power plants, or robotic spacecraft. Systems in those domains are usually best served with sophisticated and complex custom control hardware, and equally sophisticated and complex software. I will focus instead on those instruments, devices, and systems that can be easily programmed using any of a number of common interface methods.

Methodology

Using a step-by-step approach and real-world examples, we will examine the processes necessary to define the instrumentation application, select the appropriate interfaces and hardware, and create the low-level extension modules needed (if any) to interface Python with instrumentation hardware. We will also investigate the use of TkInter, wxPython, and curses for graphical and text-based user interfaces.

The book includes sections describing what is involved in writing an extension for Python in order to encapsulate a hardware vendor's DLL; how to communicate with USB-based I/O devices; and how to use industry-standard interfaces such as RS-232, RS-485, and GPIB, along with a survey of what types of hardware one might expect to find using these interfaces. It also provides references to readily available open source tools and libraries to reduce, as much as possible, the amount of time spent implementing functionality from scratch.

How This Book Is Organized

This book is organized into 14 chapters and 2 appendixes. The first 12 chapters set the stage for the implementation examples described in Chapter 14. Chapters 1 through 6 introduce basic concepts that the advanced reader may elect to skip over. Here's a closer look at what you'll find in each chapter:

Chapter 1, *Introduction to Instrumentation*
> Chapter 1 provides an overview of what instrumentation is, how control systems work, and how these concepts are used in the real world. The examples covered include automatic outdoor lights, test instrumentation in an electronics engineering environment, control of a thermal chamber in a laboratory, and batch chemical processing.

Chapter 2, *Essential Electronics*
> Because this is a hands-on book, we will need to know something about the physical hardware we want to interface to and have at least a general idea of how it works. This chapter starts off with an introduction to the basic concepts of electricity and electronics. It then explores the functional building blocks for data acquisition and control, including discrete digital interfaces, analog interfaces, and counters and timers. Lastly, it reviews the basic concepts behind serial and parallel interfaces. If you are already familiar with electric circuit theory and devices, you could skip this chapter. However, I would recommend that you still at least skim through the material, on the off chance that there might be something unique here that you can make use of later.

Chapter 3, *The Python Programming Language*
> Although this book is not a tutorial on Python, this chapter provides an introduction to the core concepts of Python and summarizes the basics of the language. The primary emphasis is on the features of Python that will be used frequently in this

book. This chapter also provides a brief overview of the tools available to make life easier for the person doing the programming, and where to go about finding them.

Chapter 4, *The C Programming Language*

Here, the C programming language is introduced in a high-level overview. The objective is to provide enough information to enable you to understand the examples in this book, without delving into the arcane details. Fortunately, C is a relatively simple language, and the information in this chapter should be sufficient to get you started on creating your own extensions for Python.

Chapter 5, *Python Extensions*

This chapter describes how a Python extension is created, and what extensions are typically used for. Examples are provided, both in this chapter and in later chapters, for you to use as templates for your own efforts.

Chapter 6, *Hardware: Tools and Supplies*

Although is it possible that one could implement an instrumentation system and never touch a soldering iron, there is a high probability that some screwdrivers, wire cutters, and a digital multimeter (DMM) will come in handy. In this chapter I provide a list of what I would consider to be a basic toolkit for doing instrumentation work. It isn't much and could all easily fit in a small box on a shelf somewhere. However, there could very well come a time when you really need to see what's going on in your system. To this end, I've included a discussion of the two pieces of test equipment that can help you eliminate the guesswork and quickly get to the root of an interface or control problem: the oscilloscope and the logic analyzer. This chapter also covers what types of instruments are available and provides some suggestions for deciding between buying new equipment or picking up something used.

Chapter 7, *Physical Interfaces*

Chapter 7 examines the types of interfaces one is most likely to encounter when attempting to interface Python to data acquisition or control instrumentation. RS-232 and RS-485, the two most commonly encountered types of serial interfaces, are examined from an instrument interface perspective. This chapter also covers the basics of USB and GPIB/IEEE-488 interfaces, along with a discussion of where one might expect to encounter them. Finally, we turn our attention to I/O hardware designed to be plugged into the bus of a PC, typically PCI-type circuit boards, and what one can typically expect in terms of API support from the hardware vendor.

Chapter 8, *Getting Started*

This chapter contains a description of a proven approach to software development. It is included here because, when implementing an instrument system in any language, it is essential to plan and define what is to be implemented, and then to test the result against the expectations captured in a set of requirements. By extending the reach of Python into the real world, we open the door for the uncertainties and vagueness of the real world to wander back in and impact—sometimes severely—the instrumentation software.

Chapter 9, *Control System Concepts*

A book on real-world data acquisition and control would be incomplete without a discussion of control systems and the theory behind them. Chapter 9 expands on the concepts introduced in Chapter 1 with detailed examinations of common control system concepts and models, including topics such as feedback, "bang-bang" controllers, and Proportional-Integral-Derivative (PID) controls. It also provides an introduction to basic control system analysis and provides some guidelines for choosing an appropriate model. Lastly, we'll look at how the mathematics of control systems translates into actual Python code.

Chapter 10, *Building and Using Simulators*

Chapter 10 examines simulators and how they can be leveraged to speed up the development process, provide a safe environment in which to test out ideas, and provide some invaluable (and otherwise unattainable) insights into the behavior of not only the instrumentation software, but also the device or system being simulated. Whether because the instrumentation hardware just isn't available yet or because the target system is too valuable to risk damaging, a simulation can be a quick and easy way to get the software running, test it, and have a high degree of confidence that it will work correctly in the real world.

Chapter 11, *Instrumentation Data I/O*

In this chapter we'll look at how to use the interfaces that were introduced in Chapter 7 to move data between the real world and your applications. We'll start with a discussion of interface formats and protocols in order to define the basic concepts we will need for the upcoming software examples, and then we'll take a quick tour of some packages that are available for interface support in Python with the *pySerial*, *pyParallel*, and *PyVISA* packages. Lastly, I'll show you some techniques to read and write instrumentation data. We'll take a look at blocking versus nonblocking I/O, asynchronous input and output events, and how to manage potential data I/O errors to help make your applications more robust.

Chapter 12, *Reading and Writing Data Files*

Chapter 12 examines some of the implementation considerations and techniques for saving instrumentation data in a variety of file formats, from plain ASCII and CSV files to binary files and databases. We'll also examine Python's configuration data file capabilities, and see how easy it is to store and retrieve configuration parameters using Python's library methods.

Chapter 13, *User Interfaces*

Unless an application is deeply embedded or specifically designed to run as a background process, it will probably need some type of user interface. Chapter 13 examines what one can do with just the command line and the `curses` screen control package for Python, and how to use an ANSI-capable terminal emulator program to display data and accept input. The chapter wraps up with a look at the TkInter GUI toolkit provided with the standard Python distribution, and also provides an overview of the wxPython GUI package.

Chapter 14, *Real World Examples*

In Chapter 14 we look at several different types of devices used for data acquisition and control applications. This chapter starts with an example of capturing the continuous data output from a digital multimeter. We then examine a common type of data acquisition device that uses a serial interface for command and data exchanges. Lastly, we wrap up with a detailed look at a data I/O device with a USB interface and its associated API DLL provided by the vendor. The selected devices illustrate key concepts shared by almost all instrumentation components, and the examples draw on earlier chapters to show how the theory is put into practice.

Two appendixes provide additional useful information:

Appendix A, *Free and Open Source Software Resources*
Appendix B, *Instrument Sources*

Conventions Used in This Book

The following typographical conventions are used in this book:

Italic
Indicates new terms, URLs, email addresses, filenames, and file extensions

`Constant width`
Used for program listings, as well as within paragraphs to refer to Python modules and to program elements such as variable or function names, data types, statements, and keywords

`Constant width bold`
Shows commands or other text that should be typed literally by the user

`Constant width italic`
Shows text that should be replaced with user-supplied values or values determined by context

This icon signifies a tip, suggestion, or general note.

This icon indicates a warning or caution.

Using Code Examples

This book is here to help you get your job done. In general, you may use the code in this book in your programs and documentation. You do not need to contact us for permission unless you're reproducing a significant portion of the code. For example, writing a program that uses several chunks of code from this book does not require permission. Selling or distributing a CD-ROM of examples from O'Reilly books does require permission. Answering a question by citing this book and quoting example code does not require permission. Incorporating a significant amount of example code from this book into your product's documentation does require permission.

We appreciate, but do not require, attribution. An attribution usually includes the title, author, publisher, and ISBN. For example: "*Real World Instrumentation with Python* by J. M. Hughes. Copyright 2011 John M. Hughes, 978-0-596-80956-0."

If you feel your use of code examples falls outside fair use or the permission given above, feel free to contact us at *permissions@oreilly.com*.

Safari® Books Online

Safari Books Online is an on-demand digital library that lets you easily search over 7,500 technology and creative reference books and videos to find the answers you need quickly.

With a subscription, you can read any page and watch any video from our library online. Read books on your cell phone and mobile devices. Access new titles before they are available for print, and get exclusive access to manuscripts in development and post feedback for the authors. Copy and paste code samples, organize your favorites, download chapters, bookmark key sections, create notes, print out pages, and benefit from tons of other time-saving features.

O'Reilly Media has uploaded this book to the Safari Books Online service. To have full digital access to this book and others on similar topics from O'Reilly and other publishers, sign up for free at *http://safaribooksonline.com*.

How to Contact Us

Please address comments and questions concerning this book to the publisher:

O'Reilly Media, Inc.
1005 Gravenstein Highway North
Sebastopol, CA 95472
800-998-9938 (in the United States or Canada)
707-829-0515 (international or local)
707-829-0104 (fax)

We have a web page for this book, where we list errata, examples, and any additional information. You can access this page at:

http://www.oreilly.com/catalog/9780596809560/

To comment or ask technical questions about this book, send email to:

bookquestions@oreilly.com

For more information about our books, conferences, Resource Centers, and the O'Reilly Network, see our website at:

http://www.oreilly.com

Acknowledgments

I would like to acknowledge some of the people who helped make this book possible: my wife, Carol, and daughter, Seren, for their patience and understanding when I needed to disappear into my office for extended periods; my friend and co-worker Michael North-Morris for his perpetual optimism; my acquisition editor, Julie Steele, for her willingness to take a chance and extend to me the opportunity to write for O'Reilly; Rachel Head, the diligent copyeditor, for catching my abuses of the English language; and all of the helpful and friendly staff at O'Reilly.

I would also like to thank the folks at LabJack Corporation for providing me with real hardware to work with and graciously offering their time and support to help make sure I got it working correctly. Thanks also to Janet Smith of Agilent for providing me with high-quality photographs of some of their products.

—John Hughes
Tucson, Arizona, 2010

## CHAPTER 1

Introduction to Instrumentation

*However far modern science and technics have fallen
short of their inherent possibilities, they have taught
mankind at least one lesson: Nothing is impossible.*

—Lewis Mumford, *Technics and Civilization*, 1934

Instrumentation is a big word, with a broad and rich set of meanings. Like most words
with multiple interpretations, the exact meaning is largely a function of the context in
which it is used, and who is using it.

Instrumentation can be defined as the application of instruments, in the form of systems
or devices, to accomplish some specific objective in terms of measurement or control,
or both. Some examples of physical measurements employed in instrumentation systems are listed in Table 1-1.

Table 1-1. Examples of physical measurements

Acceleration	Mass
Capacitance	Position
Chemical properties	Pressure
Conductivity	Radiation
Current	Resistance
Flow rate	Temperature
Frequency	Velocity
Inductance	Viscosity
Luminosity	Voltage

As natural human language is an imprecise communications medium, contextually
sensitive and rife with multiple possible meanings, the preceding definition still covers
a lot of territory. To a process engineer, it might mean pressure sensors, heater elements,
solenoid-controlled valves, and conveyors. A research scientist might think of lasers,

optical power sensors, servo-driven X-Y microscope stages, and event counters. An electrical engineer might define instrumentation as digital voltmeters, oscilloscopes, frequency counters, spectrum analyzers, and power supplies.

Generally speaking, whatever can be measured can also be controlled, although some things are more difficult to control than others (at least with our current technology). When a measured input value is used to generate a control output for a system, often referred to as the *plant*, the input may need to be modified, or transformed, in some way in order to match the operating parameters of the system. This might entail amplification, conversion from current to voltage, time delays, filtering, or some other type of transformation.

In this book, we will examine how to utilize computer-based instrumentation using readily available low-cost devices, along with the Python programming language (primarily), to perform various tasks in data acquisition and control. Using a high-level approach, this chapter introduces some of the basic concepts we will be working with throughout the rest of the book. It also shows some simple instrumentation examples. If you are not familiar with some of the concepts introduced in this chapter, don't be overly concerned about it. We will discuss them in more detail later. The primary objective here is to lay some groundwork and introduce some basic terminology.

Data Acquisition

From a computer's viewpoint, all data is composed of digital values, and all digital values are represented by voltage or current levels in the computer's internal circuitry. In the world outside of the computer, physical actions or phenomena that cannot be represented directly as digital values must be translated into either voltage or current, and then translated into a digital form. The ability to convert real-world data into a digital form is a vast improvement over how things were done in the past.

In the days of steam and brass, one might have monitored the pressure within a boiler or a pipe by means of a mechanical gauge. In order to capture data from the gauge, someone would have to write down the readings at certain times in a logbook or on a sheet of paper. Nowadays, we would use a transducer to convert the physical phenomenon of pressure into a voltage level that would then be digitized and acquired by a computer.

As implied above, some input data will already be in digital form, such as that from switches or other on/off–type sensors—or it might be a stream of bits from some type of serial interface (such as RS-232 or USB). In other cases, it will be analog data in the form of a continuously variable signal (perhaps a voltage or a current) that is sensed and then converted into a digital format.

When referring to digital data, we mean binary values encoded in the form of *bits* that a computer can work with directly. Binary digital data is said to be discrete, and a single bit has only two possible values: 1 or 0, on or off, true or false. Digital data is typically said to have a *size*, which refers to the number of bits that make up a single unit of data. Figure 1-1 shows digital data ranging from a single bit to a 16-bit *word*. The size of the data, in bits, determines the maximum value it can represent. For example, an 8-bit byte has 256 possible unique values (if using only positive values).

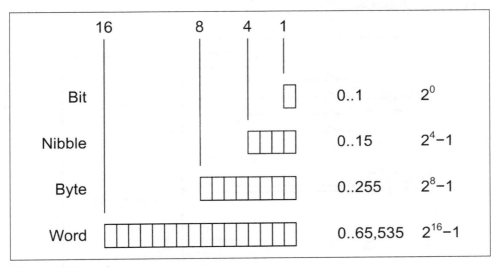

Figure 1-1. Binary data sizes

For inputs from things such as sensor switches, the size might be just a single bit. In other cases, such as when measuring analog data like pressure or temperature, the input might be converted into binary data values of 8, 10, 12, 16, or more bits in size. The number of available bits determines the range of numeric values that can be represented. Although it's not shown in Figure 1-1, binary data can represent negative values as well as positive values, and there is a standard format for handling floating-point values as well.

Analog data, on the other hand, is continuously variable and may take on any value within a range of valid values. For example, consider the set of all possible floating-point values in the range between 0 and 1. One might find numbers like 0.01, 0.834, 0.59904041123, or 0.00000048, and anything in between. The name *analog data* is derived from the fact that the data is an analog of a continuously variable physical phenomenon.

Figure 1-2 shows the various types of inputs that may be found in a computer-based data acquisition system. Switches are the equivalents of single binary digits (bits). A serial communications interface may be a single wire carrying a stream of bits end-to-end, where each set of 8 bits represents a single alphanumeric character, or perhaps a binary value. Analog input signals, in the form of a voltage or a current, are converted into digital values using a device called an analog-to-digital converter (ADC). We will take a close look at these devices—and their counterparts, digital-to-analog converters (DACs)—in Chapter 2.

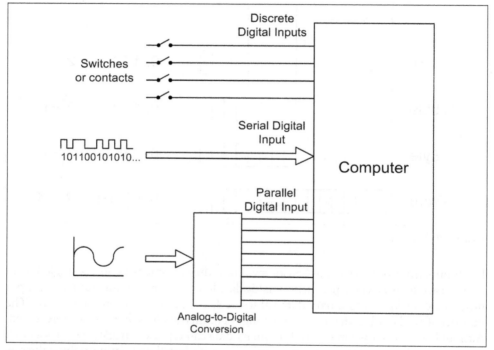

Figure 1-2. Digital and analog data inputs

Control Output

Whereas the data acquisition part of an instrumentation system senses the physical world and provides input data, the control part of an instrumentation system uses that data to effect changes in the physical world. Control of a physical device involves transforming some type of command or sensor input into a form suitable to cause a change in the activity of that device. More specifically, control entails generating digital or analog signals (or both) that may be used to perform a control action on a device or system. Linear control systems can be broadly grouped into two primary categories, *open-loop* and *closed-loop*, depending on whether or not they employ the concept of *feedback*.

Another common type of control system, the *sequential control*, utilizes time as its primary control input. In a sequential system, events occur at specific times relative to a primary event, and each event is typically discrete. In other words, a sequential event is either on or off, active or inactive. A computer is, by its very nature, a form of sequential controller, and sequential controls can usually be modeled using state machines. We'll look at state diagrams in Chapter 8.

We will encounter all three types of control systems in this book. Chapter 9 goes into the theory behind them in more detail, but for now, a high-level overview will suffice to set the stage.

Open-Loop Control

In an open-loop scheme, there is no feedback between the output and the control input of the system. In other words, the system has no way to determine if the control output actually had the desired effect. However, this doesn't prevent it from being useful. The accuracy of an open-loop control system depends on the accuracy of its components and how well the system models what it is controlling. Figure 1-3 shows a simple block diagram of an open-loop control system. The block labeled "Controlled Device" might be an electric motor, a lamp, a fan, or a valve. While it might appear that there isn't much going on here, open-loop controls can actually entail a high degree of complexity and they are fairly common.

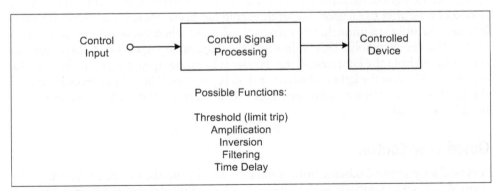

Figure 1-3. Open-loop control

Even though an open-loop control system is "blind," in a sense, it can still incorporate time into its design. An automatic light switch is one possible real-world example. A greatly simplified diagram of such a device is shown in Figure 1-4.

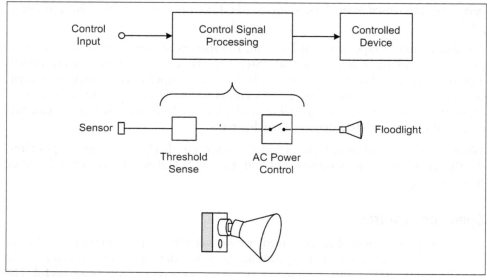

Figure 1-4. Open-loop control example

These popular devices contain a sensor (typically infrared) that will activate a floodlight if something appears in the field of view of the sensor. There is no feedback to ensure that the lights actually come on (at least, not in the typical units for residential use), nor can the sensor easily distinguish between a burglar and a large housecat.

An automatic light does, however, have a built-in time delay to hold the light on for a period of time after the sensor's input threshold has been crossed; otherwise, it would just turn on and then immediately turn back off again when the sensor input dropped back below the threshold. This is shown in the diagram in Figure 1-5. If there were no time delay to hold the lamp on, a large housecat hopping up and down in front of the sensor would cause the light to flash on and off repeatedly. This would probably annoy the neighbors (then again, automatic lights with excessive time delays can annoy the neighbors as well).

Closed-Loop Control

A closed-loop control scheme utilizes data obtained from the device or system under control, known as *feedback*, to determine the effect of the control and modify the control actions in accordance with some internal algorithm (also known as the "control laws"). Figure 1-6 shows a block diagram of a basic closed-loop control system.

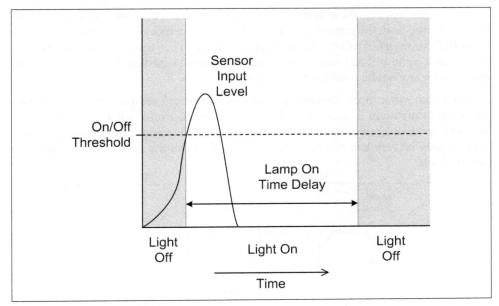

Figure 1-5. Open-loop control with time delay

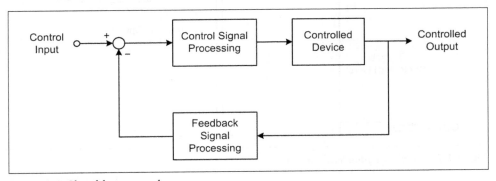

Figure 1-6. Closed-loop control

Notice that the control input and the feedback signal are summed with opposing signs at the circle symbol in Figure 1-6, which is called a "summing junction" or "summing node." The output is called the *control error*. This is because the key to a closed-loop control is the response of the controlled device to the control signal generated by the block labeled "Control Signal Processing." The control error is input to the control signal processing block, and the system will attempt to drive its control output into the controlled device to whatever extent is needed or possible in order to make the control error zero. Those readers who are familiar with operational amplifier (op amp) circuits will recognize this immediately: it's the same principle that op amp circuits are based on.

As one might suspect, there is more going on here than the system diagram in Figure 1-6 shows. Both the control and feedback processing blocks may have some degree of amplification (gain) incorporated into their design. They may also include attenuation, filters, or limit thresholds. Gain levels are selected based on the application, and responses may even be nonlinear if necessary.

Here's a somewhat more interesting closed-loop control example. Let's assume that we want to maintain a constant fluid level in a storage tank while its contents are removed at varying rates. At some times the drain rate may be quite high, while at other times it may be very low or even zero. Figure 1-7 shows the setup and its associated control loop.

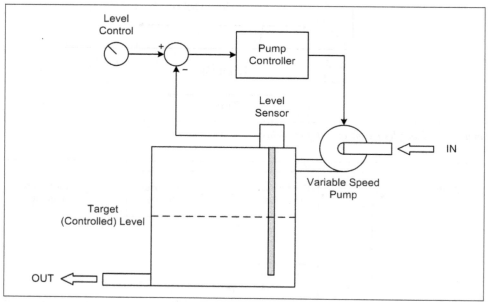

Figure 1-7. Closed-loop fluid level control

A sensor measures the fluid level in the tank, and if it is below the commanded value the rate of the input pump is commanded to increase so more fluid will enter the tank. As the fluid level approaches the target setting, the rate of the pump decreases, and once the target is reached it stops completely. This arrangement will automatically compensate for changes in how fast the fluid is drawn off from the tank, so long as the drain rate does not exceed the ability of the pump to keep up with it.

Sequential Control

Sequential controls are a very common form of control system and are straightforward to implement. Automated packaging systems, such as those used to form cereal boxes or fill plastic bags with animal feed, are typically timed sequential controls that perform specific actions using electrical or pneumatic actuators. Other sequential controls might employ some type of sensing to change sequences as necessary, or to sense a fault condition and halt the system.

Figure 1-8 shows the timing diagram for a sequential AC power controller with five devices. In this example, a delay after each device is powered on allows it to stabilize and respond to a query to verify that it is functioning correctly. In a system such as this, each device would typically have three possible states: On, Off, and Fail. In addition to commanding the devices on or off in a timed sequence, the controller would also check each device to verify that it powered up correctly. Should a device fail, the controller would either halt the sequence or begin an automatic shutdown by disabling the devices already enabled, in reverse order.

Applications Overview

Let's take a quick tour of some real-world examples of computer-based instrumentation applications. Please bear in mind that these examples are intended to show what one can do with automated instrumentation, not as specific, detailed examples of how to do something. In later chapters we will get into the specifics of interfaces, control protocols, and software algorithms.

Electronics Test Instrumentation

In an electronics laboratory, or even a well-equipped hobbyist's workshop, it wouldn't be unusual to encounter oscilloscopes, logic analyzers, frequency meters, signal generators, and other such devices. While these are useful devices in their own right, when incorporated into an automated system they can become even more useful.

In order to use a piece of test equipment in an automated setup, there must be some type of control or acquisition interface available. Many modern instruments incorporate USB, Ethernet, GPIB, RS-232, or a combination of these (these interfaces are examined in Chapters 7 and 11). In some cases, they are standard features; in other cases, the functionality must be ordered as a separate option when the instrument is purchased.

Figure 1-9 shows a simple arrangement for driving a device (the *unit under test*, or UUT) with a signal while controlling its DC power source, and acquiring measurement data in the form of logic analyzer traces and digital multimeter (DMM) readings.

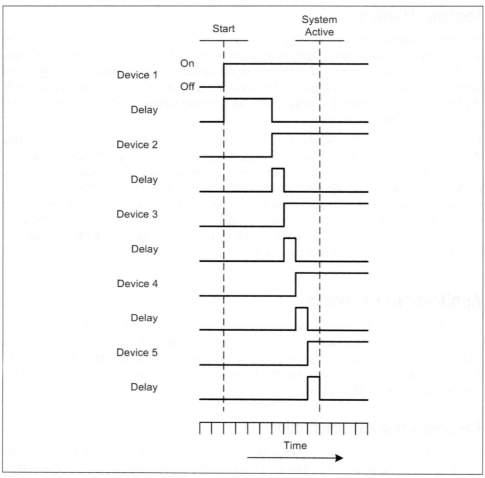

Figure 1-8. Sequential power control

The simple setup shown in Figure 1-9 has one instrument connected as a primary stimulus input to the UUT: namely, the signal generator. The signal it generates has a programmable shape (waveform) and rate (frequency). The signal level (amplitude) can also be controlled by the PC. There are two instruments connected to outputs from the UUT to capture digital logic signals (the logic analyzer) and one or more voltages (the DMM). A programmable power supply rounds out the instruments by providing a computer-controlled source of power to the UUT.

In this example, the various instruments are connected to the PC using a General Purpose Interface Bus (GPIB, also referred to as IEEE-488). There are various GPIB interface components available, ranging from plug-in PCI cards to external USB-to-GPIB adapters. Later in this book, we'll examine some of these and look at various ways to write software for them in order to control instruments and collect data.

But what does it do? What Figure 1-9 shows could well be a performance characterization setup. If the UUT generates a pattern of digital signals in response to an input from the signal generator, this test arrangement will capture that behavior. It will also capture how the UUT's behavior might change as the output from the programmable power supply is changed, or how some internal voltage might change as the frequency of the input from the signal generator changes. All of this data can be displayed on the PC's monitor and captured to disk for storage and possible analysis at a later time.

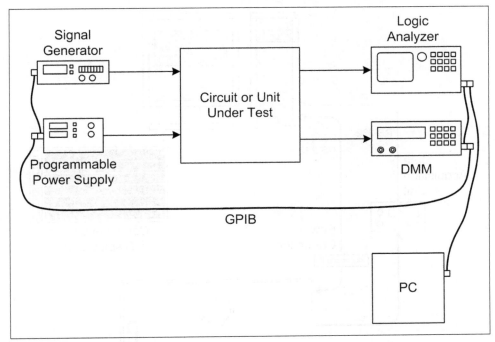

Figure 1-9. Test instrumentation example

Laboratory Instrumentation

A research laboratory might contain pH meters, temperature sensors, precision ovens, tunable lasers, and vacuum pumps (for starters). Figure 1-10 shows an example of an instrumentation system for controlling an environmental chamber.

For our purposes, it's not really important what the chamber is used for (it could be used for microbe cultures, or perhaps for epoxy curing). What is important are the instruments connected to it and how they, in turn, are interfaced to the computer. Whereas in the previous example the instrument interface was implemented using GPIB, here we have plain old vanilla serial connections in the form of RS-232 interfaces.

The data acquisition instrument is responsible for sensing and converting analog signals such as temperature, and perhaps humidity. It might also monitor the electrical status of any heaters or coolers attached to the chamber. The power controller instrument is responsible for any heaters, coolers, cryogenic valves, or other controlled functions in the chamber.

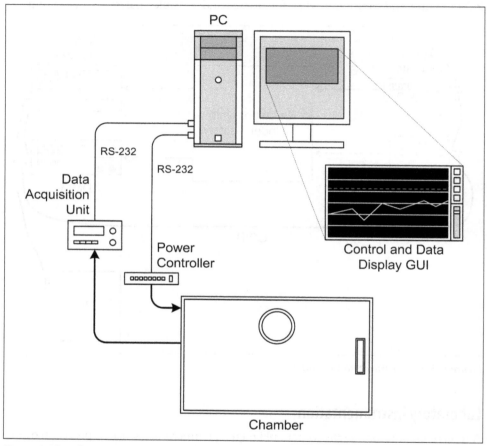

Figure 1-10. Laboratory instrumentation example

The primary objective of a setup such as this would probably be to maintain a specific temperature over time within some predefined range. It might also incorporate temperature ramp-up and ramp-down characteristics, depending on what exactly it is being used for. Generally, nothing in a system like this happens on a short time scale; significant changes may take anywhere from minutes to hours.

If implemented as a bang-bang controller, a type of on-off non-linear controller that we will look at in detail later on, there won't be any need to vary the amount of power applied to the heaters or the cooling system. It operates much like the thermostat in a house. The instrumentation can utilize the rather slow RS-232 interfaces because there is no need to run the controller with a small time constant (i.e, a fast acquisition rate).

Process Control

The diagram in Figure 1-11 is a representation of a simple automated process control system. This system might be intended for producing artificial maple syrup, or it could be some other kind of controlled chemical reaction to produce a specific output product. Note that the diagram is somewhat nonstandard, mainly because its intent is to illustrate without getting wrapped up in the details of standardized process control symbology.

In Figure 1-11, we see yet another type of interface—the USB interface module. These are common and relatively inexpensive. You can even buy one as a kit if you feel inclined to build it yourself. Many provide a set of discrete inputs and outputs, some analog inputs with 10- or 12-bit conversion, and perhaps even some analog outputs or a pulse-width modulation (PWM) channel or two.

There are four valves in the diagram shown in Figure 1-11, labeled V1 through V4, each of which is connected to one of the discrete outputs from the USB interface module. A heater is also connected to a discrete output. Note that the diagram does not show any circuitry that might be necessary to convert the 5-volt discrete signal from the USB controller into something with enough current and/or voltage to drive the valves or the heater. We'll examine how to drive external devices that utilize high currents or high voltages (or both) in Chapter 2. Three analog inputs are used to acquire liquid level, temperature, and pressure data from sensors.

As with the previous example, this probably would not be a high-speed system. It would most likely perform just fine if the sensors were read and the controls (valves and heater) updated every 1 to 5 seconds.

Summary

The domain of instrumentation applications is both broad and deep, and there is no way that a single chapter like this could possibly capture more than just a glimpse of what it is and what is possible. Some of the terms and concepts may have seemed new and strange, but they will be covered again in later chapters. The main goal here was to give you some exposure to the basic concepts. We'll fill in the details as we go along.

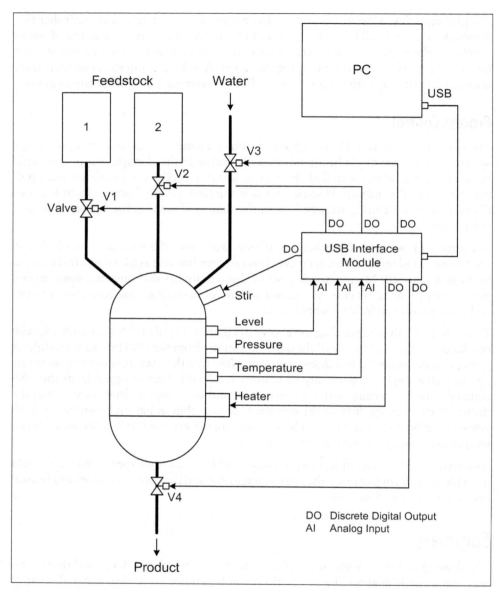

Figure 1-11. Simple chemical processing system

## CHAPTER 2

Essential Electronics

*Electricity is actually made up of extremely tiny
particles called electrons that you cannot see with the
naked eye unless you have been drinking.*

—Dave Barry, American humorist

Although this is a book primarily about instrumentation software, we must also consider what the software is interacting with in the physical world—in other words, the hardware aspects of instrumentation. This chapter is intended to provide a general high-level overview of electricity and basic electronics from an instrumentation perspective, without delving too deeply into the theory and physics behind it all.

Electronics is a deep and vast field of study. Out of a desire to avoid turning this book into a reference work on the subject, some topics are lightly glossed over here, or not even covered at all. If you're already familiar with electronics at more than just an Ohm's law level, feel free to skip over this chapter and forge ahead, but if you're not quite certain what Ohm's law is, or about the difference between a current source and a current sink, what the term "waveform" means, or how digital and analog input and output differ from one another, this chapter is for you.

We'll start off with a general description of electric charge and current, and then present some of the symbols used in schematic diagrams. Next, we'll take a look at very basic DC and AC circuits, followed by a discussion of the types of input and output found in instrumentation systems from an electrical viewpoint. In later chapters, new concepts will be introduced and explained as necessary. We'll conclude this chapter with a list of references for those who would like to learn more about electronics.

Electrical Charge

For most people, the term "electricity" typically refers to the stuff that one finds in the wires strung along poles beside the street, in a wall outlet, inside a computer, or at the terminals of a battery. But what is it, exactly?

All matter is composed of atoms. Each atom has a nucleus at its core with a net positive charge, and one or more electrons are bound to it, each of which has a negative charge (although one might hear that the electrons "orbit" the nucleus, this is not entirely accurate in the classical sense of an orbit, like, say that of the Earth around the Sun; I would refer you to a modern chemistry or physics text for a better definition than I'm prepared to deliver here). The nucleus of an atom may have one or more protons, each with a positive charge. Most atoms also have a collection of neutrons, which have mass but no charge (one might think of them as ballast for the atom's nucleus). A typical atom on a typical day in a typical chunk of matter will have a net charge of zero, because there are as many electrons, each with a unit charge of –1, as there are protons in the nucleus, each of which carries a unit charge of +1. Figure 2-1 shows schematic representations of a hydrogen atom and a copper atom.

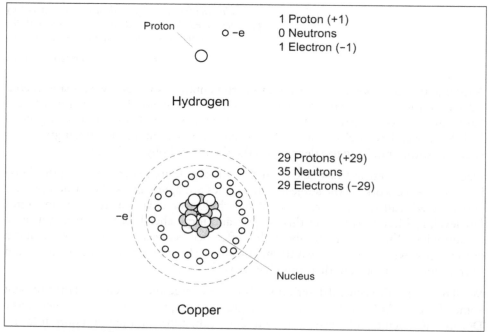

Figure 2-1. Atom organization

Some atoms have electrons that are tightly bound, whereas others can lose or gain electrons rather easily. Here's a simplistic description as to why that is.

In atoms, the electrons are arranged into what are called *orbital shells*. The outermost shell is called the *valence shell*. Elements whose atoms have only one or two electrons in the valence shell, and in which the shell is considered to be "incomplete," tend to release and gain electrons easily. Notice that the copper atom in Figure 2-1 has 29 electrons, one of which is shown outside of the main group of 28. This is copper's valence electron. Because this electron isn't very tightly bound, copper doesn't put up too much of a fuss about passing it around. In other words, copper is a good conductor. An element such as sulfur, on the other hand, does not willingly give up any electrons. Sulfur is rated as one of the least conductive elements, so it's a good insulator. Silver tops the list as the most conductive element, which explains why it's considered useful in electronics.

This should be a sufficient model for our purposes, so we won't pry any further into the inner secrets of atomic structure. What we're really interested in here is what happens when atoms do pass electrons around, and why they would do that to begin with.

Electric Current

There are two fundamental phenomena involved in electricity: electric charge and electric current. *Electric charge* is a basic characteristic of matter and is the result of something having too many electrons (negative charge) or too few electrons (positive charge), with regard to what it would otherwise need to be electrically neutral.

A basic characteristic of electric charges is that charges of the same kind repel one another, and opposite charges attract. This is why electrons and protons are bound together in an atom, although they can't directly combine with each other because of some other fundamental characteristics of atomic particles. The important thing to remember is that a negative charge will repel electrons, and a positive charge will attract them.

Electric charge, in and of itself, is interesting but not particularly useful from an electronics perspective. For our purposes, it's only when charges are moving that really interesting things begin to happen. *Electric current*, or *current flow*, is the flow of electrons through a circuit of some kind. It is also what happens when the static charge you build up walking across a carpet on a cold, dry day is transferred to a doorknob: in effect, the current flows from a high potential (you) to a lower potential (the doorknob), much like water flows down a waterfall. The otherwise uninteresting static charge suddenly becomes very interesting (at least, it gets your attention).

Current flow arises when the atoms that make up the conductors and components of electrical circuits transfer electrons from one to another. Electrons move toward things that are positive, so if one has a small lightbulb attached to a battery with some wires (sometimes known as a flashlight), the electrons move out of the negative terminal of the battery, through the lightbulb, and return back into the positive terminal. Along the way, they cause the filament in the lamp to get white-hot and glow. One way to visualize the current flow is shown in Figure 2-2, where we see a simplified diagram of some copper atoms in a wire. When an electron is introduced into one end of the wire, it causes the first atom to become negatively charged. It now has too many electrons. Assuming that we have a continuous source of electrons with a net negative charge, the new electron cannot exit the way it came in, so it moves to the next available neutral atom. This atom is now negative and has a surplus electron. In order to become neutral again (the preferred state of an atom) it passes its extra electron to the next (neutral) atom, and so on, until an electron appears at the other end of the wire.

Another way to think about current is shown in Figure 2-3. In this case, we have a tube (a conductor) filled end-to-end with marbles (electrons).

When we push a marble into one end of the tube, a marble falls out the opposite end. The net number of marbles in the tube remains the same. Note that the electrons put into one end of a conductor are not necessarily the ones that come out the other end, as one can see from Figures 2-2 and 2-3.

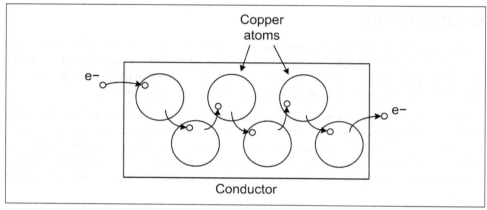

Figure 2-2. Electron movement in copper wire

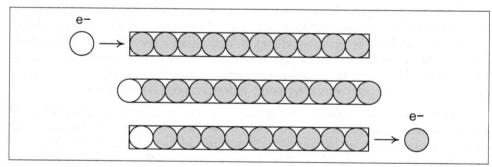

Figure 2-3. Electron movement analogy

Basic Circuit Theory

Electricity flows when there is a closed circuit that allows for the electrons to move from a high potential to a lower potential. Stated another way, in order to have current flow we need a source of electrons, and there must be a return point for the electrons. Electric current (a physical phenomenon) is characterized by four fundamental quantities: voltage, current, resistance, and power. We'll use the simple circuit shown in Figure 2-4 as our baseline for the following discussion.

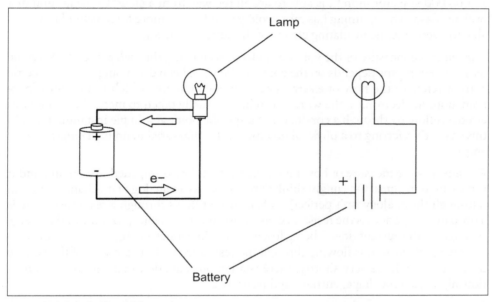

Figure 2-4. Simple electrical circuit

Current that flows in only one direction, as in Figure 2-4, is called *direct current* (DC). This is what is produced by a common battery, and by the DC power supply in a typical computer system. Current that changes direction repeatedly is called *alternating current* (AC). This is what comes out of a household wall socket (in the US, for example). It is also the type of current that drives the loudspeakers in a stereo system. The rate at which the current changes direction is called the *frequency*, and is measured in cycles per second in units of *Hertz* (abbreviated Hz). So, a 60 Hz signal is composed of a current changing direction at a rate of 60 times per second. We'll stick to DC circuits for now, and save AC for later.

By convention, current is described as flowing from positive to ground (negative), whereas in reality electrons flow from the negative terminal to the positive terminal of the power source. In Figure 2-4, the arrows show the electron flow. Although you should be aware of this, from this point onward we'll use the positive-to-negative convention for discussing current flow.

Voltage is the measure of how much electric charge, or electrical potential force, is driving electrons into a circuit. It is measured in units of *volts* (V). Electric charge is a force, in that a charge will exert a force on other charged objects. How much force is exerted depends on how much charge is present. The concepts of energy, force, and potential are described by classical mechanics, and they also apply to electric charge. The main point to remember here is that a high voltage has more force than a low voltage. This is why you don't get much more than a barely visible spark from a common flashlight battery at 1.5 volts, like the one shown in Figure 2-4, but lightning, at around 10,000,000 volts (or more!), is able to arc all the way from a cloud to the ground in a brilliant flash. The lightning has more voltage, and hence more force behind it, so it is able to overcome the insulating effects of the surrounding air.

Current is the measure of the volume of electrons moving through a circuit. What the term current means depends on the context. As we've been discussing it so far, electric current refers to the flow of electric charge in a conductor, which is a physical phenomenon. In electronics, the word "current" is usually taken to mean the quantity of electrons flowing through a conductor at a specific point at a single instant in time. In this case, it's referring to a physical quantity and is measured in units of *amperes* (A or amp).

Resistance is the measure of how much the current flow is impeded in a circuit, and it is measured in *ohms*. One might think of resistance as an analog of mechanical friction (although the analogy isn't perfect). When current flows through a resistance there is a drop in voltage across the resistance (as measured at each end), so some of the energy (voltage) in the current flow is being lost as heat. How much energy is lost is a function of how much current is flowing through the resistance and the amount of the voltage drop. As we will see very shortly, there is a famous equation that captures this relationship between voltage, current, and resistance.

Power is the measure of the amount of energy consumed in overcoming the resistance in a circuit or performing work of some sort (perhaps running a motor), and is a function of voltage and current. The common unit of measure is the *watt* (W), although one will occasionally see electric power expressed in terms of *joules* (J).

Circuit Schematics

Before moving on, we need to acquire some symbols to help describe what we're talking about. Electrical circuits are described graphically using diagrams called *schematics*. There are industry-standard symbols for every type of electrical component available, and how one graphically arranges these describes how the actual components are connected in the physical circuit. Figure 2-5 shows a small sampling of some of the more common symbols one might encounter regularly for what are called "passive" components.

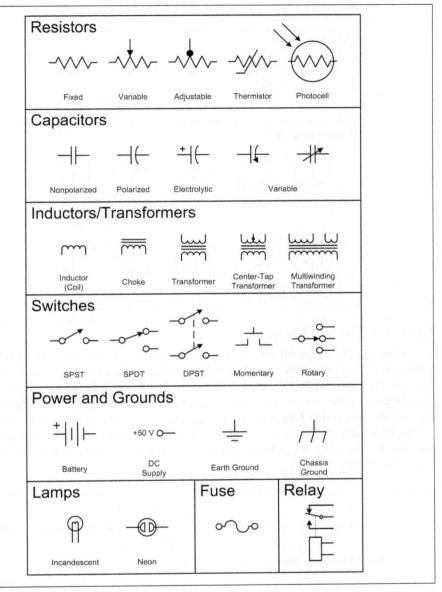

Figure 2-5. Common electronic schematic symbols

Figure 2-6 shows the symbols for diodes (rectifiers) and transistors of various types. These are referred to as *solid-state components* and are considered to be active components in that they are capable of altering the current flow in a nonlinear fashion.

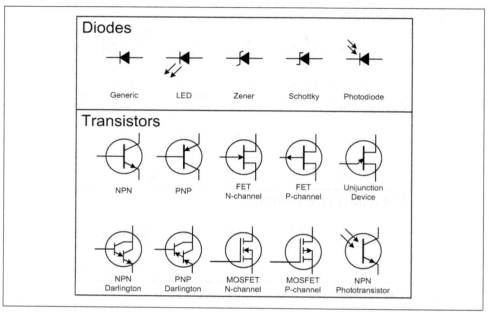

Figure 2-6. Solid-state components

The wires (or circuit board traces) in a real circuit are shown as lines in a schematic. Connections between wires are shown with a solid circle where they meet; otherwise, they simply cross. This is illustrated in Figure 2-7. Some older schematic styles use a small hump in one wire to show that it doesn't connect to the wire it is crossing, but this has become rather rare in modern diagrams. Also note that in order to avoid drawing multiple parallel lines to represent sets of associated wires, such as digital data buses, the bus is shown as a single heavy line with an indication of the number of individual wires involved.

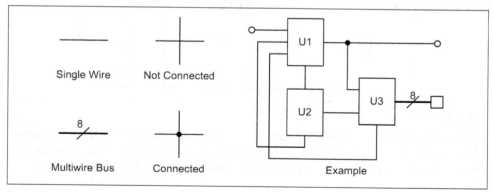

Figure 2-7. Schematic wiring notation

Digital logic has its own set of symbols, and functions within integrated circuits (ICs) such as flip-flops, timers, registers, latches, and so on, are generally shown as rectangles with input and output connections. These types of symbols are shown in Figure 2-8.

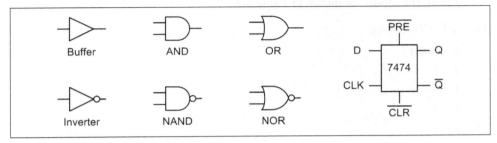

Figure 2-8. Digital logic symbols

The set of schematic symbols presented in Figures 2-5 through 2-8 is by no means complete. A full set of all currently used schematic symbols would be much more involved than what is presented here. In reality, only a small subset of those symbols are necessary for our purposes.

Also, like other specialized fields, electronics is rife with its own peculiar set of abbreviations, acronyms, and other jargon. Here is a small sampling:

DPDT
   A double-pole, double-throw switch.

DPST
   A double-pole, single-throw switch.

NPN
   A type of transistor junction. The acronym refers to the negative-positive-negative "doping" that is used to create the active junctions where modulation of current flow occurs in the device.

PNP
   The opposite of the NPN transistor. It uses positive-negative-positive junctions.

Polarity
   The positive or negative state of a terminal or device.

Polarized
   A device is said to be *polarized* when it is intended to be used such that one terminal is always more positive (or negative) than the other. Nonpolarized devices are not picky about how they are connected.

SPDT
   A switch with a single pole but two active positions. May also refer to a switch with a mechanical center-off position.

SPST
   A single-pole, single-throw switch.

The small "bubbles" used with digital logic symbols (as shown in Figure 2-8) indicate inversion. That is, if a logical True (1) encounters a bubble, it is inverted and becomes a logical False (0), and vice versa. For example, the truth table for an AND device (where A and B are the inputs) is shown in Table 2-1.

Table 2-1. AND gate logic

A	B	Output
0	0	0
0	1	0
1	0	0
1	1	1

The NAND (Not-AND) device, with a bubble on the output, produces the truth table shown in Table 2-2.

Table 2-2. NAND gate logic

A	B	Output
0	0	1
0	1	1
1	0	1
1	1	0

Don't be confused by the open circles often used to indicate terminal points in a circuit diagram. These do not indicate logical inversion. Only when the open circle is next to a digital component symbol does it mean that logical inversion is applicable.

Schematic symbols will be introduced or revisited as we go along, so there's no need to commit these to memory at this point. If you're curious, I encourage you to investigate the references found at the end of this chapter for more details on schematics and the various symbols utilized in creating them.

DC Circuit Characteristics

Now let's examine the lamp and battery circuit in Figure 2-4 more closely. It may seem simple, but there is actually quite a bit going on here.

When the lamp is connected to the battery, closing the circuit, current will flow through the lamp and then return back to the battery. If it were an open circuit, there would be no current flow and no light (switches are often used to open or close circuits). Generating current flow in a circuit requires a power source capable of producing some volume of electrons (the current) at a voltage (the electrical potential) sufficient to operate the circuit.

When electrical current flows through a circuit, there is always some amount of resistance to the flow; even wires have some resistance. A circuit with low resistance will move current more easily than a circuit with high resistance, and the high-resistance circuit will require a higher voltage to achieve the same level of current flow as the low-resistance circuit. For example, a circuit with a 10-volt supply and 50 ohms of resistance will conduct 0.2 A (also stated as 200 mA, or milliamps—thousandths of an ampere) of current. If the resistance is increased to 100 ohms and we still want to maintain 200 mA of current, the voltage will need to be increased to 20 volts. A high-resistance circuit will also dissipate more power (heat) than a low-resistance circuit at the same current. We'll have more to say about this a little later.

Ohm's Law

As you may have already surmised, there is a fundamental relationship between voltage, current, and resistance. This is called *Ohm's law*, and it looks like this:

$E = IR$

where E is voltage, I is current, and R is resistance. This simple equation is fundamental to electronics, and indeed it is the only equation that one really needs to accomplish many instrumentation implementations.

In Figure 2-4, the circuit has only two components: a battery and a lamp. The lamp composes what is called the "load" in the circuit. Incandescent lamps have a resistance that varies according to temperature, but for our purposes we'll assume that the lamp has a resistance of 2 ohms when it is glowing brightly. The battery is 1.5 volts, and we'll assume that it is capable of delivering a maximum current of 500 milliamps for one hour (this is the battery's total capacity, which is usually around 0.5 amp/hr for a typical AA type battery) at its rated output voltage.

According to Ohm's law, the amount of current the lamp will draw from the battery is given by:

$I = E/R$

or:

$I = 1.5/2$

$I = 0.75A$

Here, the value for I can also be written as 750 mA (milliamperes). If we want to know how long the battery will last, we can divide its capacity by the current in the circuit:

$0.5/0.75 = 0.67$ hours (approximately)

This might explain why those cute little single-AA-battery flashlights sometimes handed out at trade shows don't last very long before a new battery is needed.

In the simple circuit shown in Figure 2-4, the flow of electrons through the filament in the lamp causes it to heat up to the point where it glows brightly (1600 to 2800°C or so). The filament in the lamp gets hot because it has resistance, so current flows less easily through the filament than it does through the wires in the circuit. The power expended to force the current through the filament is expressed as heat. The energy converted and dissipated by a component is defined in terms of dissipated power and is expressed in watts (W). Power in a DC circuit is computed by multiplying the voltage by the current, like so:

$P = EI$

If we want to know how much power the lightbulb in our circuit is consuming, we simply multiply the voltage across the bulb by the current:

$P = 1.5 * 0.75P = 1.125$ watts

Now let's look at a slightly more complicated circuit with some new symbols. Consider the simple LED circuit shown in Figure 2-9. Here we have a resistor in series with an LED (light-emitting diode). There is a 5-volt DC power supply indicated but not shown, and a ground connection (which is the current flow return back to the power supply).

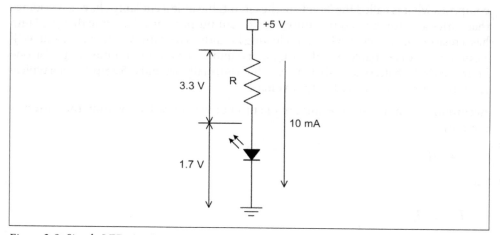

Figure 2-9. Simple LED circuit

A typical garden-variety red LED device will exhibit a drop of about 1.7 volts across its terminals. Note that this is not the same as the voltage drop across a resistor, but rather a characteristic of the solid-state "junction" that is the heart of the device. If the LED has a nominal rating of 10 milliamps (mA, or 0.01 amps) and we have a 5 V power supply, what size of resistor should we use to get 10 mA through the LED?

Since we can assume a 1.7 V drop for the LED, we can also assume a 3.3 V drop across the resistor. If we solve Ohm's law for R, we get:

$R = E/I$

$R = 3.3/0.01$

$R = 330$ ohms

So, a resistor with a value of 330 ohms will supply the 10 mA of current the LED needs to conduct and start glowing. This simple example is more important than you might think, and it will pop up again when we look into connecting LEDs to discrete digital I/O ports later.

Sinking and Sourcing

When reviewing the specifications for an interface device, one may encounter ratings for current sink and source capabilities. What this means, essentially, is that when a load is connected from the device to the positive power source, the device will be able to "sink" up to the specified amount of current before risking damage. Conversely, when the load is connected from the device to ground, it will be able to safely "source" up to the rated amount of current. Figure 2-10 shows this schematically.

The step up and step down symbols indicate how the LED will respond when the voltage from the device is high or low. When the output of the device is low with respect to the +5 V supply the LED in the current sink configuration will be active, and when it is high with respect to ground the LED will be active in the current source arrangement. The same math we used to determine the value of R for Figure 2-9 applies here as well. Note that it is important not to exceed a device's maximum sink or source ratings. For example, when a device is rated for 20 mA of current source capability, it may mean 20 mA for the whole device, not just for a single output pin.

More About Resistors

Resistors are ubiquitous in electronic circuits. A resistor can be fabricated from a piece of a poorly conductive carbon material, from a carbon film deposited on a ceramic core, or from a section of resistive wire wound inside a protective package of some type. In addition to a specific resistance value (in ohms), resistors also have a wattage rating. Typical values are 1/10, 1/8, 1/4, 1/2, 1, 2, and 5 watts, with even larger ratings available for special-purpose applications. This sets the maximum amount of power the device can safely dissipate before it risks self-destruction. Lastly, resistors are manufactured to specific *tolerances*, ranging from 20% to less than 1%, with the price rising as the tolerance tightens. The most common tolerance value is 5%.

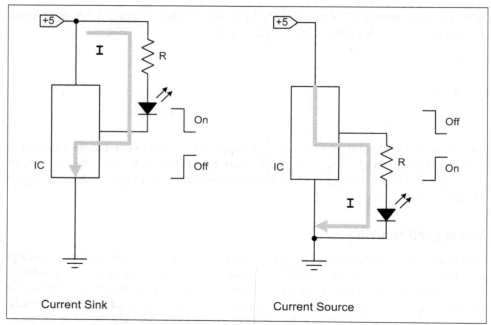

Figure 2-10. Current sink and current source

Figure 2-11 shows a generic resistor. Notice that this type of resistor uses color bands to denote its value. You can find the resistor color code in any basic electronics text, and it is explained on numerous websites, so we won't go into it here.

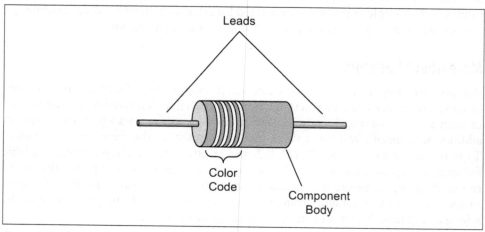

Figure 2-11. Generic carbon composition resistor

Resistors can be used to reduce a voltage level or limit the current in a circuit, among other things. Resistors are often found in instrumentation applications in circuits such as the one in Figure 2-9, in the role of current limiter. Resistors can be used singly, or they can be connected in parallel or serial configurations. Figure 2-12 shows both, and the simple math used to calculate the equivalent resistances.

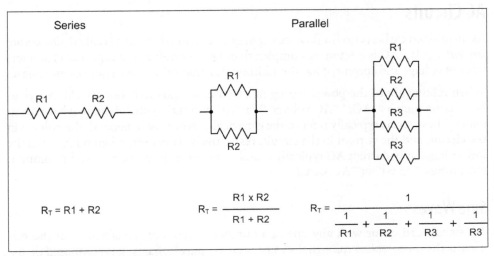

Figure 2-12. Series and parallel resistance

We now have enough pieces of the DC puzzle to start to do useful and interesting things with voltage, current, and resistance. Figure 2-13 shows a simple arrangement of two resistors called a *voltage divider*. These appear quite frequently in electronic circuits.

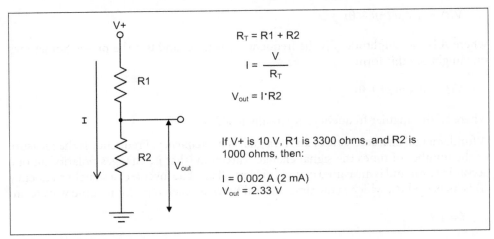

Figure 2-13. Voltage divider

The math necessary to determine the voltage across *R2* in Figure 2-13 is straightforward. Once you know the total resistance, you can find the current, and since the current through both resistors is the same it then becomes a simple matter of applying $E = IR$ to find V_{out}.

AC Circuits

As mentioned earlier, current flow that changes direction over time is called *alternating current*, or AC. AC is a bit more complex than DC. As well as the expected characteristics of voltage and current, it has the additional characteristics of frequency and phase.

When talking about the power wiring in a house, for example, one would expect to hear terms such as "AC," "AC voltage," or "AC current" (which is somewhat redundant). These terms typically refer to the electrical power type in general, the voltage in the circuit, and the current in the circuit, respectively. However, when referring to the low-voltage, low-current AC typically found in instrumentation circuits, the common term is just "signal" or "AC signal."

Sine Waves

AC signals can occur with any one of a number of types of waveforms, but the *sine wave* is the prototypical AC signal. A sine wave is "pure"; that is, it is composed of just one frequency. Other waveforms can be decomposed into a series of sine waves by means of Fourier analysis techniques (which we won't delve into here), but a pure sine wave cannot be decomposed any further.

A generic sine wave is shown in Figure 2-14. The sine wave gets its name because mathematically it is defined by the sine function:

$$V(t) = A \sin(2\pi f t + \theta)$$

where A is the amplitude, f is the frequency, t is time, and θ is the phase. Sometimes one might see this form:

$$V(t) = A \sin(\omega t + \theta)$$

where ω, the angular frequency, is actually just $2\pi f$.

A fundamental characteristic of an AC signal is its *frequency*. Frequency is the measure of the number of times the signal changes direction (that is, changes polarity) in one second of time and is measured in units of Hertz (Hz). The inverse of a signal's frequency (*f*) is its period (*t*), which is the time interval between each repetition of the waveform:

$$f = 1/t$$

$$t = 1/f$$

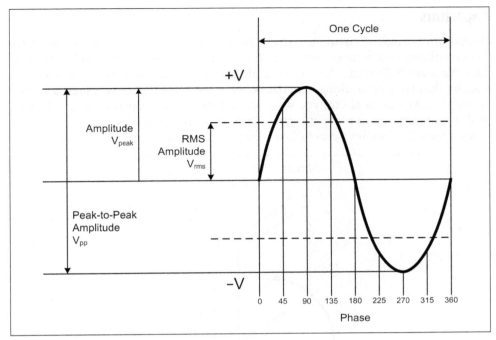

Figure 2-14. Generic sine wave

For example, if a video camera generates frames at a rate of 30 ms (milliseconds) per frame, it is operating at a frequency of 33.33 Hz. The time period of a 60 Hz signal is about 16.67 ms. A signal with a frequency of 10 KHz (kilohertz) has a time period of 100 μs (microseconds, often written as u instead of μ).

Another essential characteristic is *amplitude*. There are three ways to describe the amplitude of an AC signal: peak amplitude, peak-to-peak amplitude, and root-mean-square (RMS) amplitude. Take a look at Figure 2-14 again and notice that the peak value (the A in the sine wave equations) refers to the maximum value on either side of the zero line. When we talk about the peak-to-peak value (written as V_{pp}), we are referring to the range between the positive peak and negative peak. Lastly, the RMS amplitude is used to compute power (measured in watts, as with DC circuits) in an AC circuit. For a sine wave $V_{rms} = 0.707 * V_{peak}$, and for other waveforms it will be a different value.

Now, here's something to consider: the AC power in your house is probably something like 120 VAC (volts AC). That is its RMS value. The V_{peak} value is around 165 volts, and the V_{pp} value is about 330 volts. The V_{pp} value isn't really something to get excited about, but it might be useful to know that the actual V_{peak} value is 165 volts when selecting components for use with an AC power circuit. Just remember that the RMS value of 120 VAC is used primarily to compute power.

Capacitors

A *capacitor* is a passive component that is basically two parallel plates with a small gap between them. They come in a wide variety of materials, values, ratings, and sizes. Some capacitors are built using thin layers of aluminum as the conductive plates with an equally thin layer of insulting material between the layers; other types use a porous material soaked in an electrolytic solution as the separator between the conductors, and some incorporate a piece of ceramic material with metalized surfaces on opposite sides. Figure 2-15 shows a generalized view of a capacitor.

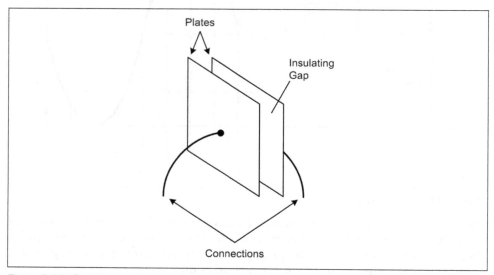

Figure 2-15. Generic capacitor

Units of capacitance are measured in *farads* (F, named after Michael Faraday). In electronics applications one will typically encounter values ranging from tens of picofarads (pF, 10^{-12} F) to upward of several hundred microfarads (µF, 10^{-6} F). Values measured in whole farads are also available for specialized applications.

Capacitors are a type of charge storage device, similar in many ways to the Leyden jar used to store electrostatic charges (the Leyden jar was invented around 1745 and named after Leyden University in the Netherlands). In a capacitor, the area of the plates and the size and type of the gap determine the capacitance of the device. The larger the plates, the more charge they can hold, and the distance between them determines how effectively the charges on the plates can interact. Capacitors can be fabricated using nothing more than metal plates separated by air: versions of this scheme with movable plates were once common in the tuning circuits of radio equipment and are still in use today. Most small capacitors found in electronic circuits use a dielectric (insulating) material that allows the plates to be very close without actually creating a directly conducting path.

When a voltage is applied to a capacitor, one of the plates will become charged in one polarity, while the other plate will take on the opposite polarity. This is illustrated in Figure 2-16.

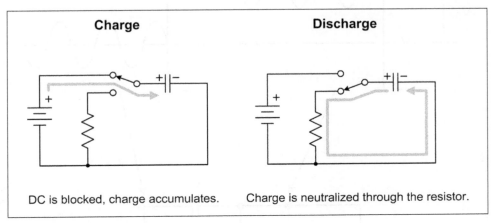

Figure 2-16. Capacitor in a DC circuit

When the switch in Figure 2-16 is set to the opposite position, the capacitor will discharge the energy it accumulated through the resistor. As one might surmise, one way to view a capacitor is as a type of short-term battery (in fact, the term "battery" was coined by Benjamin Franklin to describe an array of the Leyden jars mentioned earlier). Interestingly, there are now available capacitors with values measured in terms of whole farads that are capable of holding a large amount of charge for long enough to actually take on the role of a battery in some applications.

A capacitor will block DC but will pass AC. How well a capacitor will allow the AC signal to pass is a function of the capacitance value, any associated resistances in the circuit, and the frequency of the AC signal. In Figure 2-17, we have a circuit that combines an AC voltage source with a DC voltage source (a battery, for instance).

We can see a couple of interesting things immediately in this figure. The first is that AC and DC can exist simultaneously on the same wire (this is actually quite common in electronic circuits). Secondly, the AC signal will "ride" on top of the DC voltage, with the zero-crossing level of the AC signal at the maximum V_{DC} level. This is often referred as a DC offset or a DC bias, depending on the context.

Notice in Figure 2-17 that one can measure the composite AC-DC signal across $R1$, but the capacitor C will block the DC and allow only the AC to pass, so taking a measurement across $R2$ shows only the AC signal. Actually, we've neglected to consider the interaction between the resistors and the capacitor, which will affect how the circuit will respond to different signal frequencies. In other words, this is a type of passive filter.

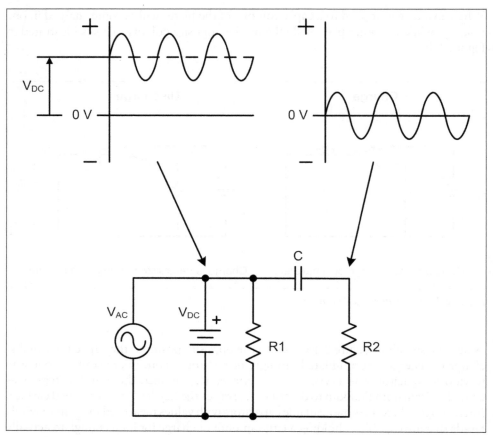

Figure 2-17. DC blocking

Like resistors, capacitors can be combined in series and in parallel, although the math involved is a little different. Figure 2-18 shows how to compute the equivalent capacitance for series or parallel arrangements of capacitors.

The ability of a capacitor to block DC can be put to use in a variety of interesting ways in instrumentation systems. Consider the situation where one might have an electromagnetic tachometer for measuring the revolutions per minute (RPM) of a rotating device. If the signal suddenly stops, how can one know if the tachometer failed, the circuitry failed, or the mechanism came to a sudden stop without actually going and looking? Figure 2-19 shows one way to do this.

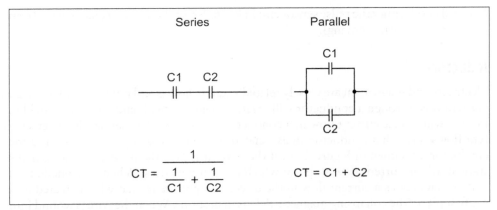

Figure 2-18. Series and parallel capacitance

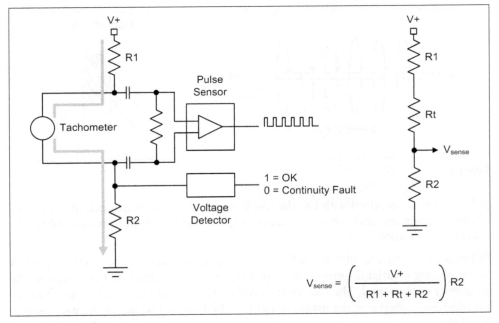

Figure 2-19. Tachometer continuity sense

In Figure 2-19 the circuit to the right is the equivalent DC circuit, where *Rt* is the DC resistance of the tachometer itself. This would probably be on the order of only a few ohms. The capacitors block the DC, and *R1*, *R2*, and *Rt* form a voltage divider. If the tachometer should fail and open the circuit, the voltage detector will indicate the fault when its input goes to zero. Conversely, if the voltage suddenly goes up, the tachometer is probably shorted. Lastly, if the signal ceases but the continuity through *R1*, *R2*, and

Rt is still good, either the pulse sensor circuit has failed or there is a mechanical problem (i.e., something isn't moving).

Inductors

Electricity and magnetism are closely related (exactly how is still not fully understood). Current flow through a conductor will create a magnetic field, and a magnetic field in motion will induce current flow in a conductor in response. Consequently, when current flows through a conductor an associated magnetic field is generated around the conductor, as shown in Figure 2-20. If the current is DC, the magnetic field remains static until the current flow stops, at which point it collapses. When a magnetic field collapses it creates a current flow in the direction opposite to that which created it in the first place (the collapsing magnetic field is in motion). When the wire is wound into a coil, the magnetic field is concentrated. The use of an iron core further increases the effect.

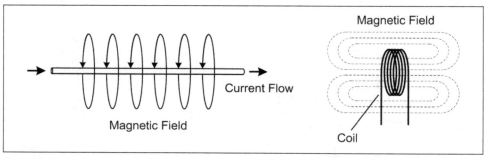

Figure 2-20. Inductor

When a coil is energized with DC the result might be an electromagnet, although AC electromagnets are also common. Electromagnets can be found in relays, solenoids, and electric motors.

When a coil is used to alter the behavior of a circuit, it can have the interesting effect of presenting a variable amount of impedance to an AC signal that depends on the frequency of the signal. The only effect a coil will have on a DC signal (other than the creation and collapse of the magnetic field) is the basic resistance of the wire used to wind the coil.

The frequency-dependent response of a coil (also called an inductor) to an AC signal is referred to as the *inductance* of the coil, and it is measured in henries (H, named after Joseph Henry). In electronic circuits, the millihenry (mH) is the unit most commonly encountered.

From the preceding description it follows that a simple length of wire is an inductor, particularly at high frequencies. This effect can degrade signals traveling over long distances, such as pulses or square waves.

In a DC circuit an inductor is basically a short (or a very, very low resistance), so it isn't all that interesting. However, in an AC circuit an inductor will impede AC (hence the term impedance) by generating a reverse current each time the signal goes from a peak amplitude (either negative or positive) back toward zero. The amount of the impedance is a function of the inductance of the coil and the frequency of the AC signal.

We won't go into the details of inductive circuits in this book, although the topic is by no means any less important than any other aspect of circuit theory. In general, we won't really need to worry too much about it, and when the need arises we will deal with it. The interested (or curious) reader should check out the references at the end of this chapter for more information.

Just as current flow creates an associated magnetic field, a moving magnetic field can generate current flow. Whenever a conductor intersects magnetic lines of force, a current flow will occur. This is shown in Figure 2-21 in the form of a simplified AC generator, also known as an alternator.

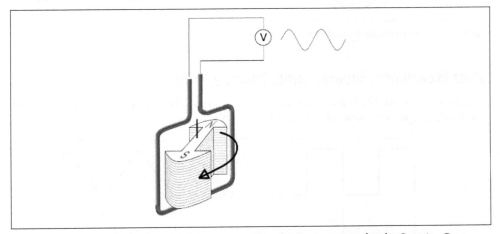

Figure 2-21. AC generator (image by Egmason, Wikipedia Commons, under the Creative Commons Attribution 3.0 Unported license: http://commons.wikimedia.org/wiki/File:Alternator_1.svg)

In Figure 2-21, an AC voltage is induced in the wire as the magnet rotates. One could also arrange the device such that the coil rotated through a stationary magnetic field. The end result would be the same. This effect has some useful applications in instrumentation, particularly when one wants to measure the rate of rotation of some mechanism. Figure 2-22 shows the basic idea behind an electromagnetic tachometer.

The output from the coil is idealized here, and in reality it may look quite a bit different. The idea, however, is the same: as the magnets pass the coil a voltage pulse or spike will be produced. Two magnets are shown here because one would usually want things to be balanced on a rotating device or shaft, especially if the mechanism spins at high revolutions per minute (RPMs). Because there are two magnets, every two output pulses represent one revolution of the mechanism.

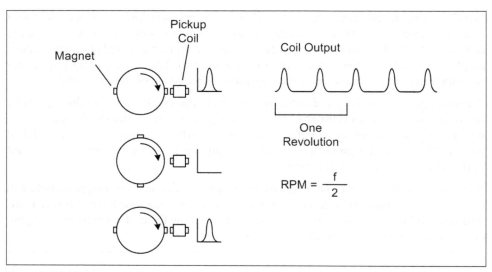

Figure 2-22. Electromagnetic tachometer

Other Waveforms: Square, Ramp, Triangle, Pulse

Besides sine waves, there are other waveforms commonly found in electronic circuits. The basic shapes are shown in Figure 2-23.

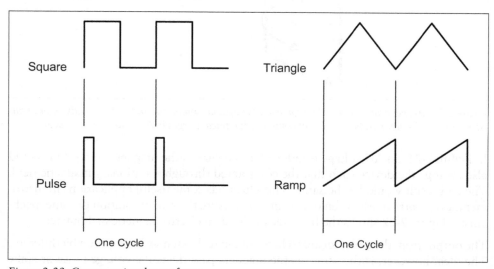

Figure 2-23. Common signal waveforms

There are, of course, very complex waveforms, such as those found in audio signals. The complexity arises because an audio signal can contain many components with different frequencies. We'll focus on the types of waveforms one is most likely to encounter in instrumentation circuits.

One of the most common (and most useful) of the nonsinusoidal waveforms is the square wave, together with its close relative, the pulse. Although a square wave is usually drawn with a shape that implies instantaneous on and off times, in reality square waves tend to be rather messy. This is shown in Figure 2-24.

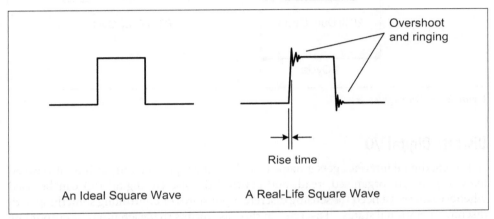

Figure 2-24. Ideal versus real square waves

The overshoot and ringing occur because of the various impedance and capacitance effects in a circuit. Because a wire has intrinsic inductance (as was stated earlier), sending a pulse or square wave over more than a few feet of unshielded wire will result in a degraded signal at the receiving end. There are ways to get around this, or at least reduce the effect, as we'll see later.

When dealing with pulses and square waves, one often refers to the *duty cycle* of the waveform. In fact, a square wave is actually a pulse with a 50% duty cycle. That is to say that it is on for one-half of a cycle. Figure 2-25 shows some pulses at various duty cycles.

Interfaces

In an instrumentation system, the interfaces are where the software meets the real world. An interface might be as simple as an input to sense the open or closed state of a switch, the voltage from a temperature sensor, or pulses from a magnetic sensor on a rotating shaft. An interface can also be a data communications channel for interfacing with a self-contained instrument or controller of some type. It could even be another computer system, as in the case of an Ethernet interface.

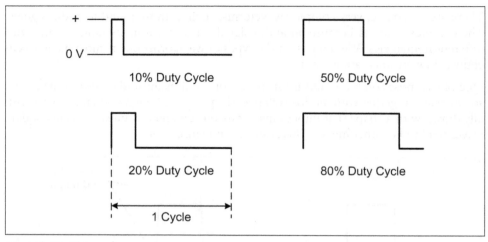

Figure 2-25. Duty cycles

Discrete Digital I/O

A discrete digital interface gets it name from how the input and output bits, also called *lines* or *pins*, are organized, read, and controlled. Discrete digital I/O can be used whenever there is a need for sensing discrete input states or controlling something with discrete operational states. "Discrete" in this case means that each input or output line has a finite number of unique discontinuous states. With a discrete digital interface, this equates to two states: on or off, 1 or 0. Discrete I/O lines may be handled in software as either singular bit values or members of a set of bits. In some cases, a particular line may be configured as either an input or an output. In other cases, an interface may provide a set of lines dedicated to output, and another set for input. As for terminology, it is common to hear "discrete I/O" or "discrete line." The digital part is understood.

Discrete I/O lines are often grouped in multiples of eight, which is the size of an 8-bit byte, but one can build interfaces with almost any number of discrete I/O lines (at least within practical limits). When a discrete interface is grouped by eight, each set of eight lines may compose what is referred to as a *port*.

There are quite a lot of indefinites in the preceding sentences, because how an interface is organized is entirely up the engineers who designed it. But from the viewpoint of a microcontroller device, the use of ports containing eight discrete lines is a natural extension of the microcontroller's internal architecture. Figure 2-26 shows how an 8-bit discrete I/O port could be implemented. Prior to the advent of low-cost microcontrollers and programmable logic devices this was a common way to implement such an interface, and it is still used today.

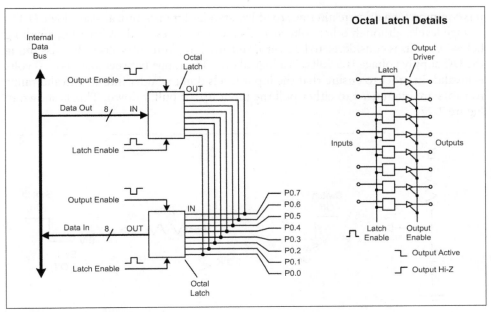

Figure 2-26. Discrete I/O port

In Figure 2-26, there are two groups of eight signals (1 byte's worth) connected to each octal output latch device (octal means eight), and another set of eight coming out of the octal input latch device. In other words, this interface will read or write 8 bits of data, or 1 byte, at a time. These are internal data buses, and they would most likely be connected to a main data bus at some point. The various signals shown going into the output and input latches are used to control when the latch should sample the input data (the latch enable signals) and when it should actually make the data available on its outputs (the output enable signals). When the outputs on either latch are not enabled they are in a high-impedance (Hi-Z) state, which is effectively an open circuit. This allows the interface to be either an input or an output, but it cannot be both at the same time. It would not make any sense to set an output line to a high level while trying to read the input from an external device, which might be low. Even if nothing overheated, it still would be a pointless thing to do. However, in the circuit shown in Figure 2-26 it would be possible to write data to the output lines and then read the data back. This is sometimes done to verify that a short to ground does not exist on any of the I/O lines.

Some interface devices, and some microcontrollers, provide the ability to assign discrete I/O pins as either inputs or outputs on an individual basis. In this case the I/O lines would be addressed in the software individually, rather than as a group of 8 bits. Assuming that the interface circuit had this capability, one could use something like the line names P0.0, P0.1, and so on, in the software to refer to specific pins (in this case, specific pins, or lines, on port 0).

It is common for a discrete interface to utilize standard transistor-transistor logic (TTL) voltage levels, although other voltage levels are sometimes used. With TTL, anything below 0.8 volts is considered to be a zero, and anything from 2.0 volts to V_{cc} (assuming the DC supply voltage is 5 volts) is a logical one. The range between 0.8 and 2.0 volts is invalid. In order to ensure that the input levels don't wander into the invalid range resistors are often used to either pull the input up, or pull it down. This is shown in Figure 2-27.

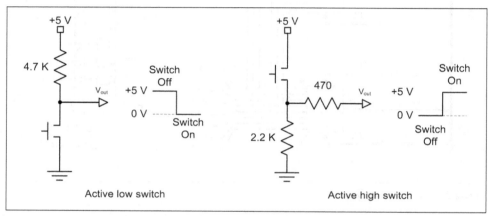

Figure 2-27. Pull-up and pull-down resistors

In Figure 2-27, the push-button switch will cause V_{out} to go to zero when the switch is closed. The 4700-ohm resistor (shown as 4.7 K) will conduct slightly more than 1 mA when the switch is closed, which is negligible in most cases. More importantly, it will provide a constant source of voltage to a digital input, thereby holding it in the logic 1 state until the switch is closed and V_{out} is pulled to ground (the switch effectively being a short). The active high switch circuit does the inverse, although here we're trying to hold V_{out} low until the switch is closed. When the switch is open, the digital input connected to V_{out} is pulled to ground through the two resistors. When the switch is closed, +5 V is applied to the input through the 470-ohm resistor and a logic 1 is sensed. The 470-ohm resistor limits the amount of current applied to the digital input to about 11 mA. While this resistor may not be absolutely necessary, it is still a good idea. Otherwise, the entire current capacity of the power supply, which may be many amperes, is present at the input of whatever the circuit is connected to. About 2 mA of current will flow through the 2200-ohm resistor when the switch is closed.

When using a mechanical switch as an input you should always keep in mind that switches have a tendency to exhibit what is called *contact bounce*, or *contact chatter*. In other words, the contact closure is seldom a clean, snap-on type of thing. Instead, the contacts inside the switch will tend to bounce off of each other for a little while after the switch is closed. This can result in a situation where a switch will generate a series of short on-off events before it finally settles down into one state or the other.

Typically this occurs over an interval ranging from just a few milliseconds to upwards of 100 ms or so, depending on the type of switch involved. To avoid reacting to contact bounce the input is "debounced," either using logic or in software.

The switches in Figure 2-27 could just as easily be limit switches on a moving part, or optical sensors detecting objects passing by on a conveyor, or even float switches in a vat or beaker. A pull-up resistor is also useful for helping to reduce signal degradation over a length of wire by making the sender actively pull the signal low, and otherwise holding it high, as shown in Figure 2-28. This helps to prevent the introduction of noise and also helps make the high to low and low to high voltage transitions more definite (i.e., the signal will have less tendency to "float" or drift between the high and low states).

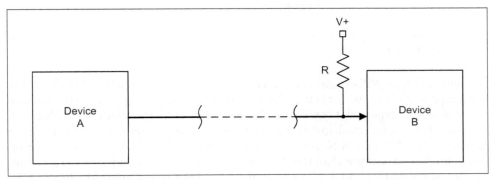

Figure 2-28. Signal pull-up

The value of R will largely depend on what type of output circuit device A happens to have. Some logic devices have what is called an *open-collector output*, which is intended to be used with an external pull-up resistor. Other devices do not have an open-collector output but can still be used with an external pull-up, provided that the value of R does not result in the device sinking more current than it is rated for.

We've already seen how a discrete digital output line can be used to directly control an LED (recall Figure 2-9), but they can also control other interesting things if the right type of interface circuit is used. Applications include relays for switching large amounts of voltage or current, solenoid valves, mechanical actuators, or electric brakes, to name but a few.

Figure 2-29 shows how one might arrange for a discrete output to drive a relay. Normally a discrete output is only capable of sourcing a small amount of current, on the order of 10 to 20 mA, and a relay might require significantly more. Connecting a relay directly to the output would result either in no operation or a damaged discrete I/O interface, or both.

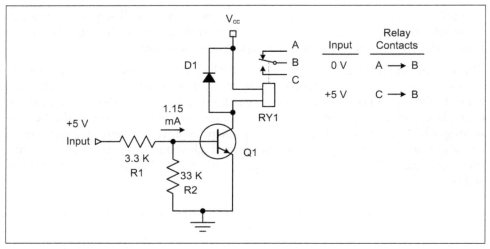

Figure 2-29. Relay driver circuit

In Figure 2-29, an NPN transistor is used as a current switch. It doesn't really matter what type of NPN transistor is used for a circuit like this, so long as it is what is called a "small signal" type and it can handle the current through the relay coil. A 2N2222A is a typical choice for small, low-power relays. When the base terminal of the transistor is positive (the "P" part of NPN), the transistor will conduct, and it is capable of handling much more current than the discrete interface alone. *R1* and *R2* form a voltage divider, supplying around 4.5 V or so at about 1.15 mA to the input (the base) of the transistor when 5 V is present on the input terminal. When there is no input voltage, *R2* acts as a pull-down to hold the transistor in an off state. *R1* is a current limiter to provide enough current to drive the transistor but not so much as to damage it. Diode *D1* is used to prevent the relay coil from sending a reverse voltage spike back into the transistor, which will almost certainly destroy it (recall from our earlier look at inductors that when current through an inductor is removed it will generate a reverse current flow as the magnetic field collapses). Now we have a circuit that can control a significant amount of current by means of the relay contacts. This same circuit could be used to drive a variety of high-current loads.

To avoid having to build such a circuit, one can purchase ready-made relay driver modules and use them with discrete outputs. This is the approach I would advocate, but it definitely doesn't hurt to have some idea of how the modules work.

Analog I/O

Analog data is converted into digital values using a device called an analog-to-digital converter (ADC). Conversely, a device called a digital-to-analog converter (DAC) is used to convert a digital value into an analog voltage or current. These functions were once quite expensive, and the necessary hardware occupied many circuit boards and a lot of cabinet space. Nowadays, many low-cost microcontrollers have ADC and DAC functions built into the chip itself. The voltage ranges and resolutions of these devices vary widely; for some applications it makes more sense to use an external high-resolution device capable of operating at high conversion rates, but even these are not excessively expensive.

Analog data is problematic for a computer. Because of the discrete digital nature of a computer, it is simply not possible to capture analog data and convert it into a digital form with a level of accuracy that will allow for a 100% faithful representation of the original signal. The same applies to converting digital data into an analog signal. This effect is called *quantization*, and it arises as a consequence of obtaining or generating a sequence of measurements of a continuously variable signal at discrete points in time.

Acquiring analog data

With analog inputs any changes in the analog signal between sample events are lost forever, and the result is only as faithful to the original as the number of samples per unit time permits. This is illustrated in Figure 2-30, which shows the difference between a signal sampled once every two seconds and the same signal sampled twice per second. Notice that the reconstructed result of the faster sampling rate is much closer to the original, but it is still not a 100% faithful reproduction.

Of course, not every application needs a high level of fidelity in order to accomplish the instrumentation objectives. In many cases it is perfectly acceptable to take data samples at intervals of several seconds, or even minutes. This is particularly true when the measured input doesn't change very much within the sample period, such as might be the case with something like an oven, an air conditioning system, or a culture incubation chamber. Other applications, such as the conversion of audio to digital form, require very high sampling rates in order to accurately capture the highest frequencies of interest and maintain a high-fidelity representation of the original input.

Analog data is typically converted to digital form with a resolution, or data size, ranging from 8 to 24 bits per sample. Resolutions of less than 8 bits or greater than 24 are not readily available, but are possible. With an 8-bit resolution, the data will range in value from 0 to 255 (or from –128 to +127 if negative values are used). Again, one does not always need a high degree of precision for every application, and sometimes less is more than sufficient.

When converting from analog to digital (or vice versa), one will encounter an inherent limitation in the conversion referred to as *quantization error*. In general terms, this is the error between the original signal and the digital values, or codes, resulting from the conversion. As shown in Figure 2-31, the lower the resolution of the ADC, the more pronounced the quantization error becomes.

According to Figure 2-31 (which is only an approximation for purposes of discussion), a 9-bit ADC with a range of 512 possible values will generate a more accurate conversion than an 8-bit ADC with a range of only 256 possible values. The sampling events (the sample rate) are shown on the time axis as T_{S0}, T_{S1}, and so on. Note that it doesn't matter if the 8-bit converter is sampled at a fast rate; it cannot do any better than its fundamental 8-bit resolution, although it will be able to detect and convert fast changes in the input that are within its resolution.

In Figure 2-30, the loss of fidelity at the slower sampling rate arose because of a lack of samples to accurately track the changes in the analog signal, not a lack of conversion resolution (the resolution isn't even mentioned, actually). In Figure 2-31, it is the lack of resolution that results in the loss of fidelity due to quantization error.

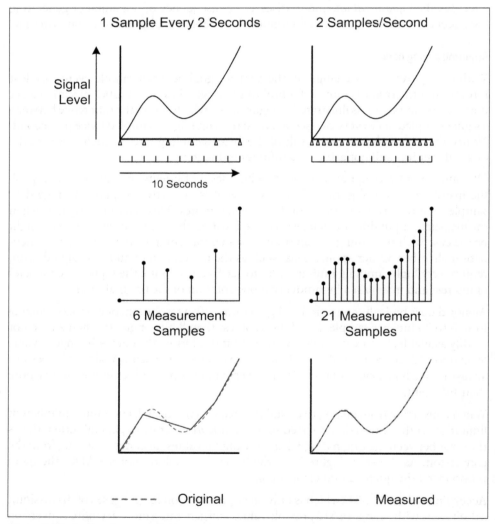

Figure 2-30. Analog data sampling

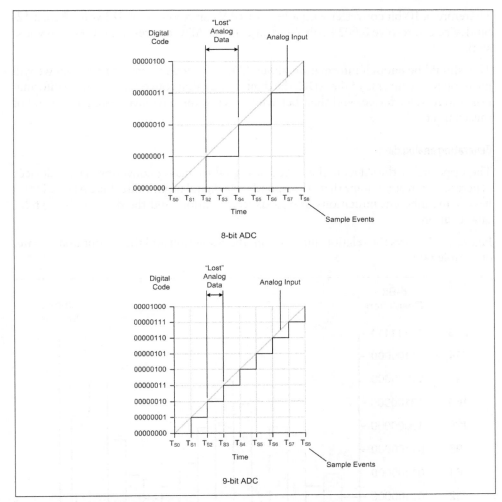

Figure 2-31. ADC quantization error

The sampling rate and the sample resolution together determine how accurately an ADC can convert an analog signal to digital form. Sample resolution can be expressed in terms of volts/step, or, in other words, the measurable voltage difference between each discrete digital value in the converter's resolution range. If we have an 8-bit converter with a maximum full-scale input range of 0 to 10 volts, each increment, or step, in the digital output code will be the equivalent of 0.039 volts. This can be expressed as:

$$Res = \frac{V_{max}}{2^n-1}$$

Therefore, a 10-bit converter with a V_{max} of 10 V can resolve 0.00978 volts/step, a 12-bit device can resolve 0.0024 volts/step, and 16-bit ADC can resolve 0.0001526 volts/step.

This should be enough information about ADCs to get us started for now, so we will move on to the inverse of the ADC, the digital-to-analog converter. For more information about ADC devices and their behavior, refer to the references listed at the end of this chapter.

Generating analog data

The opposite of the ADC is the DAC, or digital-to-analog converter. These devices generate an output voltage that corresponds to a digital input value. Like ADCs, DACs have some inherent limitations in regards to resolution, and the devices also exhibit quantization.

Figure 2-32 shows the relationship between the resolution and the output update rate, or sample rate.

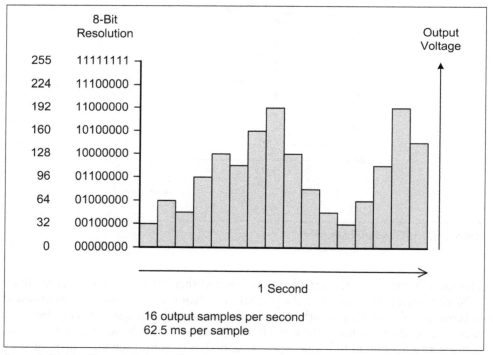

Figure 2-32. DAC output timing and resolution

For many instrumentation and control applications the output sample rate is not a critical parameter, and something on the order of once or twice a second will suffice. This is assuming, of course, that whatever the DAC is intended to control does not need to change at a faster rate.

For some DAC devices, the output voltage range is established externally using a reference voltage. In other cases, the reference voltage is built into the DAC device itself. The output resolution is determined by the number of bits used to generate the output value, and is just the output voltage range divided by the number of possible digital input values. The actual accuracy of the output is a function of the linearity of the device.

Counters and Timers

Counters and timers are essential components in many data acquisition and control implementations. Figure 2-33 shows a generic 16-bit counter with Run/Stop and Clear control inputs. When the Run/Stop input is high (true) the counter will increment an internal count value for each input pulse detected. Otherwise, it will ignore the pulse input. The Clear input allows the internal counter to be reset to zero. A counter does not need a continuous stream of input pulses; it can count random events as well. As implied in Figure 2-33, the length of time that the Run/Stop signal is in the Run state can be used to determine the rate (i.e., frequency) of the input pulses.

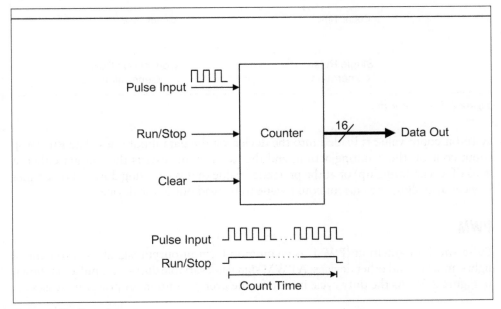

Figure 2-33. Generic counter

A timer is a device that also contains an internal counter, except that instead of counting external events it is counting either up or down until it reaches some specific value. Figure 2-34 shows a generic timer configured for single pulse output, and another version that has been configured for continuous pulse output by tying the output to the reset input.

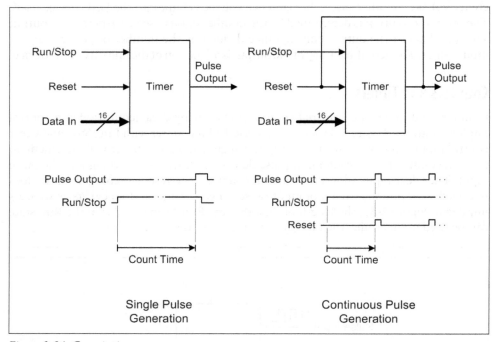

Figure 2-34. Generic timer

A 16-bit count value is loaded into the device via the data input lines. The Run/Stop input controls the counting action, and the Reset input restarts the counter either at zero (if it is counting up) or at the preloaded value (if it is counting down). Some timer devices also allow the current count value to be read out of the device.

PWM

Pulse-width modulation (PWM) is a common form of output signal used to control lights, motors, and other devices. A PWM signal is a variable duty-cycle pulse, as shown in Figure 2-35. As the duty cycle increases, the average amount of power increases.

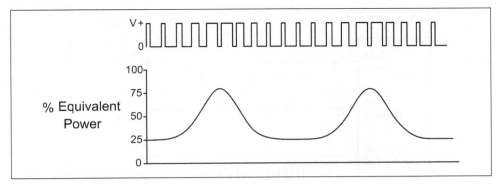

Figure 2-35. Pulse-width modulation

PWM is particularly effective for efficiently controlling DC motors. The RPM of a DC motor is proportional to the amount of power available to it. With PWM, unlike with an active linear control device such as a transistor, the average power can be modulated without wasting energy. A PWM signal can be generated directly from a digital source, with no DAC required. Figure 2-36 shows a block diagram of a PWM DC motor control.

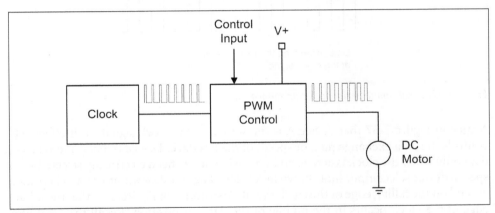

Figure 2-36. PWM DC motor control

Serial I/O

A serial interface is one wherein the data moves as a series of data bits over a single path, as shown in Figure 2-37. Serial data is typically implemented in one of two forms: synchronous or asynchronous. In a *synchronous* serial arrangement, there are one or two lines for transmitting data and a line (or two) for clock signals. The clock signals are used to inform the electronics at either end when a valid bit of data is present on the serial lines. An example of a synchronous serial interface is the low-level serial peripheral interface (SPI) feature found in some microcontroller and I/O ICs.

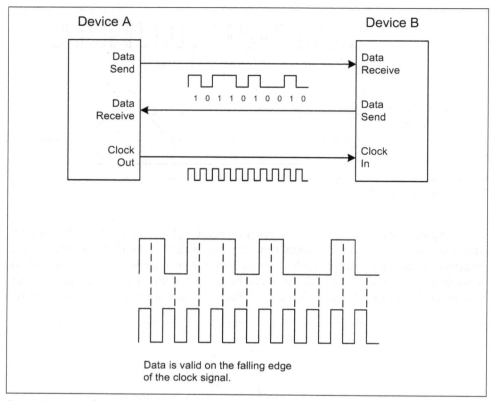

Figure 2-37. Synchronous serial data communication

Notice in Figure 2-37 that device A is the source of the clock signal, so it effectively controls the data exchange rate, or speed, of the interface. Device B sends and receives data only when the clock is active, and only when it has been electrically selected via a special device select input (not shown here). The diagram shows a situation where data is valid on the falling edge of the clock signal. Also notice in Figure 2-37 that the falling edge of the clock occurs in the middle of the data bit position. Recall the "real-life" square wave from Figure 2-24: one can see that sampling (or, "latching," as it is called) the data between the nastiness on the edges of the square waves in the data bit stream diminishes the risk of errors.

In an SPI interface, the clock is usually only active when the master device wishes to initiate communications with a peripheral device. Other types of synchronous interfaces may have the clock active all the time, and still others may utilize independent clock signals for both ends of the channel.

When connecting computing or instrumentation devices to one another, a more commonly encountered type of serial interface is the asynchronous serial interface. In this scheme there is no clock signal between the communicating devices, so the receiver electronics must synchronize on the data itself. To this end, the serial bit stream includes additional start, stop, and parity bits for each character of data. Figure 2-38 shows a greatly simplified diagram of an asynchronous communications channel using two Universal Asynchronous Receive-Transmitter (UART) devices. The RS-232 interface that was once a common feature on PCs is an asynchronous serial interface and was implemented in early versions of the PC using an Intel 8250 UART device. These types of devices can still be purchased, but it is also common to find the logical model of a more modern UART, such as the 16550, implemented within a custom gate array device as part of the chipset on a motherboard (now you know where the reference to "16550" in the serial port setup dialog box of your PC comes from, if you didn't know before—it's still there, it's just not a separate part anymore). An interesting historical tidbit is the fact that in its original form the RS-232 specification set aside signals for timing—it could also be implemented as a synchronous interface. This is still defined in the specification but is seldom used nowadays in PCs.

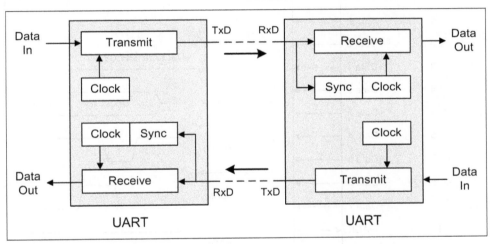

Figure 2-38. Asynchronous serial interface

A modern UART chip contains all the circuitry necessary to implement one end of an asynchronous serial interface channel. In Figure 2-38, the box labeled "Sync" is responsible for detecting the incoming data stream and adjusting the receiver section's clock to the data rate.

If an interface has signal lines for both sending and receiving data, it also has the capability for full-duplex operation. The term "full-duplex" means that an interface is capable of sending and receiving data at the same time. Interfaces that have only a single data path are typically half-duplex, meaning that the devices connected to the interface can only be a sender or a receiver at any given time, not both at the same time.

SPI and RS-232 are just two examples of serial interfaces. Some others are I²C, USB, RS-422, RS-485, MIL-STD-1553, FireWire, and Ethernet. They differ mainly in regard to how the interface operates electrically and the speed at which data can move across the channel. In Chapter 7 we will examine serial interfaces in more detail, and also explore some of the differences between full- and half-duplex operation.

Parallel I/O

Parallel I/O refers to a data communications channel where a set of discrete I/O lines is used to transfer a set of data bits in a single read or write operation. A common example of a parallel interface is the printer port on a PC, although in reality there is nothing unique about the printer port except that the pins have been preassigned to implement a printer interface. Figure 2-39 shows the pin-out and data transfer timing diagram for a PC printer port.

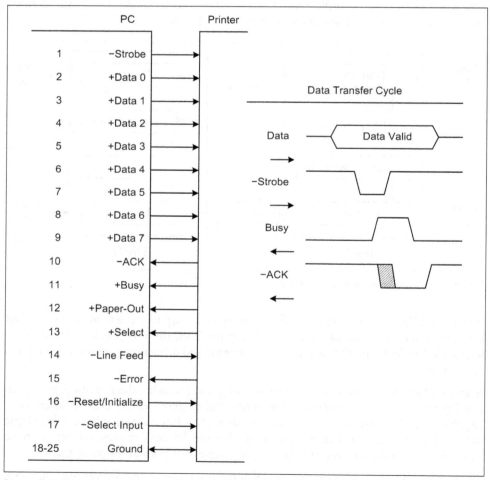

Figure 2-39. PC printer port

In Figure 2-39, the timing diagram (we'll see more of these later) shows the general relationship between the Strobe, Busy, and ACK signals. The + and – symbols indicate the active-high and active-low true states of the signals, respectively. Also notice the shaded region in the ACK waveform. This indicates that the start of the ACK signal can vary, which is OK since the sender won't attempt another transfer until ACK returns to the high state (False).

It is also possible to implement a parallel I/O channel using generic discrete I/O hardware, such as the plug-in cards available for the PC's PCI bus. This is shown in Figure 2-40.

Notice that in both cases there are signal lines set aside for "handshaking." These are the signals used to coordinate data exchanges between two devices, and are often implemented as "active-low" logic (meaning that the signal indicates True when it is low, rather than when it is high—this helps reduce false signals due to noise or other interference on the lines). In Figure 2-40, when one device has data available it will pull the DRDY (data ready) line low. The receiver will acknowledge this by pulling its ACK (acknowledge) line low and holding it low until the data transfer is complete. To initiate the transfer the sender pulls its Strobe line low, and the receiver uses this to latch the data into a buffer of some sort. When the receiver releases the ACK line, the sender is free to begin the whole process again for another set of data bits.

Parallel data interfaces have the intrinsic advantage of being able to move many bits of data at a time for every transfer cycle, and a parallel interface implemented entirely in hardware can move data at very high speeds. When implemented using software control for all of the functionality it won't run as fast as it might otherwise, but it can still be a lot faster than an RS-232 interface. Figure 2-41 shows a block diagram for a system implemented in the late 1990s that used a single board computer (an industrial-type PC on a single PCB) to communicate with a dedicated controller PC that could not use a network interface for timing and resource reasons, but could support a dedicated bidirectional parallel interface.

Summary

In this chapter we've covered the basic concepts of charge, current, voltage, and resistance, and we've looked at some examples of how these concepts are applied. We also took a brief tour of interface electronics, but realistically, we've just barely scratched the surface. Nonetheless, you should now have enough basic background knowledge to feel comfortable with the data acquisition and control devices we will encounter as we go forward.

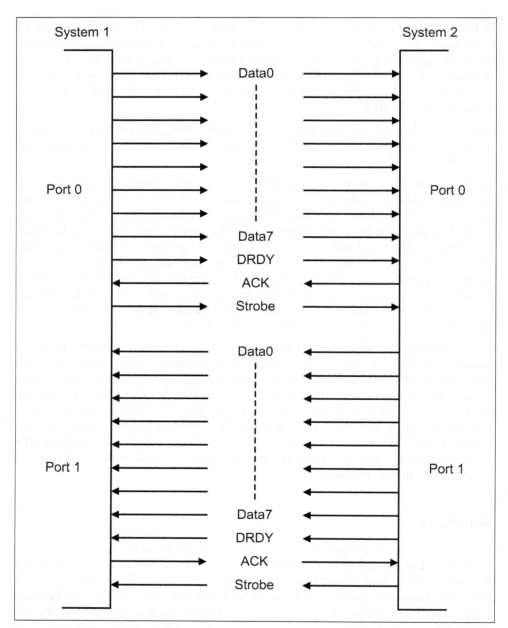

Figure 2-40. Bidirectional parallel interface

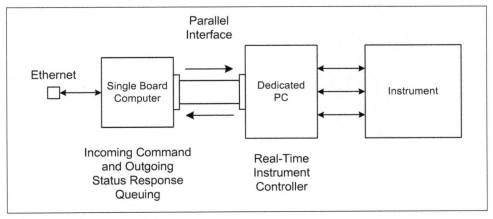

Parallel
Interface

Ethernet

Single Board
Computer

Dedicated
PC

Instrument

Incoming Command
and Outgoing
Status Response
Queuing

Real-Time
Instrument
Controller

Figure 2-41. PC-to-PC parallel interface

Suggested Reading

Electronics has become one of the cornerstones of modern civilization, and electronic devices of one type or another have now touched every corner of the globe. So it is no wonder that the field of electronics is vast and in a state of continuous change. Here are some books that I would recommend for those who would like to go deeper than what we could achieve in this chapter:

The Art of Electronics, 2nd ed. Paul Horowitz and Winfield Hill, Cambridge University Press, 1989.

This book covers everything from the basics of electronic components through the design and construction of high-speed, low-noise laboratory-grade devices. It is written in a light and easy-to-read style, with just enough math to get the point across without becoming mired in details. The book contains numerous interesting examples of electronic circuits, and a good selection of "Bad Idea" circuits to avoid.

Electronics, 2nd ed. Allan Hambley, Prentice Hall, 1999.

Suitable for use as a college text for an introductory class (or classes) in electronics theory, this book provides a formal and rigorous presentation, but the author does make a point of easing the reader into a subject, rather than dumping a pile of equations on the floor for the reader to sort out. It is a valuable resource for understanding the basics of the theory behind electronic devices and their applications.

Data Conversion Handbook. Analog Devices Inc., Newnes, 2004.

Written by the engineering staff of Analog Devices, this book represents the definitive treatment of data conversion topics by the people who have designed some of the most advanced data conversion devices currently available. It includes coverage of topics such as the history of data conversion, sampled data systems, and data converter interfaces.

## CHAPTER 3

The Python Programming Language

*I just want to go on the record as being completely
opposed to computer languages. Let them have their
own language and soon they'll be off in the corner plotting with each other!*

—Dr. Steven D. Majewski

A key requirement for automated instrumentation is the ability to describe what needs
to be done in terms that a computer, or some other type of automated control system,
can execute. While the term "programming" might immediately come to mind for some
readers, there are actually many ways to do this, some of which don't even involve a
programming language (at least, not in the conventional sense). However, in this book
we will be using Python, along with a smattering of C, to create software for automated
instrumentation.

This chapter is intended to give you a basic introduction to Python. In the next chapter
I'll introduce the C programming language, which we'll use to create extensions for
Python that will allow you to interface with a vendor's driver, or create modules for
handling computation-intensive chores. This chapter is not intended as an in-depth
tutorial or reference for Python; there are many other excellent books available that can
fill those roles (refer to the references at the end of this chapter for suggested reading).
There is also an extensive collection of documents available at the official Python website (*http://www.python.org*), ranging from beginner's tutorials to advanced topics.

Python was chosen as the primary programming language for this book for several
reasons: it's relatively easy to learn; it doesn't require a compilation step, so one can
execute programs simply by loading them (or just typing them in, if you're brave
enough); and it is powerful and full-featured. Python is also rather unique in that it
supports three different programming models—procedural, object oriented, and
functional—simultaneously. To begin, we will generally be using the procedural paradigm. Later, when we start working with graphical user interface (GUI) designs and
extensions written in C, we will encounter situations where it will be necessary to put

aside the purely procedural approach and more fully embrace objects by creating our own.

However, as we will see shortly, Python is inherently object-oriented. Even variables are actually objects, so even though Python doesn't really force the OO paradigm on the programmer, you will still be working with objects. If you're not clear on what "procedural" and "object-oriented" mean, please see the sidebar below.

Procedural and Object-Oriented Programming

The procedural paradigm is considered to be a form of imperative programming, where the primary concept is that of a set of instructions arranged in an order-specific sequence (akin to a recipe in a cookbook). Procedural programming extends the imperative model with the concept of functions (procedures) contained within a source file, or *module*. Each function performs a specific activity (an algorithm) and each can contain its own private data. Functions may also reference "global" data within the scope of the module in which they reside. Functions may call other functions, and functions may optionally return data. Modules may refer to data and functions within other modules. The idea is that programs are organized as hierarchies of modules (a technique referred to as *structured program design*). A typical nontrivial C program is an example of procedural programming. Note that here we've used "function" and "procedure" as synonyms, but in some languages they are considered to be separate entities. In both Python and C, there are just functions.

Object-oriented programming extends the procedural paradigm by employing the notion of a class of things to describe the fundamental characteristics of an object of that class (its data) and the operations that may be performed on it (an object's methods). An object is said to be instantiated using a class description or template. The class description itself is not executable; only the objects created from it may be executed. You might think of a class template as a cookie cutter and the objects based on the template as the cookies made from it. Some of the cookies might have nuts, some might have chocolate chips, and some may have frosting, but they are all members of the class of things called "cookies." You can create as many executable objects of a particular class as necessary, and each object may have some methods or data unique to it in addition to what it inherits from the parent class. An object's data is usually referred to as its *attributes* and the class functions that operate on that data are its *methods*. Objects are often described in terms of "has-a" and "is-a" relationships. For example, a rocking chair "is-a" member of the class of things called chairs; it "has-a" seat, a back, and two rockers (its attributes); and people can sit on it and rock (its methods).

Installing Python

The first step is to install Python. In this book we will be using version 2.6 (not 3.x). For the Windows environment, either the freely available ActiveState distribution, which can be found at *http://www.activestate.com/activepython/*, or the distribution from *python.org* is fine. Both include a nice help and reference tool tailored to Windows.

If you are running Linux, you should try to use your package manager (*synaptic*, *apt-get*, *rpm*, or whatever) to install version 2.6.

If you need to build and install Python from the source code, see this page for more information:

> *http://docs.python.org/using/unix.html#getting-and-installing-the-latest-version-of-python*

The Python Programming Language

Now that you have (hopefully) at least installed Python, we can take a quick tour through some of the main features of the language.

Python is an interpreted language. More accurately, it is a bytecode compiled interpreted language. What this means is that Python performs a single-pass conversion of program text into a compact binary pseudolanguage referred to as bytecode. This is what is actually executed by the interpreter, which is itself a form of virtual computer that uses the bytecode as its instruction set. This approach is common with modern interpreted languages, and if the virtual machine and its instruction set are well designed and optimized, program execution can approach some respectable speeds. Python is highly optimized internally and demonstrates good execution speeds. It will never be as fast as a compiled language that is converted into the raw binary machine language used by the underlying physical processor itself, but for most applications the speed difference is of little concern. This is particularly true when one considers that nowadays the typical processor (the CPU, or central processing unit) in an average PC is running at between 1 and 3 gigahertz (GHz). Way back in time when a CPU running at a speed of 30 megahertz (MHz) or so was considered fast, code efficiency and program execution speed were much bigger concerns.

If you are new to Python, or even if you aren't, the book *Python Pocket Reference (http://oreilly.com/catalog/9780596158095/)* by Mark Lutz (O'Reilly) is highly recommended. It provides a terse, cut-to-the-chase description of the primary features and capabilities of Python, and it is well organized and actually very readable. It is also small, so you can literally put it into a pocket and have it at hand when needed. Several other excellent books on Python are listed in the suggested reading list at the end of this chapter.

The Python Command Line

How you will start the Python interpreter in interactive mode depends on which operating system you are using. For Windows, the usual method is to first open a command prompt window (this is sometimes erroneously called a "DOS box," but Windows hasn't had a real DOS box for a long time). At the prompt (which may look different than what is shown here), type in the following command:

```
C:\> python
```

You should see something like this (assuming you've installed the ActiveState distribution, but the standard Python distribution is almost identical):

```
ActivePython 2.6.4.8 (ActiveState Software Inc.) based on
Python 2.6.4 (r264:75706, Nov  3 2009, 13:23:17) [MSC v.1500 32 bit
(Intel)] on win32
Type "help", "copyright", "credits" or "license" for more information.
>>>
```

The procedure is similar for a Linux (or BSD, or Solaris) system. Open a shell window (it shouldn't matter if the shell is *csh*, *ksh*, *bash*, or whatever) and enter python at the prompt. Assuming that Python has been installed correctly, you will see the startup message.

The >>> is Python's command prompt, waiting for you to give it something to do. To exit from the Python command line on a Windows machine, use Ctrl-Z, and on a Linux system use Ctrl-D. Typing "quit" will not work.

The Python command line is a great way to explore and experiment. You can get help for just about everything by using the built-in help facility. Just typing help(), with no arguments, results in the following display:

```
>>> help()

Welcome to Python 2.6!  This is the online help utility.

If this is your first time using Python, you should definitely check out
the tutorial on the Internet at http://docs.python.org/tutorial/.

Enter the name of any module, keyword, or topic to get help on writing
Python programs and using Python modules.  To quit this help utility and
return to the interpreter, just type "quit".

To get a list of available modules, keywords, or topics, type "modules",
"keywords", or "topics".  Each module also comes with a one-line summary
of what it does; to list the modules whose summaries contain a given word
such as "spam", type "modules spam".

help>
```

As the help display states, the tutorial material found on the official website is indeed a good place to get a feel for what Python looks like and how to use it. This chapter takes a somewhat different approach to the language, however, by introducing the reader to the concept of data objects first, and reserving things like operators and statements until a little later. I feel that the underlying object-oriented nature of the language is important enough to be dealt with first, because when creating even trivial programs in Python one will quickly encounter situations that will require the use of some of the capabilities embedded in each type of data object.

Over the years I have observed that when tutorial material on Python attempts to ignore or downplay the fundamental OO nature of the language, the result is often full of statements like "Oh, and by the way..." and "It is also like this, but we won't worry about that here..." Rather than trying to avoid the topic, we will just deal with it head-on. Having a good understanding of what is going on under the hood helps make it a lot easier to comprehend what is happening when things work correctly, and a whole lot easier to have some idea of what to look for when they don't. If you're new to Python, it would probably be a good idea to read through both this section and Python's online tutorial.

Command-Line Options and Environment

The manpage (manual page) for Python is very informative, but unfortunately it is hard to get at if you only have a Windows machine. On a Linux system, simply type man python at a shell prompt (actually, if Python was installed correctly, this should work on any Unix-ish-type system).

On Windows, you can ask Python for some abbreviated help at the command line by typing:

```
C:\> python -h
```

What you get back should look something like this:

```
usage: python [option] ... [-c cmd | -m mod | file | -] [arg] ...
Options and arguments (and corresponding environment variables):
-B     : don't write .py[co] files on import; also PYTHONDONTWRITEBYTECODE=x
-c cmd : program passed in as string (terminates option list)
-d     : debug output from parser; also PYTHONDEBUG=x
-E     : ignore PYTHON* environment variables (such as PYTHONPATH)
-h     : print this help message and exit (also --help)
-i     : inspect interactively after running script; forces a prompt even
         if stdin does not appear to be a terminal; also PYTHONINSPECT=x
-m mod : run library module as a script (terminates option list)
-O     : optimize generated bytecode slightly; also PYTHONOPTIMIZE=x
-OO    : remove doc-strings in addition to the -O optimizations
-Q arg : division options: -Qold (default), -Qwarn, -Qwarnall, -Qnew
-s     : don't add user site directory to sys.path; also PYTHONNOUSERSITE
-S     : don't imply 'import site' on initialization
-t     : issue warnings about inconsistent tab usage (-tt: issue errors)
-u     : unbuffered binary stdout and stderr; also PYTHONUNBUFFERED=x
         see man page for details on internal buffering relating to '-u'
-v     : verbose (trace import statements); also PYTHONVERBOSE=x
         can be supplied multiple times to increase verbosity
-V     : print the Python version number and exit (also --version)
-W arg : warning control; arg is action:message:category:module:lineno
-x     : skip first line of source, allowing use of non-Unix forms of #!cmd
-3     : warn about Python 3.x incompatibilities that 2to3 cannot trivially fix
file   : program read from script file
-      : program read from stdin (default; interactive mode if a tty)
arg ...: arguments passed to program in sys.argv[1:]

Other environment variables:
PYTHONSTARTUP: file executed on interactive startup (no default)
PYTHONPATH   : ';'-separated list of directories prefixed to the
```

```
                    default module search path.  The result is sys.path.
    PYTHONHOME    : alternate <prefix> directory (or <prefix>;<exec_prefix>).
                    The default module search path uses <prefix>\lib.
    PYTHONCASEOK : ignore case in 'import' statements (Windows).
    PYTHONIOENCODING: Encoding[:errors] used for stdin/stdout/stderr.
```

You will probably not have much need for the majority of the option switches, but occasionally they do come in handy (especially the -i, -tt, and -v switches). The environment variables, particularly PYTHONHOME, are important, and should be set initially according to the installation directions supplied with the distribution of Python that you are using.

Objects in Python

Generally speaking, everything in Python is an object, including data variables. An assignment is equivalent to creating a new object, and so is a function definition. If you're not familiar with object-oriented concepts, don't worry too much about it for now (see the sidebar "Procedural and Object-Oriented Programming" on page 60 for a nutshell overview). Hopefully it will become clear as we go along. For now, we just want to show what types of objects one can expect to find in Python; we'll look at how they are used later.

Table 3-1 lists the various object types most commonly encountered in Python. The type class name is what one would expect to be returned by the built-in type() method, or if an error involving a type mismatch occurs.

Table 3-1. Object types

Object type	Type class name	Description
Character	chr	Single-byte character, used in strings
Integer	int	Signed integer, 32 bits
Float	float	Double-precision (64-bit) number
Long integer	long	Arbitrarily large integer
Complex	complex	Contains both the real and imaginary parts
Character string	str	Ordered (array) collection of byte characters
List	list	Ordered collection of objects
Dictionary	dict	Collection of mapped key/value pairs
Tuple	tuple	Similar to a list but immutable
Function	function	A Python function object
Object instance	instance	An instance of a particular class
Object method	instancemethod	A method of an object
Class object	classobj	A class definition
File	file	A disk file object

We will touch on all of these before we're finished: we'll start with numeric data and work up to things like lists, tuples, and dictionaries.

Data Types in Python

If you've done any programming in a language like Pascal or C, you are probably familiar with the notion of a variable. It's a binary value stored in a particular memory location. Python is different, however, and this is where things start to get interesting. Python provides the usual numeric data types, such as integers, floats, and so on. It also has a complex type, which encapsulates both the real and imaginary parts of a complex number. The key thing is in how Python implements variables.

Numeric data as objects

When a variable is assigned a literal value in Python, what actually happens is that an object is created, the literal value is assigned to it (it becomes an attribute of the object), and then it is "bound" to a name. Objects usually have a special method called a *constructor* that handles the details of creating (instantiating) a new object in memory and initializing it. Conversely, an object may also have a *destructor* method to remove it from memory when the program is finished with it. In Python, the removal of an object is usually handled automatically in a process called *garbage collection*.

Here's an example of how Python creates a new data object:

```
>>> some_var = 5
```

This statement instantiates a new object of type int with a value attribute of 5, and then binds the name some_var to it (we'll see how name binding works shortly). One could also type the following and get the same result:

```
>>> some_var = int(5)
```

In this case, we are explicitly telling Python the object type we want (an integer) by calling the int class constructor and passing it the literal value to be assigned when the new object is instantiated. It is important to note that this is not a "cast" in a C or C++ sense; it is an instantiation of an int object that encapsulates the integer value 5.

This way of doing things may seem a bit odd at first, but one gets used to it fairly quickly. Also, most of the time you can safely ignore the fact that variables are actually objects, and just treat them as you might treat a variable in C or C++:

```
>>> var_one = 5
>>> var_two = 10
>>> var_one + var_two
15
```

You can also query an object to see what type it is:

```
>>> type(some_var)
<type 'int'>
```

Although I just stated that int() is not a cast, it can be used as something akin to that by letting the data objects do the type conversion themselves when a new object is created:

```
>>> float_var = 5.5
>>> int_var = int(float_var)
>>> print int_var
5
```

Notice that the fractional part of float_var vanished as a result of the conversion.

Octal and hexadecimal integer notation is also supported, and work as in C:

Octal integer
Use a leading 0, as in 0157.

Hexadecimal integer -
Use a leading 0x, as in 0x3FE.

Octal and hexadecimal values don't have their own type classes. This is because when a value written in either format is assigned to a Python variable, it is converted to its integer equivalent:

```
>>> foo_hex = 0x2A7
>>> print foo_hex
679
```

This is equivalent to writing:

```
>>> foo_hex = int("2A7",16)
>>> print foo_hex
679
```

So exactly what is a "data object"? In Python, things like variable names reside in what is called a *namespace*. There are various levels of namespaces, from the local namespace of a function or method to the global namespace of the Python interpreter's execution environment. For now, we won't worry too much about them; we'll just work with the concept of a local namespace.

Variable names do not have any value, other than the string that makes up the name. They are more like handles or labels that we can attach to things that do have values— namely, objects. Figure 3-1 shows how this works.

Typically objects have methods, or internal functions, that operate on the data encapsulated within them. Python's data objects are no exception. If we create an integer data object, we can ask Python to describe the object to us using the help() function, like this:

```
>>> int_var = 5
>>> help(5)
Help on int object:

class int(object)
 |  int(x[, base]) -> integer
```

```
|   Convert a string or number to an integer, if possible.  A floating point
|   argument will be truncated towards zero (this does not include a string
|   representation of a floating point number!)  When converting a string, use
|   the optional base.  It is an error to supply a base when converting a
|   non-string.  If base is zero, the proper base is guessed based on the
|   string content.  If the argument is outside the integer range a
|   long object will be returned instead.
|
|   Methods defined here:
|
|   __abs__(...)
|       x.__abs__() <==> abs(x)
|
|   __add__(...)
|       x.__add__(y) <==> x+y
|
|   __and__(...)
|       x.__and__(y) <==> x&y
|
|   __cmp__(...)
|       x.__cmp__(y) <==> cmp(x,y)
|
|   __coerce__(...)
|       x.__coerce__(y) <==> coerce(x, y)
|
|   __div__(...)
|       x.__div__(y) <==> x/y
|
|   __divmod__(...)
|       x.__divmod__(y) <==> divmod(x, y)
|
|   __float__(...)
|       x.__float__() <==> float(x)
|
|   __floordiv__(...)
|       x.__floordiv__(y) <==> x//y
|
|   __format__(...)
|
|   __getattribute__(...)
|       x.__getattribute__('name') <==> x.name
|
|   __getnewargs__(...)
|
-- More  --
```

There are more internal methods, and you can peruse them if you are so inclined (just press the space bar for another screenful, Return for another line, or q to return to the prompt), but the main point here is that in Python, data objects "know" how to manipulate their internal data using the built-in methods for a particular class. In other words, the Python interpreter handles the details of converting a statement like this:

```
5 + 5
```

into the bytecode equivalent of this, internally:

```
int(5).__add__(int(5))
```

and then executing it.

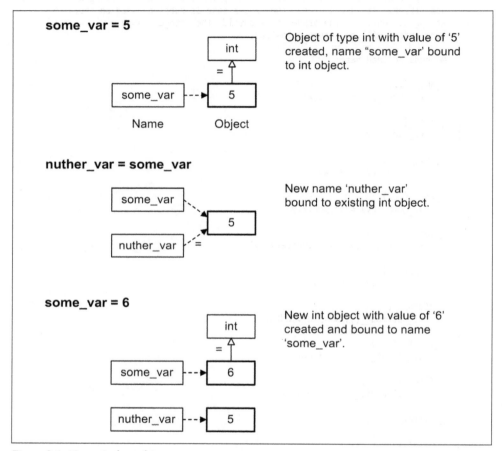

Figure 3-1. Numeric data objects

The fact that variables in Python really are objects does take a little getting used to. But it is a powerful feature of the language, and because you can selectively ignore this feature it is possible to create what look like procedural programs, when in reality Python is all about objects.

Sequence objects

Python provides three data types for ordered collections of data objects: lists (arrays), strings, and tuples (list-like objects). These are also known as *sequence objects*. The "sequence" part refers to the fact that each of these data objects may contain zero or more references to other data objects in an ordered sequence. All except for the string type allow their member elements to be any valid Python object. All have methods for manipulating their data; some methods are common to all sequence objects, and some are unique to a particular type. Table 3-2 lists the three sequence types and some of their properties.

Table 3-2. Sequence objects

Type	Mutable?	Delimiters
List	Yes	[]
String	No, immutable	' ' or " "
Tuple	No, immutable	()

Python sequence objects are either mutable (changeable) or immutable (unchangeable). A list object, for example, is mutable in that its data can be modified. A string, on the other hand, is not mutable. One cannot replace, remove, or insert characters into a string directly. A string object is an immutable collection of character values that is treated as a read-only array of byte-sized data objects.

 Actually, this applies only to 8-bit UTF-8 character encoding; other character sets (e.g., Unicode) may require something other than just single bytes for each character. In this book we'll only be working with the UTF-8 character encoding (see Chapter 12 for more on ASCII and the UTF-8 character encoding standard).

In order to make a change to a string, one must create a new string that incorporates the changes. The original string object remains untouched, even if the same variable name is reused for the new string object (which "unbinds" the original string object; unbound objects tend to evaporate through the process of garbage collection, but that's a low-level detail we don't really need to worry about).

Lists. A list is Python's closest equivalent to an array, but it has a few tricks that the arrays in C and Pascal never learned how to do. A list is an ordered sequence, and any element in the list may be replaced with something different. New elements are appended to a list using its append method (there is also a pop method, which means a list can be a queue as well), and the contents of a list can be sorted in place. Each element in a list is actually a reference to an object, just as a numeric data variable name is a reference to a numeric data object. In fact, a list can contain references to any valid Python object. Consider the following:

```
>>> import random
>>> alist = []
>>> alist.append(4)
>>> alist.append(55.89)
>>> alist.append('a short string')
>>> alist.append(random.random)
```

`alist` now contains four elements, which are composed of an integer, a floating-point value, a string, and a reference to a method from Python's `random` module called, appropriately enough, `random` (we'll discuss the `import` statement in more detail later). We can examine each member element of `alist` to verify this:

```
>>> alist[0]
4
>>> alist[1]
55.890000000000001
>>> alist[2]
'a short string'
>>> alist[3]
<built-in method random of Random object at 0x00A29D28>
```

If we want a random number, all we have to do in order to invoke `random()` is treat `alist[3]` as if it were a function by appending the expected parentheses:

```
>>> alist[3]()
0.87358651337544713
```

We can change a particular element in `alist` simply by assigning it a new value:

```
>>> alist[2]
'a short string'
>>> alist[2] = 'a better string'
>>> alist[2]
'a better string'
```

Figure 3-2 shows what is going on inside the `alist` object.

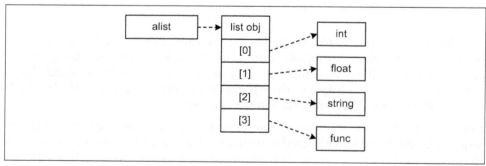

Figure 3-2. List object internal organization

We can use a list object to demonstrate Python's underlying OO nature by entering the following at the Python prompt and observing the results:

```
>>> list_name = []
>>> list_name.append(0)
>>> list_name.append(1)
>>> list_name
[0, 1]
>>> var_one = list_name
>>> var_two = list_name
```

```
>>> var_one
[0, 1]
>>> var_two
[0, 1]
>>> list_name[0] = 9
>>> var_one
[9, 1]
>>> var_two
[9, 1]
```

Because the names var_one and var_two both refer to the list object initially bound to the name list_name, when list_name is altered the change in the list object is "seen" by both of the other variable names.

Like most every other object in Python, a list has a collection of methods. These include the indexing methods we've already seen, but there are more. Lists can be concatenated and are appended end-to-end in the order specified, like so:

```
>>> alist1 = [1,2,3,4,5]
>>> alist2 = [6,7,8,9,10]
>>> alist1 + alist2
[1, 2, 3, 4, 5, 6, 7, 8, 9, 10]
```

To find the index offset of a particular item in a list, we can use the index() method:

```
>>> alist2.index(8)
2
```

We can also reverse the order of a list:

```
>>> alist1.reverse()
>>> alist1
[5, 4, 3, 2, 1]
```

And we can sort a list:

```
>>> slist = [8,22,0,5,16,99,14,-6,42,66]
>>> slist.sort()
>>> slist
[-6, 0, 5, 8, 14, 16, 22, 42, 66, 99]
```

Notice in the last two examples that the list itself is modified "in place." That is, a new object is not created as a result of reversing or sorting a list. Lists are mutable.

Strings. Strings are ordered sequences of byte-value characters. Strings are immutable, meaning that (unlike in C or C++) they cannot be altered in place by using an index and treating them like arrays. In order to modify a string, one must create a new string object. The contents of a string can, however, be referenced using an index into the string.

Here are some string examples:

```
>>> astr1 = 'This is a short string.'
>>> astr2 = "This is another short string."
>>> astr3 = "This string has 'embedded' single-quote chracters."
>>> astr4 = """This is an example
```

```
... of a multi-line
... string.
... """
...
>>>
```

Although one cannot change the contents of a string using an index value, the data can
be read using an index, and Python provides the ability to extract specific parts of a
string (or "slices," as they are called). The result is a new string object. The following
line will read the first four characters of the string variable `astr1`, starting at the zero
position and stopping before, but not at, the fourth position:

```
>>> print astr1[0:4]
This
```

We could also eliminate the 0 in the index range and just let it be assumed:

```
>>> print astr1[:4]
This
```

This form tells Python to extract everything from the start of the string up to the fourth
position. We can also extract everything from the fourth position to the end of the line:

```
>>> print astr1[4:]
 is a short string.
```

Or we can get something from the middle of the string:

```
>>> print astr1[10:15]
short
```

Figure 3-3 shows how indexing works in Python.

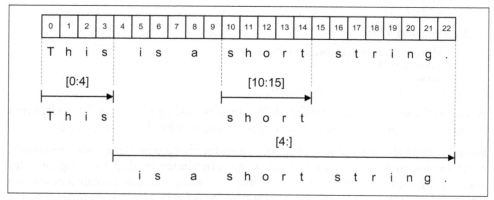

Figure 3-3. String indexing

String objects also incorporate a set of methods that perform operations such as capitalization, centering, and counting the occurrences of particular characters, among
other things, each returning a new string object.

As with lists, concatenation uses the + operator:

```
>>> str_cat = astr1 + " " + astr2
>>> print str_cat
This is a short string. This is another short string.
```

The result is, as you might expect by now, a new string object. Fortunately, Python incorporates garbage collection, and objects that are no longer bound to a name, as in the following situation, are quietly whisked away; their memory is returned to a shared pool for reuse. This is a good thing, as otherwise memory could quickly fill up with abandoned data objects:

```
>>> the_string = "This is the string."
>>> the_string = the_string[0:4]
>>> the_string
'This'
```

In this case, the name the_string is initially bound to the string object containing "This is the string.". When a section of the initial string object is pulled out, a new object is created and the name is reassigned to it. The original object, no longer bound, disappears. However, if an object is shared between two or more names, it will persist so long as one name is bound to it. This can come in handy when creating objects that need to hang around for the life of a program.

Other string methods allow you to left- or right-align a string, replace a word in a string, or convert the case of the characters in a string. Here are some examples.

The upper() method converts all alphabetic characters in a string to uppercase:

```
>>> print astr1.upper()
THIS IS A SHORT STRING.
```

find() returns the index of the first character in the search pattern string:

```
>>> print astr1.find('string')
16
```

The replace() method substitutes the new string for the search pattern:

```
>>> print astr1.replace('string', 'line')
This is a short line.
```

The rjust() method (and its counterpart, ljust()) justifies a string in a field, the width of which is the method's argument:

```
>>> print astr1.rjust(30)
        This is a short string.
```

The default fill character is a space, but one can specify an alternative as a second argument:

```
>>> print astr1.rjust(30,'.')
.......This is a short string.
```

You can get a listing of the various string methods available by typing help(str) at the Python prompt.

Tuples. The tuple is an interesting data object with many uses. Like a list object, it is an ordered set that may contain zero or more items, but unlike the list, it is immutable. Once created, a tuple cannot be directly modified. Tuples are typically referred to by the number of items they contain. For example, a 2-tuple has, as you might expect, two data objects. A shorthand way of referring to a tuple of any size is to say "*n*-tuple." Even a 0-tuple is possible in Python; it isn't particularly interesting or useful, except perhaps as a placeholder, but Python will let you create one if you really want to.

Whereas lists in Python employ square brackets as delimiters, tuples use parentheses, like this:

```
>>> tuple2 = (1,2)
>>> tuple2
(1, 2)
```

The contents of a tuple can be accessed using an index, just as with lists and strings:

```
>>> tuple4 = (9, 22.5, 0x16, 0)
>>> tuple4
(9, 22.5, 22, 0)
>>> tuple4[2]
22
>>> tuple4[0]
9
```

Like lists and strings, tuples may be concatenated (with a new tuple as the result):

```
>>> tuple2
(1, 2)
>>> tuple4
(9, 22.5, 22, 0)
>>> tuple6 = tuple2 + tuple4
>>> tuple6
(1, 2, 9, 22.5, 22, 0)
```

In this case, we can see that a new tuple object is created.

A tuple cannot be sorted, but it can be counted. To find out how many times a particular value or object occurs, we can use the count() method:

```
>>> tpl = (0, 0, 2, 2, 6, 0, 3, 2, 1, 0)
>>> tpl.count(0)
4
>>> tpl.count(2)
3
>>> tpl.count(6)
1
```

Since the contents of a tuple are actually references to objects, a tuple can contain any mix of valid Python objects, just like a list object.

Mapped objects—dictionaries

Python's dictionary is a unique data object. Instead of an ordered set of data elements, a dictionary contains data in the form of a set of unordered key/value pairs. That is, each data element has an associated key that uniquely identifies it. It is Python's one and only mapped data object.

Like any other Python data object, a dictionary can be passed as an argument to a function or method, and returned as well. It can be a data element in a tuple or list, and its values can be any valid Python object type. The types that are usable as keys are limited to integers, strings, and tuples; in other words, keys must be immutable objects.

To create a dictionary object, we can initialize it with a set of keys and associated values:

```
>>> dobj = {0:"zero", 1:"one", "food":"eat", "spam":42}
>>> dobj
{0: 'zero', 1: 'one', 'food': 'eat', 'spam': 42}
```

To get at a particular key, we can use what looks like indexing, but is not:

```
>>> dobj[0]
'zero'
>>> dobj[1]
'one'
```

If we try a key that isn't in the dictionary, Python complains:

```
>>> dobj[2]
Traceback (most recent call last):
  File "<stdin>", line 1, in <module>
KeyError: 2
```

But so long as it's a valid key, we will get a valid value back:

```
>>> dobj["spam"]
42
```

Dictionaries incorporate a set of powerful methods for manipulating their data. Table 3-3 contains a list of what's available, and we'll look at a few in detail.

Table 3-3. Dictionary methods

Method	Description
clear()	Removes all items from a dictionary.
copy()	Performs a "shallow" copy of a dictionary.
get()	Returns the data associated with a key, or a default value if no matching key is found.
has_key()	Returns True if a specified key is in a dictionary, and False otherwise.
items()	Returns a list of a dictionary's key/value pairs as 2-tuples.
iteritems()	Iterates over the key/value pairs in a dictionary.
iterkeys()	Iterates over the keys in a dictionary.
itervalues()	Iterates over the values in a dictionary.

Method	Description
keys()	Returns a list of the keys in a dictionary.
pop()	Pops off a specific item by key and removes it from the dictionary.
popitem()	Pops off a specific key/value pair and removes it from the dictionary.
setdefault()	Sets the default value to be returned should a get() fail.
update()	Updates the values with the values from another dictionary. Replaces values in matching keys.
values()	Returns a list of the values in a dictionary.

Note that there is no append() method like the one available for lists. To add a new item to a dictionary, one simply assigns a value to a new key:

```
>>> dobj[99] = "agent"
>>> dobj
{0: 'zero', 1: 'one', 99: 'agent', 'food': 'eat', 'spam': 42}
```

Notice that the new key and its associated data are inserted in the dictionary at an arbitrary location. A dictionary is not a sequence object, and data is accessed using keys, so it really is unimportant where it is actually located amongst the other key/value pairs in the data object.

This technique can also be used to modify an existing key's value:

```
>>> dobj[1] = "the big one"
>>> dobj
{0: 'zero', 1: 'the big one', 99: 'agent', 'food': 'eat', 'spam': 42}
```

A safer way to fetch a value from a dictionary is to use the get() method:

```
>>> dobj.get(99)
'agent'
```

If we attempt to get a value for a key that doesn't exist, get() will by default return the special value of None. At the Python command line, this doesn't show anything:

```
>>> dobj.get(256)
```

We can specify a default return value of our choosing, if we so desire, like this:

```
>>> dobj.get(256,"Nope")
'Nope'
```

Dictionaries are useful for keeping global data (such as parameters) in one convenient place, and the ability to return a default value allows a program to use predefined parameter values if no externally supplied values are available.

There may be times when we want to get a list of what's in a dictionary. The items() method returns all of a dictionary's key/value pairs as a list object of 2-tuples:

```
>>> dobj.items()
[(0, 'zero'), (1, 'the big one'), (99, 'agent'), ('food', 'eat'), ('spam', 42)]
```

If we want a list of the keys, we can get one using the `keys()` method:

```
>>> dobj.keys()
[0, 1, 99, 'food', 'spam']
```

Finally, if we are only interested in the values, the `values()` method comes in handy:

```
>>> dobj.values()
['zero', 'the big one', 'agent', 'eat', 42]
```

That should be enough on dictionaries for now. We will see other interesting ways to use dictionaries and the other Python data types later, but in the meantime, feel free to experiment with the Python command line. Trying out new things is one of the best ways to learn about them.

Expressions

In this book, we're going to use a mathematical-type definition of an expression. That is, an expression is a well-formed sequence of variables and mathematical or logical symbols that does not contain an equals (assignment) symbol but will evaluate to a valid logical or numerical value. A statement (which we will look at shortly) does specify an assignment or some other action, and statements may contain expressions.

Expressions make use of various operators, such as addition, subtraction, comparison, and so on. Expressions may be simple, such as:

```
a + b
```

or they may be compound expressions, as in:

```
((a + b) * c) ** z
```

Parentheses are used to indicate order of evaluation. In the previous example, the multiplication operator (*) has a higher precedence than addition (+), and exponentiation (**) has a higher precedence than multiplication, so without the parentheses the expression would be evaluated like this:

```
a + b * c**z
```

which is clearer if we put the implied parentheses back in:

```
a + (b * (c**z))
```

This is definitely not what was wanted in the original expression.

Expressions may contain things other than operators. For example, assume there is a function called `epow()` that will return the value of e raised to the power of some number or the result of some expression. An expression could contain a call to this function and use it to create a new value:

```
n + epow(x - (2 * y))
```

This would be the equivalent of writing $n + e^{(x - 2y)}$ in standard mathematical notation.

Operators

Now that we've seen the data types Python supports and what an expression is, we can look at the various things one can do with them using operators. Python provides a full set of arithmetic, logical, and comparison operators. It also includes operators for bit-wise operations, membership tests, and identity tests, and it provides various augmented assignment operators.

Arithmetic operators

Python provides the usual four basic arithmetic operators: addition, subtraction, multiplication, and division. It also has two operators that are not found in some other languages: exponent and floor division. Table 3-4 lists Python's arithmetic operators.

Table 3-4. Arithmetic operators

Operator	Description
+	Addition
–	Subtraction
*	Multiplication
/	Division
%	Modulus
**	Exponent
//	Floor division

When dealing with a mix of numeric data types, Python will automatically "promote" all of the operands to the highest-level type, and then perform the indicated operation. The type priorities are:

```
complex
float
long
int
```

This means that if an expression contains a floating-point value but no complex values, the result will be a floating-point value. If an expression contains a long and no floating-point or complex values, the result will be a long. If an expression contains a complex value, the result will be complex. So, if one has an expression that looks like this:

```
5.0 * 5
```

the result will be a floating-point value:

```
25.0
```

As I mentioned, Python also has a unique division operator called "floor division." This is used to return the quotient of a floating-point operation truncated down to the nearest whole value, with the result returned as a float. In Python, the behavior of // is like this:

```
>>> 5/2
2
>>> 5//2
2
>>> 5.0/2
2.5
>>> 5.0//2
2.0
```

Logical operators

Python's logical operators, shown in Table 3-5, act on the truth values of any object.

Table 3-5. Logical operators

Operator	Description
and	Logical AND
or	Logical OR
not	Logical NOT

Python provides the keywords `True` and `False` for use in logical expressions. Note that any of the following are also considered to be `False`:

- The `None` object
- Zero (any numeric type)
- An empty sequence object (list, tuple, or string)
- An empty dictionary

All other values are considered to be `True`. It is also common to find 1 and 0 acting as true and false values.

Comparison operators

Comparison operators evaluate two operands and determine the relationship between them in terms of equality, inequality, and magnitude (see Table 3-6).

Table 3-6. Comparison operators

Operator	Description
==	`True` if a equals b, else `False`
!=	`True` if a does not equal b, else `False`
<>	Same as ! =

Operator	Description
>	True if a is greater than b, else False
<	True if a is less than b, else False
>=	True if a is greater than or equal to b, else False
<=	True if a is less than or equal to b, else False

Python expressions that use comparison operators always return a logical true or false.

Bitwise operators

Python's AND, OR, and XOR operators map across bit-to-bit between the operands; they do not perform arithmetic operations. The bitwise operators are listed in Table 3-7.

Table 3-7. Bitwise operators

Operator	Description
&	Binary AND
|	Binary OR
^	Binary XOR
~	Binary one's complement
<<	Binary left shift
>>	Binary right shift

The AND operation will return only those bits in each operand that are true (1), whereas the OR will "merge" the bits of both operands, as shown in Figure 3-4.

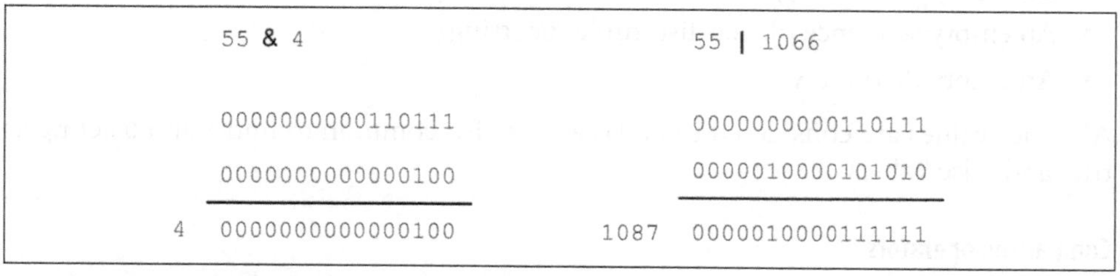

```
        55 & 4                          55 | 1066

        0000000000110111                0000000000110111
        0000000000000100                0000010000101010
      ──────────────────              ──────────────────
    4   0000000000000100          1087  0000010000111111
```

Figure 3-4. Python bitwise AND and OR operators

The bitwise operators are useful when there is a need to set a particular bit (OR) or test for a bit with a value of 1 (AND). The XOR operator returns the bitwise difference between two operands, as shown in the truth table in Figure 3-5.

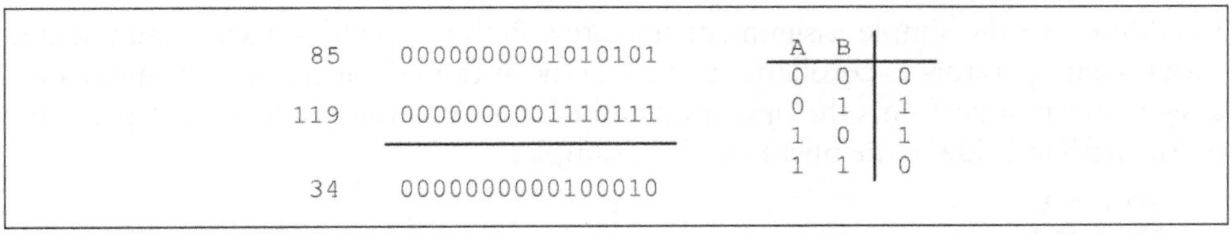

```
       85    0000000001010101        A  B
                                     ─────────
      119    0000000001110111        0  0 │ 0
             ───────────────────     0  1 │ 1
                                      1  0 │ 1
       34    0000000000100010         1  1 │ 0
```

Figure 3-5. Python bitwise XOR operator

The one's complement operator changes the value of each bit to its inverse. That is, a
binary value of **00101100** becomes **11010011**.

The binary shift operators work by shifting the contents of a data object left or right by
the number of bit positions specified by the righthand operand. The effect is the equivalent of multiplication by 2^n for a left shift or division by 2^n for a right shift (where *n* is
the number of bit positions shifted). For example:

```
>>> 2 << 1
4
>>> 2 << 2
8
>>> 2 << 3
16
>>> 16 >> 2
4
```

Assignment operators

As we've already seen, assignment in Python involves more than just stuffing some data
into a memory location. An assignment is equivalent to instantiating a new data object.
Python's assignment operators are listed in Table 3-8.

Table 3-8. Assignment operators

Operator	Description
=	Simple assignment
+=	Add *and* assignment (augmented assignment)
-=	Subtract *and* assignment (augmented assignment)
*=	Multiply *and* assignment (augmented assignment)
/=	Divide *and* assignment (augmented assignment)
%=	Modulus *and* assignment (augmented assignment)
**=	Exponent *and* assignment (augmented assignment)
//=	Floor division *and* assignment (augmented assignment)

In addition to the simple assignment operator, Python provides a set of augmented assignment operators as corollaries to each of the arithmetic operators. An augmented assignment first performs the operation and then assigns the result back to the name on the lefthand side of the operator. For example:

```
>>> a = 1
>>> a += 1
>>> a
2
```

Membership operators

The membership operators are used to determine whether a value or object exists (in), or doesn't (not in), within a sequence or dictionary object (see Table 3-9). Note that when used with a dictionary only the keys are tested, not the values.

Table 3-9. Membership operators

Operator	Description
in	Result is True if x is a member of y, else False
not in	Result is True if x is not a member of y, else False

One way to use the in operator would be like this:

```
if x in some_list:
    DoSomething(x, some_list)
```

In this case, the function doSomething() will only be called if x is in some_list. Conversely, one could test to see if something is not in an object:

```
if x not in some_dict:
    some_dict[x] = new_value
```

If the key x does not already exist in the dictionary, it will be added along with a value.

Identity operators

Python's identity operators (shown in Table 3-10) are used to determine if one name refers to the same object as another name (is), or if it does not (is not).

Table 3-10. Identity operators

Operator	Description
is	Result is True if x and y refer to the same object, else False
is not	Result is True if x and y do not refer to the same object, else False

The identity operators are handy when attempting to determine if an object is available for a particular operation. An is expression will evaluate to True if the variable names on either side of the operator refer to the same object. An is not expression will evaluate to True if the variable names on either side of the operator do not refer to the same object.

Here is a (nonexecutable) example:

```
def GetFilePath(name):
    global pathParse

    if pathParse is None:
        pathParse = FileUtil.PathParse()

    file_path = pathParse(name)
    if len(file_path) > 1:
        return file_path
    else:
        return None
```

The global name `pathParse` would be initialized (at the start of the module) to `None`, but for this function it should refer to an object of the class `pathParse` in the `FileUtil` module. If it does not (i.e., it is `None`), it is instantiated. If the function attempts to use `pathParse` with a value of `None`, it will fail.

Operator precedence

We already saw some of the precedence characteristics of operators in the earlier discussion of expressions, but now let's take a closer look. Table 3-11 lists Python's operators in order of precedence, from lowest to highest.

Table 3-11. Operator precedence

Precedence	Operator
Lowest	or
.	and
.	not x
.	in, not in, is, is not, <, <=, >, >=, <>, !=, ==
.	|
.	^
.	&
.	<<, >>
.	+, -
.	*, /, //, %
.	+x, -x, ~x
Highest	**

Parentheses are used to force the order of evaluation, as was shown earlier. If you can't remember how the evaluation order works, or the default order isn't what you want, use parentheses as necessary to get the desired result. Using parentheses for clarity is never a bad thing.

Statements

A typical program is composed of statements, comments, and whitespace (blank lines, spaces, tabs, etc.). Statements are composed of keywords and optional expressions, and specify an action. A statement might be a simple assignment:

```
>>> some_var = 5
```

Or it could be a compound set of control statements, such as an `if-else` construct:

```
>>> if some_var < 10:
...     print "Yes"
...     print "Indeed"
... else:
...     print "Sorry"
...     print "Nope"
...
Yes
Indeed
```

Python is also interesting for what it doesn't have. Those with experience in other languages may notice that there is no "switch" or "case" statement. Python's `if-elif-else` construct is usually used for this purpose. There is also nothing that looks like the structure data type in C. Dictionaries and lists can be used to emulate a structure, but it's often not necessary. Python also does not have a "do", as in `do-until` or `do-while`. It does have a `for` statement, but it doesn't work in the way that a C programmer might expect.

Indentation

When talking about program structure, one often refers to *blocks* of statements. A block can be defined as a set of one or more statements that are logically associated. Unlike C and some other languages, Python does not use special characters or reserved words to denote how statements are logically grouped into blocks. It uses indentation. For example, in C, one could write the `if-else` shown above like this:

```
if (some_var < 10) {
    printf("Yes\n");
    printf("Indeed\n");
}
else {
    printf("Sorry\n");
    printf("Nope\n");
}
```

The curly braces tell the C compiler how the statements are grouped, and C does not care how much or how little each statement is indented—in C that's considered to be "whitespace," and the compiler ignores it. In Python, however, the indentation is essential, as it tells the interpreter how the code is structured and which statements are logically associated. The amount of indentation is not critical so long as it is consistent. The recommended amount is four spaces for each level, and no tabs (tabs are generally

---

considered somewhat evil because they don't always move between different editors gracefully—one editor might interpret tabs as four spaces, whereas another might translate tabs to eight spaces).

Some people have issues with Python's use of indentation to denote blocks of code, and for those with extensive experience in C or C++ it does seem rather odd at first (although it is by no means a new idea in computer science). The advantages claimed for indentation are that it helps to enforce a consistent style across different programs by different authors and that it improves readability. Some people find that using comments such as #endif, #endfor, and #endwhile helps to make large sections of code with multiple levels of indentation easier to read, but we won't get into that discussion here.

Comments

In Python, a comment is denoted by a # character (sometimes called a *hash*), and a comment can appear anywhere on a line. The interpreter ignores everything following the hash. Use comments liberally to document your programs, but make the comments worthwhile. A comment like this:

```
a += 1    # increment by one
```

isn't very useful (although they still show up quite often), but a comment like this:

```
if (a + 1) > maxval:    # do not increment past limit
```

can help to dispel mystery.

Keywords

Python utilizes 31 distinct reserved keywords, listed in Table 3-12.

Table 3-12. Python's keywords

and	elif	if	print
as	else	import	raise
assert	except	in	return
break	exec	is	try
class	finally	lambda	while
continue	for	not	with
def	from	or	yield
del	global	pass	

We will examine some of the more commonly used keywords in the remainder of this chapter. Others will be introduced as necessary when we start developing some larger and more complex programs.

Simple statements

In Python, a simple statement (see Table 3-13) is one that consists of an assignment or keyword in a single line; there are no other components. The statement may have more than one expression, however.

Table 3-13. Simple statements

Keyword	Description
assert	assert *<expression>*; if *<expression>* is not true, an exception will be raised
Assignment (=)	Creates a new data object and assigns (binds) it to a name
Augmented assignment	See Table 3-8
pass	The null operation; when executed, nothing happens
del	Removes the binding between a name or list of names and any associated objects
print	Sends output to the standard output (*stdout*)
return	May return an optional literal value or the result of an expression
yield	Only used in generator functions
raise	Raises an exception
break	Used in for and while loops to terminate loop execution
continue	Used in for and while loops to force the loop to jump back to the top and immediately start a new cycle
import	Specifies an external module to be included in the current namespace
global	Specifies a list of names that are to be treated as global variables within the current module
exec	Supports dynamic execution of Python code

I have intentionally skipped the del, exec, raise, and yield statements in the following subsections because they really won't come into play for what we want to do in this book. A discussion of the import statement is deferred until later in this chapter, in the section titled "Importing Modules" on page 106.

assert. The assert statement is typically used to determine if some condition has been met. If not, an exception is raised. It is heavily used in unit testing and sometimes for catching off-nominal conditions (although there are other ways to do this).

Assignment. The assignment statement (=) is probably the most basic form of Python statement. As we've already seen, an assignment is essentially equivalent to instantiating an object of some type and binding it to a name. We've already made extensive use of assignment in the previous sections, so we won't belabor it any more here.

Augmented assignment. Augmented assignment statements are very useful and show up quite often in Python programs. Because an assignment of any type will create a new data object, you cannot have an augmented assignment in an expression. In other words, this won't work:

```
    if (a += 1) > maxval:
```

But this will:

```
    if (a + 1) > maxval:
```

In an augmented assignment, the arithmetic operation is performed first, followed by the assignment. For a list of Python's augmented assignment operators, see Table 3-8.

pass. The `pass` statement is a no-op statement that does nothing. It is typically used as a placeholder when a statement is required syntactically. One often finds `pass` statements in methods of a top-level class that are intended to be overwritten by methods in a child class. They may also appear in "callback" functions or methods that don't really need to do anything, but must have a statement to be syntactically complete.

print. `print` writes the values of one or more objects to *stdout*, unless *stdout* has been redirected or the output of `print` is itself redirected. If `print` is given an object that is not a string, it will attempt to convert the data to string form. By default, `print` appends a newline (/n) to the end of the output, but this can be suppressed.

return. The `return` statement is used to return control from a function or method back to the original caller. The `return` statement may optionally pass data back to the caller, and the data can be any valid Python object. As mentioned earlier, a function may return a tuple instead of just a single value, which makes it possible to return both a status code and a data value (or more). While it is possible to return a list or a dictionary, this can be problematic in large programs with large and complex data objects because of the inherently opaque nature of these data types. I'll have more to say about this kind of unintentional obfuscation in a later section.

break. The `break` statement may occur only within a `for` or `while` loop. It will terminate the nearest enclosing loop construct and skip the `else` statement, if there is one.

continue. The `continue` statement may occur only within a `for` or `while` loop. `continue` forces the loop to return to the `for` or `while` statement at the start of the loop. Any subsequent statements past the `continue` are skipped. If a `continue` causes control to pass out of a `try` construct with a `finally` statement, the `finally` is executed before the next iteration of the loop. We'll look at the `try-except` construct in more detail shortly.

global. The `global` statement is used to declare names in a module context that are modifiable by a function or method within the module. Normally such names are read-only by functions or methods, and then only if the name does not already appear in the function or method.

Compound statements

Compound statements are composed of groups of statements that are logically related and control the execution of other statements. We will take a look at the `if`, `while`, `for`, and `try` statements, but we will skip the `with` statement and save the `def` and `class` statements until the next section. Table 3-14 lists Python's compound statements.

Table 3-14. Compound statements

Keyword	Description
`if`	Conditional test with optional alternate tests or terminal case
`while`	Executes loop repeatedly while initial condition is `True`
`for`	Iterates over elements of an iterable object (e.g., a list, string, or tuple)
`try`	Defines exception handling for a group of statements
`with`	Used with context managers
`def`	Declares a user-defined function or method
`class`	Declares a user-defined class

The if statement.   Python's `if` statement behaves as one would expect. Following the keyword `if` is an expression that will evaluate to either `True` or `False`. In its simplest form it is just an `if` statement and a block of one or more subordinate statements:

```
if <expression>:
    statement
    (more statements as necessary)
```

To specify an alternative action, one would use the `else` statement:

```
if <expression>:
    statement
    (more statements as necessary)
else:
    statement
    (and yet more statement if necessary)
```

To create a series of possible outcomes, the `elif` statement (a compression of "else if") is used. It is like an `if` and requires an expression, but it can only appear after an `if`, never by itself:

```
if <expression>:
    statement
    (more statements as necessary)
elif <expression>:
    statement
    (more statements as necessary)
else:
    statement
    (and yet more statements if necessary)
```

The while statement.   The `while` statement repeats a block of statements as long as a control expression is true:

```
while <expression>:
    statement
    (more statements as necessary)
else:
    statement
    (and yet more statement if necessary)
```

The else block is executed if the loop terminates normally (i.e., the control expression evaluates to False) and a break statement was not encountered. In the following example, the loop is controlled using a Boolean variable, which is initialized to True and then assigned the value of False from within the loop:

```
>>> loop_ok = True
>>> loop_cnt = 10
>>> while loop_ok:
...     print "%d Loop is OK" % loop_cnt
...     loop_cnt -= 1
...     if loop_cnt < 0:
...         loop_ok = False
... else:
...     print "%d Loop no longer OK" % loop_cnt
...
10 Loop is OK
9 Loop is OK
8 Loop is OK
7 Loop is OK
6 Loop is OK
5 Loop is OK
4 Loop is OK
3 Loop is OK
2 Loop is OK
1 Loop is OK
0 Loop is OK
-1 Loop no longer OK
```

The else statement is completely optional.

The continue and break statements may also be used to cause a loop to re-cycle through the while statement immediately or terminate and exit, respectively. If a break statement is used to terminate a loop, the else statement is also skipped. No statements following a continue statement will be evaluated.

The for statement. Python does have a for statement, but not in the sense that one would expect to find in some other languages. In Python, the for statement is used to iterate through a sequence of values. The for statement also includes an optional else statement, just as the while statement does, and it behaves in the same way:

```
for some_var in <sequence>:
    statement
    (more statements as necessary)
else:
    statement
    (and yet more statement if necessary)
```

One way to specify a sequence of integer values is to use the built-in function range(), like this:

```
>>> for i in range(0,5):
...     print i
...
0
```

```
1
2
3
4
```

Another place where `for` comes in handy is when dealing with a sequence object such as a list:

```
>>> alist = [1,2,3,4,5,6,7,8,9,10]
>>> for i in alist:
...     print i
...
1
2
3
4
5
6
7
8
9
10
```

The values that `for` traverses don't have to be integers. They could just as well be a set of strings in a tuple:

```
>>> stuple = ("this","is","a","4-tuple")
>>> for s in stuple:
...     print s
...
this
is
a
4-tuple
```

Like the `while` statement, the `for` statement supports the `continue` and `break` statements, and these work as one might expect.

The try statement. The `try` statement is used to trap and handle exceptions, and it is similar to the `try-catch` found in C++ or Java. It is very useful for creating robust Python applications by allowing the program designer to implement an alternative to the default approach the Python interpreter takes when an error occurs (which is usually to generate what is called a traceback message and then terminate). The full form of the `try-except` construct looks like this:

```
try:
    statement
    (more statements as necessary)
except <exception, err_info>:
    statement
    (more statements as necessary)
else:
    statement
    (more statements as necessary)
finally:
```

```
    statement
    (and yet more statements if necessary)
```

The use of a specific exception type (*<exception>*) is optional, and if it is not given, any exception will invoke the statements in the except block. One way to find out what happened to cause the exception is to use the base class Exception and specify a variable for Python to write the exception information into:

```
try:
    f = open(fname, "r")
except Exception, err:
    print "File open failed: %s" % str(err)
```

In this case, if the file open fails the program won't terminate. Instead, a message will be printed to *stdout* with some information about why the open statement failed.

The else statement is executed if there was no exception, and the finally block will be executed if there is a break or continue statement in the try block of statements. Refer to the Python documentation for more information about the try statement and exception handling in Python.

Strings

The ability to create strings of formatted data is used extensively in many Python programs, and the programs we will encounter in this book are no exception. Python's string objects provide a rich set of methods, and when they are combined with string formatting Python can generate output with formatted columns, left- or right-justified fields, and specific representations of various data types. Strings are important enough to merit a separate section.

String quotes

A string literal is quoted using one of the following forms:

```
'A single-quote string.'
"A double-quote string."
'''This is a multiline string using triple single quotes.
It is a medium-length string. '''
"""This is a multiline string with triple double quotes containing many
characters along with some punctuation, and it is a very long string indeed."""
```

Multiline strings can span more than one line, and \n (newline) characters are inserted into the string automatically to preserve the original formatting.

String methods

The string type provides numerous methods, some of which we have already seen. Table 3-15 is a complete list (not including the Unicode methods) as given in the Python 2.6 documentation.

Table 3-15. String methods

capitalize	lower
center	lstrip
count	partition
decode	replace
encode	rfind
endswith	rindex
expandtabs	rjust
find	rpartition
format	rsplit
index	rstrip
isalnum	split
isalpha	splitlines
isdigit	startswith
islower	strip
isspace	swapcase
istitle	title
isupper	translate
join	upper
ljust	zfill

Some of these get a lot more use than others, but it's good to have some idea of what's available. For the methods we don't cover here, refer to the Python documentation. Also, remember that the form:

```
new_sring = "string text".method()
```

works just as well as:

```
new_string = string_var.method()
```

Also keep in mind that there needs to be a target name for the new string object created as a result of invoking the method (strings are not mutable); otherwise, the modified string data will simply vanish.

Table 3-16 lists 14 commonly used string methods. Other less commonly used methods will be described as the need arises. In the following descriptions I will use the convention used in the Python documentation to indicate (required) and [optional] parameters.

Table 3-16. Commonly used string methods

Method	Description
capitalize()	Returns a copy of the string with just its first character capitalized.
center(*width*[,*fillchar*])	Returns a copy of the text in the string centered in a new string of length *width*. If *fillchar* is specified, the new string will be padded to *width* length on either side of the string text with the *fillchar* character. The default (if *fillchar* is omitted) is to use the space character.
count(*sub*[,*start*[,*end*]])	Counts the number of unique occurrences of the substring *sub*. The arguments *start* and *end* may be used to specify a range within the original string.
find(*sub*[,*start*[,*end*]])	Locates the first occurrence of the substring *sub* within the original string and returns an index value. If the substring is not found, -1 is returned.
isalnum()	Returns True if all of the characters in the string are alphanumeric (0..9, A..Z, a..z); otherwise, returns False.
isalpha()	Returns True if all of the characters in the string are alphabetic (A..Z, a..z); otherwise, returns False.
isdigit()	Returns True if all of the characters in the string are numeric (0..9), and False otherwise.
islower()	Returns True if all of the alphabetic characters in the string (a..z) are lowercase.
isspace()	Returns True if the string consists of nothing but whitespace characters (space, tab, newline, etc.); otherwise, returns False.
ljust(*width*[,*fillchar*])	Returns a new left-justified string of length *width*. If *fillchar* is specified, the string will be padded with the specified character. The default pad character is a space. If *width* is less than the length of the original string, the original is returned unchanged.
lower()	Returns a copy of the original string with all alphabetic characters converted to lowercase.
rjust(*width*[,*fillchar*])	Returns a new right-justified string of length *width*. If *fillchar* is specified, the string will be padded with the specified character. The default pad character is a space. If *width* is less than the length of the original string, the original is returned unchanged.
split([*sep*[,*maxsplit*]])	Returns a list whose elements are the words from the string using *sep* as the delimiter. *sep* may itself be a string. If *sep* is not specified, all whitespace between words is used as the delimiter (the whitespace can be any length so long as it is contiguous). If *maxsplit* is given, only up to *maxsplit* items will be returned.
upper()	Returns a copy of the original string with all alphabetic characters converted to uppercase.

String formatting

There are basically two ways to format a string with variable data in Python. The first is to use concatenation, which we saw earlier. The second is to make use of Python's string formatting capability. Which method is most appropriate depends on what you are trying to accomplish. While concatenation is relatively easy with simple strings, it doesn't provide for a lot of control over things like the number of decimal places, and data in strings with lots of embedded characters can be cumbersome when using concatenation. Consider the following example:

```
>>> data1 = 5.05567
>>> data2 = 34.678
>>> data3 = 0.00296705087
>>> data4 = 0
>>> runid = 1
>>> outstr1 = "Run "+str(runid)+": "+str(data1)+" "+str(data2)
>>> outstr2 = " "+str(data3)+" : "+str(data4)
>>> outstr = outstr1 + outstr2
>>> outstr
'Run 1: 5.05567 34.678 0.00296705087 : 0'
```

There is an easier way. Python employs string formatting placeholders that are very similar to those used in the C `sprintf()` function. By using special formatting codes, one can specify where data is to be inserted into a string and how the data will appear in string form. Here is a string created using formatting placeholders with the same data as above:

```
>>> outstr = "Run %d: %2.3f %2.3f %2.3f : %d" % (runid, data1, data2, data3, data4)
>>> outstr
'Run 1: 5.056 34.678 0.003 : 0'
```

Notice that the variables to be used in the string are enclosed in parentheses—it is an *n*-tuple. If the parentheses are omitted, only the first variable name is evaluated and an error will result:

```
>>> "%d %d %d" % 1, 2, 3
Traceback (most recent call last):
  File "<stdin>", line 1, in <module>
TypeError: not enough arguments for format string
```

The syntax for a string format placeholder is:

`%[(name)][flags][width][.precision]type_code`

Each placeholder can have an optional name assigned to it as the first item after the `%` (the parentheses are required). Following that are optional flags for justification, leading spaces, a sign character, and 0 fill. Next is an optional *width* value that specifies the minimum amount of space to allow for the data. If the data contains a decimal part, the value of the *.precision* field specifies the number of decimal places to use. Finally, a type code specifies what kind of data to expect (string, integer, long, floating point, etc.). Table 3-17 lists the available flags. Table 3-18 summarizes the various type codes available.

Table 3-17. String format placeholder flags

Flag	Meaning
#	Use "alternate form" formatting (see the notes in Table 3-18).
0	Pad numeric values with a leading zero.
-	Left-adjust (overrides 0 flag if both are specified).
(a space)	Insert a space before positive numbers.
+	Precede the values with a sign character (+ or -). Overrides the "space" flag.

Table 3-18. String format placeholder type codes

Type code	Meaning	Notes
d	Signed integer decimal.	
i	Signed integer decimal.	
o	Signed octal value.	The alternate form prepends a leading zero to the number if one is not already present.
u	Obsolete type.	Identical to d.
x	Signed hexadecimal (lowercase).	The alternate form prepends 0x if not already present.
X	Signed hexadecimal (uppercase).	The alternate form prepends 0X if not already present.
e	Floating-point exponential format (lowercase).	The alternate form always uses a decimal point even if no digits follow it.
E	Floating-point exponential format (uppercase).	Alternate form same as e.
f	Floating-point decimal format (lowercase).	Alternate form same as e.
F	Floating-point decimal format (uppercase).	Alternate form same as e.
g	Floating-point format. Uses lowercase exponential format if exponent is less than −4 or not less than *precision*, and decimal format otherwise.	The alternate form always contains a decimal and trailing zeros are not removed.
G	Floating-point format. Uses uppercase exponential format if exponent is less than −4 or not less than *precision*, and decimal format otherwise.	Same as g.
c	Single character (accepts an integer or single-character string).	
r	String (converts any Python object using repr()).	
s	String (converts any Python object using str()).	
%	No argument is converted, results in a % character in the result.	

String methods can be applied along with string formatting in the same statement. This may look a bit odd, but it's perfectly valid:

```
>>> "%d %d".ljust(20) % (2, 5)
'2 5                 '
>>> "%d %d".rjust(20) % (2, 5)
'              2 5'
>>>
```

Because there is no assignment of the string object to a name, Python just prints it out immediately after applying the formatting.

Lastly, Python provides a set of so-called escape characters for use with strings. These are special two-character codes composed of a backslash followed by a character, as shown in Table 3-19.

Table 3-19. String escape sequences

Escape sequence	Description	ASCII
\'	Single quote	'
\"	Double quote	"
\\	Single backslash	\
\a	ASCII bell	BEL
\b	ASCII backspace	BS
\f	ASCII formfeed	FF
\n	ASCII linefeed	LF
\r	ASCII carriage return	CR
\t	ASCII horizontal tab	TAB
\v	ASCII vertical tab	VT

A backslash character (\) may also be used for line continuation if it is the last character on a line, followed immediately by a newline (LF or CRLF). This causes the newline to be ignored by the interpreter, so it treats the line and the subsequent line as a single line of code.

Program Organization

So far we've been doing things at Python's command prompt. Now we'll look at how to create program modules with functions, classes, and methods.

Scope

Earlier I obliquely referred to the notion of scope without actually defining what it is. Let's do that now.

As I've already mentioned, Python utilizes the concept of namespaces as collections of names that are bound to objects. Actually, a namespace is more like a dictionary object, where the names are the keys and the objects they reference are the values. There are three levels of namespaces in Python: local, global, and built-ins. Figure 3-6 shows the namespace scopes in a Python module.

When a name is referenced in a function or method, a search is first made of the local namespace, including enclosing functions. Next, the global namespace is searched. Finally, the built-in namespace is searched. If the name cannot be found, Python will raise an exception. Figure 3-7 shows the namespace search hierarchy.

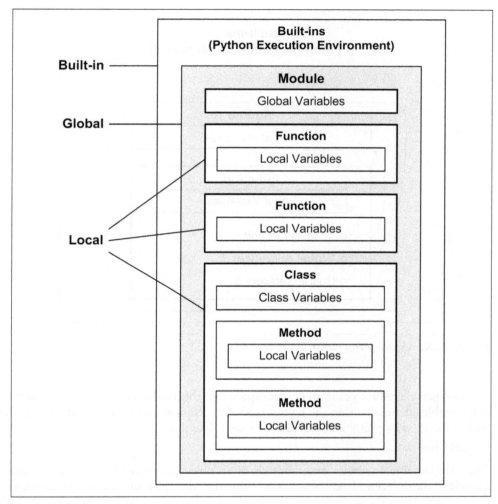

Figure 3-6. Python's namespaces

Local scope. The local scope is the namespace of a particular function, class, or method. In other words, any variables defined within a function are local to that function and are not visible outside of it. The local scope also includes the nearest surrounding function (if any). We will look at nested functions shortly.

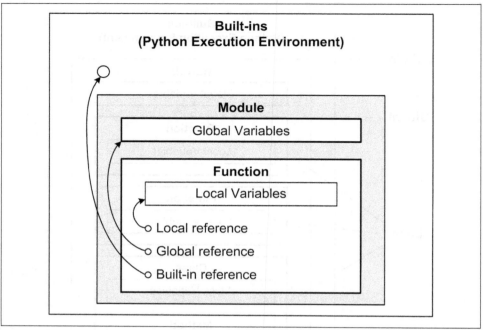

Figure 3-7. Namespace search hierarchy

Class objects introduce yet another namespace into the local context. In a class object, any variables defined within the namespace of the class are accessible to any method within the class by prefixing the name with `self`, like this:

```
self.some_var
```

The data variable attributes and methods of an object instance of a class are visible outside of the object and may be accessed using the "dot notation" we've already seen:

```
SomeObj = SomeClass()
SomeObj.var_name = value
```

This will assign a value to the attribute `var_name` in the object instance `SomeObj`. If `var_name` does not exist, it will be created in the object's context. This leads us to an interesting observation: Python objects do not have truly private data or methods in the sense that they cannot be accessed from outside of the object. Everything is accessible, although some things are not as readily available as others. You can prefix the name of a function, class, or variable with a leading underscore to prevent it from being included in a wildcard import, but that doesn't hide it. Using two leading underscore characters will "mangle" the object's name, but even then it is still accessible if you know how. So, while nothing is really hidden, the onus is on the programmer to be polite and not look.

If you're not sure exactly what this means, don't worry about it for now. We'll address objects in more detail later, when we start building user interfaces for our instrumentation applications.

Global scope. The global scope is the namespace of the enclosing module. Functions cannot modify the module's global variables unless the `global` statement is used. The following example, named `globals.py`, illustrates this:

```
# globals.py

var1 = 0
var2 = 1

def Function1():
    var1 = 1
    var2 = 2

    print var1, var2

def Function2():
    global var1, var2

    print var1, var2

    var1 = 3
    var2 = 4

    print var1, var2
```

To try it out, we will need to load it using the `import` statement. This tells Python to read the module and populate the command line's namespace using what it finds there:

```
>>> import globals
```

Once `globals` is imported, we can use the `help()` function to see what is inside:

```
>>> help(globals)
Help on module globals:

NAME
    globals

FILE
    globals.py

FUNCTIONS
    Function1()

    Function2()

DATA
    var1 = 3
    var2 = 4
```

If we execute Function1, we can verify that the global instances of **var1** and **var2** are not changed:

```
>>> globals.var1
0
>>> globals.var2
1
>>> globals.Function1()
1 2
>>> globals.var1
0
>>> globals.var2
1
```

However, Function2 will change the values assigned to var1 and var2:

```
>>> globals.Function2()
0 1
3 4
>>> globals.var1
3
>>> globals.var2
4
```

If a function assigns values to variables with names identical to those in the global namespace, the global statement must be used if the names are referenced before the assignments are made. This example, called globals2.py, illustrates this:

```
# globals2.py

var1 = 0
var2 = 1

def Function1():
    print var1, var2

def Function2():
    var1 = 1
    var2 = 2

    print var1, var2

def Function3():
    print var1, var2

    var1 = 1
    var2 = 2

    print var1, var2
```

Observe what happens when we execute the three functions:

```
>>> import globals2
>>> globals2.Function1()
0 1
>>> globals2.Function2()
```

```
1 2
>>> globals2.Function3()
Traceback (most recent call last):
  File "<stdin>", line 1, in <module>
  File "globals2.py", line 14, in Function3
    print var1, var2
UnboundLocalError: local variable 'var1' referenced before assignment
```

Function1() succeeded because there was no conflict between its local variables and the module's global variables. In Function2() the local variables var1 and var2 are defined within the function, so again, there is no problem. However, Function3() causes Python to emit an error message. In this case the use of the global names is blocked because identical names have already been placed into the function's local namespace, but the names aren't yet bound to an object containing a value when the print statement is invoked. Hence the UnboundLocalError exception. If the print statement were preceded by a global statement, the error would not have occurred.

Built-in scope. The built-in namespace is the Python runtime environment. It includes things like abs(), print, and various exception names. If you want a list of the built-in names, just type dir(__builtins__) at the Python prompt. I won't list the output here because it's rather large (144 names at least).

Modules and packages

A Python source code file is called a *module*. It is a collection of statements composed of variable definition statements, import statements, directly executable statements, function definition statements, and class definition statements, with the variables and methods that go with them.

Modules are contained within *packages*. A package is, in effect, a directory that contains one or more modules. Packages may contain other packages. Figure 3-8 shows this graphically.

A module is an object, and as we've already seen, it has its own namespace. A module also has attributes just like any other Python object. A module's attributes include the functions, classes, methods, and variables defined in its namespace.

Functions, classes, and methods

The def statement is used to define both functions within modules and methods within classes:

```
def SomeName (parameters):
    """ docstring goes here.
    """
    local_var = value

    statement...
    statement...
    more statements...
```

When used to define a function, the def statement begins at the leftmost column and all of the function's statements are indented relative to it. When used to define a method in a class, the def statement is indented relative to the class statement.

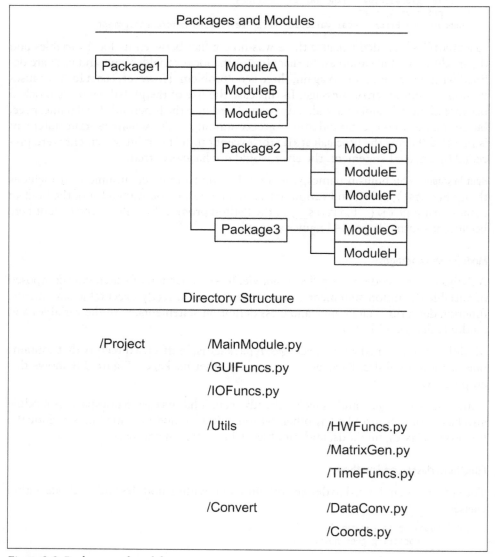

Figure 3-8. Packages and modules

Functions and methods may be nested. When this is done, the internal functions are not accessible from outside of the enclosing function. Here is a rather contrived example of nested functions called subfuncs.py:

```
#subfuncs.py

def MainFunc():
    def SubFunc1():
        print "SubFunc1"
    def SubFunc2():
        print "SubFunc2"
    def SubFunc3():
        def SubSubFunc1():
            print "SubSubFunc1"
        def SubSubFunc2():
            print "SubSubFunc2"
        SubSubFunc1()
        SubSubFunc2()
    SubFunc1()
    SubFunc2()
    SubFunc3()
```

We can only execute the function `MainFunc()`; none of the other functions nested within it are directly accessible from outside of the scope of `MainFunc()`. If you import `subfuncs` and try to get help on it, this is all you will see:

```
>>> import subfuncs
>>> help(subfuncs)
Help on module subfuncs:
NAME
    subfuncs
FILE
    subfuncs.py
FUNCTIONS
    MainFunc()
```

However, if we execute `MainFunc()` we can see that the subfunctions do get executed:

```
>>> import subfuncs
>>> subfuncs.MainFunc()
SubFunc1
SubFunc2
SubSubFunc1
SubSubFunc2
```

The `class` statement defines a class object, which in turn is used to create object instances of the class. The following class defines a timer object that may be used to get elapsed times during program execution:

```
import time

class TimeDelta:
    def __init__(self):
        self.tstart = 0
        self.tlast  = 0
        self.tcurr  = 0

        self.Reset()

    def GetDelta(self):
```

```
            """ Returns time since last call to GetDelta(). """
            self.tcurr = time.clock()
            delta = self.tcurr - self.tlast
            self.tlast = self.tcurr
            return delta

    def GetTotal(self):
        """ Returns time since object created. """
        return time.clock() - self.tstart

    def Reset(self):
        """ Initializes time attributes. """
        self.tstart = time.clock()
        self.tlast = self.tstart
```

Objects of this class can be instantiated in the code wherever one might want to check on elapsed times, and multiple occurrences may exist simultaneously. This would be rather awkward to do if `TimeDelta` was a function in a module, but as a class each instance can maintain its own data for when it was started and when it was last checked.

Docstrings

Docstrings are used to document modules, classes, methods, and functions. A multiline string that appears at the start of a module, function, class, or method is seen by Python as a docstring, and it is stored in the object's internal __doc__ variable. This is what you are seeing when you type `help()` for a specific function at the command-line prompt.

The following example shows how docstrings are used. The `pass` statement has been used so that we can import this code and use `help()` to display the embedded documentation:

```
#docstrings.py

""" Module level docstring.

    This describes the overall purpose and features of the module.
    It should not go into detail about each function or class as
    each of those objects has its own docstring.
"""

def Function1():
    """ A function docstring.

        Describes the purpose of the function, its inputs (if any)
        and what it will return (if anything).
    """
    pass

class Class1:
    """ Top-level class docstring.

        Like the module docstring, this is a general high-level
        description of the class. The methods and variable
        attributes are not described here.
```

```
"""

    def Method1():
        """ A method docstring.

            Similar to a function docstring.
        """
        pass

    def Method2():
        """ A method docstring.

            Similar to a function docstring.
        """
        pass
```

When the `help()` function is used on this module, the following output is the result:

```
>>> import docstrings
>>> help(docstrings)
Help on module docstrings:

NAME
    docstrings - Module level docstring.

FILE
    docstrings.py

DESCRIPTION
    This describes the overall purpose and features of the module.
    It should not go into detail about each function or class as
    each of those objects has its own docstring.

CLASSES
    Class1

    class Class1
     |  Top-level class docstring.
     |
     |  Like the module docstring, this is a general high-level
     |  description of the class. The methods and variable
     |  attributes are not described here.
     |
     |  Methods defined here:
     |
     |  Method1()
     |      A method docstring.
     |
     |      Similar to a function docstring.
     |
     |  Method2()
     |      A method docstring.
     |
     |      Similar to a function docstring.

FUNCTIONS
```

```
Function1()
    A function docstring.

    Describes the purpose of the function, its inputs (if any)
    and what it will return (if anything).
```

Importing Modules

Python modules can bring in functionality from other modules by using the `import` statement. When a module is imported Python will first check to see if the module has already been imported, and if it has it will refer to the existing objects by including their names in the current namespace. Otherwise, it will load the indicated module, scan it, and add the imported names to the current namespace. Note that "current namespace" may refer to the local namespace of a function, class, or method, or it might be the global namespace of a module.

Statements in a Python module that are not within a function or method will be executed immediately when the module is loaded. This means that any `import` statements, assignments, `def` or `class` statements, or other code will be executed at load time. Code within a function or method is executed only when it is called, although an object for it is created when the `def` or `class` statement is processed.

Import methods

The `import` statement comes in several different forms. This is the most common, and safest, form:

```
import module
```

The objects in *module* are added to the current namespace as references of the form *module.function()* or *module.class()*. To access data attributes within a module, the notation *module.variable* is used.

A variation on this is the aliased `import` form:

```
import module as alias
```

This is identical to the `import module` statement, except now the alias can be used to reference objects in *module*. This is handy when a module has a long name. For example:

```
import CommonReturnCodes as RetCodes
```

One can also specify what to import from a module:

```
from module import somename
```

This form imports a specific function, class, or data attribute from a module. The function or attribute *somename* can then be used without a module prefix.

The wildcard form imports everything from the external module and adds it to the current namespace:

```
from module import *
```

The wildcard import is generally considered to be a bad idea except in special cases, such as when importing a module that has been specifically designed to be used in this fashion and contains only unique names that are unlikely to conflict with existing names. It is considered problematic because it imports *everything* from the imported module unless special precautions are taken. If the imported module happens to have attributes with the same names as those in the current module, the current names will be overwritten.

There is, as one might expect from Python, a way to control what is exported by using single or double leading underscore characters for attribute names. An attribute name of the form:

    _some_name

will not be included in a wildcard import, but it can still be referenced using the module prefix notation. A double leading underscore of the form:

    __some_name

is about as close as Python gets to data hiding. It can still be accessed from outside the parent module, but its external name is "mangled" to make it more difficult to get at.

Import processing

Because Python executes any import statements that are not within the scope of a function immediately when a module is imported, it will descend through the import statements in each module in a depth-first fashion until all imports have been processed. Figure 3-9 shows graphically how this works.

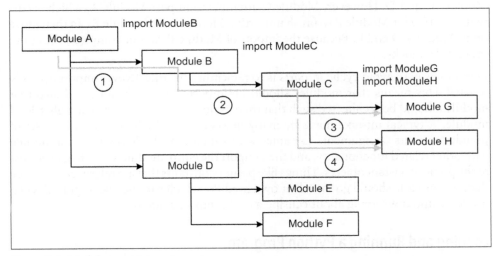

Figure 3-9. Module import sequence

The import sequence in Figure 3-9 is indicated by numbers in circles. Module A imports module B, which imports Module C, which in turn imports modules G and H. Module D and the modules it imports will be next in line after module H is processed.

Cyclic imports

One drawback to Python's import scheme is that it is possible to create situations where imports can become "hung." This is called a *cyclic import*. Consider the diagram in Figure 3-10.

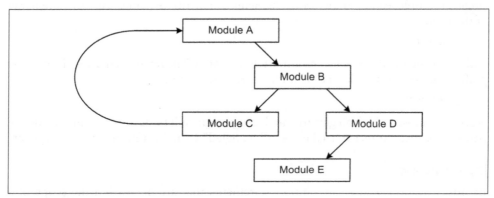

Figure 3-10. Cyclic import situation

Here we have a situation where Module A imports Module B, which in turn imports Modules C and D. However, Module C attempts to import Module A, which is currently waiting for Module B to finish importing Module C, so Module B can then move on to Modules D and E. Because the import of Module B cannot complete, the entire process deadlocks.

One sure way to avoid cyclic imports is to remember the rule "Never import up, only down." This means that modules should be imported hierarchically, and also that modules should be architected such that there is no need to import from a higher-level module. A typical mistake made by many newcomers to Python is to place a set of pseudoconstants (assignments to names with values that don't change) in a module with other related functionality, and then import the entire module solely to gain access to the pseudoconstant objects. Things like pseudoconstants that are referenced by more than one module should go into their own module, which can then be imported when needed without worrying about causing a cyclic import situation.

Loading and Running a Python Program

The following example is a complete Python program that contains no function or class definitions—it is what is commonly referred to as a "script." It will generate a PGM format image file consisting of random data. The result looks like an old-style TV screen tuned to an empty channel—it's a lot of "snow." The main point here is to get a look at what a small Python program looks like. Any image viewer capable of handling PGM files should be able to load and display the image (ImageJ, a free tool from *http://rsbweb.nih.gov/ij/*, works quite well for this, and check out *http://netpbm.sourceforge.net* for information about the PGM image format.)

Executing this program doesn't require that you start the Python interpreter first. Just run *python* from the command line with the program filename as its only parameter, like this:

```
C:\samples\> python pgmrand.py
```

or, on Linux:

```
/home/jmh/samples/% python pgmrand.py
```

The prompt will most likely look different on your system (unless you're keeping your Python samples in a directory called "samples").

If you are using Linux, you'll probably need to put the following line at the top of the program file:

```
#! /usr/bin/python
```

On some systems you may need to modify this to point to where Python is actually installed. A likely alternate location is */usr/local/bin/python*.

Here's the source code:

```
""" Generates an 8 bpp "image" of random pixel values.

The sequence of operations used to create the PGM output file is as follows:
    1. Create the PGM header, consisting of:
        ID string (P5)
        Image width
        Image height
        Image data size (in bits/pixel)
    2. Generate height x width bytes of random values
    3. Write the header and data to an output file
"""
import random as rnd    # use import alias for convenience

rnd.seed()        # seed the random number generator

# image parameters are hardcoded in this example
width  = 256
height = 256
pxsize = 255      # specify an 8 bpp image

# create the PGM header
hdrstr = "P5\n%d\n%d\n%d\n" % (width, height, pxsize)

# create a list of random values from 0 to 255
pixels = []
for i in range(0,width):
```

```
    for j in range(0,height):
        # generate random values of powers of 2
        pixval = 2**rnd.randint(0,8)
        # some values will be 256, so fix them
        if pixval > pxsize:
            pixval = pxsize
        pixels.append(pixval)

# convert array to character values
outpix = "".join(map(chr,pixels))  ❶

# append the "image" to the header
outstr = hdrstr + outpix

# and write it out to the disk
FILE = open("pgmtest.pgm","w")
FILE.write(outstr)
FILE.close()
```

❶ The string join() method and the map() function are used to create an output string
that is written to the image file.

It would be a worthwhile exercise to review the program and look up the things that
don't immediately make sense to you. The only really "tricky" part is the use of the
string join() method and the map() function to create the output string. This was done
because Python does not have a native byte type, but it does have a chr type for use
with strings. If one wants an array of bytes, one way to get these is to create a string by
scanning through a list of integers, converting each to a chr type, and then joining it to
an empty string (the "" in the "".join(map(chr,pixels)) statement). Note that all the
parameters one might want to change to experiment with the output file are hardcoded
in this example.

Basic Input and Output

In order to be generally useful, a program must have some means to input data and
output results. Python provides several ways to achieve both objectives using the console, the command line, and file objects. Later on we will examine things like serial
ports, USB interfaces, network sockets, and data acquisition hardware, but for now
let's look at what can be done with Python as it comes right out of the box.

User input

Getting user input from *stdin* (standard input) is straightforward. Python provides the
raw_input() function for just this purpose.

The module `getInfo.py` contains a simple example of how `raw_input()` can be used:

```
# getInfo.py

def ask():
    uname = raw_input("What is your name? ")
    utype = raw_input("What kind of being are you? ")
    uhome = raw_input("What planet are you from? ")
    print ""
    print "So, %s, you are a %s from %s." % (uname, utype, uhome)
    uack = raw_input("Is that correct? ")
    if uack[0] in ('y', 'Y'):
        print "Cool. Welcome."
    else:
        print "OK, whatever."
```

To see how this works, we can import the module `getInfo` and then call its function `ask()`:

```
>>> import getInfo
>>> getInfo.ask()
What is your name? zifnorg
What kind of being are you? Zeeble
What planet are you from? Arcturus III

So, zifnorg, you are a Zeeble from Arcturus III.
Is that correct? y
Cool. Welcome.
```

The `raw_input()` function accepts an optional prompt string and always returns the data from *stdin* as a string. If the program is looking for a numeric value, it will need to be converted. A safe way to do this is by using the **try-except** construct. Here is `getInfo2.py` with the try-except modification:

```
def ask2():
    uname = raw_input("What is your name? ")
    utype = raw_input("What kind of being are you? ")
    uhome = raw_input("What planet are you from? ")
    getgumps = True
    while (getgumps):
        intmp = raw_input("How many mucklegumps do you own? ")
        try:
            ugumps = int(intmp)
        except:
            print "Sorry, you need to enter an integer number."
            continue
        else:
            getgumps = False
    print ""
    print "So, %s, you are a %s from %s, with %d mucklegumps."\
        % (uname, utype, uhome, ugumps)
    uack = raw_input("Is that correct? ")
    if uack[0] in ('y', 'Y'):
        print "Cool. Welcome."
    else:
        print "OK, whatever."
```

Before we move on, there are a few things to consider about this simple function. First, it will only accept an integer value for the number of "mucklegumps." Strings and floats will be rejected. Secondly, there is no way for the user to gracefully abort the input process. This could be easily handled by checking for a special character (a ., for example), or just detecting null input (just pressing the Enter key with no input). Speaking of null input, if the user does press the Enter key in response to the last question, Python will raise an exception:

```
Is that correct? <enter>
Traceback (most recent call last):
  File "<stdin>", line 1, in <module>
  File "getInfo2.py", line 18, in ask2
    if uack[0] in ('y', 'Y'):
IndexError: string index out of range
```

The expression in the if statement is attempting to match whatever is in uack[0] with either of the values in the 2-tuple ('y', 'Y'), and just pressing Enter returns a zero-length string, which causes the exception. Using a try-except here will prevent this from happening:

```
uack = raw_input("Is that correct? ")
try:
    if uack[0] in ('y', 'Y'):
        print "Cool. Welcome."
    else:
        print "OK, whatever."
except:
    print "Fine. Have a nice day."
```

When dealing with user input (that is, whatever a human being types in response to a prompt), one must always be aware of possible input errors or exceptions. Humans can, and often will, type in erroneous data, values that are out of range, unexpected words or phrases, or even nothing at all. Users are unpredictable, so building in safeguards to catch bad input values is always a good idea.

Command-line parameters

Program parameters entered at the command line are captured by the operating system and passed to the program via the Python interpreter as a list. The first item in the list (at index 0) is always the name of the program itself. Python's included sys module contains methods for dealing with this data.

This simple program (argshow.py) will print out all the items from the command-line parameter list:

```
import sys

print "%d items in argument list\n" % len(sys.argv)

i = 1
for arg in sys.argv:
```

```
    print "%d: %s" % (i, arg)
    i += 1
```

And here is what happens when we run it:

```
C:\samples> python argshow.py 1 2 3 4 -h -v
7 items in argument list

1: argshow.py
2: 1
3: 2
4: 3
5: 4
6: -h
7: -v
```

Python also provides tools for detecting specific arguments and extracting values from command-line parameters, which we won't cover at this point. We will see them in action in later chapters.

Files

Python has a basic built-in object type for dealing with files that provides methods to read and write data from and to a disk file, among other actions. We've already seen a little bit of it with the pgmrand.py script we looked at earlier.

The open() method is used to create an instance of a file object:

```
>>> fname = "test1.txt"
>>> fmode = "w"
>>> f = open(fname, fmode)
```

Of course, you could also write:

```
f = open("test1.txt", "w")
```

and get the same result.

Once we have a file object, we can write something to it using its write() method:

```
>>> f.write("Test line 1\n")
>>> f.write("Test line 2\n")
>>> f.close()
```

The resulting file should now contain two lines of text:

```
Test line 1
Test line 2
```

Notice that the strings to be written to the file end with a \n (the code for a newline character). The file write() method does not append a newline to the end of a string like print does, so it must be explicitly included in the string.

Table 3-20 lists the most commonly encountered file modes.

Table 3-20. File I/O modes

Mode	Meaning
r	Read
rb	Read binary
w	Write
wb	Write binary
a	Append
ab	Append binary

Table 3-21 lists some commonly used file object methods. For a description of the other file object methods that are available, refer to the Python documentation.

Table 3-21. File methods

Method	Description
close()	Close a file.
flush()	Flush the internal buffer.
read(*[size]*)	Read at most *size* bytes from the file.
readline(*[size]*)	Read an entire line from the file.
write(*str*)	Write a string to the file.

Console output using print

We've already seen Python's print function in action. Its primary purpose is to send output to whatever is currently defined as *stdout* (standard output). The print function is capable of handling conversions between numeric types and strings for console output in a transparent fashion. The string formatting discussed earlier works with the print statement to create nicely formatted output.

Redirecting print

By default, the output of print is sent to whatever is currently defined as *stdout*. By using the "chevron" (>>) operator this behavior can be modified, and print can send output to any object that provides a write() method. Typically this would be a file object, as shown here:

```
>>> datastr = "This is a test."
>>> f = open("testfile.txt", "w")
>>> print >> f,datastr
>>> f.close()
```

Hints and Tips

Here is a semirandom collection of observations that may prove useful to you.

Module global variables

It is usually a good idea to initialize module global `variables at the start of a module file. Attempting to check a global variable that does not yet exist will result in an exception, and taking care of this beforehand can save some aggravation later.

Latent defects

Because Python does not execute the internal statements (i.e., the body) of functions or methods when a module is imported, only the `def` statement, it is always possible for bugs to be lurking there that will not become apparent until the code is invoked. In such situations the `try` statement is a powerful ally, but it is not a cure-all. Good unit testing is key to detecting and removing such defects before they can cause problems.

Deferred imports

Sometimes you may encounter code where the original author attempted to resolve a cyclic import by deferring the import of the problematic module by placing the `import` statement within a function or method, instead of at the top of the module file. While this is syntactically allowed in Python it is considered to be bad form, and it's a sure sign that someone didn't think the design through before sitting down at the keyboard and hammering away at it. However, when dealing with legacy code (or just poorly written code) it may not be possible to avoid using this trick. Use it sparingly, only when you really have to, and test it thoroughly.

Dictionaries as function parameters

Although Python allows any data object to be used as a parameter to a function or method, resist the temptation to use dictionary objects unless you have a compelling reason to do so. If a dictionary object is used as a parameter, document it in detail and try to avoid altering its structure dynamically as it gets passed from function to function. Code that dynamically alters the structure of a shared dictionary object can be very difficult to understand and a nightmare to debug. It could even be considered a form of obfuscation, albeit (hopefully) unintentional. The same common-sense rationale applies to lists.

Function return values

Tuples are a handy way to return more than one value from a function. For example, one could return a tuple containing both a status code value and a data value by using a 2-tuple. To see if the function succeeded one would examine the status code, and if it is OK one would then get the data value.

Think of modules as objects

Of course, in Python a module actually is an object (everything is, as you may recall), but the tendency seems to be to treat a module as something akin to a source code module in C or C++. One can achieve some neat and tidy data encapsulation using just a module with nothing in it but assignment statements to associate names with values. Here is part of a module that contains nothing but event ID values for use with a wxPython GUI, which we will get to in a later chapter:

```
# ResourceIDs.py

import  wx

# File
idFileSave                      = wx.NewId()
idFileSaveAs                    = wx.NewId()
idFileNew                       = wx.NewId()
idFileOpen                      = wx.NewId()
idFileOpenGroup                 = wx.NewId()
idFileClose                     = wx.NewId()
idFileCloseAll                  = wx.NewId()
idFilePrint                     = wx.NewId()
idFilePrintPreview              = wx.NewId()
idFilePrintSetup                = wx.NewId()
```

The wxPython package includes a function called `NewID()` that automatically assigns a new ID number each time it is called. When `ResourceIDs` is imported, every statement is evaluated and a value is assigned to each data object. To use these one simply imports the module (perhaps using an alias, as shown here):

```
import ResourceIDs as rID

event_id = rID.idFileSave
```

This comes in handy in large programs, especially those that employ a GUI with lots of event ID names. A data-only module can also be imported from any other module without worrying about creating a cyclic import, provided that it does not itself import anything else (except perhaps system-level modules). If the attribute names in a data-only module are unique (using, say, a special prefix on each name), it could also be safely imported using the wildcard import style.

Use docstrings and descriptive comments

Once upon a time, a physics professor told me: "Document everything you do in the lab like you were going to get struck with amnesia tomorrow." Sage advice, to be sure, but many people are loath to spend the time necessary to include docstrings and descriptive comments in their code. This is silly, because no one can be expected to remember exactly what something does or why it's even there 12 months or more down the road (some might say that even a couple of months is a stretch). It also says something about how the author of the software feels about those who might come along later and try to fix or maintain the code.

Coding style

The document known as "PEP-8" (available from *http://www.python.org*) contains some suggested coding style guidelines. You may not agree with all of it, but you should at least read it and be familiar with it. There is a lot of good advice there. In any case, you should attempt to arrive at some type of consistent style for your code, if for no other reason than that it improves readability and makes things a whole lot easier when there is a need to revisit old code.

Python Development Tools

A good development environment can make the difference between success and frustration. The development environment must, at a minimum, provide some way to create and edit Python source code as a standard ASCII text file. Additional tools, such as debuggers, automatic documentation generators, and version control are all good, but one could get by without them if absolutely necessary. Fortunately this isn't necessary, given that there are a lot of excellent FOSS (Free and Open Source Software) tools available, and some very good and inexpensive commercial tools as well.

In this section we'll take a brief look at what is available, with a primary emphasis on FOSS tools. It doesn't really matter what tools you use, and most people have (or develop over time) their own preferences and work habits. The important thing to take away here is that there are many paths available, and choosing the right one is simply a matter of picking the tools that feel right and selecting the right tools for the job.

Editors and IDEs

At the very least, you will need a text editor or integrated development environment (IDE) of some sort for entering and editing Python source code. You may also want to use the editor for your C source code when writing extensions (which we will delve into in Chapter 5), so it may be a good idea to pick something that's language-neutral, or perhaps language-aware with syntax highlighting.

The primary difference between an editor and an IDE lies in how much one can accomplish from within the tool itself. An editor typically allows you to do just one thing: editing. An IDE, on the other hand, lets you do much more—from editing, to compiling, debugging, and perhaps even metrics and version control. An IDE is intended to be an environment the developer doesn't need to leave until either it's time to quit and go home, or the program is complete.

With some editors there is also the capability to launch another program from within the tool and then capture and display program output, but this is usually more of an add-on capability, not something that is inherently part of the editor tool, and some editors support this capability better than others. A full-featured IDE incorporates all of this functionality in some form or another, although some IDEs also require functionality from external tools and applications. In other words, the line between an editor with lots of bells and whistles and an IDE is sometimes blurry.

Using an IDE with Python is probably not necessary (although there are a few available), since it is not a compiled language, and most of what happens with Python is either happening at the command line or within the Python application's GUI (if it uses one).

Editors

If you think you would prefer to use a standalone editor (which is what I use, by the way), there are several excellent packages to choose from. Table 3-22 lists a few of the more popular ones to consider.

Table 3-22. Short list of text editors

Name	OS	FOSS?	Pros	Cons
Emacs	Linux Windows Others	Yes	Supports sophisticated editing functions, scripting, syntax highlighting, and multi-window displays.	Has a somewhat steep learning curve and uses some nonintuitive multikey commands that must be memorized.
vi/vim	Linux Windows Others	Yes	The basic functions are easy to learn, and *vi* is very widespread across different Linux- and Unix-like platforms. *vim* also provides a GUI interface in addition to the conventional command-line operation.	Learning the more complex and sophisticated functionality can be a slog. Nonintuitive key combinations and codes are a holdover from the days of mainframes, minicomputers, and terminals.
nano	Linux	Yes	Very simple. Provides some syntax highlighting.	Based on the Pico editor and its Control-key commands. Limited capabilities.
Slickedit	Linux Windows Others	No ($$$)	Lots of features, full GUI interface, programmable macros, and syntax highlighting. Capable of emulating other editors.	Lots of knobs and dials to learn—may be overkill for most development tasks. Rather hefty price tag.
UltraEdit	Linux Windows	No ($)	Very easy to learn with a full GUI interface. Multiple tabbed text windows, programmable macros, and syntax highlighting.	Has lots of features that the average developer will probably never use. Requires some effort to figure out how to adjust the default settings and disable some unnecessary defaults. It costs money (but not a whole lot).

This is only a partial list, and there are other editors available, including some good FOSS ones. If you don't already have a favorite editor (or even if you do), it would probably be worthwhile to try to compare what's available for your development platform. But, a word of caution: some people seem to become rather attached to a particular editor, even to the point of being somewhat fanatical about it. This is particularly apparent in the *Emacs* versus *vi* debate that has been going on now for well over 20 years (refer to *http://en.wikipedia.org/wiki/Editor_war* for details). Just keep an open mind, select the right tool for the job, and see the editor war for what it really is: free entertainment.

IDE tools

An IDE attempts to integrate everything a programmer might need into a single tool. The first popular and low-cost IDE for the PC was Borland's Turbo Pascal, developed by Philippe Kahn in the mid-1980s. Most modern IDEs provide a text editor for source code, an interface to a compiler or interpreter, tools to automate the build process, perhaps some support for version control, and a debugger of some sort. In other words, it's a one-stop shopping experience for software development. Not every IDE will provide all the functionality we've listed here, but at the very least you should expect a text editor and the ability to run external tools and applications such as a compiler, interpreter, and debugger. In this sense even editors such as UltraEdit and *Emacs* (listed in Table 3-22) could be used as IDEs (and often are, actually). Table 3-23 lists some readily available IDE tools suitable for use with Python.

Table 3-23. Short list of IDEs

Name	OS	FOSS?	Pros	Cons
Boa	Any that Python and wxPython support	Yes	Excellent tool for creating and maintaining wxPython GUI components and applications. Includes a decent editor and a basic Python debugger.	Targeted for the wxPython GUI add-on package. It does a lot but isn't as full-featured as a dedicated editor.
Idle	Any that Python supports	Yes	Provided with Python and coded entirely in Python. Provides multiple editing windows, function/method lists, a Python shell window, and a rudimentary debugger.	Idle's multiple editing windows are free-floating, and it is sometimes annoying trying to track down a particular window.
Eclipse (with PyDev)	Linux Windows Others	Yes	A very flexible multilanguage IDE written in Java. Additional functionality and language support are provided by plug-in modules such as PyDev for Python development.	A rather steep learning curve and a project/package model for capturing project components that may not be suitable for everyone.
PythonWin	Windows	Yes	Provided with the ActiveState Python distribution. Includes most of the same capabilities as Idle.	Specifically for the Windows platform.
WingIDE	Linux Windows Others	No ($$)	Lots of functionality specifically geared toward Python development and debugging.	Python-specific, although the editor can, of course, be used with other languages. The interface can be somewhat busy and cluttered, so spending time with the configuration is usually necessary.

Debuggers

Debuggers allow a software developer to see inside the software, so to speak, while it is running. While one could perhaps argue that a debugger is seldom, if ever, actually necessary, they can save a lot of time and quickly expose serious problems in a program. However, as with any addictive substance, a debugger may be good in moderation, but it can develop into a serious dependency problem if one is not careful.

What, exactly, can one do with a debugger? For starters, a debugger allows the developer to set "breakpoints" in the code by selecting a particular line in the source listing. When the program execution reaches that point, it is halted and the local variables may be examined. A debugger also provides the ability to step through the code, one line at a time. If the debugger supports the concept of a "watch," specific variables may be selected and their values displayed to the developer at breakpoints or while stepping through the code.

A debugger is, by necessity, language-specific—there is no "one size fits all" debugger currently available, although there are some "shells" that provide a similar interface across several languages.

For Python, the Boa, Idle, Eclipse, and WingIDE tools provide capable debuggers. A standalone Python debugger, *Winpdb*, is also available, and Python itself ships with an integrated command-line debugger, *pdb*.

Summary

This concludes our brief tour of Python. You should now have a general feel for what Python looks like and what it is capable of. I have intentionally glossed over many aspects of the language, because, after all, this book is not a tutorial on Python. As I stated going in, there are many excellent books available that can provide copious amounts of detail, and the official Python website is the authoritative source of all things Python. As we go along we will encounter other features of the language, and we will examine them when the need arises.

Suggested Reading

If you would like to get deeper into the realm of Python programming, the following books would be good places to start:

Python in a Nutshell, 2nd ed. (http://oreilly.com/catalog/9780596100469/) Alex Martelli, O'Reilly Media, 2006.
> A compact reference that's very handy to have on the desk when you're working with Python. Well organized and easy to use, this is an essential reference work when you need to look up something in a hurry and want more than a pocket reference, but less than a massive tome.

Programming Python, 3rd ed. (http://oreilly.com/catalog/9780596009250) Mark Lutz, O'Reilly Media, 2006.

A comprehensive introduction to Python and a massive reference, this 1,600-page book covers everything from string methods to GUI programming. The one book anyone working with Python should have.

In addition to the URL references already provided in this chapter, there are numerous other online resources available for Python, including the following:

http://diveintopython3.org

This site hosts the complete text of Mark Pilgrim's book *Dive Into Python*, also available as a PDF download. The book takes a learn-by-doing approach and uses numerous examples to illustrate key concepts and techniques.

http://effbot.org

Fredrik Lundh's blog site. Here you can find hundreds of articles on Python, downloadable and viewable books, and some software to examine and try. The articles are well written and interesting to browse, and they are useful for the insights they provide into the language and its uses.

## CHAPTER 4

The C Programming Language

*Low-level programming is good for the
programmer's soul.*

—John Carmack, cofounder of Id Software

The C programming language was created at Bell Laboratories by Ken Thompson and others between 1969–1973 as part of the early development work on Unix. C has been an integral part of Unix ever since, and Unix is itself written mostly in C (with a few parts written in assembly language where necessary). Linux, Solaris, BSD, and other modern operating systems are also written primarily in C. In this book we will use ANSI C, standardized in the mid-1980s and described in the book *The C Programming Language*, Second Edition, by Brian Kernighan and Dennis Ritchie (Prentice Hall).

This chapter is not intended to be a comprehensive tutorial on the C programming language; it is merely intended to provide enough detail to enable you to effectively apply the C language later, when you need to create extensions for Python. If you happen to be familiar with the original version of C (sometimes called "K&R"), you may notice that things have changed somewhat, but it shouldn't be difficult to grasp the new features.

Installing C

The *gcc* compiler is a popular and widely used C compiler. Unfortunately, it doesn't work with Windows (at least, not directly). Those working in a Linux or Solaris environment with access to *gcc* are ready to go with nothing else to install, and if *gcc* is not installed a short session with a package manager can usually solve the problem. If you will be using a Windows machine, you'll need to do some extra work, or spend some money, to get a C compiler installed and running.

One solution is to obtain a copy of Microsoft's Visual Studio, but I would recommend against this. It's not that Visual Studio is a bad tool—it's not. It is, however, so heavily integrated with the Microsoft GUI paradigm that just compiling a simple C program can involve a lot of mouse pushing and button clicking. If you're going to start a major project developing a Windows application, that's not such a big deal, but we really don't need to go through all that just to write a simple Python extension. The alternative is to bypass the Visual Studio environment completely.

Although one can use the Microsoft C compiler and linker from the Windows command line, this is not an exercise for the faint of heart. An easier alternative is to install the MinGW (Minimalist GNU for Windows) compiler for Windows. It isn't hard to install and provides a *gcc* experience for creating Python extensions. A detailed step-by-step description of how to install and configure MinGW can be found here:

http://boodebr.org/main/python/build-windows-extensions

Developing Software in C

C is a purely procedural compiled language. All functionality is encapsulated into functions, and C programs are structured such that they are collections of functions grouped into files (roughly the equivalent of Python's modules). Each file may also include some global variables and various preprocessor directives. In a C source file global variables can be designated as *static*, which effectively hides them from functions outside of the current file.

A C source code file is compiled into an object file, which in turn is linked with other object files (either part of the immediate program or perhaps system library object files) to produce a final executable object. I should point out that the terms "object file," "library object," and "executable object" have nothing to do with object-oriented programming. These are historical terms from the days of mainframes and refrigerator-size minicomputers.

In the procedural paradigm a program's functions are the primary focus and are distinct from the data they operate on, whereas in object-oriented programming the data and the methods unique to that data are encapsulated into an object. Figure 4-1 attempts to illustrate this graphically.

Unlike Python programs, C programs are compiled directly into a binary form (machine language) that is executed by the CPU. There is no conversion into an intermediate bytecode form, and no virtual processor to interpret the bytecode. C is thus considered to be "close to the metal," and it is commonly used in applications where performance and compactness are primary considerations. Operating systems are a primary example. C and its OO cousin C++ are also typical first choices for creating *libraries*, which are collections of functions that can be reused in other programs. In fact, C is so close to the underlying hardware that it has sometimes been jokingly referred to as an assembler with fancy clothing, and most C compilers have an option to output the assembly language that corresponds to the original source code.

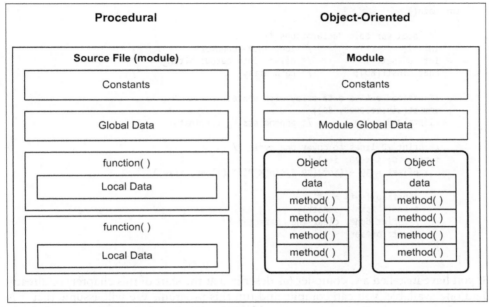

Procedural	Object-Oriented
Source File (module)	**Module**
Constants	Constants
Global Data	Module Global Data
function( ) / Local Data	**Object** data / method( ) / method( ) / method( ) / method( ) **Object** data / method( ) / method( ) / method( ) / method( )
function( ) / Local Data	

Figure 4-1. Procedural versus OO functional organization

A Simple C Program

Most tutorials on C start off with the infamous "hello world" program example. I would prefer to start with something a bit more substantial, but still (hopefully) comprehensible. My selection for this is a simple program that generates a plot of a sine wave using nothing more than simple printable characters. If you've ever taken a college-level programming class, you may well have encountered something very much like this.

Every standalone C program has a starting point in the form of a function named main(). Some C programs are not intended to be standalone modules, but rather are libraries (collections) of functions for other modules to use. In those cases, there is no main() function; it is provided by some other part of the application. For a quick peek at a small C program, consider the following example:

```
/*  sine_print.c
    Print a sideways sine wave pattern using ASCII characters

    Outputs an 80-byte array of ASCII characters (otherwise
    known as a string) 20 times, each time replacing elements
    in the array with an asterisk ('*') character to create a
    sideways plot of a sine function.
*/

#include <stdio.h>      /* for I/O functions        */
#include <math.h>       /* for the sine function    */
#include <string.h>     /* for the memset function  */
```

```
int main()
{
    /* local variable declarations */
    int  i;              /* loop index counter        */
    int  offset;         /* offset into output string */
    char sinstr[80];     /* data array                */

    /* preload entire data array with spaces */
    memset(sinstr,0x20, 80);
    sinstr[79] = '\0';   /* append string terminator  */

    /* print 20 lines to cover one cycle */
    for(i = 0; i < 20; i++) {
        offset = 39 + (int)(39 * sin(M_PI * (float) i/10));

        sinstr[offset] = '*';
        printf("%s\n", sinstr);
        /* print done, clear the character */
        sinstr[offset] = ' ';
    }
}
```

If you have installed a C compiler (as described at the start of this chapter) or already had one available, you can compile and run this program. We will assume that it is named *sine_print.c*. On Linux, one would do the following:

```
% gcc sine_print.c -o sine_print
% chmod 775 sine_print
% ./sine_print
```

The output should look like that shown in Figure 4-2.

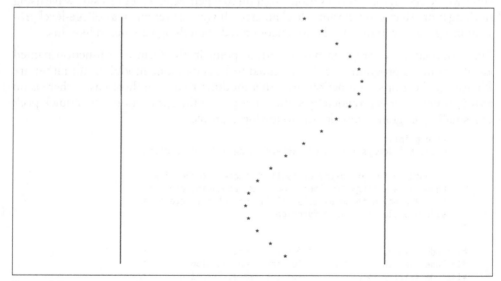

Figure 4-2. sine_print output

I chose to start with this example rather than "hello world" because it illustrates several key features of the C language. We'll go through them quickly here, and then examine them in more detail in later sections.

The first eight lines are a comment block. In C, comment blocks begin with /* and end with */. A comment block may span more than one line.

 Although you may see the // comment notation in ANSI C programs (I have, many times), it is not part of the ANSI C standard. // is valid comment notation for C++ programs, and most modern ANSI C/C++ compilers also honor it. However, its use in pure C programs is not recommended.

Next, we have three #include statements. These specify external files to be included in the program, that is, separate files that will be read in and merged into the existing code before the compiler is invoked. The #include statement is not actually part of the C language itself: it is a preprocessor directive. The preprocessor recognizes a number of reserved words; in fact, preprocessor directives could be considered a minimal language in their own right. The preprocessor also removes all comments from the source code before it is passed on to the compiler.

Next comes the declaration of the function main(). In C, a function's return type is declared before the function name, and if it has no return type specification the int type is used by default. As in Python, the use of arguments is optional, so here we have an empty set of parentheses.

C uses curly brackets (the { and } characters) to mark the start and end of blocks of code. A block may contain zero or more statements. C is a free-format language, and so long as the syntax is correct and there is at least one whitespace character between names (or *tokens*, as they are called), the compiler doesn't care how much additional whitespace there is. As a result, one can create perfectly valid programs in C that are almost impossible for a human reader to decipher. There is even an annual contest to write the most obfuscated C program. We will endeavor to avoid writing code like that.

The *sine_print* program declares three local variables, i, offset, and sinstr. The variables i and offset are integers, and sinstr is an array of characters (bytes). These variables persist only for as long as *sine_print* persists, and they are actual memory locations, not objects as in Python.

Next up is a call to the standard C library function memset(). This sets all the elements of sinstr to space characters. Notice that it has three parameters. The first is the target memory location, which in this case is sinstr. The second is the character value we want to write into memory starting at the location of the first element of the array sinstr, which is an ASCII space character (its value is 0x20 in hexadecimal notation, or 32 in decimal). Finally, there is an integer that specifies how many elements sinstr has (that is, its size—in this case, 80). Notice that although sinstr is an array, we didn't write it like one. This is because of the close relationship in C between arrays and pointers, which we'll get to shortly. For now, you can safely assume that using the name of an array variable without an index is equivalent to specifying the memory address of the zeroth element in the array. So, in a nutshell, memset() will fill 80 consecutive memory locations with the space character starting at the address of the zeroth element of the character array sinstr.

Now notice the assignment statement on the following line. In C, a string is always terminated with a so-called *string null*. This is really nothing more than an 8-bit zero value. As you may recall, Python does not use string terminators, because a Python string object "knows" how big it is when it is instantiated. In C, a string is just another type of array, and without the terminator it is very possible for code to "walk off the end" of the string.

Now that the string array has been initialized, the fun can start. The for loop modifies sinstr 20 times and prints each modification to *stdout*. Within the for loop, the first statement computes where to place an asterisk using C's sin() function from the math library and writes this value to the variable offset. The index counter i is divided by 10 and used to divide up the value of *pi* from the math library. The constant value 39 in the offset calculation statement determines where the output will start relative to the start of the string array.

The variable offset is used as an index into sinstr to change the space character at that location to an asterisk. The entire string in sinstr is then printed, including the newly inserted asterisk. After the string has been printed, the asterisk in the string array is replaced by a space and the process is repeated again.

Finally, the program returns a value of zero and terminates.

Preprocessor Directives

C provides a preprocessor that supports capabilities such as file inclusion (#include) and named literals (#define), to name the two most commonly used functions. The #define preprocessor directive is commonly referred to as a *macro*. The preprocessor also provides a basic conditional test and control capability (#if, #elif, #ifdef, #ifndef, #else, and #endif), and the ability to "undefine" a macro definition (#undef). Notice that the preprocessor directives begin with a pound (hash) symbol. These are not comments, as in Python.

In some C implementations, the preprocessor is a separate program that is invoked as the first step in the compilation sequence, but can also be run by itself if necessary. The preprocessor scans the source file, acting on any directives encountered and stripping out comments. What comes out the other end will usually look quite different from what goes in (sometimes radically so). The output is in a form that the compiler can deal with directly: pure C language tokens, whitespace characters, and nothing more.

For most of what we'll be doing, we won't need the more advanced capabilities of the preprocessor. We just need to be able to include files in our code, define some constants, and then let the compiler have at it.

#include

The #include directive, as its name implies, is used to include the contents of one file into another. For example, it is often used to include the contents of a header file, which, as *its* name implies, is included at the start of a source file. Header files typically contain things like function definitions for code in other modules or library objects, and macro definitions related to those functions. The #include directive could also be used to include one source file into another, but this is generally frowned upon. We will look at header files and how they are used when we discuss the structure of a C program.

An #include statement must appear before the contents of the file that it refers to are used, and it is common practice (and a Very Good Idea) to place these statements at the start of a source file. In the example program we looked at earlier (*sine_print.c*), there are three #include directives at the top of the listing:

```
#include <stdio.h>      /* for I/O functions        */
#include <math.h>       /* for the sine function    */
#include <string.h>     /* for the memset function  */
```

These tell the preprocessor to include the contents of the files *stdio.h*, *math.h*, and *string.h* into our program. These are part of the standard library for C, and all three of these files contain #define statements, function declarations, and even more #include statements. They contain everything necessary to make use of the standard I/O functions (printf(), memset(), and the value of *pi*) and the sin() function from the basic math facilities available in the libraries that come with the C compiler.

#define

The #define macro directive associates a name (a string) with a substitution string. Anywhere in the source code where the macro name occurs, it will be replaced with the substitution string. #define macro names can appear anywhere where it would be valid to type in the substitution string. Consider the following example:

```
#define UP    1
#define DOWN  0

if (avar < bvar) {
    return DOWN;
}
else {
    return UP;
}
```

After the source has been through the preprocessor, it will look something like this:

```
if (avar < bvar) {
    return 0;
```

```
    }
    else {
        return 1;
    }
```

The #define macro is commonly used to define constants that are used in various places in one or more source modules. This is much preferable to using literal values as "naked numbers" typed directly into the source. The primary reason is that if a program has a constant used in calculations in multiple places, using one macro in a common included file makes it much easier to change and is less error-prone than hunting through the code for each occurrence of the literal value and replacing it. Also, unless there is a comment specifically stating that some literal value is a special constant, it might be difficult to tell the difference between two constants of the same value that are used for completely different purposes. Changing the wrong literal value could lead to highly annoying results.

#define is also sometimes used to define a complex statement or set of statements, and supports the ability to accept variables. This is really where it gets the macro moniker. Here's a simple example:

```
#define MAX(a, b)    ((a) > (b)?(a) : (b))
```

The ternary conditional (?:) is a shorthand way of testing the (a) > (b) expression. If it evaluates to true, the value of (a) is returned; otherwise, (b) is the result. This is a somewhat risky macro, however, because if a happened to be of the form ++a (which we will discuss shortly) it would get evaluated twice—once in the comparison and once when it is returned as the result—and its value would be incremented twice. This might not be the desired result.

If we were to put the two #define statements from this example into their own file, called *updown.h*, it could then be included in any other C source file that needed those definitions:

```
/* updown.h */

#define UP     1
#define DOWN   0
```

And here is how it is used:

```
#include "updown.h"

if (avar < bvar) {
    return DOWN;
}
else {
    return UP;
}
```

When *updown.h* is included into the program source, the result is the same as if the two #define statements had been written into the code from the outset.

As a final example before we move on, here is what *sine_print.c* looks like if #define macros are used instead of simple literals in the code (I've named this version *sine_print2.c*):

```
/*  sine_print2.c
    Print a sideways sine wave pattern using ASCII characters

    Outputs an 80-byte array of ASCII characters (otherwise
    known as a string) 20 times, each time replacing elements
    in the array with an asterisk ('*') character to create a
    sideways plot of a sine function.

    Incorporates #define macro for constants.
 */

#include <stdio.h>         /* for I/O functions        */
#include <math.h>          /* for the sine function    */
#include <string.h>        /* for the memset function  */

#define MAXLINES    20
#define MAXCHARS    80
#define MAXSTR      (MAXCHARS-1)
#define MIDPNT      ((MAXCHARS/2)-1)
#define SCALEDIV    10

int main()
{
    /* local variable declarations */
    int  i;                  /* loop index counter       */
    int  offset;             /* offset into output string */
    char sinstr[MAXCHARS];   /* data array               */

    /* preload entire data array with spaces */
    memset(sinstr, 0x20, MAXCHARS);
    sinstr[MAXSTR] = '\0';   /* append string terminator */

    /* print MAXLINES lines to cover one cycle */
    for(i = 0; i < MAXLINES; i++) {
        offset = MIDPNT + (int)(MIDPNT * sin(M_PI * (float) i/SCALEDIV));

        sinstr[offset] = '*';
        printf("%s\n", sinstr);
        /* print done, clear the character */
        sinstr[offset] = ' ';
    }
}
```

This version makes it much easier to see what happens if one changes the maximum line length from 80 to, say, 40 characters. The #define macros for MAXSTR and MIDPNT are computed from the value defined by MAXCHARS, so all one needs to do is change MAXCHARS to 40. It should be noted that when the macro substitutions for MAXSTR and MIDPNT occur in the code, it will look like this when the C compiler gets it from the preprocessor:

```
    sinstr[(80-1)] = '\0';
```

and:

```
    sinstr[((80/2)-1) + (int)( ((80/2)-1) * sin(3.14159265358979323846 \
    * (float) i/10))] = '*';
```

The M_PI macro is supplied by the included file *math.h*, and in this case is defined as:

```
    3.14159265358979323846
```

Try changing MAXCHARS to 40 or 20 and then recompile the program to see for yourself how this works.

Standard Data Types

C has only four fundamental numeric data types. These are listed in Table 4-1.

Table 4-1. Basic C data types

Type	Description
char	A single byte (8 bits). Signed unless specified as unsigned.
int	An integer, which is typically the size of native integer values on the host system. Commonly found in either 16- or 32-bit sizes. Signed unless specified as unsigned.
float	A single-precision floating-point value, typically expressed in 32 bits (4 bytes). Always signed.
double	A double-precision floating-point value, typically expressed in 64 bits (8 bytes). Always signed.

In addition, there are four modifiers that can be applied to the basic types to specify the amount of storage that should be allocated and the expected range. They are short, long, signed, and unsigned.

Putting it all together yields the type definitions shown in Table 4-2.

Table 4-2. Extended C data types

Type	Bytes	Range
unsigned char	1	0 to 255
signed char	1	−128 to 127
char (same as signed char)	1	−128 to 127
short (int)	2	−32,768 to 32,767
unsigned short (int)	2	0 to 65,535
unsigned int	4	0 to 4,294,967,295
signed int	4	−2,147,483,648 to 2,147,483,647
int (same as signed int)	4	−2,147,483,648 to 2,147,483,647
unsigned long	4	0 to 4,294,967,295
long (int)	4	−2,147,483,648 to 2,147,483,647

Type	Bytes	Range
float	4	approximately +/– 3.4 E +/–38
double	8	approximately +/– 1.798 E +/–308
long double	12	(Note: 12 bytes, not 16)

 These are typical range values. Actual ranges depend on machine architecture and implementation. Refer to your C compiler documentation for details.

There is no string type in C; a string is just an array of type char with the last element containing a zero as a terminator value. In C, strings are alterable (or mutable, to borrow Python's terminology) arrays just like any other array.

One will often encounter the use of short and long without the int portion of the type name. When specifying a short or long integer type, the int is implied, and although the compiler will (or at least, should) accept the int keyword, it is not necessary. Also, unless specifically stated otherwise, all integer types are assumed to be signed.

Lastly, we should mention the void keyword. It's not a type in the conventional sense, but rather serves as a placeholder that indicates an undefined type. It is typically used to indicate that a function returns nothing (the default expected return type for a function is int), or as a placeholder for a pointer that can refer to any valid memory location (we'll discuss pointers later).

User-Defined Types

C allows the programmer to define an identifier that represents an existing data type or a construct that incorporates existing data types. For example:

```
typedef signed short    int16_t;
typedef unsigned short  uint16_t;
typedef float           float32_t;
typedef double          float64_t;
```

These are actually found in the header file */usr/include/sys/types.h*.

If these are defined, one can write:

```
int16_t var1, var2;
```

and it will mean the same thing as:

```
short var1, var2;
```

typedef can also be used to create new type definitions for things like pointers and structures.

Operators

C provides the usual selection of arithmetic, logical, and comparison operators. It also has some rather unique unary (single-operand) operators such as pre- and post-increment, pre- and post-decrement, logical negation, and unary plus and minus (arithmetic negation).

Some operators appear more than once in the following tables to reflect their status as members of more than one class of operations.

Arithmetic operators

The arithmetic operators (see Table 4-3) in C are much like the arithmetic operators in any other language.

Table 4-3. C arithmetic operators

Operator	Description
+	Addition
-	Subtraction
*	Multiplication
/	Division
%	Modulus

One does need to be careful, however, when performing operations on variables of different types. For example, when two integer types are used, the smaller type is "promoted" to a size equal to that of the larger type. Thus, if a short integer is added to a long, the short is promoted to a long for the operation.

Unary operators

C's unary operators (shown in Table 4-4) perform a specific action on one, and only one, variable. They will not work on expressions, but they can appear in expressions.

Table 4-4. C unary operators

Operator	Description
+a	Unary plus
-a	Unary minus (arithmetic negation)
++a	Pre-increment
a++	Post-increment
--a	Pre-decrement
a--	Post-decrement
!a	Logical negation (NOT)

Operator	Description
~a	Bitwise one's complement (NOT)
*	Pointer dereference (see section on pointers)
&	Memory address (see section on pointers)

These operators might need a few words of explanation. The unary plus and minus operators change the sign of a variable. Consider the following bit of code:

```
#include <stdio.h>
void main() {
    int a, b;

    a = 5;
    printf("%d\n", a);
    b = -a;
    printf("%d\n", b);
}
```

When this code is compiled and executed, the following output is generated:

```
5
-5
```

The increment and decrement operators increase or decrease the value of a variable by 1. When this occurs is determined by the location of the operators. If the ++ or -- operator appears before the variable, the increment or decrement operation occurs before any subsequent operations using that variable. If the ++ or -- operator appears after the variable name, the increment or decrement occurs after the indicated operation. The following code shows how this works:

```
#include <stdio.h>

void main()
{
    int a = 0;
    int b;

    b = ++a;
    printf("a: %d, b: %d\n", a, b);
    a = 0;
    b = a++;
    printf("a: %d, b: %d\n", a, b);
}
```

The output looks like this:

```
a: 1, b: 1
a: 1, b: 0
```

In the first case, the value of a is incremented and then assigned to b. In the second case, the assignment occurs before the increment (the increment is a post-increment), so b gets a's original starting value, not the incremented value.

The ! and ~ operators work as one might expect. It is common to see expressions of the form:

```
a = !(b > c);
```

which means that if b is greater than c, the result will be false, even though the b > c part of the expression is true. It is logically negated. The binary negation (~, one's complement) operator inverts the sense of each bit in a variable, so that a variable with a bitwise value of:

```
00100010
```

becomes the complement of the original value:

```
11011101
```

We will discuss the * and & operators when we get to pointers, so we'll put those aside for now.

Assignment and augmented assignment operators

The C language provides a number of useful assignment operators. These are shown in Table 4-5.

Table 4-5. C assignment operators

Operator	Description
=	Basic assignment
+=	Addition *and* assignment
-=	Subtraction *and* assignment
*=	Multiplication *and* assignment
/=	Division *and* assignment
%=	Modulus *and* assignment
<<=	Assignment by bitwise left shift
>>=	Assignment by bitwise right shift
&=	Assignment by bitwise AND
|=	Assignment by bitwise OR
^=	Assignment by bitwise XOR

The assignment operator in C works by copying a value into a memory location. If we have two variables and we write:

```
x = y;
```

the value contained in the memory location called y will be copied into the memory location called x. Note that both x and y must have already been declared before an assignment can take place, so that the compiler can allocate memory space for the variable ahead of time.

As in most other modern programming languages, C's augmented assignment operators work by performing the indicated operation using the values of the variables on either side of the operator and then assigning the result back into the lefthand variable. So, if we have an expression that looks like this:

```
cnt += 10;
```

we can expect that the value cnt will have 10 added to it and the sum will then be assigned back to cnt.

Comparison operators

C's comparison and relational operators (shown in Table 4-6) only work on numeric values. They don't work on strings, structures, or arrays, although it is possible to compare two characters, as in ("a" < "b"). In this case the result will be true, since the numeric ASCII value of "a" is less than the numeric value of "b". C simply treats them as byte values.

Table 4-6. C comparison and relational operators

Operator	Description
<	Less than
<=	Less than or equal to
>	Greater than
>=	Greater than or equal to
!=	Not equal to
==	Equal to

Expressions that use comparison operators always return a logical true or false. In C, false is defined as zero (0), and anything else is considered to be true (although the value 1 is typically given this honor). The operands may be single variables or other expressions, which allows for some rather complex compound expressions.

Logical operators

C provides three logical operators, shown in Table 4-7.

Table 4-7. C logical operators

Operator	Description
!a	Logical negation (NOT)
&&	Logical AND
||	Logical OR

C's logical operators act on the truth values of the operands. Thus, a statement such as this:

```
tval = !x && (y < z);
```

has a truth table that looks like Table 4-8.

Table 4-8. Truth table for tval

tval	x	(y < z)
F	F	F
T	F	T
F	T	F
F	T	T

In this case, `tval` will be assigned a true value if and only if x is false and the expression (y < z) evaluates to true.

Bitwise operators

The rich set of bitwise operators found in C is a legacy of its long history as a systems-level language, and these operators are ideally suited to applications that are "close to the metal." Table 4-9 lists C's bitwise operators. Manipulating the bits in a hardware register is much easier to do in a low- to mid-level language like C than in a high-level language such as Python.

Table 4-9. C bitwise operators

Operator	Description
<<	Bitwise left shift
>>	Bitwise right shift
~a	Bitwise one's complement (NOT)
&	Bitwise AND
		Bitwise OR
^	Bitwise XOR
<<=	Assignment by bitwise left shift
>>=	Assignment by bitwise right shift
&=	Assignment by bitwise AND
|=	Assignment by bitwise OR
^=	Assignment by bitwise XOR

C extends the concept of augmented assignment by including bitwise operations. The shift-assign operators shift the value of the lefthand operand in a bitwise fashion either left or right by the number of bits specified in the righthand operand, and assign the result to the lefthand operand.

If we have a variable that contains the value 1 and we shift it left by 2, the result will be the value 4. This is shown graphically in Figure 4-3.

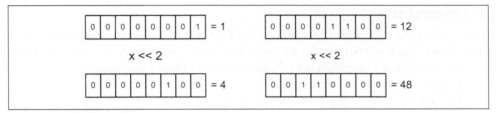

Figure 4-3. Bitwise left shift

In the first case (on the left), the original value of 1 becomes 4. In the second case, the original value of 12 becomes 48. A left shift is, in effect, multiplication by powers of 2 wherein the original value is multiplied by 2^n, where n is the number of bit positions shifted. Conversely, a right shift is equivalent to division. And, yes, one can do some speedy math tricks using shifts, but only if it works out that a power of 2 is suitable for the operation.

The AND, OR, and XOR bitwise operators map across bit-to-bit between the operands. The AND and OR operators are used fairly heavily in situations where one must manipulate the individual bits in a hardware register, such as might be found in an interface circuit of some kind. The bitwise AND is often used to isolate a particular bit in an integer value, which may have been read from a hardware register. The following code snippet shows how the AND operator can be used (we'll assume that the variables have all been properly defined elsewhere):

```
regval = ReadReg(regaddr);
if (regval > 0) {
    if (regval & 0x08)
        SetDevice(devnum, SET_ON);
    else
        SetDevice(devnum, SET_OFF);

    regval &= 0xf7;
    WriteReg(regaddr, regval);
}
```

The first step is to obtain the current contents of a hardware register and write the data into the variable **regval**. Next, **regval** is checked to see if any bits are set (it will be > 0). If so, then the bit at position 2^3 (0x08) is tested by "masking" all the other bits. With the AND operator, if the 2^3 bit is 1, the result will be nonzero (it will be 0x08, actually) and the TRUE portion of the second if statement will be executed. Otherwise, the

FALSE portion of the if will be executed. Lastly, the snippet clears the 2^3 bit by applying the one's complement of 0x08 (which is 0xf7) and writes the value back into the hardware register. If the bit at the 2^3 position in regval is already 0, it will remain 0. This could have the effect of resetting a trigger condition or perhaps terminating some action in the external physical world. Figure 4-4 shows how the snippet operates on the bits in regval.

Operator precedence

To complete our overview of operators in C, we need to consider the subject of operator precedence. Each operator in C has a specific priority, or precedence, in the order of execution when an expression is evaluated. Consider these two expressions:

```
2 * 4 + 12
2 * (4 + 12)
```

They may look similar, but they will give very different results. The first expression will yield a value of 20. The second will yield a value of 32. The reason is that the multiplication operator has a higher precedence than the addition operator, so unless the compiler is told otherwise by mean of parentheses grouping, it will perform the multiplication first.

Associativity also affects how an expression will be evaluated. In general terms, associativity defines how evaluation of an expression associates operands with operators, and in which direction, for operators of the same precedence. For example, if we have the following:

```
3 + 5 + 7 - 2 + 6
```

the addition and subtraction operators associate left to right. The result is the same as if the expression had been written as:

```
((((3 + 5) + 7) - 2) + 6)
```

Now consider this expression:

```
3 + 2 * 6 + 8 / 4
```

Multiplication and division also associate left to right, but they are of a higher precedence than addition or subtraction, so this expression could be stated as:

```
((3 + (2 * 6)) + (8 / 4))
```

If a different outcome is desired, parentheses can be used to group the operands accordingly.

In general, it is a good idea to use parentheses to make the original intent clear rather than relying on the precedence and associativity rules of a language. The result is more readable and less prone to misinterpretation.

Table 4-10 lists the operators available in C in order of precedence, from highest to lowest, along with the associativity of each.

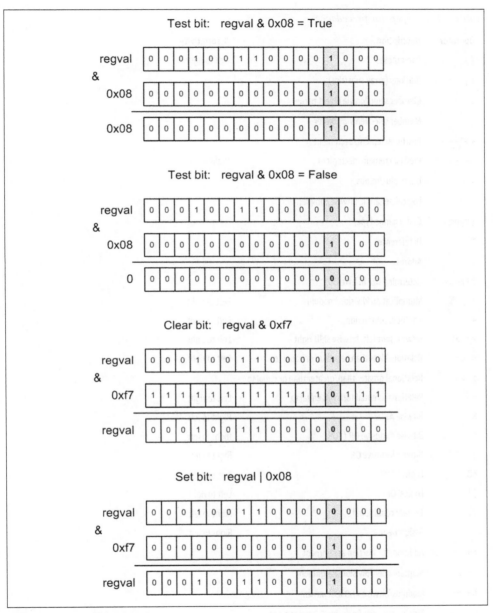

Figure 4-4. Using C's AND operator

Table 4-10. C operator precedence

Operator	Description	Associativity
()	Parentheses	Left to right
[]	Brackets (array subscript)	
.	Member selection via object name	
->	Member selection via pointer	
++ --	Postfix increment/decrement	
++ --	Prefix increment/decrement	Right to left
+ -	Unary plus/minus	
! ~	Logical negation/bitwise complement	
(type)	Cast (change type)	
*	Dereference	
&	Address	
sizeof	Determine size in bytes	
* / %	Multiplication/division/modulus	Left to right
+ -	Addition/subtraction	Left to right
<< >>	Bitwise shift left, bitwise shift right	Left to right
< <=	Relational less than/less than or equal to	Left to right
> >=	Relational greater than/greater than or equal to	
== !=	Relational is equal to/is not equal to	Left to right
&	Bitwise AND	Right to left
^	Bitwise exclusive OR (XOR)	Right to left
|	Bitwise inclusive OR	Right to left
&&	Logical AND	Left to right
||	Logical OR	Left to right
?:	Ternary conditional	Right to left
=	Assignment	Right to left
+= -=	Addition/subtraction assignment	
*= /=	Multiplication/division assignment	
%= &=	Modulus/bitwise AND assignment	
^= |=	Bitwise exclusive/inclusive OR assignment	
<<= >>=	Bitwise left/right shift assignment	
,	Comma (separate expressions)	Left to right

Expressions

An expression in C makes use of one or more of the available operators to define a computational action. This might be as straightforward as a comparison, or as complex as a multivariable Boolean equation. When used within control statements (which we will examine shortly), an expression is always enclosed in parentheses. Expressions used in an assignment statement may have optional parentheses to help establish the desired order of operations to be performed. Parenthesized expressions always return a value as a side effect, which may or may not be useful.

Statements

A C program is composed of statements. A statement is executable code, such as an assignment, a function call, a control statement, or a combination of these. Statements consist of tokens (variable and function names), expressions, and possibly other statements. C is a logically rich language and allows for a great deal of flexibility in how statements are assembled by the programmer.

Assignment statements copy the value of whatever is on the right side of the assignment operator to the token on the left side. The lefthand token must be a variable (either a single variable, an element in an array, or a member of a structure), whereas the righthand operand may be any valid variable name, a constant, an expression, or a statement that returns a value. One cannot assign a value to a function or a constant, but one can assign the return value of a function or the value of a constant to a variable.

A function call statement transfers program execution to another function. It might be within the same module as the calling function, or it in another module altogether. When the external function finishes and returns, control resumes at the next statement following the call statement. It is common to see a combination of an assignment with a function call, like this:

```
ret_val = ext_function();
```

The control statements of a C program control program execution. There are various types of control statements available to perform branching, implement loops, and directly transfer control to another part of the program.

Groups of statements are referred to as *statement blocks*, and are delimited using the curly brace characters ({}).

if-else statement

The if statement is used to direct control flow, or the path of execution, through the code. The test expression will be evaluated as either true (any nonzero value) or false (a zero). The basic form of if statement looks like this:

```
if (expression) {
    statement(s)
}
```

If only a single statement is used, the curly braces are optional.

In a simple `if` statement, when (*expression*) is true, the statement or statements associated with the `if` are executed. Because C is an unstructured language, one could also write a simple `if` like this:

```
if (expression) statement;
```

or:

```
if (expression) {statement; statement;}
```

While there are situations where this might make the intent of the code more readable and concise, it should be used sparingly, if at all.

The `else` statement allows for an alternative to handle the condition where (*expression*) evaluates to false and some alternative action is necessary:

```
if (expression1) {
    statements(s)
}
else {
    statements(s)
}
```

If (*expression*) is true, the first block of statements is executed; otherwise, the second block of statements is executed.

Multiple conditional tests may be grouped into a set of alternative actions by using the `else if` statement:

```
if (expression1) {
    /* block 1 */
    statements(s)
}
else if (expression2) {
    /* block 2 */
    statements(s)
}
else if (expression3) {
    /* block 3 */
    statements(s)
}
else {
    /* block 4 */
    statements(s)
}
```

If (*expression1*) is true, the statements in block 1 are executed. If *expression1* is not true, (*expression2*) is evaluated, and if it is true the statements in block 2 are executed. The same applies to (*expression3*). If none of the expressions are true, the statements in block 4 under the final `else` are executed. Note that the use of the last `else` is optional.

switch statement

The `switch` statement is used to select an execution path based on the value of an expression. The value of the expression is compared to a constant and, if it matches, the statement or statements associated with that branch are executed:

```
switch (expression) {
    case constant:    statement;
    case constant:    statement;
    case constant:    statement;
    default:          statement;
}
```

The constant may be a `char`, an `int`, a `float`, or a `double`, and all case values must be unique. The optional `default` statement is executed if none of the `case` statements are matched.

If more than one statement is used with a `case` statement, the statements do not need to be grouped into a block using curly braces, although it is syntactically legal to do so:

```
switch (expression) {
    case constant:
        statement;
        statement;
    case constant: {
        statement;
        statement;
        statement;
        }
}
```

One tricky—and often misunderstood—behavior of a `switch` statement is called fall-through. Consider the following example program, *c_switch.c*:

```
/* C switch example */
#include <stdio.h>

int main(void)
{
    int c;

    while ((c = getchar()) != EOF) {
        if (c == '.')
            break;

        switch(c) {
            case '0':
                printf("Numeral 0\n");
            case '1':
                printf("Numeral 1\n");
            case '2':
                printf("Numeral 2\n");
            case '3':
                printf("Numeral 3\n");
        }
```

```
        }
    }
```

This compiles just fine, and when a period (.) is entered the `while` loop is exited using a `break` statement as it should, but the output looks like this:

```
0
Numeral 0
Numeral 1
Numeral 2
Numeral 3
1
Numeral 1
Numeral 2
Numeral 3
2
Numeral 2
Numeral 3
3
Numeral 3
.
```

What is happening here is that when a `case` statement matches the variable `c`, it not only executes its statement, but then execution "falls through" and all subsequent statements are executed. This may not be what was intended (although there are some cases where this behavior might be desirable). In order to prevent fall-through, the `break` statement can be used. Here is the revised version of *c_switch.c* with `break` statements:

```c
/* C switch example */
#include <stdio.h>

int main(void)
{
    int c;

    while ((c = getchar()) != EOF) {
        if (c == '.')
            break;

        switch(c) {
            case '0':
                printf("Numeral 0\n"); break;
            case '1':
                printf("Numeral 1\n"); break;
            case '2':
                printf("Numeral 2\n"); break;
            case '3':
                printf("Numeral 3\n");
        }
    }
}
```

The output now looks like what we would expect:

```
0
Numeral 0
1
Numeral 1
2
Numeral 2
3
Numeral 3
1
Numeral 1
3
Numeral 3
2
Numeral 2
.
```

One should always use `break` statements in a `switch` construct unless there is a very good and compelling reason not to do so. The `default` statement is also a good idea. In some coding style requirements, such as those employed in the aerospace industry, a `default` statement is always required, even if it does nothing. One use for a `switch` construct with a `default` statement is as an input verifier. Suppose a function expects a specific set of input parameter values, and anything else is an error that must be trapped and handled. Here's a simple example code snippet:

```
switch(inval) {
    case 0:
    case 1:
    case 2:
    case 3:
        rc = OK;
        break;
    default:
        rc = BAD_VAL;
}
```

This will set the variable `rc` (i.e., the return code) to whatever the macro `OK` is defined to be if the input value (`inval`) is between 0 and 3, inclusive. If it is anything else, `rc` is set to `BAD_VAL`. It is assumed that `rc` will be checked further down in the code to handle the invalid input condition. Although one could have written an equivalent bit of code using an `if` and comparison operators, like so:

```
if ((inval >= 0) && (inval <= 3)) {
    rc = OK;
else
    rc = BAD_VAL;
```

the `switch` method also handles noncontiguous sequences of values quite nicely without resorting to long and complex combinations of logical and comparison operators.

while loop

The while loop executes a statement or block of statements so long as a test expression evaluates to true:

```
while (expression) {
    statement(s)
}
```

Because the test expression is evaluated before the body of the loop, it is possible that it may not execute any of its statements at all.

do-while loop

The do-while loop is similar to while, but the loop test expression is not evaluated until the end of the loop's statement block:

```
do {
    statement(s)
} while (expression);
```

The statement or statements in the body of a do-while loop will always be executed at least once, whereas in the while loop they might not be executed at all if the test expression evaluates to false.

for loop

The for loop is typically used as a counting loop, although it is not restricted to using just numeric types:

```
for (<initialization expression>, <test expression>, <iteration expression>) {
    statement(s)
}
```

The for statement contains three distinct components, all of which are optional. When the test expression is omitted, the logical value is assumed to always be true. The initialization and iteration expressions are treated as no-ops when either or both are omitted. The semicolons in the syntax are sufficient to indicate the omission of one or more of the expressions.

For example, a for loop can omit the initialization and test expressions:

```
int i = 0;

for (; ; i++) {
    if (i > 9)
        break;
}
```

To emulate an unbounded loop, all of the for loop's expressions can be omitted:

```
int i = 0;

for (;;) {
    if (++i > 9)
```

```
        break;
    }
```

"Unbounded" in this case simply means that there is no implicit way for the loop to terminate. If the internal test never becomes true, the loop will execute forever.

C's **for** loop is very flexible, but it is typically found in the role of a counting loop (by way of contrast, a **for** statement in Python is designed to iterate through a range of values or data objects). The initialization expression establishes the starting value of a loop counter variable, the test expression controls execution of the loop (it will execute so long as the test expression is true), and the iteration expression is invoked each time through the loop immediately after the test expression is evaluated. The following code snippet illustrates this:

```
int i;

for (i = 0; i < 10; i++) {
    /* statements go here */
};
```

The loop starts with the value of the counter variable **i** set to **0**. The statements in the body of the loop are then executed and the counter variable is incremented by 1. It is then tested and, if the result is true, the loop repeats.

break statement

The **break** statement is used to terminate, or break out of, a loop (**while**, **do**, or **for**) or a **switch** construct. When it is encountered, it will cause the surrounding loop to terminate. No further statements in the loop's statement block will be executed. The *c_switch.c* example shown earlier demonstrated the use of **break** in both a loop and a **switch** context.

continue statement

The **continue** statement forces execution to immediately branch back to the top of a loop. It is used only with **while**, **do**, and **for** loops. No statements following the **continue** statement are executed.

goto statement

The C language provides a statement that is inherently dangerous, potentially evil, and prone to much abuse and misuse. This is the **goto** statement, which, as you might surmise, causes program execution to abruptly jump to a labeled location in the code. As Kernighan and Ritchie put it: "Formally, the **goto** is never necessary, and in practice it is almost always easy to write code without it." Sage advice. We won't be using **goto** in any of the C code in this book.

Arrays and Pointers

Arrays and pointers are closely related in C; both refer to contiguous areas of memory set aside for data storage. Arrays have an inherent structure imposed by the type and the size (number of elements) specified when the array is declared. A pointer also references an area of memory that has structure and size, although how this is achieved differs from an array declaration, as we'll see shortly. Because of this close relationship, it is possible, for example, to refer to the contents of an array using a pointer. Conversely, an array index might be thought of as a pointer into a specific memory space.

In this section, we'll look at arrays and pointers and see how they are related. We'll also see exactly what pointers are and how they are used.

Arrays

An *array* is an ordered set of data items in a contiguous region in memory. Arrays are defined with a type when they are declared, and all the data elements in the array must be of that type. As we've already seen, a string in C is an array of char (byte) type data items. One can also have arrays of int, float, and double values, as well as pointers.

In C, an array is fixed in size. Its size cannot be changed once it is defined (actually, this is not entirely true if one is using pointers, but we'll get to that in a moment). Each element, or cell, in an array occupies the amount of memory required to hold a variable of the type of the array.

Here is a contrived example that will print each element in a string array on its own line of output:

```
#include <stdio.h>

int i;
char cval = ' ';

int main(void)
{
    char str[16] = "A test string\0";

    for (i = 0; cval != '\0'; i++) {
        cval = str[i];
        if (cval != '\0') printf("%c\n", cval);
    }
}
```

Notice that the string in str has a char zero value at the end. Without this, the for loop would run off the end of the array and into some other part of memory. Also notice that if cval contains the null character (\0), it is not printed.

Lastly, there is the array of pointers, which are treated as unsigned integer values of a size corresponding to the native address size of the underlying machine (typically 32 bits).

When an array is accessed using an index, the actual position in the array's memory space is based on the size of the data type of the array, as shown in Figure 4-5.

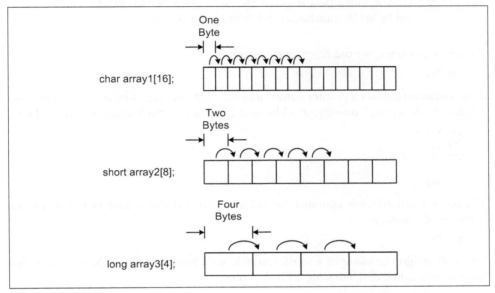

Figure 4-5. Array indexing

When the index of `array1` is incremented, it advances one byte (char). When the index of `array2` is incremented, it advances by two bytes. For `array3`, the index advances by four bytes. Note that in C array indexing is zero-based.

Pointers

A *pointer* is a variable that contains a memory address. This address might be that of another variable, or it could point to a contiguous region of memory. It might also be something like the address of a control register in an I/O device of some type. Pointers are a powerful concept, and they make some classes of problems much more tractable than would otherwise be possible. For this reason, C has sometimes been called "the language of pointers." Understanding what a pointer is and how to use it effectively is key to writing efficient and powerful programs in C. Occasionally one hears criticism leveled at C because of pointers, and while it is true that a stray pointer can cause serious problems, it is also true that if pointers are used carefully and with some discipline, the result is as safe and robust as any code written in a language that lacks the concept of a pointer.

For a real-life example of how pointers in C can be used to manage memory for image data processing on a spacecraft, see Chapter 3 of the book *Beautiful Data* (*http://oreilly.com/catalog/9780596157128/*), edited by Jeff Hammerbacher and Toby Segaran (O'Reilly).

To define a pointer, we use the * unary operator:

```
int *p;
```

This statement defines a pointer named p of type int, and it can be used to point to an integer data location. To assign an address to it, we can use the & unary operator, like so:

```
int x = 5;
int y;
int *p;

p = &x;
```

The pointer variable now contains the address of the variable x, and we can access the contents of x using p:

```
y = *p;
```

This will assign the value of x to the variable y. When the * operator is used in this fashion, it is called *dereferencing*, or *indirection*.

Pointers can be passed as parameters to functions. This allows a C function to manipulate data in some location outside of itself, or return more than just a single value. Here's a common swap function:

```
void swap (int *x, int *y)
{
    int tmp;
    tmp = *y;
    *y = *x;
    *x = tmp;
}
```

The parameters x and y are pointers provided by a calling function, like so:

```
int a = 10
int b = 20;

swap(&a, &b);
```

Note that when swap() is called, the & address operator is used to pass the addresses of the two variables a and b. When swap() returns, a will contain 20 and b will contain 10.

We stated earlier that arrays and pointers are related, and this is a good time to explore that relationship a bit further. In C, the first element in an array is the base address of the array's memory space. We can assign the base address of an array to a pointer using the & operator, like so:

```
int anarray[10];
int *p;
p = &anarray[0];
```

Since both `anarray` and `p` are defined as int types, these two statements are equivalent:

```
anarray[5];
*(p+5);
```

Both refer to the value stored at index position 5 in the `anarray` memory space. With the pointer form, the address it contains is incremented by five, not the value it is pointing to. If we had written *p+5, the array element at `anarray[0]` would have had 5 added to it instead. One can also assign the base address of an array to a pointer, like this:

```
p = anarray
```

This form implies `&anarray[0]` and is usually how an array base address is assigned to a pointer. The `&anarray[0]` form is not necessary; unless there is a specific need to reference the address of a particular array element other than the zeroth element, one would just use the array name.

Pointers can be used to point to things other than simple variables and arrays. A pointer can refer to a structure (discussed in the next section), or it can point to a function. Pointers in C take a little getting used to if one has never dealt with them before, but it is worth the effort to learn them as they allow for compact and efficient expressions that would otherwise be difficult, or even impossible, to achieve.

Structures

A *structure* in C is a collection of variables of different types. A structure has a unique name, and structures may include substructures.

Figure 4-6 shows a graphical representation of structure syntax.

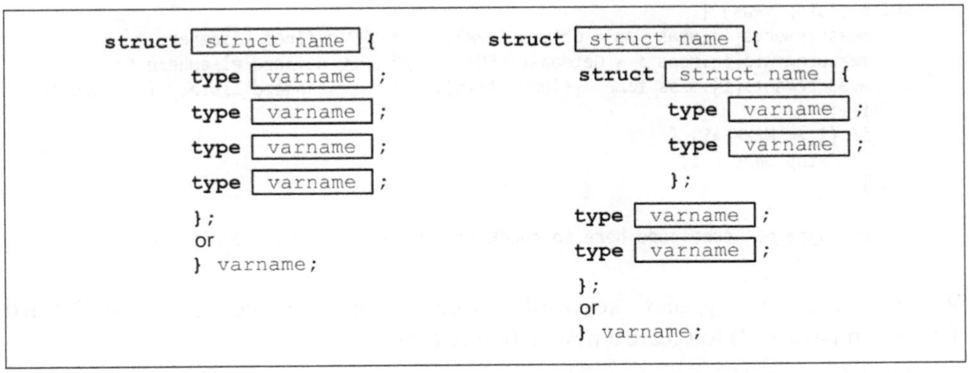

Figure 4-6. C structure syntax

Here is a definition for a simple structure that contains three variables that hold the result from a single input measurement of some sort:

```
struct measdata {
    float meas_vpp;
    float meas_f;
    long curr_time;
};
```

This, by itself, isn't particularly interesting, but if we had an array of these structures we would have a set of measurements:

```
struct measdata measurements [100];
```

Note that the structure definition does not allocate storage space—it is just a definition. In other words, it's a new programmer-defined type. We can also skip the extra step of declaring a variable of the structure type by appending one or more variable names to the structure definition:

```
struct measdata {
    float meas_vpp;
    float meas_f;
    long curr_time;
} measurements[100], single_meas;
```

The so-called "dot notation" is used to refer to a structure member. If we wanted the value of meas_vpp from the 47th measurement, we would use:

```
vpp_value = measurements[46].meas_vpp;
```

Here is a more fully realized example that will obtain up to 100 measurements from an input source:

```
#define MAXMEAS 100

struct measdata measurements [MAXMEAS];
int stop_meas = 0;
int i = 0;

while (!stop_meas) {
    measurements[i].meas_vpp = GetMeas(VPP);     /* VPP defined elsewhere */
    measurements[i].meas_f = GetMeas(FREQ);      /* FREQ defined elsewhere */
    measurements[i].meas_time = (long) time(); /* use standard library function */
    i++;
    if (i >= MAXMEAS) {
        stop_meas = 1;
    }

    /* maybe put some code here to check for an external stop condition */
}
```

We can use the typedef keyword (discussed in the section "User-Defined Types" on page 133) to create a new structure type:

```
typedef struct dpoint {
    int unit_id;
```

```
        int channel;
        float input_v;
} datapoint;
```

When used with **typedef**, the structure name is optional. This form works just as well:

```
typedef struct {
        int unit_id;
        int channel;
        float input_v;
} datapoint;
```

The new type may then be used to create new variables:

```
datapoint input_data;
```

Before moving on, we need to look at pointers to structures and how the contents of a structure are accessed via a pointer. The follow example program shows how one can create an array of pointers to structures, acquire memory for the structure data, and then reference the contents of the structures:

```
#include <stdio.h>
#include <stdlib.h>

typedef struct {
        int unit_id;
        int channel;
        float input_v;
} datapoint;

int i;

datapoint *dpoint[10];

int main(void)
{
        for (i = 0; i < 10; i++) {
                dpoint[i] = (datapoint *) malloc(sizeof(datapoint));
                dpoint[i]->unit_id = i;
                dpoint[i]->channel = i + 1;
                dpoint[i]->input_v = i + 4.5;
        }

        for (i = 0; i < 10; i++) {
                printf("%d, %d: %f\n", dpoint[i]->unit_id,
                                        dpoint[i]->channel,
                                        dpoint[i]->input_v);
        }

        for (i = 9; i > 0; i--) {
                free(dpoint[i]);
        }
}
```

When we execute this code, the following output is generated:

```
0, 1:  4.500000
1, 2:  5.500000
2, 3:  6.500000
3, 4:  7.500000
4, 5:  8.500000
5, 6:  9.500000
6, 7:  10.500000
7, 8:  11.500000
8, 9:  12.500000
9, 10: 13.500000
```

There are some new things here, so now would be a good time to look at them. First, notice that an array of pointers of type `datapoint` is created and called `dpoint`. When a pointer or array of pointers is defined in this fashion, the pointer values are not yet valid—they point to nothing because no memory addresses have been assigned.

In the `main()` function, the first `for` loop handles the chore of assigning a `datapoint`-sized chunk of memory to each of the elements in the array of pointers by calling the standard library function `malloc()`. The `malloc()` function requests a block of memory of a specified size (in this case, large enough to hold an instance of a `datapoint` structure) from the operating system. The first `for` loop also assigns values to locations in that memory allocation that map to the structure defined in the `datapoint` type.

Since `dpoint` is of type `datapoint`, the memory block provided by `malloc` will be treated just like a `datapoint` structure. Figure 4-7 shows this graphically.

To access individual elements in each structure, the so-called *arrow notation* is used. This notation is used in C to relate pointers to structures with the defined data elements within the structure type.

The second `for` loop reads out the data in structures and prints it, while the last `for` loop works backward through the array of pointers and frees the memory for each entry.

Functions

In C, all executable statements are contained within functions (preprocessor directives are not executable parts of the compiled code). C does not support the use of immediate execution statements such as those found in Python modules. Also, every executable C program must have a function named `main()`. This is the primary entry point when the program is started. Utility, support, and library modules that are intended to be compiled and then "linked" with other modules (more on this in a bit) do not have a `main()` function.

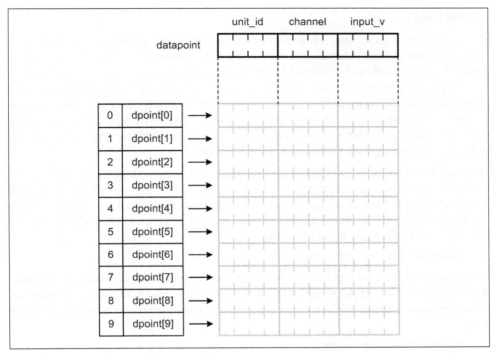

Figure 4-7. Structure mapping to allocated memory

Function syntax

The basic syntax of a C function looks like this:

```
[type] name (parameters)
{
    statements...
}
```

The optional *[type]* qualifier specifies the return type of the function, and if it is not present the compiler typically assumes that the function will return an integer (some compilers, such as *gcc*, may generate a warning message about it). The function name is composed of alphanumeric characters; how they are utilized is largely a stylistic issue. The function name is followed by zero or more parameters enclosed in parentheses. Parameters also have type qualifiers, and may be either values or pointers. On the next line, there is a left curly brace ({), followed by zero or more statements, and then a final closing right curly brace (}).

Functions cannot normally be nested in standard ANSI C, although some compilers do allow functions to be nested as a nonstandard extension (hint: don't do it—you will most likely hate yourself for it later). Each function is treated as a single unique entity with its own local scope.

Function prototypes

A *function prototype* defines a function to the C compiler in a format that can be used to resolve forward and external references. Because C requires that things like variables, typedefs, and functions be defined before they are used, it is convenient to place the prototypes for the functions in a module at the top of the module, or in an external file. This allows the functions in the module itself to appear in any order. The alternative is to arrange the functions such that they appear and are defined before they are called. This might be acceptable for a small module, but it can quickly become a major headache with a large module containing many functions.

A function prototype is just the function definition statement terminated with a semicolon (;). A C function prototype defines a reference to an as-yet-undefined function within the current source file, or an external function within a separate object module. Prototypes are used to create placeholders in the compiled code that will be filled in later by a tool called a *linker*. For example:

```
void bitstring(char *str, long dval);
```

The function prototype specifies the function's return type (**void** in this case), its name, and the number and types of its parameters. The use of parameter names is optional, which means we could just as easily have written the following and it would work just fine:

```
void bitstring(char *, long);
```

The Standard Library

An ANSI-compliant C compiler comes with a number of header files and library modules that provide support for math operations, string processing, memory management, and I/O operations, among many others. Table 4-11 gives an abbreviated listing of what is available. For more information, refer to the documentation supplied with your particular C compiler.

Table 4-11. ANSI C standard library components

Filename	Description
assert.h	Defines the assert() macro. This is used to assist with testing and detection of errors in a debug version of a program. If debugging is not active, the assert() macro is disabled.
ctype.h	Declares functions for testing and classifying characters, such as isalpha(), isdigit(), and so on.
errno.h	Captures error codes generated by other functions in the standard library.
float.h	Defines macro constants for use with floating-point math operations.
limits.h	Defines macro constants that are implementation-specific values for things such as the number of bits in a byte and the minimum and maximum values for integer types.
locale.h	Defines things like local currency representation and decimal point formatting. Declares the setlocal() function.

Filename	Description
math.h	Declares mathematical functions such as `sin()`, `log()`, `pow()`, and `floor()`. Macro definitions include `M_PI`, `M_TWOPI`, `M_SQRT2`, and `M_LOG2E`, among others.
setjmp.h	Declares the macro `setjmp()` and the function `longjmp()`, which are used for nonlocal exits.
signal.h	Provides a means to generate and handle various system-level signals, such as `SIGTERM` and `SIGSEGV`.
stdarg.h	Defines the `va_start()`, `va_arg()`, and `va_end()` macros for accessing a variable number of arguments passed to functions.
stddef.h	Defines several useful types and macros that are used in other standard library headers.
stdio.h	Provides input and output functionality, including `printf()`, output formatting, input formatting, and file I/O operations.
stdlib.h	Contains declarations for a variety of utility functions, including `atoi()`, `rand()`, `malloc()`, and `abs()`. The functions and macros declared in *stdlib.h* support a variety of operations, including conversions, random numbers, memory allocation, process control, environment variables, and sorting.
string.h	Defines string-manipulation functions such as `strcpy()`, `strcat()`, and `strcmp()`, and memory-manipulation functions such as `memcpy()` and `memset()`.
time.h	Provides several functions useful for reading and converting the current time and date. Some behavior of the functions declared here is defined by the `LC_TIME` category of the location setting.

The most commonly used standard library components are *math.h*, *stdio.h*, *stdlib.h*, and *string.h*. I would advise you to take a look at these components so you can get an idea of what is available.

Building C Programs

A nontrivial C program is usually a collection of files. Some of these may contain source code directly related to the program, while some might be local files containing function prototypes and macro definitions. Still other files may reside in a common library directory. When the program is compiled it is all pulled into the compiler, converted into object files, and then linked into a complete executable program. Figure 4-8 shows the steps involved in compiling C source code into an executable program file.

Header files

In C, one will typically see two types of file extensions: *.c* and *.h*. The *.h* extension is used to denote a *header file*, so called because one typically includes all necessary *.h* files at the start of a module, before any of the actual code.

Header files are included in their entirety via the `#include` directive. They typically contain function prototypes, macro definitions, and `typedef` statements, and a header file can—and often does—include other header files. However, it is considered both bad form and bad practice to place executable function code in a header file. Since it is rather trivial to build execution-safe linkable object files in C, there really is no reason to do this.

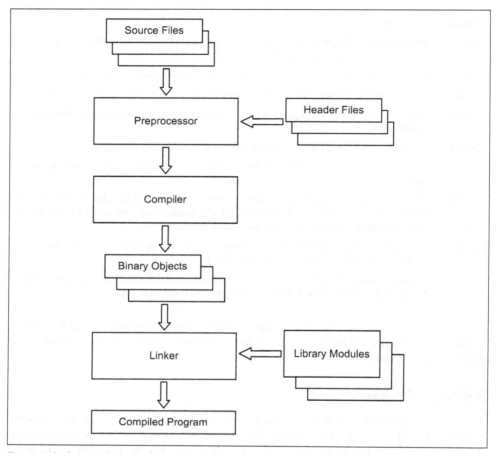

Figure 4-8. C program compilation

Object files

The C compiler does not itself generate executable output. It generates what are referred to as *object files*, which is an ancient term from the land of mainframes that refers to the notion of a binary object consisting of machine-code instructions. Actually, however, an object file is an intermediate product. In order to execute, it still needs some additional code, and this is provided by the linker.

If an object file references other binary objects outside of itself, the compiler inserts a placeholder and creates a list of these in the object file. The linker then reads this data in order to resolve the external references. Some C compilers (most notably Microsoft C) also automatically incorporate a runtime object to allow a program to access Windows system functionality.

Libraries

Library files are collections of binary objects that may be incorporated into other programs. Binary library files have specific formats, and there really isn't a universal format. Figure 4-9 shows a generic example of the internal format of a library file.

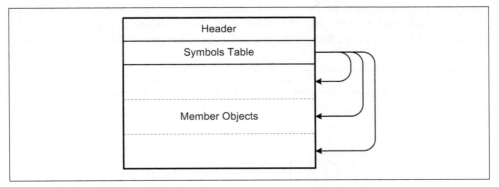

Figure 4-9. Generic library file internal format

The header identifies the type of library file, which may be either static or dynamic. The symbol table contains a list of the object names in the file along with address offset values that point to each object. Lastly, there are the binary objects themselves.

Linking

The linker is a standalone utility that links program binary objects to external library modules. It uses the external reference placeholders in the program binary object to determine what is needed and where the address reference for the external object should be inserted. Figure 4-10 shows how the linking works.

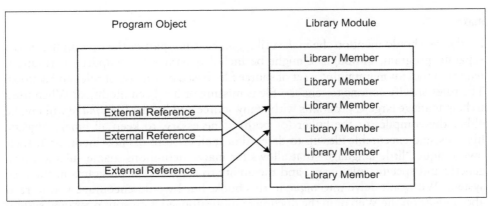

Figure 4-10. Program binary object linkage

The linker is typically language-independent. So, for example, one could link a binary object originally created using FORTRAN with an object created using C, provided that the compilers for both objects create binary objects that adhere to the same format as that expected by the linker. Figure 4-11 shows a generic linked executable with one program binary object, two library modules, and a runtime object to interface with the underlying operating system. Not every C implementation uses or requires a runtime object module, and in some implementations the functionality to support things like the printf() function is included automatically, even if it isn't used in the program.

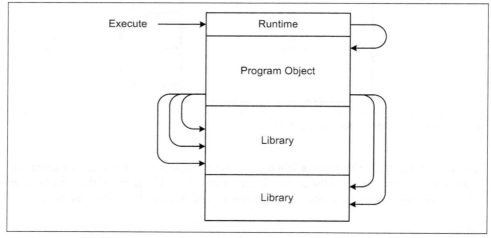

Figure 4-11. Linked executable

Program execution always begins with the main() function, and this is where the default runtime code will point the CPU when the program is loaded.

make

Lastly, we should mention the *make* utility. *make* is not part of the C compiler; it is a separate program, although it might be included with a C compiler distribution. *make* is a tool for maintaining a set of source files based on the use of rules and actions. The rules specify actions to take if a file is missing or has been modified. When used to help manage large C programs with many source and header files, *make* will invoke either the compiler or the linker (or both) as necessary, to keep all binary objects, libraries, and executable files up-to-date. Almost all versions of *make* incorporate their own unique "little language" that allows for macro definitions, name substitutions, generic and specific rule forms, and the ability to access other programs in the host system. We won't delve into *make* in this book, but I would encourage you to read about *make* on the Web or in the documentation supplied with your operating system or C compiler.

C Language Wrap-Up

C is a procedural language originally used for system-level programming. It has since evolved into a general-purpose language that occupies a niche just above assembly language and well below high-level languages such as Python, Java, or Lisp. Because of C's low-level nature, it is well suited to tasks that involve direct interaction with system hardware and the underlying operating system. These capabilities are a double-edged blade, however, and it's easy to write C code that can do very unpleasant things to the host system. Care and discipline are required to write solid, safe, and reliable C code.

C Development Tools

As with Python, you will need a text editor or IDE of some sort for entering and editing C source code.

Whereas Python handles the chores involved with keeping the various packages and modules up-to-date dynamically at runtime and provides capabilities like introspection as built-in functionality, a C program must be compiled and linked from its component parts as a separate step in the development process.

Also, C does not support the ability to dynamically examine a running program, nor does it output messages stating what modules are being loaded (unless the programmer explicitly writes this functionality into the code). The end product for a C program is a binary executable object, so debugging requires a specialized tool that is capable of reading the various headers and symbol tables found in binary objects and matching these to the original source code. If you want visibility into the compiled code, it must be compiled with debugging enabled. This generates a larger object file because it includes various symbol tables and other data for a debugger to use.

For a list of some of the editors that are available, see Chapter 3. As for IDE tools, the Eclipse IDE offers a plug-in for C as well as one for Python, and of course Microsoft's Visual Studio supports C and C++ right out of the box.

For C on Linux- and Unix-like systems, the classic GNU debugger, *gdb*, is supplied with most *gcc* distributions. If your system has *gcc*, the odds are very good that *gdb* is also present. On a Windows platform with either Cygwin or MinGW installed, *gdb* should also be available. Microsoft's Visual Studio has an excellent symbolic debugger with a GUI interface. For Linux platforms, the DDD debugger is an excellent tool that provides a GUI "wrapper" for the *gdb* debugger used with *gcc*. It also supports several other C debuggers on Unix systems.

Summary

C is a fascinating language, so low-level that it removes almost all of the constraints on the programmer by opening up the internals of the computer system to examination and manipulation. At the same time, it fits comfortably in the role of a mid-level procedural language. We have only touched on some of the capabilities of the language, but we've still managed to cover quite a bit. With what you've seen here, you should be able to write your own extensions to the Python language to give it new functionality and new interfaces into the real world.

Suggested Reading

C is now almost 40 years old, and mountains of books, papers, essays, and presentations have accumulated over the years. The following is just a minute sample of what is available:

C Programming Language, 2nd ed. Brian W. Kernighan and Dennis M. Ritchie, Prentice Hall, 1988.
> Written and reviewed by the people at Bell Labs who invented C, this is considered to be the original definitive reference for the C language. It has been updated since it was first published and now incorporates the ANSI standard version of the language. Short, to the point, and easy to follow, this little book made an indelible impact on a generation (or two) of C programmers and software engineers. A must-have for anyone working with C.

The Standard C Library. P. J. Plauger, Prentice Hall, 1991.
> A detailed and handy resource the covers the standard C library components. This is definitely a reference work, and it's a good thing to have on the bookshelf.

Practical C Programming, 3rd ed. (http://oreilly.com/catalog/9781565923065/) Steve Oualline, O'Reilly Media, 1997.
> A straightforward, no-nonsense approach to the C language in particular, and software engineering best practices in general. Examples help to illustrate the types of pitfalls commonly encountered in C programming, and there are numerous insights into the whys and wherefores of writing code in C.

As one might expect, the Internet is brimming with websites devoted to the C language. Entering the search phrase "C programming language" into Google returns something on the order of 15 million results. Here are a few highlights:

http://cm.bell-labs.com/cm/cs/who/dmr/chist.html
> An interesting account of the early history and development of the C language by Dennis Ritchie that outlines some of the thinking that went into the language as it came into existence in the early 1970s.

http://cprogramminglanguage.net
> Contains lots of brief but useful introductory material neatly organized like chapters in a book.

http://www.gnu.org/s/libc/manual/html_node/index.html
> Online documentation for the libraries supplied with the GNU *gcc* compiler suite. Also includes a very useful "concept index" that groups related subjects by specific topic.

http://en.wikipedia.org/wiki/C_(programming_language)
> Wikipedia has a large entry on the C language, along with many links to other sources of information.

http://www.acm.uiuc.edu/webmonkeys/book/c_guide/
> The student chapter of the ACM at UIUC (University of Illinois at Urbana/Champaign, home of the NCSA) has an online version of *The C Library Reference Guide* by Eric Huss available, with a comprehensive up-front index into the various pages.

http://citeseerx.ist.psu.edu
> An incredibly useful site chock-full of research papers and technical publications. Although almost none of the documents are at the tutorial level, there is still a lot of fascinating and useful material to be found here.

## CHAPTER 5

Python Extensions

Simplicity, carried to the extreme, becomes elegance.

—Jon Franklin

The main objective of this chapter is to show you how you can extend Python to take advantage of existing binary library modules. Python provides a couple of ways to achieve this, and we'll take a look at both of them.

Out of the box, Python cannot directly access the underlying hardware, nor can it interface directly with the software library modules provided by most hardware vendors. Python can, however, communicate with anything connected to a serial port or to a USB device that utilizes what is referred to as a virtual serial port (many USB–to–RS-485 converters use this technique). For those types of applications, an extension module typically isn't necessary.

One way to give Python access to the real world, or just add some faster or specialized functionality, is to use the C programming language to create *extensions*. These are basically dynamically linked library (DLL) objects that give Python capabilities beyond what is included in its own libraries. We'll mainly be using extensions as "wrappers" for the DLL modules supplied with commercial instruments and interfaces, but they might also be used to optimize a particular part of a Python program to improve on processing speed.

Another approach is to use Python's *ctypes* library, which contains methods to directly access the functions in an external DLL. The *ctypes* library can be used directly from within a Python program without the need to write any C code, and it supports both the Linux and Windows environments. The downside is that if you need additional functionality in the interface between your program and the external library object, it will need to be written in Python, and it won't be as fast as the equivalent code written in C as a wrapper for the external library. *ctypes* also imposes a processing penalty in that it is not particularly fast. But, if your application doesn't have a need for speed, it might be the easiest way to go.

Which method to use depends largely on what you want to accomplish with the interface. If the external DLL already does everything you need, there's probably no good reason to go through the process of writing your own extension wrapper in C. On the other hand, if you need to incorporate some additional functionality, such as error checking, buffer handling, or custom capabilities based on the functions in the external DLL, you should probably consider writing a custom wrapper in C.

Throughout this chapter I'll be using the acronym *DLL* to refer to both Windows-style DLL objects and Linux-type *.so* (shared object) dynamic libraries. Python's shared library objects typically have a *.pyd* extension. Also, bear in mind that most discussions about vendor DLL modules that provide an API for data acquisition and control hardware will, by default, be referring to the Windows environment. The reality is simply that there isn't much available (yet) for Linux. The electronics engineering world is very Windows-centric, and that's just something we'll have to deal with when working with plug-in cards for data acquisition and control signal output.

Creating Python Extensions in C

In order to use Python for an automated instrumentation application, we will need to build a bridge between an instrument or interface hardware and the Python application that will access it. In some cases the application program interface (API) DLL supplied by the vendor provides all the necessary functionality; the Python program just needs to be able to access it. In a situation like this you might want to consider using the *ctypes* library, discussed in a later section. In other cases, however, the vendor's DLL may not supply the necessary functionality, or it may be architected such that it is difficult to use without helper functions of some sort. This is where C comes into the picture. Figure 5-1 shows the relationships between a low-level API library object, an extension module, and a Python application.

This section is an overview of the basic steps involved in creating a Python extension module. In some ways this might seem like a big step from the overviews of Python and C presented in the preceding chapters, but not to worry. The intent here is to take a look at what is entailed, and not get too wrapped up in the gory details. Later, when we explore some specific applications in detail, we will go through the steps involved and explain each one. By that point you should be comfortable enough with Python that it will all make a lot more sense. Of course, if you already know Python or C, or both, this won't be much of a stretch for you: it's just a new library API to learn and some caveats to observe.

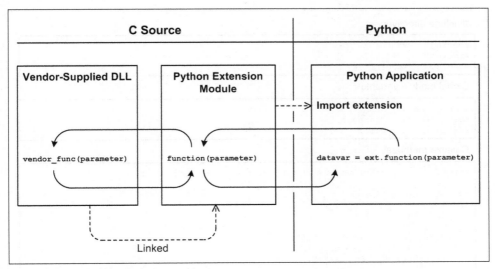

Figure 5-1. Python extension hierarchy

Python's C Extension API

Adding new functionality to Python is straightforward and fairly painless. Python provides an API for just this purpose that defines the types, macros, and external variables and functions needed to allow a Python application to import an extension module written in C and treat it as if it had been written in Python from the outset. The Python API is incorporated into a C source file by including the header file *Python.h* and then linking the module with the Python libraries.

The intent of this section is to provide an overview of what an extension module looks like and how it is structured, since in this book we will be building most of our extensions by hand. While something like the SWIG tool (available from *http://www.swig .org*) can help automate the process of creating a C extension module, using the header files for the external module or modules to create (most of) the necessary extension code, most of what we will need extensions for won't really warrant this approach. SWIG does, however, have some interesting uses, one of which is using Python to test C code. A description of this can be found here: *http://www.swig.org/papers/Py96/py thon96.html*.

Extension Source Module Organization

The internal layout of an extension source module typically follows a pattern like the one shown in Figure 5-2.

```
#include <Python.h>
#include <stdio.h>
#include <VendorAPI.h>
```

Global module variables

```
static int dev_handle;
static int dev_channel;
static int dev_port;
```

Callable methods

```
static PyObject *ExtFunction1(PyObject *self, PyObject *args)
{
    int ret_val = 0;
    int port;
    int state;

    PyArg_ParseTuple(args, "ii", &port, &state);
    /* more statements here */
    return Py_BuildValue("i", ret_val);
}
```

```
static PyObject *ExtFunction2(PyObject *self, Pyobject *args)
{
    /* statements */
}
```

```
static PyObject *ExtFunction3(PyObject *self, Pyobject *args)
{
    /* statements */
}
```

```
static PyObject *ExtFunction4(PyObject *self, Pyobject *args)
{
    /* statements */
}
```

Method table

```
static PyMethodDef ExtMethods[] = {
    {"ExtFunction1", ExtFunction1, METH_VARARGS, "Extension function 1"},
    {"ExtFunction1", ExtFunction1, METH_VARARGS, "Extension function 2"},
    {"ExtFunction1", ExtFunction1, METH_VARARGS, "Extension function 3"},
    {"ExtFunction1", ExtFunction1, METH_VARARGS, "Extension function 4"},
    {NULL, NULL}
};
```

Module initialization

```
void initExtAPI(void)
{
    Py_InitModule("ExtAPI", ExtMethods);
    dev_handle = -1;
}
```

Figure 5-2. Python extension module internal layout

The primary sections shown in Figure 5-2 are described in Table 5-1.

Table 5-1. Python extension module sections

Section	Purpose
#include directives	*Python.h* must be the first header file included. One would also want to include whatever C standard library headers are necessary and the vendor-supplied API header file.
Global module variables	Any necessary global module variables are declared here, and are defined as static. In fact, just about every variable and function in the module is defined as static, with the exception of the initialization function.
Callable methods	An extension module may have any number of methods available to a Python program. Although Python treats these as methods, they are written as functions in the C source module. Each is defined as static with a type of PyObject. Parameters are also defined as pointers to data objects of type PyObject.
Method table	The method table provides the dynamic linkage between the methods in the compiled extension module and whatever Python program is importing it.
Initialization	The initialization function always begins with the "init" prefix. This is what Python will expect to execute when the extension is imported.

Python API Types and Functions

The skeleton example shown in Figure 5-2 utilizes the following types from the Python API:

PyObject
> Represents an arbitrary Python data object.

PyMethodDef
> Defines the methods declared in the extension module as a NULL-terminated array. This table is passed to the Python interpreter by the extension module's initialization function.

It also uses the following API functions:

PyArg_ParseTuple()
> Parses the arguments in the list pointed to by the *args parameter according to a format definition string and sets the values of the variables following the parameter definition string.

Py_BuildValue()
> Builds a Python return value according to a format definition string.

Py_InitModule
> Passes the address of the method table to the interpreter.

The Method Table

The method table defines the entry points for accessing the internal functions in the extension, and it deserves a bit more explanation. The full syntax of an entry in the table is as follows:

```
{method_name, method_function, method_flags, method_docstring}
```

The fields are defined in detail in Table 5-2.

Table 5-2. PyMethodDef table fields

Field	Description
method_name	A C char * type that defines the name of the extension function as it will be seen by the Python code that imports this module. A literal string is commonly used here.
method_function	A pointer to a function within the extension module that is called when the name is invoked. It is of the type PyCFunction.
method_flags	A bit field used to indicate either a calling convention or a binding convention. METH_VARARGS is probably the most commonly used, although in some cases no flags are needed at all. This field is explored in more detail in the following section.
method_docstring	An optional string that will be used as the docstring for the function. In other words, this is what will appear if you type help(extension) after importing the extension.

Method Flags

The *method_flags* entry is a bit field. Its value depends on what flags are specified, and each flag is defined to be a value that is the equivalent of setting a unique bit within an integer variable. Although this implies that the flags can be combined without overwriting each other, in actuality only the calling convention flags METH_VARARGS and METH_KEYWORDS can be used at the same time, although they can be combined with a binding flag. For a detailed discussion of the method flags, refer to the Python documentation (you can view it online here: *http://docs.python.org/c-api/structures.html*).

We will be using only a few of the available method flags. The rest are more useful when dealing with complex interfaces that we won't be using. Table 5-3 lists the three most common method flags. In reality, if you are writing your own extension it is usually possible to design the extension functions such that the more esoteric flags are not necessary.

Table 5-3. Common method flags

Field	Description
METH_VARARGS	This defines the typical calling convention. In this case, the extension functions are of the type PyCFunction and the functions use two input parameters of type PyObject*. The first parameter is PyObject *self (by convention), and the second is PyObject *args (although you can name this whatever you wish). A call to PyArg_ParseTuple (or one of the other related functions) is used to extract parameter values from args.

Field	Description
METH_KEYWORDS	If you want to use functions with predefined keyword values (i.e., a Python-style parameter of the type *varname = value*), you will need to specify the METH_KEYWORDS flag. In this case, the function will take three parameters: PyObject *self, PyObject *args, and PyObject *kwargs, which is a dictionary containing the keywords and their associated default values.
METH_NOARGS	Functions that take no parameters still need to define two input parameters, although the functions don't need to check them. The first parameter, PyObject *self, is required. The second argument is effectively a NULL.

METH_VARARGS example

We can use PyArg_ParseTuple() to extract the parameter values and write the data into variables defined within the function:

```
static PyObject *ex_varargs(PyObject *self, PyObject *args)
{
    int param1;
    double param2;
    char param3[80];

    PyArg_ParseTuple(args, "ids", &dev_handle, &param2, param3);

    return PyString_FromFormat("Received %d, %f, %s" % (param1, param2, param3));
}
```

Notice that we don't need the address operator with the string (although we could have used &param3[0] to achieve the same effect). Also note that if the function takes three parameters, it needs to receive three parameters when called; no more, no less.

METH_KEYWORDS example

A function using the METH_KEYWORDS calling convention uses the Python C API method PyArg_ParseTupleAndKeywords() to extract parameter values and associate parameter keywords with names. The syntax of PyArg_ParseTupleAndKeywords() is defined as:

```
int PyArg_ParseTupleAndKeywords(PyObject *arg, PyObject *kwdict,
                                char *format, char **kwlist, ...);
```

The parameter kwdict is a pointer to a dictionary object passed in from the Python runtime when the function is called, and kwlist is a null-terminated list of strings containing the names of the parameters. METH_KEYWORDS is useful when you want to assign a value to a specific parameter by name. In other words, a METH_KEYWORDS function supports both positional and named parameters. The PyArg_ParseTupleAndKeywords() function is used as follows:

```
static PyObject *ex_keywords(PyObject *self, PyObject *args, PyObject *kw)
{
    int param1;
    double param2;
    char param3[80];
```

```
        static char *kwlist[] = {"param1", "param2", "param3", NULL}

        if (!PyArg_ParseTupleAndKeywords(*args, *kw, "ids", kwlist,
                                &dev_handle, &param2, param3);
            return NULL;

        return PyString_FromFormat("Received %d, %f, %s" % (param1, param2, param3));
    }
```

METH_NOARGS example

A function using the METH_NOARGS calling convention can simply ignore the args
parameter:

```
    static PyObject *ex_keywords(PyObject *self, PyObject *noargs)
    {
        return PyString_FromFormat("No arguments received or expected");
    }
```

Passing Data

Passing integers between an application program and a wrapper is fine, but what if we
want to work with things like strings, floating-point values, lists, or other Python objects? The methods PyArg_ParseTuple(), PyArg_ParseTupleAndKeywords(), and Py_Build
Value() can handle the common Python data types, and there are also other methods
available, such as PyArg_VaParse(), PyArg_Parse(), PyArg_UnpackTuple(), and
Py_VaBuildValue(). Refer to Python's C API documentation for details.

The key to PyArg_ParseTuple() and PyArg_ParseTupleAndKeywords() lies in understanding the various format codes that are used. Table 5-4 lists some of the more commonly
used codes.

Table 5-4. PyArg_ParseTuple type codes

Code	Python type	C type	Description
b	integer	char	Converts a Python integer to a small (byte-sized) int.
c	string of length 1	char	Converts a Python character (a string of length 1) to a C char.
d	float	double	Converts a Python floating-point number to a C double.
D	complex	Py_complex	Converts a Python complex number to a C Py_complex structure.
f	float	float	Converts a Python floating-point number to a C float.
h	integer	short int	Converts a Python integer to a C short int.
i	integer	int	Converts a Python integer to a default C int.
l	integer	long int	Converts a Python integer to a C long int.
s	string	char *	Creates a pointer to a string. The string may not be None or contain any null bytes.

Code	Python type	C type	Description
s#	string	char *, int	Generates two values: the first is a pointer to the string, and the second is its length.
z	string or None	char *	Creates a pointer to a string, which may be None (if None, the result is a pointer to NULL).
z#	string or None	char *, int	Same as s#, but accepts None or a string with null bytes.

For example, if we had an extension function that expected a floating-point value as an input parameter, like, say, an analog output function, we could write something like this:

```
static PyObject *WriteAnalog(PyObject *self, PyObject *args)
{
    int     dev_handle;
    int     out_port;
    float   out_value;

    PyArg_ParseTuple(args, "iif", &dev_handle, &out_port, &out_pin, &out_value);
    rc = AIOWriteData(dev_handle, out_port, out_pin, out_value);

    return Py_BuildValue("i", rc);
}
```

In this example, the function AIOWriteData() would be supplied by the vendor's DLL. In reality, analog I/O tends to be somewhat more complex than this, because there are often parameters for things like the output range (+/- V), the reference source, a conversion clock, and so on.

Using the Python C Extension API

There are many other functions and types available in Python's API that we have not covered here. However, what we have already seen should be sufficient for most of the extension modules we will need to create.

Generic Discrete I/O API

Let's take a look at what an extension written in C for a hypothetical discrete digital I/O card would look like. First off, the device uses a DLL to access the hardware via the PCI bus, so we need to know what API functions the DLL exposes. These are defined in the header file supplied with the DLL. This is a very simple piece of hardware, so just eight basic functions are needed. Here is the hypothetical header file (*PDev.h*) we'll be using:

```
/* PDev.h - API for a simple discrete digital I/O card */

typedef int dev_handle;
```

```
#define PDEV_OK  1
#define PDEV_ERR 0

/*
 * Open Device Channel
 *
 * Opens a channel to a particular I/O device. The device is specified
 * by passing its unit number, which is assigned to the device by a
 * setup utility. dev_handle is an int type.
 *
 * Returns:   If dev_handle is > 0 then handle is valid
 *            If dev_handle is = 0 then an error has occurred
 */
dev_handle PDevOpen(int unit_num);

/* Close Device Channel
 * Closes a channel to a particular I/O device. Once a channel is
 * closed it must be explicitly re-opened by using the PDevOpen API
 * function. Closing a channel does not reset the DIO configuration.
 *
 * Returns:   If return is 1 (true) then channel closed OK
 *            If return is = 0 then an error has occurred
 */
int PDevClose(dev_handle handle);

/*
 * Reset Device Configuration
 *
 * Forces the device to perform an internal reset. All
 * configuration is returned to the factory default
 * setting (All DIO is defined as inputs).
 *
 * Returns:   1 (true) if no error occurred
 *            0 (false) if error encountered
 */
int PDevCfgReset(dev_handle handle);

/*
 * Configure Device Discrete I/O
 *
 * Defines the pins to be assigned as outputs. By default all
 * pins are in the read mode initially, and they must be
 * specifically set to the write mode. All 16 I/O pins are
 * assigned at once. For any pin where the corresponding binary
 * value of the assignment parameter is 1, then the pin will
 * be an output.
 *
 * Returns:   1 (true) if no error occurred
 *            0 (false) if error encountered
 */
int PDevDIOCfg(dev_handle handle, int out_pins);

/*
 * Read Discrete Input Pin
 *
```

```
 * Reads the data present on a particular pin. The pin may be
 * either an input or an output. If the pin is an output the
 * value returned will be the value last assigned to the pin.
 *
 * Returns:    The input value for the specified pin, which
 *             will be either 0 or 1. An error is indicated
 *             by a return value of -1.
 */
int PDevDIOReadBit(dev_handle handle, int port, int pin);


/*
 * Read Discrete Input Port
 *
 * Reads the data present on an entire port and returns it as a
 * byte value. The individual pins may be either inputs or outputs.
 * If the pins have been defined as inputs then the value read
 * will be the value last assigned to the pins.
 *
 * Returns:    An integer value representing the input states
 *             of all pins in the specified port. Only the
 *             least significant byte of the return value is
 *             valid. An error is indicated by a return value
 *             of -1.
 */
int PDevDIOReadPort(dev_handle handle, int port);


/*
 * Write Discrete Output Pin
 *
 * Sets a particular pin of a specified port to a value of either
 * 0 (off) or 1 (on, typically +5V). The pin must be defined as
 * an output or the call will return an error code.
 *
 * Returns:    1 (true) if no error occurred
 *             0 (false) if error encountered
 */
int PDevDIOWriteBit(dev_handle handle, int port, int pin, int value);


/*
 * Write Discrete Output Port
 *
 * Sets all of the pins of a specified port to the unsigned value
 * passed in port_value parameter. Only the lower eight bits of the
 * parameter are used. If any pin in the port is configured as an
 * input then an error code will be returned.
 *
 * Returns:    1 (true) if no error occurred
 *             0 (false) if error encountered
 */
int PDevDIOWritePort(dev_handle handle, int port, int value);
```

Our hypothetical device has two 8-bit ports, and the pins (bits) of each port may be set to be either inputs or outputs. Pins may be read or written either individually or as a group of eight bits (a port).

Generic Wrapper Example

Let's create a simple wrapper for the device's DLL. We won't try to be clever here, although there are some things that could be implemented if we wanted to give the wrapper extended capabilities. I'll talk about those a little later.

The first step is to determine what we will need to import, and define any global variables the wrapper will need:

```
#include    <Python.h>
#include    <stdio.h>
#include    <PDev.h>
```

Notice that in this example we don't really need any static global variables.

So, now that we have the top of the file, let's do the bottom. The second step is to create the initialization function, which is what Python will execute when the wrapper DLL (a *.pyd* file) is loaded, and define the function mapping table:

```
static PyMethodDef PDevapiMethods[] = {
    {"OpenDevice",      OpenDev,    METH_VARARGS,
                        "Open specific DIO device."},
    {"CloseDevice",     CloseDev,   METH_VARARGS,
                        "Close an open DIO device."},
    {"ConfigOutputs",   ConfigDev,  METH_VARARGS,
                        "Config DIO pins as outputs."},
    {"ConfigReset",     ConfigRst,  METH_VARARGS,
                        "Reset all DIO pins to input mode."},
    {"ReadInputPin",    ReadPin,    METH_VARARGS,
                        "Read a single specific pin."},
    {"ReadInputPort",   ReadPort,   METH_VARARGS,
                        "Read an entire 8-bit port."},
    {"WriteOutputPin",  WritePin,   METH_VARARGS,
                        "Write to a specific pin."},
    {"WriteOutputPort", WritePort,  METH_VARARGS,
                        "Write to an entire port."},
    {NULL, NULL}
};


/****************************************************************************/
/*  initPDevapi
 *
 *  Initialize this module when loaded by Python. Instantiates the methods table.
 *
 *  No input parameters.
 *
 *  Returns nothing.
 ****************************************************************************/
void initPDevAPI(void)
{
    Py_InitModule("PDevapi", PDevapiMethods);

    dev_handle = -1;
}
```

There's nothing fancy here; I've basically just mapped the functions in the API to wrapper functions on a one-to-one basis. This does mean, however, that the Python code that calls this module will need to be responsible for keeping track of the device ID and the device handle, at a minimum.

Lastly, we define the interface functions. Here's the entire extension, which I've called *PDevAPI.c*:

```c
#include     <Python.h>
#include     <stdio.h>
#include     <PDev.h>

static PyObject *OpenDev(PyObject *self, PyObject *args)
{
    int     dev_num;
    int     dev_handle;

    PyArg_ParseTuple(args, "i", &dev_num);
    dev_handle = PDevOpen(dev_num);

    return Py_BuildValue("i", dev_handle);
}

static PyObject *CloseDev(PyObject *self, PyObject *args)
{
    int     dev_handle;
    int     rc;

    PyArg_ParseTuple(args, "i", &dev_handle);
    rc = PDevClose(dev_handle);

    return Py_BuildValue("i", rc);
}

static PyObject *ConfigDev(PyObject *self, PyObject *args)
{
    int     dev_handle;
    char    cfg_str[32];
    int     rc;

    memset((char *) cfg_str, '\0', 32);    /* clear config string */

    PyArg_ParseTuple(args, "is", &dev_handle, cfg_str);
    rc = PDevDIOCfg(dev_handle, cfg_str);

    return Py_BuildValue("i", rc);
}

static PyObject *ConfigRst(PyObject *self, PyObject *args)
{
    int     dev_handle;
    int     rc;

    PyArg_ParseTuple(args, "i", &dev_handle);
    rc = PDevCfgReset(dev_handle);
```

```
        return Py_BuildValue("i", rc);
}

static PyObject *ReadPin(PyObject *self, PyObject *args)
{
    int     dev_handle;
    int     in_port;
    int     in_pin;
    int     in_value;

    PyArg_ParseTuple(args, "iii", &dev_handle, &in_port, &in_pin);
    in_value = PDevDIOReadBit(dev_handle, in_port, in_pin);

    return Py_BuildValue("i", in_value);
}

static PyObject *ReadPort(PyObject *self, PyObject *args)
{
    int     dev_handle;
    int     in_port;
    int     in_value;

    PyArg_ParseTuple(args, "iii", &dev_handle, &in_port);
    in_value = PDevDIOReadPort(dev_handle, in_port);

    return Py_BuildValue("i", in_value);
}

static PyObject *WritePin(PyObject *self, PyObject *args)
{
    int     dev_handle;
    int     out_port;
    int     out_pin;
    int     out_value;

    PyArg_ParseTuple(args, "iii", &dev_handle, &out_port, &out_pin, &out_value);
    rc = PDevDIOWriteBit(dev_handle, out_port, out_pin, out_value);

    return Py_BuildValue("i", rc);
}

static PyObject *WritePort(PyObject *self, PyObject *args)
    int     dev_handle;
    int     out_port;
    int     out_value;

    PyArg_ParseTuple(args, "iii", &dev_handle, &out_port, &out_value);
    rc = PDevDIOWritePort(dev_handle, out_port, out_value);

    return Py_BuildValue("i", rc);
}

static PyMethodDef PDevapiMethods[] = {
    {"OpenDevice",      OpenDev,    METH_VARARGS,
```

```
                      "Open specific DIO device."},
    {"CloseDevice",    CloseDev,   METH_VARARGS,
                      "Close an open DIO device."},
    {"ConfigOutputs",  ConfigDev,  METH_VARARGS,
                      "Config DIO pins as outputs."},
    {"ConfigReset",    ConfigRst,  METH_VARARGS,
                      "Reset all DIO pins to input mode."},
    {"ReadInputPin",   ReadPin,    METH_VARARGS,
                      "Read a single specific pin."},
    {"ReadInputPort",  ReadPort,   METH_VARARGS,
                      "Read an entire 8-bit port."},
    {"WriteOutputPin", WritePin,   METH_VARARGS,
                      "Write to a specific pin."},
    {"WriteOutputPort", WritePort,  METH_VARARGS,
                      "Write to an entire port."},
    {NULL, NULL}
};

/****************************************************************************/
/*  initPDevapi
 *
 *  Initialize this module when loaded by Python. Instantiates the methods table.
 *
 *  No input parameters.
 *
 *  Returns nothing.
 ****************************************************************************/
void initPDevAPI(void)
{
    Py_InitModule("PDevapi", PDevapiMethods);
}
```

And that's it.

I should point out that this API uses integers and strings only as parameter values, and the functions return only integers. The extension code shown is just a translation wrapper between the device API and Python, nothing more. In many cases, however, that's all a wrapper really needs to be.

Calling the Extension

In a real-life situation, you would probably want to create a Python module with functions for opening the device channel and saving the handle the API returns in a persistent variable object, writing to specific bits and then verifying that the bits changed state as expected, and even setting up an output pattern playback capability, among other things.

Let's assume that we want to get the value of a particular input pin and write an 8-bit value to a port to set the status of some external hardware based on the true or false state of that particular input pin. Here's a simple example:

```
import PDevAPI

PDdevID = 1
```

```
        PDev = 0

        # open device, check for error return
        PDev_handle = PDevAPI.OpenDevice(PDevID)

        if PDev_handle:
            # define port 0 as inputs, port 1 as outputs
            PDevAPI.ConfigOutputs(PDev_handle, 0xFF00)

            pinval = PDevAPI.ReadInputPin(PDev_handle, 0, 2)
            if pinval:
                portval = 49
            else:
                portval = 0
            PDevAPI.WriteOutputPort(PDev_handle, 1, 42)
            PDevAPI.CloseDevice(PDev_handle)
            return 1
        else:
            print "Could not open device: %d" % PdevID
            return 0
```

The example starts by attempting to open the interface to the hardware. If it succeeds, the handle value contains some positive integer, which is equivalent to True in Python. Should it fail and return 0, we can treat it as False.

Next, we want to define the inputs and outputs. The call to PDev.ConfigOutputs does this. The value of 0xFF00 indicates that we want the uppermost 8 bits of the 16 bits available in the hardware to be outputs:

$0xFF00_{16} = 1111111100000000_2$

Now that we have a valid device handle and the I/O has been configured, we can read a specific bit and take action based on its returned value. In this case we will write the decimal value 42 to the output port if the input bit is true; otherwise, we write all 0 bits to the output port.

The number 42 is interesting in its own right, but in this case it is the decimal equivalent of 00101010_2. These might be control signals for a bank of heater elements, a set of valves, perhaps some lights, or just about anything else that could be controlled effectively in an on/off fashion.

Lastly, let's look at some of things I didn't put into this code.

For starters, there's no error return checking for the ConfigOutputs(), ReadInput Pin(), WriteOutputPort(), and CloseDevice() calls. I left this out just to keep things simple, but in reality you would probably want to include this, especially if whatever this interface is controlling could possibly do something that could cause damage in the real world. In fact, it's not uncommon for high-reliability software to have as many, or even more, lines of code dedicated to error checking and fault handling than lines of code that deal directly with the control logic. It's easy to set an output value, but it can take some effort to detect a problem after the value has been set, when something doesn't work correctly. The software must then take action to try to recover from the fault, or at least put the system into a safe state to minimize any possible damage. In a later chapter I'll show you how to do a simple fault analysis so you can get an idea of what might go wrong, and the possible actions the software could take to deal with the problem.

The example also doesn't provide any support for dealing directly with bits. We could easily write a couple of utility functions that would allow us to enable or disable a specific bit without disturbing any other bits in the byte that makes up a port. A time-honored way to do this is called *read-modify-write*. Here's how to set a particular bit:

```
def SetPortBit(PDev_handle, portnum, bitpos):
    # read the current port state
    portval = PDevAPI.ReadInputPort(PDev_handle, portnum)

    if portval >= 0:
        insval = 1 << bitpos
        # change the designated bit
        newval = portval | insval
        # write it back out
        rc = PDevAPI.WriteOutputPort(PDev_handle, portnum, newval)
    else:
        rc = 0
    return rc
```

The shift operation generates a value that is a power of two (2^n). So, a bit at position 2^0 is 1, 2^4 is 16, and so on. The resulting value, or *mask*, is then ORed into the value read from the port (most discrete digital I/O devices will allow you to read from any port or pin, even those designated as outputs), and the mask value is applied. It doesn't matter what is already at the designated bit position, it will be set to 1. The rest of the bits in the mask value are 0s, so a 1 in the original data in portval stays 1, and a 0 stays 0. (Refer back to Chapter 3 for an overview of how Python's bitwise operators work.)

Clearing a bit (setting it to 0) involves creating a mask with all the bits except the one we want to clear set to 1, and then using an AND instead of an OR. Here's an example:

```
def ClearPortBit(PDev_handle, bitpos):
    # read the current port state
    portval = PDevAPI.ReadInputPort(PDev_handle, portnum)

    if portval >= 0:
        insval = 1 << bitpos
        newval = ~insval & portval
        rc = PDevAPI.WriteOutputPort(PDev_handle, portnum, newval)
    else:
        rc = 0
    return rc
```

The function ClearPortBit() reads the current output port state, creates a bit value using a left shift, and then applies the one's complement of the bit value to the current port value using Python's bitwise AND operator. If bitpos is 2 and the resulting value of insval is 4, the bit at position 2^2 is 1, or 00000100 in binary. Inverting this results in 11111011, or 251. When this is ANDed with the port bit values in portval, any port bit that is a 1 will remain 1, 0s will remain 0s, and the bit we want to clear at 2^2 will always end up as 0.

You might be concerned about the output port glitching, or outputting a short spike when the new value is written back, but not to worry. A correctly designed discrete digital I/O port will not do this, so you can safely assume that the hardware will do what you expect. If you do happen run across some hardware that behaves this way, well, you might want to consider using something else instead. The reason you don't have to worry is that almost every discrete digital I/O device made utilizes latches. The data is loaded into the latch, and the latch drives the output pins. The result is that any latched output that is already a 1 will remain a 1. (See Chapter 2 for a schematic of a latched discrete digital I/O port.)

You could, of course, write utility functions to handle bit manipulation in C and put them into the extension, rather than writing them in Python, as I've done. The resulting code would execute faster than native Python, but it might not be worth the trouble. It is often easier to keep the core low-level I/O functions in the wrapper module, and then create a module specifically to interface with the low-level wrapper. The Python interface module could also implement error checking and parameter verification, and provide additional utilities that aren't speed-critical. In effect, the wrapper would have two parts: one part in C to interface with the hardware, and one part in Python to provide extended capabilities to the application that uses it. Figure 5-3 shows this concept in block diagram form.

Python's ctypes Foreign Function Library

There is another way to get at the functions exposed by a DLL: *ctypes*, Python's library for accessing external DLL objects. This section provides a general overview of *ctypes*.

The *ctypes* library gives Python programs the ability to directly access the functions within an external DLL without the need to create interface code in C. *ctypes* is part of the standard distribution with Python 2.5 and later, and it supports both Linux and Windows environments, with the usual caveats concerning the fundamental differences between the two platforms.

Loading External DLLs with ctypes

ctypes exports three primary interface classes: cdll, windll, and oledll. cdll is used for both Linux and Windows and supports library modules that use the cdecl calling convention. The windll class supports Windows libraries that use the stdcall convention. oledll also uses the stdcall convention, but it assumes that the library functions return an HRESULT error code. cdecl is the default for C programs, so most library objects on Linux will use this convention. On a Windows system you should check the appropriate Windows technical documentation to see what the various library objects use as their calling convention.

Using *ctypes* is straightforward. Here is what happens when the Windows C runtime library, *msvcrt* (Microsoft Visual C Run-Time), is accessed using *ctypes*:

```
>>> from ctypes import *
>>> msvcrt = cdll.msvcrt
>>> msvcrt
<CDLL 'msvcrt', handle 78000000 at 97b0f0>
>>> msvcrt.printf("Testing...\n")
Testing...
11
>>> rc = msvcrt.printf("Testing...\n")
Testing...
```

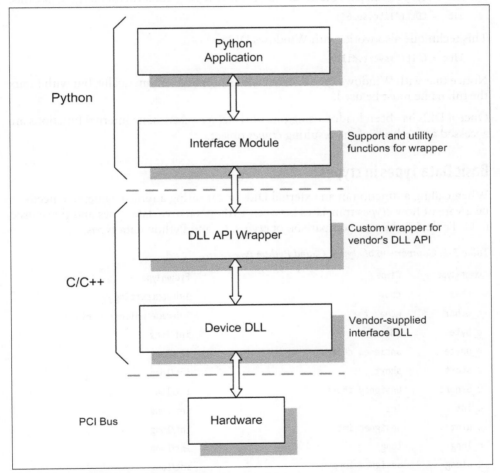

Figure 5-3. DLL wrapper extension and support module

This calls the trusty `printf()` function, which behaves exactly like you might expect. Note that the call returns the number of characters passed to `printf()`. If you look up the documentation for the `printf()` function you will see that this is exactly what it is supposed to do, although in most cases the return value is simply ignored. In order to catch the return value and prevent it from showing up on the console, I used the variable `rc`.

On a Linux system, you will need to specify the full name of the shared library object:

```
libc = cdll.LoadLibrary("libc.so.6")
```

Alternatively, you can pass the library name into the class constructor method, like this:

```
libc = CDLL("libc.so.6")
```

This technique also works with Windows DLLs:

```
libc = CDLL("msvcrt.dll")
```

Notice that with Windows the *.dll* extension is supplied automatically, but with Linux the full name must be used.

Once a DLL has been loaded using one of the *ctypes* classes, its internal functions are accessed as methods of the resulting *ctypes* object.

Basic Data Types in ctypes

When calling a function in an external DLL or capturing a return value, one needs to be aware of how *ctypes* translates between Python's native data types and those used in C. Table 5-5 shows a comparison of *ctypes*, C, and Python data types.

Table 5-5. Comparison of ctypes, C, and Python types

ctypes type	C type	Python type
c_char	char	1-character string
c_wchar	wchar_t	1-character unicode string
c_byte	char	int/long
c_ubyte	unsigned char	int/long
c_short	short	int/long
c_ushort	unsigned short	int/long
c_int	int	int/long
c_uint	unsigned int	int/long
c_long	long	int/long
c_ulong	unsigned long	int/long
c_longlong	__int64 or long long	int/long
c_ulonglong	unsigned __int64 or unsigned long long	int/long
c_float	float	float

ctypes type	C type	Python type
c_double	double	float
c_longdouble	long double	float
c_char_p	char * (NULL-terminated)	string or None
c_wchar_p	wchar_t * (NULL-terminated)	unicode or None
c_void_p	void *	int/long or None

Understanding how *ctypes* handles the conversion between Python and C is essential. For example, if we want to pass a floating-point value to a DLL function from Python, it must be converted into the appropriate type. Just handing off a float value from Python won't work.

Let's assume that a DLL has been loaded and we now have an object called someDLL to reference it. If it contains a function called someFunc() that we want to use, and this function accepts an integer parameter and a floating-point parameter, we might think that the following would work:

```
int_var = 5
float_var = 22.47
someDLL.someFunc(int_var, float_var)
```

Unfortunately, this won't work, and Python will issue an exception traceback. The reason for this is that all Python types except for integers and strings have to be wrapped with the appropriate *ctypes* type, like this:

```
someDLL.someFunc(int_var, c_double(float_var))
```

This will now work as expected.

The native Python object types None, integer, long, and string are the only types that can be used directly as parameters via *ctypes* to functions in a DLL. A None object is passed as a NULL pointer. A string object is passed as a pointer to the location in memory where the data resides. Integer types (both integer and long) are passed as whatever the platform's default C int type happens to be. Note that a long data object will be masked to fit into the default C int type.

Using ctypes

Although *ctypes* may appear to be simple, it can quickly become rather complex if you want to do things like pass pointers, define a callback function, or get the value of a variable exported from a DLL. We will stick with the basic capabilities in this book, but I would encourage you to take a look at the *ctypes* documentation located at *http://docs.python.org/library/ctypes.html*. Also, the various data types in ctypes are useful for more than just accessing an external DLL. In Chapter 12 I'll show you how to use ctypes to handle binary data directly in a Python program, including C structures, and in Chapter 14 we'll see how ctypes is used in a commercial API for a USB interface device.

Summary

In this chapter we've seen the basics of what is involved with creating an interface between a Python program and an external device via a vendor-supplied DLL. Fortunately, adding functionality to Python is not necessarily a painful process; it just requires some up-front planning. This means that reading the available documentation on designing and implementing Python extensions is really not optional, which is why this chapter is peppered with URLs to sources of information.

Reading and understanding the API for a foreign DLL is also essential. When creating a wrapper extension for an existing DLL, the biggest obstacle one typically encounters is the API for the DLL. Occasionally it will be necessary to contact the vendor directly and request some technical support. Be forewarned, however, that many vendors either don't have a clue about Python or don't want to be bothered with it, so you may need to invest some time experimenting to find the best approach for creating a working interface.

With what we've covered here, you should be able to see where you want to go from where you are, and have a general idea about how to get there. In Chapter 14 we'll see a working extension wrapper for real hardware using ctypes, and we'll fill in more of the details in the process.

Suggested Reading

Interestingly, it seems that there are no books devoted solely to the subject of creating extensions for Python. There are, however, resources available at various websites, the foremost being Python's primary documentation site:

http://docs.python.org/release/2.6.5/
> The official Python documentation for version 2.6.5 contains several sections on the topic of extending Python using C or C++. This should be your first stop when looking for additional information.

http://docs.python.org/release/2.6.5/extending/index.html
http://docs.python.org/release/2.6.5/c-api/index.html
> These two sections of the online Python documentation provide a detailed discussion of extension modules and the functionality available for creating them.

http://docs.python.org/library/ctypes.html
> This is essential reading if you want to use the *ctypes* library.

## CHAPTER 6

Hardware: Tools and Supplies

> *Byrne's Law: In any electrical circuit, appliances and
> wiring will burn out to protect fuses.*
>
> —Robert Byrne

Although it may be possible that one could implement a complex instrumentation system and never touch a tool more complicated than a screwdriver, there is a high probability that a soldering iron, wire cutters, and a digital multimeter (DMM) will come in handy at some point—particularly if things don't work quite right from the outset, or if there's a reason to be concerned should something accidentally be damaged.

In this chapter, we'll look at what might go into a basic toolkit for doing instrumentation work. It isn't much and could all easily fit in a small box on a shelf somewhere. Additionally, as there may very well come a time when you really need to see what's going on in your system, I've included a short discussion of the two pieces of test equipment that can help eliminate the guesswork and get to the root of an interface or control problem: the oscilloscope and the logic analyzer.

The Essentials

First and foremost, one needs some decent hand tools. These can be had *à la carte* from the local hardware store, or in a kit form in a nice zippered carrying case. Having even a modest set of hand tools available can make the difference between getting the job done quickly and efficiently, or having to trudge down the hall, or across town, to try and find the right tool. Even if they are only used once for one project, the expense is minimal, and they will be there should a need arise again in the future.

A digital multimeter is an essential item for dealing with instrumentation interfaces. It is handy for determining whether a voltage is present on an input or output terminal and whether DC power is enabled (and at the correct voltage), and some models come with a built-in interface that allow the meter to serve as single-channel data acquisition device.

Hand Tools

Your toolkit should contain a selection of Phillips and regular screwdrivers, mostly on the small side. Many hardware and "big box" home improvement stores sell kits of these. A basic toolkit should also have a set of miniature screwdrivers like those used by jewelers. These are essential for dealing with the tiny screws used with multipin connectors and with the terminals of many interface modules. At least one pair each of needle-nose pliers and diagonal cutters are essential for dealing with wires. A 6" adjustable wrench and a combination wire stripper and crimping tool would round out a very basic kit. These tools can often be found in prepackaged sets, and electronics-production-grade tools can be ordered from several online sources. Figure 6-1 shows a basic set of hand tools.

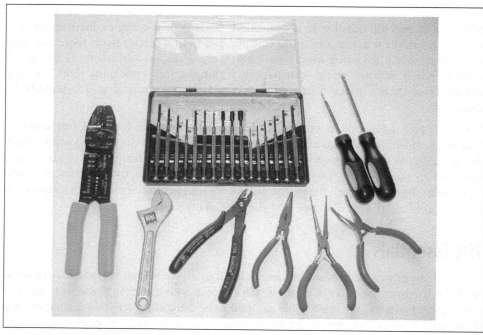

Figure 6-1. Basic hand tools

Of course, one could go all out and assemble a fully stocked toolkit. Figure 6-2 shows an overstuffed kit with a lot of miles on it. This would definitely be overkill for a one-time job, but if you have a consistent need for tools and odd small parts, a toolkit like this is essential.

Figure 6-2. Overstuffed toolkit

Be kind to your tools

Never use a pair of pliers on things like nuts if you can avoid it. Pliers will usually slip and round off the edges of the nut that define its six-sided shape. It only takes a few moments of effort with pliers to make it impossible to remove a nut with even the correct tool, which is a wrench or a socket.

Also, try to avoid using something like the black-handled wire cutters shown in Figure 6-1 to cut heavy wire. The thin, sharp blades of the cutters can easily become nicked and render the tool useless. It's also best not to use the cutters as wire strippers. Although this is possible with some practice, it is very difficult to control the amount of pressure sufficiently to avoid nicking the wire inside, or even cutting it. Damaged wires tend to break easily at the nick location. Use a wire-stripping tool for removing insulation. The large tool in Figure 6-1 with the lettering on it is a combination wire stripper, lug crimper, and screw cutter. For fine-gauge wire (in the 18- to 32-gauge range) consider the purchase of a dedicated wire-stripping tool with adjustable sizing. These range from just a few dollars to upwards of $100 or more for production-grade models, depending on the quality and features.

Where to purchase tools

Apart from the local hardware store, there are numerous places to purchase tools. Some of these are retailers specializing in discount tools imported from Asia, which you might also find in the "bargain bins" in some home improvement stores. Professional-grade tools are available from electronic supply houses and various distributors. In most cases there's nothing wrong with the bargain-bin tools, but be careful to check for smooth operation, sharp blades, evenly machined surfaces, and sharp—not rounded—angles on the insides of sockets and the outside of hex wrenches.

Table 6-1 is just a representative sampling of possible sources for tools, and is in no way meant as an endorsement of any particular brand or distributor.

Table 6-1. Electronics tool sources

Source	Description	URL
Allied Electronics	Online electronics components and tools distributor	*http://www.alliedelec.com*
Digi-Key Corporation	Online electronics components and tools distributor	*http://www.digikey.com*
Electronic Toolbox	Offers a variety of low-cost tools and supplies	*http://www.electronictoolbox.com*
MCM Electronics	Carries a range of parts, supplies, kits, and tools	*http://www.mcmelectronics.com*
RadioShack	Carries a good selection of tools and supplies online; availability varies from store to store	*http://www.radioshack.com*
Stanley Supply and Services	Carries a range of tool brands for electronics	*http://www.stanleysupplyservices.com*
Techni-Tool	Supplier of tools and supplies to the electronics industry	*http://www.techni-tool.com*

One of the best ways to get information about tools is to ask someone who has been working in the electronics industry for a while. Most technicians and engineers will have their favorites, and also some opinions about which tools they don't like (and why). Spending some time online browsing websites is also a good way to get a feel for what is available and the price ranges one can expect.

Digital Multimeter

The modern digital multimeter has evolved over the years from its humble beginnings into a complex and capable instrument. Prices vary widely, depending on factors such as accuracy, ruggedness, and features. A simple and usable handheld DMM can be had for as low as $20, while some of the professional high-accuracy models can run to upwards of $500. Figure 6-3 shows both a low-cost model and a more expensive unit that includes an output port for data acquisition.

Both of the units shown can measure DC voltage, AC voltage, DC current, AC current, and resistance. The unit on the left in Figure 6-3 has a socket for testing small transistors, while the fancier instrument on the right has the ability to measure frequency and capacitance. It can also capture and hold a measurement. DMM instruments also come in bench models, like the one shown in Figure 6-4.

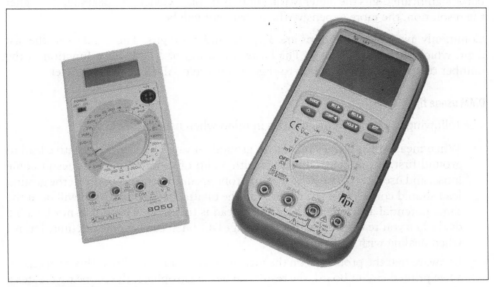

Figure 6-3. Digital multimeters

Figure 6-4. Bench model precision DMM (Agilent 34405A)

The high-end instruments can range to upwards of several thousand dollars in price, but they do offer accurate operation, high reliability, and a selection of data and control interfaces. We will be referring to instruments like the one shown in Figure 6-4 in Chapter 11, when we look at instruments with serial and GPIB interfaces.

With the high-end DMM units you also get a certificate of calibration, and most professional-grade instruments are calibrated periodically using a commercial or in-house calibration service. Unless what you will be doing involves requirements for high precision and repeatable measurements, this is not really necessary, although it is a good idea to occasionally cross-check one meter against another using the same voltage source and resistance reference.

DMM resolution

DMMs come in several different resolutions. In this case, resolution refers to the number of significant digits the meter will accurately display. Generally speaking, the higher the resolution, the more expensive the instrument will be.

Commonly available resolutions are 3½, 4½, and 5½ digits. The ½ refers to the last digit, which shows only 0 or 1. The basic resolution of a DMM is a function of the number of bits used in the analog-to-digital converter (ADC) inside the meter.

DMM usage tips

The following is a list of things to keep in mind when using a DMM:

- When measuring voltages relative to ground, always connect the negative lead to ground first. If possible, connect it with a clip of some kind so it doesn't come loose, and use only the positive lead to probe around. Remember that if the ground lead should come loose, the meter (and the unattached ground lead) will be at the same potential as whatever the positive lead is touching. This might not be a big deal when you're working with low-voltage DC, but it can become a definite hazard when dealing with high voltages.

- Be aware that the probe tips on the measurement leads can slip. If this happens on a live printed circuit board, the result can be catastrophic if the probe tip creates a short between the pins on a connector or an integrated circuit. A probe slip can also bring your hands into contact with potentially lethal voltages, which is another justification for clipping the ground lead and just using the positive lead to poke around. The old "keep one hand behind your back" rule applies when dealing with voltages that could injure or kill, such as AC wall voltage or high-voltage DC circuits.

- Never measure resistance in a circuit of any kind with power applied. A meter set to a resistance measurement mode will usually not tolerate a voltage input for very long before something fails.

- Never connect the meter to a voltage source greater than its rated maximum. Since most modern DMMs are capable of handling input voltages of up to 600 volts, this is usually not a problem. If you need to measure more than the meter's maximum rating, consider purchasing a special high-voltage probe. Also remember that AC voltages are often given as the RMS value, not the peak value.

- Always check the meter's settings before attempting to take a measurement. Although almost every DMM has internal fuses on the inputs, it is still a very bad idea to try to measure a voltage when the meter is set to the current measurement mode. This is effectively a short between the positive and negative terminals (with a low-value series shunt resistor), and if one of the probes is connected to ground it can blow the meter's fuse, damage its internal circuitry, or even damage the circuit being measured.

- The meter leads have resistance. It is usually very low, on the order of 0.5 ohms or so, but if you are trying to measure something like a wire-wound power resistor with a low resistance (0.1 ohms, for example), the meter leads can contribute more to the reading than the part being measured. Some DMMs have the ability to compensate for the lead resistance, but with others you should measure the leads first and then subtract that from whatever the meter indicates. For things like current shunts, with resistances on the order of a few milliohms, one would typically use something like a Wheatstone or Carey Foster bridge to measure a very low resistance. As a historical footnote, Figure 6-5 shows a vintage bridge test set.

Figure 6-5. Vintage Leeds and Northrup Resistance Bridge Test Set

Soldering Tools

Soldering is the application of a molten low-temperature alloy to join two wires or make a connection between the leads of a component and the copper paths on a printed circuit board (among other uses). An alloy of tin and lead (typically 60% tin and 40% lead, although other formulations are available) was once the most commonly used solder, but with the recent push to move away from materials containing lead, new alloys are starting to appear. However, when one purchases solder for occasional use, the most readily available type is still tin-lead. It is relatively safe (the lead is bound to the tin in the alloy), and so long as one takes reasonable precautions it should not present a significant health hazard.

Solder for electrical use typically comes in the form of a very pliable thick silvery wire that also incorporates a hollow core filled with a rosin flux material. The flux melts and flows before the solder melts, and helps to remove oxidation from the solder and the surfaces being soldered. Some people prefer a paste flux, which is a thick, sticky brown paste that is supplied in small tins. It is applied to the pieces to be soldered before the actual soldering starts, and is also sometimes used in conjunction with flux-core solder wire to help make solid connections on printed circuit boards. A solder with a 60/40 composition melts at about 188°C.

Soldering irons come in a variety of sizes, temperatures, and prices. The low-cost models typically found at local electronics and hardware stores are around 15 watts and have small pencil-point tips. These can handle most small-gauge wires and circuit board work, and cost anywhere from $10 to $25. They are not, however, temperature-controlled, so the tip can sometimes get too hot, resulting in a weak solder joint or a burned circuit board. They also have a tendency to cool off rapidly when one is attempting to solder large objects or heavy-gauge wire. If you plan on doing more than just occasional soldering work, it is worthwhile to invest in a unit with temperature control and interchangeable tips. These can range in price from $50 to $300, depending on the wattage and the features included (operator-controlled temperature, digital temperature readout, internal grounding, and so on). Figure 6-6 shows a low-cost 15 W pencil-type soldering iron. You might also have noticed a similar unit in the top tray of the toolbox shown in Figure 6-2.

Figure 6-6. Pencil-type soldering iron

You will also need something to clean the tip and some way to hold the soldering iron when it's not in use (just laying it down on the bench or table is generally not a good idea). Wire stands are available that include a small tray for a damp sponge to clean residue and oxidation from the tip. There are also tip cleaners in the form of small tins filled with a loosely coiled wire that require no water, and a paste-like material is available that will clean and brighten a soldering iron's tip (it also comes in a small tin). Both are commonly used in electronics manufacturing, but they are not very common in the toolkit of the occasional user.

There are numerous resources available online that deal with solder, soldering irons, and how to solder. It is a good idea to get some scrap wire or a defunct printed circuit board and practice a bit before tackling a real project. Soldering may sound easy and look simple, but getting it right takes a degree of skill that only practice can provide.

Soldering Guns Versus Soldering Irons

A word of caution: do not purchase a soldering gun unless you really have a need for such a thing. Soldering guns can produce a significant amount of heat, and are intended for working with thick and heavy materials like heavy-gauge wires and copper tubing. They are not suitable for small wires, connectors, or printed circuit boards, and even a skilled operator can inadvertently do some serious damage with a soldering gun.

Nice-to-Have Tools

In addition to the tools we've already discussed, there are some other tools that are incredibly useful, if not essential, for certain types of work. They aren't used as frequently as the more common hand tools, but when they are needed there is really nothing that can do the work as well. Consider acquiring the following:

Lineman's pliers
>These heavy, square-jawed pliers are designed to bend, twist, and cut heavy-gauge wires. They can also be used to bend thin strips of sheet metal, or cleanly break off pieces of plastic. Lineman's pliers are available at most well-stocked hardware stores, and inexpensive imported versions can occasionally be found in bargain bins.

Hex wrench set
>Also sometimes called *hex keys* or *Allen wrenches*, these are simple tools with a hexagonal cross-section used to drive bolts and screws with a hexagonal socket in the head. These types of fasteners are commonly found in electronic devices and laboratory equipment, and there is nothing else that can deal with them. Hex wrenches also tend to be relatively inexpensive, and they are available in both SAE and metric sizes.

Nut drivers
>As the name implies, these tools are designed to handle nuts. They typically look like screwdrivers with a socket instead of a screwdriver tip, and some have a "T" handle to enable more torque to be applied to a nut. They are available in both SAE and metric sizes, and can be purchased as kits containing from four to eight or more tools in various sizes.

Miniature socket set
>Like nut drivers, sockets are designed to drive hex nuts and hex-head bolts, but they use a right-angle ratcheting handle to apply much more torque than is possible with a nut driver (too much, sometimes). Small, compact sets with a selection of sockets, a drive extension, and a ratchet handle are available in both SAE and metric sizes (often combined in the same set). These tools are intended for larger nuts and bolts, and typically range from 3/16" to 9/16" for SAE sizes, and from 4 mm to 14 mm for metric sizes.

Advanced Tools

There is a lot one can do with a tool like a DMM, but there are some things it simply cannot do. One application the DMM cannot handle is the direct measurement of electrical waveforms. Another is the visualization of logic signals on multiple parallel lines. For these situations, tools such as an oscilloscope and a logic analyzer can make the difference between knowing and just guessing.

The Oscilloscope

The oscilloscope is a very old instrument, and has been around in one form or another for at least 80 years (perhaps longer, depending on how one defines what an oscilloscope is). The reason for its success is its inherent usefulness for examining changing electrical signals over time. Early electronic oscilloscopes used vacuum tubes for signal amplification, and a specialized type of tube called an *electrostatic cathode ray tube* (CRT) for the primary display. An oscilloscope CRT is similar in operation to the CRT found in older computer monitors and television sets, except that it typically uses electrical fields rather than magnetic deflection fields to guide the beam onto the screen.

Modern oscilloscopes are digital instruments with LCD displays like those found in flat-screen monitors—the days of vacuum tube amplifiers are long past, and the CRT is quickly heading for obsolescence. Figure 6-7 shows the front panel of a simplified generic dual-trace digital oscilloscope.

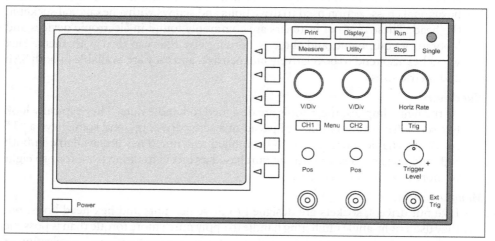

Figure 6-7. Generic digital oscilloscope

Dual-trace oscilloscopes with the ability to display two simultaneous signals are the most common, although single-trace instruments are available. Instruments capable of displaying four or more channels are also available. The latest high-end models provide color displays, advanced built-in signal processing and measurement capabilities, and network interfaces.

The vertical input channels amplify the input signals and cause the display point to move either up or down relative to a horizontal line defined as zero, or ground. The horizontal section of the instrument drives the display point across the screen from left to right, which is referred to as the *horizontal sweep*. A trigger circuit synchronizes the horizontal sweep with the incoming signal from either of the vertical channels in order to generate a waveform display that doesn't "walk" or wander across the screen.

One fundamental characteristic of an oscilloscope is its bandwidth. Low-end instruments are usually limited to a 25 MHz bandwidth, meaning that they will start to attenuate signals above 25 MHz. This comes into play when a signal has harmonic components above its fundamental frequency. For example, if a 25 MHz signal is measured by a 25 MHz oscilloscope, it will probably display the fundamental waveform, but it will not accurately display harmonics above that, so some key features of the signal will not be shown. This can become an issue when examining square waves, which may contain higher-order components that are causing problems, as these will not appear on a slow oscilloscope. This is shown in Figure 6-8.

As a general rule of thumb, one should try to use an oscilloscope with a bandwidth at least four times the fundamental frequency of the signal of interest. If the only oscilloscope available has a bandwidth around the frequency of the fastest signal of interest, you should expect that there are probably things going on in the signals that you cannot see.

Figure 6-9 shows an image of a digital oscilloscope screen. This image shows two channels, one with a 0 to 3 V range and the second with a 0 to 12 V display range. Measurement cursors (the *x* and *o* symbols) are used to determine the time interval between the cursor locations, which in this case is 36.3 seconds. This particular instrument is an older model that uses a CRT display.

If you are not very familiar with oscilloscopes, then it is worthwhile to spend a little time and read up on how they work and how to use them. There are lots of excellent sources of information available online. The thing to remember is that an oscilloscope (and most other test instruments, for that matter) can only present data within the range of its capabilities, and attempting to interpolate missing data, or assuming that what is shown is completely accurate, can lead to erroneous conclusions.

Logic Analyzers

The logic analyzer is a very useful instrument for measuring and monitoring activity within digital circuits. Logic analyzers capture a set of digital inputs simultaneously and store the binary values in a short-term trace memory. The contents of the trace memory are then read out and displayed in the form of a timing diagram. We saw these types of diagrams in Chapter 2, and we will be seeing more of them in later sections.

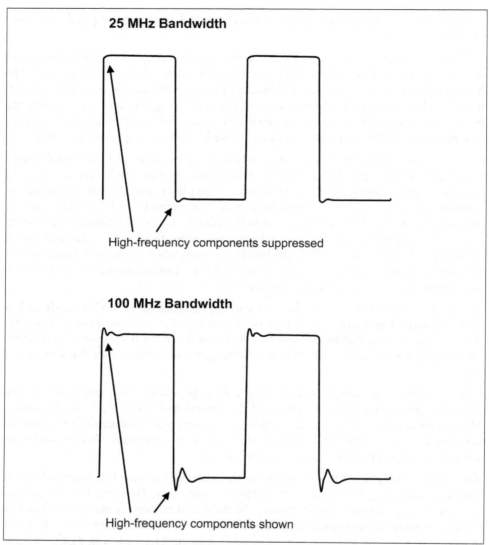

Figure 6-8. Effect of oscilloscope bandwidth

Figure 6-10 shows a block diagram of a simple logic analyzer. This diagram would be applicable to a self-contained instrument, but there are other ways to achieve a similar result. For example, if the signals are changing relatively slowly, one can use the parallel printer port on a PC as a simple four-channel logic analyzer (the PC parallel port has four input lines available).

One can also purchase inexpensive USB logic analyzer modules that use the PC's display rather than providing one of their own. An example is shown in Figure 6-11.

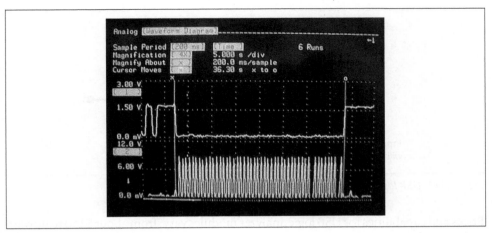

Figure 6-9. Digital oscilloscope display

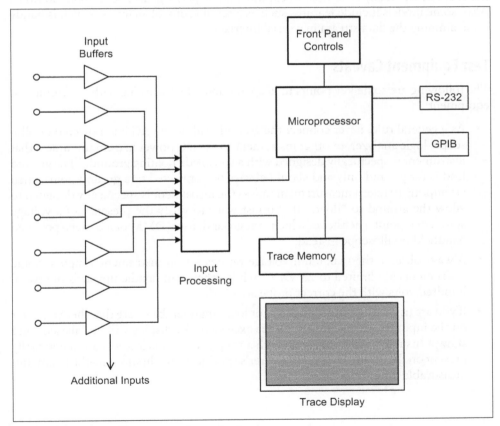

Figure 6-10. Logic analyzer internal organization

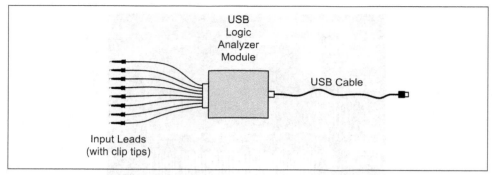

Figure 6-11. USB logical analyzer module

Prices and capabilities for USB logic analyzer modules vary, from about $150 to upward of $6,000. For most instrumentation applications, a low-cost unit will do all that is needed, as there really is no need to capture and display signals above about 50 MHz. Also, some models include features such as a serial protocol analyzer, which is handy for examining the data stream in a serial interface.

Test Equipment Caveats

The following are some key points to keep in mind when working with electronic test equipment:

- As a general rule, never connect the ground lead of any AC line-powered oscilloscope, logic analyzer, or other instrument to the DC power in a circuit, unless that instrument is specifically designed with a so-called "floating ground." The ground lead is for ground only and should always be connected to a ground point when attempting to take a measurement unless the instrument is specifically designed to allow the ground to "float." If you just want to verify the presence of a voltage across two points, neither of which is at ground, use a DMM or a battery-powered handheld oscilloscope instead.

- Always observe the maximum voltage ratings for an instrument's inputs. Some instruments are limited to 25 V DC, while others can handle upwards of several hundred volts with the correct probe attached.

- If you are using a digital oscilloscope or logic analyzer, be aware that there is a limit on the input frequency. If this limit is exceeded, the display will be "aliased" and show a (usually) distorted signal with a frequency that is lower than that actually present on the input. The manufacturer's specifications should state the maximum measurable input frequency.

Supplies

Having a supply of items such as wire, wire nuts, electrical tape, and so on, readily available can make things a whole lot less frustrating and help to ensure that the end result will be both reliable and professional-looking. Table 6-2 shows a list of suggested supplies to keep handy.

Table 6-2. Suggested supplies

Item	Description
Insulated hookup wire	#22 stranded, various colors
	#20 stranded, various colors
	#18 stranded, various colors
	#16 stranded, various colors
Shielded coaxial cable	RG-58, 50 ohms impedance
Wire nuts	Small (#18–14 size)
Electrical tape	Black
Kapton tape	1/4″ wide
Heat-shrink tubing	Various diameters (from 3/32 to 1/2″)
Resistors	1/4 watt; 100, 330, 1K, 2.2K, 4.7K, and 10K ohms
Wire lugs	#18 to #16 wire gauge size

Wire and cable typically come on spools in lengths from 10 feet to over 1,000 feet. For hookup wire, 25 feet is a good length, and a selection of standard colors (red, black, white, blue, and green) allows one to readily identify power (red), ground (black), and signal wires. Some types of wire, particularly in the smaller gauges, will have only a single copper conductor instead of multiple strands. Single-conductor wire is not recommended unless there is a specific reason to use it, as the single conductor can break if bent too far or nicked when the insulation is removed. Stranded wire is much more flexible and durable.

The Kapton tape mentioned in Table 6-2 deserves a brief explanation, as most folks outside of the aerospace and electronics production realms may not have heard of it. Basically, Kapton is a polyimide film with excellent temperature tolerance (–273 to +400°C). Among other applications, it is used to make flexible printed circuit boards, as insulation for wiring, as a protective wrap for the cable bundles on spacecraft, and as one of the outer layers of spacesuits. It is much better than electrical tape for many applications, as it leaves virtually no residue. It is also suitable for many uses in environments where low outgassing is a consideration (such as in vacuum chambers). Lastly, Kapton tape is a transparent golden color, which makes it useful for applying labels to already fabricated cabling.

Most of the supplies listed in Table 6-2 can be purchased from the suppliers listed in Table 6-1, with the possible exception of the Kapton tape. One place to purchase Kapton in small quantities is *http://www.kaptontape.com*.

New Versus Used

For most instrumentation projects, the demands placed on test equipment are very modest. Data sampling and control update intervals are relatively long (100 ms to many minutes), so having the latest expensive high-speed equipment really isn't necessary. This means that the old oscilloscope that's been gathering dust on the shelf in the storage room is probably more than adequate (assuming that it still works, of course).

It also means that there is no reason not to look into buying used test and instrumentation equipment. eBay is one possible source for used items, provided that you bear in mind that you should be prepared to unpack a broken or nonfunctional item when it arrives. This is a relatively rare occurrence, but it does happen.

 There is buyer protection available through PayPal (eBay's preferred payment system) just in case your item does get drop-kicked somewhere in shipping, or doesn't work as advertised, but there's no way to recover the wasted time.

A local electronics store might also carry a selection of used or surplus equipment at discounted prices. The secret to putting older equipment to work is knowing what it will need to measure. For example, 100 MHz would be a reasonable lower limit for the bandwidth of an oscilloscope. A DMM should have at least enough digits to satisfy the accuracy requirements of the voltages you might want to measure in your system. While 3½ digits are usually acceptable for most purposes, 4½ digits are necessary for verifying the basic operation of an ADC or DAC.

Summary

You should now have some ideas for a shopping list of at least the basic tools you will need, and some idea of where to find them. We've also covered some of the basic electronics test equipment that you might need, and briefly discussed the pros and cons of buying new versus acquiring used tools and equipment.

Beyond the basic hand tools and a decent DMM, there isn't much else you should need to get started, except perhaps some specialized tools for working with connectors.

Suggested Reading

If you would like to explore test equipment and measurement topics in more depth, I would suggest the following book as a good place to start:

Electronic Test Instruments: Analog and Digital Measurements, 2nd ed. Robert A. Witte, Prentice Hall, 2002.
> This book provides a solid introduction to basic measurement theory, followed by a very readable and informative survey of modern electronic test instruments and their applications. Each topic is supported with real-world examples drawn from the author's own experiences.

You can also find appendixes in books on electronic circuit theory that describe the basic theory and applications of instruments such as DMMs and oscilloscopes.

Finally, many test equipment manufacturers offer excellent online tutorials for their products, so I would suggest that you look there first for more information when searching the Web.

## CHAPTER 7

Physical Interfaces

> Connectors usually cause more failures than any other
> type of component. Many of these failures are not
> reported because they can be "fixed" by reseating
> the connector.
>
> —W. Ireson, Clyde Coombs, and Richard Moss,
> *Handbook of Reliability Engineering and
> Management*, Second Edition, 1995

In this chapter we will examine the types of interfaces, both physical and software, that one is most likely to encounter when attempting to interface Python to data acquisition or control instrumentation. We looked briefly at some of these in Chapter 2, but here we'll start to get into the details.

But first we'll take a look at physical connectors, and in particular the types commonly used with the interfaces found in PC-based instrumentation. By the end of this chapter you should be able to determine what type of interface you might expect to find with a given connector type, or at least be able to readily identify the connector. You should also bear in mind that the conventions for connector usage aren't always followed, so don't be surprised to find a DB-9 connector being used in an interface for motor control signals, or an aerospace-style circular connector serving as an Ethernet connection.

We will then turn our attention to serial interfaces—namely, RS-232 and RS-485, the two most commonly encountered types of serial interfaces. We then cover the basics of the USB and GPIB/IEEE-488 interfaces, along with a discussion of where one might expect to encounter them.

Finally, we will look at I/O hardware designed to be plugged into the bus of a PC—typically, PCI-type circuit boards—and what one can usually expect in terms of software support from the hardware vendor.

Connectors

Physical interfaces are implemented with a connector of some type. It might be one of the common 9- or 25-pin DB-type serial and printer connectors found on PCs, or perhaps a 4-pin USB connector. It might be a circular connector with anywhere from 2 to 100 or more pins, like those commonly found in industrial and aerospace equipment. Connectors also come in sizes and shapes suitable for use on printed circuit boards (PCBs), and even some types that directly accept the edge of a PCB, such as the plug-in cards on the motherboard of a PC. Terminal blocks are used to connect single wires, and come in a variety of types for different applications. A quick glance through the "Connectors" section of a major electronics distributor's catalog will give you some idea of what is available.

Figure 7-1 shows the business end of a gadget that uses both circular connectors and terminal blocks. We'll look at both of these types of connectors in just a bit.

Figure 7-1. A gadget with various connector types

DB-Type Connectors

Figure 7-2 shows the female version of a DB-9 connector, and Figure 7-3 shows its male counterpart. These are commonly used for RS-232 interfaces, although they are also used as DC power connectors, RS-485 connectors, and even instrument-specific interface signal connectors.

Figure 7-2. DB-9 female connector

Figure 7-3. DB-9 male connector

Another commonly encountered connector is the DB-25. It has the same general shape as the DB-9, with the main difference being that it is wider in order to accommodate 25 pins instead of 9. The DB-25 is the connector most commonly used with the full implementation of the RS-232 standard. It is also commonly used for the parallel data printer output port on desktop PCs (and some older notebook/laptop machines). The DB-9 has generally replaced it because it is smaller and not all of the original RS-232 signals are necessary in order to implement a serial interface. Figure 7-4 shows a female DB-25 connector with "solder cup" connections on the back for wiring (more on this in a bit).

Note that all of the DB-type connectors shown so far are panel-mount or shell types. In other words, they are designed to either be mounted in a metal or plastic panel by way of screws through the holes in the flanges on either side of the connector body, or be used with what is called a "backshell," as shown in Figure 7-5.

The fully assembled connector looks like the one shown in Figure 7-6.

Both male and female DB-style connectors are available in PCB-mount versions as well. The DB-9 and DB-25 connectors on a PC motherboard connect directly to the circuit traces on the motherboard. As for pin counts, DB-type connectors are also available in 15, 37, and 50 pin types. Finally, several types of high-density D-type connectors are available, such as those used with analog video display monitors. These utilize three or more rows of pins or sockets in the connector body.

Pin numbering for a DB-9 connector is shown in Figure 7-7. Notice that the pins are reversed between the male and female connectors when viewed from the face of the connector.

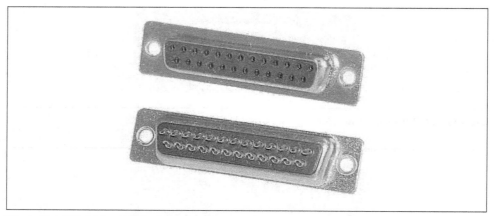

Figure 7-4. DB-25 front and rear views

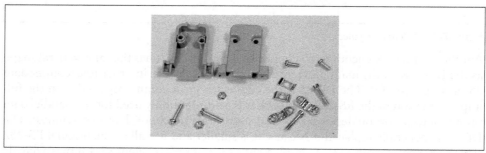

Figure 7-5. DB-9 backshell parts

Figure 7-6. DB-9 connector with backshell assembly

USB Connectors

Universal Serial Bus (USB) connector shapes and sizes are defined by the USB standards. They all have four contacts: two for the data signals (D+ and D–) and the other two for power (+5 V) and ground. Typically these are premolded, so (hopefully) you won't need to assemble any of them. What you should be aware of are the different types of connectors defined by the USB standard.

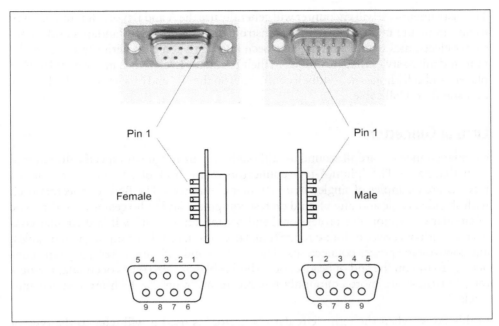

Figure 7-7. DB-9 pin and socket numbering

There are four basic USB connector types, as shown in Table 7-1.

Table 7-1. Basic USB connector types

Type		Description
Type A		Used primarily at the host or controller end of a USB connection. On a PC, these are used to connect keyboards, mice, drawing tablets, cameras, printers, and hubs, among other things.
Type B		A square-shaped connector with beveled exterior corners on one side to orient it to a socket. This connector is typically found on external devices such as hubs and printers.
Mini USB		This type is commonly found on consumer digital cameras and other mobile devices.
Micro USB		Similar to the mini USB but slimmer. The micro USB connector is designed to be more resistant to wear than the mini USB type.

The instruments we will encounter will generally use the A and B types. It is uncommon to find mini and micro connectors on instrumentation devices. Standards aside, consumer electronics manufacturers have been known to come up with variations of the mini and micro styles that are unique to their products. Even today, many popular MP3 players and cell phones use oddball connectors on the "B" end of what would otherwise be a standard USB cable.

Circular Connectors

Circular connectors are all around us, although they are not always specifically referred to by that name. The "phono"-type connectors on the back of a TV monitor or stereo receiver are examples of single-circuit circular connectors. The BNC connectors used with shielded cable and often found on test equipment and radio gear are another type of circular connector. For professional audio applications, one will find circular connectors with one, two, or four circuits (pins) used for microphone inputs, patch cables, and low-voltage power connections. The 2.5 mm and 3.5 mm stereo-plug-type connectors found on the end of headset or earbud cables are also types of circular connectors, but these are more commonly referred to as "plugs," which are inserted into "jacks."

In this book, when the term "circular connector" is used it will refer to the type of connector shown in Figure 7-8.

Figure 7-8. MIL-type circular connector

The connector shown in Figure 7-8 is known as a "MIL-type" connector. The reason for this is that these types of connectors were originally intended for military and aerospace applications. As such, they are very robust and can endure harsh environments. Some types, made entirely of plastic, are inexpensive but still relatively robust. Other types, made from aircraft-grade materials and assembled to order by manufacturers with facilities for handling custom orders of various sizes, can be quite expensive (over $200 is not uncommon for a connector built to military standards). Both types are available with pin counts from two to over a hundred.

Figure 7-9 shows the AN/ARC-220. This is a mobile radio system used by the US military that utilizes circular connectors of various types and configurations to interface with an aircraft's power and avionics systems.

Figure 7-9. AN/ARC-220 radio set (image credit: US Army)

Although you might never encounter the AN/ARC-220 in the wild, it is possible that you might come across some ruggedized instrumentation equipment that looks something like this.

Wiring a MIL-type circular connector involves either soldering the wires into solder cups on the ends on the pins or sockets, or using a special (and typically rather expensive) crimping tool with specially machined pins and sockets. Some of the low-cost multipin circular connectors use stamp-formed pins and sockets rather than solid machined parts, and although they're not as rugged or reliable, they can be considerably less expensive.

Terminal Blocks

Terminal blocks are ancient (in a technology time sense). They started to appear in common use in the early part of the 20th century, replacing the threaded binding posts and clip-type connectors of the late 19th century. World War II provided a major incentive for the development of more robust and reliable connectors, and the pace of innovation hasn't slowed since that time.

The name "terminal block" actually refers to a number of different styles of termination devices. A barrier terminal block, like the one shown in Figure 7-10, uses screws to hold down a wire or crimp-on lug-type connector.

Figure 7-10. Barrier terminal block

Although one can simply loop bare wire under the screw head, this is not an optimal method. The wire may slip out, especially if it is multistranded. When using bare wire, single-conductor copper wire works best with a barrier-type terminal block. However, because the screw head can create an immobile pressure point where wire flexing is concentrated, there is also a possibility that it will break off. A lug connector is the optimal way to connect a wire to a barrier terminal block. A typical lug connector suitable for use with a barrier-type terminal block is shown in Figure 7-11. You can also see them on the gadget shown in Figure 7-1.

Figure 7-11. Crimp-type spade lug

This type of connector does require the use of a crimping tool, but these are common and easily obtainable at any well-stocked hardware store or automotive parts supplier.

A type of compact terminal block more commonly encountered in instrumentation devices is the PCB-mount type shown in Figure 7-12. These are designed to be soldered directly onto a circuit board, and provide a convenient and reliable way to interface with a circuit.

Figure 7-12. Typical PCB-mount terminal block

These types of compact connectors are very common in instrumentation devices intended for use with a PC, such as the USB-based interface devices we will examine later. It is also common for interface cards installed in a PC to connect to a module with compact terminal blocks by way of a special multiconductor cable, shown in Figure 7-13.

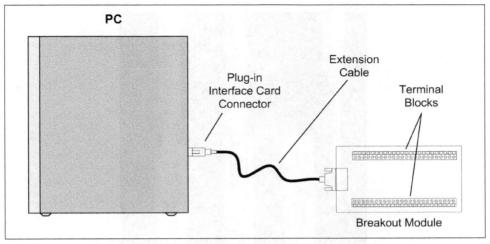

Figure 7-13. PC interface card breakout module example

Wiring a compact terminal block simply involves stripping about 1/4 to 3/16 of an inch of insulation from the end of a wire, inserting the bare wire into the hole below the screw, and then tightening the screw until it clamps the wire firmly in place. No soldering or crimping is required. The downside is that terminal blocks take up more space than some other connector types, and they aren't always suitable for environments where ruggedness is a primary concern.

Wiring

Wiring a connector correctly the first time can save an immense amount of time, and possibly money, further down the road. As you have probably gathered by now, the two primary means of connecting wires to a connector other than a terminal block are soldering and crimping, and for terminal blocks either a bare wire is inserted into a terminal position or a crimp-on lug is secured under a terminal screw. Regardless of the connector type, there are correct (and incorrect) ways to wire a connector, and we'll look at a few of them here.

Soldering

If you are new to soldering, it is probably a good idea to get in some practice before tackling a connector. Spending some time with some scrap wires and old circuit boards will pay dividends later. US government publications are an excellent source of information on soldering techniques and standards. For example, NASA STD 8739.3 describes solder connections and contains a wealth of useful information.

Connectors that are designed for solder connections have a special feature called a "solder cup" machined or formed into the end of the pin where the wire is attached. Figure 7-14 shows how NASA defines a good solder cup connection.

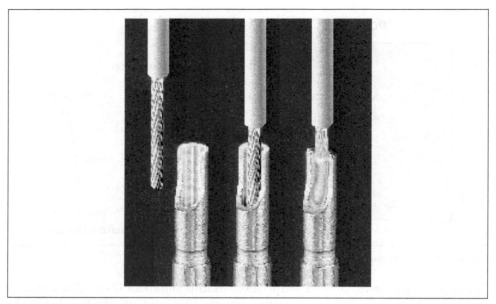

Figure 7-14. Solder cup connection (image credit: NASA)

Crimping

Crimp-type connectors are easier to assemble than solder-cup connections, and for some applications they provide for a more robust connection, but only if the crimp is made according to the manufacturer's specification using the correct tool. Figure 7-15 shows a machined crimp pin for a circular connector. Once the wire is crimped into the pin it is inserted into the connector from the back using a special tool, where it locks into place within the connector body. It can be removed using another special tool. Of course, for each pin there is a matching socket in the female connector. These are also crimped and inserted into the connector body. Crimped pins and sockets require unique tools that are specifically made for a particular type and size of connector. Crimping tools for MIL-type connectors can cost upwards of $500 (or more) apiece. Other types of crimping tools, such as those used with DB-type connectors or low-cost rectangular connectors such as those made by Molex or Hirose, are usually not as expensive, but nonetheless they still aren't cheap.

Crimped pins and sockets are inherently strain-relieved by virtue of the design of the crimped part. A crimp-style pin or socket not only "bites" into the bare wire but also has a second area, near the open end of the pin or socket, that clamps down on the wire's insulation. When assembled correctly and combined with the appropriate backshell, a crimp-style circular or DB-type connector is a very rugged item—which is why you can find a lot of them in aircraft, spacecraft, military field gear, and harsh industrial environments.

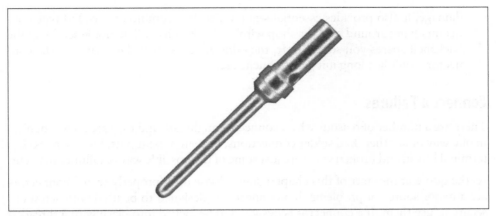
Figure 7-15. MIL-type crimp pin

Wiring caveats

Here are a few points to keep in mind when wiring a connector:

- As a general rule, do not tin the end of a stranded wire when it's used with a screw-type terminal block. This might seem like a good idea, but it creates a situation that can lead to metal fatigue and broken wires. Leave the wire bare, twist it tightly, and let the screw in the terminal block do its job.

- You really want to avoid soldering a wire to a connector that wasn't originally intended to be soldered. In other words, if a connector uses inserted pins and sockets designed for a crimping tool, attempting to solder a wire to the pin or socket will often result in a connection that is mechanically fragile. It may also turn out to be the case that while a soldered pin or socket can be inserted into a connector body, any stray bits of solder hanging over the sides may jam it in place. It will then be next to impossible to ever remove it should the need arise. This could result in the entire connector ending up in the trash can.

- Always use the right wire for the job. Don't use grossly undersized wire, and don't try to cram a heavy-gauge wire into a terminal block or lug meant for a smaller gauge. By the same token, if the solder cups on a connector are designed for, say, 18- to 22-gauge wire, trying to solder a 14-gauge wire to it probably won't allow the wire to seat completely within the cup, and the connection may cause a short with adjacent pins.

- Keep things neat. Bundle individual wires with related signals using nylon or plastic cable ties as much as possible. If there are a lot of cable bundles, labeling them can save time and reduce frustration in the future when you have to follow a cable and figure out what each line is supposed to be connected to.

- Always use a backshell with connectors on the end of a cable. This goes for circular as well as DB-type connectors. The backshell not only protects the wiring from damage, it also provides essential strain relief. It is common to see DB-type connectors lying around a lab or shop with no backshells. While not assembling the backshell spares you some effort, the odds are good that the wiring on the connector won't last long if it gets frequent use.

Connector Failures

There are a number of reasons why a connector might fail, and they are all mechanical in one way or another. Bad solder connections, broken or bent pins, loose screws on a terminal block, and broken wires are just some of the possible ways a failure can occur.

As the quote at the start of this chapter states, loose or improperly seated connectors are a major source of problems. If a connector is designed to be used with screws to secure it, use them. If a connector is designed to be locked into place with a threaded or bayonet-type outer shell, by all means use that. Some connectors, such as RCA phono plugs or USB connectors, are designed to be plugged in without any additional hardware to physically secure them, but just plugging in a connector that is meant to be secured and then letting it go at that is an excellent way to increase the odds of experiencing mysterious intermittent failures later.

If a connector is carrying low-level signals, especially in high-impedance circuits, corrosion or dirt can cause the connection to introduce noise into the signal, or cause intermittent failures that mysteriously appear and disappear. Corrosion can occur due to oils and acids from fingertips. Using connectors not intended for harsh environments can also cause problems.

Lastly, you should be aware that connectors are often rated in terms of the number of "insertion cycles" they can tolerate before things become worn and the connection becomes unreliable. Each time a connector is "mated" to its matching part, it counts as an insertion cycle. Some inexpensive DB-type connectors may only be good for around 50 insertion cycles (or less, if they're really cheap connectors). Other types, such as USB connectors, may have ratings of over 5,000 cycles before the connector starts to experience noticeable wear-related issues.

Serial Interfaces

The three most common types of serial interfaces you are likely to encounter when dealing with instrumentation device interfaces are RS-232, RS-485, and USB. The RS-232 and RS-485 standards were originally given the RS (Recommended Standard) designation by the Electronic Industries Alliance (EIA). When the maintaining organization changed its name the prefix changed as well, first to EIA-232 and finally to TIA-232. The standards are currently revised and maintained by the Telecommunications Industry Association, but since the RS nomenclature is so deeply ingrained in the history of electronics engineering and telecommunications, it has refused to go away. In this book I will use the RS-232 and RS-485 names for these standards.

USB interfaces have become very common over the past decade, to the point where USB has largely supplanted the RS-232 interface once found on just about every PC. Only desktop or rack-mounted PCs still provide serial interfaces (and even some of the thin rack-mount units have done away with them). The latest models of notebooks and so-called netbook computers now have only USB ports.

There are a variety of different types of special-purpose, high-reliability serial interfaces used in specific applications. These include CAN (Controller Area Network), FieldBus, and Profibus. The MIL-STD-1553 serial bus found in military applications and some avionics is yet another example. These are specialized interfaces that are not often encountered outside of limited domains, so we won't cover them here. However, the basic concepts behind serial communications apply to all serial interfaces, and the RS-485 interface is the underlying framework on which some industrial interfaces are based.

Half- and Full-Duplex

The terms "half-duplex" and "full-duplex" refer to the data transfer modes used with a pair of devices (or people) communicating over a channel of some sort. In a half-duplex system, the devices on either end take turns as either sender or receiver and do not talk simultaneously. A common example of a half-duplex communication channel is two-way radio (e.g., walkie-talkies), where the person on each end waits for the other to finish before talking back. This is where the terms "10-4," "over," "roger," and "over and out" come into play: they indicate whose turn it is to speak so that the people at the ends of the communication channel know when to talk. Otherwise, they would be talking on top of each other, and no one would be able to understand what was being said. In terms of serial interfaces, a half-duplex channel will have one set of wires. The direction of data flow between the endpoint devices is determined by the communications protocol the devices employ.

In a full-duplex system there are two channels, and each end of the channel can send whenever there is data ready to transmit. For example, an RS-232 connection may have only one cable, but inside there are two wires, one per data direction (actually, there are more than two wires, but we'll get to that later). Each wire is its own communications channel. Ethernet is another full-duplex type of interface, although it can also operate in half-duplex mode as well. RS-485, on the other hand, is often implemented as a half-duplex interface. In a basic RS-485 interface there is only one pair of wires to support a single interface channel, and the devices at each end must take turns being the transmitter and receiver during a data exchange.

RS-232/EIA-232

RS-232 is a voltage-based interface; that is, the difference between a logical 0 and a logical 1 is determined by the voltage level present on the signal lines. The standard does not specify the data encoding, only the hardware interface, but it is so closely associated with ASCII character encoding (discussed in detail in Chapter 12) that the two standards have become deeply intertwined. RS-232 has some limitations to be aware of. For example, there cannot be more than one device connected to a single "port" on a PC or other system (usually). In other words, it's a point-to-point interface, as shown in Figure 7-16. It also has line length and speed limitations because of the use of voltage swings to perform the signaling, and RS-232 tends to be susceptible to noise and interference from the surrounding environment.

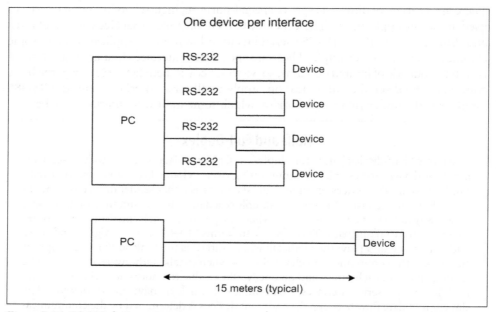

Figure 7-16. RS-232 device connections

RS-232 data formats

As we just mentioned, RS-232 is a voltage-based interface. That is, it uses one voltage level to signify a logical true (1), and another for logical false (0). Figure 7-17 shows how this works.

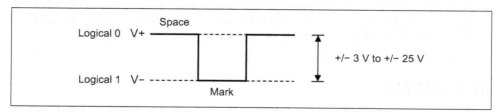

Figure 7-17. RS-232 signal levels

Notice that RS-232 data signals employ negative logic. That is, a logical true (1) is a negative voltage level, and a logical false (0) is a positive level.

When using ASCII encoding, an RS-232 character consists of a start bit (a mark), followed by 5 to 9 data bits, an optional parity bit, and 1 or 2 stop bits (a space). Figure 7-18 shows the format for 8 data bits with no parity and 1 stop bit, and 7 data bits (true ASCII) with even parity and 1 stop bit. In both cases the actual number of bits sent or received for each character or byte is 10 bits. Each unit of data, from the start bit to the stop bit (if used), is referred to as a "frame."

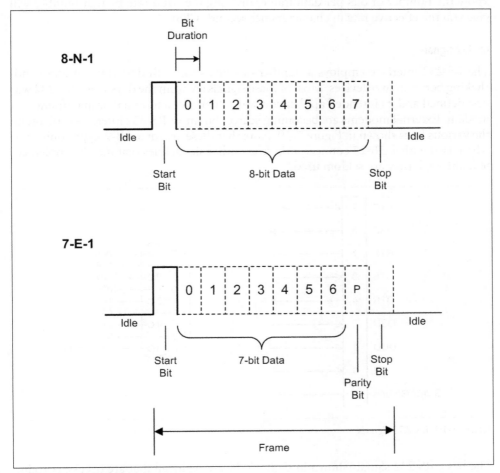

Figure 7-18. RS-232 data formats

In order for a specific format to work correctly, both ends of the communications channel must be configured correctly from the outset. Attempting to connect a device configured as 8-N-1 to a device set up for 7-E-1 won't work, even though both ends are sending and receiving 10 bits of data per frame. It will, at best, result in erroneous data at the 8-bit end, and a lot of parity errors at the 7-bit end.

The speed, or data transmission rate, of an RS-232 interface is measured in *baud*, which is the number of bits per second. What this means is that a serial interface running at 9,600 baud will not send or receive 1,200 bytes or characters per second (9600/8), because at least 2 of the 10 bits in the frame are taken up by the start and stop bits. That is, only 80% of the frame contains actual data. The actual maximum rate just happens to work out to 960 characters per second in this case. As a general rule, if you know the number of bits per data frame, dividing the baud rate by that number will give you the effective rate in characters per second (CPS).

RS-232 signals

The RS-232 interface employs a number of signals for both data transfer and handshaking between two devices. Most of these signals are from the days when RS-232 was first defined and its intended application was to connect a terminal or mainframe to a modem. External modems are becoming scarce, but most RS-232 interfaces still retain the various lines shown in Figure 7-19. Note that these are for a DB-9–type connector; when used with a DB-25 connector there are other signal lines that may be implemented, although they are seldom used.

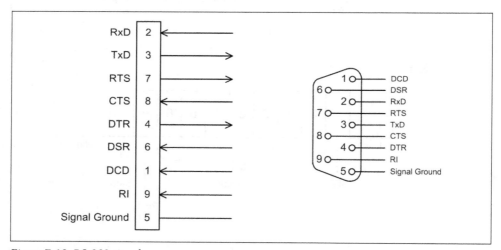

Figure 7-19. RS-232 signals

The basic RS-232 signals shown in Figure 7-19 are really all that are necessary to implement a full RS-232 interface with hardware handshaking. The signals are defined in Table 7-2.

Table 7-2. RS-232 DB-9 pin definitions

Signal	Definition
RxD	Received Data
TxD	Transmitted Data
RTS	Request to Send
CTS	Clear to Send
DTR	Data Terminal Ready
DSR	Data Set Ready
DCD	Data Carrier Detect
RI	Ring Indicator

RS-232 is a full-duplex interface, meaning that data may move in both directions simultaneously. It is also asynchronous, and all data clock synchronization is derived from the incoming data stream itself, not from an additional clock signal line in the interface (there is, of course, an exception to this—RS-232 can be implemented as a synchronous, or clocked, interface—but it is seldom used). RS-232 can also be used in half-duplex mode. See the sidebar "Half- and Full-Duplex" on page 219 for more information.

In many cases all one really needs are the RxD (receive) and TxD (transmit) data lines, and some instruments are indeed wired this way. Most instruments with an RS-232 interface will work fine when connected to a PC using the correct cable (typically supplied with the instrument), and no modifications to the interface wiring should be necessary.

DTE and DCE

When working with RS-232 interfaces you will no doubt encounter the acronyms DTE (Data Terminal Equipment) and DCE (Data Communications Equipment). Hailing from the days of mainframes and acoustic coupler modems, these terms were used to define the endpoints and link devices of a serial communications channel. The terms were originally introduced by IBM to describe communications devices and protocols for its mainframe products.

In the context of RS-232, DTE devices are found at the endpoints of a serial data communications channel. The "terminal" in DTE does not refer to a device with a roll of paper and a keyboard (a teletype terminal, or TTY), or a CRT and a keyboard (an old-style computer terminal, or "glass TTY" as they were once known). It literally means "the end." Figure 7-20 shows this arrangement graphically.

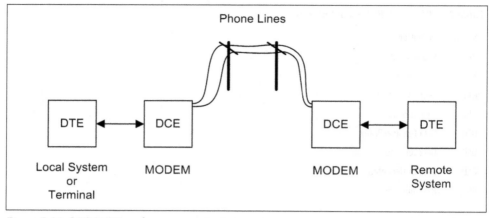

Figure 7-20. DTE/DCE modem communications

Another way to look at it is in terms of "data sink" and "data source." A data sink receives data, and a data source emits it. Either end of the channel (the two DTE devices) can be a sink or a source. The DCE devices provide the channel between the endpoints using some type of communications medium. For a system using modems, this would typically be a telephone line.

Nowadays modems are becoming something of an endangered species, although they are still used for data communications in some remote parts of the US and around the world that lack high-speed Internet services. However, the wiring employed in RS-232 cables and connectors still reflects that legacy, which is why it's important to understand it in order to correctly connect things using RS-232.

The signals described in the previous section are named with reference to the DTE. In other words, on a DTE device, TxD is a data source, or output. On a DCE, it is a sink, or input, for the TxD of the DTE. This also applies to the RxD line. In effect, the DCE's data source and sink connections are functionally inverted with respect to the DTE's TxD and RxD lines, even though they have same names. This may seem confusing, but the upshot of it all is that when connecting a DTE to a DCE, the interface is wired pin-to-pin between them (1 to 1, 2 to 2, and so on).

If you need to connect two devices that happen to be DTEs, you will need to use what is called a *crossover cable* or, if you don't need the handshake lines, a *null-modem cable*. Figure 7-21 shows how the TxD and RxD lines would cross over for a DTE-to-DTE interface. It does not show how the handshake lines would need to be connected.

Most devices with a serial port are wired as DTE devices, although some do have the ability to be configured as DCEs. This can be done using jumpers, small PCB-mounted switches, a front-panel control, or even via software. The built-in serial port on a PC is typically implemented as a DTE.

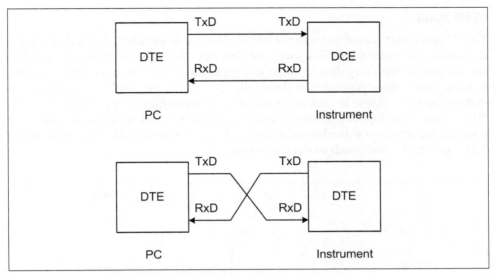

Figure 7-21. Crossover or null-modem interface

For devices with low-speed interfaces, or when the communications protocol is strictly a command-response format, you probably don't need the rest of RS-232's handshaking lines. In this case, you can use a ready-made commercial null-modem cable or a null-modem adapter. Such an adapter is shown in Figure 7-22.

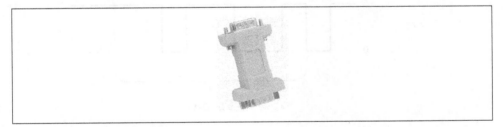

Figure 7-22. DB-9 null-modem adapter

RS-485/EIA-485

RS-485 is commonly found in instrument control interfaces and in industrial settings. Like its predecessor, RS-422, it has a high level of noise immunity, and cable lengths can extend up to 1,200 meters in some cases. RS-485 is also faster than RS-232. It can support data rates of around 35 Mbit/s with a 10-meter cable, and 100 Kbit/s at 1,200 meters.

RS-485 signals

RS-485 owes these capabilities to the use of differential signaling. Instead of using a dedicated wire to carry data in a particular direction, there are two wires that are electrically paired that carry data in either direction, but not at the same time. The two wires in a differential interface are always the opposite of one another in polarity. The state of the lines relative to each other indicates a change from a logic value of "1" to a "0," or vice versa. Figure 7-23 shows a typical situation involving asynchronous serial data that incorporates a start bit and a stop bit. For comparison, it also shows the digital TTL input that corresponds to the RS-485 signals.

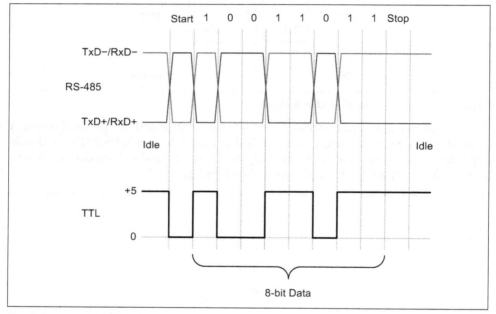

Figure 7-23. RS-485 signal levels

Note that the + and – signals always return to the initial starting state at the completion of the transfer of a byte of data.

Line drivers and receivers

In an RS-485 interface, each connection point uses a pair of devices consisting of a differential transmitter and a differential receiver. This is shown in Figure 7-24.

RS-485 may be implemented as a two-wire half-duplex interface or a bidirectional four-wire full-duplex interface, but for many applications full-duplex operation is not required. A four-wire arrangement is shown in Figure 7-25.

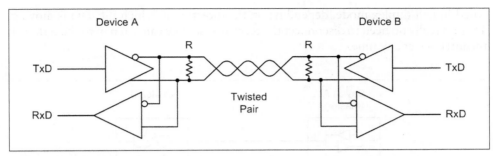

Figure 7-24. RS-485 interface drivers in two-wire mode

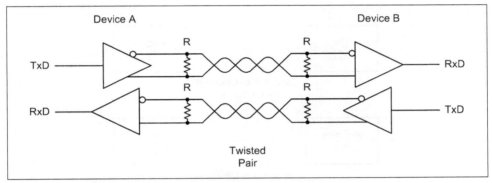

Figure 7-25. RS-485 interface drivers in four-wire mode

RS-485 multi-drop

RS-485 also allows for more than one device, or *node*, to be connected to the serial "bus" in what is called a *multidrop configuration*. This is shown in Figure 7-26. In order to do this, the transmitter (output) section of an RS-485 driver must be capable of being placed into a Hi-Z, or high impedance, mode. This capability is also essential when RS-485 is connected in two-wire mode.

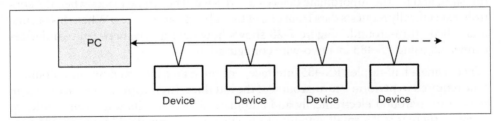

Figure 7-26. RS-485 multidrop

The reason for this is that if the transmitter was always actively connected to the interface it could conflict with another transmitter somewhere along the line. In Figure 7-27 you can see how the drivers take turns being "talkers," or data sources, when wired in half-duplex mode, depending on the direction in which the data is moving. There is really no need to disconnect the receivers, so they can listen in to the traffic on the interface at any time.

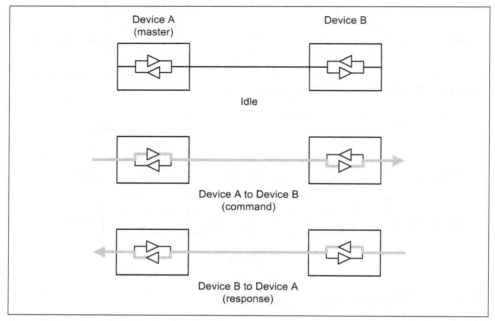

Figure 7-27. RS-485 half-duplex data flow

In a typical multidrop configuration, one device is designated as the controller and all other devices on the RS-485 bus are subordinate to it, although it is possible to have multiple controllers on an RS-485 network. The default mode for the controller is transmit, and for the subordinate devices it is receive. They trade places when the controller specifically requests data from one of the subordinate devices. When this occurs, it is called "turn-around." Figure 7-28 shows how data moves between two devices connected using RS-485 in a two-wire configuration.

When using a half-duplex RS-485 interface, one must take into account the amount of time required to perform a turn-around of the interface. Even with an interface that can sense a turn-around electronically and automatically change its state from sender to receiver, there is still a small amount of time involved. Some RS-232–to–RS-485 converters can use the RTS line from the RS-232 interface to perform the turn-around as well. Figure 7-29 shows how this works.

Notice that when either device in Figure 7-29 is in the receive mode, there is an explicit wait involved while the device listens for a response from the other end of the channel.

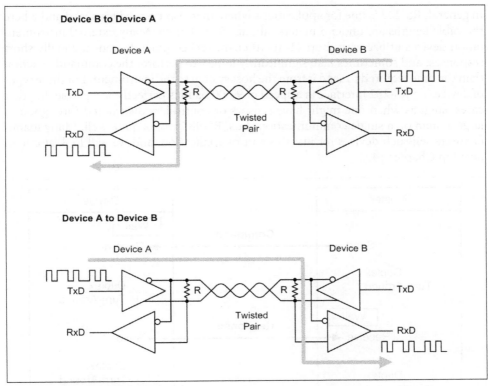

Figure 7-28. RS-485 half-duplex operation

RS-232 versus RS-485

Table 7-3 contains a comparison of some of the electrical characteristics of RS-232 and RS-485.

Table 7-3. RS-232 versus RS-485

Characteristic	RS-232	RS-485
Differential	No	Yes
Max. number of drivers	1	32
Max. number of receivers	1	32
Modes of operation	Half- and full-duplex	Half- or full-duplex
Network topology	Point-to-point	Multidrop
Max. distance	15 m	1,200 m
Max. speed at 12 m	20 kbit/s	35 Mbit/s
Max. speed at 1,200 m	n/a	100 kbit/s

In general, RS-232 is fine for applications where there isn't a need for speed and where the cable lengths are under 5 meters (about 15 feet) or so. Many external instrumentation devices utilize very short (2- to 10-character) commands, return equally short responses, and sometimes take significantly longer to perform the commanded action than the time required to send it from the host system to the instrument. For these types of devices an RS-232 interface at a speed of 9,600 baud is perfectly acceptable. In other cases, such as when one might have sensors or controllers distributed throughout a large system on a single communications bus, RS-485 works quite well. Many manufacturers sell such devices for just this sort of application, and we will look at one in detail in Chapter 14.

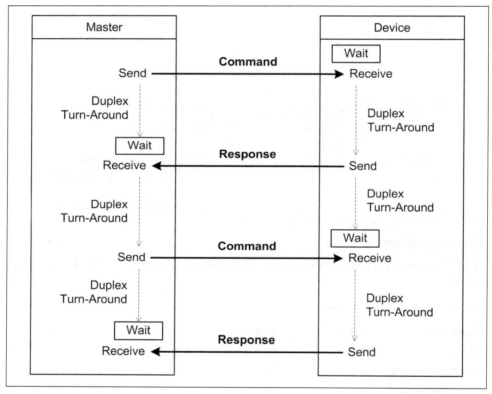

Figure 7-29. RS-485 command-response sequence

USB

Universal Serial Bus is yet another form of half-duplex asynchronous serial interface. It is similar in some respects to RS-485 in that data is carried as a differential signal on a pair of wires in the USB cable. The cable also includes wires for power and ground. Also, in a USB network only one interface can act as the controller (or host), and all other devices are subordinate.

Figure 7-30 shows a USB network consisting of a host system with an internal hub, two external hubs, and eight USB devices.

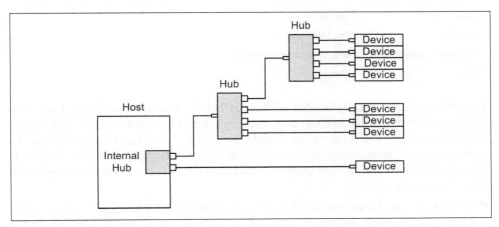

Figure 7-30. USB network

For the most part, we don't need to worry about the low-level details of the USB interface itself. Both the Windows and Linux operating systems incorporate low-level drivers to handle the host chores, and instruments that utilize USB at a low level are provided with software that deals with the communications. In some cases, the vendor may also provide a library module that supports access from user-written application programs. This is more common for Windows than it is for Linux, although some Linux interface drivers are available as well.

USB classes

The USB standard defines various classes of devices that utilize USB interfaces. Some of the more common classes that you might encounter on a regular basis are listed in Table 7-4.

Table 7-4. Common USB device classes

USB class	Example(s)
Communications	Ethernet adapter, modem
HID (Human Interface Device)	Keyboard, mouse, etc.
Imaging	Webcam, scanner
IrDA	Infrared data link/control
Mass Storage	Disk drive, SSDD, flash memory stick
PID (Physical Interface Device)	Force feedback joystick
Printer	Laser printer, etc.
Smart Card	Smart card reader
Test & Measurement (USBTMC)	Test and measurement devices
Video	Webcam

You are most likely already familiar with the HID and Mass Storage classes. These two classes include things like keyboards, mice, simple joysticks, outboard USB disk drives, and flash memory sticks (so-called thumbdrives). The HID class is relatively easy to implement, and most operating systems come with generic HID class drivers, so it is not uncommon to find devices implemented using the HID class that don't look at all like a keyboard or mouse.

If a USB device uses a unique interface (there's a USB class for this, too), it is up to the vendor to supply the necessary interface drivers, including any low-level drivers needed by the operating system. In cases like this you typically need to install the driver software before attaching the device so that it will be available to the operating system when the new device is detected.

Since we won't be writing any low-level USB driver software, we won't delve any deeper into USB classes. The working assumption here is that the device will come with whatever software is needed.

USB data rates

When working with USB devices, it is good to know what to expect of the interface in terms of performance. One potential downside to USB interface devices is speed: many are not particularly fast when compared to what can be achieved using a PCI bus–based interface or a dedicated standalone data acquisition system.

The maximum data rate for a USB interface can vary from 1.5 Mbit/s (megabits/second) to 4 Gbit/s (gigabits/second), depending on the standards compliance level of the interface. The data transfer rates for USB are defined in terms of a revision level of the USB standard. In other words, devices that are compliant with USB 1.1 have a theoretical maximum data rate of 12 Mbit/s in full-speed mode, whereas USB 3.0–compliant devices have a maximum data transfer rate of 4 Gbit/s. Table 7-5 lists the specification levels and the associated maximum data transfer rates.

Table 7-5. USB versions

Version	Release date	Maximum data rate(s)	Rate name	Comments/features added
1.0	1996	1.5 Mbit/s	Low speed	Very limited adoption by industry
		12 Mbit/s	Full speed	
1.1	1998	1.5 Mbit/s	Low speed	Version most widely adopted initially
		12 Mbit/s	Full speed	
2.0	2000	480 Mbit/s	High speed	Mini and micro connectors, power management
3.0	2007	4 Gbit/s	Super speed	Modified connectors, backward compatible

USB 3.0 is still rather new, and most USB devices that one will encounter will either be 1.1- or 2.0-compliant. You should also know that even if a device claims to be a USB 2.0 high-speed type, the odds of getting sustained rates of 480 Mbit/s are slim. The time required for the microcontroller in the USB device to receive a command, decode it, perform whatever action is requested, and respond back to the host can be considerably slower than what one might expect from the data transfer rate alone. In addition, the ability of the host controller to manage communications can contribute to slower than theoretical maximum data rates. If the host is busy with other tasks, it may be unable to service the USB channel fast enough to sustain a high data throughput.

How USB devices and hubs are connected can also play a big part in how responsive the communications will be. A USB 1.1 network using 1.1 hubs and devices is only as fast as the slowest device in the network. USB 2.0 hubs deal with this by separating the low/full-speed traffic from the high-speed data. When purchasing new USB components, you should avoid 1.1 hubs and stick to 2.0 units. That way, you can avoid having a high-speed 2.0 device run into a bottleneck due to 1.1 devices on your USB network (assuming that the host controller is itself USB 2.0 high-speed capable).

But speed isn't everything, and in many instrumentation systems it's not critical so long as the basic response time requirements are met. Because of the appeal of low cost and ease of use, we will examine various low-cost USB instrumentation devices in the following sections.

USB instrumentation

A generic version of the type of USB instrumentation device we can expect to encounter is shown in Figure 7-31. This is similar to several readily available commercial devices and is intended to illustrate the types of inputs and outputs one can expect to find.

Many USB interface devices also incorporate a high degree of internal functionality and configuration options. For example, the hypothetical device shown in Figure 7-31 has discrete I/O lines that may be configured as either inputs or outputs on an individual basis, analog inputs and outputs, and some counter and timer ports. These are typical and are found on many devices of this type. The PWM outputs should be able to accept control parameters to determine the base clock rate and the duty cycle. Some devices may even incorporate the ability to control the duty cycle directly through one of the analog inputs.

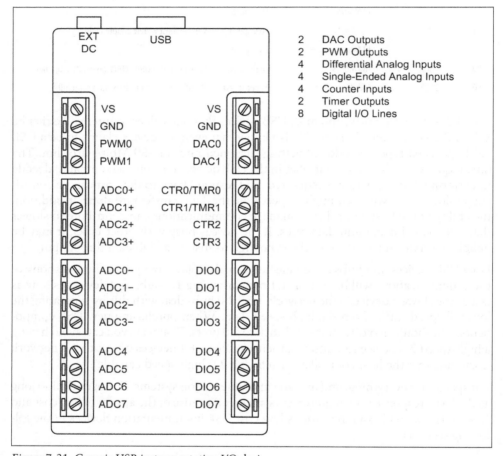

Figure 7-31. Generic USB instrumentation I/O device

Now let's look at a real USB interface device. Figure 7-32 shows one type of commercially available USB instrumentation device, the LabJack U3. This is a low-cost (around $110) unit that features configurable discrete I/O; analog input and output channels; timers; counters; and support for SPI, I2C, and asynchronous serial protocols. The U3 employs a full speed (12 Mbit/s) USB interface.

Figure 7-32. LabJack USB interface device

Windows Virtual Serial Ports

Under Windows, one can implement what is known as a *virtual serial port* (VSP) or *virtual COM port* (VCP). An aspect of "port redirection," VSPs have been a part of Windows for quite a long time. A virtual serial port supports most or all of the functionality normally found with any other Windows serial port interface. You can set the baud rate and the number of data bits, and read and write data just as you would with a "real" serial port. The virtual port also emulates the control lines used in a physical serial port, such as RTS, CTS, and so on.

One primary application for a virtual serial port is to provide a common and convenient interface to a physical USB port and the devices that might be connected to it. Figure 7-33 shows a simplified diagram of a VSP-to-USB interface.

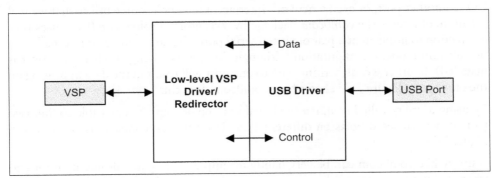

Figure 7-33. Virtual serial port interface

In some cases, a virtual serial port is used with a USB-to-serial converter. USB converters for RS-232 and RS-485 interfaces are readily available, and Figure 7-34 shows a generic diagram of such a device used to interface a serial instrument with a USB port on a PC. ICs from vendors such as FTDI and Silicon Labs are available that incorporate all of the necessary functionality to implement a USB-to-serial interface. With the demise of the RS-232 serial port on the latest computers, particularly notebook and netbook machines, many manufacturers are turning to these types of interfaces for products that would otherwise use RS-232 or RS-485 as their primary control and data interface. In other cases it might serve as the primary connection to an instrument or device that has only a USB interface incorporated into its design, but includes a driver that can translate between serial data and the interface protocol used by the device. The USB-to-GPIB interface we will look at later is one such device.

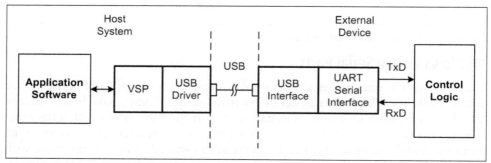

Figure 7-34. USB-to-serial interface

USB redirection is just one application for a virtual serial port and port redirection. A Windows virtual serial port can be used just like a regular serial interface to redirect I/O to another port, or even a network interface. One open source utility that we will see more of later is the *com0com* package by Vyacheslav Frolov. com0com uses port redirection to implement a pair of virtual serial ports that are connected internally in a default null-modem configuration (although this can be changed when the driver is installed). In other words, writing data to one port will result in the data appearing on the other port. Figure 7-35 shows how com0com does this.

By using a utility called *com2tcp* (included with com0com) it is possible to link two pairs of virtual serial ports on different PCs via a network connection, as shown in Figure 7-36.

A utility like com0com can be very handy for implementing a real-time monitor and trace facility or a command-line-type user interface, or to simulate an instrument that utilizes a serial interface. The ability to redirect serial interfaces is a powerful tool for working with instrumentation devices.

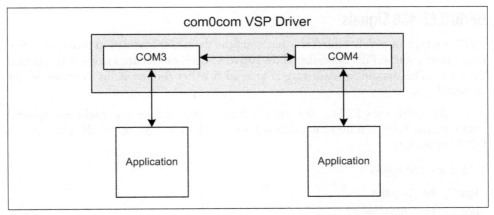

Figure 7-35. The com0com VSP utility

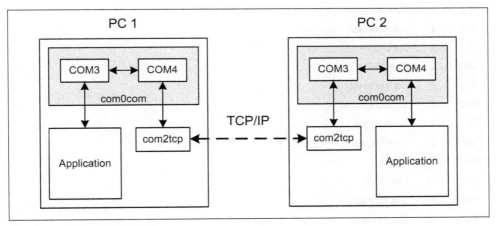

Figure 7-36. com0com over TCP/IP

GPIB/IEEE-488

The General Purpose Interface Bus (GPIB) was developed by Hewlett-Packard in the late 1960s to interface HP test equipment with other test instruments, HP printers, and HP's line of laboratory minicomputers and mass data storage devices. Originally known as the Hewlett-Packard Interface Bus (HPIB), it was given an IEEE standards designation in 1975.

Although GPIB (HPIB at the time, actually) was used in the late 1970s with some HP computer equipment to interface large external disk drives and line printers, it never really caught on as a data peripheral interface standard. It was, and still is, most commonly found in test and data acquisition equipment.

GPIB/IEEE-488 Signals

GPIB is a type of parallel interface that contains data, command, and interface signal lines in one cable. GPIB addressing allows up to 15 devices to share a single 8-bit parallel data bus. The maximum data rate is around 8 MB/s for the latest versions of the standard.

Internally, GPIB uses 12 lines for various signals and 12 lines for shield and ground connections. Table 7-6 lists the GPIB signals, and Figure 7-37 shows the pin-out of a GPIB connector.

Table 7-6. GPIB signals

Signal	Pin	Function
DIO1	1	Data/command
DIO2	2	Data/command
DIO3	3	Data/command
DIO4	4	Data/command
EOI	5	End or identity
DAV	6	Data valid
NRFD	7	Not read for data
NDAC	8	Not data accepted
IFC	9	Interface clear
SRQ	10	Service request
ATN	11	Attention
Shield	12	Cable shield
DIO5	13	Data/command
DIO6	14	Data/command
DIO7	15	Data/command
DIO8	16	Data/command
REN	17	Remote enable
Ground	18	Ground
Ground	19	Ground
Ground	20	Ground
Ground	21	Ground
Ground	22	Ground
Ground	23	Ground
Ground	24	Ground

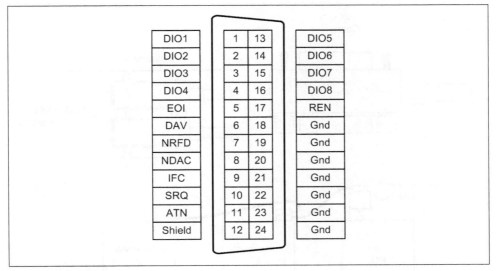

DIO1		1	13		DIO5
DIO2		2	14		DIO6
DIO3		3	15		DIO7
DIO4		4	16		DIO8
EOI		5	17		REN
DAV		6	18		Gnd
NRFD		7	19		Gnd
NDAC		8	20		Gnd
IFC		9	21		Gnd
SRQ		10	22		Gnd
ATN		11	23		Gnd
Shield		12	24		Gnd

Figure 7-37. GPIB connector pin assignments

GPIB Connections

GPIB uses a special 24-pin connector that allows connections to be stacked. The slowest device on the bus sets the maximum data transfer rate. Figure 7-38 shows an outline of a GPIB/IEEE-488 connector and how the connectors are stacked to connect two or more devices in a sequential arrangement.

GPIB devices may also be connected in a star configuration, as shown in Figure 7-39.

GPIB via USB

Although one can install a GPIB PCI interface card in a full-sized computer, there are now inexpensive USB-to-GPIB interface modules available. One of these is shown in Figure 7-40. These work well with notebook-class computers, and most include interface software for use with custom applications, as well as drivers with an application program interface (API) for custom software.

The Prologix interface shown in Figure 7-40 uses the FTDI FT245R USB interface chip, and you have a choice of two interface modes: Windows virtual serial port/Linux serial driver, or direct access via a library module. FTDI provides drivers for both Windows and Linux. It is also useful to note that the Prologix device can be connected directly to the GPIB port of an instrument, so one can avoid purchasing a GPIB cable if only one GPIB instrument is involved. It is also possible to equip multiple instruments with their own converters and use a USB hub instead of daisy-chaining GPIB cables between instruments.

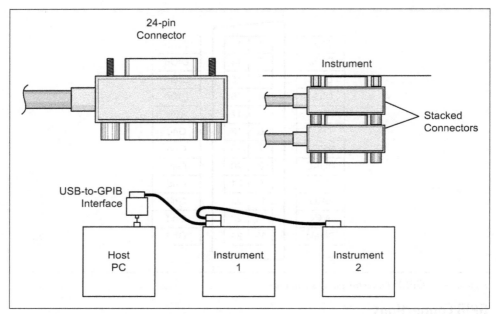

Figure 7-38. *GPIB instrument interface*

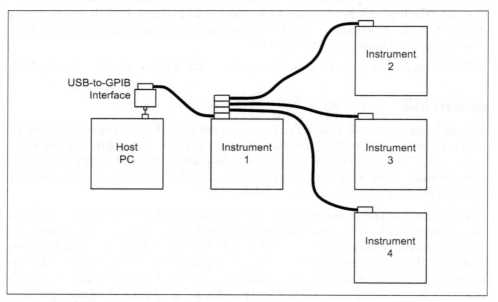

Figure 7-39. *GPIB star connection configuration*

Internally, a USB-to-GPIB interface will typically have two main sections: the USB interface hardware and a GPIB interface processor, as shown in Figure 7-41.

Figure 7-40. USB-to-GPIB interface

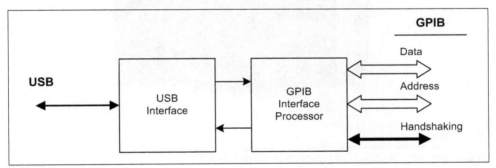

Figure 7-41. USB-to-GPIB converter block diagram

With a USB-to-GPIB converter, you are basically using a serial port (USB) to communicate with a parallel instrumentation bus (GPIB). Internal logic in the converter handles the GPIB handshaking and data transfer operations. If the converter utilizes a virtual serial port, everything that applies to serial programming applies here as well.

PC Bus Interface Hardware

A device designed to connect directly to the internal bus of a computer doesn't usually have a command-response protocol in the same sense that one would find with the serial or GPIB-type device. Instead, the interface protocol is embodied in the form of callable functions provided by driver software. They are also typically somewhat more difficult to use due to a higher level of software interface complexity.

You can buy various interface cards for a PC that are capable of capturing high-frequency signals in real time, whereas there are no such devices for RS-232 or RS-485, and only a handful with high-speed USB interfaces (and the USB devices often employ some type of buffering, or temporary storage, to help move data between the device and the host system).

The most common type of bus-based interface cards utilize the industry-standard Peripheral Component Interconnect (PCI) bus and the newest variant, the PCI Express (PCIe) bus. A typical PCI multifunction data acquisition (DAQ) card is shown in Figure 7-42. There are also add-on cards available for the industrial VME bus and the instrumentation PXI bus, but we won't get into those in this book as most of what we will want to do can be done with PCI- or PCIe-type cards.

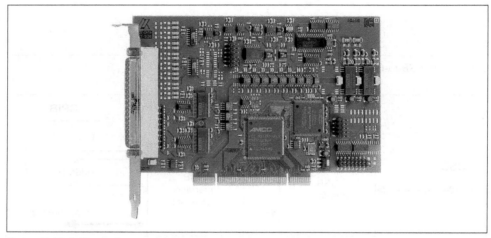

Figure 7-42. PCI interface card (ADDI-DATA APCI-3001)

Pros and Cons of Bus-Based Interfaces

Bus-based interfaces have a couple of inherent advantages over serial-interface-type devices:

- The bus-based interface is always faster than a serial interface, since it has direct access to the internal data bus in the computer. Data can be moved to and from the device in parallel at full (or almost full) bus speed, thereby avoiding the serial interface bottleneck.

- The internal settings of the device are directly accessible and the device can generate internal interrupt signals to get the attention of the host system, which makes it possible to incorporate functionality that would otherwise be difficult to build into a device connected using a serial interface.

Figure 7-43 shows the relationship between various types of PCI interface cards and the rest of the host computer system.

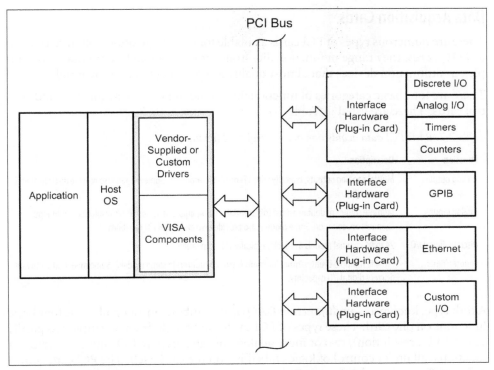

Figure 7-43. PCI interface cards

The main thing to notice in Figure 7-43 is that a PCI card always requires additional driver software to interface between the operating system, the application, and the hardware of the interface card itself. A driver will present an API that defines various functions for accessing the interface hardware, such as read, write, set a parameter, return a status value, and so on. We will discuss VISA drivers for instrumentation in Chapter 11.

The driver requirement is one downside to plug-in interface hardware. One cannot just pass ASCII strings back and forth via a serial port. You have to either create software that can interact with the driver's API, or use the application software provided by the card vendor. The other downside is that the back of a PC can get very crowded very quickly, and some cards use special high-density connectors that are somewhat fragile and must be used with strain-relief brackets so as to prevent them from being pulled or twisted (which can result in a damaged connector, a damaged card, or both). In addition, a PC loaded with interface cards isn't very portable, whereas a PC that uses serial, USB, or GPIB interfaces can (usually) be unplugged and moved without too much effort.

Data Acquisition Cards

There are numerous types of PCI cards available for data acquisition. Often referred to as *DAQ cards*, they range in functionality from simple discrete I/O interfaces to complex multifunction devices that almost qualify as computers in their own right.

There are four basic categories of functionality found in PCI data acquisition and control cards. These are listed in Table 7-7.

Table 7-7. Basic PCI data acquisition and control card functions

Function	Description
Analog output	Multiple analog outputs, typically with 12- or 16-bit resolution. Some models also provide discrete digital I/O capability.
Analog input	Multiple single- or double-ended (differential) analog inputs at 12- or 16-bit resolution. Eight input channels are common. Some models also provide discrete digital I/O capability.
Discrete digital I/O	24 to 96 channel models available, typically TTL-compatible.
Counter/timer	Provide multiple counter/timer functions (up to 20 counters in some models). Some models also provide discrete digital I/O capability.

A fifth type, known as a *multifunction DAQ card*, combines most or all of the four basic functions on one card. These types of PCI cards might include analog inputs (typically 12- or 16-bit resolution), two or more analog outputs, discrete I/O, and counter/timer functions, all under control of logic embedded on the card itself. The PCI card shown in Figure 7-42 is a multifunction DAQ card.

GPIB Interface Cards

Several manufacturers produce PCI GPIB interface cards. These cards are accessed through driver software supplied by the manufacturer, and most provide a programming interface that exposes functions for configuration, addressing, and data exchange.

Given that GPIB has a maximum data throughput of 8 MB/s, or 64 Mbit/s, a GPIB interface running at its theoretical maximum is over five times faster than a full-speed USB interface (but not as fast as a high-speed USB interface at 480 Mbit/s). Consequently, while a full-speed USB-to-GPIB interface may be convenient and easy to use, it becomes less useful as the need for high-speed data transfers over GPIB increases. There are some high-speed USB-to-GPIB interfaces available, but they tend to cost several times what a full-speed device costs.

One example of a plug-in GPIB interface card for the PCI bus is the 82350B from Agilent, shown in Figure 7-44.

A PCI interface card will often provide features such as buffering for high-speed data transfers and a full suite of IVI standard interface functions.

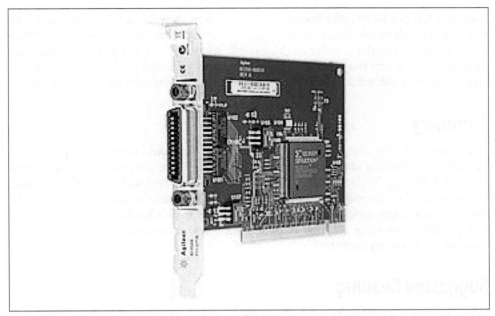

Figure 7-44. Agilent 82350B GPIB PCI interface card

Old Doesn't Mean Bad

Just as with used test equipment, there are a lot of used instrumentation and interface devices available. Most of them are still perfectly usable—they're just not likely to be as fast as newer equipment, or to have the bells and whistles that the newer units offer. Realistically, this shouldn't matter when you're working with systems that exhibit changes and responses that take anywhere from seconds to minutes (or even hours). What does matter is how easily the older equipment can be interfaced to a PC, and what kind of software interface it will need.

One downside to the older items is that they usually won't have any USB support. But that's really not a big deal in many cases. Unless a device uses a special custom interface, it should still have either a serial or GPIB interface available.

Older devices that employ a custom interface using a plug-in card won't work with modern computers if the interface card uses an ISA-type bus connection. Other than some models of industrial rack-mount computers, it is simply impossible to buy a new computer with ISA bus slots. Although it is possible to acquire an older PC with a decent CPU and run Python on it, the effort required to assemble the system and then write custom interface software is usually not worth it. It would make more sense to purchase a newer piece of equipment with a more modern type of interface.

That still leaves a lot of older instruments available with serial or GPIB interfaces, and these could well be worth the effort of incorporating them into a system rather than consigning them to the recycler or the landfill. As we will see in Chapter 11, communicating with an external instrument can be readily accomplished with a suitable interface, and the software necessary to achieve this isn't that difficult to implement.

Summary

We've covered a lot of ground in this chapter, and we should now be in a position to actually start thinking about how to select and use the physical interfaces of an instrumentation system. We've seen how different connectors are used with different interface types, and we learned the basics of assembling a connector. We then reviewed the various types of interfaces we'll be dealing with later, from a hardware perspective. We will put this knowledge to good use when we start discussing real instruments and systems in upcoming chapters.

Suggested Reading

While there are some books available on the topics we've covered in this chapter, you can probably find everything you need to know on the Web. There is a large amount of information available for RS-232, RS-485, USB, and GPIB. For example:

http://www.omega.com/techref/pdf/rs-232.pdf
> Omega Engineering has made available a compact one-page summary of the RS-232 standard. It's a handy thing to keep on the workbench or in your lab binder for quick reference.

Also, as you might expect, Wikipedia has entries on all manner of serial communications topics.

Some of the best places to look for technical information on connectors and the specialized tools that go with them can be found on distributors' websites. Here are a few:

> *http://www.DigiKey.com*
> *http://www.alliedelec.com*
> *http://www.mouser.com*

Federal and military standards are another good resource. Many of these documents go into great detail concerning assembly and interface techniques, and while you probably won't need all of the information, they also typically include some high-level material, and some even have what can only be described as tutorials. The NASA document referenced here is one such standard, and there are many more available:

NASA STD 8739.3, *"Soldered Electrical Connections." NASA Technical Standards Program, NASA, 1997.*

One of many technical standards freely available from NASA through its Technical Standards Program, this is a concise guide to high-reliability soldering techniques. It is available from *http://www.hq.nasa.gov/office/codeq/doctree/87393.htm.*

A catalog of available NASA technical standards can be found at *http://standards.nasa.gov/documents/nasa.*

## CHAPTER 8

Getting Started

The secret of getting ahead is getting started. The secret of getting started is breaking your complex overwhelming tasks into small manageable tasks, and then starting on the first one.

—Mark Twain

In this chapter we will look at some things that have been shown, time and again, to contribute to successful software projects of any size. I am, of course, talking about planning. This includes defining what you intend to do in the form of requirements and a design description, documenting how you plan to test it in order to catch as many bugs as possible, and then verifying that it actually meets the requirements and does what the original design called for. Lacking or unclear requirements are by far one of the leading causes of software project failures. Another big factor is inadequate testing.

With a small project, not having things work out as expected is annoying, but it may not be a major disaster. For larger projects, though, the result can be catastrophic. For substantial or logically complex programs, it is essential to have some solid requirements and a good testing strategy in place before coding ever starts. Also, one should be mindful of the fact that extending the reach of Python into the real world opens the door for the uncertainties and ambiguity of the real world to creep back in and impact, sometimes severely, the instrumentation software. Having a clear path and a well-defined set of goals to guide the effort is especially critical.

The reason for this chapter is simple: I want you to succeed. I am assuming that you could well be writing software for something that, while perhaps simple in and of itself, is a critical part of some other activity. Perhaps it is a controller for a piece of lab equipment, or maybe a data acquisition system to be used during research activities. It might be an automated test system for a production environment, or it could be a sprinkler control system for a world-class golf course. Whatever it is, if it doesn't work, or doesn't work reliably, it could mean lost time, lost revenue, or unusable data. Or worse.

Over the years I've become convinced that requirements, of some kind, are essential. I don't believe that anyone can sit down at the keyboard and start whacking away and expect to produce anything more complex than just a trivial application that is bug-free and feature-complete. Yet, many times I've encountered people who actually do seem to think that it is possible (a lot of whom really should know better), or worse, who don't understand that the trivial exercises they learned in college programming classes don't scale into full-size applications without some significant extra effort. These are the same people who can't understand why the software doesn't do what they (or their customers) expect and why it's so buggy. It doesn't have to be that way.

I hope this chapter will show you how easy it really is to define some basic requirements and create a plan for the software you want to create. The time and effort you spend up front doing this will pay dividends at the end of the project. Instead of fixing bugs or wondering why the data looks wrong, you can be proudly demonstrating your handiwork, secure in the knowledge that you've taken the right steps to ensure that it will work as intended.

Defining the Project

So, what is it, exactly, that you want to create? This is an important question that too often doesn't get much more consideration than a doodle on a whiteboard or some vague handwaving during a meeting. One of the most often cited reasons for the failure of software projects (as it currently stands, somewhere between 50 and 70% of all significant software projects are failures—depending on how one defines "failure") is the lack of a solid set of requirements and a plan for translating those requirements into working code. Try entering the terms "poor requirements software failures" into Google to see how much has been written about this.

All projects begin with a *statement of need* of some kind or another. It might be just an informal idea, or perhaps a request in an email. In some cases it might even be a formal document. From this starting point the project objectives are developed, usually in the form of a *statement of work* (SOW). The SOW captures details that the statement of need does not. Then come the various requirements, and finally the software design specification. Figure 8-1 shows the progression of each step from statement of need to design specification.

At each step, the level of detail increases. The level of detail eventually culminates in the *software design description* (SDD), which should (ideally) contain sufficient detail to generate the necessary software that will meet the requirements. In the following sections we will examine each step leading up to the SDD.

Requirements-Driven Design

Just so you know up front, what we're going to be looking at here may be defined as a relative of the so-called "waterfall" software life-cycle model for software development. If you're not familiar with the term "waterfall," don't be too concerned about it; it's just one way of conceptualizing and organizing development activities. Or, to put it another way, the waterfall model is one way of describing the software development life cycle (SDLC). Figure 8-1 is basically the frontend of a waterfall model diagram, and we'll see more a little later. There are, of course, other approaches that have been advanced as superior for one reason or another, and it is true that for some problem domains there are other models that are perhaps better. However, I'm not hard-over one way or the other with regard to models, nor do I believe that it is sacrilege to go back and modify requirements in order to synchronize them with reality. The major problem with modifying requirements is minimizing the impact the changes may have on work that's already been accomplished. Changes create a ripple effect, and if the ripples are too large they can turn into really big waves. In large projects this can be a major issue, but for small projects like the ones we will be dealing with it's not such a big deal.

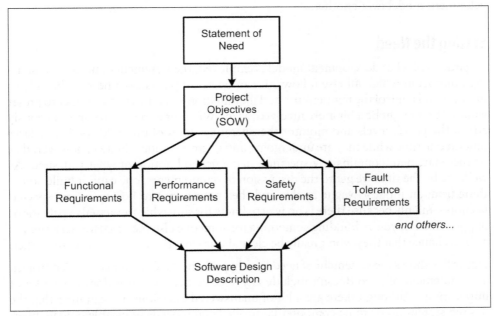

Figure 8-1. Evolution of requirements

The approach I will be using throughout this book is what is often called *requirements-driven design* (RDD). RDD works best when the requirements can be established early on, without much chance of major changes. Some types of projects—particularly those that deal with human-oriented transactions (e.g., banking, medical records, and other "fluid" domains)—may need more flexibility than is afforded by an RDD model. In our case, however, we are going to be discussing systems that incorporate "black boxes" in the form of commercial instruments or devices, use established interface and control protocols, and are intended to accomplish very specific tasks, usually over and over again until either something wears out or someone flips the power switch. The main challenge lies in defining how all the parts will fit together and what will become of the data collected, if any is collected at all.

Software development models are like tools in a toolbox: you always (I would assume) want to use the appropriate tool for the job at hand. Screwdrivers don't work well on nails, and hammers are useless for dealing with screws. It makes sense to use the most appropriate tool for the job, and in our case I believe that tool happens to be the RDD paradigm. The same thinking applies to programming languages, editors, and platforms. As Abraham Maslow, a well-known 20th century sociologist, once said: "If the only tool you have is a hammer, you tend to see every problem as a nail." If you'd like to know more about other software development models, I would encourage you to explore, as there is a lot of information available. There are also some rather amusing debates that have raged both online and at conferences on the advantages of one development model over another.

Stating the Need

Regardless of what development model is employed, the statement of need is the starting point from which all else follows. It can be as simple as "We need to be able to monitor and control the temperature and illumination levels in a test chamber to preset values," or it might be a bit more involved, as in "We want to be able to simultaneously adjust the power levels and monitor the operating states of up to 20 solid-state laser units at one time while they are undergoing initial stress testing." Notice, however, that neither statement contains any specifics, just a general notion of what is desired. As we'll see by the time we get to the discussion of requirements, one cannot build something from an input as vague as this and then count on it to behave in an expected fashion—mainly because there is no way to know for sure what the actual expectations happen to be. If you're building something for someone else (i.e., a customer), there is a good chance that they won't really be clear about what their expectations are, either.

Figure 8-2 shows the statement of need for a hypothetical AC power controller project. This statement of need doesn't include any specific details, but it does have a lot of implications. Although there are a lot of unanswered questions, we can infer that the desired system needs to be computer-controlled and it needs to be able operate unattended. A few moments of thought should also lead to the conclusion that if it is going to run automatically on a 24-hour basis, it should also be able to detect when something is wrong, take appropriate action, and alert an operator somehow.

The important point to remember is that a statement of need is not the same thing as a requirement. In some circles it is sometimes humorously referred to as a "desirement." It is only the outline of the foundation; it is not the whole structure, but carefully considering what is stated and asking some questions shows the way forward to acquiring the necessary details.

Statement of Need

The test group needs a way to automatically control the AC power to various units under test in the burn-in room. The current method of manually controlling the power at predetermined intervals is both cumbersome and prone to error. For 24-hour (or longer) test cycles it also means that an operator must be on duty during the entire test period. An automated system would allow the testing to go on unattended during evening hours.

Figure 8-2. Statement of need

Project Objectives

The next level of detail lays out the project objectives, also known as the statement of work. These still aren't requirements in the strictest sense, but rather definite goals that can be translated into requirements. For example, the project objectives for our hypothetical AC control system might look like the statement of work shown in Figure 8-3.

The primary thing to notice here is that the objectives still don't contain any definite values for parameters such as time durations, what constitutes an anomaly, or data communication protocols. What they do contain are specific statements about the desired high-level functional characteristics of the finished system (i.e., the general behavior), and those are what the specific functional requirements will be derived from. The SOW defines what will be the basis for determining the ultimate success or failure of the project from an end user's point of view (or from your point of view, if you happened to write the SOW for your own project).

Requirements

Requirements come in many levels of detail. The next level after the SOW might be high-level project objectives, science requirements, operational requirements, and so on, descending in ever-increasing levels of detail until finally arriving at the software implementation requirements contained in the SDD.

Statement of Work

The test group desires an automated AC power control system for use in the burn-in room. The system should demonstrate the following features:

1. The ability to control up to 64 devices (a unit under test, or UUT) using commercially available AC power control devices;

2. The ability to enable or disable any single device via software control;

3. The ability to receive status data from the test monitoring system and immediately shut down a particular UUT to prevent catastrophic damage;

4. The ability to execute power-on and power-off events at predetermined intervals;

5. The ability to sense the state of a UUT after a power-on event and determine if the UUT has failed to respond correctly;

6. The ability to display the current status of all AC power control channels in real time using a GUI.

The system should consist of rack-mounted AC power control units and a dedicated rack-mounted control PC with LCD monitor. The control interface for the AC power control units may be RS-232 serial, USB or GPIB (whichever is the least costly). The control and data interface to other test systems may be either RS-232 or Ethernet.

The system must be capable of operating 24 hours a day, seven days a week, without operator supervision. It must have the ability to alert an operator, either locally or via a network connection, should an anomaly be detected. The system must have the ability to assign levels of severity to anomalies in order to minimize alerts from non-critical events.

Figure 8-3. Statement of work

Lower levels of requirements are derived from the requirements above them, in a top-down fashion. At each level more details emerge and are incorporated into the requirements set in a process known as *requirements decomposition*, which is a part of the requirements analysis activity. How much time and effort one spends doing requirements decomposition depends on the type of project; some projects are simple enough that a basic set of testable functional requirements will suffice, while others (like the full-authority digital engine controls on jet aircraft, or the guidance and propulsion control systems on spacecraft) might require extensive requirements analysis and decomposition to ensure that all the relevant requirements have been captured, all the off-nominal conditions have been accounted for, and all the low-level implementation requirements necessary to build and program the system are defined and reviewed. The requirements documents for these types of projects can easily run to hundreds of pages. One of the trickier parts of the requirements analysis activity is knowing when enough is enough, and when to keep going to fill in necessary details.

Why Requirements Matter

Without requirements, or at least a statement of work, there is really no way to get a clear idea of exactly what the end result is supposed to be or how it should behave. Sure, there might be some vague notion of what the system is supposed to do, but it is only that—a vague notion—and it's a sure bet that your vague notion isn't going to be the same as someone else's vague notion. A doodle on a napkin during lunch is not a requirement, and neither are the notes jotted down on a whiteboard during a meeting. These types of things are insufficient as requirements, not only because they don't meet the criteria for verifiability, but also because they are only the tops of the waves in what might actually be a very deep ocean.

Requirements, even a minimal set, allow us to define what is desired in clear and specific terms. A good set of requirements is something that everyone should be able to agree on. They are also the yardstick against which the behavior of the finished product is measured to verify success, or perhaps failure.

A True Requirements Story

Once upon a time I was tasked with creating a real-time filter array data acquisition system for a large radio telescope. The filter array was an old thing that someone had hauled out of storage, but it had 640 discrete channels, each narrowly tuned to a specific frequency. My job was to obtain a set of high-speed analog-to-digital converters for acquiring data from each channel, integrate various pieces of new hardware with the old filter array system, and then program the whole thing using a real-time operating system. An RF engineer was lined up to tune the beast once it was running. All good so far. The fun started when I tried to get the person who was to be in charge of operating the filter array to agree to any specific requirements.

"What is the maximum allowable conversion time for each channel?" I asked. "Well, as fast as possible," was the response. That wasn't going to work, so I tried again by rephrasing the question. Still the vague answer. Things went on like this for at least 30 minutes, with me getting more frustrated and the other person getting increasingly annoyed at my attempts to pin down some actual numbers. I finally did manage to get a few basic numbers to work with, but I still had to interpolate some of the missing values and just make educated guesses at the others.

In the end, the resulting system met, and even exceeded, the timing and stability expectations. In fact, it did its job a little too well. The first time we tried to run it at full speed and stream all 640 channels' worth of data into the telescope's control and data processing system, we managed to crash it. The entire multimillion-dollar radio

---

telescope was dead. It took something like two hours for the operators to bring it all back up again. Fortunately it happened during allocated engineering time, otherwise we would probably have had to deal with an irate scientist. The moral of the story: don't ever assume that the person who needs to supply the baseline values for the requirements actually knows the answers (and is willing to admit he doesn't know). Be prepared to fill in the blanks yourself and double-check your assumptions. It's also a good idea to give the people from whom you need answers some advance warning as to the type of information you will be looking for. At least that way they can't reasonably accuse you of springing a pop quiz on them.

Well-Formed Requirements

A requirement describes, in a clear, precise, and unambiguous manner, what characteristics something must possess and what behaviors it must demonstrate in order to meet one or more project objectives. A requirement almost always contains the word "shall." Here is an example of a functional requirement statement:

> The system shall be capable of detecting a nonresponsive UUT within 100 milliseconds after AC power is commanded to the ON state for any particular UUT.

One key characteristic of a good requirement is that it is verifiable. In other words, it defines specific values for rates, limits, and exceptions (if any) that can be verified by testing. The preceding example functional requirement is testable—it states a specific event and a time interval. However, it is easy to write a requirement that is not testable, even if it does contain the word "shall." For example:

> The system shall incorporate the ability to detect and handle invalid data appropriately.

By itself, this requirement isn't really a requirement; it's a desirement. For instance, what exactly does it mean? What is "invalid data"? What does "handle" mean? What is appropriate? There are no definitions, so therefore there is nothing specific to test for. The bottom line is that this "requirement" is not a requirement, and it cannot be verified.

There are basically five essential characteristics of a well-formed requirement, and these are listed in Table 8-1.

Table 8-1. Essential requirements characteristics

Characteristic	Description
Necessary	Requirements must only address the functionality or characteristics necessary in order for the system to meet the objectives defined in the SOW. In other words, there should be no "bells and whistles" requirements.
Unambiguous	A requirement may have only one possible interpretation. Requirements with multiple possible interpretations may result in a system that does not meet the SOW objectives. Requirements must be clear and concise.
Consistent	Requirements must not introduce conflicting objectives, parameters, or functionality. Within the requirements set for a project, requirements must support one another.

Characteristic	Description
Traceable	Every requirement must have a reason to exist, and traceability establishes that reason. It defines the link between a requirement and the higher-level item that it was derived from, which may itself be a requirement or an element in the SOW. In other words, requirements flow downward, and traceability flows upward.
Verifiable	A requirement must be capable of being verified by testing, analysis, inspection, or, in some cases, demonstration. A requirement that cannot be verified cannot be implemented with confidence, because there will be no way to know for sure that the software is in compliance.

There are other criteria in use, but these five are usually considered to be the most important.

The Big Picture

Now that we've examined the basics of requirements, this would be a good time to see how things fit in with the software development and verification activities. Figure 8-4 shows how requirements progress from the SOW (project description and objectives) through to the actual software, and also how testing is dependent on requirements.

Requirement Types

Let's discuss Figure 8-4 a little, since there's a lot going on here, and we'll be referring back to it later. We already know about the SOW ("Project Description and Objectives"), so we can move past that. If we follow the flow, the next thing we encounter are three primary types of requirements in a box, labeled "Integration," "Performance," and "Functional." These are all closely related, and may even appear together in the same document. There is also something hovering up above called "Derived Requirements." Let's take a closer look at these different types of requirements:

Functional requirements
> Functional requirements, and any associated performance and integration requirements, typically deal with the overt external behavior of a device or system. Or, to put it another way, they deal with what should happen when the power switch is set to "On" and the system is stimulated with some type of input. Functional requirements can be defined as the required behaviors of a system or device from a "black box" perspective. In other words, for any given input it must generate a specific output. Exactly how it does this is not within the scope of the functional requirements; that is covered by the implementation requirements in the SDD.

Performance requirements
> Performance requirements describe how well a system must perform. Typically these requirements are concerned with characteristics such as speed (i.e., amount of data transferred per some unit of time), capacity (how much data can be stored), and real-time display update rates (live video, live data graph displays, etc.), among

other things. Performance requirements complement the functional requirements, and the two are sometimes merged into a single requirements document.

Integration requirements

Integration requirements define how the system will interact or interoperate with other systems. These requirements deal with things like communications protocols, command and data formats, and physical interfaces. Sometimes requirements of this type are contained in the functional requirements document along with the performance requirements. Alternatively, the integration requirements may be in a separate *Interface Control Document* (ICD).

Derived requirements

A derived requirement is a requirement that was not explicitly stated in the functional, performance, or integration requirements, but was instead derived during the requirements analysis or perhaps during the creation of the design documentation. For example, a communications interface may need to have error detection and reporting capabilities that are not explicitly captured anywhere else, but that need to be taken into account when the low-level design is developed. A derived requirement "plugs the hole," so to speak, in the other high-level requirements and provides a traceable justification for a design element.

For the most part, the example requirements we'll be looking at are what are sometimes known as *contract-style requirements*. That is, each requirement is a single statement containing a "shall," and each is written in a rather stiff and formal style intended to be concise, unambiguous, and verifiable. They are organized such that they form a sort of checklist. For many years this was the standard way to capture and document requirements, and it is still in use today, particularly in the aerospace and defense industries. However, current trends in requirements engineering for commercial software and systems have moved away from this model in favor of use cases and other techniques. Figure 8-5 shows an example of this type of requirements style. We'll look at use cases in the next section.

For a small set of requirements (between, say, 20 and 50), there is really nothing wrong with the contract style. It is when the requirements set becomes very large that it can become a problem. For one thing, a set of contract-style requirements tends to abstract the requirements away from the SOW and other sources that originally drove them, so the context can get lost and it can be difficult to perceive how the requirements relate to one another.

Use Cases

Contract-style requirements are not the only way to capture requirements. In addition to the issues already mentioned, contract-style requirements tend to get a bit unwieldy when dealing with things like graphic user interfaces or other aspects of human-machine interaction. The *use case* type of requirement definition may be more appropriate for some aspects of a system's requirements.

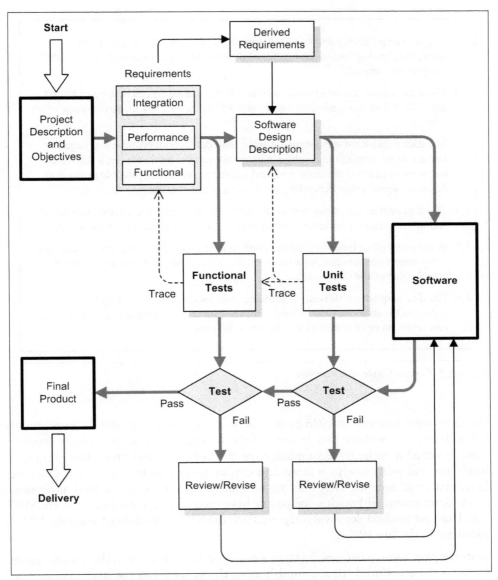

Figure 8-4. Software requirements in the development flow

 Conversely, use cases are not well suited to capturing things like algorithmic or mathematical requirements, nor do they work well for nonfunctional characteristics such as performance, timing, or safety requirements.

1.1 The data acquisition subsystem software shall be capable of acquiring and converting analog data as 16-bit signed data samples at a sustained rate of 1,000 samples per second.

1.2 The data acquisition subsystem software shall generate values between −32,768 and +32,767 across a nominal input range of −10 to +10 V with an accuracy of +/- 1 bit.

1.3 The data acquisition subsystem software shall detect both positive and negative voltage input over-range conditions in the conversion hardware, set a software status bit to indicate the condition, and return the maximum possible positive or negative digital value depending on the sign of the over-range condition.

1.4 The data acquisition subsystem software shall incorporate the ability to set upper and lower limits for acceptable input values via a configuration parameters file.

1.5 In the event of an input beyond the configurable range limits, the data acquisition subsystem software shall set a status bit to indicate the condition, and return the actual value of the conversion.

1.6 The data acquisition subsystem software shall incorporate the ability to detect a failure in the data conversion hardware, set a status bit to indicate the condition, and return an error code value in lieu of valid data.

Figure 8-5. Contract-style requirements

Use cases were invented in 1986 by Ivar Jacobson as a way to model the interactions between a system and the user or users of the system (which might be real people or other systems) in order to accomplish a specific task. Use cases treat the system as a black box and focus solely on input and output actions. In this sense, use cases are functional requirements. They may not be appropriate for use as low-level implementation descriptions, although some people have tried to coerce use cases into the SDD role. Use-case methodology was integrated into the Unified Modeling Language (UML) paradigm in the late 1990s.

In its simplest form, a use case has four primary features: the actor, the system, a goal for what the actor needs to accomplish using the system, and the steps necessary to achieve the goal. Use cases can refer to other use cases in a hierarchical arrangement, starting with a set of general high-level use cases and descending into greater levels of detail. A use case can also refer to other use cases at the same level when two or more use cases are necessary to describe the actions required to meet a common goal.

Figure 8-6 shows an (admittedly somewhat contrived) example of a use case for a hypothetical greenhouse control system. In this example the use case has six elements, which are listed in Table 8-2.

Table 8-2. *Basic use case elements*

Element	Description
Identification	A unique identifier for the use case. May be whatever format makes sense for the project, just so long as it can be used to unambiguously refer to a specific use case.
Title	A title for the use case. This, along with the identification, might appear in a listing of use cases for the project, so the title should be short yet descriptive.
Description	Also known as the "goal" of the use case. This describes, briefly and at a high level, what the use case is attempting to define.
Actors	The agents (biological or otherwise) that need to accomplish the goal or goals stated in the description.
System	The thing that will respond to the actor(s) to allow for the realization of the goal.
Assumptions	The conditions that must exist in order in order for the goal to be accomplished.
Steps	The sequence of events (which may be just one) that must occur to accomplish the goal.

If you've had only limited exposure to use cases, you might think they are just the cartoons known as "use-case diagrams." They are not. Use-case diagrams are intended as a way to present a high-level view of how a system will be used and by whom; they are not intended to define functional requirements. What is shown in Figure 8-6 is typically referred to as a *formal use case*, or sometimes as a *traditional* or *concrete use case*.

Another thing to note about use cases is that the criteria we looked at for well-written requirements also apply to use cases. They are, after all, requirements. In fact, a formal use case is somewhat like a set of one or more contract-style requirements grouped under a single heading, the goal.

The finer points of use-case generation and organization are outside the scope of this book, so if you're interested I would suggest that you look into some of the titles in the "Suggested Reading" section at the end of this chapter, or just peruse the Web. Wikipedia has a good introduction at *http://en.wikipedia.org/wiki/Use_case*.

I would recommend using plain ASCII text files for use cases, because you can place text files under version control using a tool like CVS or Subversion. Both CVS and Subversion have the ability to automatically modify specially tagged lines in the files to note things like the last author, the version number, and the date of the last check-in.

Traceability

Traceability refers to the linkage that must exist between a requirement and whatever drove it to exist in the first place. It doesn't matter what form the requirement takes, be it contract-style or use case, it must still have a reason to exist.

Figure 8-7 is a graphical illustration of traceability, starting with the SOW, then the functional and derived requirements, on to the SDD, and finally the software itself. This is also indicated in Figure 8-4 by the dashed lines labeled "Trace."

Identification:	UC-GH-021
Title:	Obtain Periodic Temperature Data from the Greenhouse Control System
Description:	A monitor system (the actor) periodically queries the control system and obtains temperature data for display with a GUI. The transactions between the control system and the monitor system are accomplished using a custom communications protocol over a network connection.
Actors:	One actor consisting of an outboard computer system used to monitor the primary control system and display data such as temperature over time and error notifications using a GUI.
System:	A dedicated control system for control of temperature, humidity, watering and illumination within the greenhouse.
Assumptions:	The communications protocol used to exchange commands and data between the actor and the system is defined in the project ICD, and implemented in both the monitor and control systems.
	The control system is powered on and running correctly.
	The monitor system is powered on and running correctly.
	An Ethernet connection has been established between the control and monitor systems.
Steps:	1. Actor sends query to system requesting current greenhouse temperature.
	2. Control system responds with a string of ASCII characters as defined in the ICD.
	3. Actor parses the response from the system and either plots a new data point or displays an error message, as appropriate.
	4. If the control system is nonresponsive then the monitor displays an appropriate error message.

Figure 8-6. Example formal use case

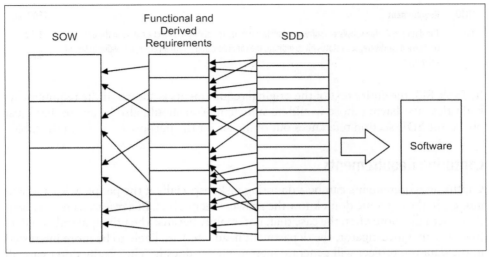

Figure 8-7. Requirements traceability

Establishing traceability is essential for verifying that there is "requirements coverage" at each level. In other words, do the functional and derived requirements cover everything in the SOW? Does the SDD cover everything in the functional and derived requirements? Without traceability it might be impossible to know for certain, particularly in cases where there are more than just a few requirements to deal with.

A requirements traceability matrix like the one shown in Table 8-3 is a document that shows exactly how each functional requirement is mapped to the SDD. A similar table, called the *verification matrix*, is used to map the requirements to the tests used to verify each one.

Table 8-3. Requirements traceability matrix

FR ID	Requirement	SDD ref.
1.1	The data acquisition subsystem software shall be capable of acquiring and converting analog data as 16-bit signed data samples at a sustained rate of 1,000 samples per second.	3.2.1
1.2	The data acquisition subsystem software shall generate values between −32,768 and +32,767 across a nominal input range of −10 to +10 V with an accuracy of +/− 1 bit.	3.2.2
1.3	The data acquisition subsystem software shall detect both positive and negative voltage input over-range conditions in the conversion hardware, set a software status bit to indicate the condition, and return the maximum possible positive or negative digital value depending on the sign of the over-range condition.	3.3.1 3.7.3
1.4	The data acquisition subsystem software shall incorporate the ability to set upper and lower limits for acceptable input values via a configuration parameters file.	3.3.2
1.5	In the event of an input beyond the configurable range limits, the data acquisition subsystem software shall set a status bit to indicate the condition, and return the actual value of the conversion.	3.4.1 4.2.4

FR ID	Requirement	SDD ref.
1.6	The data acquisition subsystem software shall incorporate the ability to detect a failure in the data conversion hardware, set a status bit to indicate the condition, and return an error code value in lieu of valid data.	3.4.2 4.2.5

In Table 8-3, the entire text of the original requirements is shown. If the requirements had titles, just having those would be sufficient. You should also be aware that I just pulled the SDD section references out of the air for the purpose of filling in the table.

Capturing Requirements

Capturing requirements can be a daunting task, especially if the people with a vested interest in the outcome don't know the answers themselves. In a research environment this is actually more often the case than not, mainly because the principal stakeholders (the principal investigator, the department head, etc.) are likely to be more interested in the data the project will generate than in how it does it. They really don't care all that much about the details of how a device does what it does, so long as it does it reliably and accurately, so asking specific questions about data conversion rates, bit resolution, over-voltage limits, and so on, is often not a very productive exercise.

A similar situation can exist in a commercial setting where requirements for a product are driven by marketing desirements. The folks in the marketing department may know, in general functional terms, what features the product needs in order to be competitive, but asking them specific low-level questions is typically not appropriate or fruitful.

Of course, there are situations where specific requirements for functionality, performance, error handling, and so on, have already been worked out in advance to some level of detail. This is common in the aerospace and defense industries, and in some industrial processing situations, but outside of these domains it is more the exception than the rule. Even in cases where detailed requirements are provided, they should not be blindly accepted. Someone will need to review them for consistency and feasibility, as they will be a major driver in determining the level of effort, and hence the cost, of the project.

What this really boils down to is that in most situations, if you want to have solid requirements to work from (and this is something you really should want), you will need to help create them. To this end, you may need to conduct interviews with the various stakeholders to determine what their primary objectives are for the project. If a statement of need does not exist, it should be created, and everyone with a vested interest will need to agree to it (or, in biz-speak, you will need to get "buy-in"). Once that key piece is in place, the rest of the requirements-creation effort is a matter of defining successively greater levels of detail until there is enough to design, build, and test the desired system.

When attempting to capture low-level details, it is a good idea to write up a list of questions and provide it in advance to the people whom you will be interviewing to obtain the answers. If you think you already know some of the answers, or they can be surmised from information already on hand, you should also write up your deductions and assumptions and provide those as well.

While there are specialized commercial tools available for formal requirements capture and documentation, a word processor or even a spreadsheet is often more than sufficient for most small- to medium-size projects. If you elect to use another approach, such as use cases, there are open source tools available to help with that too, but a decent word processor will again work pretty well.

Designing the Software

Now that you have some functional requirements, in whatever format, it's time to think about designing the software to meet those requirements. How much latitude is available in the design will depend on how detailed the functional requirements happen to be. If they are extremely detailed, you won't have as much leeway as with a loose set of functional requirements.

The Software Design Description

In Figure 8-4 the last thing in line before the software is the software design description, also known as the SDD. The SDD is, in effect, a set of low-level implementation requirements. Often the SDD is written in a more narrative form than the functional-level requirements. It typically contains things like definitions of return code values, flowcharts, block diagrams, inheritance diagrams, message sequence charts, and so on. The SDD is the theory of operation document for the system to be built, and it should contain enough details such that a programmer can translate it directly into working code. Typically, the SDD is organized along the same lines as the software. In other words, there might be a section describing data acquisition, another dealing with data processing, one that describes the user interface, and so on. A comprehensive SDD may also contain one or more introductory overview sections that reiterate the SOW in a more technical context and lay the groundwork for the detailed descriptions in subsequent sections of the document.

For small projects an SDD may not even be necessary, but unless you are the only person who will be working on the software it is essential to make sure everyone involved understands what is required and how the software will meet the requirements. The SDD fulfills that role, and serves as the implementation requirements for creating both the software and the unit tests.

An important thing to keep in mind regarding the SDD is that it is driven by the requirements preceding it, not the other way around. Each distinct descriptive item in the SDD must be traceable back to one or more of the functional-level requirements.

In an RDD development model, if something can't be traced back to a higher-level requirement, it doesn't belong in the design. If something really needs to be in the design, but there is no requirement for it, a derived requirement must be created to cover it.

If nothing else, the presence of an SDD shows that some thought went into the design of the software—i.e., it wasn't just pulled full-grown from some nebulous place and assumed to be complete and accurate. Such an assumption is seldom, if ever, borne out.

Graphics in the SDD

An SDD can be a simple thing with only a few pages, but it can help make things clearer if there is something graphical for a reader (maybe you, at some later date) to illustrate some of the key aspects of the architecture of the software. Graphical representations also allow you, the designer, to see your design from new angles. It's not uncommon for the designer to discover that the approach originally adopted won't work as intended when it's modeled using some type of diagramming methodology. Not only do graphical representations and models help make problems in the design more visible, they can also help identify inefficiencies and suggest better ways of doing things.

This section is by no means a tutorial on any of the graphical representation and modeling techniques presented here. It is an overview, and I am assuming that the reader will be able to infer how these tools are used from the material presented in this book. There is also a vast amount of information freely available on the Web. The main point here is to introduce the terms and concepts.

Block diagrams

A block diagram is intended to show how different functional sections of a system— be it software, hardware, or both—relate to one another. In fact, we have already seen a lot of block diagrams in this book. Figure 8-4 is a block diagram, for instance (actually, it's something of a hybrid that combines elements of both a block diagram and a flowchart). If done correctly, a block diagram can convey a tremendous amount of information in a very compact format.

A block diagram showing an overview of the system to be built is a good starting point for writing an SDD. In fact, a good block diagram, along with a page or two of text, might make up the entire SDD for a simple project.

Flowcharts

The concept of the flowchart is older than computers themselves, and predates the advent of programming languages by at least 30 years. Flowcharts were originally developed to represent and model the flow of activities in industrial processes. At IBM around 1947 Herman Goldstine and John von Neumann created what we know today as the software flowchart. The ISO standard 5807:1985 contains the latest definitions for flowcharts; unfortunately, ISO wants over $100 for it, but an older document from IBM (GC20-815-1, "Flowcharting Techniques," 1969) can be found online without too much searching and downloaded for free.

Figure 8-8 shows a simple flowchart for a simple controller. The flowchart not only shows the essential functionality of the algorithm, but also shows where there might be some room for improvement. Notice, for example, that there is no provision to handle an error from Sensor 1. There is also no check to determine if the Output (whatever that might be) is actually responding.

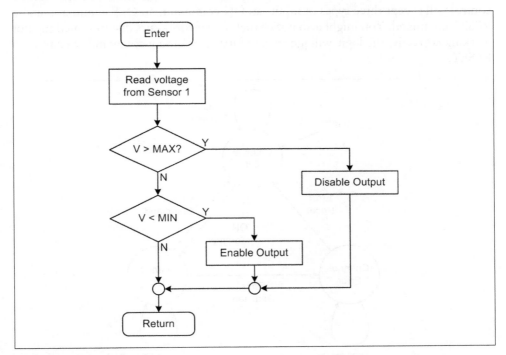

Figure 8-8. Example flowchart

Some people may scoff at flowcharts and claim they are obsolete, but in reality flowcharts are very much alive and well. In UML the equivalent to a flowchart is called an *activity diagram*. A flowchart is an effective way to visualize decision paths through a program, but it starts to become bogged down when dealing with control flow constructs such as switches or loops. Still, a flowchart can illustrate a section of program logic in a visually intuitive fashion, and should not be overlooked if it will benefit the SDD.

State diagrams

A state diagram is a powerful tool for modeling state changes. In fact, state diagrams have evolved to the point where there are tools available that can translate a state diagram directly into program code ready for compilation. In addition, a tool of this type can usually create a simulation based on the state diagram and execute it to allow the developer to observe its behavior.

Figure 8-9 shows the state diagram for a simple on-off control. The channel might be an AC power control, or it could be a relay. From the diagram we can see that the control will accept three types of input: an ON command, an OFF command, and a RESET command. You might also notice that if an error occurs due to something not working correctly, the logic will ignore any further incoming commands except for a RESET.

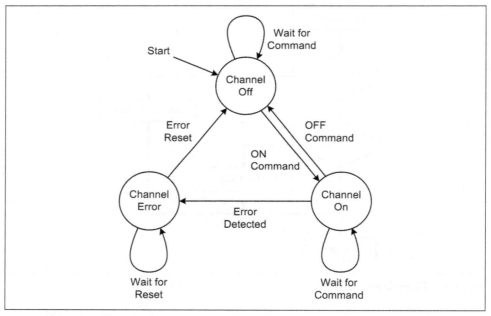

Figure 8-9. Example state diagram

Message sequence charts

The *message sequence chart* (MSC) is defined by the guidelines document Z.120, maintained by the International Telecommunication Union (ITU). In its current form, an MSC is a powerful tool for modeling command-response transactions between multiple entities. The UML equivalent of the MSC is the sequence diagram. A simple MSC is shown in Figure 8-10.

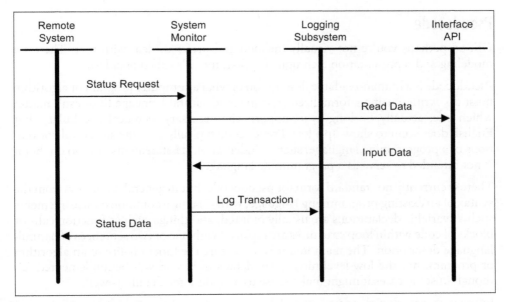

Figure 8-10. MSC example

An MSC models the transactions that may occur between entities such as users, processes, or services. The transactions typically involve exchanges in the form of requests, commands, or data. In the simple MSC shown in Figure 8-10 there are four processes: a remote system, the primary system monitor, a logging subsystem, and the data acquisition hardware (represented by the interface API process). When the remote system wants to obtain data, it sends a request to the system monitor. This, in turn, passes a command to the interface API, which then interacts with the hardware and returns the data requested. The system monitor logs the response from the interface API and completes the transaction cycle by responding to the remote system's original request.

Even with a simple MSC like that shown in Figure 8-10 there are some things that may have caught your eye. First, a status request takes a finite amount of time to process. What the MSC does not show is just how long that finite amount of time might be. In a more detailed MSC this could be indicated as an upper limit on acceptable response time. Secondly, our simple MSC doesn't show the alternate scenario where an error occurs at the interface API level, although it could have done so if the full syntax for an MSC had been used.

The latest revision of Z.120 contains a large amount of detail on the syntax of MSCs, and if you're interested in using them it's worth looking through it to get an idea of just what these diagrams are capable of. There are also various tools available for creating MSC diagrams, both commercial and open source.

Pseudocode

OK, so perhaps you're not visually inclined and prefer to deal with text. There's a modeling and representation technique for that, too: it's called *pseudocode*.

Pseudocode is a human-readable description of what a computer program or algorithm must do, written using a formalized style in some natural language (it doesn't matter which one, actually, so long as it supports the necessary technical vocabulary, but English does seem to show up a lot). Pseudocode typically uses the structural conventions of a programming language, such as indentation, if statements, and so on, but it is not intended to serve as a programming language.

There is currently no standard form for pseudocode, but in general it borrows from the syntax of an existing programming language, with C being a common choice. Elements such as variable declarations are usually omitted, and things such as function calls or blocks of code within loop structures are replaced with one or two sentences of natural-language description. The main intent is to capture the functionality of an algorithm or program, not the low-level nitty-gritty details of how it will be implemented, although in some cases it might make sense to include some details as well.

In practice, pseudocode may vary widely in style, depending on who is writing it and the environment in which it is used. It can range from something that looks like a real programming language at one extreme, to a description approaching something like an essay at the other. Ideally the writer should strive to strike a balance somewhere in between.

Figure 8-11 shows a sample of pseudocode for a function to read analog data from a lower-level function. As you can see, the main intent of ReadAnalog is to wrap the lower-level function ReadAnalogChan with parameter checking, and also replace the return code from the driver API with something the higher-level program can understand (actually, it simplifies the return code, because some API calls might return 20 or 30 different values primarily of interest to hardware engineers, depending on what went wrong with the hardware).

Pseudocode should be detailed enough to capture the essential functionality of a program or algorithm, but still be easily readable by someone who is not familiar with the programming language that will be used to implement it. This allows it to be inspected and reviewed as a way to ensure that the final program will meet design specifications, and that there are no lurking deficiencies that the original author may have overlooked (which happens all the time, since humans tend to overlook errors in their own writing).

Divide and Conquer

Now that we've looked at some of the tools available for creating an SDD, let's look at how an SDD might be organized. Figure 8-12 shows how we can use a high-level block diagram of a system to create the outline structure for an SDD.

```
Function ReadAnalog

Inputs:     device, channel

Outputs:    exit code, data value


Begin
    Set exit code to NO_ERR
    Set data value to zero

    If channel < 0 or channel > maximum allowable channels, then
        Set exit code to ERR_BAD_PARAM
    Endif

    If device < 0 or device > maximum allowable devices, then
        Set exit code to ERR_BAD_PARAM
    Endif

    If exit code is NO_ERR, then
        Call ReadAnalogChan, returns status code and data value
        If call returns error in status code, then
            Set data value to zero
            Set exit code to DEV_FAULT
        Else
            Set exit code to status code from call
        Endif
    Endif

    Return exit code and data value
End
```

Figure 8-11. *Pseudocode example*

The idea here is very simple: just write a section for each major functional block in the system diagram. You will also need some words and maybe a diagram or two describing how the functional blocks integrate into the overall system. The integration details can be included in the appropriate sections, or they might be a section of their own; that's up to you.

As I stated earlier, the SDD doesn't need to be a tome of detailed minutiae, but it does need to have enough information to allow someone reading it to understand how to implement the software, and why the software was written the way it was. It also demonstrates that the software was planned, rather than just being hacked into existence. This, by the way, isn't just a "warm and fuzzy" sort of thing. Should something not work as planned, or if a problem should occur months, or even years, after the software was created, the SDD will be invaluable in helping to determine why the problem occurred and what options might be available to deal with it. If the software is generating data for research purposes, it can also come in handy should a question ever arise as to the accuracy of the data and the methods used to process it. Should you ever find yourself defending the data generated by software that you wrote, an SDD could be worth its weight in gold.

Handling Errors and Faults

Unfortunately we don't live in a perfect world, and I've yet to meet a perfect software developer, so a design document must plan for the unexpected and describe how the software will deal with errors or faults, should they occur. And it's a safe bet that even if the obvious bugs in the software are found and dealt with, nonobvious things like off-nominal input values, hardware errors, or unplanned sequences of events can still occur when least expected.

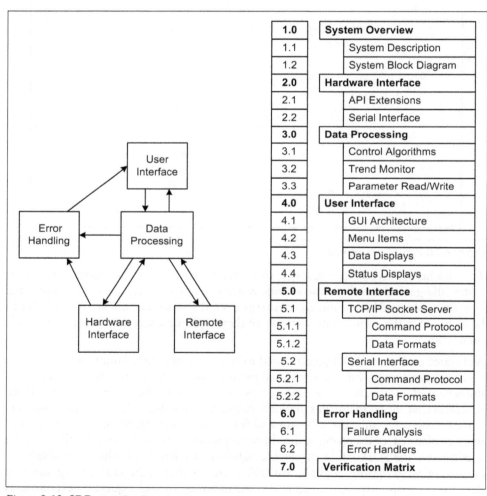

1.0	**System Overview**	
1.1	System Description	
1.2	System Block Diagram	
2.0	**Hardware Interface**	
2.1	API Extensions	
2.2	Serial Interface	
3.0	**Data Processing**	
3.1	Control Algorithms	
3.2	Trend Monitor	
3.3	Parameter Read/Write	
4.0	**User Interface**	
4.1	GUI Architecture	
4.2	Menu Items	
4.3	Data Displays	
4.4	Status Displays	
5.0	**Remote Interface**	
5.1	TCP/IP Socket Server	
5.1.1		Command Protocol
5.1.2		Data Formats
5.2	Serial Interface	
5.2.1		Command Protocol
5.2.2		Data Formats
6.0	**Error Handling**	
6.1	Failure Analysis	
6.2	Error Handlers	
7.0	**Verification Matrix**	

Figure 8-12. SDD organization

Identifying potential failures

One way to identify potential failures is by doing a basic failure analysis. A failure analysis is a simple and effective way to list all of the possible ways a system might fail, and then identify how the software might deal with the failures. It is, in essence, a set of "what if?" questions, along with your best attempt at a reasonable answer for each. Table 8-4 shows a simple failure analysis table.

Table 8-4. Simple failure analysis

Failure	Cause	Response
Input hardware error	Invalid input channel specified	Notify user and log error. System does not halt.
	Invalid input port specified	Notify user and log error. System does not halt.
	Hardware nonresponsive	Notify user and halt system.
Output hardware error	Invalid output channel specified	Notify user and log error. System does not halt.
	Invalid input port specified	Notify user and log error. System does not halt.
	Hardware nonresponsive	Notify user and halt system.
Invalid user input	User-supplied parameter or command code is invalid	Notify user and log error. System does not halt.

This type of analysis can easily be done using a spreadsheet. With a little thought (and a real system to work from), Table 8-4 could most likely be expanded to cover more possible failure cases, but the idea here is that for every possible failure listed, a response is defined. You should also be aware of the temptation to say, "Nah, that could never possibly happen" when reviewing potential failures. Such assumptions have resulted in some spectacular software failures over the years.

Failure responses

Failure conditions can generally be categorized into three groups: fatal, nonfatal, and trivial. It is important to plan out how the system will respond to each class of failure. For example, should a fatal error occur, will the system try to shut itself down gracefully, or will it just drop dead (i.e., crash)? If a nonfatal error crops up, what functionality, if any, will or should be disabled? Will the system still be usable? And what of trivial failures? Should the system try to send some type of notification, silently log the event for later review, or just ignore it completely? These are the kinds of things you should consider when formulating your responses.

Functional Testing

We now have some requirements and hopefully a design document, but before the first line of code is written we need to think about testing. Here I am referring to functional testing, as opposed to unit testing; they are very different things, with different objectives and methods. We'll get to unit testing in just a bit, but for now, let's look at functional testing and see why it's an essential (and arguably the only) method for verifying compliance with the requirements.

Testing to the Requirements

A functional test, as the name implies, tests the functionality of a system against the requirements that defined the system in the first place. Creating functional test cases from the requirements is actually very straightforward. A well-written requirement should contain all the information necessary for the test case. For example, assume we have a requirement that reads:

> The data acquisition subsystem software shall be capable of acquiring and converting analog data as 16-bit signed data samples at a sustained rate of 1,000 samples per second.

From this we can see that we'll need an input that will result in the system generating values between −32,768 and 32,767. We will also need to be able to count the samples generated in a one-second window. If the software has the ability to determine its actual sample rate in real time and display it (or at least record it), we're basically done. If it doesn't, maybe this is something that should go into a derived requirement and then into the SDD (this example is one way that derived requirements are discovered).

But even without a new derived requirement, it may still be possible to determine the sample rate. Perhaps the system saves data samples, along with timestamps, to a buffered file. It doesn't have to save each sample, but perhaps it will save data every 100 samples. If a logging capability is incorporated into the software, it may be possible to obtain the necessary verification data that way. Finally, it may be possible to connect instrumentation to the hardware and observe the timing of the data acquisition and conversion pulses while it is running.

This, by the way, is why it's a Good Idea to start working on the functional tests before the coding starts. In the process of designing the test cases it is very possible that deficiencies in the design will become apparent, and now is the time to deal with them, not later, when the code is already written. Writing the test cases before the code can illuminate dark corners and stimulate thinking in ways that will save time (and probably money) later on in the development process.

Test Cases

A functional test case describes the context and procedures necessary to test a particular aspect of the system against a particular requirement. Requirements drive test cases, and test cases in turn are used to define or generate the methods that will actually perform the tests. A functional test case may also be part of a use case, but in this book I will treat use cases and functional tests as two separate entities.

The block diagram in Figure 8-13 shows the relationship between a test case and the requirement that drives it, along with the procedures that will execute it, and finally the data that is used to determine the pass/fail status of the test.

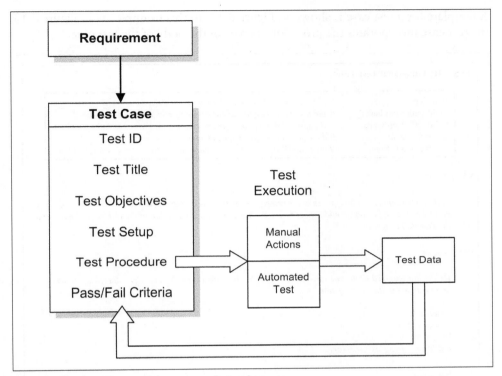

Figure 8-13. Requirement and test case relationship

In some environments one might hear of "test procedures," or perhaps a "test procedures document." These are just the "scripts," or series of actions, that need to occur in order to perform the tests. They might actually be something like a script that an actor (the tester) would follow (e.g., Step 1, Step 2, Step 3, etc.), or they could be scripts in the sense of being some type of programmatic test procedure (e.g., a Python script, say, or a control script for a communications simulator). This would be the box labeled "Automated Test" in Figure 8-13.

Separating out the tests into two separate but related documents, cases and procedures, is not really necessary in most situations. However, with some projects the level of complexity may be such that it makes sense to separate the nonexecutable description of the test (the test case) from the executable portion (the test procedure) for verification and tracking purposes. Abstracting out the test cases from the procedures makes it possible to independently write, verify, execute, and modify the procedures without disturbing the associated test cases any more than is absolutely necessary. This also has the effect of adding more effort (and cost) to the whole process, because now there are two documents to manage instead of one. But regardless of how the tests are structured, it is the test procedure that is "buying off" the requirement, because it is the test procedure alone that determines if the test is marked as a pass or fail.

A template for a test case is shown in Figure 8-14. In this example, as in Figure 8-13, the test case incorporates the procedure as part of the body of the test case.

TEST_ID Functional Test Title

Test Type:	*Is the test manual, scripted, or externally driven?*
Valid with Simulator:	*Is the test valid with the software running in simulation mode?*
Valid with Hardware:	*Is the test valid with the software running on the actual hardware?*
Script Utilized:	*If the test is automatic, what script is used?*
External C&C Source:	*If the test utilizes an external command/control source, what is it?*

Objectives

> *This is where the driving requirement is referenced as the reason for this test, and also where you describe what the tester should expect to see during and at the completion of the test. It does not define the pass/fail criteria.*

Pretest Setup

> *Define the required pretest actions here. These are the steps necessary in order to perform the test actions listed in the next section.*

A. Procedure
B. Procedure
C. Procedure
   (additional items as necessary)

Test Procedure

> *This is where the actual test procedure is defined. A procedure may consist of multiple steps. Each step should be a verifiable action (e.g. "Set switch S1 to the ON position and verify that the channel 1 light is illuminated" or "Start the test script and verify that no error messages appear during script startup").*

A. Step description
B. Step description
C. Step description
D. Step description
   (additional steps as necessary)

Pass/Fail

> *This section defines the pass/fail criteria for this test. A test that passes would exhibit the behavior defined by the driving requirement without exceeding nominal ranges or limits, or generating any errors during the execution of the test. A test failure might be a value that is too high or too low or a function taking too long to execute. Any error that occurred during the test that resulted in an error message is an obvious failure.*

Figure 8-14. Generic test case template

Also notice that the template in Figure 8-14 has a little something extra up at the top. I like to put a block at the top of each of my test cases that shows, in a nutshell, what type of test it is and what it needs in the way of a script or program if it happens to be scripted (i.e., automatic). The summary block also states whether the test is valid with the software running in a simulation mode, or if it needs the actual hardware in order to be executed. Note that it is possible to have a "Yes" for "Valid with Simulator" and a "No" for "Valid with Hardware." This scenario can arise when the software's internal simulation capabilities, if it has any, allow some functionality to be exercised that cannot be performed on a live system (e.g., during error-handling tests that use fault injection). Next, if an automated script is used, it is named here. Lastly, if an external source of commands and/or control signals is utilized for the test, that is noted here.

Test cases may reside in a larger document as subsections, or they might be single entities created as text files. Both approaches have their pros and cons. One large document puts everything in one convenient place. Separate text files allow the test cases to easily be placed under version control and revised independently.

You will need some way to record the pass/fail status of each test case, along with the date on which it was last executed. A spreadsheet works well for this, as does a printed listing of the test case IDs along with space to record the test results.

Testing Error Handling

One aspect of testing that too often gets overlooked is fault detection and error handling. We touched on this briefly earlier when we discussed failure analysis, and here we'll see why it's essential not only to test for correct functionality, but also to test for the appropriate responses when things don't go as planned.

The problem with testing error handling in software is that it is often much harder to do than success testing. How, for instance, does one instigate a fault condition in a communications channel? And how can a fault be simulated in the interface between the software and an analog-to-digital converter? These are the types of errors that can, and will, rear their ugly heads when least expected, so it's to everyone's benefit to test them before the software is turned loose on the world.

A common approach to testing error handling is called "fault injection." As the name implies, this involves incorporating some functionality into the code that will allow the tester to reach inside, so to speak, and set an internal variable that will induce the fault. One way to do this is via a network socket connection that is used only for this purpose and must be specifically enabled via a configuration parameter before it will communicate. A serial port connection can also serve in this role.

If the test involves an external device, just disconnecting it will inject a fault, but only one type of fault. This approach won't inject errors arising from corrupted data; it will only simulate a complete lack of communications.

It is important to remember that the purpose of testing the system's response to error conditions isn't necessarily to simulate the errors themselves, but rather to stimulate the code that is supposed to handle the errors. An approach that I've found useful is to create a collection of global state variables, perhaps in their own module, that are used to record error conditions as the software executes. For example, the low-level function that reads data from some hardware might record its success or failure in the set of global state variables, and it should not overwrite an existing error indication. The error state can then be checked by code further up that needs to obtain the data from the hardware, and if an error is indicated it will initiate the appropriate action. With a scheme like this it is possible to simply set the error condition by modifying the appropriate global variable externally. The low-level code won't override it, and the upper-level code will see it and respond as if an actual error had occurred. Only the lowest-level portions of the code will not be tested by this approach, but they can be handled separately using other testing techniques.

We will leave error handling and fault injection at that for now, but we'll return to it later on. Of course, the usual caveat applies: there's more than one way to get there from here, and what I've described here is just one way to do it.

Regression Testing

The idea behind regression testing is simple: the question to ask is "Did any recent changes break anything?" Any time you make a change to the code, whether to fix an existing problem or to implement new functionality, you should do regression testing. In order to perform regression testing, you would typically take some or all of the existing set of functional tests and run them again on the modified software. A partial regression test will focus on the functionality in the software where changes have occurred. A full regression test will execute all available functional tests.

It is a well-established fact that changes to software will frequently introduce defects, perhaps by allowing a previously dormant bug to manifest itself, or perhaps by creating a new execution path that contains previously unknown defects. There is always the possibility that the "fix" won't turn out to be as good as hoped. Maybe it's "brittle" because it doesn't account for things like range errors or off-nominal and unexpected inputs. Regression testing can help uncover these and other problems before they become unwieldy or, worse, before they escape into the wild as part of the released software.

Regression testing isn't, and shouldn't be, just something one does with functional tests. It also applies to unit tests, which we will get to shortly. Regression testing is also something that can be automated in many cases, which means that it's possible, and often practical, to run a full suite of tests on the software overnight on a daily basis. A quick review of the test results first thing in the morning will let you know if there's something from the day before that needs attention.

Tracking Progress

If you were to track the results from each round of functional testing over the life of the project, you would probably end up with something like the series of bar graphs shown in Figure 8-15. This is fairly typical for projects that rely heavily on functional testing for verification, in that things start out a little rough and then start to improve as the project progresses. If the project activities also include extensive unit testing and code reviews, this scenario can be improved, and the overall level of functional test failures should drop toward zero much sooner than what is shown here. But, in any case, the ultimate objective is to have zero test failures and 100% requirements coverage by the time the project wraps up.

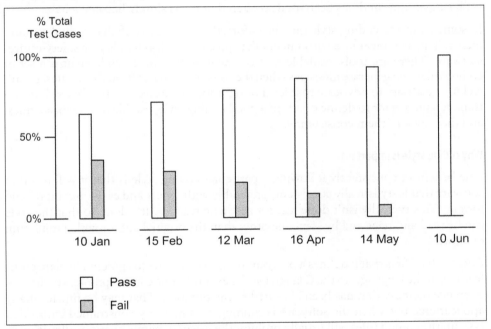

Figure 8-15. Functional testing pass versus fail results over time

Implementation

Now, at last, we come to the fun part: writing the software. We've covered requirements, the design, and the functional tests, so now we can turn our attention to some of the activities that go into creating the code.

What the code should do should already have been defined by the requirements and the SDD. This section deals with how it is organized, formatted, reviewed, and tested using unit test methods. These aspects are sometimes overlooked or pushed aside as trivial matters, but that is a mistake that can come back to haunt the developer months or even years later. Careless programming can also make life miserable for those who come along after the code has been written and released, if there is a need to do maintenance or just to try to understand what the software really does.

Coding Styles

A coding style has been created for almost every programming language. Sometimes there are different styles for the same programming language. It's not uncommon to find that different companies, government agencies, research groups, open source projects, and individual developers have their own styles. In some cases the coding might be formalized in a document, whereas in other cases it's just something that evolved over time and has been used so often that it has simply become a habit.

In some cases the coding style may be enforced by a set of verifiable coding requirements. This is typical in environments that produce high-reliability or safety-critical software. There are tools available that can analyze the source code against a set of coding rules and generate messages when the software deviates from those rules. I don't feel it's necessary to advocate that level of rigor for the projects in this book, but I do think it's important to define or adopt a good coding style, establish some basic rules, and then stick to them consistently.

Why coding style is important

One benefit of consistently following a particular coding style is that it will result in software that is stylistically consistent, preferably with a clear and easy-to-comprehend format. This typically isn't done just for aesthetic reasons. It's done so that the code can be read and reviewed by someone other than the original author with a minimum of effort.

Another benefit is that it defines a programming style that avoids potentially dangerous features in the language. In the C language, for example, one can use pointers to directly reference memory that has been allocated to the program. That may be fine for many applications, but when the software is running on a memory-constrained embedded system, the coding rules will usually prohibit the use of dynamic memory allocation in order to avoid fatal pointer errors and memory "leaks." In an embedded system, with no one around to push a reset button, these situations can produce effects that are much worse than just having the program crash. As another example, the Python language allows the programmer to create dictionary objects on the fly, pass them around as both parameters and return values, and modify them dynamically along the way. After a dictionary object has been tweaked by multiple functions or methods, it can become difficult to know just what's in it, where it came from, and what it does.

Adopting existing coding style guidelines

The good folks at Python.org have documents available online that define a set of basic coding style guidelines. The primary document is PEP-8, "Style Guide for Python Code"; PEP-257, "Docstring Conventions," also contains useful information.

Style is about consistency, primarily in the layout, names, and organization of your code. To quote from PEP-8: "A style guide is about consistency. Consistency with this style guide is important. Consistency within a project is more important. Consistency within one module or function is most important."

If you're new to Python, or programming in general, I would suggest that you stick to PEP-8 as much as possible. This is the best way to find out what works, and what doesn't. After you've gained more experience, or if you already have a lot of experience, you might be in a position to make a case for using your own variations.

While there are some guidelines for C programming style floating around, there also seem to be a large number of variations. Some programmers use the K&R "ANSI C" reference book as their style guide. In other cases, a style guide might already exist, or there may be explicit coding style requirements. Regardless of the style you select, be consistent with it.

Organizing Your Code

If you have a good SDD to start with, the organization of the code should be obvious from the organization presented in the SDD. Applying some basic guidelines can also help keep things neat, tidy, and easy to read.

First off, avoid the temptation to wedge everything into a single source module. There is no penalty for having multiple modules, each containing functions or classes with related functionality. This is a good thing because it helps keep things comprehensible, and it can help make it easier to change something without impacting other parts of the code. So, even if the SDD implies that 20 different functions (for example) could reside in the same module, you might want to consider having two, three, or four modules instead, each containing closely related functions.

Python's concepts of packages and modules help to keep things neatly organized, and you should take a little time and read up on them if you aren't already familiar with the concepts. C has no corresponding source code organization, but it too can easily be modularized into header files, source files, and library modules.

Figure 8-16 shows a block diagram of just one way that the source code for an instrumentation application might be organized. This is only one way to do it, and other approaches are certainly possible. The main point here is that the code is divided into levels based on functionality, and each block in the diagram pertains to a particular group or class of functions.

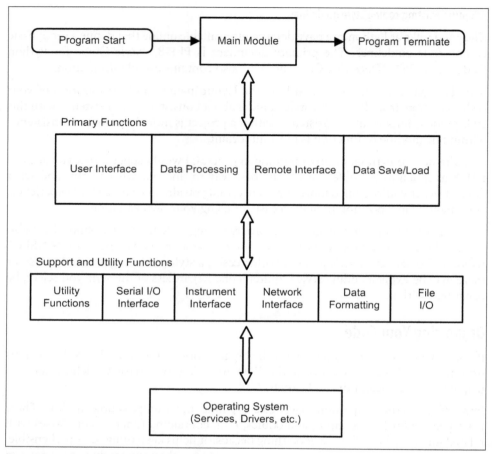

Figure 8-16. Code organization example

Code Reviews

Code reviews can be incredibly useful, particularly for helping to maintain stylistic consistency and for spotting errors that the original author of the code may have continually overlooked, or just not been aware of. Code reviews cannot, however, take the place of testing—the two activities are the opposite sides of the same coin.

Code reviews can also be a monumental chore if they aren't done correctly. I once participated in a series of code reviews that lasted for almost eight days. Why? Because the other people participating in the review hadn't bothered to read through the code beforehand or review the SDD, so they didn't know the structure, didn't know the intent of the functionality, and had to be walked through it line by line and have every little detail explained to them as if it was a detailed design walk-through. The really aggravating part was that this was code we'd all seen before, so there was really no excuse for the waste of time.

A code review can be as simple as two people going over the code, or as formal as a meeting with a moderator, a secretary, several reviewers, and the author of the software. It all depends on the complexity of the software, how critical it is, and how complete the SDD is from the outset. For most of the projects in this book, just having someone else look it over will be very useful. Even if you have to walk the other person through it (maybe she's not a programmer), the activity of verbalizing what you've done can often shed light on things you might have overlooked before.

Here are some ground rules for code reviews that I've found useful:

- Everyone should have at least skimmed through the code beforehand. If someone shows up who hasn't read through the code, call off the review and reschedule it, or just carry on without that person (if possible).
- Everyone participating in the code review should have read the relevant parts of the SDD before showing up.
- Focus on the things that are best suited for a code review: stylistic consistency, obvious logical errors (a problem with an `if-elif-else` structure, for example), uninitialized variables, a mismatched number of `malloc` and `free` calls (for C code), or improper placement of class variables in module scope (and vice versa) are just some examples.
- Use a checklist and try to stick to it. A code review checklist should contain the key things to look for during the review. Try not to deviate too far from the checklist, as this could end up wasting time better spent somewhere else.

The last item is particularly important. A basic checklist can save time and effort by helping to focus attention and effort during the review, and it provides a convenient way to keep track of results from the review. A minimal checklist might look something like Figure 8-17.

Let's look at the items in Figure 8-17 a bit more closely:

1. Has the design been correctly implemented in accordance with the SDD?

   The code must follow the SDD to the maximum extent possible (this depends, of course, on how well defined the SDD happens to be). Assuming that the intent is to comply with the requirements (initial or derived), code that does not follow the SDD is most likely not in compliance with the requirements. Bells and whistles may be cool and all that, but if there's no requirement for them, at best the programmer has wasted time building them into the software. At worst, undocumented, noncompliant features may introduce all sorts of evil defects into the code that unit testing may not catch.

1.	Has the design been correctly implemented in accordance with the SDD?
2.	Are there any obvious misspellings and typos?
3.	Does the software follow the project coding guidelines and conventions?
4.	Do the comments make sense? Are they necessary? Are there enough comments, or too many?
5.	Are data objects (e.g. structures, dictionaries, arrays, etc.) adequately defined?
6.	If literal values are used, are they the correct values?
7.	Are the same constant values used in multiple places when they should be defined in a common location?
8.	Are there any obvious repeated sections of the code that could be encapsulated as a function or method?
9.	Is there any code that, just on inspection, appears that it will never be executed?
10.	Are all the variables and constants defined in the code actually used in the code?

Figure 8-17. Minimal review checklist

2. Are there any obvious misspellings and typos?

While unit testing may catch some misspelled variable names, it won't catch all of them, especially with a language like Python that allows the code to create variables dynamically. A variable may have been defined at the start of a module, function, or method and then misspelled further down, and the code might still pass a unit test. This is something to watch for if a module or class has a variable that is used to track some internal state, and that variable is only set inside the code and only read by code somewhere outside of the class or module. It might never change if it's misspelled, and the external caller will never know the difference.

3. Does the software follow the project coding guidelines and conventions?

This one is rather obvious, and it's even more obvious during a review. If a coding style is going to be used, it should be used consistently.

4. Do the comments make sense? Are they necessary? Are there enough comments, or too many?

Comments are sometimes used as a way to cover up poor coding (perhaps there was a lack of understanding, or a section of code was a bit of a stretch when it was written). They can also be overused (commenting a line like a += 1, for example—

it happens quite often, actually). Comments should only appear when necessary to explain something that might not otherwise be obvious, including what a function or method is supposed to do.

5. Are data objects (e.g., structures, dictionaries, arrays, etc.) adequately defined?

   All data objects should have a comment unless their use is immediately obvious. This is especially true for compound objects like Python's dictionaries or structures in C. A variable used as a simple index counter in a loop probably doesn't need a comment.

6. If literal constant values are used, are they the correct values?

   Whenever a literal constant value is used it is "cast in stone," so to speak, so it really needs to be right from the outset. Mistyping a value can result in some decidedly unwanted behavior on the part of the software.

7. Are the same constant values used in multiple places when they should be defined in a common location?

   If the same literal value is used in two or more places, it should be converted into a global literal of some form and its name should be used in the code instead of the "naked number." This allows it to be changed in just one place, and that change will then take effect wherever the name appears. The alternative is to try to track down every place where it appears, and as the number of occurrences increases, so too does the chance that it will be missed somewhere and will cause grief later.

8. Are there any obvious repeated sections of the code that could be encapsulated as a function or method?

   If the code contains what essentially amounts to the same functionality repeated in multiple locations, that functionality should probably be a function or method that can be called whenever it is needed.

9. Is there any code that, just on inspection, appears that it will never be executed?

   So-called "dead code" is something to be avoided. It clutters up the software, making it difficult to determine what it is really supposed to do. It might also be inadvertently activated later by someone who doesn't fully understand why it's there, or through an untested path that occurs only under very unique circumstances. In other words, it presents a risk and a potential place for bugs to lurk. If it's not used, take it out. To really ensure that all the code is executed you need to use a code coverage tool, but catching the obvious during a review is a good start.

10. Are all the variables and constants defined in the code actually used in the code?

    If a module, function, method, or class defines variables, it should be used. If it is not used, like sections of dead code, it should be removed.

You could, of course, have a checklist with many more items than this, but I feel that this is a good place to start. It's short enough that you could feasibly review your own code (if there is no one else available to review it with you), although having a second pair of eyes (or more) is always better.

Unit Testing

The intent of unit testing is to exercise the functionality of a small portion of the overall software. A unit might be a function, a class, or a single method within a class. It is typically the smallest possible logical unit of code capable of execution on its own. For example, a function that accepts a raw binary data value from an external instrument, performs some scaling and range checking, and returns a binary value along with a return code would be a unit. It can be tested by supplying it with both nominal and off-nominal input values. While a Python unit is being tested, the code coverage can also be determined. This is a bit more difficult in C, particularly if the code is part of a low-level extension module, but it is doable. However, we'll stick to Python unit testing in this book.

Defining a unit test

A unit test doesn't necessarily map directly to a requirement, but it does map directly to the SDD. Assume the SDD defines a function that scales the data. It might look like this somewhat trivial example:

```
def ScaledInput(data):
    rc = NO_ERR

    scaled_data = data

    if data >= DATA_MIN and data <= DATA_MAX:
        scaled_data = (data * data_scale) + data_offset
        if scaled_data > SCALE_MAX:
            scaled_data = SCALE_MAX
            rc = ERR_MAXSCALE
        elif scaled_data < SCALE_MIN:
            scaled_data = SCALE_MIN
            rc = ERR_MINSCALE
    else:
        rc = ERR_OVER

    return (rc, scaled_data)
```

For our purposes, we can assume that `data_scale` and `data_offset` are set elsewhere (perhaps when the software initializes itself). `DATA_MIN`, `DATA_MAX`, `SCALE_MIN`, `SCALE_MAX`, `NO_ERR`, `ERR_MAXSCALE`, and `ERR_MINSCALE` are "constants" that do not change during program execution and that have hardcoded values, perhaps in another module where such things reside by themselves.

Lastly, note that the data return value is initialized to the value of the raw input data. Should an input range error occur, the function will still return data, but it won't be scaled or otherwise adjusted. If a scaling error occurs, the data returned will be either the scaled maximum possible or the minimum. It is the responsibility of whatever called this function to check the return code (`rc`) portion of the returned 2-tuple to see if an error has occurred.

A unit test is constructed such that all possible inputs are used to force the execution to traverse all possible paths. One way to achieve this is to create a test table. In the case of `ScaledInput()`, we can see that there are three obvious input cases: too low, too high, and within range. Table 8-5 shows these three test cases for this function.

Table 8-5. ScaledInput() test cases

Test	Input	RC	Output
1	data < DATA_MIN	ERR_OVER	Raw input data
2	data > DATA_MAX	ERR_OVER	Raw input data
3	min <= data <= max	NO_ERR	Processed data

This is a good start, but it's incomplete: there are no tests for the cases where `scaled_data` might exceed the scaling limits, so there are paths in the code that may not be exercised by the original three test cases. We need something more. Table 8-6 shows the complete suite of test cases for this deceptively simple function.

Table 8-6. ScaledInput() test cases (complete)

Test	Input	data_scale	data_offset	RC	Output
1	data < DATA_MIN	1.0	0.0	ERR_OVER	Raw input data
2	data > DATA_MAX	1.0	0.0	ERR_OVER	Raw input data
3	min <= data <= max	2.0	0.0	NO_ERR	Processed data
4	min <= data <= max	10.0	0.0	ERR_MAXSCALE	SCALE_MAX
5	min <= data <= max	−10.0	0.0	ERR_MINSCALE	SCALE_MIN
6	min <= data <= max	1.0	1000.0	ERR_MAXSCALE	SCALE_MAX
7	min <= data <= max	1.0	−1000.0	ERR_MINSCALE	SCALE_MIN

The actual values for `data_scale` and `data_offset` would, of course, depend on the values of `SCALE_MAX` and `SCALE_MIN`, but for our purposes here we can assume that they are appropriate for the results defined in the table of test cases. This also applies to `DATA_MIN` and `DATA_MAX`.

Although it might be argued that the last two cases aren't really necessary, they do provide complete coverage of all possible inputs to the function. I should also point out that the table describes the expected behavior, which includes the cases where `rc` contains something other than `NO_ERR`. In a unit test a failure would be any result that, given the specified inputs, does not conform to the table, not just the presence of an error value in the return code. A unit test case document should contain a table like Table 8-6 for every unit test to be performed. It would also define any necessary conditions for the tests.

Creative Time Wasting—Testing Without Justification

Even though unit tests do not necessarily map directly to driving requirements in the same way that functional tests do, they still need to have some kind of documentation to describe what they are intended to demonstrate and how to execute them. Implementing any tests, either unit or functional, without some kind of justification for their existence and a description of the pass/fail criteria is usually just a waste of time, even if it's just a simple test. If you don't know what a test is supposed to demonstrate, how can you tell if it really succeeds or not?

It is also worthwhile to consider this tidbit of wisdom: code that includes undocumented tests is actually worse than code that includes no tests at all. Why? Well, with untested code you can be fairly certain that it has bugs, whereas code that contains meaningless tests may lull you into a false sense of security, even though the odds of the code containing serious defects remains high. Or, to put it in a nutshell (and repeat what has been said many times before by many others): testing badly done is worse than no testing at all.

Implementing unit tests

With a table of test cases, we can now write the actual unit test. Fortunately, Python includes a built-in unit test facility, and code coverage capability as well (as the Python folks say: batteries included). The following is a module called InputUtils.py containing just one function, ScaledInput(). There is no reason it couldn't contain more utility functions for input verification and processing, but for now, this is it.

The return code "constants" used by ScaledInput() are defined within the same module, although in reality you would probably want to put them in a module by themselves (and with nothing else) so they can easily be imported and used by other parts of your application. Because we know that using a wildcard import is generally to be avoided, I haven't put leading underscore characters on any of the variable names, but in practice it would be a good idea to do so because you don't know what someone may decide to do with your code at a later date.

That said, let's take a look at the module code:

```
""" InputUtils.py

    A collection of input verification and processing functions.

    Just have one (ScaledInput) for now.
"""
NO_ERR = 0
ERR_OVER = -1
ERR_MAXSCALE = -2
ERR_MINSCALE = -3

DATA_MIN = -10.0
DATA_MAX = 10.0
```

```
SCALE_MIN = -50.0
SCALE_MAX = 50.0

data_scale = 1.0
data_offset = 0.0

def ScaledInput(data):
    rc = NO_ERR
    scaled_data = data

    if data >= DATA_MIN and data <= DATA_MAX:
        scaled_data = (data * data_scale) + data_offset
        if scaled_data > SCALE_MAX:
            scaled_data = SCALE_MAX
            rc = ERR_MAXSCALE
        elif scaled_data < SCALE_MIN:
            scaled_data = SCALE_MIN
            rc = ERR_MINSCALE
    else:
        rc = ERR_OVER

    return (rc, scaled_data)
```

Now we just need some way to exercise `ScaledInput()` using the test parameters listed in Table 8-6. Python's `unittest` facility is the tool of choice for this.

As with just about everything else in Python, there are several ways to use the Python `unittest` facility, and this is just one of them. I prefer this approach because it's straightforward and (at least to me) rather obvious. Let's look at the code, which resides in the module `test_001.py`, and then we'll walk through it and see what it does:

```
import unittest
import InputUtils as UUT

class test_001_UT(unittest.TestCase):

    def test_001_UT_01(self):
        UUT.data_scale = 1.0
        UUT.data_offset = 0.0
        data = -11
        rc, sdata = UUT.ScaledInput(data)
        assert rc == UUT.ERR_OVER
        assert sdata == data

    def test_001_UT_02(self):
        UUT.data_scale = 1.0
        UUT.data_offset = 0.0
        data = 11
        rc, sdata = UUT.ScaledInput(data)
        assert rc == UUT.ERR_OVER
        assert sdata == data

    def test_001_UT_03(self):
        UUT.data_scale = 2.0
        UUT.data_offset = 0.0
```

```
            data = 5
            rc, sdata = UUT.ScaledInput(data)
            assert rc == UUT.NO_ERR
            assert sdata == data * UUT.data_scale

    def test_001_UT_04(self):
        UUT.data_scale = 10.0
        UUT.data_offset = 0.0
        data = 10
        rc, sdata = UUT.ScaledInput(data)
        assert rc == UUT.ERR_MAXSCALE
        assert sdata == UUT.SCALE_MAX

    def test_001_UT_05(self):
        UUT.data_scale = -10.0
        UUT.data_offset = 0.0
        data = 10
        rc, sdata = UUT.ScaledInput(data)
        assert rc == UUT.ERR_MINSCALE
        assert sdata == UUT.SCALE_MIN

    def test_001_UT_06(self):
        UUT.data_scale = 1.0
        UUT.data_offset = 1000.0
        data = 10
        rc, sdata = UUT.ScaledInput(data)
        assert rc == UUT.ERR_MAXSCALE
        assert sdata == UUT.SCALE_MAX

    def test_001_UT_07(self):
        UUT.data_scale = 1.0
        UUT.data_offset = -1000.0
        data = 10
        rc, sdata = UUT.ScaledInput(data)
        assert rc == UUT.ERR_MINSCALE
        assert sdata == UUT.SCALE_MIN


suite = unittest.TestLoader().loadTestsFromTestCase(test_001_UT)
unittest.TextTestRunner(verbosity=3).run(suite)
```

The first thing to notice is that it imports only two things: the unittest library from Python and the module to be tested, InputUtils, which is aliased to the name UUT. The next step is to declare a class that inherits from the generic test case template, TestCase. Within this new class we create seven member methods, one for each of the test cases in Table 8-6.

Each test case method is identical with the exception of the data, scale, and offset parameters. The variables data_scale and data_offset reside in the UUT module, whereas the input data is passed directly to the function ScaledInput() by each test case method.

After a test case method sets up the initial conditions, it calls ScaledInput(). The return code and the processed data are captured in the variables rc and sdata, respectively.

The returned values are then tested using Python's **assert** statement. If the expression is `True`, the assertion passes; both assertions in each test case method must be `True` for the test case to pass. The resulting output looks like this:

```
>>> import test_001
test_001_UT_01 (test_001.test_001_UT) ... ok
test_001_UT_02 (test_001.test_001_UT) ... ok
test_001_UT_03 (test_001.test_001_UT) ... ok
test_001_UT_04 (test_001.test_001_UT) ... ok
test_001_UT_05 (test_001.test_001_UT) ... ok
test_001_UT_06 (test_001.test_001_UT) ... ok
test_001_UT_07 (test_001.test_001_UT) ... ok


----------------------------------------------------------------------
Ran 7 tests in 0.000s

OK
```

assert versus assertEqual() and friends

The `unittest` library has its own collection of `assert`-type methods in the `TestCase` class that have been tailored specifically to unit testing. Two of the more commonly used are `assertEqual()` and `assertNotEqual()`. As an example, we can rewrite test_001_UT_07 using these methods to look like this:

```
    def test_001_UT_07(self):
        UUT.data_scale = 1.0
        UUT.data_offset = -1000.0
        data = 10
        rc, sdata = UUT.ScaledInput(data)
        self.assertEqual(rc, UUT.ERR_MINSCALE)
        self.assertEqual(sdata, UUT.SCALE_MIN)
```

Why use `assertEqual()` and not just `assert`? There are two possible reasons: first, if the code is run with optimization enabled (the -O command-line switch), `assert` statements are ignored; second, the `assertEqual()` method generates some additional information that `assert` does not (at least, not without some extra work, as we'll see shortly). Let's say that test case 07, using the vanilla `assert` statement, encounters an error and the last assertion fails. Here's what the output of the test run would look like:

```
>>> import test_001
test_001_UT_01 (test_001.test_001_UT) ... ok
test_001_UT_02 (test_001.test_001_UT) ... ok
test_001_UT_03 (test_001.test_001_UT) ... ok
test_001_UT_04 (test_001.test_001_UT) ... ok
test_001_UT_05 (test_001.test_001_UT) ... ok
test_001_UT_06 (test_001.test_001_UT) ... ok
test_001_UT_07 (test_001.test_001_UT) ... FAIL


======================================================================
FAIL: test_001_UT_07 (test_001.test_001_UT)
----------------------------------------------------------------------
Traceback (most recent call last):
```

```
      File "test_001.py", line 61, in test_001_UT_07
        assert sdata == data
    AssertionError


    -----------------------------------------------------------------------
    Ran 7 tests in 0.050s

    FAILED (failures=1)
```

While this does indicate that test 7 failed, it doesn't tell us why. If we replace the assert statements with assertEqual() and run the test again, it will still fail, but the assertEqual() method will display the values of the two variables that failed the equality check:

```
    >>> import test_001
    test_001_UT_01 (test_001.test_001_UT) ... ok
    test_001_UT_02 (test_001.test_001_UT) ... ok
    test_001_UT_03 (test_001.test_001_UT) ... ok
    test_001_UT_04 (test_001.test_001_UT) ... ok
    test_001_UT_05 (test_001.test_001_UT) ... ok
    test_001_UT_06 (test_001.test_001_UT) ... ok
    test_001_UT_07 (test_001.test_001_UT) ... FAIL


    =======================================================================
    FAIL: test_001_UT_07 (test_001.test_001_UT)
    -----------------------------------------------------------------------
    Traceback (most recent call last):
      File "test_001.py", line 61, in test_001_UT_07
        self.assertEqual(sdata, data)
    AssertionError: -50.0 != 10


    -----------------------------------------------------------------------
    Ran 7 tests in 0.000s

    FAILED (failures=1)
```

Here we can plainly see what caused the problem, and on what line it occurred.

> To be fair, I should point out that I rigged this test to illustrate a test failure by comparing the processed data value from the ScaledInput() function to the original data input parameter, not to UUT.ERR_MINSCALE, which is what it actually is.

There have been arguments made about the merits of assert versus assertEqual(), some better than others, but I think that in the end it comes down to what you need to accomplish with your unit testing and what makes sense for you. If you are never planning to run your unit tests under optimization, and you don't have a compelling need to see the test parameters for every failure, go ahead and use the plain old vanilla assert statement. That being said, there is a way to see what failed; it just requires a bit more typing. I should point out that I'm showing you this just to be complete—it's not something I think you should actually do on a regular basis.

The formal syntax for assert (as stated in Section 6.3 of the Python 2.6.5 documentation) is:

```
assert_stmt ::=  "assert" expression ["," expression]
```

The second expression can be used to append a message to the exception's output, like so:

```
>>> var1 = 1
>>> var2 = 2
>>> assert var1 == var2, "%s != %s, at least not in this universe!" % (var1, var2)
Traceback (most recent call last):
  File "<stdin>", line 1, in <module>
AssertionError: 1 != 2, at least not in this universe!
```

This is just a bird's-eye view of what unittest can do, but we'll leave it at that for now. And, of course, there is much more information about unittest and its methods in the Python documentation.

Unit testing is something that should be done as a normal part of software development. As soon as a new function or method is complete you should create a unit test for it, and then run it often. In some environments other people may be responsible for creating the functional tests and setting up the test environment, but the person who wrote the code is uniquely qualified to create the unit test. This is also more efficient than having someone try to figure out what the code does and then create the tests for it after the fact.

Code coverage

While unit testing is good for performing basic low-level tests, it can also serve another equally important purpose: code coverage analysis.

If you're not familiar with code coverage analysis, the idea is actually very simple. Every line of code in a program must be executable. Or, to put it another way, you don't want any "dead code" in your software that might come back to haunt you later. Code coverage analysis also tells you if your unit tests are complete. Incomplete unit tests can leave dark corners in the software where evil things may be lurking, so you really want to touch everything while you're testing.

Figure 8-18 shows the flowchart for the ScaledInput() function. If you compare this to the test cases listed in Table 8-6, you should be able to readily identify the paths of execution that each of the test cases will follow (just look for the return codes). I've changed some of the variable names so things will fit nicely.

As we discussed earlier, one way to find dead code is through code reviews. Another way is to use a tool that can follow along with the execution of the software and keep track of which statements have been executed and which have not. I recommend the coverage package from Ned Batchelder, which is available at *http://nedbatchelder.com/code/coverage/*.

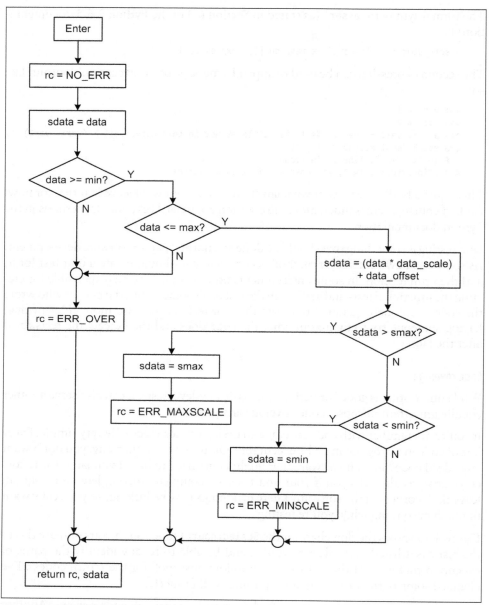

Figure 8-18. ScaledInput() flowchart

Once you've installed it, you can run it by simply typing `coverage` along with a command parameter and a source filename at the command prompt (note, not `python coverage`, just `coverage`). This command will execute the specified program module and generate some coverage statistics. Using our example unit test, we would enter:

```
coverage -x test_001.py
```

The -x command-line switch tells *coverage* to execute the program and collect coverage data. The newer run parameter is also available. Type coverage help at the command line to see what the newer-style parameters look like, and coverage help classic to see alternate older-style command-line parameters. I prefer the older style, myself. The output should look exactly like what you would expect to see when running the unittest module as we did previously, but *coverage* has generated something extra for us: a coverage metrics data file.

Using *coverage*'s report function, we can see the code coverage data in a nice tabular format. The -m switch tells *coverage* to also show the line numbers of code that wasn't executed:

```
coverage report -m
```

The output looks like this:

```
Name          Stmts   Exec  Cover  Missing
------------------------------------------
inpututils       23     23   100%
test_001         54     54   100%
------------------------------------------
TOTAL            77     77   100%
```

This demonstrates that all of the statements in ScaledInput() are executed by the test cases, and that every possible path in Figure 8-18 has been taken. No dead code here! *coverage* has also tracked the execution of the test_001 wrapper, but you can exclude that from the analysis if you wish, as explained in the documentation for *coverage*.

Connecting to the Hardware

There comes a point during the development of software when you will need to see if it will actually play nice with the hardware. Hopefully this point will come sooner rather than later, because what you really don't want is to get close to the end of the effort and then discover that the hardware doesn't really work like you thought it did, or that your code has a bug—or two, or more—that doesn't appear until the interface is active (I've been faced with both of these situations in the past, and they weren't the least bit fun). These types of bugs typically involve things like data representation, bit order, timing, or some other subtle thing that unit testing may have a hard time catching. It is even possible that the hardware has a problem, and you really don't want to be on the phone at the eleventh hour trying to get your hardware repaired or replaced after it's been sitting on a shelf for months waiting for you to use it.

Start with small, manageable low-level modules and build on them. In other words, if your application uses a serial port to communicate with an external device, first test just the serial interface module with the hardware (or a simulator, which we will discuss in Chapter 10). Once that is working correctly, add on more functionality. One of the biggest mistakes people make when attempting to implement a new system is to immediately throw all of the software at the hardware in one go. If you're really lucky it might work, but the odds are good that it won't. The real problem with the all-or-nothing approach is that you might have more than one thing going wrong at once, and it can be very difficult to determine what is causing which error because they can mask one another. Worse yet, there may be nothing wrong with the individual units of the software, but there may be some major issues when you attempt to integrate them all at once.

You may need to do things a little differently in your project, but here's one suggested integration order:

1. Low-level extensions (driver wrappers and such)
2. Communications (serial interface handlers and remote communications, for example)
3. Utility functions and classes (like the InputUtils.py module we saw earlier)
4. Data-processing and error-handling functionality

In other words, start integrating the software to the hardware, and to itself, from the bottom up. The following is a summary of the benefits of early integration:

- Low-level supporting functionality is tested and verified first, providing a solid foundation on which to add more complex functionality.
- If the code is correctly and sufficiently modular, the low-level (and even some of the mid-level) modules can go into your "software parts box" for possible reuse on future projects.
- Errors can be easily identified and resolved while they are small and manageable, hopefully before they appear and propagate anomalous behavior throughout the rest of the software.

Once you have all the underlying functionality in place, the last steps involve integrating the upper-level functionality, such as the data-processing and user interface, with the modules that have already been tested and verified.

Documenting Your Software

While the SDD may constitute a plan for your software, it doesn't necessarily take the place of code-level documentation. Depending on the level of detail in the SDD, it may describe the architecture of the application only in general terms, without specific details such a function or method parameters, global variables, and so on. In fact, it typically makes sense to not put an excessive amount of detail into the SDD, because invariably things will change as result of unit testing and integration activities. So where do we put things like descriptions of function parameters? In the code, of course.

Python includes the embedded documentation concept known as the *docstring*. My recommended tool for extracting docstrings and generating nicely formatted and indexed HTML pages of code documentation is the Epydoc tool from Edward Loper. You can download it from *http://epydoc.sourceforge.net*.

To illustrate how it works, here is the InputUtils module again, only this time I've added docstrings and renamed it to InputUtils2.py:

```
""" InputUtils.py

    A collection of input verification and processing functions.

    Just have one (ScaledInput) for now.
"""
NO_ERR          = 0        #: No error
ERR_OVER        = -1       #: Overrange error code (+ or -)
ERR_MAXSCALE    = -2       #: Maximum + output value exceeded
ERR_MINSCALE    = -3       #: Maximum - output value exceeded

DATA_MIN        = -10.0    #: Maximum - input value
DATA_MAX        = 10.0     #: Maximum + input value
SCALE_MIN       = -50.0    #: Maximum - output value
SCALE_MAX       = 50.0     #: Maximum + output value

data_scale      = 1.0      #: scaling coefficient
data_offset     = 0.0      #: offset coefficient


def ScaledInput(data):
    """ Input data checking and scaling.

        Uses global coefficients to scale a data value and apply an offset to it.

        The operation is, in effect, the common y = mx + b slope intercept form,
        where m is the scaling coefficient, b is the offset, and x is the input
        data. The values of m and b are provided via adjustable global variables.

        The input data is checked against predefined range limits. The result is
        also checked to ensure that it does not exceed predefined output range
        limits.

        If the input is out of range then ERR_OVER (overrange) is returned.

        If the output is out of range then the maximum possible value (+ or -)
        is returned.

        The output is a 2-tuple consisting of the return code and the result value.

        @param data:    The input data value

        @return:        Returns a 2-tuple with the return code and the modified
                        input data if no range errors occur. Otherwise returns
                        the unmodified input data value.
    """
    rc = NO_ERR
    scaled_data = data
```

```
    if data >= DATA_MIN and data <= DATA_MAX:
        scaled_data = (data * data_scale) + data_offset
        if scaled_data > SCALE_MAX:
            scaled_data = SCALE_MAX
            rc = ERR_MAXSCALE
        elif scaled_data < SCALE_MIN:
            scaled_data = SCALE_MIN
            rc = ERR_MINSCALE
    else:
        rc = ERR_OVER

    return (rc, scaled_data)
```

Epydoc generates a set of HTML files by default. If we open the top-level file, *index.html*, the result looks like Figure 8-19. Notice that the module global variables are also documented.

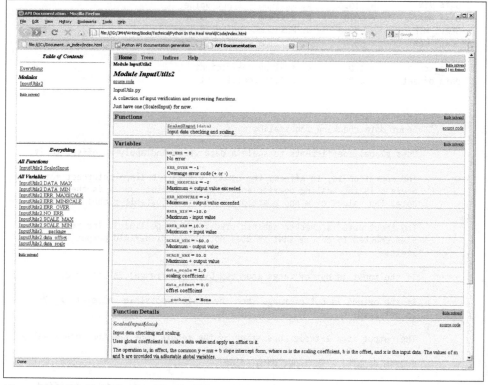

Figure 8-19. Example Epydoc output

Epydoc is a very useful and powerful tool. For C or C++ there is a similar tool, Doxygen, by Dimitri van Heesch, that also generates HTML output and uses markup tags in the comment text. It is available from SourceForge at *http://sourceforge.net/projects/doxygen/*.

Version Control

Version control is a critical part of any design and development activity. A good version-control tool allows you to track changes and maintain a history for a particular file. It also gives you a way to "step back" to an earlier revision if you find that something didn't work quite as planned. Even if you are the only software developer, having a version-control tool available can make the difference between wails of anguish and "Oh, no problem, I'll just go back to the previous version."

My tool of choice for version control is CVS. Granted, it's starting to show its age, but it's still in widespread use. Newer tools, such as SubVersion, have appeared, but I go back far enough to remember learning to use RCS and SCCS, so I just happen to feel more comfortable with CVS (which, by the way, is descended from RCS). I advocate using it for any text file, be it source code, use cases, or HTML files. It doesn't work quite as well with binary or mixed-mode files, such as those generated by Word, but there are open source tools available that can handle Word and Excel documents and maintain a version history.

There is much that can be said about version control, and whole books have been written about it. This book is not one of those, but I would encourage you to seek them out and read them. The book *Essential CVS (http://oreilly.com/catalog/9780596527037/)*, by Jennifer Vesperman (O'Reilly), is an excellent place to start. The home of CVS is *http://www.nongnu.org/cvs/*, and of course Wikipedia has a write-up on it, which is located at *http://en.wikipedia.org/wiki/Concurrent_Versions_System*.

Lastly, I have found that the manpages for CVS on most Linux installations have a massive amount of well-organized information. In fact, my favorite CVS "manual" is a binder with a printout of the CVS manpages and a few extra pages of notes.

Defect Tracking

Bug-tracking tools, also known as defect trackers, are essential in a team environment, where one person (a tester, perhaps) may be finding defects that another person (usually the person who wrote the code) will then attempt to resolve. For a one-person project, a full-on defect tracker might not be necessary if you are good at taking notes and keeping track of your "to-do" items, and you use a version-control tool. Because the focus of this book is on small projects with one or perhaps two software developers, I won't spend a lot of time on defect tracking. I will, however, try to provide enough information to give you an idea of what is involved, and provide some URLs you can check out for more information and software packages.

The idea behind a defect tracker is simple. First, a defect is discovered. It is then entered into the system, and the resulting "ticket" is assigned to someone. The defect entry then goes through a series of states, typically along the lines of *unread, working, testing, verified,* and *resolved.* It might also transition from working to testing and back to working again a few times before it is finally ready to be verified and marked as resolved.

Most open source defect trackers utilize a web-based interface, and some require a web server. I happen to prefer the Roundup tool, which is available on SourceForge, because it's simple to set up, easy to use, and it doesn't require a web server (although you can use it with one, if you want to). It's also written entirely in Python.

If you want to learn more about Roundup, you can check out its home page: *http:// roundup.sourceforge.net*.

Finally, Steve McConnell has an interesting paper on how defect tracking can be used to determine if software is really ready for release. It is available at *http://www.stevemc connell.com/ieeesoftware/bp09.htm*.

User Documentation

At some point, your project will (hopefully) be done. All the requirements have been defined, the SDD is complete, the code is written and the testing is finished, and it all seems to work as intended. If everything has gone according to plan, you should have working software as the end result of your hard work and diligent attention to detail. But there is one last step that needs to be completed before it is really done: the user documentation.

Even if you've created something primarily for your own use, you still should have some kind of documentation that describes how to use your creation. For projects with a limited distribution, I often use a three-ring binder and clear sheet protectors. I print out key procedures, parameter values, error codes, and other essential information on single sheets and slip them into the protectors. In essence, this is a highly condensed version of what a full-on user manual might contain. The advantage to this approach is that I can create each page as it's needed, put them into the notebook as they become available, and easily replace them if things change (as they almost always will). The binder then lives in the lab with the system so that anyone, including myself, who might need a quick refresher on how to use it can grab the binder and look it up.

If the system is intended for broad distribution, though, you'll need to consider creating an actual user manual for it. This may seem daunting, but a good place to start is to look at other user manuals. Which ones do you like (or not like), and why? Pick one or two that you think are well written and model your documentation on those.

Summary

In this chapter we've covered requirements, design, implementation, testing, and documentation. It should be obvious now why a software project without requirements is a like a ship without a rudder. Without at least some basic requirements, it's all too easy to create something that doesn't do what was originally intended, or doesn't work correctly at all. We have also seen how testing, when done to the requirements, not only helps to identify defects in the code, but also helps to ensure that the code stays on track and meets the requirements. Writing, in the form of documentation, has been stressed throughout the discussion, and in all honesty, if you aspire to achieve recognition for your work you need to document it so that others (who may not have your depth of understanding) can readily understand and appreciate it. However, the main point in this chapter isn't about rigorous adherence to a particular process or life-cycle model, nor is it about creating massive tomes of technical details. It's about knowing where you want to go by knowing what you need to do in order to get there, knowing when you've arrived, and creating a map of your journey in the form of documentation so that others can follow the path.

Suggested Reading

There are hundreds of good books available on the topics we've covered in this chapter, but in the interest of keeping things brief I'll list a few that I particularly like:

Code Complete, Second Edition. Steve McConnell, Microsoft Press, 2004.
I have both the first and second editions of this book, and I think they're both excellent. McConnell does a good job of laying out the steps necessary to successfully define and implement quality software, and he does it in a semiformal way that's engaging and enjoyable to read. I can only hope to encourage more people to read and apply the material in his book.

Software Requirements: Objects, Functions and States, 2nd ed. Alan Davis, Prentice Hall, 1993.
This is one of my favorite books on the subject of software requirements. I've been known to take it with me to meetings and quote from it now and again. The author discusses different approaches to requirements analysis and capture in a clear and lucid style, and also includes useful examples of different approaches. An extensive list of references provides numerous paths for further exploration and discovery.

Software Testing. James McCaffrey, Booksurge, 2009.
This book provides a good overview of the skills and techniques directly applicable to software testing, gleaned by the author from interviews and conversations with test managers in a number of settings. Short, simple, and to the point, it is a good starting place for someone new to software testing, and a useful quick refresher for the seasoned practitioner.

Writing Effective Use Cases. Alistair Cockburn, Addison-Wesley, 2001.
A well-written guide for writing well-written use cases, this book describes what constitutes a good use case and points out some of the pitfalls one might encounter while collecting the information necessary to craft a useful description of the intended behavior of the software. While I'm not a big fan of use cases (I prefer formal hierarchical requirements), if you are planning to employ use cases, you owe it to yourself to read this book.

Essential CVS, Second Edition. (http://oreilly.com/catalog/9780596527037/) Jennifer Vesperman, O'Reilly, 2006.

> This book starts with an introduction to the basic concepts behind CVS and builds from there, with discussions of tagging, branching, merging, and logging, among other topics. It helps to fill the gaps in the formal reference documentation found in CVS's online documentation, and to clarify some of the more opaque features and functions of CVS.

When it comes to online resources, well, they are legion. Entering the phrase "software requirements" will provoke Google into returning something like 1 million hits. Here are a few from my own bookmarks that I think are noteworthy:

http://software.gsfc.nasa.gov

> NASA has many documents available online in the Process Assets Library at the Goddard Space Flight Center. While a lot of these will be far too complex and detailed for the typical small project, the overall concepts and methods are universally applicable. It's worth a look to see if there's something here that you can apply to your own activities.

http://www.techwr-l.com/techwhirl/magazine/writing/softwarerequirementspecs.html

> TECHWR-L, a website oriented toward technical communicators, hosts this overview of what is entailed in writing a software requirements specifications document.

http://www.aspera-3.org/idfs/APAF_SRS_V1.0.pdf

> This is the SRS for the Aspera-3 project (part of the Mars Express mission) from the Swedish Institute of Space Physics. It's not often that one gets to see what a real SRS looks like (particularly not from recent NASA projects, thanks to ITAR), but here is one you can examine at your leisure.

## CHAPTER 9

Control System Concepts

If everything seems under control,
you're just not going fast enough.

—Mario Andretti

A book on real-world data acquisition and control systems would be incomplete without a discussion of the basics of control systems and the theory behind them. Although this chapter is not intended as a detailed or rigorous treatment of control systems, it will hopefully provide enough of a foundation, if you should need it, to enable you to start assembling usable control systems of your own.

Building on the material presented in Chapter 1, this chapter further explores common control system concepts and introduces additional essential details in the form of slightly more formal definitions. It also provides an introduction to basic control system analysis, and gives some guidelines for choosing an appropriate model.

Our primary focus in this chapter will be on simple control systems based on software and electromechanical components. These types of systems would ideally be constructed from readily available instrumentation and control devices such as DMMs, data acquisition units, motor controller modules, power supplies, and power control modules. You shouldn't have to design and assemble any circuit boards (unless you really want to, of course), or deal with esoteric devices and interfaces—everything you need should be available in an off-the-shelf form. In fact, it might already be on a shelf somewhere gathering dust.

We'll start off the chapter with an overview of linear, nonlinear, and sequential control systems, followed by definitions of some of the terms and symbols used in control system design. Next, we'll explore block diagrams and how they are used to diagram control systems. We'll then take a quick look at the differences between the time and frequency domains, and how these concepts are applied in control systems theory. I won't go into things like Laplace transfer functions, other than to introduce the concepts, mainly because the types of control systems we'll be working with can be easily modeled and implemented using garden-variety math.

The next section covers a selection of representative control systems, and shows how the terminology and theory presented in the first section can be applied to them. I'll present descriptions and examples of open-loop, closed-loop, sequential, PID, nonlinear bang-bang, and hybrid control systems.

To wrap up this chapter, we'll look at what goes into designing and implementing a control system in Python. We'll see examples of a proportional control, a nonlinear bang-bang control, and a simple implementation of a proportional-integral-derivative (PID) control.

Basic Control Systems Theory

We are surrounded by control systems, and we ourselves are a form of control system, albeit of a biological nature. A control system may be extremely simple, like a light switch, or very complex, like the autopilot device in an aircraft or the control system in a petrochemical refinery.

Broadly speaking, a *control system* is any arrangement of components, be they biological, mechanical, pneumatic, electrical, or whatever, that will allow an *output action* to be regulated or controlled by some form of input. Control systems with the ability to monitor and regulate their own behavior utilize what is called *feedback*, which is based on the ability to compare the input to the output and generate an error value that is the difference between the two. The error value is used to correct the output as necessary.

A control system isn't always a single thing in a box by itself. It may contain multiple subsystems, each of which might use a different control paradigm. When assembled together, the subsystems form a cohesive whole with well-defined behavior (ideally, anyway). The overall size of a control system, in terms of its scale and complexity, is a function of its scope. On that basis we could even say that the Earth's atmosphere is a largely self-regulating climate control and hydraulic distribution system, itself a subsystem of the entire system that is the planet. On a slightly smaller scale, a large ship, like a freighter, is a system for carrying cargo. It contains many subsystems, from the engines and their controls to the helm and the rudder.

If you look around at the various control systems in your immediate environment, you might notice that they are either rather simple or are composed of simple subsystems acting in concert to produce a particular (and perhaps complex) result.

In this chapter we'll be dealing primarily with three types of control systems: linear, nonlinear, and sequential. A linear control system utilizes a variable control input and produces a variable output as a continuous function of the input. Nonlinear controls, on the other hand, produce a response to a linear input that does not exhibit a continuous relationship with the input. A sequential system, as the name implies, is one that moves through a specific series of states, each of which may produce a specific external output or a subsequent internal state. We won't be delving into things like fuzzy logic, adaptive controls, or multiple-input/multiple-output control systems. These are deep subject areas in modern control systems research, and they're way beyond the scope of this book.

Linear Control Systems

As I stated in the introduction to this section, a linear control system produces a variable output as a continuous linear function of the input. For example, consider the following simple equation:

$$y = mx + b$$

This is the well-known slope intercept equation, and it defines a linear proportional relationship between x and y as a result of m (the slope). The b term applies an optional offset to the output. Could this be used in a control system? Absolutely. In fact, by itself it could be applied as a form of proportional control. Equation 9-1 shows the same equation recast in control system notation.

Equation 9-1.

$$u = K_p * e + P$$

For discrete-time applications, Equation 9-1 can be written as Equation 9-2.

Equation 9-2.

$$u(t) = K_p e(t) + P$$

In Equation 9-2, $u(t)$ is the control output, $e(t)$ is the system error, K_p is the proportional gain applied to the error, and P is the steady-state bias (which could well be zero). The symbol t indicates instantaneous time, otherwise known as "right now." It doesn't actually do anything in the equation except to say that the value of u at some time t is a function of the value of e at the same time t.

Don't worry about what the error is or about the symbols used here for now; we'll get to them shortly. The important thing to notice is that this is just the slope intercept equation in fancy clothes.

Control systems are typically grouped into two general categories: closed-loop and open-loop. The primary difference between the two involves the ability (or lack thereof) of the system to sense the effect of the controller on the controlled system or device (i.e., its response to the control signal) and adjust its operation accordingly. Closed-loop control systems are also called *feedback controllers*.

Figure 9-1 shows the response we would expect to see from Equation 9-1. Here I've used the error variable as the input, but it's actually the difference between a reference or control input and the feedback from the device under control (we'll get into all this in just a bit). The main point here is that it is ideally linear.

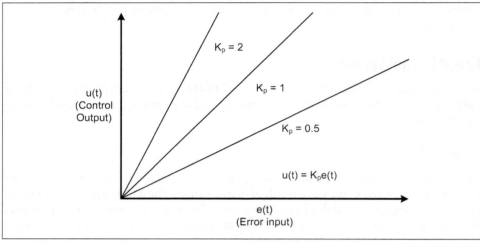

Figure 9-1. Linear control system proportional response

I should point out that while linear models are used extensively in control system analysis and modeling, in reality there are no truly linear systems. For various reasons, every system will exhibit some degree of nonlinear behavior under certain conditions. Also, in a closed-loop feedback system the output response of the controller is dependent on the feedback, and as we will see a little later, feedback from devices with mass, inertia, and time delays can and often do create situations where the resultant graph of the system is not a nice straight line.

Nonlinear Control Systems

A nonlinear control system is one where the input and the output do not have a continuous linear relationship. For example, the output might vary between two (or more) states as a function of a linear input level, as shown in Figure 9-2.

Mathematically, the basic behavior of the system responsible for the graphs in Figure 9-2 can be written in piecewise functional notation, as shown in Equation 9-3.

Equation 9-3.

$$f(V_{in}, S_{low}, S_{high}, H) = \begin{cases} 1, & V_{in} \leq S_{low} - H \\ 0, & V_{in} \geq S_{high} + H \end{cases}$$

$S_{low} - H < V_{in} < S_{high} + H$
is indeterminate (current state unchanged)

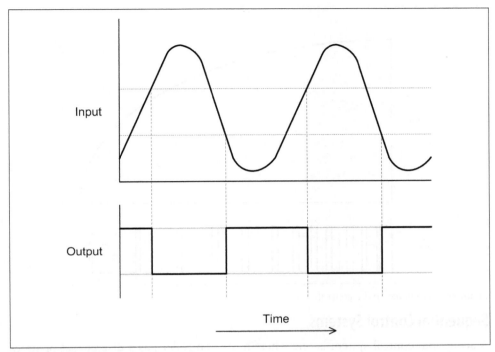

Figure 9-2. *Nonlinear control system response*

This is typical of the behavior of what is called a *bang-bang* or *on-off* type of controller. If the input exceeds a particular high or low limit, the output state changes. Otherwise, it remains in its current state. We'll take a closer look at this class of controller shortly, and see where it is commonly used in real-life applications.

Now let's consider a system where a control action occurs for only a specific period of time, like a short burst, and in order to realize a continuous control function both the burst rate and burst duration must be controlled during operation. This is shown in Figure 9-3.

This type of control is found in various applications, such as the antilock braking systems on late-model automobiles, and as the control paradigm for the variable-duty-cycle rocket engines used on robotic planetary landers. In this case the engines are either on or off, and they can only be active for a certain amount of time before they will need to be shut down in order to cool off (otherwise, they will overheat and self-destruct).

Note that the ability to perform continuously variable control of a system is a property of both linear and nonlinear systems. The distinction lies in how the output is manipulated in response to the input in order to achieve control. As we'll see a little later, the result of a nonlinear control can be a smooth change in the system response, even though the output of the controller itself is definitely not smooth and linear.

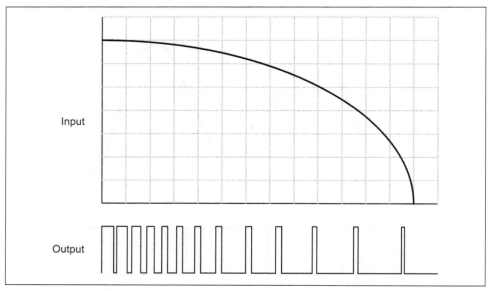

Figure 9-3. Nonlinear pulse control

Sequential Control Systems

A sequential control system is one wherein the controller has a discrete set of states with inputs and outputs consisting of discrete control signals. The controller might enable or disable devices that themselves utilize discrete states, or they could be linear (or nonlinear) subsystems. The main point is that the devices under control will be either active or inactive, on or off, in a predefined sequence.

Sequential control systems are often found in applications where a series of timed steps are performed in a specific sequence. An example would be an automatic sprinkler system. Internally the sprinkler controller is based on a model composed of sprinkler zones, which typically define groups of commonly plumbed sprinkler heads in certain areas of a yard (or golf course, park, etc.).

Figure 9-4 shows the timing chart for a five-zone sprinkler system. The system is programmed to activate each zone at a certain time on a specific day of the week, and to stay active for some specific duration.

In this example the sequence starts at 2200 hours (10 p.m.) and ends at 0400 (4 a.m.). A typical automatic sprinkler control system is a form of sequential control that relies solely on the current time; it has no other inputs to regulate its behavior. It doesn't matter if the soil is already damp, or if it is pouring rain; the grass will get watered anyway at the designated times.

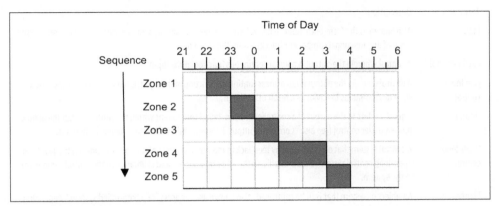

Figure 9-4. Sprinkler system sequential control

Terminology and Symbols

Before we get too much further into control systems, we need to have some terminology to work with, and some symbols to use. Control systems engineering, like any advanced discipline, has its own jargon and symbols. Table 9-1 lists some of the basic terms commonly encountered when dealing with control systems.

Table 9-1. Control systems terminology

Term	Description
Closed-loop control	A control system that incorporates feedback from the process or plant under control in order to automatically adjust the control action to compensate for perturbations to the system and maintain the intended process output.
Continuous time	A control system with behavior that is defined at all possible points in time.
Control signal	Also referred to as the "output." This is the signal that is applied to a controlled plant or process to make it respond in a desired way.
Control system	A system with the ability to accept an input and generate an output for the purpose of modifying the behavior of itself or another system. See "System."
Controlled output	The response generated by the system as the result of some input and, in a closed-loop control system, the incorporation of feedback into the system. Designated by the letter u in block diagrams.
Discrete time	A control system with behavior that is defined only at specific points in time.
Error	The difference between the reference input and the feedback from the plant.
Feedback	A type of input into the control system that is derived from the controlled plant and compared with the reference input to generate an error value via a summing junction. Designated by the letter b in block diagrams.
Gain	A multiplier in a system that is used to alter the value of a control or feedback signal. Gain can be changed, but in a conventional control system it is usually not a function of time. In some types of adaptive or nonlinear control systems, gain may be a function of time.

Term	Description
Input	Also known as the "reference input" when referring to the controller as a whole; otherwise, it can refer to the input of any functional component (block) within the controller.
Linear control	A control wherein the output is a linear continuous function of the input.
Nonlinear control	A control wherein the output is not a linear continuous function of the input, but may instead exhibit discrete-state discontinuous behavior as a result of the input.
Output	Typically refers to the output of a controller or a functional component within the controller, not the plant or process under control (see also "Controlled output"). Designated by the letter c in block diagrams.
Open-loop control	A control system that does not employ feedback to monitor the effect of the control signal on the plant. An open-loop control system relies primarily on the inherent accuracy and calibration of the control components in the system.
Plant	An object or system that is to be controlled. Also known as a "process" or a "controlled system," depending on the type of device or system being controlled.
Reference input	A stimulus or excitation applied to a control system from some external source. The reference input represents the desired output or behavior of the controlled plant. Designated by the letter r in block diagrams. See also "Input."
Sampled data	Data values obtained at specific intervals, each representing the state of a particular signal or system at a discrete point in time.
Summing node	The point in the control system where the feedback signal is subtracted from the reference input to obtain the error. Can also refer to any point where two or more signals or values are arithmetically combined.
System	A collection of interconnected functional components that are intended to operate as a unit.

Some of the alphabetic symbols commonly encountered when working with control system diagrams are listed in Table 9-2.

Table 9-2. Common control system diagram symbols

Symbol	Meaning
b	Feedback variable (or signal)
c	The controlled output of the system
e	The error derived from $r - b$
K	A gain value
r	The reference input to the system
u	The controlled variable (i.e., the input to the plant)

Control System Block Diagrams

Block diagrams are used extensively in control system design and analysis, so I'd like to introduce some of the basic concepts here that we will use throughout the rest of this chapter. Figure 9-5 shows the block diagrams for both an open-loop and a closed-loop control system, along with typical notation for the internal variables.

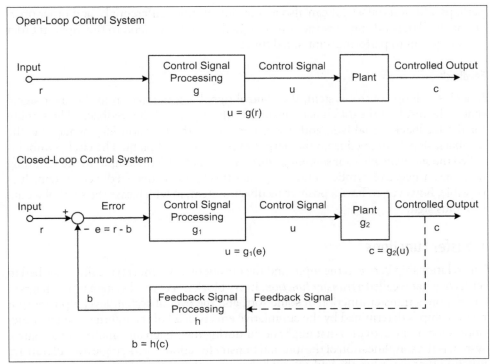

Figure 9-5. Control system block diagrams

Every control system has at least one input, often called the *reference input*, and at least one output, referred to as the *control signal* or the *controlled variable*. The final output from the plant is called the *controlled output*, and in a closed-loop system this is what is measured and used as the input to the feedback path. The relationship between the input and the controlled output defines the behavior of the system. In Figure 9-5, the reference input is denoted by the symbol r, the control signal is u, and the controlled output is c. The symbols are historical and still in common use, so I'll use them here as well.

Input-output relationships

The blocks in a block diagram define processing functions, and each has an input and an output. There may also be auxiliary input variables for things such as bias or external disturbances.

The output may or may not be equal to the response implied by the input. Actually, it is common to find some kind of math going on between the input and the output of a block, which in Figure 9-5 is indicated by the block labeled "Control Signal Processing." Notice that this block has a symbol for its internal function, which in this case is g (or g_1 in the closed-loop system). This might be as simple as multiplication (gain), or perhaps addition (offset). It can also involve integration, differentials, and other operations. It all depends on how the control signal needs to respond to the input in order for the system to perform its intended function.

Feedback

In a closed-loop control system, the control signal is generated from the error signal that is the result of the difference (or sum) of the input and the feedback. The symbol for the feedback signal is b, and it is generated by the function $h(c)$, where c is the feedback signal obtained from the output of the controlled plant. The circle symbol is called the *summing node*, or *summing junction*. In Figure 9-5 the b input to the summing node has a negative symbol, indicating that this is a negative feedback system. It is possible, however, to have a positive feedback system, in which case the symbol would be a plus sign.

Transfer Functions

The relationship between the input and the output of a system is typically described in terms of what is called a *transfer function*. Every block in a control system block diagram can denote a transfer function of some sort, and the overall system-level input/output relationship is determined by the cumulative effects of all of the internal transfer functions. One of the activities that might occur during the design and analysis of a control system is the simplification of the internal transfer functions into a single overall transfer function that describes the end-to-end behavior of the system.

Mathematically, a transfer function is a representation of the relationship between the input and output of a time-invariant system. What does that mean? We'll get to the definition of time-invariant shortly, but for now what this is saying is that transfer functions are applied in the frequency domain and that the functional relationship does not depend directly on time, just frequency.

In control systems theory the transfer functions are derived using the *Laplace transform*, which is an integral transform that is similar to the Fourier transform. The primary difference is that the Fourier transform resolves a signal or function into its component frequencies, whereas the Laplace transform resolves it into its "moments." In control systems theory the Laplace transform is often employed as a transformation from the time domain to the frequency domain. When working with complex or frequency-sensitive systems, the Laplace forms of the transfer functions are usually much easier to deal with and help to simplify the system model.

Although Laplace transforms are widely used, their use is not mandatory. In this chapter I won't be using Laplace transforms, mainly because much of what we'll be doing is very straightforward, and also because we will be working almost exclusively in the time domain with systems that are slow enough to not have significant issues with frequency response. For our purposes, basic algebra and calculus will serve just fine.

Time and Frequency

Time and frequency are key components in control system design. Activities occur for specific periods of time, events might occur at some set rate or at varying rates, and AC signals have a particular frequency (or a number of frequencies, in complex signals). The processing operations within a digital control system also require a finite amount of time, and this too must be accounted for in the system design.

Time and frequency domains

When discussing things such as mathematical functions or electrical signals with respect to time, we are dealing with what is called the *time domain*. If, on the other hand, our main concern is analyzing and processing AC signals in terms of frequency, we will be working in the *frequency domain*. The two terms refer to how one might perform the mathematical analysis and modeling of a function within a system, and which one is more appropriate depends on what one is looking for as a result of the analysis.

These distinctions may apply to an entire system, but they are more commonly applied to specific subfunctions within a system. For example, a clock or timing subsystem operates in the time domain, whereas a filter or phase-shifting subsystem operates in the frequency domain.

One way to think of the distinction between the time and frequency domains is to consider how you might go about graphing variable data in each domain. Figure 9-6 illustrates what one might expect to see on the displays of an oscilloscope (which we discussed briefly in Chapter 6) and a frequency spectrum analyzer (FSA).

The important point here is that the oscilloscope operates in the time domain, and the FSA operates in the frequency domain. The key is what is being used for the x-axis of the display. With the oscilloscope, the x-axis of the display is time and the y-axis is the amplitude of the signal at any given point along the x-axis. An oscilloscope can be used to determine the time interval between waveforms and the amplitude of the waveforms, but it can't directly tell you how the component frequencies are distributed within the signal. For that, you'll need to use the FSA.

The x-axis of the FSA display is frequency, and in Figure 9-6 it ranges from 0 to 50 KHz. I've shown the display as a vertical bar graph, but there are other ways to generate the graph. The FSA works by extracting the component frequencies from a signal (perhaps using a set of discrete filters, or by processing the signal using a Fourier analysis technique). The result is a set of values representing the relative amplitudes of the component frequencies within the signal.

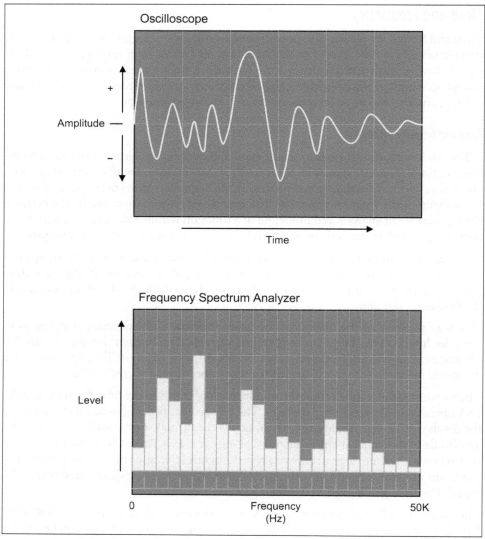

Figure 9-6. Time and frequency domain graphs

We can move back and forth between domains as needed, because time and frequency are just the inverse of one another. It all depends on your perspective. So, given a signal with a period of 20 ms between waveforms, its frequency would be the inverse, or 50 Hz. In other words:

$f = 1/t$

and:

$$t = 1/f$$

Another example might be a system where pulses from some type of sensor are arriving every 500 μs. If we take the inverse of 0.0005 we get 2,000 Hz, or 2 KHz. This is important to know if we're thinking of using a data acquisition device with an upper input frequency limit of 1 KHz.

Time and control systems behavior

The behavior of a control system over time is determined by how time affects its operation. The terms time-invariant and time-variant are used to categorize a system's sensitivity to time.

A *time-invariant* system is one wherein the output does not depend explicitly on time, and the relationship $y_{t0} = f(x_{t0})$ at time $t0$ will produce the same value for y as the relationship $y_{t1} = f(x_{t1})$ at time $t1$. In other words, the value of y will always be the same for any given value of x regardless of the time.

Time-invariant systems, and particularly linear systems (referred to as linear time-invariant systems, or LTIs), operate primarily in the frequency domain. Each has an input/output relationship that is given by the Fourier transform of the input and the system's transfer function. An amplifier is an example of an LTI. It doesn't matter what time it is when a signal arrives at the input; it will be processed according to its frequency and the transfer function embodied in the circuitry, and for any given signal an ideal amplifier will always produce the same output.

A *time-variant* system is one that is explicitly dependent on time. Time, in this sense, may also be a component of velocity (recall that velocity = distance/time), so a system that is moving is a time-variant system. For example, the autopilot and flight management systems in an aircraft must take time and airspeed into account in order to determine the aircraft's approximate position as a function of both its velocity and its heading. All of these factors are dependent on time.

Discrete-time control systems

Lastly, we come to discrete-time control systems. This class of control system may be linear or nonlinear, and it is this type of control that we will be working with directly when we're not using a sequential control scheme. Virtually all control systems that incorporate a computer and software to implement the control and signal processing are discrete-time systems.

In a traditional analog control system, the relationship between the input and output is immediate and continuous—a change in the input or the feedback is immediately reflected in the output. In a discrete linear control system, the input data acquisition (both reference and error), control processing, and output processing occur in discrete steps governed by a clock, within either a computer or some other type of digital control circuitry. To illustrate this, Figure 9-7 shows the block diagram of a discrete-time closed-loop control system.

In Figure 9-7, the block labeled "Clock" drives some sequential control logic. This could be a microprocessor, or it could be some software. This, in turn, activates the input, processing, and output functions in sequence, as indicated by the signals labeled t_1, t_2, and t_3. It is important to note that just because this is a discrete-time system does not mean that it is also a time-variant system. In this case, any given set of values for r and b at any time t will produce the same values for u and c that would be produced at time $t + n$, given the same input conditions. It is a discrete-time LTI control.

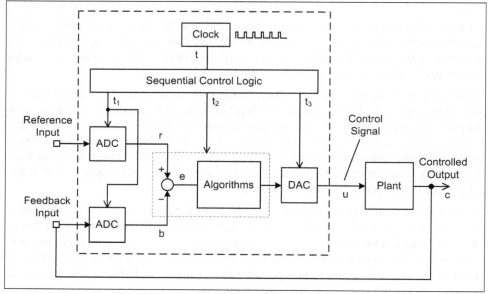

Figure 9-7. Discrete-time closed-loop control system

 There is a technique for modeling and analyzing discrete-time systems, referred as the *z-transform*. This is similar in application to the Laplace transforms used with systems in the continuous domain. When a system contains a mix of both continuous and discrete components, it is not uncommon to map from one domain to the other as necessary for the analysis. We won't be getting into z-transforms in this book, but I wanted you to be aware of them. What we will be concerned with is discrete system timing and how it can affect a control system's responsiveness.

In a discrete-time control system, when data is acquired and when control outputs are generated or updated is a function of the overall time required for the controller to complete a full cycle of input, processing, and output activities.

The system under control also has an element of time in the form of a *system time constant*. The system time constant is the amount of time required for a change to occur over some specific range. In other words, small changes (such as noise) may not be of any concern, but large changes need to be sensed and controlled. How often the control system will need to go through a complete control cycle is a function of the time constant of the system it is controlling.

Figure 9-8 shows a simplified block diagram of the primary software functions in a computer control system, which is composed of the three key functions from Figure 9-7: ADC data acquisition (the "Acquire" block), data-processing algorithms (the "Process" block), and DAC control output (the "Control" block). In the discrete-time environment of the computer these steps occur in a fixed order, and each requires a specific amount of time to execute (as indicated by t_a, t_p, and t_o).

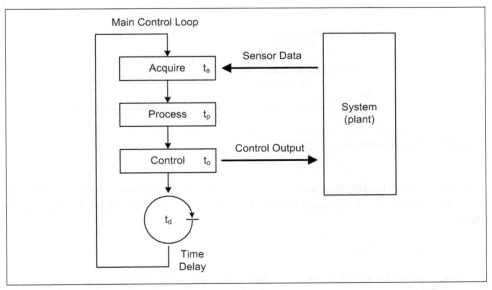

Figure 9-8. Control system software flow

There is also a circular symbol that stands for a time delay of duration t_d. After the output has been generated, the delay allows the external system to respond before the process is repeated and new control outputs are generated. The delay time would typically be "tuned" to accommodate the time constant of the system it is controlling.

Also notice that the diagram shows an endless loop. This is typical of computer programs for instrumentation applications. Once the steps required for the application have been defined and implemented, the resulting control program runs in a loop, repeating the acquire/process/control steps until either the loop or the entire application is terminated.

Figure 9-9 shows a timing chart representation of the block diagram in Figure 9-8. Here we can see that each activity consumes a specific amount of time. When the line is up, the step is active, and when it's down, that step is inactive.

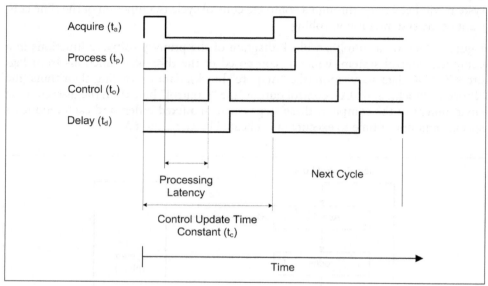

Figure 9-9. Control system software timing

In Figure 9-9 the fundamental time constant for the control system, or the *control cycle time*, is equivalent to the interval between acquire events. From Figure 9-9 we can see that:

$$t_c = t_a + t_p + t_o + t_d$$

This may seem like a trivial equation, but as we will soon see, the values assigned to these variables can have some profound effects on the system under control. In many cases the delay will contribute the most to the overall control cycle time, although the acquisition time can also be a major factor if external devices are slow in responding.

Control System Types

Up to this point we've seen only the basic outline of the domain of things called control systems. In this section we'll take a look at some specific examples, and apply some of the concepts and terminology. We'll start by examining examples of open-loop systems, then move on to closed-loop controls, sequential controls, and nonlinear controls. Ultimately we'll end up at proportional-integral-derivative (PID) controls, the most common form of closed-loop linear control in use today.

Open-Loop Control

In Chapter 1, an automatic outdoor light was used as an example of a nonlinear open-loop system. Linear and nonlinear open-loop control systems operate on the basis of a specific relationship between a control input and the resulting output, and as we've already seen, an open-loop controller has no direct "knowledge" of what the actual system is doing in the form of feedback. The accuracy and repeatability of the input/output control relationship is solely dependent on the initial accuracy and calibration of the components in the system.

A gas stove is a familiar example of the input/output relationship in an open-loop control system. The amount of heat applied to a frying pan is determined by the gas control valve on the front of the range top (the control input), and the gas pressure at the valve might be limited by a pressure regulator somewhere in the line (usually at the gas meter outside the house). Once the burner is lit it will produce a flame with an intensity proportional to how the valve is set, but it cannot determine when the pan reaches some specific temperature and regulate the flame accordingly. Some older stoves cannot even determine if the burner is actually lit, and will readily spew raw gas into the kitchen (which is why natural gas has an odor added to it before it is piped to the customer). It is a linear relationship, more or less, but it is a purely open-loop relationship. If the operator (i.e., the cook) sets the flame too high, the scrambled eggs might get a bit too crunchy or the pasta will get scorched. The stove will burn the food just as readily as it will cook it to perfection.

Open-loop controls are useful for applications where the relationship between the input and the output is well defined, and where feedback is not critical for acceptable operation under nominal conditions. However, an open-loop control system cannot respond to continuously changing conditions in the system under control, nor can it deal with transient disturbances or errors. Manual intervention is necessary to adjust the operation of the system as conditions change.

Closed-Loop Control

A closed-loop controller employs feedback to achieve dynamic automatic system control. Closed-loop control systems are also known as feedback control systems, and they may be linear, nonlinear, or even sequential.

Controlling position—Basic feedback

In a closed-loop feedback control system, one or more sensors monitor the output and feed that data back into the system to affect the operation of the controlled system, or *plant*. In a system that employs negative feedback the objective of the controller is to reduce the error from the summing node to zero (recall the closed-loop part of Figure 9-5).

For example, Figure 9-10 shows the water tank control system from Chapter 1.

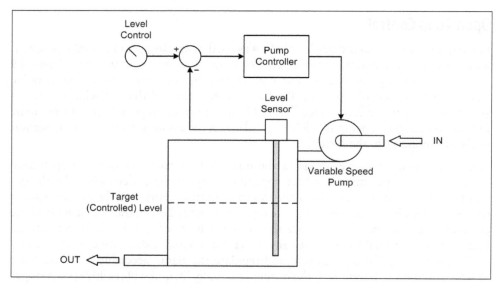

Figure 9-10. Closed-loop water tank level control

In this system time is irrelevant and the functionality is for the most part linear, so it's an LTI-type system. As with the other examples in this chapter, it is assumed that the control times are slow enough that the frequency response of the system is not a significant concern. The level control setting and the level sensor feedback are the sole inputs to the pump controller.

Let's take a closer look at this seemingly simple linear system. Figure 9-11 shows the system in block diagram form, and Figure 9-12 shows a pair of graphs depicting the behavior of the pump in response to changes in the water level.

The system block diagram includes additional details such as amplifiers with adjustable gain inputs and an AC power controller for the motor. Since this is a proportional control system, the amount of gain applied to the amplifiers will determine the responsiveness of the system (recall Figure 9-1). The gain variables K_m and K_f have a cumulative effect on the system. With the gains set too low, the system will not be able to command the pump to run fast enough to keep up with outflow from the tank. With the gains set too high, the water level will tend to overshoot the target level. In this system, K_m is the master gain and K_f is the feedback gain.

The upper graph in Figure 9-12 shows how the level changes as water is drawn off from the tank. The lower graph depicts the behavior of the pump motor in response to a change in the water level. There is a direct inverse linear relationship between the water level and the pump speed.

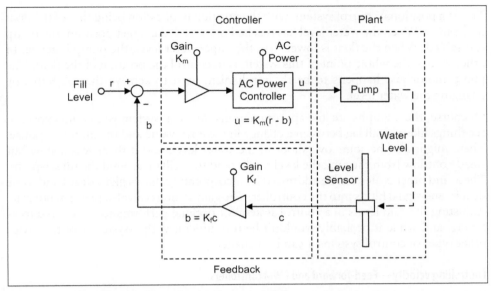

Figure 9-11. Closed-loop water tank control system details

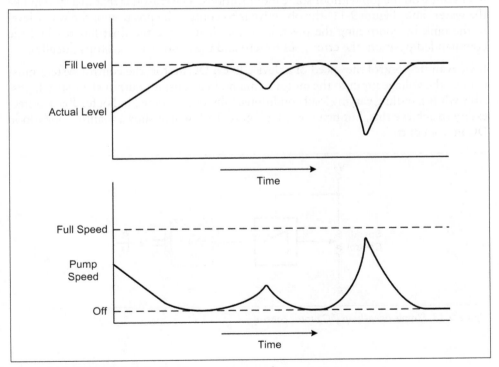

Figure 9-12. Water tank control system response graphs

This is a positional control system, with the position in question being that of the float in the tank. When the water level has reached or exceeded a target position, the pump is disabled. When the float is lower than the target water level, the pump is active. In other words, the whole point of this system is to control the position of the float. The pump motor just happens to be the mechanism used to achieve that objective by changing the water level.

Of course, these graphs are just approximations. In a real system you could expect to see things like a small lag between a change in the error value and the motor response. There might also be some overshoot in the water level, and if there was a slow but steady outflow from the tank the level might tend to oscillate around the fill set-point. These and other issues can be addressed by incorporating things like a deadband, time delays, and signal filters into the controller. The gain settings can also play a major role. Adjusting the gain levels in a control system for optimal performance is referred to as *tuning*, and while it probably wouldn't be too difficult with a system like this, with other types of control systems it can be a challenge.

Controlling velocity—Feed-forward and PWM controllers

When dealing with systems that involve velocity or speed, the basic closed-loop control won't quite do the job without some modifications. The reason is that in a system like the water tank (Figure 9-11) the objective is to control the position of the water level in the tank by controlling the position of the float. Once the float has reached the commanded position, the error goes to zero and the control action stops (ideally).

If we want to control the speed of a device like a DC motor, the control system must control the voltage input to the motor to maintain a constant output shaft speed, possibly while handling varying load conditions. Obviously, some kind of feedback is necessary to achieve this, but first consider Figure 9-13, which shows a simple open-loop DC motor control.

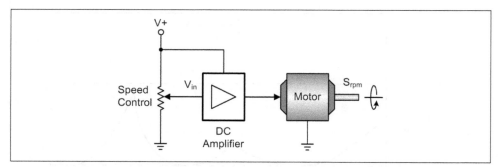

Figure 9-13. Simple open-loop DC motor control

This is a linear control, meaning that the voltage supplied to the motor is a linear function of the voltage at the input of the DC amplifier (V_{in}), and the shaft speed S_{rpm} is proportional to the input voltage to the motor. The amplifier is an essential component because a typical potentiometer won't handle the current that a DC motor can draw, and it can also provide gain if needed.

In its simplest form, the equation for Figure 9-13 would be:

$$S_{rpm} = M_r G V_{in}$$

where:

S_{rpm}
    Is the motor output RPM
M_r
    Is the motor's response coefficient
G
    Is the gain of the amplifier
V_{in}
    Is the input to the amplifier

In the open-loop motor control equation, the M_r coefficient indicates that there are some other factors involving the motor itself. These include the electrical characteristics of the motor as a function of load and shaft RPM, but for our purposes we can lump all these into M_r.

If we want to be able to set the motor speed and then have the system maintain that speed, some type of feedback is required. Assuming that we have some kind of tachometer on the motor shaft that produces a voltage proportional to the motor's speed, we can use that as the input to the feedback loop.

An arrangement like the closed-loop control shown earlier in Figure 9-11 can be made to work, but it would require some tweaking in terms of the gain values for r, b, and e. Stability is also an issue, and any changes in the load on the motor may result in oscillations in the shaft output speed. Depending on how the various gains are set, the oscillations may take a while to die out.

Another solution is to incorporate a feed-forward path in the control system along with the ability to sense the load on the motor. In a feed-forward type of controller, a control value is passed directly to the controlled device, which then responds in some deterministic and predictable way. Does that sound familiar? It should. Feed-forward is essentially an open-loop control scheme like the one shown in Figure 9-13. In fact, another name for feed-forward is open loop.

To implement a stable velocity control system, we can add one or more feedback loops for load compensation and speed stability, and use these to adjust the motor's operation by summing them with the feed-forward input. This arrangement is shown in Figure 9-14. Here, the feedback from a DC tachometer (essentially, a small DC generator) is used to provide stability. The feed-forward input is summed with the velocity error and feedback from a current sensor to compensate for changing torque loads on the motor.

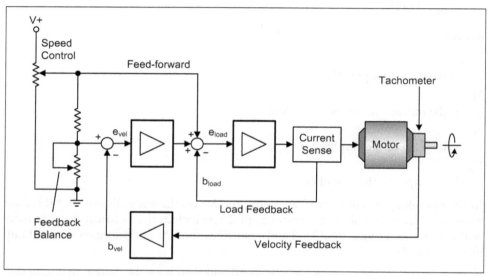

Figure 9-14. Feed-forward DC motor velocity controller

The velocity error b_{vel} will converge to zero so long as the motor's output RPM matches the reference input. Notice that the reference input is proportional to the speed input. If the load on the motor should change, b_{load} will act to compensate by adjusting the voltage to the motor to hold the speed constant (a motor with no load draws less current at a given RPM than one with a heavy load). Figure 9-15 shows how the error value e_{vel} acts to help stabilize the system.

Another way to achieve velocity control is to use pulses for both the motor control and the velocity feedback, as shown in Figure 9-16. For motor velocity control, a pulse-width modulation (PWM) type of control offers better electrical efficiency than a variable voltage controller. A PWM control is also simpler to implement and doesn't require a DAC component to generate the control signal. A pulse-type encoder that emits one, two, or even four pulses per shaft revolution can be used to determine the rotation speed of a motor's output shaft by counting the number of pulses that occur within a specific time period. As with the PWM output, this is electrically simple, but notice that a controller of this type, while capable of continuously variable control, is a nonlinear controller. As such, it is heavily dependent on internal processing to read the encoder input, determine the output RPM of the motor, and then modulate the PWM input to the motor to maintain velocity control. The end result is much like what is shown in Figure 9-3.

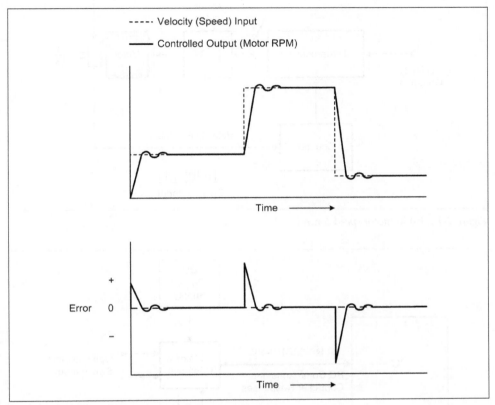

Figure 9-15. Error versus command input response

I've shown what is involved in a basic motor control so you will have an idea of what goes into one. These types of controllers are typically implemented as electronic circuits or microcontroller-based modules. Should you encounter a need to control the speed of a motor, I would suggest purchasing a commercial motor speed control unit. Figure 9-17 shows a block diagram with a commercial motor control module.

The commands sent to the motor controller in Figure 9-17 would, of course, be in whatever format the manufacturer designed into the controller. In general, a motor controller that accepts ASCII strings will use one character per parameter (direction, velocity, time, and so on), along with the appropriate numeric data for each parameter. The use of RS-232 or RS-485 interfaces for communication with the controller is common, although there are some motor controllers available that are sold as plug-in cards with bus interfaces.

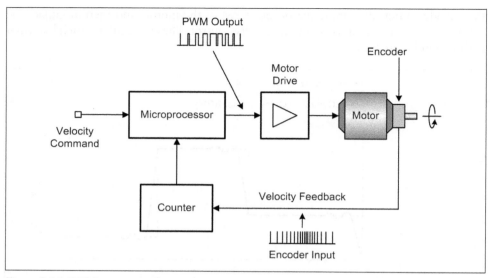

Figure 9-16. PWM motor speed control

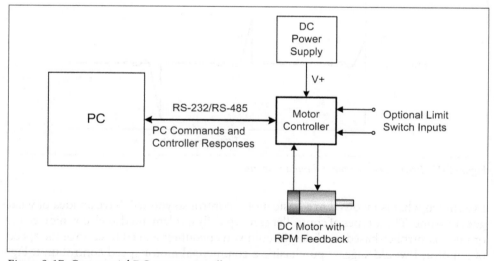

Figure 9-17. Commercial DC motor controller

Nonlinear Control: Bang-Bang Controllers

Bang-bang controllers, also known as on-off controllers, are a very common and simple type of nonlinear control system. Bang-bang controllers are so named because the control output responds to a linear input by being either on or off, all or nothing. In pre-electronic times this type of control might have been built with a control arm moving between two mechanical stops, which would result in a "bang" each time the arm moved from the off position to the on position, or vice versa. The thermostat for a typical residential heating and air conditioning system is the control for a closed-loop bang-bang control system. The automatic floodlight we looked at in Chapter 1 is an example of an open-loop bang-bang control system.

Nonlinear control systems often incorporate a characteristic referred to as *hysteresis*—in effect, a delay between a change in a control input and the response of the system under control. The delay can apply to both "ON" actions and "OFF" actions. In mechanical terms, one can think of it as a "snap action." A common example of mechanical hysteresis can be found in a typical three-ring notebook, with rings that suddenly open with a "snap" when pulled apart with some amount of force, and then close with a similar snap when moved back together. If the rings simply opened or closed as soon as any force was applied, they would be useless.

In a bang-bang controller, hysteresis is useful for moderating the control action. Figure 9-18 shows the hysteresis found in a common thermostat for an air conditioning unit. It also shows what would happen if there was no built-in hysteresis in the thermostat: the rapid cycling of the air conditioner would soon wear it out.

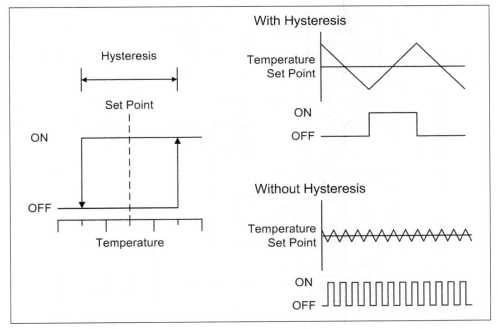

Figure 9-18. Hysteresis

Because of the hysteresis shown in Figure 9-18, the air conditioner won't come on until the temperature is slightly higher than the set-point, and it will remain on until the temperature is slightly below the set-point. While this does mean that the temperature will swing over some range around the set-point, it also means that the unit will not continuously and rapidly cycle on and off. Without hysteresis the thermostat would attempt to maintain the temperature at the set-point, which it would do by rapidly cycling the power to the air conditioner. Generally, this is not a good thing to do to a compressor in a refrigeration system.

Electromechanical bang-bang controllers are simple, robust devices that rely mainly on hysteresis in the controller mechanism to achieve a suitable level of responsiveness. However, if a bang-bang control is implemented in software as a discrete-time control system, the various time constants in the software will play a major role in determining how the system responds to input changes and how well it maintains control.

The flowchart in Figure 9-19 shows a simple controller for an air conditioning system. In this implementation hysteresis is determined by the offset constant H, which is applied to the set-point variable s. If the sensed temperature (t) is above or below the set-point with the hysteresis offset applied, the A/C unit will be either powered on or powered off, respectively.

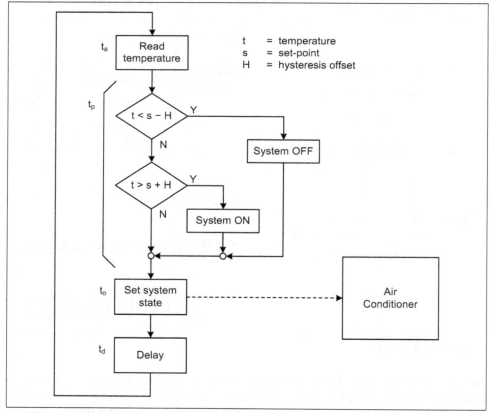

Figure 9-19. Software bang-bang controller

If we refer back to Figure 9-9 and examine Figure 9-19, we can see that in the overall scheme of things, times t_a, t_p, and t_o in this system should be negligible. What really counts here is the controller's cycle time, t_c, which is largely composed of the delay time, t_d.

The control cycle time should be as short as possible (the meaning of short is relative to the system under control, and could well be on the order of many milliseconds). This is a discrete-time control, so it will not have the continuous input response that we would expect from an electromechanical or analog electronic controller. The input needs to be sampled fast enough to avoid situations where the controlled output will overshoot or undershoot the set-point by excessive amounts. With a high sampling rate, the hysteresis coefficient becomes the dominating factor in determining the controlled-output duty cycle.

When determining the optimal value for t_c, one must take into account the responsiveness of the system being instrumented. Figure 9-20 shows the idealized response of a bang-bang controller with a relatively high control-sampling rate. The timing for t_a, t_p, and t_o is not shown, but we can assume that it's only a small fraction of t_c.

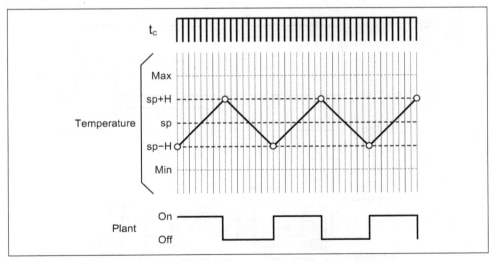

Figure 9-20. Bang-bang control response

The controller's cycle time and the amount of hysteresis in the system interact to determine the overall control responsiveness of a discrete-time bang-bang controller. In real applications, a bang-bang controller shouldn't be used where changes occur rapidly, because the controller will be unable to track the changes. If the time interval between t_a and t_o becomes large relative to the rate of change in the controlled system, the controlled output may continue to change significantly during that time. This can result in overshoot and undershoot, possibly exceeding allowable limits.

Sequential Control Systems

Sequential control systems are typically straightforward to implement, and they can range in complexity from very simple to extremely complex. They are commonly encountered in applications where a specific sequence of actions must be performed to achieve a deterministic result. Earlier, we looked at a simple example of a sequential control system in the form of an automated sprinkler system. Now I'd like to examine a slightly more complex and more interesting example.

Figure 9-21 shows a sequentially controlled robotic device. Here we have a mechanism consisting of a horizontally mounted rail, a fixed-speed electric motor, a couple of limit sensors, and a tool head of some sort. This system might be used to transfer biological samples from one station to another, string wires across a frame, or perhaps do something at one position while another robotic mechanism does something at the other position.

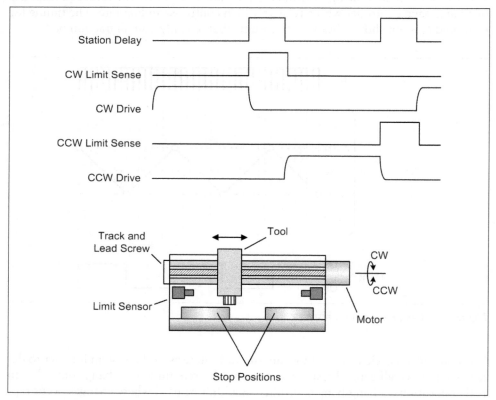

Figure 9-21. Sequentially controlled robotic system

The mechanism has only one degree of freedom (one range of motion), either left or right, which in Figure 9-21 is shown as CW (clockwise) or CCW (counterclockwise) to indicate the rotation of the motor driving the lead screw. It doesn't keep track of where the tool head is during travel; it only senses when the tool head is at one of the stop positions. The stop positions are determined by the physical positions of each of the end limit sensors.

In Figure 9-21, the motor activity indicated in the timing chart for CW Drive and CCW Drive has no sharp corners. This is because electric motors have inertia, and it takes some finite amount of time for the motor to come up to full speed, and some time for it to come to a complete stop when the power is removed. Notice that the state of the limit sensors changes as soon as the motor moves the tool off the limit in the opposite direction, but not when the motor starts, since it may take a little time to move off the limit sensor. Finally, we can assume that if the system is moving CW it doesn't need to check the CCW limit sensor (which should be active), as it's already there at the start of the movement. The same reasoning applies to CCW motion and the CW limit sensor.

I mentioned earlier that a sequential control system can often be modeled as a state machine, and this is shown in the simplified state diagram in Figure 9-22. When the tool head reaches a limit sensor the motor (and motion) stops, and the system then waits (delays) for some period of time before sending the tool head back in the opposite direction. This cycle will repeat continuously until intentionally stopped.

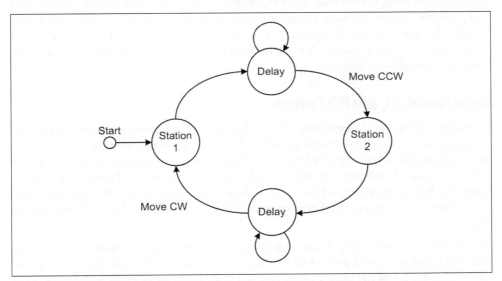

Figure 9-22. Sequential control system states

In a real system, you would also want to incorporate some type of error checking: say, a timeout to determine if the motor has stalled and the tool head is stuck somewhere between the two limit sensors. If a fixed-speed motor is used, the time required for the tool head to move from one station to the other should be consistent to within a few tens of milliseconds, so you could also put in a time limit for moving the tool head between station positions. If the limit sensor takes too long to report a stop, there is probably something wrong that needs attention.

Sequential control systems are common in industrial process environments, and they are often implemented using programmable logic controller (PLC) devices. State diagrams are a common way to describe a sequential control system, and PLC technology has its own types of diagrams, known as ladder diagrams and sequential function charts (SFCs). Flowcharts can be used to model sequential systems, but they are actually too verbose for anything but the most trivial designs.

If you will be implementing sequential controllers, it would be worthwhile to explore what's available in terms of diagram methodologies. Personally, I happen to prefer the SFC-type diagrams. They provide a slightly higher level of abstraction than a ladder diagram and are much more compact than a flowchart. Figure 9-23 shows an IEC 61131-3–type SFC.

In Figure 9-23, the heavy bars across the lines indicate a *gating condition*, which is some condition that needs to be true in order for the execution to proceed down a particular path. At each step there are actions that can be taken that will provide the inputs to a subsequent conditional test, or perform some system function.

An important thing to take away from Figure 9-23 is that a sequential controller doesn't just perform a series of steps in a fixed order; it can have branches to alternate sequences as well. In other words, a sequential system can incorporate if-then-type decision points and conditional loops. A sequential control system can also incorporate feedback in a closed-loop fashion.

Proportional, PI, and PID Controls

Proportional control is a key component in linear feedback control systems. A proportional controller is slightly more complex than a bang-bang controller, but it offers some significant advantages in terms of its ability to automatically accommodate a changing control environment and provide smooth, continuous linear control functionality. Purely proportional controls do have some drawbacks, though, including what is known as "droop," and poor response behavior to sudden changes in the control input.

We've already seen some basic examples of proportional controls (e.g., in Figure 9-11), but now we'll look at them in a bit more detail. We will then look at how the shortcomings of the purely proportional controllers can be dealt with by incorporating integral and derivative control modes into a system in the form of PI (proportional-integral) and PID (proportional-integral-derivative) controllers.

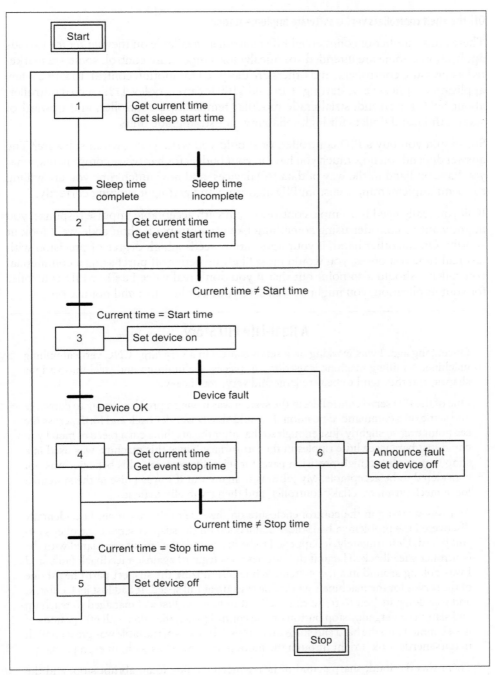

Figure 9-23. Example SFC diagram

Off-the-shelf controllers versus software implementation

There are a number of commercial PID controllers available on the market for various applications. Some are intended specifically for temperature control, some are marketed as pressure controllers, and others are designed for motion control, to name a few applications. Prices vary, starting at around $100 for an entry-level PID servo controller, about $400 for an industrial-grade modular temperature controller, and upward of several thousand dollars for high-reliability industrial-grade units.

So, should you buy a PID controller, or should you write your own in software? The answer depends on how much you have in your budget for hardware components, what you have on hand in the way of data I/O devices, and how much time you are willing to spend implementing a custom PID algorithm and getting it running correctly.

If all you really need is a simple control system with acceptable impulse response, you might want to consider using something like the example Python code we'll look at shortly. On the other hand, if your application needs a high degree of precision with fast real-time responses, you would most likely be better off purchasing a commercial controller. I should also point out that if you don't really need a PI or PID controller for your application, you might as well save yourself the effort and not use one.

A Real-Life PID Story

Once, long ago, I was working on a servo control in a very large CNC vertical milling machine. A milling machine is used to cut pieces of aluminum and steel into various shapes, and they tend to be very large and very, very heavy.

One of the PID servo controllers in the system was having a problem trying to converge and settle on a commanded position. It would slowly wander back and forth across the set-point ever so slightly, just enough so that after the machine cut a piece of metal you could just barely see little ripples in the cut surface. Since this machine was used in a shop that produced high-precision parts for scientific research, this behavior was not considered to be acceptable. My job was to figure out if it was noise in the system, a loose mechanism, or a flaky controller, and then try to eliminate it.

As I was working in the control enclosure on the side of the machine, I accidentally discovered the problem: a bad solder connection on the suspect servo controller's circuit board. Unfortunately, it happened to be in a part of the circuit associated with the controller's feedback. The unit did not have a safeguard against a feedback fault, and I was poking around in a live system. While scrutinizing the suspect part I heard one of the servos for the machine's worktable start up at full speed. It had lost its feedback, and was doing its best to try to run itself out to infinity. Just as I managed to reach up and slap the emergency stop button on the control panel, the table—all 600 pounds of it—slammed into the hard end stops on its rails. The mass of the table was great enough that its inertia took it right through the motion limit switches without even pausing.

There was the loud, sharp sound of heavy metal coming to an abrupt stop, and the whole two-ton milling machine jumped slightly. Part of that sound was the table's lead screw drive nut meeting an untimely end. It just so happened that it was a very expensive

---

type of drive nut filled with ball bearings, and it shattered. I was showered with hundreds of little ball bearings, and pieces of the shattered drive nut clattered onto the floor. The machinists in the shop all gathered and stared at the mess, and at me sitting on the floor staring at the huge steel table hanging above my head while I tried to comprehend what had just happened. Later, after I'd replaced a one-inch-diameter stainless steel lead screw (it was bent), the drive nut, the limit switches, the table's hard end stops, and the servo controller, the machine behaved fine. For me, it was a valuable (and expensive) lesson in how not to design a potentially dangerous system, and what to watch out for when working with live motion controllers.

PID overview

In industrial control applications the most commonly encountered controller type is the PID, in both linear and nonlinear forms. Linear PID-type controls have been around in one form or another for over 100 years. In the earliest incarnations they were implemented as mechanical, hydraulic, or pneumatic devices based on levers, gears, valves, pistons, and bellows. As technology progressed, DC servos, vacuum tubes, and transistors were used. All of these designs operated in the continuous linear time domain. With the advent of computer-controlled systems the analysis and implementation of PID controls moved into the nonlinear and discrete-time domains, and topics such as sampling intervals and sample resolution became important design considerations. We'll start here by looking at the basic theory behind PID controls in the continuous-time domain. Later we'll see how a PID control can be implemented in software by translating it into the discrete-time domain.

A full PID controller is composed of three basic parts, or *terms*. These are shown in the block diagram in Figure 9-24.

The output of a PID control is just the sum of three terms:

$$u = P + I + D$$

Each has a specific role to play in determining the stability and response of the controller.

Mathematically, the control function for an ideal PID control can be written as shown in Equation 9-4.

Equation 9-4.

$$u(t) = K_p e(t) + K_i \int_0^t e(\tau)d\tau + K_d \frac{de(t)}{dt}$$

where:

e

    Represents the system error $(r - b)$

K_p

Represents the proportional gain

K_i

Represents the integral gain

K_d

Represents the derivative gain

t

Represents instantaneous time

u

Is the control output

τ

Is the integral interval time (which may, or may not, be the same as t)

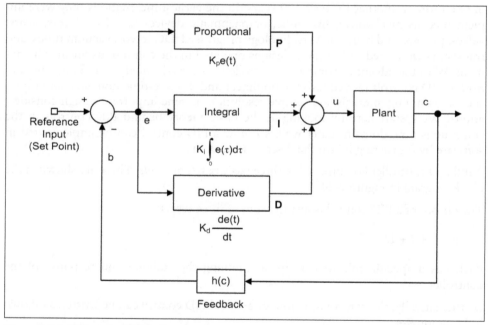

Figure 9-24. PID control block diagram

In practice, though, it's more common to find the PID equation written like Equation 9-5.

Equation 9-5.

$$u(t) = K_c e(t) + \frac{K_c}{T_i} \int_0^t e(\tau)d\tau + K_c T_d \frac{de(t)}{dt} + u_o$$

Equations 9-4 and 9-5 both describe a PID control in the continuous-time domain. The primary difference between them is that in Equation 9-5 the gain parameter K_c is applied to all three terms, and the independent behavior of the I and D terms is determined by T_i and T_d, which are defined as the integral time and the derivative time, respectively. I mention this because you may come across a PID description that uses a single gain variable, in what is called the standard form (Equation 9-6).

Equation 9-6.

$$u(t) = K_c \left[e(t) + \frac{1}{T_i} \int_0^t e(\tau)d\tau + T_d \frac{de(t)}{dt} \right]$$

In a PID controller, the proportional term is the primary contributor to the control function, with the integral and derivative terms providing smaller (in some cases, much smaller) contributions. In fact, a PI controller is just a PID controller with the D term set to zero. You can also make a PID controller behave like a purely proportional control by setting the I and D terms to zero.

The proportional control term

A proportional control is a type of linear feedback control system, and we've already seen some examples of these types of systems (see "Linear Control Systems" on page 305). What I want to discuss here are some of the shortcomings of proportional controls as a prelude to the introduction of the I and D terms.

A proportional control works pretty well when the input changes slowly over time and there are no sudden jumps in the input level or in the feedback from the plant. However, proportional controls don't handle sudden changes or transient events very well, and tend to exhibit overshoot, undershoot, and a reluctance to converge on the set-point (the reference input) if things are changing too rapidly. This is shown in Figure 9-25 for different values of K_p with a step input.

A step input is useful for control system response analysis, even if it will never be experienced by a control system in its operational setting. The main thing to take away from Figure 9-25 is how the gain variable K_p affects the ability of the control to respond to a quickly changing input and then damp out any swings around the set-point. A high gain setting will make for a more responsive system, but it will tend to overshoot and then dither around the set-point for a while. If the gain is set high enough it may never completely settle, and if the gain is set too high the entire system can go into oscillation. Conversely, if the gain is too low, the system will not be able to respond to input changes in a timely manner and it will have significant droop.

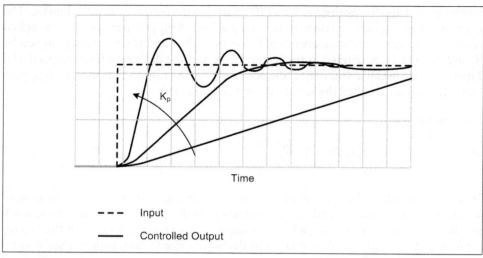

Figure 9-25. Proportional term control response

"Droop" is a problematic characteristic of proportional control systems wherein the output of the controller may never settle exactly at the set-point, but will instead exhibit a steady-state error in the form of a negative relative offset from the set-point. This is due largely to the difference between the gain of the controller and the gain of the process (or plant). Droop can be mitigated by applying a bias to the output of the controller, or it can be dealt with by using an integral term, as in a PI- or PID-type controller. Figure 9-26 shows the effect of droop.

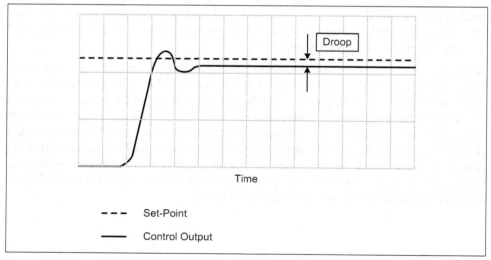

Figure 9-26. Proportional controller droop

There are also other external factors that affect how well a proportional control term will respond to control inputs. These include the responsiveness of the plant, time delays, and transient inputs.

PI and PID controls

The integral term, also known as the *reset*, is in effect an adaptive bias. The purpose of adding the integral term to the output of the controller is to account for the accumulated offset in the output and accelerate the output toward the set-point. Consequently, the proportional gain, K_p, must be lowered to account for the inclusion of the I term into the output.

If we recall that the error is the result of $r - b$, it should be apparent that the value of the integral term will increase rapidly when the error is largest, and then slow as the output converges on the reference input set-point and the error value goes to zero. So, the effect of the integral term will be to help to drive the system toward the set-point more rapidly than occurs with the P term alone. However, if K_i is too large, the system will overshoot, and it may become unstable. The effect of the integral term is dealt with when the controller is tuned for a particular application.

The derivative term in a full PID controller acts to slow the rate of change in the output of the controller. The effect is most pronounced as the control output approaches the set-point, so the net result of the derivative term is to limit or prevent overshoot. However, the derivative term also tends to amplify noise, and if K_d is too large, in the presence of transients and noise the control system may become unstable.

When all three terms are active and the controller is correctly tuned, it will exhibit a response like that shown in Figure 9-27.

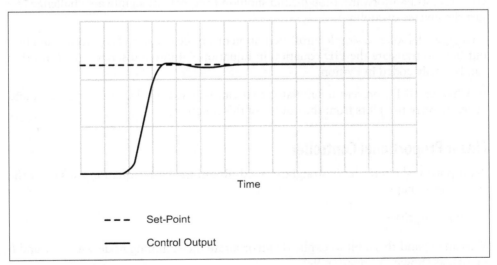

Figure 9-27. Tuned PID controller response

Hybrid Control Systems

The distinction between sequential and linear control systems is not always clear-cut. It is not uncommon to find control systems that are a mix of various paradigms, because of the different subsystems that are incorporated into them.

Consider the control system one might find in a brewery for beer bottling. Such a system could be composed of various subsystems. One subsystem might control the bottle conveyor, and its function would be to ensure that empty bottles appear under a nozzle at specific times. In order to do this it must control the speed of the conveyor precisely, taking into account the weight of different bottle styles. Another subsystem might control the filling operation. It would need to sense when a bottle is under the nozzle and then dispense a specific amount of beer. The amount of beer to dispense could be a function of time (valve open for some number of seconds). You can extend this thought experiment further if you like, and it will soon become apparent that the beer-bottling part of a brewery is actually a rather complex system, itself consisting of many inter-related subsystems (some operating as sequential controls, others operating as linear controls, and perhaps even some nonlinear controls).

Implementing Control Systems in Python

We'll start off by creating a simple linear closed-loop proportional control function. It may not look like much, but it has everything a basic proportional control requires. Next up is a nonlinear control in the form of a basic bang-bang controller. It has enough functionality to find immediate application as the controller for an air conditioning system, but it doesn't handle heating. Adding the ability to control heating as well as cooling is straightforward, though, and shouldn't present any significant challenge (it's just the inverse of cooling).

Finally, we'll look at a simple implementation of a basic linear PID controller, and find out how to translate the PID equation in Equation 9-4 into a discrete-time form that can be easily coded in Python.

In Chapter 10 I'll present a simulator that can be used to obtain realistic data and generate response plots from the output of this function.

Linear Proportional Controller

A proportional controller is straightforward. Recall the basic equation we saw at the start of this chapter:

$$u(t) = K_p e(t) + P$$

We can expand this a bit to explicitly incorporate the summing node with its r and b inputs, as shown in Equation 9-7.

Equation 9-7.

$$u(t) = K_p(r(t) - b(t)) + P$$

Here is the code to implement Equation 9-7:

```
""" Simple proportional control.

    Obtains input data for the reference and the feedback, and
    generates a proportional control value using the equation:

    u = Kp(r - b) + P

    b is obtained from c * Kb, where c is the output of the
    controlled device or system (the plant), and Kb is a gain
    applied to scale it into the same range as the r (reference)
    input.

    The gain parameters Kp and Kb should be set to something
    meaningful for a specific application. The P parameter is
    the bias to be applied to the output.
"""
# local global variables. Set these using the module.varname
# external access method.
Kp = 1.0
Kb = 1.0
P  = 0

# replace these as appropriate to refer to real inputs
rinput = 0
cinput = 1

def PControl():
    rval = AnalogIn(rinput)
    bval = AnalogIn(cinput) * Kb
    eval = rval - bval
    return (Kp * eval) + P
```

In this example, the function `AnalogIn()` is just a dummy placeholder. You will need to replace it, and the `rinput` and `cinput` variables, with something that makes sense for your application.

Bang-Bang Controller

Recall from earlier that a bang-bang controller is a type of nonlinear control wherein the output is nonlinear, but it is a function of a linear input. In this example we'll assume that the nonlinear output response is determined by two set-point values, one high and one low. When examining the following code, you might wish to refer to Equation 9-3 as a reference:

```
import time      # needed for sleep

# pseudo-constants
OFF = 0
```

```
    ON   = 1

    H = 2.0             # hysteresis range
    delay_time = 0.1    # loop delay time

    # replace these as appropriate to refer to real input and output
    temp_sense = 0
    device     = 0

    def BangBang():
        do_loop = True
        sys_state = OFF

        while (do_loop):
            if not do_loop:
                break

            curr_temp = AnalogIn(temp_sense)      # dummy placeholder

            if curr_temp <= set_temp - H:
                sys_state = OFF

            if curr_temp >= set_temp + H:
                sys_state = ON

            # it is assumed that setting the port with the same value isn't
            # going to cause any problems, and the output will only change
            # when the port input changes
            SetPort(device, sys_state)            # dummy placeholder

            time.sleep(delay_time)
```

This function maps directly to Equation 9-3, and it will behave as I described earlier, when we first looked at nonlinear controls. As with the other examples in this section, it doesn't have error detection, and it could be extended to include the ability to handle both heating and cooling. Also, the functions `AnalogIn()` and `SetPort()` are dummy placeholders, and the variables `temp_sense` and `device` will need to be replaced with something that matches the real execution environment.

Simple PID Controller

The first step in creating PID algorithms suitable for use with software is to convert from the continuous-time domain PID form in Equation 9-4 to a form in the discrete-time domain.

First, we formulate a discrete approximation of the integral term (Equation 9-8).

Equation 9-8.

$$\int_0^t e(\tau)d\tau \approx T_s \sum_{i=0}^t e(i)$$

In this equation:

e(i)
> Is the error at integration step *i*

i
> Is the integration step

T_s
> Is the time step size (Δt)

Now for the derivative term (Equation 9-9).

Equation 9-9.

$$\frac{de(t)}{dt} \approx \frac{e(t) - e(t-1)}{T_s}$$

In this equation:

t
> Is the instantaneous time

e(t – 1)
> Is the previous value of *e*, which is separated in time from *e(t)* by T_s

Just remember that we're now in the discrete-time domain, and the *t* is there as a sort of placeholder to keep things temporally correlated.

We don't really need to do anything with the proportional term from Equation 9-4; it's already in a form that can be translated directly into code.

We can now substitute the discrete-time approximations in Equation 9-4 to obtain Equation 9-10.

Equation 9-10.

$$u(t) = K_p e(t) + K_i \left(\frac{T_s}{T_i} \sum_{i=0}^{t} e(i) \right) + K_d \frac{T_d\,(e(t) - e(t-1))}{T_s}$$

In Equation 9-10:

T_i
> Is the integral time substep size

T_d
> Is the derivative time substep size

T_s
> Is the time step size (Δt)

While this form does allow for fine-grained control in regard to time in order to generate better approximations of the integral and derivative term values, it often isn't necessary to divide the overall T_s period into smaller slices for the integral and derivative terms. If we have a relatively fast control loop and we assume a unit time interval for all terms, Equation 9-10 can be simplified to Equation 9-11.

Equation 9-11.

$$u(t) = K_p e(t) + K_i \sum_{t=0}^{t} e(t) + K_d \frac{e(t) - e(t-1)}{t - (t-1)}$$

The following code listing shows a simple PID controller that implements the unit step time form from Equation 9-11:

```python
class PID:
    """ Simple PID control.

        This class implements a simplistic PID control algorithm. When
        first instantiated all the gain variables are set to zero, so
        calling the method GenOut will just return zero.
    """
    def __init__(self):
        # initialize gains
        self.Kp = 0
        self.Kd = 0
        self.Ki = 0

        self.Initialize()

    def SetKp(self, invar):
        """ Set proportional gain. """
        self.Kp = invar

    def SetKi(self, invar):
        """ Set integral gain. """
        self.Ki = invar

    def SetKd(self, invar):
        """ Set derivative gain. """
        self.Kd = invar

    def SetPrevErr(self, preverr):
        """ Set previous error value. """
        self.prev_err = preverr

    def Initialize(self):
        # initialize delta t variables
        self.currtm = time.time()
        self.prevtm = self.currtm

        self.prev_err = 0

        # term result variables
        self.Cp = 0
        self.Ci = 0
        self.Cd = 0
```

```
def GenOut(self, error):
    """ Performs a PID computation and returns a control value based
        on the elapsed time (dt) and the error signal from a summing
        junction (the error parameter).
    """
    self.currtm = time.time()          # get t
    dt = self.currtm - self.prevtm     # get delta t
    de = error - self.prev_err         # get delta error

    self.Cp = self.Kp * error          # proportional term
    self.Ci += error * dt              # integral term

    self.Cd = 0
    if dt > 0:                         # no div by zero
        self.Cd = de/dt                # derivative term

    self.prevtm = self.currtm          # save t for next pass
    self.prev_err = error              # save t-1 error

    # sum the terms and return the result
    return self.Cp + (self.Ki * self.Ci) + (self.Kd * self.Cd)
```

Tuning a PID controller by adjusting the values of K_p, K_i, and K_d is often considered to be a black art. There are several approaches used for PID tuning, including the Ziegler-Nichols method, software-based automated tuning, and the trial-and-error method.

Here are some general rules of PID behavior that are useful for tuning a controller:

- K_p controls the rise time. Increasing K_p results in a faster rise time, with more overshoot and longer settling time. Reducing K_p results in a slower rise time with less (or no) overshoot. The K_p term by itself is subject to droop.

- K_i eliminates the steady-state error (droop). However, if K_i is set too high the control output may overshoot and the settling time will increase. K_i and K_p must be balanced to obtain an optimal rise time with minimal overshoot.

- K_d provides a minor reduction in overshoot and settling time. Too much K_d can make the system unstable and cause it to go into oscillation, but a small value for K_d can improve the overall stability.

To use the PID control shown previously, you would first instantiate the controller and set the K_p, K_i, and K_d parameters:

```
pid = PID()
pid.SetKp(Kp)
pid.SetKi(Ki)
pid.SetKd(Kd)
```

A simple loop is used to read the feedback, call the PID method GenOut(), and then send the control value to the controlled device (the plant):

```
fb = 0
outv = 0
```

```
PID_loop = True

while PID_loop:
    # summing node
    err = sp - fb      # assume sp is set elsewhere

    outv = pid.GenOut(err)
    AnalogOut(outv)

    time.sleep(.05)

    fb = AnalogIn(fb_input)
```

Note that the set-point, sp, must be set somewhere else before the loop is started. Alternatively, you could call the PID control as part of a larger control loop, which would then make it possible to change sp on the fly while the system is running:

```
def GetPID():
    global fb

    err = sp - fb

    outv = pid.GenOut(err)
    AnalogOut(outv)

    time.sleep(.05)

    fb = AnalogIn(fb_input)
```

The system loop could also perform other functions, such as updating a user interface, processing acquired data, checking for errors, and so on:

```
while sys_active:
    # do some stuff
    UpdateUI()      # get sp from user
    GetPID()
    # do more stuff
```

If sp is a global variable in the context of the system loop, the GUI might allow the user to change it, and GetPID() will use it the next time it is called.

Summary

This has been a very lightweight introduction to control systems theory and applications, and it is by no means complete. We have only skimmed the surface of the field of control systems theory and applications. This is a deep topic in engineering, drawing upon years of experience by an uncountable number of engineers and researchers.

It is my hope that you now have a general idea of what types of control systems can be built, how they work, and how to select the one that makes sense for your application.

Suggested Reading

If you would like to learn more about control systems and their applications, I would suggest that you pick up one (or more) of the following books:

Advanced PID Control. Karl Åström and Tore Hägglund, ISA—The Instrumentation, Systems, and Automation Society, 2005.

> If you want to dig deeper into control systems theory, and PID controls in particular, this book is a good place to start. It covers nearly every aspect of using PID controllers, and combines discussions of real-world examples with a solid presentation of the mathematical theory behind PID control technology. With chapters dealing with topics such as process models, controller design, and predictive control, it is a valuable resource for anyone working with control system technology.

Introduction to Control System Technology, 7th ed. Robert Bateson, Prentice Hall, 2001.

> I would recommend this book as a good starting point to learning about control systems and their applications. The math doesn't require much more than first-year calculus, and the author employs numerous real-world examples to help illustrate the concepts. It also contains extensive definitions of terms in the form of chapter-specific glossaries and a section on basic electronics.

Computer-Controlled Systems, 3rd ed. Karl Åström and Bjorn Wittenmark, Prentice Hall, 1996.

> While it is well written (albeit a bit terse) and contains examples for Matlab® and Simulink®, this is probably not a book I would recommend as a first read on the subject of control systems. It is, however, a good reference once you've gotten your feet wet and need to find insight into specific problems. If you work with control systems on a regular basis (or you're planning on it), I'd recommend this book as a handy reference and for advanced study.

Real Time Programming: Neglected Topics, 4th ed. Caxton C. Foster, Addison-Wesley, 1982.

> Foster's book is a short, concise treatment of various topics relevant to real-time data acquisition and control systems. Well written with a light and breezy style, the book contains several short chapters dealing with basic control systems theory using a minimal amount of mathematics. It also covers the basics of digital filters, signal processing, and constrained communications techniques, among other topics. It has been out of print for a long time, but it is still possible to find used copies.

There are also numerous websites with excellent information on control systems, and even some software available for free. Here are a few to start off with:

http://citeseerx.ist.psu.edu/viewdoc/download?doi=10.1.1.129.1850&rep=rep1&type= pdf

> PDF version of the book *Feedback Control Theory*, by John Doyle, Bruce Francis, and Allen Tannenbaum (Macmillan, 1990). It can also be purchased in paperback form. Oriented toward classical control theory and transfer function analysis, this book is a good introduction to advanced concepts. Its particular emphasis is on robust performance.

http://aer.ual.es/modelling/

> Home site for a set of excellent interactive learning modules from the University of Almeria (Spain). Check this out after you've spent some time reading through one of the books cited previously; the interactive applets are very useful for dynamically illustrating various control system concepts. The module on PID controls is a companion resource for the book *Advanced PID Control*. Note that the commercial site for the Swiss company Calerga Sarl at *http://www.calerga.com/contrib/index.html* hosts the same learning modules.

http://www.cds.caltech.edu/~murray/amwiki/index.php/Main_Page

> Karl Åström's and Richard Murray's wiki. Contains the complete text of the book *Feedback Systems: An Introduction for Scientists and Engineers* (Princeton University Press), along with examples and additional exercises. This is a good introduction to feedback control systems that doesn't shy away from the necessary mathematics. But even if your memories of calculus are a bit fuzzy, you should still find plenty to take away from this book.

http://www.me.cmu.edu/ctms/controls/ctms/pid/pid.htm

> A collection of control system tutorials written for use with Matlab and Simulink.

And, of course, Wikipedia has numerous articles on control systems topics.

CHAPTER 10

Building and Using Simulators

Is that some kind of a game you are playing?

—C. A. Chung, *Simulation Modeling Handbook: A Practical Approach*

So far in this book we've covered the basics of programming in Python, reviewed some essential electronics, and explored the tip of the iceberg of control systems theory. We've covered a lot, to be sure, but there is still one major topic left before we take on the challenges of actually connecting a computer to an instrument or a control system and turning it loose: *simulation.*

In engineering, simulation can be applied to many things, from a simple device to an entire complex system. In electronics engineering, circuit simulations are used to explore and analyze analog and digital designs well before an IC is fabricated or a soldering iron comes into play. Systems engineers build complex simulations of industrial systems to evaluate various control strategies and process flow models long before the pipes are laid out and the conveyors are installed. Military and commercial pilots are trained in realistic aircraft simulators where procedures and techniques can be learned and practiced with no risk to an actual vehicle or the people in it (or on the ground).

The primary objective of this chapter is to equip you with extensible simulation tools that you can reuse in other projects later, as well as an understanding of when and where simulation is useful, and where it is not. To this end, we'll examine a couple of complete simulators written entirely in Python. We'll wrap up by looking at some ways to leverage commonly available (and free) software tools to create other simulators.

The first example we will consider is a simulation of a generic multifunction device with both analog and discrete I/O. The second simulator example is an eight-channel AC power controller. Although the simulators in this chapter will touch on topics such as data I/O, data capture, and user interfaces, we will defer in-depth discussions of those topics to later chapters. Chapter 11 will examine data I/O in detail, and in Chapter 12 we will look at some ways to load and save data using files. In Chapter 13 we'll explore user interfaces in more detail, including the TkInter and wxPython GUIs. It is my hope that you will take the initiative to return to these simulators and extend their usefulness with the knowledge you gain later.

What Is Simulation?

If you've ever played a video game, you've used a simulator. One of the first commercially successful video games, Atari's *Pong*, was a simulation (albeit crude by today's standards) of a ping-pong game. In fact, all video games are simulations of something—what they simulate might not actually exist in the real world, but they're still simulations. By the same token, a simulation of a control system that doesn't really exist allows us to try out different novel ideas, invent worst-case scenarios to evaluate system behavior, and explore various behavioral models, all without risking any hardware or jeopardizing personal safety.

The key concept of simulation is that all simulators are based on a model of some sort. Models can be simple, or they can be complex. A model may be event- or time-series-based (automated handling of luggage at a large airport), purely mathematical (optical performance of lenses and mirrors), or some combination of these and other factors. One way to think of the core model in a simulation is as a dynamic virtual system. If, for example, you have a high-fidelity simulator for some type of chemical processing system, there is, in essence, a virtual chemical processing system in the simulation software that will exhibit as many of the responses and characteristics of the real thing as the fidelity of the simulation will allow. A truly high-fidelity simulation might even produce a simulated chemical product.

Figure 10-1 shows how a simulation corresponds to its real-world counterpart. The instrumentation system (which would typically be what we are developing or testing in this book) uses a simulated interface to interact with a model. The model allows us to observe and analyze how the instrumentation software will behave when connected to a system (in this case, a virtual system). We can implement a crude simulation model with basic behavior, or we could build something that has a very high degree of fidelity. We can also inject simulated faults into the model and examine the response of the instrumentation system.

When implementing data acquisition and control systems, simulations of the devices connected to the control PC can be used to speed up the development process and provide a safe environment to test out ideas. Simulation can also provide some invaluable, and otherwise unattainable, insights into the behavior of the instrumentation software and the device or system being simulated. Whether it's implemented because the instrumentation hardware just isn't available yet or because the target system hardware is too valuable to risk damaging, a simulation is a good way to get the software running, test it, and have a high degree of confidence that it will work correctly in the real world.

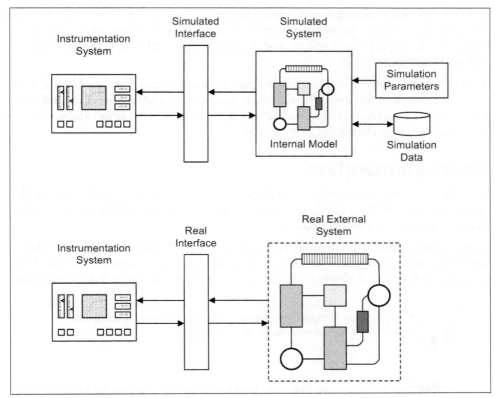

Figure 10-1. Simulation versus the real world

Low Fidelity or High Fidelity

When talking about simulation, one of the first considerations to come up is the issue of fidelity. The fidelity of a simulation defines how accurately it will model a real system. The cost and effort of implementing a simulation can rise significantly with each increase in the level of fidelity, so you'll have to decide when it's good enough and resist the temptation to polish it up too much.

A common error made when attempting to write a simulator for the first time is to throw everything into it. Even seasoned pros with access to lots of real data from a real system don't usually do this. There are too many unknowns at the outset. Subtle behavioral interactions can be surprising and might never have been seen in a real system, and assumptions made about the more opaque parts of a system may contain all sorts of traps and pitfalls.

This is why simulations are typically built up incrementally. First, the software interface, or API, is defined. A generic interface may use different names for the API functions, but it should accept and return data that looks as much like real API data as possible. In other words, the simulation should support the basic algorithmic functionality of the control or instrumentation system you are building in terms of the data that needs to pass through the interface. Once the interface simulation is at a point where it can support initial testing and development, simulation fidelity can be improved as necessary.

That being said, sometimes a low-fidelity simulator consisting of just an API will work fine. For example, if all you really want to do is verify that a proportional control function is working correctly, a simple data source to drive the simulation and some way to capture and save the output may be all that's necessary.

Simulating Errors and Faults

In addition to simulating the functionality of a working system, a simulation may also need to have the ability to simulate an error. In other words, it should be able to simulate being broken in some predefined way.

If you've done a failure analysis, as outlined in Chapter 8, you should have an idea of what types of errors might occur and how they will cause the system to fail. The ability to simulate those errors allows you to see how well your software will deal with them.

 If you do want to include the ability to do fault injection in a simulation, a preliminary failure analysis is an essential first step.

In general terms, there are two primary classes of faults (not including bugs that may be lurking in the instrumentation code itself) that come into play: *interface faults* and *system faults*. The line between these two classes of faults isn't always distinct, but in a simulated environment it's usually possible to treat them as separate classes. This, in turn, makes it much easier to clearly distinguish cause and effect without the complexity and messiness of dealing with real physical components.

Interface faults

An interface fault results in an error that, as the name implies, occurs in the API layer between the system under development or in test, and the system simulation behind it. These types of faults might manifest as communications errors, such as corrupt data or no response. In other words, an interface fault occurs in between the instrumentation software and the simulated system. In the real system, errors in the interface might arise as a result of broken wires, corroded connections, a defective electronic component, or spurious noise.

Simulating interface faults typically involves things like disabling a communications channel or injecting random data into a channel. You can also simulate a fault in a piece of bus interface hardware (e.g., a plug-in I/O card), although this falls into that gray area I alluded to earlier and may be better dealt with as a system fault.

Figure 10-2 shows a diagram of an interface simulation with basic fault injection capabilities. Notice that the TxD (transmit) output from the instrumentation software to the instrument simulator doesn't have a disable capability. This isn't an oversight. If the instrument employs a command-response type of control interface, disabling the TxD link between it and the instrumentation software doesn't really accomplish much. The instrument (or simulated instrument) should just sit and wait for a command, and it won't have any way to detect whether the link is broken or not.

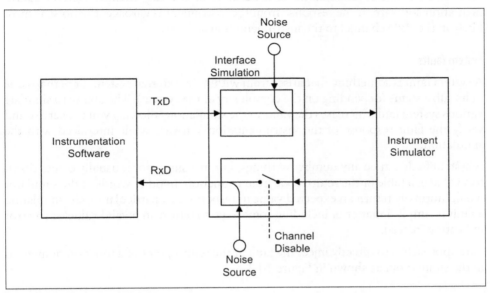

Figure 10-2. Interface fault injection

The path from the instrument to the instrumentation software is another matter. In this case, the instrumentation software should be able to detect when it has not received a response from the instrument and react in a predefined manner.

A reasonable question to ask at this point would be: why not just simulate the disabled communications in the instrument simulator, instead of using an interface simulation? The reason is that the instrument, or control system, may interact with some other component in the system that the instrumentation software can sense even if the primary link to the instrument is disabled. In other words, clever instrumentation software can sometimes get verification from another source (e.g., sensing a power state change) indicating that a correct command action has occurred, and thereby determine that the interface is the probable cause of the problem.

Figure 10-2 also indicates that both the TxD and RxD (receive) channels have noise injection capabilities. In the context of a communications channel that handles streams of ASCII characters, this could involve the injection of random characters to simulate line noise. Anyone who has ever had to use a modem to communicate with a remote computer system has mostly likely seen examples of line noise when the modem connects to or disconnects from the remote host.

Instrumentation software that is able to deal with corrupted data will most likely have the ability to retry an operation, or at least issue a query to determine whether a command was accepted correctly. It is also possible to determine where the noise occurred by examining the response from the instrument. If the instrument complains that it received an invalid command, the noise occurred on the TxD channel from the instrumentation software. If the response from the instrument is garbage, the noise is most likely in the RxD channel to the instrumentation software.

System faults

A system fault is something that arises from within the external system, or perhaps one of its subsystems (depending on the complexity of the system). The ability to simulate various system faults increases the value of the simulation, allowing you to exercise and verify the fault response of the instrumentation software while interfaced with the simulation.

A system fault can be any number of things, but in a simulator it usually comes down to a value in a table or the return code from a function. In other words, if the simulator would normally return an expected value in response to a particular input, simulating a fault is simply a matter of including some logic to return an invalid value or an error indication instead.

One approach is to directly inject the fault at the return point of a function or method in the simulation, as shown in Figure 10-3.

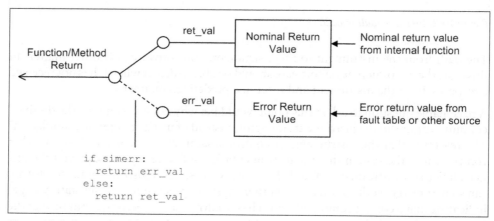

Figure 10-3. System-level fault injection

Assuming that `ret_val` in Figure 10-3 holds the nominal value that the function or method would normally return, setting `simerr` to `True` will result in the error return value (`err_val`) being passed back to the caller instead. The error value could be set via an accessor method, loaded from a fault table, or even entered manually from a user interface of some sort.

Another approach is to establish a fault condition using a module global variable or an object variable, as shown in Figure 10-4.

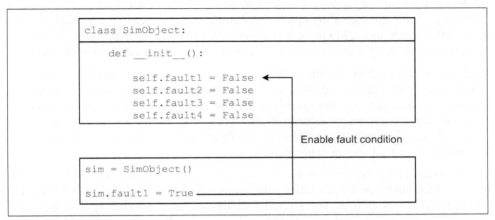

Figure 10-4. Simulator fault injection using object variables

In Figure 10-4, the class definition for SimObject has been designed to specifically expose key variables used by the methods in the class. In a simplistic scenario these would be read-only variables, set once at object instantiation and not modified by the class methods. It is possible to implement a lockout capability to prevent methods from modifying shared object variables, but that usually entails a level of complexity that's not always necessary.

If you're experienced with unit testing techniques, you might be thinking that all this sounds rather familiar, and you would be correct (we also discussed this in Chapter 8). In unit testing, a primary objective is to exercise all possible paths of execution to achieve complete statement coverage. If the unit under test has paths that can be executed only when an error occurs, the unit test environment must be able to set variables or coerce inputs to stimulate the appropriate error responses. A simulation that has fault injection capabilities does much the same thing, although for a somewhat different reason.

As a test environment, a simulator can be used to create fault scenarios that would otherwise be difficult (or even near impossible) to replicate with real hardware, at least not without the possibility of risking some serious (and expensive) physical damage. Simulation with fault injection allows you to observe the behavior of the control or data acquisition system you are building to see how it will respond to various error conditions and, if you have been following some requirements that define error responses, to determine whether it meets those requirements.

Using Python to Create a Simulator

In this section we will examine two complete simulators written in Python: DevSim and the Simple Power Controller (SPC). Later, we'll look at some other ways to achieve simulation using free and open source software. The sources for the simulators are located in the resource repository for this book, which can be accessed from the book's web page. While these are fully functional simulators, they are also only examples, not production-grade tools. My hope is that you will use them as inspiration, or perhaps as starting points, to create your own simulator tools to meet your particular needs.

Python is well suited to creating simulators. It is easy to use, very flexible, and allows you to easily implement things such as plug-in modules. Working simulators can often be gotten up and running very quickly, and once in place they can be readily extended and revised as necessary. In addition, Python is capable of some impressive math tricks when add-on libraries such as *SciPy* or *NumPy* are installed, and as we'll see shortly, generating graphical output is not that difficult.

On the other hand, Python is not as fast as code written in C or C++. That's just the nature of the language and its underlying interpreter. If you need high-speed data generation and fast responses, you should probably consider another approach. Fortunately, most instrumentation applications have rather long time constants to begin with, so speed is usually not an issue.

Package and Module Organization

The simulators we'll examine in this chapter are DevSim and SPC. Each can reside in its own package (subdirectory). This is how I've arranged them, with SPC residing in the ACSim directory. DevSim imports the FileUtils module that we'll see in Chapter 12 for reading and writing ASCII data files. It also imports a module called RetCodes, which contains a set of pseudoconstants for return code values. It is intended to be a read-only shared file. Typically the FileUtils and RetCodes modules would reside in a separate package called SimLib, as shown in Figure 10-5, along with any other modules that your simulators and utilities might need to share.

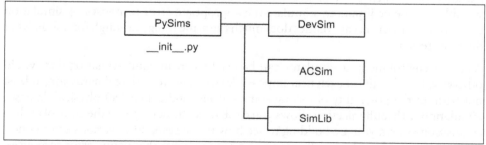

Figure 10-5. Simulation package structure

If you have not already done so, now would be a good time to pause and download the source code for this book from its website. There's more there than what you'll see here, and it's all already neatly organized with installation instructions.

Notice that the top-level package, PySims, has a file called __init__.py. This establishes PySims as the "anchor" of the package hierarchy; it may contain a docstring, package initialization code, or nothing at all. When we look at *gnuplot* later, we'll see how one developer elected to use __init__.py to handle package initialization.

Data I/O Simulator

First up is a rather substantial simulator that is intended to stand in for a bus-based multifunction I/O card. Right out of the box it can be used with the PID control code we saw in Chapter 9 (and I'll show you how to do that in just a bit). It also has the ability to incorporate user-defined functions as part of the response data processing, which is useful for simulating things like mechanical inertia or applying a filter function.

DevSim internals

Although the DevSim API may look daunting, it's mainly just a collection of accessor methods to set simulation parameters and return the current values. In its basic form, it doesn't actually simulate any particular external device or system. That functionality is added by you, in the form of user-definable functions or additional software to meet project-specific needs.

Rather than list it all here (it's almost 1,000 lines of code), I'm going to describe its internal structure, list the various methods available, show some highlights, and discuss how the simulator is used. You should have the source listing handy for reference, if possible.

Internally, DevSim is the most complex thing we've seen so far, but keep in mind that it's mostly just data routing. Figure 10-6 is an IC data-sheet-style logic diagram for DevSim.

Data is buffered as it moves though DevSim, and each activity is synchronized so as to occur in a lock-step fashion. DevSim is also multithreaded: four threads handle cyclic functions (waveform generation), another four manage file input, and a ninth thread handles the simulator's primary sequencing in a main loop.

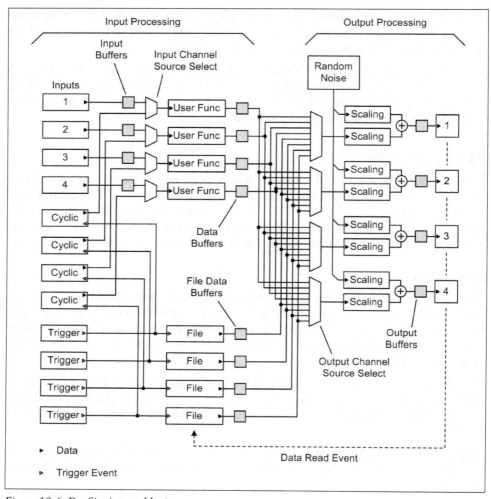

Figure 10-6. DevSim internal logic

The DevSim class's __init__() method presets the internal parameters to default values, and then calls the internal method _run() as its final action. The code for _run() follows:

```
#-------------------------------------------------------------------
# Simulator launch
#-------------------------------------------------------------------
def _run(self):
    """ Simulator start.

        Instantiates the main loop thread, sets up the cyclic and
        file I/O threads, and then waits for the start flag to go
        True. When the start flag becomes True the main loop
```

```
        thread is started.
    """
    # input thread object lists
    cycThread  = [None, None, None, None]
    fileThread = [None, None, None, None]

    simloop  = threading.Thread(target=self.__simLoop)

    # create the cyclic and file input handling threads,
    # four of each
    for inch in range(0,4):
        cycThread[inch]  = \
            threading.Thread(target=self.__cyclic, args=[inch])
        fileThread[inch] = \
            threading.Thread(target=self.__fileData, args=[inch])

        # start the cyclic and file I/O threads just created
        cycThread[inch].start()
        fileThread[inch].start()

    # wait for start signal then start the main thread
    wait_start = True
    while wait_start:
        if self.startSim == True:
            wait_start = False
        else:
            time.sleep(0.1)      # wait 100 ms
    simloop.start()              # start it up
```

First, the primary thread, `simloop()`, is created. Next, the eight input threads are instantiated in a pair of lists. As each thread is created, it is subsequently started. The `__run()` method then waits for a start signal, and finally starts the `simloop()` main thread.

The simulator is designed to start running when a Boolean variable (`startSim`) is set to `True`. You can set the various parameters before enabling the simulator, or they can be set "on the fly" while it is running. The simulation is stopped by setting the value of the Boolean object variable `stopSim` to `True`.

The four cyclic threads and the four file input threads each load data into a buffer when an "event" occurs. In the case of DevSim, an event is simply a flag variable that is set and reset to control activity; it is not a true event in the sense of a low-level message such as one would find in a GUI. Figure 10-7 shows how the threads are used to obtain input data and place it into buffers for eventual routing to the outputs. Notice that the `__cyclic()` threads can each select from one of five possible inputs: DC (constant value), sine wave, pulse (square wave), ramp, and sawtooth. The cyclic data is updated at a rate set by the parameter accessor `setCyclicRate()`, and each cyclic input may have a unique rate value. The cyclic inputs are very useful for generating a fixed DC-like value or periodic waveforms that the instrumentation software connected to the simulator can read and process.

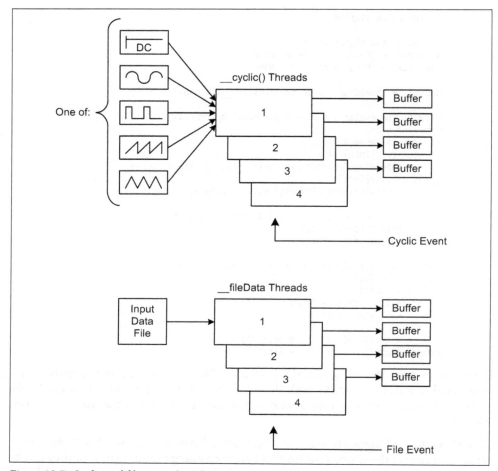

Figure 10-7. Cyclic and file input threads

Using threads for the cyclic inputs allows them to run at different rates than the simulator's main thread, and this in turns allows them to create waveform data at specific frequencies. If they weren't implemented as threads they would generate changes in the simulated waveforms at the main loop rate of the simulator, which wouldn't be suitable for a lot of situations. Allowing the cyclic data generators to run asynchronously is an example of timing decoupling. The buffers are necessary to capture the asynchronous data as it is generated.

Threads of Execution

Modern operating systems support multiple processes, running more or less at the same time, by quickly switching the CPU between processes. A *process*, in this context, refers to a program and its memory space, its system environment variables, and possibly whatever I/O resources it is assigned when it is created. These make up the *execution environment* of the process, and it can be a lot of baggage for a process to haul around with it.

A *thread*, on the other hand, is also sometimes called a *lightweight process* because threads typically execute within the context of a parent process. In other words, the threads within a process share the memory space and execution environment of the parent process. One way to look at threads of this type is to think of them as functions that are capable of independent execution. Because they execute in a shared environment, it is possible for one thread to interfere with the global variables used by another within the parent process context. This type of data coupling can result in some nasty data corruption or deadlock situations, so some careful thought needs to go into where and how threads are implemented.

The __fileData() threads are used to obtain data values from a file and pass them through to the instrument software under test. This feature allows you to replay a set of input data over and over again. It is useful when evaluating the instrumentation software under test against a known set of input values, to observe its behavior.

The main loop thread, shown next, is where all the data is collected and routed to the output buffers:

```python
def __simLoop(self):
    """ Simulator main loop.

        The main loop continuously checks for input data (either
        from an external caller or from a cyclic source) for each
        input channel. If data is available it starts the
        processing chain that will ultimately result in the data
        appearing in the output buffers.

        The main loop runs forever as a thread. All externally
        supplied data is buffered, and all output data is buffered.
        When running in cyclic mode the output buffers will be
        overwritten with new data as it becomes available.
    """
    while self.stopSim != True:
        # scan through all four input channels, get available data
        for ichan in range(0, 4):
            if self.in_src[ichan] == DS.EXT_IN:
                indata = self.inbuffer[ichan]
            else:
                indata = __getCycData(ichan)

            # if a user-supplied function is defined, then apply
            # it to the data
```

```
                self.databuffer[ichan] = self.__doUserFunc(ichan, indata)

        # fetch file data (if configured to do so)
        self.__getFileData(ichan)

        # step through each output channel, move data as nesc
        for ochan in range(0,4):
            if (self.out_src[ochan] >= DS.INCHAN1) and \
               (self.out_src[ochan] <= DS.INCHAN4):
                outdata = self.databuffer[ochan]
            else:
                outdata = self.filebuffer[ochan]

            randdata = self.__getRandom()

            oscaled = self.__scaleData(outdata, self.outscale[ochan])
            rscaled = self.__scaleData(randdata, self.randscale[ochan])

            self.outbuffer[ochan] = oscaled + rscaled
            self.outavail[ochan] = True

        time.sleep(self.simtime)
```

Reading through the code for the __simloop() method is equivalent to following the data flow through Figure 10-6 from left to right. The first step is to get either externally supplied data (via the sendData() method, described in the following section), or from one of the cyclic data sources. Next the data is passed to a user-defined function, if one exists. It is then written to a buffer (databuffer).

If the data input is a file, the data is read from the file and stored in another buffer. Note that although a method is called, this doesn't mean that anything will actually happen. An input method might be quiescent and therefore skipped internally, depending on how the simulator is configured.

Once the input data is in one of the two input buffers, it is read out and passed to the output. Along the way random data is obtained (for noise simulation), and the data is optionally scaled before it is summed with scaled random data. Finally, the data ends up in the output buffers for each channel.

DevSim methods

The DevSim class contains 26 public methods and 15 internal methods. Most of the public methods are devoted to setting or retrieving internal parameter values. The public methods are described in the following lists.

 When used, the parameters *inchan* and *outchan* may be any channel number from 0 to 3.

Parameter accessor methods:

getCyclicLevel(*inchan*)
>   Returns a 2-tuple with either NO_ERR and the current cyclic level of the specified channel, or BAD_PARAM and None if *inchan* is out of range.

setCyclicLevel(*inchan, level*)
>   Sets the output value for a cyclic source in CYCNONE mode for a specific input channel. Returns NO_ERR if successful or BAD_PARAM if *inchan* is out of range.

getCyclicOffset()
>   Returns the current cyclic offset value.

setCyclicOffset(*offset*)
>   Sets the current cyclic offset value for all cyclic data. The offset is the shift of the peak-to-peak range of the output relative to zero, otherwise known as the *bias*.

getCyclicRate(*inchan*)
>   Returns a 2-tuple with either NO_ERR and the current cyclic rate of the specified channel, or BAD_PARAM and None.

setCyclicRate(*inchan, rate*)
>   The parameter rate defines the cyclic rate in fractional seconds for a specific input channel. Note that this is the period of the cyclic data, not the frequency. The frequency is the inverse of the rate. Returns NO_ERR if successful or BAD_PARAM if *inchan* is out of range.

getCyclicType(*inchan*)
>   Returns a 2-tuple with either NO_ERR and the current cyclic wave shape of the specified channel, or BAD_PARAM and None.

setCyclicType(*inchan, cyctype*)
>   Defines the output wave shape of a cyclic data source. The available wave shapes are sine, pulse, ramp, and sawtooth. A cyclic source may also be set to generate a constant output value, and the value may be changed at any time while the simulator is active. This, in effect, emulates a variable voltage source. Table 10-1 lists the five cyclic data types available.

Table 10-1. Simulator cyclic data types

Cyclic type	Data value	Description
CYCNONE	0	Constant output level
CYCSINE	1	Sine wave
CYCPULSE	2	50% duty-cycle pulse (i.e., a square wave)
CYCRAMP	3	Ramp wave shape with leading slope
CYCSAW	4	Sawtooth wave with symmetrical rise/fall

Returns NO_ERR if successful or BAD_PARAM if *cyctype* is invalid or *inchan* is out of range.

setDataFile(*infile, path, filename, recycle=True*)

Defines and opens a data file for input as a data source specified by the *infile* index. If *path* is not specified (empty string or None), the default path is assumed to be the current working directory. The input file must contain data in one of the four formats supported by the ASCIIDataRead class in the module FileUtils.

If the parameter *recycle* is True, the file will be reset to the start and reread when an EOF is encountered. The default behavior is to recycle the data file. If a data source file is already opened for a given input channel and this method is called, the currently open file will be closed and the new file will be opened.

Returns OPEN_ERR if the file open failed or BAD_PARAM if *infile* is invalid; otherwise, returns NO_ERR.

getDataScale(*outchan*)

Returns a 2-tuple with either NO_ERR and the current data scaling for a specific channel, or BAD_PARAM and None.

setDataScale(*outchan, scale*)

Sets the output channel's input data scaling factor. Each output channel may have an optional unique multiplicative scaling factor applied. Returns NO_ERR if successful or BAD_PARAM if *inchan* is out of range.

getFunction(*inchan*)

Returns a 2-tuple with either NO_ERR and the current function string for the specified channel, or BAD_PARAM and None.

setFunction(*inchan, funcstr=' '*)

Applies a user-supplied function expression to the data stream of a specified input data channel using two predefined variables:

x0

Input data

x1

Previous (1/z) data

The function is a string. It may reference the x0 and x1 variables but may not contain an equals sign (an assignment). The result is used as the data input to the output channels. Passing None or an empty string disables the application of a function to the data. Returns NO_ERR if successful or BAD_PARAM if *inchan* is out of range.

getInputSrc(*inchan*)

Returns a 2-tuple with either NO_ERR and the input source for a specific channel, or BAD_PARAM and None.

setInputSrc(*inchan, source*)

Selects the data source for an input channel. *inchan* may be any valid input channel number from 0 to 3. The *source* parameter may be one of EXT_IN (default) or CYCLIC. The input source may be changed on the fly at any time. Returns NO_ERR if successful or BAD_PARAM if *inchan* is out of range or *source* is invalid.

`getOutputDest(outchan)`

Returns a 2-tuple with either NO_ERR and the current output channel data source, or BAD_PARAM and None.

`setOutputDest(outchan, source)`

Selects the data source for an output channel. *outchan* may be any valid output channel number between 0 and 3. The *source* parameter may be one of INCHAN1, INCHAN2, INCHAN3, INCHAN4, SRCFILE1, SRCFILE2, SRCFILE3, or SRCFILE4. Returns NO_ERR if successful or BAD_PARAM if *inchan* is out of range or *source* is invalid.

`getRandScale(outchan)`

Returns a 2-tuple with either NO_ERR and the current random data scaling multiplier, or BAD_PARAM and None.

`setRandScale(outchan, scale)`

Sets the output channel's random data scaling factor. Each output channel may have an optional multiplicative scaling factor applied to the random data. If the scaling is set to zero, no random values are summed into the data. Returns NO_ERR if successful or BAD_PARAM if *inchan* is out of range.

`getSimTime()`

Returns the current simulator cycle time.

`setSimTime(time)`

Sets the overall cycle time of the simulation. This is, in effect, the amount of time for which the main loop will be suspended between each loop iteration. The time is specified in fractional seconds. Returns nothing.

`getTrigMode(inchan)`

Returns a 2-tuple with either NO_ERR and the current trigger mode for the specified channel, or BAD_PARAM and None.

`setTriggerMode(inchan, mode)`

Sets the trigger mode for a particular channel. The trigger mode may be one of NO_TRIG (0), EXT_TRIG (1), or INT_TRIG (2).

In NO_TRIG mode, all cyclic sources run continuously at the clock rate set by the setCyclicClock() method, and data source file reads do not occur until an output channel is accessed.

In EXT_TRIG mode, cyclic sources perform a single operation and file sources are read once for each trigger occurrence.

In INT_TRIG mode, cyclic sources perform a single cycle and data source files are read once each time an output channel is accessed.

Returns NO_ERR if successful or BAD_PARAM if *inchan* is out of range or *mode* is invalid.

Simulator control and I/O methods:

```
genTrigger(inchan)
```
Generates a trigger event. Depending on the trigger mode, a trigger event will result in one iteration of a cyclic data source, or one record read from a data input file. Returns NO_ERR if successful or BAD_PARAM if *inchan* is out of range.

Input/output methods:

```
readData(outchan, block=True, timeout=1.0)
```
Returns the data available for the specified output channel from the output buffer. If blocking is enabled, this method will block the return to the caller until the data becomes available or the specified timeout period has elapsed.

Returns a 2-tuple consisting of the return code and the data value from the output channel. Returns NO_ERR if successful or BAD_PARAM if *outchan* is out of range. If the return code is anything other than NO_ERR, the data value will be zero.

```
sendData(inchan, dataval)
```
Writes caller-supplied data into the specified channel. The data in the input buffer will be read on each cycle of the simulator. Returns NO_ERR if successful or BAD_PARAM if *inchan* is out of range.

For all its apparent complexity, the simulator really boils down to just two main methods: readData() and sendData(). Everything else just sets the stage for what will occur between the inputs and the outputs.

Some simple examples

The following example code demonstrates the data flow from an input to an output in the simulator. It doesn't use the optional user function, nor does it apply scaling or noise to the data:

```python
#! /bin/python
# TestDevSim1.py
#
# Echos data written into the simulator back to the output.
#
# Source code from the book "Real World Instrumentation with Python"
# By J. M. Hughes, published by O'Reilly.

from    DevSim import DevSim
import  SimLib.RetCodes as RC
import  DevSimDefs as DS

def testDevSim1():
    simIO = DevSim.DevSim()

    # set up the simulated device
    simIO.setInputSrc(DS.INCHAN1, DS.EXT_IN)
    simIO.setOutputSrc(DS.OUTCHAN1, DS.INCHAN1)

    loopcount = 0
    while loopcount < 10:
```

```
            simIO.sendData(DS.INCHAN1, (5.0 + loopcount))
            print simIO.readData(DS.OUTCHAN1)
            loopcount += 1

    simIO.stopSim = True    # set the stop flag
```

Referring to the code and to Figure 10-6, the first points of interest are the
setInputSrc() and setOutputSrc() statements. In both method calls, the first parameter
identifies the input or output channel to use and the second parameter specifies where
the data will come from. The first call states that the data for input channel 1 will be
obtained from the channel 1 external input, which occurs when the sendData() method
is called. In other words, it controls the "Input Channel Source Select" (the small two-
input trapezoid symbol in Figure 10-6). The second method call (setOutputSrc()) determines where the data that will appear on output channel 1 will be obtained. In this
case, the selection parameter governs the behavior of the eight-input source selector,
and it specifies input channel 1. Note that input channel 1 could mean either a direct
input from an external source, or one of the internal cyclic data sources. If we follow
the data path in Figure 10-6 we see that it goes through the user function block in the
input side, and then through a scaling block and a summing junction for random data
(noise) on the output side. This example does not use any of those features, so it's
effectively a straight connection between the input and the output.

The second example uses a data file as the input to the simulator:

```
#! /bin/python
# TestDevSim2.py
#
# Reads data from an input file and passes the data to the output. A
# data file containing 10 values in ASCII form must exist in the
# current directory.
#
# Source code from the book "Real World Instrumentation with Python"
# By J. M. Hughes, published by O'Reilly.

from    DevSim import DevSim
import  SimLib.RetCodes as RC
import  DevSimDefs as DS

def testDevSim2():
    simIO = DevSim.DevSim()

    # define the source file to use
    rc = simIO.setDataFile(DS.SRCFILE1, None, "indata1.dat")
    if rc != RC.NO_ERR:
        print "Error opening input data file"
    else:
        # set up the simulated device
        simIO.setOutputSrc(DS.OUTCHAN1, DS.SRCFILE1)

        loopcount = 0
        while loopcount < 10:
            # read and print data from file
```

```
print simIO.readData(DS.OUTCHAN1)
loopcount += 1

simIO.stopSim = True
```

The call to the method setDataFile() defines the data file that will be associated with the index SRCFILE1. Note that setDataFile() also opens the file, and will return an error value of OPEN_ERR if the open fails. In this simple example we're not checking the value of the error code, except to determine whether it's anything other than NO_ERR. The call to setOutputSrc() associates OUTCHAN1 with the data file. Whenever the readData() method is called, the file is accessed and a single entry is read. The data is then passed through the eight-input source selector (see Figure 10-6) to the output scaling and random data summing stages, and finally appears on the output. Calling readData() is, in effect, a trigger event for the internal data file read operation.

Since there is no scaling and no random data "noise" applied to the values from the input file, this is basically just a way to open and read a data file. However, it's also a useful building block for creating a more complex simulation setup, as shown in Figure 10-8. Here, DevSim is used to read data from an input file, process the data by applying a user-defined function and scaling, and then drive some test code with the resulting stimulus. This is just one way that DevSim can be leveraged to provide enhanced test and simulation functionality.

User-defined functions

DevSim incorporates the ability to insert a simple user-defined function into the input data stream just after the input source selector. A user-defined function is a string containing a valid Python statement. It is processed internally using Python's built-in eval() method, and two predefined variables, x0 and x1, are provided. x0 is the current input data value, and x1 is the last current data value (a $1/z$ unit delay). You can actually do quite a bit with just these two variables. The result of the statement evaluation becomes the output to the eight-channel source selector. If the function string is empty, it is ignored.

For example, the statement x0 * 2 will multiply the input data by 2; it's a simple scaling function. However, the statement (x0/(x0**2))+x1 is rather more interesting. It is an exponential expression, and given a linear series of input values (say, 0 to 10) it will generate an output that will produce a graph like the one shown in Figure 10-9.

The main restrictions on what you can do with a user-defined function are as follows:

1. A user-defined function cannot refer to any variables other than x0 and x1.
2. The x0 and x1 variables are read-only (i.e., inputs).
3. A user-defined function cannot contain an assignment.
4. A user-defined function must be a single statement; multiple statements and conditionals are not allowed.

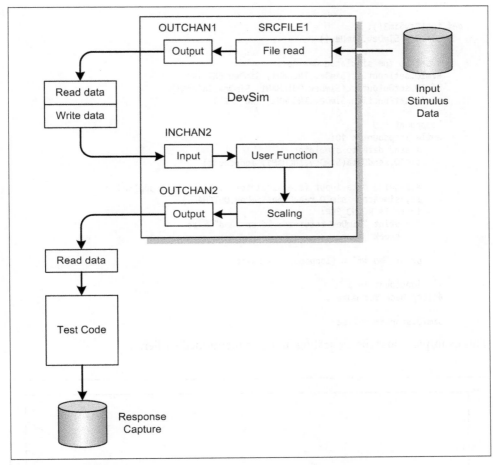

Figure 10-8. DevSim usage example

Even with these restrictions there is quite a lot that can be accomplished with user-defined functions, including the simulation of physical characteristics such as inertial lag or a simple digital filter.

The following example shows how a user-defined function is used:

```
#! /bin/python
# TestDevSim3.py
#
# Demonstrates the use of a user-defined function string.
#
# Source code from the book "Real World Instrumentation with Python"
# By J. M. Hughes, published by O'Reilly.

from    DevSim import DevSim
import  SimLib.RetCodes as RC
import  DevSimDefs as DS
```

```
def testDevSim3():
    simIO = SimDev.SimDev()

    # set up the simulated device
    simIO.setInputSrc(SimDev.INCHAN1, SimDev.EXT_IN)
    simIO.setOutputSrc(SimDev.OUTCHAN1, SimDev.INCHAN1)
    simIO.setFunction(SimDev.INCHAN1, "x0 * 2")

    loopcount = 0
    while loopcount < 10:
        # send data to simulator
        simIO.sendData(SimDev.INCHAN1, loopcount)

        # acquire data input from simulator with function applied
        rc, simdata = simIO.readData(SimDev.OUTCHAN1)
        if rc != RC.NO_ERR:
            print "SimDev returned: %d on read" % rc
            break

        print "%d %f" % (loopcount, simdata)

        loopcount += 1
    # loop back for more

    simIO.stopSim = True
```

This example is just the 2x scaling function mentioned earlier.

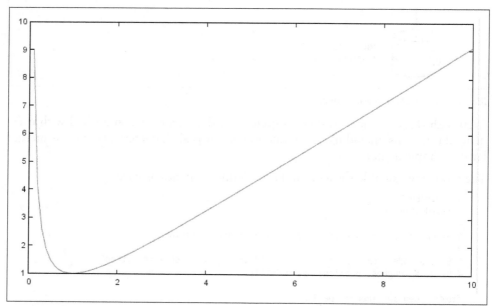

Figure 10-9. Plot of (x0/(x0**2))+x1

Cyclic functions

The cyclic functions of the simulator provide a convenient source of predictable cyclic data. You have complete control over the wave shape and the timing, so you can, for example, set up a simulation using the pulse mode to evaluate the response of a control algorithm. The other cyclic functions might be used to simulate the velocity feedback from a mechanism, to simulate temperature change over time, or as a source of data to check limit sensing.

Because the cyclic functions have the ability to run in an asynchronous mode, you need to make sure that you don't end up with a situation where the cyclic data is aliased because the data read rate is too slow, as shown in Figure 10-10. In this case, either the sample rate needs to be increased or the cyclic rate needs to be decreased so that the sample data read rate is no less than four times the cyclic rate.

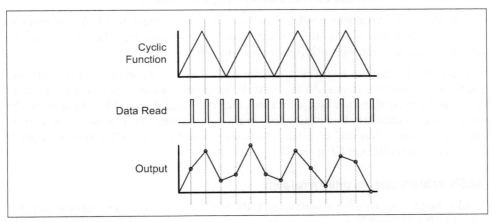

Figure 10-10. Aliased cyclic data readout

Noise

Lastly, there is the random data injection that occurs just before the output. The relative range, or level, of both the data and the random "noise" are controllable. This allows you to set the balance between the two. Note that the random data is summed into the data stream, not simply injected. It won't allow for the simulation of discrete transient events, but it does simulate modulation noise, such as might be found in a noisy voltage source (or a corroded connector).

AC Power Controller Simulator

The next example we'll look at is a simulation of an eight-channel AC power control unit of the type often found in large server installations, laboratories, and industrial facilities. This example is intended to show how a simple command-response-type instrument behaves, and also to provide some insight into instruments that employ a serial interface. The concepts introduced here can also be seen in devices such as laser controllers, electronic test equipment, temperature controllers, and motion control units. We'll also look at how to communicate with a serial interface simulator without using a second computer and a physical cable.

The SPC model

This simulation models a hypothetical device called the Simple Power Controller (SPC). It doesn't have some of the bells and whistles found on real units, such as password protection, controller unit ID assignment, and so on, mainly because these features aren't really necessary to control power. It does, however, simulate the inclusion of electronic circuit breakers (ECBs) for each AC channel. These are similar to the power control devices found in aerospace applications. They protect each channel from an over-current condition and can be reset remotely if necessary.

A diagram of the hypothetical SPC controller is shown in Figure 10-11. As you can see, it's rather simple electrically (most devices like this are, actually). The "smarts" of the unit are contained entirely within its microcontroller.

In Figure 10-11, the blocks labeled SSR are solid state relays, and the microcontroller could be any suitable device. Notice that the diagram does not show any front-panel controls, because the simulator won't be concerned with them. The objective of the simulator is to emulate the functionality of the microcontroller in terms of the remote control interface. You are, of course, welcome to add a nice GUI if you wish (we'll discuss user interfaces in Chapter 13).

The SPC serial interface and virtual serial ports

Unlike the DevSim simulator with its API, the SPC simulator uses a serial interface. It's a simple 9,800-baud N-8-1–type interface that is implemented using the *pySerial* library, which we will examine in detail in Chapter 11. For now we can assume that *pySerial* provides all the necessary functionality to open a serial port, set the serial port parameters, and read and write data.

There's a catch to using a simulator that employs a serial interface, and that is interfacing with it. One way is to use two computers with a null-modem cable between them (as shown in Chapter 7), but a second computer is not always a viable option, and some machines don't even have a serial port available (such as notebook and netbook PCs).

The solution is to use what are called "virtual ports" to create a link between two applications that utilize a serial interface. One such utility for the Windows environment is Vyacheslav Frolov's *com0com* package. You can download it from *http:// com0com.sourceforge.net*.

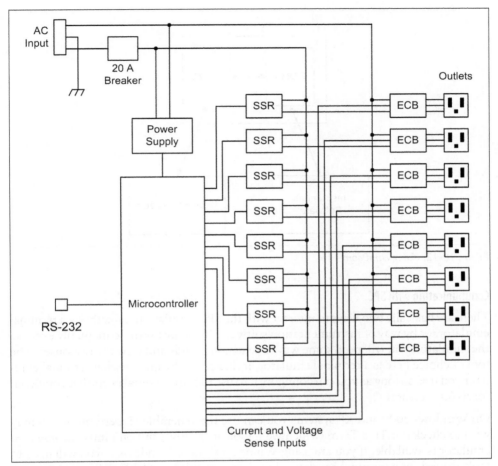

Figure 10-11. AC simulator block diagram

com0com works by creating a pair of virtual serial ports configured as a null-modem connection. You can assign standard names to the ports when they are created in order to accommodate applications that can only deal with names like COM1, COM2, COM3, and so on, and from an application's perspective these ports will behave exactly like real physical interface ports. You can set the baud rate, query the status, and in general do just about anything that can be done with a normal serial port. Figure 10-12 shows how instrumentation software can communicate with a serial interface–type simulator using two virtual serial ports.

Linux users can instead use *tty0tty*, which is available from *http://tty0tty.sourceforge .net*. It's rather minimal, and the documentation is somewhat thin, but the user-level version worked just fine for me on Ubuntu 10.04 after compilation.

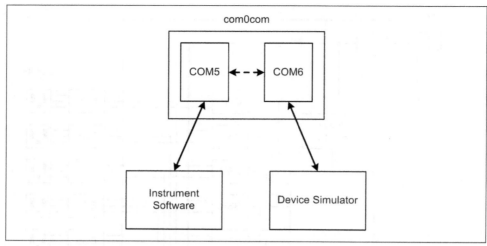

Figure 10-12. Using com0com

Communicating with SPC

There are basically two ways to interact with the SPC simulation: directly via a terminal emulator, or by way of instrumentation software. If you just want to manually exercise the simulator, you will need some way to send commands and view the responses. The tool of choice here is a terminal emulator. It doesn't really matter what terminal emulator you use, so long as you can configure it to use the virtual serial ports that com0com (or tty0tty) creates.

On Windows 2000 and XP systems you can use the venerable Hyperterm or you may wish to check out Tera Term (which we'll look at shortly), and on Linux the *minicom* emulator is available. If you are using Windows Vista or Windows 7, you will need to look around for a terminal emulator, but there are many available. When using a terminal emulator and virtual serial ports the setup will be basically the same as that shown in Figure 10-12, but with "Instrument Software" replaced by "Terminal Emulator."

The SPC command set

SPC utilizes 10 simple commands to control outputs, check status, and set configuration parameters. All commands are three characters in length, with no exceptions, and all commands take at least one parameter. The commands are listed in Table 10-2.

Table 10-2. SPC commands

Command	Parameters	Description
ALL	state	Enables or disables all eight AC channels at once
POW	ch, state	Sets the power state of a specific channel to either On or Off
SEQ	state	Starts either a power-up or a power-down sequence

Command	Parameters	Description
STM	*time*	Sets the delay time between sequence steps, in milliseconds
SOR	*ch, ch, ch, ch, ch, ch, ch, ch*	Defines the power-up and power-down sequence
SEM	*mode*	Sets the sequence error-handling mode
CHK	*ch*	Returns the on/off status of a specific channel or all channels
ECB	*ch*	Returns the OK/error status of a specific ECB or all ECBs
LIM	*ch, amps*	Sets the ECB current limit for a specific channel
RST	*ch*	Resets the ECB for a specific channel

Command descriptions

Here are a few general notes on the SPC commands:

- All commands require at least one parameter. There are no zero-parameter commands.
- Channels are identified by ASCII digits between 1 and 8, inclusive. The value 0 is used to indicate all channels with the CHK command.
- The ASCII digits 1 and 0 are used to indicate On and Off, respectively, for the ALL and POW commands, and startup and shutdown for the SEQ command.
- The sequence mode command, SEM, takes a single ASCII digit (0, 1, or 2) to indicate the mode selection.
- Time and current limit values used with the STM and LIM commands are whole integer values in ASCII form, and are limited to two digits (0 to 99) for current limits (in amps) and three digits (0 to 999) for time (in seconds).
- The SOR command takes a comma-separated list of one to eight channel numbers.
- All commands return a response; there are no silent commands. Command responses are either 1 or 0. A 1 indicates either On or OK, and a 0 indicates either Off or an error.

Now, let's take a closer look at the commands:

ALL *state*
> Enables or disables all eight AC channels in sequence order without a dwell delay.
>
> The *state* parameter may be 1 (On) or 0 (Off).
>
> Responds with 1 (OK) if successful, or 0 (error) if the ECB is tripped for any channel at power-up. Returns immediately (does not wait for command completion).

POW *ch, state*
> Sets the power state of a channel to either On or Off.
>
> *ch* is a channel number, and *state* may be 1 (On) or 0 (Off).
>
> Responds with 1 if successful, or 0 if the ECB is tripped at power-up or some other error occurred. Waits for command completion before returning.

SEQ *state*

Commands the controller to start either a power-up or power-down sequence. If no sequence order has been defined using the SOR command, the startup order will be from lowest to highest and the shutdown order will be the inverse.

The parameter *state* may be 1 (startup) or 0 (shutdown).

Responds with 1 if successful, or 0 if the ECB is tripped for any channel at power-up. Returns immediately (does not wait for command completion).

STM *time*

Sets the amount of time to pause between each step in a power-up or power-down sequence. The default pause time is 1 second, and the time is specified as an integer value.

Responds with 1 if successful, or 0 if the time value is invalid.

SOR *ch, ch, ch, ch, ch, ch, ch, ch*

Defines the startup and shutdown sequence order. Shutdown is the inverse of startup. The list may contain from one to eight channel ID entries. Any channel not in the list will be excluded from sequencing, and unused list positions are marked with a 0.

Responds with 1 if successful, or 0 if a sequence parameter is invalid.

SEM *mode*

Sets the error handling for power-up sequencing, where *mode* is defined as follows:

0

Normal (default) operation. If the ECB for any channel trips, the controller will disable power to any channels that are already active, in reverse order.

1

Error hold mode. If the ECB for any channel trips, the controller will halt the startup sequence but will not disable any channels that are already active.

2

Error continue mode. If the ECB for any channel trips during a startup sequence, the controller will continue the sequence with the next channel in the sequence list.

Responds with 1 if successful, or 0 if the mode is invalid.

CHK *ch*|0

Returns the on/off/error status of channel *ch* as either 1 or 0. If *ch* is set to 0, the statuses of all eight channels are returned as a comma-separated list of channel states. Also returns a 0 character for a channel if that channel's ECB is tripped. Use the ERR command to check the ECB state.

ECB *ch*|0

Returns the ECB status of channel *ch* as either 1 (OK) or 0 (error). If *n* is set to 0, the ECB statuses of all eight channels are returned as a comma-separated list of states.

LIM *ch*|0, *amps*

Sets the current limit of the ECB for channel *ch*. If 0 is given for the channel ID, all channels will be assigned the limit value specified by *amps*.

Responds with 1 if successful, or 0 if the channel ID or current limit value is invalid.

RST *ch*

Attempts to reset the ECB for channel *ch*.

Responds with 1 if successful, or 0 if the ECB could not be reset.

SPC simulator internals

The SPC is a simple command-response-type device. It will never initiate communications with the host system. This means that it can be effectively simulated using a simple command recognizer. Also, since the SPC is a discrete state-based simulator, it needs a set of data to define the state of each of the power control channels. How and when a channel transitions from one mode to another is determined by the commands described in the previous section. Figure 10-13 shows the internal data that the SPC simulator needs in order to model a physical system.

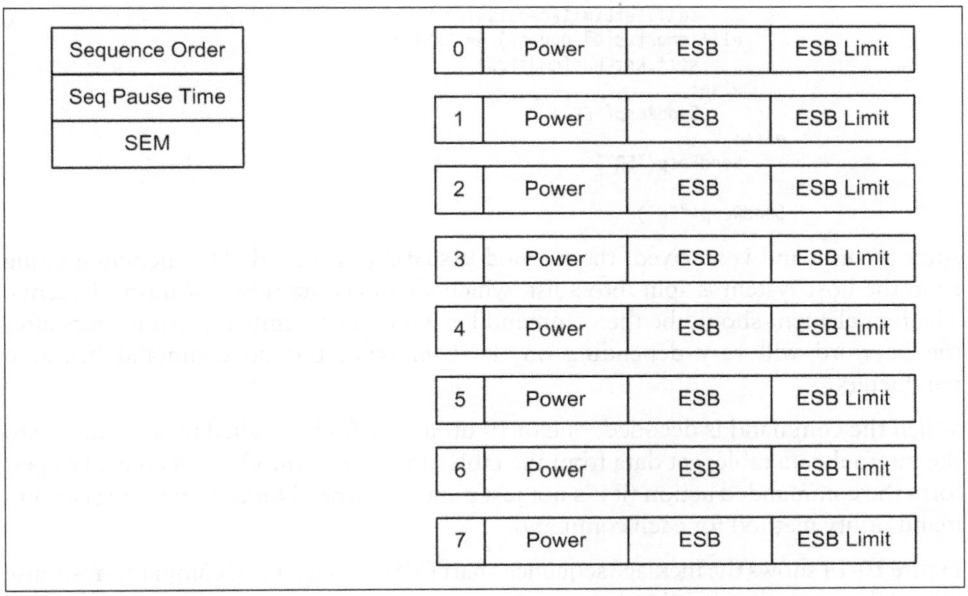

Sequence Order	0	Power	ESB	ESB Limit

Figure 10-13. SPC internal data

The sequence control data objects apply to all channels, and each channel has three attributes: power state (1 or 0), ECB state (1 or 0), and a current limit for the channel's ECB.

Next up is the command recognizer, which is very simple:

```
def Dispatch(self, instr):
    cmdstrs = instr.split()

    if len(cmdstrs) >= 2:
        if len(cmdstrs[0]) == 3:
            if cmdstrs[0].upper() == "ALL":
                self.SetAll(cmdstrs)
            elif cmdstrs[0].upper() == "POW":
                self.SetPower(cmdstrs)
            elif cmdstrs[0].upper() == "SEQ":
                self.SetSeq(cmdstrs)
            elif cmdstrs[0].upper() == "STM":
                self.SetSTM(cmdstrs)
            elif cmdstrs[0].upper() == "SOR":
                self.SetOrder(cmdstrs)
            elif cmdstrs[0].upper() == "SEM":
                self.SetSEM(cmdstrs)
            elif cmdstrs[0].upper() == "CHK":
                self.ChkChan(cmdstrs)
            elif cmdstrs[0].upper() == "ECB":
                self.ChkECB(cmdstrs)
            elif cmdstrs[0].upper() == "LIM":
                self.SetLimit(cmdstrs)
            elif cmdstrs[0].upper() == "RST":
                self.RstChan(cmdstrs)
            else:
                SendResp("ER")
        else:
            SendResp("ER")
    else:
        SendResp("ER")
```

After a command is received, the method `Dispatch()` is called. The incoming string from the host system is split into a list, which should contain two or more elements. The first element should be the command keyword. The number of parameters after the keyword will vary depending on the command, but no command has zero parameters.

When the command is decoded, one of 10 utility methods is called to write data into the internal data table, get data from the table, and invoke the channel control to perform the commanded action (if it's not just a status query). Notice that there is a command utility method for each command.

Figure 10-14 shows the message sequence chart (MSC) for a typical command-response interaction with the SPC simulator.

There are two possible return paths from the SPC command processor back to the host (the terminal emulator or instrumentation software), depending on the command. Some commands provide an immediate response and do not wait for the channel control logic to complete an activity. Other commands will wait and then return an indication of success or failure.

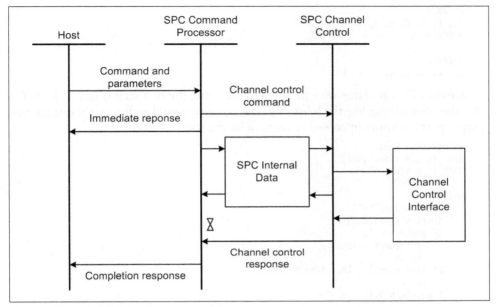

Figure 10-14. SPC command-response MSC

Configuring the SPC

The SPC simulator uses a configuration file, also known as an "INI" file, to hold various configuration parameters that are read in at startup. Here is what *spc.ini* might look like:

```
[SPC]
SPORT=COM4
SBAUD=9600
SDATA=8
SPAR=N
SSTOP=1
ECB1=2.5
ECB2=2.5
ECB3=5.0
SOR=[3,2,1,4,5,8,7,8,6]
STM=2.0
SEM=0
```

The values from the INI file will be loaded into the internal data table, but they may be overwritten with new values using the SPC commands. Parameters not defined in the INI file will assume their default values.

Interacting with the SPC simulator

When the SPC simulator is started, it will first attempt to open the serial port defined in the INI file. If successful, it will start its primary loop and wait for incoming commands. When the SPC receives a carriage return (CR) and nothing else, it will return the prompt character (>). Here's an example session that enables power channel 1:

```
> CHK 0
[0, 0, 0, 0, 0, 0, 0, 0]
> POW 1, 1
1
> CHK 0
[1, 0, 0, 0, 0, 0, 0, 0]
```

To use the SPC simulator with instrument software, the first step is to get the SPC's attention. Something like the following code snippet should suffice (we'll assume that a serial port is already open and referenced by the **sport** object):

```
gotprompt = False
last_time = time.time()
MAXWAIT = 5.0

while True:
    sport.write("\r")
    instr = sport.read(2)
    if instr=="> ":
        gotprompt = True
        break
    if time.time() - last_time > MAXWAIT:
        break
    time.sleep(0.5)
```

This snippet will send a carriage return character every 500 milliseconds until the SPC responds or five seconds has elapsed, whichever comes first. When the SPC responds with a prompt, it exits the loop, and the system is ready to communicate.

Using the SPC as a framework, you can create a simulator for just about any simple device or instrument with a serial control interface. The SPC simulator also shows how a simulation can be used to evaluate a device or instrument that does not (yet) exist in the real world. There is no substitute for working with a live system, be it real or simulated, to get a feeling for what it can, and cannot, do.

Serial Terminal Emulators

When working with instruments and subsystems that employ a serial interface, it is sometimes possible to repurpose some commonly available tools to create a perfectly usable simulator.

One such tool for Windows systems is called Tera Term; this is the tool I will focus on in this section. Originally written by T. Teranashi in the mid-1990s (and last updated in 1999, when version 2.3 was released), Tera Term supports Telnet logins as well as serial I/O, but the original release of 2.3 does not support SSH.

Although there is no longer a big demand for serial terminal emulators, and Tera Term is getting rather dated, it has something that makes it particularly interesting: a powerful scripting language. When combined with a tool such as com0com, it is possible to use Tera Term to create a respectable simulation of a serial I/O instrument and

---

communicate with it from your instrumentation software during development and testing. Tera Term works well at the other end of the communications link as well, and I've used it as a functional test driver for an embedded imaging system and a laser interferometer system, among other applications. Of course, I have also used it many times as just a terminal emulator.

You can download Tera Term and get more information about it from *http://hp.vector .co.jp/authors/VA002416/teraterm.html*. The source code is freely available, and there are some add-ons available as well. Check the website for details.

Installing Tera Term is easy. After downloading the archive, unzip it into a temporary location. Then find and run the file *setup.exe*. This will install Tera Term in *c:\Program Files\TTERMPRO* (unless you specify a different location). After the installation is complete, you can delete the contents of the temporary directory.

The installation will create a subsection in the Windows Start→Programs menu called "Tera Term Pro." You can use the right mouse button to drag the program icon labeled "Tera Term Pro" out onto the desktop and create an icon. Tera Term is known to work with Windows 2000 and Windows XP.

Almost all Linux installations come with a serial terminal emulator tool called *minicom*, and there are other emulators available as well. Some like, *minicom*, are rather limited in terms of their scripting capability, whereas others are more feature-complete. I tend to view Tera Term as a model of what a free and open source serial terminal emulator should be able to do, so I will stick to that for the rest of this discussion. If you are using a Linux system, by all means explore the options available to you. Given the huge amount of software available for Linux, I'm sure there is something that will meet your needs. In any case, after seeing what Tera Term can do you should have some idea of what to look for.

Using Terminal Emulator Scripts

The main focus of terminal emulator scripts is the conditional test. In other words: *if something is this, then do that, else do another thing*. Although a terminal emulator may have a lot of bells and whistles, a basic script to dial a number and announce a connection boils down to something like this:

```
:dial
send string "555-1212"
if busy then goto dial
wait connected
if connected print "CONNECTED"
if not connected print "ERROR - COULD NOT CONNECT"
exit
```

If we accept that the wait statement is actually a form of IF-ELSE statement, we can see that this simple script is really just a sequence of conditional tests.

I'm making a point of this because once you understand the paradigm behind the scripting languages employed in terminal emulators it becomes much easier to leverage these tools into roles for which they were never originally intended.

The Tera Term scripting language (Tera Term Language, or TTL as the author calls it) is a full-featured language that not only provides the basic commands for handling IF-THEN decisions in a communications context, but also includes commands for generating dialog windows, writing data to files, reading from files, string conversions, and executing external applications. The language provides flow control statements such as IF-THEN (plus ELSEIF and ELSE), FOR, and WHILE. It does not have a complete set of math functions, and it supports only two data types: integers and strings. But, given what it was originally intended to do, this makes perfect sense, and it really isn't a major hurdle. You can view the online documentation included with Tera Term by selecting the Help menu item (there is no user manual). Note that the main help display refers to the scripting facility as "MACRO."

Here is the connection test for the SPC that we saw earlier in Python, translated into TTL:

```
waitcnt = 0

:connect
; check for max attempts
if wantcnt > 9 then
    goto noconnect
endif

send ""
recvln
; recvln puts its return into "inputstr"
strcompare inputstr  "> "
; strcompare sets "result" based on the comparison
if result = 0 then
    goto start
else
    ; pause only uses whole numbers
    pause 1
    ; jump back and try it again
    goto connect
endif

:start
; skip over the error dialog display
goto endconnect

:noconnect
messagebox "SPC not responding" "Error"

:endconnect
; at this point the user can start entering commands
```

If you've ever worked with BASIC, or the so-called batch files on an MS-DOS or Windows system, this should look familiar. Tera Term's TTL does support subroutines (`CALL-RETURN`), and it has a perfectly usable `WHILE` statement, but I elected not to use them in this example.

Like most terminal emulators, Tera Term handles only one external connection at a time, so it's not really possible to employ Tera Term as the control logic in an instrumentation system (at least not easily—this can be done using external programs and data files). Where Tera Term is useful is in creating a simulation of an instrument or device for a Python instrumentation application to communicate with. One could, in fact, implement the SPC simulator entirely in TTL using Tera Term. Almost any other simple instrument with a serial interface could also be a candidate for simulation using Tera Term.

Tera Term is also useful for driving other systems for repetitive testing. In fact, during the development of the image acquisition and processing software for a space probe, Tera Term was used to push tens of thousands of test images through the image compression software and log the results of each test. It worked flawlessly, and generated a mountain of data to sift through.

Displaying Simulation Data

A simulation can generate a lot of useful data, but just looking at a file with a list of numbers isn't as intuitive as seeing a graph of the data. In this section I will show you how to use the data generated by a simulator to create interesting and useful graphical output in the form of data plots.

We'll focus on *gnuplot (http://www.gnuplot.info)*, a venerable tool that has been available for Unix and Linux systems for many years. There is also a Windows version available, and both can work with Python to display dynamically generated data. Later, in Chapter 13, we'll look at user interfaces and more sophisticated ways to generate graphical output, but this is a good place to begin.

gnuplot

gnuplot is a powerful and well-established graphical plotting tool that is capable of generating graphical output ranging from simple line graphs to complex data visualizations. Although it was originally developed for Unix, there is a Windows version available as well. *gnuplot* has a serviceable built-in command-line-style user interface and the ability to load plot command and data files. It can also use so-called *pipes* for its command input, thus allowing other applications to drive the plot display. This section briefly describes two methods to allow Python programs to send data and commands to *gnuplot* for display. The first is a simple demonstration of Python's `popen()` method. While this method is straightforward and easy to implement, it does nothing to assist you with *gnuplot*; it just sends commands. Consequently, the programmer needs to have a good understanding of the *gnuplot* application and its various command and configuration options. The second method uses Michael Haggerty's `gnuplot.py` package, which implements a wrapper object for *gnuplot* that handles some of the details of the command interface for the programmer. The documentation for *gnuplot* is contained in a set of HTML pages included with the distribution, and is also available online at *http://gnuplot-py.sourceforge.net/doc/Gnuplot/index.html*.

The first step is to install *gnuplot*, if it isn't already installed on your system. If you're running Linux, there's a good chance it's already available. If it isn't, a quick session with a package manager (*apt-get*, *rpm*, *synaptic*, etc.) can be used to do the installation. If you're running Windows, you'll need to download the *gnuplot* installation package from SourceForge. If you are so inclined, you can also download the source code and build it from scratch (not recommended unless you really know what you're doing and your system doesn't have a package manager tool available). The current version of *gnuplot* (at the time of publication) is 4.4.2. It is available from *http://gnuplot.source forge.net*.

Installing gnuplot on Windows

I will assume that Linux users will install *gnuplot* using a package manager, so I won't describe the process here. This procedure applies only to Windows users.

If installing the support packages for the first time, perform the setup in the following order:

1. Unzip the archive file *gp440win32.zip* to your *C:* drive, or somewhere else where you would like it to live permanently. You might even put it under "Program Files" on the *C:* drive. A directory called *gnuplot* will be created when the archive is unzipped.

2. Open the environment variables dialog (on Windows 2000 and XP) by using Settings→Control Panel→System→Advanced→Environment Variables, or right-clicking on the "My Computer" icon on the desktop and selecting "Properties." Set the GNUPLOT environment variable (as a system variable, not a user variable) to refer to the directory *binary* in the *gnuplot* directory structure. See the *INSTALL* file in the *gnuplot* directory for more information about the various environment variables available.

   Using the Environment Variables dialog, put the *gnuplot\binary* directory into the Windows search path (the PATH environment variable). For example, if you put *gnuplot* in the root of the *C:* drive, you would add *C:\gnuplot\binary* to the search path string. Note that entries in the path string are separated by semicolons.

3. Optionally, you can also create an icon on the desktop to launch *gnuplot* using the file *wgnuplot.exe*. Make sure that the "Start in" parameter refers to the *gnuplot \binary* directory (right-click on the icon and select Properties from the menu that appears).

4. Look through the documentation found in the directory *gnuplot\docs*, and the file *gnuplot-4.4.0.pdf* in particular. Also read *README.windows*, located in the root directory of the *gnuplot* directory tree.

The *gnuplot* package for Windows contains the following executable files:

wgnuplot.exe
> A Windows GUI version of *gnuplot*. Provides the same command-line console interface as the non-GUI version, but uses a GUI text-editor-type display for the command line and includes a menu bar and buttons to click for common operations.

wgnuplot_pipes.exe
> Same as *wgnuplot*, but with the advantage of support for internal pipe specifications of the form:
>
> ```
> plot `<awk -f change.awk data.dat`
> ```

gnuplot.exe
> The classic text (console) interface version of the *gnuplot* executable, with all the associated pipe functionality as found on other platforms. This means that this program can also accept commands on *stdin* (standard input) and print messages on *stdout* (standard output). This is the preferred executable to use when integrating *gnuplot* with other programs, such as Python applications.

pgnuplot.exe
> A "helper" program that will accept commands on *stdin* (standard input) and pipe them to an active (or newly created) *wgnuplot.exe* console window. Command-line options are passed on to *wgnuplot*.

wgnuplot is what you would typically put on the Windows desktop as an icon, and *gnuplot* is what a Python program would open when creating a pipe.

Using gnuplot

As I stated earlier, we are going to look at two ways to interface with *gnuplot* from a Python application. The first is simple, but requires a solid grasp of the *gnuplot* command set. The second method handles a lot of the details for you, but it also hides some of those command details from you, and it implements someone else's notion of what a Python-*gnuplot* interface should be. It's up to you to pick the path of least resistance to accomplish your objectives, and you should at least skim through the available documentation for *gnuplot* and gnuplot.py before deciding which method makes the most sense for your application.

Method 1: Using Python's popen() method

If you want to be able to use a pipe to send commands to *gnuplot* running under Windows, you must use the *gnuplot* version, not *wgnuplot*. This is because Windows GUI applications (such as *wgnuplot*) do not accept input from *stdin*. You can tell Python to use *gnuplot* when creating the pipe using popen(). Alternatively, you can use *pgnuplot* to achieve the same results with *wgnuplot*. On a Linux system this is not an issue (there are no *wgnuplot* or *pgnuplot* binaries).

The following example, gptest.py, will launch *gnuplot* and display a series of plots:

```
#! /usr/bin/python
# gptest.py

import os
import time

f=os.popen('gnuplot', 'w')

print >> f, 'set title "Simple plot demo" 1, 1 font "arial, 11"'
print >> f, 'set key font "arial, 9"'
print >> f, 'set tics font "arial, 8"'

print >> f, "set yrange[-20:+20]"
print >> f, "set xrange[-10:+10]"
print >> f, 'set xlabel "Input" font "arial,11"'
print >> f, 'set ylabel "Output" font "arial,11"'

for n in range(100):
    # plot sine output with zero line (the 0 term)
    print >> f, 'plot sin(x * %i) * 10, 0' % (n)
    time.sleep(0.1)

f.flush()

# pause before exit
time.sleep(2)
```

To run this example, just save the code to a file (gptest.py, for example) or load the file from the source code for this book. On a Windows machine, type in the following at a command prompt:

python gptest.py

Under Linux you can just enter the script's name, assuming that the file is marked as executable and the Python interpreter resides in */usr/bin*:

% gptest.py

When it runs, you should see a sine wave that expands and contracts several times. What is actually happening is that *gnuplot* is regenerating the plot across the *x* range of –10 to +10 each time the plot command is called. The result appears as an animated image, but in fact it is a series of plots presented in rapid succession. Note that the *gnuplot* window will close as soon as the script completes and Python terminates.

The following lines from the Method 1 example are possible candidates for inclusion into the *gnuplot.ini* file, which should be located in the binary directory with the *gnuplot* executables:

```
set key font "arial, 9"
set tics font "arial, 8"
```

Refer to the *gnuplot* documentation for more about the *gnuplot.ini* file and its uses.

Method 2: gnuplot.py

The second method uses Michael Haggerty's `gnuplot.py` package (version 1.8), which is available from *http://gnuplot-py.sourceforge.net*. You will also need the *NumPy* package (version 1.4.1), available from *http://numpy.scipy.org*. For Windows, you should download and install *numpy-1.4.1-win32-superpack-python26.exe* (just execute the file to start the installation).

To install `gnuplot.py`, follow these steps:

1. Unzip *gnuplot-py-1.8.zip* into a temporary directory. It will create a directory called *gnuplot-py-1.8*.
2. Open a command window, and from within the command window change to the directory *gnuplot-py-1.8* in the temporary directory where *gnuplot-py-1.8* was unpacked. You should see a file called *setup.py*.
3. At the command prompt, type:

    ```
    python setup.py install
    ```

During the execution of the setup script, you should see many lines of output go by on the screen. If an error is encountered, the setup script will halt; otherwise, you should now be ready to go.

Testing gnuplot.py

In the directory *<python>\Lib\site-packages\Gnuplot* run the file *demo.py*, like so:

```
python demo.py
```

<python> is where you installed Python 2.6, and on a Windows system it may be something like *C:\Python2.6*.

If all goes well, you'll see a plot display. Pressing the Enter key from within the command window will cause a series of graphs to be displayed.

Using gnuplot.py

`gnuplot.py` is somewhat unusual in terms of how it is imported into your application. If you look at *demo.py*, you'll see that it is importing *Gnuplot* and *Gnuplot.funcutils*. But there is no "Gnuplot.py" in the *Gnuplot* directory where the package resides. What is happening here is that the package initializer, `__init__.py`, is imported. It, in turn, imports the rest of the necessary modules. The __init__.py module also contains a top-level docstring with lots of information. If you examine __init__.py you may also notice that it contains the following code at the bottom of the file:

```
if __name__ == '__main__':
    import demo
    demo.demo()
```

What this means is that you can type in:

```
python __init__.py
```

from the *Gnuplot* directory, and the demo will execute.

This approach is interesting in that when the gnuplot.py package is imported the __init__.py module will be evaluated immediately, and the necessary imports will be in place and available from that point onward in your application.

To import gnuplot.py into your application, you must at least import the main module:

```
import Gnuplot
```

You can import additional modules using dot notation, like so:

```
import Gnuplot.funcutils
```

Plotting Simulator Data with gnuplot

This next couple of examples will plot the contents of a data file containing a set of records with a single field (we will look at ASCII data files in more detail in Chapter 12).

We'll use the PID class introduced in Chapter 9, and create a data file to graph the impulse response of the controller.

First, here's how to do it using the pipe method:

```
#! /bin/python
# PIDPlot.py
#
# Uses gnuplot to generate a graph of the PID function's output
#
# Source code from the book "Real World Instrumentation with Python"
# By J. M. Hughes, published by O'Reilly.

import time
import os
import PID

def PIDPlot(Kp=1, Ki=0, Kd=0):
    pid = PID.PID()

    pid.SetKp(Kp)
    pid.SetKi(Ki)
    pid.SetKd(Kd)

    time.sleep(.1)
```

```
f = open('pidplot.dat','w')

sp = 0
fb = 0
outv = 0

print "Kp: %2.3f Ki: %2.3f Kd: %2.3f" %\
        (pid.Kp, pid.Ki, pid.Kd)

for i in range(1,51):
    # summing node
    err = sp - fb

    # PID block
    outv = pid.GenOut(err)

    # control feedback
    if sp > 0:
        fb += (outv - (1/i))

    # start with sp = 0, simulate a step input at t(10)
    if i > 9:
        sp = 1

    print >> f,"%d  % 2.3f  % 2.3f  % 2.3f  % 2.3f" %\
                (i, sp, fb, err, outv)
    time.sleep(.05)

f.close()

gp=os.popen('gnuplot', 'w')
print >> gp, "set yrange[-1:2]"

for i in range(0, 10):
    kpval = 0.9 + (i * .1)
    PIDPlot(kpval)
    print >> gp, "plot 'pidplot.dat' using 1:2 with lines, \
                    'pidplot.dat' using 1:3 with lines"

raw_input('Press return to exit...\n')
```

This will generate a series of graphs, with a K_p value ranging from 0.9 to 1.8. The last graph is shown until the user presses the Enter key, and when the program terminates *gnuplot* closes. The output for the last graph ($K_p = 1.8$) is shown in Figure 10-15.

As you may recall from Chapter 9, if the proportional gain is too high the system will exhibit instability in response to a sudden input change, and there it is in Figure 10-15.

Now here's the gnuplot.py way to plot the data:

```
# PIDPlot.py
#
# Uses gnuplot to generate a graph of the PID function's output
#
# Source code from the book "Real World Instrumentation with Python"
# By J. M. Hughes, published by O'Reilly.
```

```
import Gnuplot, Gnuplot.funcutils

import time
import os
import PID

def PIDPlot(Kp=1, Ki=0, Kd=0):
    pid = PID.PID()

    pid.SetKp(Kp)
    pid.SetKi(Ki)
    pid.SetKd(Kd)

    time.sleep(.1)
    f = open('pidplot.dat','w')

    sp = 0
    fb = 0
    outv = 0

    print "Kp: %2.3f Ki: %2.3f Kd: %2.3f" %\
            (pid.Kp, pid.Ki, pid.Kd)

    for i in range(1,51):
        # summing node
        err = sp - fb

        # PID block
        outv = pid.GenOut(err)

        # control feedback
        if sp > 0:
            fb += (outv - (1/i))

        # start with sp = 0, simulate a step input at t(10)
        if i > 9:
            sp = 1

        print >> f,"%d  % 2.3f  % 2.3f  % 2.3f  % 2.3f" %\
                    (i, sp, fb, err, outv)
        time.sleep(.05)

    f.close()

gp = Gnuplot.Gnuplot()
gp.clear()
gp.title('PID Response')
gp.set_range('yrange', (-1, 2))

for i in range(0, 10):
    kpval = 0.9 + (i * .1)
    PIDPlot(kpval)
    gp.plot(Gnuplot.File('pidplot.dat', using=(1,2), with_='lines'),
            Gnuplot.File('pidplot.dat', using=(1,3), with_='lines'))
```

```
raw_input('Press return to exit...\n')
```

The output looks the same as before, except that now there is a title above the graph. For some examples of the other things that gnuplot.py can do, see the demo.py and test.py files included with gnuplot.py and located in the *gnuplot* directory where the package was installed (usually *python26/Lib/site-packages*).

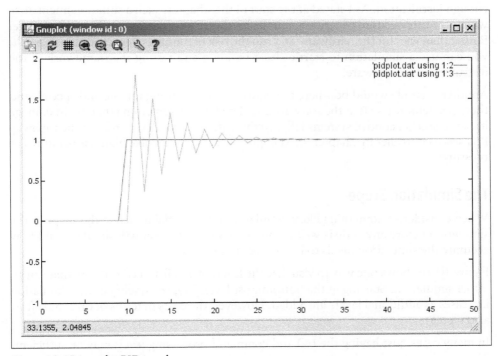

Figure 10-15. gnuplot PID graph

Creating Your Own Simulators

Now that we've touched on what simulators are and seen some ways they can be used, it's time to consider what goes into creating such a thing. I'm a big fan of simulators, but I also try to temper my enthusiasm with some realism. It's all too easy to eat up a big chunk of the time and budget for a project just fiddling with the simulation. So, before starting to build your own simulator, there are three key questions you should ask yourself:

1. Why do you want to use a simulator?
2. What do you want to simulate?
3. How much time and effort can you expend to create a simulator?

How you answer these questions will help you avoid spending time on something you don't really need (even if it is fun to build and play with).

Justifying a Simulator

First and foremost, there must be a real need for a simulation. If it is really not possible to develop the instrumentation or control software without one, that is probably enough justification. As I stated at the start of this chapter, such a situation might arise when software needs to be written, but the hardware won't arrive until some later date. Rather than wait for the hardware, and run the risk of running over schedule as a result, you can use a simulation to start at least building and testing the framework of the instrumentation software.

Another example would be where the hardware is something unique and special, and there is a definite risk that the software could make it do something that might damage it. Some motion control systems fall into this category (recall the story of the runaway PID servo controller in Chapter 9), as might systems that involve high temperatures or pressures.

The Simulation Scope

When considering something like a simulator, it is essential to define the scope of the simulation before any code is written: in other words, what it will simulate, and how accurate the simulation needs to be in order to be useful.

Figure 10-16 shows one way to visualize the levels of detail and complexity that can go into a simulation. Starting at the bottommost level, I/O, the fidelity of the simulation increases as additional layers are added. However, the costs in terms of time and effort also increase.

In many cases, just having the I/O and command processing levels may be sufficient. The simulators we've already seen in this chapter really aren't much more than this, with a little bit of functionality to handle setting and recalling states and parameters. As the size of the blocks in Figure 10-16 implies, the more capabilities you add, the more complex and costly the simulator becomes.

Although each simulator you might contemplate must be evaluated based on the specific needs of the project, it is generally safe to say that if you can accurately simulate the interface and the command processing, it's probably good enough to get you started. You can always add details in the behavior level later if it turns out that they are really necessary.

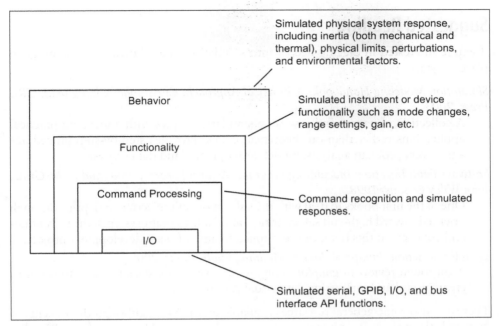

Figure 10-16. Simulation levels

Time and Effort

Writing a simulator takes time and effort. Sometimes this can be significant, and it is not uncommon to have a situation where creating and verifying the simulator takes as much (or more) effort than that required to implement the system being developed. This might be justified if the system is something critical (like part of an experimental aircraft), if the simulator is generic enough to be reused on other projects, or if it can be used later in a production environment for product testing. If it's just a one-time thing for a simple system, it shouldn't be any more complicated than it really needs to be. It might even turn out that a simulator isn't really necessary at all if a good debugger is available, and you're willing to use simple files to capture data.

Summary

When used appropriately, simulation is a powerful tool that can help save effort and avoid costly mistakes and delays later on, when the software meets real hardware. It is also a potential time-sink and source of development delays, so deciding when and how to employ simulation is important.

Suggested Reading

If you're interested in digging deeper into simulation, the following books are good places to start:

Simulation Modeling Handbook: A Practical Approach. Christopher Chung (ed.), CRC Press, 2003.
> A collection of papers and essays on simulation topics with a focus on practical applications rather than on theoretical issues. Provides step-by-step procedures and covers problem analysis, model development, and data analysis.

Software Fault Injection: Inoculating Programs Against Errors. J. Voas and G. McGraw, John Wiley & Sons, 1998.
> One of the first books to deal with the subject of fault injection in depth. Although oriented toward high-end safety-critical and fault-tolerant systems, the techniques and concepts in this book can be applied to any software development project.

Gnuplot in Action. Philipp K. Janert, Manning Publications, 2009.
> A thorough review of *gnuplot*, along with a wealth of ideas for how to use it to create useful and interesting data visualization displays.

There are also some general resources available on the Web, although there seems to be very little in the way of introductory material available. Here are a few URLs that may be of interest to you:

http://www4.ncsu.edu/~hp/simulation.pdf
> This link points to the PDF version of *Computer Simulation Techniques: The Definitive Introduction!*, by Harry Perros. While not quite as broad in scope as the title might suggest, this book introduces traditional Operational Research (OR)–type simulations and contains extensive discussions of randomness, sampling theory, and estimation techniques.

http://sip.clarku.edu/index.html
> The companion website for the book *Introduction to Computer Simulation Methods*, by Harvey Gould, Jan Tobochnik, and Wolfgang Christian (Addison-Wesley). While the book itself is not available here, there are lots of useful notes, tutorials, and a couple of sample chapters in PDF format. The main focus of the book itself is on computational physics and the simulation of physical systems. I've recommended it here mainly for the examples it provides of ways to approach various simulation problems using mathematical techniques.

CHAPTER 11
Instrumentation Data I/O

It is a capital mistake to theorize before one has data.

—Sir Arthur Conan Doyle

In Chapter 7 we looked at the various physical interfaces and signal protocols that you might encounter with instrumentation systems. Now we'll look at how to use those interfaces to move data between the real world and our applications.

The data an instrumentation system collects or generates comes in a variety of formats and fulfills a wide range of needs. We'll start this chapter with a discussion of interface formats and protocols, defining the basic concepts we will need for the upcoming software examples. Then we'll take a quick tour of some packages that are available for interface support in Python: namely, the *pySerial*, *pyParallel*, and *PyVISA* packages.

Lastly, I'll show you some techniques to read and write instrumentation data. We'll take a look at blocking versus nonblocking I/O, asynchronous input and output events, and how to manage potential data I/O errors to help make your applications more robust.

Data I/O Interface Software

Over the years, computer interface hardware has evolved from simple devices using serial communications and I/O registers mapped into a computer's memory address space to complex subsystems with their own built-in processors, onboard logic, advanced protocols, and complex API definitions. As the complexity grew, the number of unique interface methods and protocols also began to grow. As you might imagine, if a large system had to support more than just two or three unique interfaces, each with its own unique way of doing things, this could result in a significant hassle.

Early on, people began to realize that it didn't make much sense for each device to have a custom interface, especially when many devices shared common internal functions and had similar capabilities. In order to rein in the impending chaos and establish consistent interfaces across different application domains, various industry standards organizations were formed. These organizations began to define guidelines and rules for interfaces and the software that would use them. These could then be applied to different types of equipment in a wide variety of situations. The Electronics Industries Association (EIA) published its initial definition of RS-232 in 1962, and after several revisions, it is still in use today. Various common standards have also been developed by other organizations, such as the American National Standards Institute (ANSI), the Institute of Electrical and Electronics Engineers (IEEE), and the Interchangeable Virtual Instrument (IVI) Foundation.

That being said, one must occasionally deal with exceptions. Although there are a number of common standards for communications and instrumentation interfaces, not every manufacturer follows them, and sometimes a device just doesn't fit easily into an existing framework. If you want to use a device in your system that does things in its own special way, you'll need to be able to accommodate that device. This is particularly true if you are planning to use an older instrument or device that might predate a more current standard.

Interface Formats and Protocols

Regardless of the type of connector used for a particular interface, or even the way in which data moves through an interface, the key thing is that data is moving between a host system (the master controller, if you will) and whatever devices or instruments are connected to it.

Naturally, when it comes to data acquisition and instrument control, there are multiple ways to get there from here. One approach is to use custom software with common interfaces to external instruments, such as serial and USB interfaces. Another way is to utilize industry-standard drivers and protocols that provide a consistent API across a range of physical interfaces, including serial, USB, GPIB, and bus-based hardware. Interface drivers that are based on the IVI standards are one example of this approach. In this section we'll take a brief look at how various command and data protocols are implemented, at some of the more common standards and guidelines used to implement them, and at the physical interfaces commonly found in instrumentation devices.

The simplest way to interface a computer with the real world is through a serial or parallel port interface of some sort. The apparent simplicity is a result of the physical simplicity: the computer already (usually) has a serial or parallel interface of some sort, so the physical connection is typically just a cable. However, from a software viewpoint it may be anything but simple, especially with USB or GPIB. We'll get to that in just a bit.

The other method, which we saw in Chapter 7, is the plug-in circuit board that is connected directly to the computer's internal data and address buses. With an arrangement like this, the circuit board (or "circuit card," as it's often called) appears to the CPU (central processing unit) as just another address or set of addresses in memory space, I/O space, or both. Figure 11-1 shows how this works with a generic CPU that does not provide a separate I/O bus for peripherals (such as the Motorola 68000 family), and a CPU that incorporates a bus specifically for I/O functions (like the Intel processors found in most modern PCs).

The first generation of PCs used the Industry Standard Architecture (ISA) bus for add-on circuit boards. The earliest incarnations of the ISA bus, also known as the *AT bus* (it appeared in AT class PCs from IBM), took advantage of the Intel CPU's built-in I/O bus and directly exposed the various add-on boards to the CPU in the form of registers. Later bus schemes, such as VESA Local Bus, EISA, and PCI, used special circuitry (called "chipsets") to act as intermediaries between the CPU and the I/O devices. This resulted in more addressing flexibility, better support for direct memory access, and faster data rates. But regardless of the bus type, plug-in circuit boards still use registers to pass command and response data between the board's circuitry and the CPU.

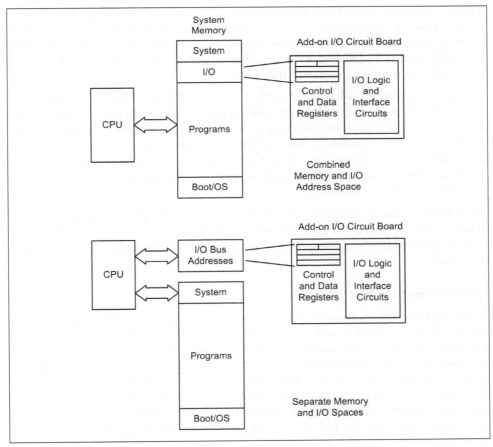

Figure 11-1. CPU I/O addressing schemes

When working with I/O hardware that uses registers, a piece of software called a *driver* is employed to handle the low-level details of the interface. The driver provides an interface to programs that use the hardware, and it typically handles things like interrupts and bulk data transfers in a more or less transparent fashion. From the viewpoint of the application software, the driver appears as a set of function calls. From the viewpoint of the driver, the hardware appears as a set of registers in memory or I/O address space. Another characteristic of a driver is that it can be integrated into the operating system as an extension to its basic functionality. In modern operating systems, programs running at what is called the *user level* cannot usually access the underlying hardware directly, for various security and system-stability reasons. The operating system needs to be able to coordinate access to the hardware in the system to avoid conflicts and possible system failure.

Drivers might also be used to access a standard serial or parallel port, and they are always used with USB- or GPIB-type interfaces. In some cases, such as with a standard serial interface, the stock driver supplied with the operating system might be sufficient. In other cases, a special driver is needed to handle the interface. In those cases where software is provided to communicate with an external device using a common interface, I will refer to it as an *I/O handler*, rather than as a device driver. You can think of an I/O handler as something akin to a translator.

The upshot here is that whatever form the I/O takes, there is a driver or I/O handler of some type acting as an intermediary between the hardware and the application software. At the other end, in the hardware or external instrument, there are functions for handling the physical interface and communicating with the device's hardware logic and control circuitry. Figure 11-2 shows the more common functional components one might encounter when interfacing with an external instrument or bus-based device connected to a host controller PC.

We will define the various acronyms in the figure and look at each component more closely in the following sections. For now, think of Figure 11-2 as a reference. I will refer back to it in later sections as we explore the various functional components within each level.

IVI—Interchangeable Virtual Instrument

In the instrumentation industry, the IVI suite of standards is becoming commonplace for Windows platforms, and many instrument manufacturers now provide IVI-compliant drivers. Aimed mainly at instrumentation applications, the IVI defines a standard set of instrument interfaces and commands. Prior to the creation of the IVI suite of standards, there were multiple standards in use, with the most notable being the Standard Commands for Programmable Instruments (SCPI, sometimes pronounced "skippy") and the newer Virtual Instrument Software Architecture (VISA) standards. Each vendor could, and sometimes did, do things a little differently in its own special way.

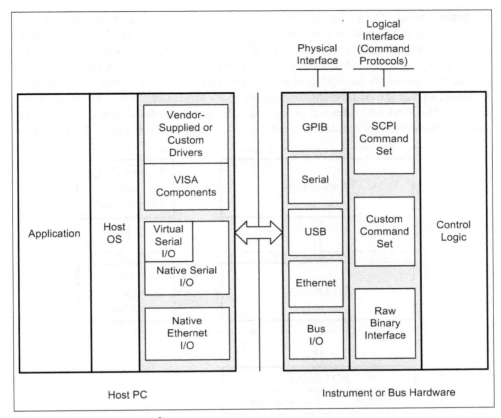

Figure 11-2. Instrument interface components

The SCPI standard defines a standard set of commands for instrumentation, and VISA defines a common API usable with different I/O interfaces, such as GPIB and VXI. SCPI and VISA are now both part of the IVI suite. The primary focus of these standards is to define common interfaces that help to reduce, or eliminate, the necessity of treating each instrument as a unique programmable object. Note that while SCPI and VISA are now part of the overall IVI suite, they are actually two different things.

If you will be using instruments such as DMMs and counters in your instrumentation setup with GPIB interfaces, the odds are good that you will need to know about SCPI. If you want to take advantage of a manufacturer's VISA drivers, you'll need to know about those as well. In just a bit we'll take a look at how to use VISA drivers with Python for both Windows and Linux systems.

There are, of course, situations where things like SCPI or VISA simply aren't available. In these cases there may be no choice but to either try to use whatever interface software the manufacturer did provide or, lacking that, just write your own. That said, I should point out that writing a device driver or I/O handler is often a nontrivial task, and you really should avoid it if at all possible.

IVI-compliant drivers. Depending on the complexity of the project and the operating system on the host PC, it may make more sense to adopt something like the IVI drivers instead of attempting to "roll your own" API. The IVI Foundation standards define the driver architecture for various classes of instruments and interface hardware. The IVI approach is based on the notion of shared software components with common functionality, so that the API for one instrument looks much like the API for another. It is based on the VISA I/O standard (which we will encounter shortly), and also incorporates the SCPI protocol standard. Figure 11-3 shows an overview of the IVI architecture.

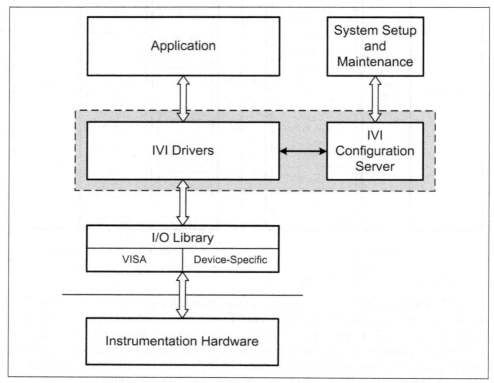

Figure 11-3. IVI architecture overview

IVI-compliant software can offer some significant advantages. These include state caching, multithreaded drivers, simulation capabilities, and instrument interchangeability. One of the claims made for IVI is that its standardized interface handles the details between different instrument types, thus allowing the system implementer to focus on the data handling and display software, rather than having to deal with unique interface code for each instrument in the system. For the most part this is true, but only insofar as it applies to commercial off-the-shelf (COTS) software that is IVI-compliant. If you need to access an instrument using a programming language that isn't supported (such as Python), or use data capture and analysis tools that don't come with IVI interface capabilities already built in, you will need to do some work to get things to play nice with one another.

One potential downside to IVI is that fully IVI-compliant (and IVI-certified) drivers are available only for the Microsoft Windows platform. This is stated clearly in the IVI specifications published by the IVI Foundation. Although some instrumentation vendors have created "IVI-style" drivers for their products that will work with Linux systems, if you're looking for true cross-platform compatibility across a variety of vendors you may want to take this into consideration.

VISA—Virtual Instrument Software Architecture

VISA is a widely used interface I/O API specification for communicating with instruments connected to a PC using GPIB, VXIbus, serial, Ethernet, or USB-type interfaces. The VISA standard is also a core component in the IVI suite.

The VISA library defines a standardized API using a Windows DLL module, typically named *visa32.dll*. VISA also supports the Microsoft Component Object Model (COM) technology. If applications are written against the VISA standard, they should be generally interchangeable with VISA driver implementations from different vendors.

Not all instruments come with VISA drivers, and for some VISA support may be an optional add-on at the time of purchase. GPIB-interface products, such as the plug-in cards sold by National Instruments (NI), usually do come with VISA drivers, and a Linux version is readily available as well. Agilent also sells GPIB interfaces with VISA components, and Agilent recommends a VISA interface for Linux that is available from a third-party source.

SCPI—Standard Commands for Programmable Instruments

The SCPI standard defines the syntax, command structure, and data formats for use with programmable instruments. SCPI does not define the actual physical interfaces (GPIB, RS-232, USB, etc.), meaning that it is an interface-neutral standard. SCPI was preceded by the IEEE-488.2 standard, which is similar but with a more limited scope.

SCPI commands are ASCII strings. Responses may also be ASCII strings, although in some cases they are binary data (for example, when transferring bulk measurement data). SCPI commands are organized into instrument classes, each of which defines a baseline set of commands. Instruments that support the SCPI protocol do not require the low-level VISA I/O functions so long as there is some way available for the host system to communicate with the instruments (remember that SCPI is a command protocol, so it is interface-neutral). Figure 11-4 shows the instrument model employed by the SCPI standard. The SCPI functionality resides in the logical interface layer in the instrument interface, as shown previously in Figure 11-2.

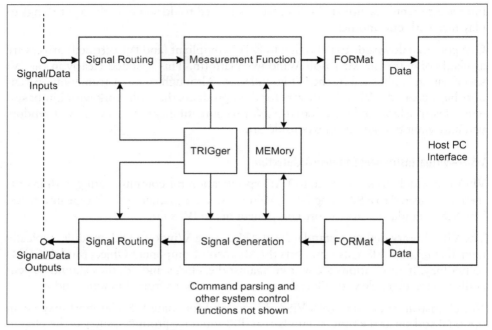

Figure 11-4. SCPI instrument model

Not all of the functions shown in Figure 11-4 are used in all instruments. Some instrument types, such as temperature sensors or digital multimeters, may be input-only devices. For these, there would be no signal generation section. Others, such as some types of spectrum analyzers, might incorporate both input and output functions, so they could include all of the SCPI model (or at least a good portion of it).

The commands available for a given instrument are based on the instrument type, or class. The SCPI 1999 standard defines eight instrument classes, each of which utilizes a particular subset of the SCPI commands:

- Chassis Dynamometers
- Digital Meters
- Digitizers
- Emissions Benches
- Emission Test Cell
- Power Supplies
- RF & Microwave Sources
- Signal Switchers

Some of the terminology in these class names might not be intuitively obvious. In SCPI parlance, a *digitizer* is a device designed to measure voltage waveforms over time—in other words, an oscilloscope or a logic analyzer. A *signal switcher* is an instrument designed to control the path of signals through some kind of routing or switching network. This might be as simple as an on-off switch, or as complex as a multipath input-output switch matrix. Several instrument manufacturers produce devices that incorporate signal-switching capabilities along with optional data acquisition or control functions. The Agilent 34970A Data Acquisition Switch Unit and the Keithley 3706 System Switch/Multimeter are examples of these types of devices.

SCPI commands are organized as related groups of instructions. A group is composed of a primary, or *root*, command, and each root command has a number of optional parameters. One example of a command group is the MEASure command. (SCPI allows commands to be abbreviated, as indicated by the use of capitalization; so, for example, instead of using MEASure one could use MEAS.)

Figure 11-5 shows a simplified command tree diagram for the MEASure command as it might be used with a digital multimeter. To build up a command string, you would start at the left side with MEASure and then move to the right through the tree, picking up the necessary parameter keywords as you go.

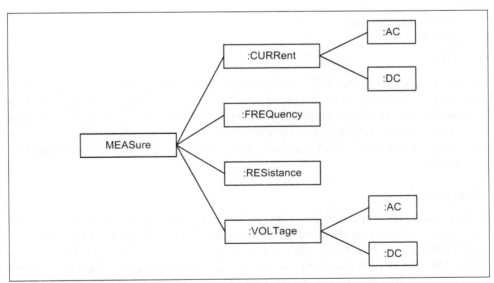

Figure 11-5. SCPI MEASure command tree example

Here is an example of a SCPI command for use with a digital multimeter, such as an Agilent 34405A DMM (refer to Figure 6-4) with a GPIB interface:

    MEASure:VOLTage:DC?

Assuming that access to the GPIB port or interface device has already been established, and the instrument has been correctly initialized, this command instructs the instrument to take a DC measurement using whatever autoranging is appropriate and return the result (as implied by the question mark at the end of the command string).

Here is an alternate command sequence for the Agilent 34405A DMM to set the DC input range and then acquire a measurement:

```
CONFigure:VOLTage:DC 1, 0.0001
TRIGger:SOURce IMMediate
INITiate
FETCh?
```

This command sequence configures the DC input for the 1 V input range with a 0.1 mV resolution and sets the measurement trigger mode to immediate. The INITiate command places the instrument in the "wait for trigger" mode, which in this case is immediate, so the instrument begins taking continuous readings. The FETCh command returns the most recent voltage reading.

As mentioned earlier, the SCPI commands can be abbreviated. Here's what the preceding command sequences look like in short form:

```
MEAS:VOLT:DC?
```

and:

```
CONF:VOLT:DC 1, 0.0001
TRIG:SOUR IMM
INIT
FETC?
```

A description of the entire SCPI specification would be beyond the scope of this book. For more information, consult the section "Suggested Reading" on page 436. You should also refer to the programming documentation supplied with each instrument you intend to use to determine exactly how it implements SCPI. While many instrument manufacturers follow the SCPI standard, there may be variations to accommodate special features.

Unique protocols

Some instruments (e.g., some low-cost DMMs) use command and data protocols that are unique to that particular model. For example, the tpi 183 has a 3.5 mm jack built into the side of the meter and continuously outputs a stream of RS-232 data at 1,200 baud. The type of data is determined by the meter's manual control settings (a large rotary switch)—there is no way to set it via the serial interface. The output is a string of ASCII characters, and the format is defined as FAR DDDDDDT. The character in the F position is the function code (0 to B), A is the manual or autorange mode (0 or 1, respectively), and R is the range code (0 to 5). This is followed by a space character (which is somewhat unusual) and six ASCII characters for data in floating-point format (the DDDDDD part of the format string). The T character indicates the end of the output string.

Although this interface may be unique to the tpi 183, it is by no means a singular example. Many instruments—especially older units—have unique interface protocols. Even some modern USB-type devices have their own unique command and data interface protocols.

Another example is the command and response protocol used with devices connected to an RS-485 bus. A common scenario is where one device is designated as the master (typically the host PC), and the other devices respond only when they receive commands addressed specifically to them. In this case, a device identifier must be included with each command on the RS-485 bus, alerting the relevant device that this command is intended for it. The other devices will "hear" the command, but they will not respond to it. One possible format for the command and response messages s shown in Figure 11-6.

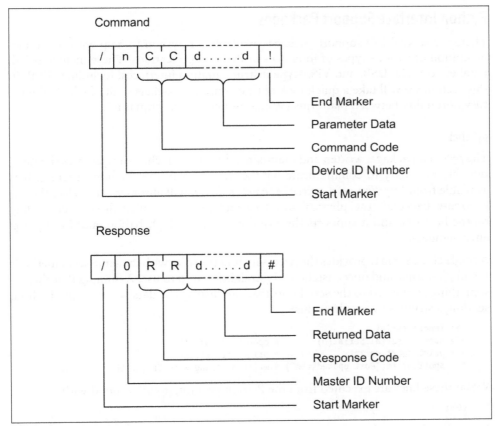

Figure 11-6. Command and response formats

Notice in Figure 11-6 that the response always begins with /0, because in a scheme like this the master controller is typically assigned a device ID of zero. Since there is only one ASCII digit available for the device ID number, this protocol will only be able to support 15 unique devices, addressed as 1 through F. From Figure 11-6 we can also infer that there are 256 possible command or response codes (assuming that hexadecimal notation is used, i.e., 00 through FF). The number of characters sent as command or parameter data or returned as response data is variable and is defined by the command type. A command message is terminated with a ! character, and a response is terminated with a # character. Remember that this is just one possible protocol, although it is actually modeled on real products that are commercially available. How the command and response messages are defined is ultimately up to the engineers designing the product.

Python Interface Support Packages

There are several I/O support packages available for Python to help with the implementation of various types of interfaces in Python applications. These include serial, parallel port I/O, USB, and VISA-type instrumentation interfaces, including GPIB. In this section we will take a quick look at three different packages, all of which aim for easy portability between platforms (Windows and Linux, primarily).

pySerial

The *pySerial* package, written and maintained by Chris Liechti, encapsulates the functionality necessary to communicate with a serial port from a Python program. It is available from *http://pyserial.sourceforge.net*. *pySerial* will automatically select the appropriate backend (the physical interface and its OS-supplied driver), depending on the host OS, and it supports the Windows, Linux, BSD, Jython, and IronPython environments.

A single class, Serial, provides the necessary functionality with the same set of methods for all platforms, and once installed it is straightforward to use. Assuming that there is something connected to the serial port that can display the data written from Python, sending a string is as simple as this:

```
>>> import serial
>>> sport = serial.Serial(0)      # open a serial port
>>> print sport.portstr           # print port string
>>> sport.write("Port opened\r\n") # write a string with CR and LF
```

When these lines are executed from the Python prompt, it will respond with:

```
COM1
```

(assuming that COM1 was used, of course), and at the other end of the connection you should see:

```
Port Opened
```

When we're done with the serial port we can close it gracefully (it can be reopened later on, if need be):

```
>>> sport.close()                    # close port
```

pySerial also supports various port configuration parameters and timeout values, and it provides methods such as `read()`, `write()`, and `readln()`.

If there is no serial port available, which is typical with notebook and netbook computers, you'll see an error traceback that looks something like this:

```
Traceback (most recent call last):
  File "<stdin>", line 1, in <module>
  File "c:\APython26\lib\site-packages\serial\serialwin32.py", line 30,
  in __init__
    SerialBase.__init__(self, *args, **kwargs)
  File "c:\APython26\lib\site-packages\serial\serialutil.py", line 201,
  in __init__
    self.open()
s File "c:\APython26\lib\site-packages\serial\serialwin32.py", line 56,
  in open
    raise SerialException("could not open port %s: %s" % (self.portstr,
    ctypes.WinError()))
serial.serialutil.SerialException: could not open port COM1: [Error 2]
The system cannot find the file specified.
```

You can also create a serial port instance without actually opening the port by simply not passing any parameters to the `Serial` object's initialization method:

```
>>> import serial
>>> sport = serial.Serial()
>>> sport.baudrate = 19200
>>> sport.port = 0
```

Now that the serial port object has been instantiated and some basic parameters defined, it can be opened and closed as necessary. The `isOpen()` method is used to check the state of the serial port:

```
>>> sport.open()
>>> sport.isOpen()
True
>>> sport.close()
>>> sport.isOpen()
False
```

Tables 11-1 through 11-6 provide a summary of some of the methods available with *pySerial*, organized by functional category. In all likelihood you won't need more than a handful of these, but *pySerial* does provide a fairly comprehensive suite of methods for dealing with serial communications. Even some of the more arcane capabilities of RS-232 are supported.

Table 11-1. pySerial port open/close methods

Method	Description
open()	Opens (or reopens) the port using the current settings.
close()	Closes the port but does not destroy the port object. It may be reopened later.
isOpen()	Returns True if the port is open; otherwise, returns False.

Table 11-2. pySerial port read/write methods

Method	Description
read(*size=1*)	Reads size bytes from the serial port. If a timeout is set, it may return fewer characters than requested. With no timeout enabled, this method will block until the requested number of bytes is read.
readline(*size=None*, *eol*='\n')	Reads a string of characters until an end-of-line (eol) character (a \n by default) is received, or until a read timeout occurs.
readlines(*sizehint=None*, *eol*='\n')	Reads a list of lines until the read timeout occurs. The sizehint parameter is ignored.
write(*data*)	Outputs the given string over the serial port.
writelines(*lines*)	Writes a list of strings to the serial port.

Table 11-3. pySerial data buffer management methods

Method	Description
flushInput()	Clears the input buffer, discarding all data currently in the buffer.
flushOutput()	Clears the output buffer, aborting the current output and discarding all remaining data currently in the buffer.
inWaiting()	Returns the number of characters currently in the input buffer.
outWaiting()	Returns the number of characters waiting in the output buffer.

Table 11-4. pySerial port parameter methods

Method	Description
getBaudrate()	Returns the current baud rate setting.
setBaudrate(*baudrate*)	Sets the port's baud rate. This method cannot be used if the port is already open.
getByteSize()	Returns the current byte size setting.
setByteSize(*bytesize*)	Sets the data character bit size.
getDsrDtr()	Returns the current DSR/DTR flow control setting.
setDsrDtr(*dsrdtr=None*)	Sets the DSR/DTR flow control behavior.
getParity()	Returns the current parity setting.
setParity(*parity*)	Sets the port parity.
getPort()	Returns the current port setting.

Method	Description
setPort(*port*)	Sets the port number or name.
getRtsCts()	Returns the current RTS/CTS flow control setting.
setRtsCts(*rtscts*)	Sets the RTS/CTS flow control behavior.
getStopbits()	Returns the current stop bits setting.
setStopbits(*stopbits*)	Sets the number of stop bits to use.
getTimeout()	Returns the current timeout setting.
setTimeout(*timeout*)	Sets the read timeout period.
getWriteTimeout()	Returns the current write timeout setting.
setWriteTimeout(*timeout*)	Sets the write timeout period.
getXonXoff()	Returns the current XON/XOFF setting.
setXonXoff(*xonxoff*)	Sets the XON/XOFF flow control behavior.

Table 11-5. pySerial port capabilities methods

Method	Description
getSupportedBaudrates()	Returns a list of baud rates supported by the serial port.
getSupportedByteSizes()	Returns a list of the character bit sizes supported by the serial port.
getSupportedParities()	Returns a list of parity bit settings supported by the serial port.
getSupportedStopbits()	Returns a list of stop bit settings supported by the serial port.

Table 11-6. pySerial hardware handshake line status methods

Method	Description
getCD()	Returns the state of the Carrier Detect line.
getCTS()	Returns the state of the Clear To Send line.
getDSR()	Returns the state of the Data Set Ready line.
getRI()	Returns the state of the Ring Indicator line.
setDTR(*level=1*)	Sets the Data Terminal Ready line to the specified state.
setRTS(*level=1*)	Sets the Request To Send line to the specified state.

pySerial does not support RS-485 interfaces directly, but it works fine with RS-232–to–RS-485 converters that provide half-duplex auto-turnaround capability. It will also work with USB-to–RS-485 converters, provided that they use a virtual serial port (for Windows) or a *tty*-type device entry in the */dev* directory (for Linux). An experimental implementation of an RFC 2217 server is also provided with the *pySerial* package.

For installation and additional usage instructions, refer to the *pySerial* website.

pyParallel

pyParallel (http://pyserial.sourceforge.net/pyparallel.html) is a companion project to *pySerial* by the same author. The purpose of *pyParallel* is to encapsulate access to a parallel port by a Python program in a platform-independent manner (refer back to the discussion of parallel ports in Chapter 2 if you need a refresher). At present, it supports only Windows and Linux.

Unlike *pySerial*, *pyParallel* has no open or close methods. If instantiated with no port parameter, *pyParallel* will attempt to use the first available parallel port. Optionally, you can specify a particular port name as a string.

Here's a simple example of how it can be used:

```
>>> import parallel
>>> pport = parallel.Parallel()      # open first available parallel port
>>> pport.setData(0x55)
>>> pport.setData(0xAA)
```

This will write the value 0x55 to the parallel port, followed immediately by the value 0xAA. Table 11-7 lists the methods available.

Table 11-7. pyParallel methods

Method	Description
setData(*value*)	Applies a byte value to the data pins of the parallel port
setDataStrobe(*level*)	Sets the Data Strobe line to *level* (0 or 1)
setAutoFeed(*level*)	Sets the Auto Feed line to *level* (0 or 1)
setInitOut(*level*)	Sets the Initialize line to *level* (0 or 1)
getInSelected()	Reads the state of the Select line
getInPaperOut()	Reads the state of the Paper Out line
getInAcknowledge()	Reads the state of the Acknowledge line

Notice that *pyParallel* does not provide functions to read the Busy or Error inputs. However, *pyParallel* does allow you to directly manipulate the handshaking output lines on the port.

On Windows machines, *pyParallel* requires direct access to the physical port hardware. It cannot be used with USB parallel port adapters, so it won't work on a notebook or netbook with only USB ports. It also does not support Extended Parallel Port (EPP) functionality.

Sending data to an external device via *pyParallel* involves outputting byte values one at a time under software control. This may sound clumsy, but there really is no other way to do it, short of using smart hardware with built-in flow control management and internal buffering capabilities. When communicating with a printer the program must, at a minimum, set and clear the Data Strobe and check the Acknowledge line coming back from the printer.

The parallel port on a PC isn't restricted to just sending data to a printer, however. An interesting example of how you can drive an LCD display from a parallel port can be found at *http://pyserial.svn.sourceforge.net/viewvc/pyserial/trunk/pyparallel/examples/*.

Other interesting uses for a parallel port include controlling a DAC device, sensing discrete digital inputs, and using the 8 bits of output to control relays or other devices. The downside is that the port circuitry isn't designed to handle very much current, so external interface circuitry is often required.

PyVISA

The *PyVISA* package provides a Python API for an IVI-standard VISA driver on Windows, or an IVI-compatible VISA driver for Linux systems. It uses a driver DLL or library file provided by an instrument vendor. On Windows machines, the package expects to find a DLL by the name of *visa32.dll* in the path, typically in *C:\WINNT \system32*. For Linux systems, National Instruments (NI) supplies an IVI-compliant VISA driver as a shared object library module (the Linux equivalent of a DLL on Windows systems), called *libvisa.so.7*. This file usually resides in */usr/local/vxipnp/linux/bin*.

The NI Linux version of *visa32* specifically supports the following distributions:

- Red Hat Enterprise Linux Workstation 4
- Red Hat Enterprise Linux Desktop + Workstation 5
- SUSE Linux 10.1
- openSUSE 10.2
- Mandriva Linux 2006
- Mandriva Linux 2007

Refer to the section "Suggested Reading" on page 436 for more information about the NI VISA driver.

For Windows, you shouldn't have to do a lot of digging to find what you need. Modern instruments with IVI-compliant interface capabilities typically come with a VISA driver for the Windows platform, so if you don't have the original CD that came with an instrument you may want to look around and see if you can locate it, or perhaps one from a similar instrument. You may also be able to download the VISA components from an instrument vendor's website.

VISA, and by extension *PyVISA*, supports serial, GPIB, GPIB-VXI, VXI, TCP/IP, and USB interfaces. We will be using VISA primarily to interface with GPIB-capable devices. A simple example of *PyVISA* in action looks like this:

```
>>> import visa
>>> dmm = visa.instrument("GPIB::2")
>>> print dmm.ask("*IDN?")
```

This tells the VISA driver that we want to use the instrument with GPIB address 2 as the object dmm. The dmm.ask method sends the string specified ("*IDN?", in this case). It then returns the instrument's response, which should be the device's internal identification string.

You can find more information about *PyVISA* at the project's home page, located at *http://pyvisa.sourceforge.net*.

VISA provides far too many different functions to go into all of them here. For a detailed look at VISA itself, the VPP-4.3 VISA library reference is available from the IVI Foundation.

Alternatives for Windows

There is an OSS project called *PyUniversalLibrary* that is developing a wrapper for Measurement Computing's Universal Library API. According to the website it is not 100% complete, but it does have enough functionality to be useful. You can find out more about it here: *https://code.astraw.com/projects/PyUniversalLibrary*.

The UNC Python Tools package contains, among other things, a wrapper for National Instruments's older NI-DAQ drivers. It is available from *http://sourceforge.net/projects/uncpythontools/*.

Using Bus-Based Hardware I/O Devices with Linux

Plugging an interface into a Windows machine is usually straightforward, and vendors typically supply interface drivers with their products. With Linux, an instrumentation device that uses a serial, GPIB, or USB port to communicate isn't really a problem in most cases. However, when it comes to the cards that plug into the PC's internal PCI bus, things get more complicated. In Chapter 5 we looked at what goes into an extension to allow it to serve as a wrapper for a DLL used with Windows to access a device connected to the internal bus of a PC. In the realm of Linux, each I/O device requires a driver written specifically for the Linux environment, along with whatever tools and utilities the device might need to configure its internal settings. Many instrumentation manufacturers simply don't support Linux, at least not directly. This usually isn't an intentional snub; there just aren't enough Linux systems being used in instrumentation applications (yet) to justify the effort and expense of supporting two different versions of the interface software. There is, however, a project called Comedi that aims to provide a way to connect instrumentation interface hardware to PCs running Linux.

The Comedi project

The Comedi project was started in 1996 by David Schleef as a collection of low-level drivers to allow a Linux system to communicate with various types of data acquisition and digital interface cards. It is an open source project and is currently hosted at its own website, *http://www.comedi.org*.

The *comedi* package is a combination of three complementary software components. The first component is a generic, device-independent API. This interacts with a collection of Linux kernel modules that provide the interface support for the generic API (the second component), and lastly there is a library of functions that provides an interface to configure various cards (the third component). The Comedi team works with hardware vendors (whenever possible) to gather information, obtain hardware for test and verification, and develop the drivers. In one sense, you might say that Comedi is the Linux corollary to the IVI suite of drivers.

If you want to download and build Comedi yourself, make sure you get both the *comedi* and *comedilib* packages. You might also want to get the *comedi_examples* file.

Comedi hardware support

Comedi supports the following interface hardware manufacturers, to one degree or another:

- ADLink
- Advantech
- Amplicon
- Analog Devices
- ComputerBoards
- Contec
- Data Translation
- Fastwel
- General Standards Corporation
- ICP
- Inova
- Intelligent Instrumentation
- IOTech
- ITL
- JR3
- Keithley Metrabyte
- Kolter Electronic
- Measurement Computing
- Mechatronic Systems, Inc.
- Meilhaus
- Micro/sys
- Motorola
- National Instruments

- Quanser Consulting
- Quatech
- Real Time Devices
- Sensoray
- SSV Embedded Systems
- Winsystems

Not every card from every vendor is supported, but with over 400 different types (and growing), Comedi covers a lot of territory. For a complete list, see the Comedi website.

Using comedi with Python

comedi is shipped with the ability to use the Simplified Wrapper and Interface Generator (SWIG) to generate a wrapper for *comedilib*. You can learn more about SWIG at *http://www.swig.org*. There is also a discussion group on Google that is a good first place to look if you encounter problems with *comedi*.

Data I/O: Acquiring and Writing Data

Now that we have some idea of what to expect in terms of the software we'll need to interact with instrument hardware, let's take a look under the hood and see how we can put it to work for us.

Basic Data I/O

When considering data acquisition, there are basically two types of data sources: external instruments, and data acquisition hardware installed in the computer itself. In both cases there is a transaction that occurs between your application software and the device. Sometimes the transaction is direct, such as when accessing the hardware registers of a device directly from the application-level code. This style of interface programming is rather rare nowadays, as the underlying operating system tends to prohibit direct hardware access by user-level code. In most cases, it will involve an intermediary such as a driver with a vendor-defined API (recall Chapter 5), or an interface library (e.g., *pySerial*).

When acquiring data from an external device, or sending data (e.g., a command) to a device, there are several ways to get there from here. If you want to send data, the first, and most obvious, approach is to just write the data to the port or device and let it go at that. When you want to read data, the obvious approach is to simply read the data on demand.

Both of these methods assume that when the device is sent a command or queried for data it will automatically and immediately perform whatever hardware functions are necessary to convert the data into an internal register address, an internal command code, or a return value. For the most part, this is a valid assumption. But there can be situations where things don't work out like you might expect. Instead of a successful write operation, an error might occur, or the device's driver API function might take a while to return or, worse still, not return at all.

Reading data

When reading data from a bus-based device, the device's interface will typically return a binary value that can be used immediately. There is no need to send a command, *per se*; you can just use a function call. With an external instrument, on the other hand, the commands and data are typically in the form of ASCII strings and utilize a command-response format. ASCII-to-binary conversions can be handled fairly easily in Python.

Instruments that utilize SCPI will typically return strings containing a numeric value, or multiple numeric values separated by commas. Fortunately, Python can easily deal with numeric data in a string format. Assume that we have an instrument that returns something like "+4.85510000E-01" when queried for a measurement. In the following code snippet, the hypothetical function getDataResponse() will return a string containing the instrument response string, or it will return None. We can use Python's float type object constructor to do the necessary conversion for us:

```
raw_data = getDataResponse(instID)
if raw_data:
    data_val = float(raw_data)
```

If raw_data is not None, the variable data_val will contain 0.48851, as expected.

Let's look at another example, this time involving more than one return value in response to a measurement command. Assume that an instrument returns four values when queried, as the string "+5.50500000E00, -2.66000000E-01, +8.24000000E01, -6.34370000E00". In Python, it is very easy to convert a string of comma-separated values into a list of strings. The following code snippet can be used to deal with a situation like this:

```
data_val = []
data_str = getDataSet(instID)
raw_vals = data_str.split(",")
for raw_data in raw_vals:
    data_val.append(float(raw_data))
```

After this, the list variable data_val will contain four floating-point values:

```
[5.5049999999999999, -0.26600000000000001, 82.400000000000006,
 -6.3437000000000001]
```

The numbers look a bit odd due to the way that Python handles the string–to–floating-point value conversions, but they are essentially the same numbers as in the original string. The oddness is a result of the way that floating-point values are handled in the CPU (Python doesn't make it pretty unless you ask it to do so).

If you are acquiring data from an instrument that returns an ASCII string that contains something other than just numeric data, you may need to do some type of parsing to extract the specific sections of interest from the returned string. The ASCII data will also need to be converted into a binary format of some type. The RS-485 interface we looked at earlier is an example of this type of situation.

In some cases the return string may contain a mix of numeric and nonnumeric characters, and not always in a fixed format. The tpi 183 DMM we looked at earlier generates a fixed-format data string. This is very easy to deal with, as all you need to do is extract a slice from the string that contains the data (see Chapter 3 for more on slices in Python). However, this is not always the case; sometimes the length of the data portion, and even the leading header characters, of the return string can vary.

If you're dealing with an instrument or device that employs a format with a fixed starting position for the data and uses an end marker character, you can obtain the position of the end marker in the string and use a slice to pull out what you need. If the starting position is not fixed, you'll need to scan through the string and find the start of the data field before you can use a slice to extract it.

Writing data

As mentioned earlier, accessing a bus-based device typically involves just calling a function in the device's API. There are no commands, as such, but it is common to write parameter values to the device, or call a function to start or stop some action (such as, say, a timer or clock function).

Writing ASCII data (i.e., commands and parameter values) to an external instrument that utilizes SCPI, or a unique command format, involves creating the necessary command string, writing it, and then waiting for the instrument to respond. In this command-response scenario the instrument returns data only when requested to do so; it does not spontaneously send data on its own. Also, in some cases there is no response.

For example, let's assume that we have a GPIB instrument such as a programmable power supply. This example is based on the Agilent E364xA series, which includes some non-SCPI commands that I won't cover here. For now, I'll just use the following commands:

```
OUTPut
    [:STATE] {ON|OFF}
    [:STATE]?

[SOURce:]
    CURRent
    CURRent?
    VOLTage
    VOLTage?

MEASure
    :CURRent?
    [:VOLTage]?
```

The curly braces around the `ON|OFF` parameters indicate a choice. Also, notice that some of the items are in square brackets, including the key command `SOURce`. This indicates that these are optional, and whatever parameter is in square brackets is the default. So, in the case of the `MEASure` command, if the command is given as:

```
MEAS?
```

it will return the voltage at the outputs of the power supply. To get the current, the command must explicitly specify it:

```
MEAS:CURR?
```

Since the `SOURce` command is optional, the following set of command strings will set the output to 5.1 volts DC and the current limit to 1.0 amperes:

```
VOLT 5.1
CURR 1.0
```

If we wish, we can also control the output from the supply using the `OUTPut` command, like so:

```
OUTP:OFF
SOUR:VOLT 5.1
SOUR:CURR 1.0
OUTP:ON
```

This disables the output before changing the `V` and `I` parameters.

To read back the settings, we can use the `SOURce:VOLTage` or `SOURce:CURRent` commands with a question mark to indicate a query:

```
VOLT?
```

This will return a response like this:

```
5.00000
```

To see what is really happening on the output terminals we can use the `MEASure` command, like so:

```
MEAS:CURR?
```

This returns (for example):

```
0.20000
```

This command will read the output voltage:

```
MEAS?
```

and it returns:

```
5.00000
```

Finally, we can check to see whether the supply's output is enabled or not using the query form of the `OUTPut` command:

```
OUTP?
```

If the supply is enabled, it will return an ASCII "1"; otherwise, a "0" is returned.

I haven't indicated how the commands are sent and the response returned because there are several ways to do this, such as serial, USB, and GPIB. But let's assume that there is a function called sendCommand() that will take care of this for us. For this example we'll create a function called setPowerSupply() that will accept the voltage and current parameters and send them to the instrument:

```
def setPowerSupply(volts, current):
    rc = OK
    volts_str = "%2.2f" % float(volts)
    current_str = "2.2f" % float(current)

    cmd_str = "VOLT " + volts_str
    rc = sendCommand(instID, cmd_str)
    if rc == OK:
        cmd_str = "CURR ", current_str
        rc = sendCommand(instID, cmd_str)

    return rc
```

This seems rather straightforward, but there are some things going on that might not be readily obvious.

After rc (the return code) is preset to OK (to be optimistic), the input parameters volts and current are converted to string representations. Notice that the format is specified as %2.2f. This will create a string representation that the instrument can easily handle. Also notice that the input parameters are used to create float variable objects, which are then inserted into the string variables. If the input parameters are given as floats, nothing changes, but if the input parameters are integers they will be converted. Also, this function will accept string representations of integer or floating-point values for either parameter.

This, by the way, is a very handy and powerful trick. It will deal with almost any numeric value, in any valid format, that you might care to throw at it, and gracefully convert it to a floating-point type. It will fail if an input parameter is a nonnumeric string, a hex value in string format, an *n*-tuple, or a dictionary, but these cases can easily be trapped and handled using a try-except construct.

Next, the sendCommand() function is called. This might use GPIB, or it might be the access function for serial I/O. It really doesn't matter how the command is sent, as long as the instrument gets it.

So now that we've seen how to send a command, how can we tell if the instrument actually accepted the command and did what the command specified? In the case of a power supply, we would mainly be interested in knowing if the output is active and what the output values actually are. Sensing the output state (On or Off) is straightforward, as we've already seen, but determining if the output levels are at, or near, the commanded values can be somewhat challenging.

The reason is that we've now made the leap from digital to analog, and the analog world is full of subtle variations. Depending on the accuracy of the instrument, if we command it to generate a 5.000 V DC output, in reality the voltage on the output terminals might be 4.999 V DC, or anything within the tolerance range of the device. The following snippet shows one way to implement a return value check with upper and lower tolerance bounds:

```
def testDelta(testval, targval, tolerance=0.001):
    testval_float = float(testval)
    targmax = float(targval) * (1 + tolerance)
    targmin = float(targval) * (1 - tolerance)
    if (testval_float >= targmax) or (testval_float <= targmin):
        return False
    else:
        return True
```

The float object conversion is also used here, as in the previous example. This ensures that all the internal variables will be float types.

If the value passed to `testDelta()` is within some +/- range of the target value (`targval`), the function will return `True`; otherwise, `False` is returned. The tolerance check is symmetrical around the target value, as shown in Figure 11-7.

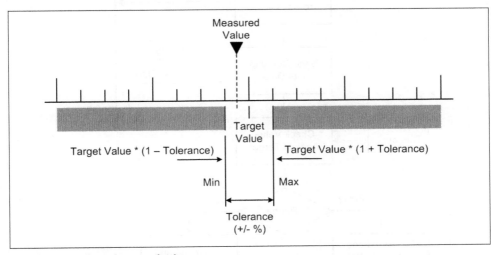

Figure 11-7. Value tolerance checking

If we wanted an asymmetrical tolerance check, we would need to specify an offset relative to the target value. Between the tolerance range and the offset, we could move the acceptance window to any position and width necessary.

Figure 11-8 shows a flowchart for a function used to set the output of an instrument (such as a power supply or some other type of analog output), and then read the output and compare the value returned to the original commanded value. Depending on the system, just checking the actual output value and then reporting an error (if any) might be sufficient, but as we'll see in a just a bit we could also attempt to retry the command, or initiate a system shutdown.

Now, at this point you may be wondering: "Why would I want to go to all that trouble?" Good question, and here's an example of why you might want to do that.

With a programmable power supply you can set the maximum current as well as the output voltage. What happens when the current exceeds the programmed limit? Some power supplies can be configured to go into what is called "constant current" mode. What this means is that the supply will endeavor to maintain the output current at the preset limit, even if that means that the voltage begins to fall toward zero as the load gets closer to being a short. The same can apply if the output voltage is commanded to a point where the load draws more current than the present limit.

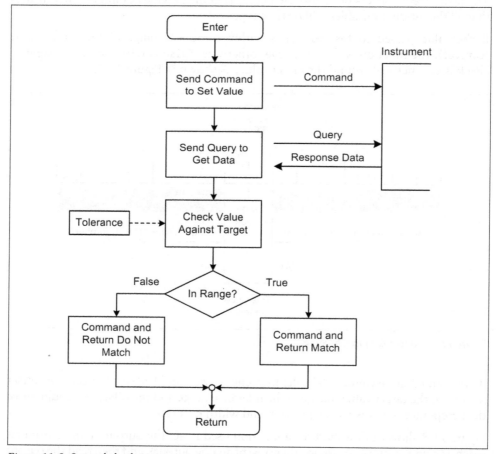

Figure 11-8. Set and check instrument output

For example, if you command the current limit to something like 1.0 amps and the output voltage to 5.0 volts DC, and there is a 10-ohm load connected to the supply, the actual current will be 500 mA. At 500 mA the voltage should stay at 5.0V, since it's well below the 1 A limit. However, if the load resistance is reduced to 4 ohms, the supply cannot deliver more than 1 amp (the commanded maximum), and the voltage decreases to 4 V DC while the current holds steady at 1 A. This is just a simple application of Ohm's law, which we covered in Chapter 2. So, if the current limit is set at or near the maximum you would ever expect the supply to experience in a system, you can sense the voltage to detect a problem. In such a case, the control software might send an OUTP OFF command immediately upon detecting a voltage set failure.

Blocking Versus Nonblocking Calls

Now it's time to introduce some concepts that you will need to use later to build robust and reliable software. We'll start with a discussion of blocking and nonblocking function calls, and then take a look at some basic techniques for handling errors.

One way to describe the behavior of a function or method is in terms of how quickly it will return after it has been invoked. Some only return after a result of some type is obtained, while others may return immediately without waiting for something else downstream to produce a particular response. In other words, functions may be either *blocking* (the calling code must wait for a response), or *nonblocking* (the call returns immediately, usually with a response that indicates success or failure).

Actually, all software functions (and methods, too) can be classified as either blocking or nonblocking, and the majority of functions within a typical software application are of the blocking variety—that is, they don't return until the intended action is complete or an error is detected. You can see this in the message sequence chart (MSC) shown in Figure 11-9. Here we have Function1() calling Function2(), which in turn calls Function3() and finally Function4(). The time required for Function1() to receive a response from Function2() is dependent on how long it takes for functions 2, 3, and 4 to complete their processing and return. During this entire time, Function1() is blocked. (In an MSC diagram, events in a function or process occur in a top-to-bottom order, and transactions between functions or processes are the horizontal lines.)

Blocking allows functions to maintain synchronization and honor the intended flow of execution through the code. The action or data that the call is requesting may or may not be available at the time the call is made, so a blocking call will wait for the other end to respond in some fashion before returning to the caller. As a side effect, it will also effectively suspend your application until it returns.

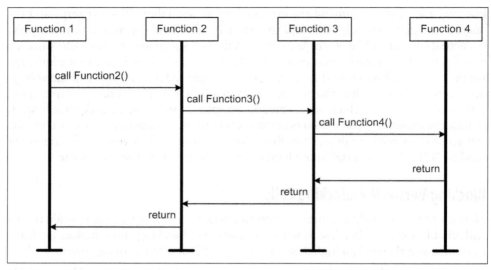

Figure 11-9. Function blocking

The type of blocking we're most interested in is when an application process is forced to wait for an interface, which in turn waits for a hardware device to respond. This is shown in Figure 11-10. Notice that there is a timer symbol in this diagram. This means that if the hardware does not respond within some preset period of time, the interface process will terminate and return an error.

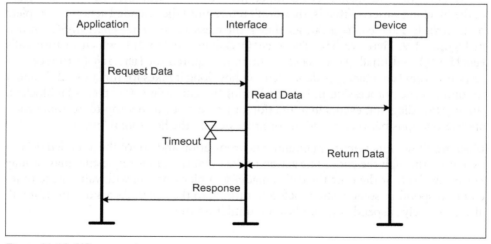

Figure 11-10. I/O transaction

In some cases it may not matter if a blocking call waits for a bit before returning to the caller, and allowing this is more convenient than writing the necessary code to support continual query and retry actions. But, there is a warning in order here: when working with I/O devices, a blocking call without a timeout of some sort can potentially hang forever. This is usually a bad thing, and often the only way to get out of the situation is to shut down Python and restart the application. If your code is running on an unattended machine somewhere in the middle of nowhere, a fault that hangs a blocking call can be really, really bad.

One way to deal with this is to use nonblocking function calls. This entails some additional code, but it's very useful when dealing with network communications and data acquisition. We'll look at some ways to use this approach shortly.

Data I/O Methods

Now that we've seen what blocking and nonblocking functions entail, let's look at how these concepts are involved with various operational modes of interface I/O. We'll start with the simplest form, on-demand I/O, then proceed to polled I/O, and finally take a quick a look at multithreaded I/O.

On-demand data I/O

As I stated earlier, the two most obvious ways to move data into or out of your application are just a matter of reading from or writing to a port or device. When sending (writing) data using a serial (RS-232 or RS-485) or GPIB-type interface, there usually is no need to worry about the use of a blocking call. In the case of an RS-232 interface that does not use hardware handshaking, the data is sent out through the hardware port immediately. An RS-485 interface with a single master and multiple listeners should never block on a write by the master device, but the listeners may be unresponsive for a period of time. GPIB can also get into a situation where there are no listeners responding to the sender, but most GPIB interface APIs and the associated hardware can detect this and return an error code. Writing to a hardware interface API for a device such as a PCI interface card is usually not a problem in terms of blocking, but the call might still return an error code if something is amiss.

If your software uses on-demand calls to read data, they should be blocking calls, and your software should always check the return codes. If timeout parameters are available for a blocking function call they should definitely be used, but not every API provides blocking calls with timeouts (perhaps it was assumed that a timeout couldn't possibly happen). For those situations you'll need to use a nonblocking version of the API function and employ a different approach to implement a timeout in your own software.

Polled data I/O

A nonblocking call will return immediately, and its return code or return value will (hopefully) let the caller know whether or not it succeeded. A nonblocking call can be used to avoid an I/O hang, but it requires more code to support it. For example, let's assume that the API we're using has both blocking and nonblocking versions of I/O functions to read data from a device, or perhaps that the I/O functions have a parameter that can be set to control blocking. You can then put a nonblocking call into a loop that also checks for a timeout, like this:

```
def GetData(port_num, tmax=5.0):
    checking = True
    tstart = time.time()
    while checking:
        rc, data = ReadNonBlocking()
        if rc == ERR:
            break
        if time.time() - tstart > tmax:
            checking = False
            rc = TIMEOUT
        else:
            time.sleep(0.05)      # wait 50 ms between checks

    return rc, data
```

This is an example of polling: this function will attempt to get data from a specific data acquisition device by continually polling the port (using the ReadNonBlocking() function call) until valid data appears. In between each read attempt it will sleep for 50 milliseconds. The delay is mainly for the benefit of the device being read, as many devices can't tolerate being hammered continuously for data.

In order to actually have a polling function that doesn't cause the rest of an application to suspend while it's active, you need to use a thread.

Acquiring data using a thread

So far we've looked at on-demand and polled data I/O. Now let's take a quick look at how we might check for incoming data without bogging down the entire system in a continuous polling loop.

There are two API functions in the following skeleton example that we haven't seen before: SendTrigger() and GetData(). It is assumed that these exist as part of the API for the data acquisition hardware, and they do what their names imply. Also, the type of data being acquired isn't specified, primarily because it doesn't really matter for this example. It could be anything, just so long as the specified number of samples are acquired and no errors occur:

```
class AcqData:
    def __init__(self, port_num, timeout):
        self.timeout = timeout
        self.dataport = port_num
        self.dvals = []          # list for acquired data values
        self.dsamps = 0          # number of values actually read
        self.get_rc = 0          # 0 is OK, negative value is an error
        self.get_done = False    # True if thread is finished


    def Trigger(self):
```

```
        SendTrigger(self.dataport)

    def _get_data(self, numsamples):
        cnt = 0
        acqfail = False

        while not acqfail:
            self.get_rc, dataval = GetData(self.dataport, self.timeout)
            if self.get_rc == OK:
                self.datasamps = cnt + 1
                self.dvals.append(datavalue)

                cnt += 1
                if cnt > numsamples:
                    break
            else:
                acqfail = True
        self.get_done = True


    def StartDataSamples(self, samplecnt):
        try:
            acq_thread = threading.Thread(target=self._get_data, args=(samplecnt))
            acq_thread.start()

            self.Trigger()        # start the data acquisition

        except Exception, e:
            print "Acquire fault: %s" % str(e)

    def GetDataSamples(self):
        if self.get_done == True:
            return (get_rc, self.dsmaps, self.dvals)
        else:
            return (NOT_DONE, 0, 0)
```

This bit of code uses a thread, in the form of the function _get_data(), to continuously
read the external device to obtain some number of data samples. Notice that the hypothetical API function GetData() supports the use of a timeout parameter, and we can
assume that it will return an error code if a timeout does occur.

The key things in this simple example are how the thread is created, and how we can
check to see if the data acquisition is complete. Python's threading library includes a
thread object method called join(), which accepts an optional timeout parameter and
is typically used to block the execution of one thread while it is waiting for another to
complete. In this case we won't use join(), so the thread is allowed to run on its own.
The accessor function GetDataSamples() checks the variable self.get_done to determine if the thread has finished. If so, GetDataSamples() will return the data collected.
If the thread is still running, it will return a 3-tuple with the first item set to NOT_DONE.
It is up to the caller to determine if the sample count returned matches the sample count
requested.

This is just one way to do this, but it illustrates a fundamental issue that is often encountered when working with threads; namely, at what point does the program come to a halt and wait for something else to finish what it's doing? In a program that is designed to run continuously, this can be dealt with by placing the call to `GetData Samples()` in a single main loop in the application. This allows it to be checked each time through the loop if data is expected, with the results read back if they are available. Otherwise, the program could just continue to use the last known results.

Handling Data I/O Errors

No matter how unlikely it may seem, errors can still happen, especially when dealing with interfaces to the real world. They might be the result of spurious noise on a serial interface, an out-of-range voltage level on an analog input, or a fault in an external instrument. How the software detects and handles errors is directly related to its robustness. Another way to put it would be to say that robust software tends to exhibit a high degree of fault tolerance.

Faults, Errors, and Failures

Here are some terms commonly used when discussing and describing fault-tolerant systems. Although these are common terms, often used interchangeably, they have special and specific meanings when used in a fault-tolerant context:

Fault
> A defect in the code, the electronics, or the mechanisms of a system. A fault only becomes apparent when it is encountered and an error occurs. A fault that is not encountered is called a *latent fault*.

Error
> Some abnormal behavior that results when the system encounters a fault. The abnormal behavior might be an erroneous result in a computation, unexpected or missing data in a communications channel, or an unwanted (and potentially disastrous) physical behavior. Errors are generally categorized as being either fatal or nonfatal in terms of the continued operation of the software.

Failure
> The nonperformance of an expected action as the result of an error, typically expressed as a deviation from the required behavior as defined in the system specification.

In summary, faults cause errors, and errors cause failures. It is well known that it is extremely unlikely that all possible faults in complex systems will be identified, and even seemingly simple systems can harbor latent faults. The objective of fault-tolerant design is to create systems that can continue to function at some level, even in the presence of faults.

For a system (be it software, hardware, or a combination of the two) to be called fault-tolerant implies that it has the ability to detect a fault condition, take action to correct or bypass the fault, and continue to function (perhaps at a reduced level of functionality) instead of just crashing or abruptly halting. The ability to continue to function at reduced levels of capability in the presence of an increasing level of errors is called *graceful degradation*. Of course, if the errors continue to mount, at some point the system will eventually come to a halt, but the idea is that it will do so after giving ample notice and it will not do it in a catastrophic fashion.

The reality is that there are almost always faults, and most things will eventually break or wear out. How much planning you should do for the mostly likely faults and the resulting errors is largely down to how much of a problem a failure will create. It might be insignificant (just ignore it and move on), or it could be a really big deal (something might explode, catch fire, or otherwise fail to stop an impending disaster). If you've done your up-front planning, as discussed in Chapter 8, you should be able to identify the nastiest scenarios and give some thought to how your system might deal with them should they arise.

Classes of errors

Errors can be grouped into two broad categories: nonfatal and fatal. A *nonfatal error* might be something like an intermittent communications channel, perhaps due to noise or other perturbations in the medium, or someone's foot occasionally kicking a connector under a desk. Depending on the speed of the system and the duration of the failure, it may be possible to continue operation without adverse effects until communications can be reestablished. Another example might be an instrument that occasionally does not respond in a timely fashion, for whatever reason. If the command or query can be retried successfully with no ill effect, the error could be considered nonfatal. (Note that nonfatal does not mean nonannoying!)

A *fatal error* is one that requires significant intervention if the system is to continue functioning. Lacking that, it will need to perform a complete shutdown. An example of a fatal error would be the loss of control for the primary DC power supply used in an experiment. Unless there is a backup supply available that can automatically take over, the system will need to shut down until the problem can be resolved. Another example might be the failure of the control system for the liquid nitrogen supply used for the sorption pumps on a vacuum chamber, perhaps due to a failure in the control interface electronics, or a failure in the command communications channel. In either case, the system will begin to lose vacuum and potentially damage things like ion gauges or sputter emitters. At the very least, the current activity should be stopped until the problem is resolved.

Error retry and system termination

Sometimes it may make sense to retry an operation if an error is detected, perhaps after altering a parameter to compensate for the error. While this might sound clever (and it can be), it's not something that should be done without some serious consideration of the context, cause, and consequences of the error. Blithely attempting to retry a failed operation can sometimes cause serious damage.

The more error-detection and self-recovery capabilities one attempts to build into a system, the more complicated the system becomes. This is fairly obvious, to be sure, but what isn't obvious is how that complexity will manifest, and the subsequent implications it might have, not only for a particular subsystem, but for the system as a whole. As complexity increases, so too does the chance of new defects being introduced. Increased complexity can also increase the number of possible execution paths in the software, some of which may be unintended.

Figure 11-11 shows a scheme for handling a data I/O error in a fault-tolerant fashion. While this approach may not be suitable for every application, it does show why robust or fault-tolerant software tends to be an order of magnitude (or more) more expensive to implement than something that just does the I/O operation and returns either pass or fail. This is particularly true when performing testing to verify the fault-tolerant behavior. In Figure 11-11, there are three possible paths that can be taken should an error occur. In addition to the I/O operation itself, each of these paths must be tested by simulating the I/O and the error context. This rigorous testing involves a lot of work, but if you need that level of robustness there really is no other way to achieve it.

An interesting point to note about Figure 11-11 is the amount of code it implies. The data I/O operation and its return code (pass or fail, perhaps) are simple and straightforward, and might take no more than a line or two of code to implement. With the error handling included in the design, the code for performing a data I/O operation will grow by anywhere from 10 to 100 times in size. This is typical of fault-tolerant software. A large portion of it is concerned with error detection and handling, and only a fraction actually deals directly with the I/O. Also note that the last decision block, "Backup active?," means that if the backup is already in use (i.e., the test is True), there are no more options left except to fail.

When detecting and attempting to deal with an error, the system has to make a decision as to whether to attempt to recover from the error (and what recovery strategy to use) or just try to shut down gracefully. The logic making that decision must have inputs in the form of data describing the context in which the error occurred and the current state of the system, and there may also be a need to define excluded operations that should not be used.

For example, it may not be a good idea for a system controlling a pressure vessel to just relinquish control of the system without first performing some kind of check to determine if the pressure needs to be released. If the pressure continues to build even after the pumps and heaters are disabled (this can happen), there is a risk that the vessel may explode, especially if the error involved an over-pressure-related situation to start with. A graceful shutdown could possibly involve some type of venting action before control is completely terminated.

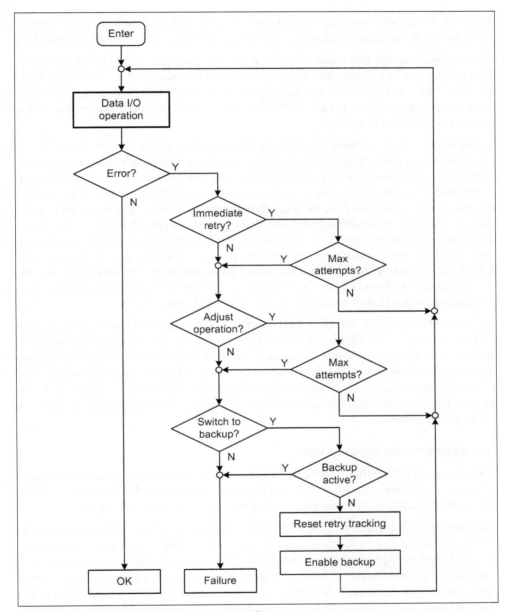

Figure 11-11. Fault-resistant data I/O error handling

Similarly, if an error occurs in a system that is moving a mass of some type, does it make sense for the system to just stop? If the action of lifting or moving the mass entails control of power to a motor or servo, it might not be a good idea to just kill the power.

The system may need to engage some type of braking or locking mechanism, or it might make sense for the mass to be lowered to a safe position prior to shutdown (if possible).

These considerations also come into play when attempting to retry a failed operation. Retries may not be appropriate after some types of failures, such as the loss of direct positional feedback, or the failure of a temperature sensor. Other failures may be known to be transient, and the operations can be retried some number of times before the situation is declared hopeless.

Consider the situation where the position of a secondary mechanism is dependent on the position of a primary mechanism, both of which are moving at a slow and relatively continuous rate for extended periods of time. The link between the two is a communications channel that is known to occasionally drop out due to system load or other factors. In a situation like this, the secondary mechanism that is following the primary one might be able to predict where it should be over short periods of time. This allows it to continue to function without an update from the primary mechanism. If after some period of time the communications with the primary mechanism cannot be reestablished, the secondary mechanism will enter an error condition. If it does reestablish the communications channel with the primary mechanism before the timeout period, it can update its position, if necessary, and reset the timeout.

Failure analysis, which we discussed briefly in the section "Handling Errors and Faults" on page 272 in Chapter 8, comes into play when making decisions like these. If done correctly, it can provide the guidance needed to make the decision to terminate abruptly, terminate gracefully, or attempt to recover. Lacking a failure analysis, the best choice is often to just terminate gracefully, and provide sufficient information (typically in a crash log or something similar) to allow someone to go back and ascertain the cause of the problem later.

Error/warning message single-shot logic

It sometimes happens that something in a system will occasionally generate a nonfatal error or warning message, and while you do want to know that the error has occurred, you probably don't want to see the warning messages over and over again.

An example of this might be a high-speed data acquisition device that, depending on whatever else is going on, might miss a data acquisition operation every now and again. The author of the API library might have considered this to be bad, but you might not, especially if your software is clever enough to toss out a bad sample and simply try it again (as we just discussed). So long as your software is applying a timestamp to the data and there are no specific requirements that the data be acquired at precise intervals (having an accurate timestamp can help with this), you can often just ignore the error and try for another sample.

Here's one way to handle this:

```python
# somewhere in the module's global namespace, we define some control
# variables and assign initial values (these could also be object
# variables):

msglock   = False
errcnt    = 0
errcntmax = 9    # this will result in 10 counts before lockout

# And here is the function/method that does the actual data
# acquisition and error message lockout:

def grabData():
    global msglock, errcnt

    rc = Acquire()

    if rc != OK:
        if msglock == False:
            errcnt += 1
            if errcnt > errcntmax:
                print "ERROR: Data acquisition failed %d times" % (errcntmax + 1)
                msglock = True
    else:
        msglock = False
        errcnt  = 0

    return rc
```

The idea here is to not emit an error message unless some number of consecutive errors have occurred. When errors occur back-to-back, the variable `errcnt` will be incremented. When it reaches a threshold count, an error message will be printed, but it will only be printed once. The first nonerror return from the `Acquire()` call will reset the error count and the lockout variable, `msglock`.

It is also possible to put the error count and lockout logic into a separate function, but remember that a function or method call takes time, and if you have a need for speed it might make more sense not to try to encapsulate this functionality, but just to leave it as inline code.

Handling Inconsistent Data

When attempting to acquire data, you may occasionally run into a situation where the quantity being measured exhibits some type of instability. This often occurs with devices that need time to stabilize after power-on before they begin to provide consistent readings. In other cases, the values being measured are so small that just the inherent noise in the system can introduce significant errors into the data.

Waiting for stability

Sometimes an instrument or external device needs a period of time to stabilize before it will return valid data. If you happen to know what that time period is in advance, all you need to do, theoretically, is wait until it has elapsed before attempting to take a reading. However, if the time period is variable (perhaps due to changes in the ambient temperature of the operating environment), a deterministic timeout period cannot necessarily be relied upon.

Figure 11-12 shows how a series of measurements can be used to determine when an input is stable.

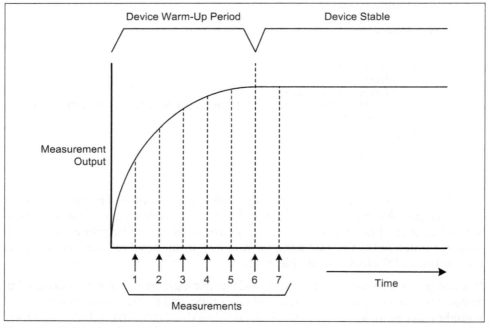

Figure 11-12. Waiting for stability

Depending on the inherent behavior of the instrument, the *delta*, or difference, between measurements may decrease as the instrument warms up, until it is close to zero. Hence, the difference between measurements 1 and 2 will be large, but it will be small (close to zero) between measurements 6 and 7. Due to noise or conversion errors, the delta may never be exactly zero.

In other cases the data may vary widely at first and then start to converge on a stable (more or less) output value, as shown in Figure 11-13. Precision solid-state laser controllers sometimes exhibit this type of behavior when attempting to measure the wavelength of the output beam. Until the controller and the laser head have both achieved an optimal operating temperature, the wavelength and the power of the beam may jump around, sometimes considerably.

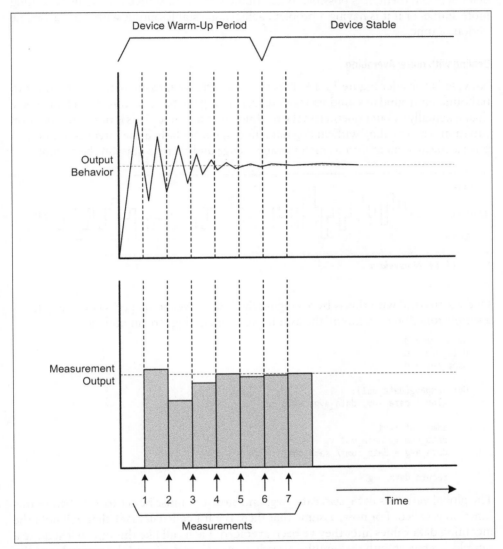

Figure 11-13. Warm-up convergence

The delta test function shown earlier (in the section "Writing data" on page 416) is a good candidate for checking warm-up stability convergence. A little additional logic could be used to set the delta match acceptance to something like two or three consecutive readings within tolerance.

The warm-up read and test approach offers a notable advantage over a simple timed wait in terms of fault detection. By taking a series of test readings and examining the delta between them, it is possible to determine if the data source is actually becoming more stable, or if it is having a problem achieving a stable output within a reasonable period of time.

Dealing with noise: Averaging

Now, let's consider Figure 11-14. This shows a series of measurements that appear to be bouncing around in a random fashion. Depending on the scale, this might look worse than it actually is, but nonetheless the readings are not stable. This is not an uncommon situation when dealing with analog data inputs, particularly if the intent is to obtain a precise measurement over a small variance range and there is noise in the system.

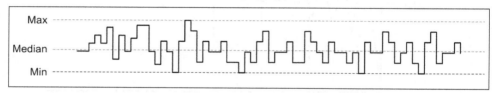

Figure 11-14. Noisy data

One way to deal with this is by averaging the inputs over some period of time. Here's a simple function to compute the average of an incoming stream of data:

```
data_sum = 0
data_avg = 0
samp_cnt = 0

def sampAvg(data_val):
    global data_sum, data_avg, samp_cnt

    samp_cnt += 1
    data_sum += data_val
    data_avg = data_sum / samp_cnt

    return data_avg
```

The global variables data_sum, data_avg, and samp_cnt must be set to zero before this function is called. For now, assume that there is a list called dataset that will hold the incoming data values after they've been averaged. Each call like this one will acquire a sample, average it with the samples already acquired, and append the new value to the list:

```
dataset.append(sampAvg(readInputData()))
```

Averaging works best with data that is changing with each input sample. Figure 11-15 shows how averaging can help smooth out data that is fluctuating very rapidly.

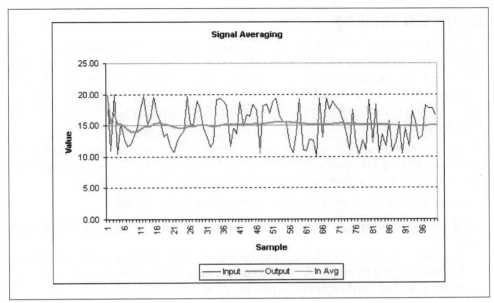

Figure 11-15. Rapidly changing averaged data

Of course, this isn't real data (to produce data this nasty, something would have to be seriously wrong), but it shows how averaging fares with this type of input.

By the way, the averaging function used in this example is not optimal; it's just there to illustrate one way of doing this. It would be better if the function calculated a continuous running average, so that there would be no need to worry about the summation variable eventually becoming a monstrous number.

Averaging can handle a lot of cases where data is changing on a small scale around a stable or very slowly changing mean, but it should be used with caution. An averaged signal that is trending either positive or negative will pull the average along with it, but if a change happens rapidly—say, a short-term variance that returns to the original level—the change will tend to be averaged out.

Summary

With the material that we've covered in this chapter, you should now have a good idea of what is involved when using an external instrument or device with Python, and the various tools that are available to help make everything work together. We've looked at serial, parallel, USB, GPIB, SCPI, and VISA interfaces, and at the basics of how one can implement an interface that is both robust and fault-tolerant. There are, of course, many deeper levels that we didn't cover, but with what we've seen so far we can move forward into some working examples using real hardware.

Suggested Reading

In terms of books, USB is probably the most popular topic. With a little digging, you might be able to turn up a book or two dealing with RS-232 or RS-485. There really isn't a whole lot available in the way of contemporary books about GPIB (or IEEE-488), but there are a lot of useful sources of information available via the Internet. Entering either "GPIB" or "IEEE-488" into Google will return numerous documents, some better than others.

Most of the books on Python that have already been referenced contain information concerning writing extensions in C or C++, and reviewing the API documentation for a particular piece of hardware is essential in order to use it effectively.

As a starting point, here are a few references you might find useful:

Real Time Programming: Neglected Topics, 4th ed. Caxton C. Foster, Addison-Wesley, 1982.
> Contains a brief but useful overview chapter on GPIB interfaces and the hardware handshaking GPIB employs. This book has long been out of print, but it is still possible to find used copies (also referenced in Chapter 9).

USB Complete: The Developer's Guide, 4th ed. Jan Axelson, Lakeview Research, 2009.
> If you want to learn more about USB, you might want to consider this book. Axelson does a good job of explaining the low-level details of USB interfaces, with a particular focus on Human Interface Device (HID) class implementation. If you want to implement your own USB interface or just learn more about USB in general, this is a good place to start.

http://www.ivifoundation.org/docs/SCPI-99.PDF
> This link points to a PDF document that contains the complete SCPI specification. It is available free of charge through the IVI Foundation.

http://www.ivifoundation.org/specifications/default.aspx
> The IVI Foundation also has the VPP-4.3 VISA library reference available at no charge. If you're going to use a VISA-compliant interface, you should have a copy of the documentation at hand.

http://joule.ni.com/nidu/cds/view/p/id/852/lang/en
> The NI-VISA 4.2 driver suite is available as an ISO file, ready to burn to CD. You can download it via this link.

The following semiconductor companies offer free application notes that cover a wide variety of topics of interest to instrumentation system implementers:

- Analog Devices, Inc. (*http://www.analog.com*)
- Maxim/Dallas Semiconductor (*http://www.maxim-ic.com/appnotes10.cfm*)
- National Semiconductor (*http://www.national.com/apnotes/*)
- Texas Instruments (*http://www.ti.com*)

## CHAPTER 12

Reading and Writing Data Files

Two people were examining the output of the new computer in their department. After an hour or so of analyzing the data, one of them remarked: "Do you realize it would take 400 people at least 250 years to make a mistake this big?"

—Anonymous

Being able to acquire data is good, but being able to save it in a file so it can be analyzed and archived is even better. Simple applications, such as an electronic thermostat, might not have an obvious need to save data, but data acquired and saved by even the simplest applications may provide valuable insight into long-term trends. In Chapter 10 we saw how to use a simulator that could save the results of a simulation into an ASCII file for later review and analysis. In this chapter we'll take a closer look at how that can be accomplished, and we'll also look at some other ways to save data.

For example, consider what you might be able to learn if the thermostat in your home could record the outside ambient temperature, the inside temperature, the set-points, the activity of the heater and air conditioner units, and the control settings. With this data you would be able to see how well your heater or air conditioner is handling temperature control, what kind of duty cycle it has, and if someone is overriding the fan on a regular basis. What it could tell you might just surprise you, especially if you could collect the data continuously for a year or two.

Data can exist in many different forms. In some cases it's just a series of numbers in the form of ASCII (character) strings. Other types of data might have information such as the time and date associated with a measurement, and some data might consist of multiple measurements and associated parameters in a structured binary format. But regardless of the format used, the whole point of saving data is to be able to readily recall it later, and hopefully do something useful with it.

"Useful" is a broad term, but for our purposes I'm going to apply the notion of usefulness to data that can be easily accessed in a variety of contexts—in other words, data that has a consistent and logical structure and contains enough auxiliary information to allow it to be associated with a particular source and time, and perhaps a location as well. ASCII data, with its text-based representation of numeric values, fits these requirements quite nicely.

Python works well with ASCII data, and that will be a primary focus in this chapter. In general, systems that don't need to deal with things like images, large numeric arrays, or complex compound data objects can use ASCII files and do just fine. But not all data can be efficiently handled as ASCII. This is particularly true if you need the ability to exchange binary data with other applications or transfer it over a network connection. The second main focus of this chapter will be on creating, saving, and reading binary data objects using only Python.

In this chapter we'll be seeing a lot of code, including several complete utility functions. By the end of this chapter we will have created a collection of reusable functions and classes that we can integrate with the simulators we saw in Chapter 10 and use later, when creating instrumentation and control software.

ASCII Data Files

Data that has been encoded to represent the characters of a natural alphabet is the *lingua franca* of computers, and has been for over 40 years. Commonly referred to as *text data*, or as *text files*, this is data that can be sent directly to a printer; displayed on a terminal; and edited, sorted, and searched with just the native capabilities of the host computer system. In order to achieve this level of cross-platform compatibility, the ASCII standard was developed and later incorporated into the UTF family of standards.

The ASCII character encoding standard is now almost 50 years old. The acronym ASCII stands for American Standard Code for Information Interchange, and it originally encoded 33 nonprintable control characters and 95 printable characters, for a total of 128 character codes. As you might surmise from this, it was also a 7-bit encoding scheme ($2^7 = 128$). When ASCII was originally defined the use of 8-bit characters was considered, but it was ultimately rejected due to data transmission costs and parity-bit considerations. Another factor was that the devices that needed to use it, such as teletype machines and paper tape reader/punch units, typically only worked with 7-bit data. For a historical perspective on the relationship of ASCII to early network communications, you might want to take a look at "RFC20—ASCII format for network interchange," written by Vint Cerf in 1969 (see the section "Suggested Reading" on page 485).

Today, the most common character encoding is UTF-8. This is an encoding scheme that preserves the original 128 ASCII characters and adds room for 128 more, plus additional bytes of data (depending on the encoding extension employed). The additional data bits and bytes are used to encode special symbolic characters, and character sets other than the English alphabet that require two or more bytes for encoding. We'll be dealing with the original 7-bit ASCII part of UTF-8, although the full UTF-8 specification is an interesting topic for exploration in its own right.

The Original ASCII Character Set

Since ASCII was originally intended for devices and applications that no longer exist today, it contains some oddities that, for the most part, you can safely ignore, such as most of the control characters. Figure 12-1 lists the nonprintable ASCII control characters. The codes for BEL, BS, LF, CR, and FF are still in common use. The rest of the codes are seldom used nowadays, but there's nothing that says you can't use them if you really want to.

Most of the control characters might seem like anachronisms, but they can have a role to play in some situations. If you are using older instruments for a project, you might find that the ACK, NAK, and perhaps EOT and ETB characters are used to synchronize communications between the instrument and whatever it is connected to. If you are designing your own system, you might also have a use for these characters. But, a word of warning: if you use nonprintable characters other than CR and LF, your interface may no longer be easily usable by a human operator using a terminal emulator (e.g., the Tera Term communications application and terminal emulator we saw in Chapter 10).

You should also bear in mind that there are differences between how lines of text are terminated in different operating systems. MS-DOS and Windows use a pair of characters, CR and LF, as the EOL (end-of-line) terminator. Unix, Linux, AIX, and other Unix-like systems use a single LF character. Older Apple products used a single CR (the BSD-based OS X uses an LF character).

The printable characters define symbols for punctuation, numerals, and both lower- and uppercase characters from the American English alphabet. Figure 12-2 lists the printable ASCII characters.

Python's ASCII Character-Handling Methods

You may have noticed that the upper- and lowercase alphabetic characters in Figure 12-2 differ from one another by a value of 32 (or 0x20 in hexadecimal). So, if you want to do a lower- to uppercase conversion, you need only check to see if a character's ASCII value is greater than or equal to 0x61 and less than or equal to 0x7A, then subtract 0x20.

Although this technique, or some variation of it, is sometimes seen in C code and is very common in assembly language programming, it isn't really necessary with Python. Built-in functions are included to do things like character to ordinal value (integer) conversion and integer to character conversion, and Python provides various string methods to handle common operations like case conversion.

Dec	Hex	Symbol	Control Character Definition
0	0	NUL	Null
1	1	SOH	Start of Heading
2	2	STX	Start of Text
3	3	ETX	End of Text
4	4	EOT	End of Transmission
5	5	ENQ	Enquiry
6	6	ACK	Acknowledge
7	7	BEL	Bell (audible or attention signal)
8	8	BS	Backspace
9	9	TAB	Horizontal Tabulation
10	A	LF	Line Feed
11	B	VT	Vertical Tabulation
12	C	FF	Form Feed
13	D	CR	Carriage Return
14	E	SO	Shift Out
15	F	SI	Shift In
16	10	DLE	Data Link Escape
17	11	DC1	Device Control 1
18	12	DC2	Device Control 2
19	13	DC3	Device Control 3
20	14	DC4	Device Control 4
21	15	NAK	Negative Acknowledge
22	16	SYN	Synchronous Idle
23	17	ETB	End of Transmission Block
24	18	CAN	Cancel
25	19	EM	End of Medium
26	1A	SUB	Substitute
27	1B	ESC	Escape
28	1C	FS	File Separator
29	1D	GS	Group Separator
30	1E	RS	Record Separator
31	1F	US	Unit Separator
127	7F	Del	Delete

Figure 12-1. ASCII control characters

For dealing with the value of ASCII characters, the chr() and ord() functions are available. Here is what the Python documentation has to say about these functions (from the Python Standard Library document, Section 2, "Built-In Functions"):

chr(*i*)

Return a string of one character whose ASCII code is the integer *i*. For example, chr(97) returns the string 'a'. This is the inverse of ord(). The argument must be in the range [0..255], inclusive; ValueError will be raised if *i* is outside that range. See also unichr().

ord(*c*)

Given a string of length one, return an integer representing the Unicode code point of the character when the argument is a unicode object, or the value of the byte when the argument is an 8-bit string. For example, ord('a') returns the integer 97, ord(u'\u2020') returns 8224. This is the inverse of chr() for 8-bit strings and of unichr() for unicode objects. If a unicode argument is given and Python was built with UCS2 Unicode, then the character's code point must be in the range [0..65535] inclusive; otherwise the string length is two, and a TypeError will be raised.

Dec	Hex	Symbol	Dec	Hex	Symbol	Dec	Hex	Symbol
32	20	(space)	65	41	A	98	62	b
33	21	!	66	42	B	99	63	c
34	22	"	67	43	C	100	64	d
35	23	#	68	44	D	101	65	e
36	24	$	69	45	E	102	66	f
37	25	%	70	46	F	103	67	g
38	26	&	71	47	G	104	68	h
39	27	'	72	48	H	105	69	i
40	28	(	73	49	I	106	6A	j
41	29	)	74	4A	J	107	6B	k
42	2A	*	75	4B	K	108	6C	l
43	2B	+	76	4C	L	109	6D	m
44	2C	,	77	4D	M	110	6E	n
45	2D	-	78	4E	N	111	6F	o
46	2E	.	79	4F	O	112	70	p
47	2F	/	80	50	P	113	71	q
48	30	0	81	51	Q	114	72	r
49	31	1	82	52	R	115	73	s
50	32	2	83	53	S	116	74	t
51	33	3	84	54	T	117	75	u
52	34	4	85	55	U	118	76	v
53	35	5	86	56	V	119	77	w
54	36	6	87	57	W	120	78	x
55	37	7	88	58	X	121	79	y
56	38	8	89	59	Y	122	7A	z
57	39	9	90	5A	Z	123	7B	{
58	3A	:	91	5B	[	124	7C		
59	3B	;	92	5C	\	125	7D	}
60	3C	<	93	5D	]	126	7E	~
61	3D	=	94	5E	^			
62	3E	>	95	5F	_			
63	3F	?	96	60	`			
64	40	@	97	61	a			

Figure 12-2. ASCII printable characters

In essence, these are byte-to-integer conversions. Since, unlike C, Python has no char type, you can't just pluck out a character from a string and expect to get a sensible 8-bit value. For example:

```
>>> foo = "ABCD"
>>> foo[0]
'A'
>>> int(foo[0])
Traceback (most recent call last):
  File "<stdin>", line 1, in <module>
ValueError: invalid literal for int() with base 10: 'A'
```

That didn't work out too well, but if we use the `ord()` function we will get the integer value of the ASCII character 'A':

```
>>> ord(foo[0])
65
```

If we want to go in the other direction, the `chr()` function is what we need to use:

```
>>> chr(65)
'A'
```

Or, in hex notation:

```
>>> chr(0x41)
'A'
```

`chr()` returns a single character string object.

Once we have a string, there are other operations available in the form of string methods. We first saw these in Chapter 3, and in this chapter we'll take a closer look at how they can be put to use for operations such as case conversion, alignment, and parsing.

Reading and Writing ASCII Flat Files

An ASCII flat file is defined as a file that is composed of one or more lines of ASCII text called *records*. Each record may consist of one or more data elements, or *fields*, each separated by one or more spaces, commas, slashes, or whatever character makes the most sense for the application. Each record is a complete data entity unto itself. The term "flat" refers to the fact that the data resides in a single file, the records represent rows and columns in a two-dimensional table, and there are no relationships between the records other than the fact that they all reside in the same file. Flat-file databases are as old as computers themselves, and they still serve an important role in a variety of applications.

Records

A record is a single line of characters, terminated by an EOL (end-of-line) character (or characters, in the case of Windows systems). Each record is organized into fields, with separators of some type between each field. In some cases the separators can be dispensed with if the fields will always be the same size, but I don't recommend this, as it makes the data difficult to read and use by a human being. Also, the use of separator characters allows the data fields to be variable-width, so long as the number of fields in a record matches the expectations of whatever is reading the data. Fixed-width fields are fine, but I believe that separators are also a very good idea.

Here is an example of a record that might be used for data acquisition:

```
0021 080728 101829 02  4.99
```

This is a columnar record that contains five fixed-width fields in each record with space characters used as separators. The fields (from left to right) are used for a sequence number, the date in YYMMDD format, the 24-hour time in HHMMSS format, the input port number, and the voltage read from the port. Although space characters are used as separators in this case, any other characters that will never, ever appear in the data fields could also be used (commas, colons, vertical bars, equals signs, and even dollar signs have all been spotted in ASCII data files). The "extra" space in front of the voltage value is reserved for a negative sign, should it be needed.

Writing dates in YYMMDD formats allows the values to be easily sorted and extracted. Using the more common DDMMYY format (or even the DD MMM YY style, where MMM is a three-letter abbreviation of the month) may be a little easier to read, but it can be awkward to sort and may require extra code to process.

Microsoft's Excel spreadsheet can handle flat ASCII data files using either fixed-width fields or user-specified separators (it knows how to deal with a CSV file, which we'll look at shortly, without any need for the user to intervene). Here's a subset of data collected from a hypothetical instrumentation system:

```
0000 080728 101808 02  4.78
0001 080728 101809 02  4.82
0002 080728 101810 02  4.80
0003 080728 101811 02  4.84
0004 080728 101812 02  4.86
0005 080728 101813 02  4.83
0006 080728 101814 02  4.86
0007 080728 101815 02  4.87
0008 080728 101816 02  4.85
0009 080728 101817 02  4.88
0010 080728 101818 02  4.89
0011 080728 101819 02  4.90
0012 080728 101820 02  4.91
0013 080728 101821 02  4.90
0014 080728 101822 02  4.91
0015 080728 101823 02  4.92
0016 080728 101824 02  4.94
0017 080728 101825 02  4.95
0018 080728 101826 02  4.97
0019 080728 101827 02  4.96
0020 080728 101828 02  4.98
0021 080728 101829 02  4.99
0022 080728 101830 02  4.98
0023 080728 101831 02  5.00
0024 080728 101832 02  5.01
0025 080728 101833 02  5.03
0026 080728 101834 02  5.04
0027 080728 101835 02  5.02
0028 080728 101836 02  5.05
0029 080728 101837 02  5.06
0030 080728 101838 02  5.08
```

We can see that the input activity started at 10:18:08 a.m. on the 28th of July, 2008, and the data covers a 30-minute time period. Figure 12-3 shows the graph generated by the input voltage data. The graph was created by using Excel to import the data and then plot it as a simple line graph.

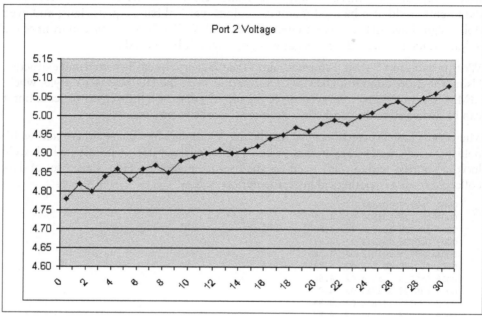

Figure 12-3. Sample input data plot

Writing ASCII data files

Saving ASCII data in Python is simply a matter of formatting the data into a string and then writing it to the file. First, we open a file to receive the data:

```
fout = open("datafile.txt", "a")
```

A couple of observations about this are in order. First, the filename is hardcoded here, which is probably not something you will always want to do. It would be better if it was a string variable defined elsewhere, as was done in the I/O device simulator in Chapter 10. Secondly, there's no way to tell if the open call succeeded.

We can add these missing features and get the following:

```
dataname = "datafile.txt"
datamode = "a"

try:
    fout = open(dataname, datamode)
except Exception, e:
    print "Output file open error: %s" % str(e)
```

There are, of course, other ways to do this, but this is fine for our present purposes.

Once the file is open, we can write data to it. I'll assume that Python's `time` and `datetime` library modules have already been imported so we can generate the timestamp data:

```
# get current date and time from the system
t = datetime.datetime.now()
currdatetime = t.timetuple()
currutime = time.mktime(t.timetuple())
yr = str(currdatetime[0])
curr_date = "%02d"%int(yr[2:]) + "%02d"%currdatetime[1] + "%02d"%currdatetime[2]
curr_time = "%02d:"%currdatetime[3] + "%02d:"%currdatetime[4] + "%02d"%currdatetime[5]
tstamp = curr_date + " " + curr_time
```

`tstamp` is a string that contains the year in YYMMDD format and the current time in HHMMSS format, with a space character in between. Lastly, we format the data to look like the sample data we just saw and then write the line to the output file:

```
outstr = "%d %s %d %4.2f" % (seq_num, tstamp, port_num, dataval)
fout.write(outstr+"\n")
```

In this example the variables `seq_num`, `port_num`, and `dataval` would be supplied from elsewhere.

Note that the `write()` method of a file object does not automatically append an EOL, so it must be explicitly added with a \n escape character.

There's another way to write the data (there's almost always another way with Python) that uses the `print` statement and doesn't require the EOL character (`print` supplies it for us, in this case):

```
print outstr >> fout
```

You would most likely want to put the timestamp and output code into a function or method that could then be called whenever your application needs to write data to the output file.

Reading ASCII data files

Reading data from an ASCII file is about as straightforward as writing it. Python provides some very useful methods for dealing with strings, including the ability to parse a string into its component parts based on a specific delimiter character.

Let's assume that we want to read the contents of an ASCII data file that look like this:

```
0.000    0.000    0.000    0.000
0.000    0.000    0.000    0.000
0.000    0.000    0.000    0.000
1.000    0.000    0.000    0.000
1.000    1.085    1.000    1.250
1.000    0.839   -0.085   -0.106
1.000    0.908    0.161    0.201
1.000    0.900    0.092    0.116
```

```
1.000    0.909    0.100    0.125
1.000    0.914    0.091    0.113
1.000    0.919    0.086    0.108
1.000    0.923    0.081    0.101
1.000    0.927    0.077    0.096
1.000    0.930    0.073    0.091
1.000    0.934    0.070    0.087
1.000    0.936    0.066    0.083
1.000    0.939    0.064    0.079
1.000    0.941    0.061    0.076
1.000    0.944    0.059    0.073
1.000    0.946    0.056    0.070
1.000    0.948    0.054    0.068
1.000    0.950    0.052    0.065
```

We can use something like the following code snippet to read each line from a columnar-format ASCII data file and print each field. Granted, it's not particularly useful as it stands, but it does help to illustrate some key points:

```
fin = open('testdata.dat', 'r')
for line in fin:
    lineparts = line.split()
    for i in range(0, len(lineparts)-1):
        print lineparts[i],
        print " ",
    print lineparts[i + 1]
```

There are a couple of things to notice about this little bit of code. First, it doesn't matter how many columns the file has, just so long as there are one or more whitespace characters between each field. Second, the data is printed out as lines organized into columns by using a comma at the end of the print statement in the for loop to suppress the newline character, except for the last print, which does generate a newline character. That's why the for loop stops one field short of the last field in a line. Here's what the output looks like:

```
0.000    0.000    0.000    0.000
0.000    0.000    0.000    0.000
0.000    0.000    0.000    0.000
1.000    0.000    0.000    0.000
1.000    1.085    1.000    1.250
1.000    0.839   -0.085   -0.106
1.000    0.908    0.161    0.201
1.000    0.900    0.092    0.116
1.000    0.909    0.100    0.125
1.000    0.914    0.091    0.113
1.000    0.919    0.086    0.108
1.000    0.923    0.081    0.101
1.000    0.927    0.077    0.096
1.000    0.930    0.073    0.091
1.000    0.934    0.070    0.087
1.000    0.936    0.066    0.083
1.000    0.939    0.064    0.079
1.000    0.941    0.061    0.076
1.000    0.944    0.059    0.073
```

```
1.000    0.946    0.056    0.070
1.000    0.948    0.054    0.068
1.000    0.950    0.052    0.065
```

Based on what we've already seen, we can make a general-purpose ASCII columnar data file reader to extract specific columns of data values. With a tool like this, we could easily pipe its output to another tool (perhaps to plot it), or save it in a temporary file for use later. On a Linux system you may need to change the first line to point to where your Python interpreter resides if it's not in *usr/bin*:

```python
#! /usr/bin/python
#==================================================================
# readascii
#
# A simple utility to extract data from an ASCII file containing
# columnar data.
#
# Includes the ability to extract a specific column or range of
# columns. Can also skip over an arbitary number of non-columnar
# header lines. Output is printed to stdout.
#==================================================================
import sys
import getopt

startcol = 0     # default start is column zero (first)
colspan  = -1    # default span is all columns
hdrskip  = 0     # default header line skip is zero (no header lines)
fname    = ''    # Empty string as default input file name

def usage():
    print "Usage: readascii [options] file_name"
    print "        Options:"
    print "            -c  Start column (default is zero)"
    print "            -s  Column span (default is all columns"
    print "            -h  # of header lines to skip (default is zero)"
    sys.exit(1)

# get command-line arguments
if len(sys.argv) > 1:
    try:
        clopts, clargs = getopt.getopt(sys.argv[1:], ':c:s:h:')
    except getopt.GetoptError, err:
        print str(err)
        sys.exit(2)
    #endtry

    for opt, arg in clopts:
        if opt == "-c":
            startcol = int(arg)
        elif opt == "-s":
            colspan = int(arg)
        elif opt == "-h":
            hdrskip = int(arg)
        else:
            print "Unrecognized option"
```

```
            usage()
    if len(clargs) > 0:
        fname = clargs[0]
else:
    usage()

# attempt to open input file
try:
    fin = open(fname, 'r')
except Exception, err:
    print "Error: %s" % str(err)
    sys.exit(2)

# see if header needs to be skipped
if hdrskip > 0:
    for i in range(0, hdrskip):
        fin.readline()

# read, parse, and output the designated fields from the input file
for line in fin:
    lineparts = line.split()
    if colspan == -1:
        colspan = len(lineparts)
    for i in range(startcol, (startcol + colspan)):
        print lineparts[i],
        print " ",
    print ""
```

To use this utility under Windows, simply invoke it from the shell command line like so:

```
python readascii.py datafile.dat -c1 -s1 -h3
```

Under Linux, just type the script name (the script file needs to be marked as executable). Either method will launch Python, which then loads and executes readascii.py using the input file *datafile.dat*. The options specify that the tool should extract just the second column (the column numbering starts at zero, by the way) and skip over three header lines at the top of the input data file.

CSV files

A CSV (comma-separated values) file is a type of flat file that has become more or less a standard way to exchange data between various application programs. CSV has been around for a long time, even before the advent of personal computers. Most spreadsheet applications support CSV, and Python even has a set of methods in its standard library for handling CSV data provided by the csv library module.

Unfortunately, there is no "standard" for CSV files. Instead, there are multiple variations on the CSV theme, referred to as "dialects." Microsoft's Excel is one example of a particular dialect of CSV. RFC 4810, "Common Format and MIME Type for Comma-Separated Values (CSV) Files" (see the section "Suggested Reading" on page 485), defines a recommended standard for CSV files. PEP 305 defines the API for Python's standard CSV module, which has the ability to support various dialects of CSV. Additional information on the CSV format can be found on Wikipedia.

If you only need a simple CSV to export data into something like Excel, and you're not concerned about headers, field names, and such, you can easily create a data file using the string formatting techniques we've already examined in this chapter. However, if you need something fancier, you should take a look at Python's CSV capabilities.

Python's `csv` library comes with two preregistered dialects: *excel-tab* and *excel*. You can define and register a new dialect by using the `csv.register_dialect()` method. The `csv` module supports things like quoted strings and empty columns, and its main benefit is that it takes care of a lot of little details for you. If you don't need this level of control, though, there's nothing wrong with just doing it yourself.

Configuration Data

Configuration data files are a common and convenient way to collect application control parameters into one place. On the Windows platform they are usually called "INI" files and are still in use by various applications, although Microsoft has been actively encouraging developers to abandon them in favor of the Windows Registry scheme. The configuration data files on a Windows system usually have a *.ini* extension (hence the name "INI"). On Unix-type systems configuration data files are often referred to as "config" files and can have any extension, although the most commonly encountered are **.conf* and **.rc*. I'll use the term "config file" from here on out to mean both types.

A config file is an ASCII flat-file database with only two fields per record, in what is called a key/value pair (KVP) organization. The separator on Windows systems is usually the equals sign (=). On Linux systems the configuration files for various applications might use a colon instead.

Although often treated as an afterthought, or created ad hoc as the code is hacked into existence, an application's configuration parameters play a big role in how well it can be tested, tuned, and maintained. Overly large config files can make life difficult when it doesn't need to be, and can lead to crashes or strange behavior. Take a moment and plan how your config files will be utilized up front: set some initial guidelines for size, context, and content type, and then stick to them. You'll be glad you did.

Basic configuration file organization

Simply put, a config file contains one or more key/value pairs, one pair per line record, usually separated with an equals sign or perhaps a colon. Here's an example from an INI file in my *C:\Windows* directory:

```
[Window]
Xpos=0
Xright=640
Ypos=0
Ybottom=1024
```

```
[Font]
Height=10
Weight=400
Italic=0
CharSet=0
Pitch=49
Name=Times New Roman
```

and here are a few lines from one of the *.conf* files on my Linux machine that utilizes colons as separators:

```
wordlist_extend: true
minimum_word_length: 1
maximum_word_length: 25
wordlist_cache_size: 10485760
wordlist_page_size: 32768
wordlist_compress: 0
wordlist_wordrecord_description: NONE
```

Config files can contain other features as well, such as section headers, comments, and so on. Note that not all platforms and library packages support all of the possible variations. To find out more about how Python supports config files, check out this section of the Python documentation: *http://docs.python.org/library/configparser .html*. Wikipedia also has a nice write-up on the subject, which can be found at *http:// en.wikipedia.org/wiki/INI_file*.

Using configuration files

Over time, I've learned that there are some good ways to use config files, and some bad ways. Here is a collection of guidelines that I employ in my work and that you might find useful as well. They are rather Python-centric (since that's what I'm using a lot these days), but they also apply to other languages:

1. Multiple small config files are better than one big file.

    Small files are easier to manage from within the code. Changing the behavior of a particular subsystem requires only that its (hopefully small) config be changed, not an entire monster config file.

    Small files are also easier to document and easier to comprehend, which makes it easier for the user to edit them manually if necessary.

    Small files are less risky to modify from within the code. Small files isolate potential configuration file errors and prevent catastrophic errors from spreading across a large number of parameters. Case in point: when modifying a value in a config file corrupts everything past the point where the value was modified because there was a system glitch while the file was open for writing.

2. Avoid the Windows Registry (if you can).

    Try not to use the Windows Registry to store configuration data if you think there's even the slimmest chance that the code will ever get ported to a different platform someday, or if a user may need to be able to easily inspect or modify the data manually. If there's even a shred of doubt, use text-based INI-type files instead. This will help to ensure easier portability across multiple platforms, and an easier time for the user.

3. Use simple strings for keys and values.

   If a value cannot be represented easily as a simple string, it probably doesn't belong in a config file. In other words, if the code can't figure out if the value part of the KVP is supposed to be a single integer; a float; a long; a string; or, in Python, a tuple, list, or dictionary object, it should probably be in a custom format data file. Python provides the pickling mechanism for serializing objects, and there are other options for binary data available, which we will look at later in this chapter.

4. Pair related data elements.

   When a parameter requires additional information, such as a unit of measurement, use a Python tuple or store the unit value as a separate parameter in the config file. For example, as a Python tuple:

   ```
   output_lambda:          (687, nm)
   ```

   or as separate parameters:

   ```
   output_lambda:          687
   output_lambda_units:    nm
   ```

   Do not store the value as:

   ```
   output_lambda:          687 nm
   ```

   A Python utility such as an autoconvertor (discussed in the next section) can easily handle all of the standard Python types, but it won't handle a value like "687 nm". For that you'll need to write your own custom parser, and personally I'd rather spend my time doing something else. Using separate parameters for values and units can make things easier to process in any language.

5. Don't overload the config file.

   Store data that is more properly represented in binary in a binary file. In other words, it's not a good idea to convert a 2D image (even a really small one) into a 2D array of values in ASCII just so it can be stored in a config file. Don't snicker, I've seen this done.

Module AutoConvert.py—Automatic String Conversion

The following utility function will take a string representation of a valid Python data type and attempt to convert it to an actual data object. It was originally created to handle value strings (the V in KVP) from a config file, but it will also process just about anything you might care to throw at it (with a few exceptions—see the comments in the code). If the input is already a nonstring type, it will simply be passed through as is.

Here is the source code for AutoConvert.py:

```python
def AutoConvert(input):
    """ Attempts to identify and convert any type of input to a standard
    Python type.

    Useful for dealing with values stored in a configuration data
    file (i.e., an 'ini' file) where the values read from the KV pairs
    are always in string format.

    Returns the converted value (or just the input value, if no
    conversion took place) along with the data type as a 2-tuple.
    Always returns valid data, even if it's just a copy of the
    original input. Never returns None.

    Note that Boolean value characters ('t', 'T', 'TRUE', etc.) are
    converted to 0 or 1. They are not returned as Boolean values using
    Python's True or False values. This can be changed easily enough
    if you really want Boolean values as the output.
    """
    if type(input) == str:
        if input.isalpha():
            # convert T and F characters to 1 and 0
            if len(input) == 1 and input.upper() == 'T':
                ret_val = 1
            elif len(input) == 1 and input.upper() == 'F':
                ret_val = 0
            else:
                if input.upper() == "TRUE":
                    ret_val = 1
                elif input.upper() == "FALSE":
                    ret_val = 0
                else:
                    ret_val = input
                #endif
            #endif
        elif input.isdigit():
            # integer in string form, convert it
            ret_val = int(input)
        elif input.isalnum():
            # mixed character string, just pass it on
            ret_val = input
        else:
            # see if string is a float value, or something else
            try:
                ret_val = float(input)
            except:
                # No, so see if it's a tuple, list or dictionary. The code
                # below will exclude most attempts to invoke internal
                # functions or built-in methods masquerading as parameter
                # values.
                try:
                    ret_val = eval(input, {"__builtins__":{}}, {})
                except:
                    # eval choked, so just pass it on
                    ret_val = input
```

```
        #endif
    else:
        # We'll assume that input is a valid type not captured in a string.
        # This might be problematic, since a value from a conventional
        # *.ini file should be a string.
        ret_val = input
    #endif

    ret_type = type(ret_val)

    return ret_val, ret_type


if __name__ == "__main__":
    print "%s  %s" % AutoConvert("T")
    print "%s  %s" % AutoConvert("F")
    print "%s  %s" % AutoConvert("t")
    print "%s  %s" % AutoConvert("f")
    print "%s  %s" % AutoConvert("[0, 4, 1, 8]")
    print "%s  %s" % AutoConvert("5.5")
    print "%s  %s" % AutoConvert("-2")
    print "%s  %s" % AutoConvert("42")
    print "%s  %s" % AutoConvert("Spam, spam, spam")
    print "%s  %s" % AutoConvert("(1, 2, 3)")
    print "%s  %s" % AutoConvert("{1: 'fee', 2: 'fie', 3: 'foe'}")
    print "%s  %s" % AutoConvert(1)
    print "%s  %s" % AutoConvert(99.98)
    print "%s  %s" % AutoConvert([1, 2,])
    print "%s  %s" % AutoConvert((9, 8, 7))
```

When you run AutoConvert.py like so:

python AutoConvert.py

you should get the following output:

```
1  <type 'int'>
0  <type 'int'>
1  <type 'int'>
0  <type 'int'>
[0, 4, 1, 8]  <type 'list'>
5.5  <type 'float'>
-2.0  <type 'float'>
42  <type 'int'>
Spam, spam, spam  <type 'str'>
(1, 2, 3)  <type 'tuple'>
{1: 'fee', 2: 'fie', 3: 'foe'}  <type 'dict'>
1  <type 'int'>
99.98  <type 'float'>
[1, 2]  <type 'list'>
(9, 8, 8)  <type 'tuple'>
```

For the most part, AutoConvert.py does a pretty good job of figuring out what the input is supposed to be and then doing the right thing with it.

One thing I'd like to point out is the use of the eval() method, which in Auto Convert.py is coded like this:

```
ret_val = eval(input, {"__builtins__":{}}, {})
```

Normally eval() isn't something to take lightly. It is considered a security risk, because it will execute any valid Python statement. In order to deal with this I've written it such that it will not execute built-in functions or methods, and it will not be able to access local names. eval() is a powerful feature, but be careful with it.

Module FileUtils.py—ASCII Data File I/O Utilities

Next we'll look at a utility module for reading and writing ASCII data files using fixed format definitions. The library module FileUtils.py defines two classes for reading and writing ASCII data records using text files: ASCIIDataWrite and ASCIIDataRead. In FileUtils.py, we can see working examples of the topics we have been discussing. It can also serve as a framework for you to build upon by adding your own functionality.

I chose to implement these utilities as classes instead of functions primarily because an object maintains its own internal variables (also called attributes), and each instance object of the class is associated with a particular file. In essence, the objects wrap the file in a set of functions that handle formatting, error checking, and, of course, reading and writing. This allows for multiple self-contained instances of each class to be created for different purposes without worrying about conflicts over shared global variables or file access issues.

Each class provides methods for opening, closing, and either reading data from or writing data to an ASCII file:

```
class  ASCIIDataWrite()
    openOutput(self, path, file_name, reset_file=False)
    closeOutput(self)
    writeData(self, dataval, use_sn=False, use_ts=False)

class  ASCIIDataRead()
    openInput(self, path, file_name)
    closeInput(self)
    readDataRecord(self)
    readDataFields(self)
```

The module also contains a shared function to handle closing a file object:

```
closeFile(file_id)
```

The data is in the form of single-line records with one of four specific formats, as shown in Table 12-1.

Table 12-1. ASCIIData formats

Number of fields	Format
4	[sequence number] [date] [time] [data]

Number of fields	Format
3	[date] [time] [data]
2	[sequence number] [data]
1	[data]

With this scheme it is possible to know what fields a record contains simply by counting the number of fields in the record. The order will always be as shown in Table 12-1. (Note that the timestamp is actually two fields: [date] and [time].) For example, records with either two or four fields will contain a sequence number. Records with only three fields will contain the timestamp fields, but no sequence number. All record formats contain the [data] field, and it is always written to a file as the string representation of a floating-point value. In other words, integers will be written with the fractional part set to zero.

The ASCIIDataRead class methods are described in Table 12-2, and Table 12-3 shows the ASCIIDataWrite class methods.

Table 12-2. ASCIIDataRead class methods

Method	Description
closeInput (self)	Closes an already opened input file. If file is not already open, an error is returned. Calls the module function closeFile() to do the actual file close.
openInput(self , path, file_name)	Opens a file for ASCII data input. If path is not specified (an empty string is given as the path), the function will attempt to open the named file in the current execution directory.
readDataFields (self)	Reads fields from a record in an ASCII data file, one record at a time, and returns each record as a list object with one list element per field. An EOF returns an empty list. The data for each field is converted from strings to the appropriate data type based on the number of fields in the record. Returns a 2-tuple consisting of a return code and the field's list object.
readDataRecord (self)	Reads a complete record string one record at a time and returns the entire record string as-is from the file. An EOF returns an empty record string. Returns a 2-tuple consisting of a return code and the record string.

Table 12-3. ASCIIDataWrite class methods

Method	Description
closeOutput(self)	Closes an already opened output file. If file is not open, an error is returned.
openOutput(self, path, file_name, reset_file=False)	Opens a file for ASCII data output. If path is not specified (an empty string is given as the path), the file will be opened in the current execution directory. If the reset_file parameter is False, the file will be opened in append mode. If True, the file will be opened in write mode and any existing data will be deleted if the file already exists.
writeData(self, dataval, use_sn=False, use_ts=False)	Generates a string containing a data value in ASCII. If use_sn is False, a sequence number will not be inserted into the record string. Otherwise, the object will maintain a sequence count and prepend this to the data record string. If use_ts is False, no timestamp is applied. Otherwise, a timestamp will be obtained and applied to the output string.

Figure 12-4 shows how the objects defined by `ASCIIDataRead` and `ASCIIDataWrite` can be used to access the contents of ASCII files. In this case the diagram illustrates a situation where an input file (file 1) contains data that is used to stimulate a system—say, values that are converted into analog output voltages. The response data is captured and stored in file 2 and file 3 by `ASCIIDataWrite` objects.

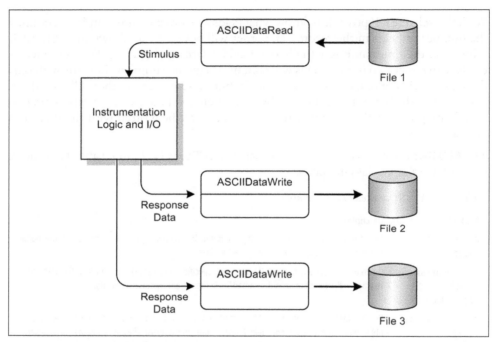

Figure 12-4. Accessing data files using ASCIIData classes

Here is the source code for `FileUtils.py`:

```
#! /usr/bin/python

""" ASCII Data File R/W Utility Classes.

Defines two classes for reading and writing ASCII data records
using text files.

The methods in this module support opening, closing, reading,
and writing ASCII data in the form of single-line records. The
class ASCIIDataWrite handles data record writing, and
ASCIIDataRead handles the reading chores. The instantiated
objects maintain their own file object references, and more
than one instance of either class may be active at any one
time.

There are four record formats available, as follows:
```

```
4 fields:    [sequence number] [date] [time] [data]
3 fields:    [date] [time] [data]
2 fields:    [sequence number] [data]
1 field:     [data]
```

Note that the timestamp is actually two fields: [data] and
[time]. Records with either 2 or 4 fields will contain a
sequence number. Records with only 3 fields will contain the
timestamp fields, but no sequence number. All record formats
contain the data field, and all fields are written as strings.

The [data] field is always written to a file as the string
representation of a floating-point value. In other words,
integers will be written with the fractional part set to zero.
"""

import os

import TimeUtils   # time and data utilities
import RetCodes   as RC   # shared return code definitions

class ASCIIDataWrite:
    """ Methods for writing ASCII data records to a file.

        Defines an object for writing ASCII data records to a
        standard "text file". Each object is unique, and more than
        one object may be in use at any one time.
    """
    def __init__(self):
        self.seq_num = 0
        self.file_ref = None

    def openOutput(self, path, file_name, reset_file=False):
        """ Opens a file for ASCII data output.

            If path is not specified (an empty string is given as
            the path), the file will be opened in the current
            execution directory.

            If the reset_file parameter is False, file will be
            opened in append mode. If True, file will be opened
            in write mode and any existing data will be deleted if
            the file already exists.
        """
        rc = RC.NO_ERR

        if len(file_name) > 0:
            # create the fully qualified path name
            file_path = os.path.join(path, file_name)

            if reset_file:
                fmode = "w"
            else:
```
```

```
            fmode = "a"

        try:
            self.file_ref = open(file_path, fmode)
        except Exception, e:
            rc = RC.OPEN_ERR
            print "%s" % str(e)
    else:
        rc = RC.NO_NAME

    return rc


def closeOutput(self):
    """ Closes an already opened output file.

        If file is not open, an error is returned.
    """
    rc = RC.NO_ERR

    if self.file_ref and self.file_ref != None:
        rc = closeFile(self.file_ref)
    else:
        rc = RC.NO_FILE

    return rc


def writeData(self, dataval, use_sn=False, use_ts=False):
    """ Generates a string containing a data value in ASCII.

        If use_sn is False, a sequence number will not be
        inserted into the record string. Otherwise, the object
        will maintain a sequence count and prepend this to the
        data record string. If use_ts is False, no timestamp is
        applied. Otherwise, a timestamp will be obtained and
        applied to the output string.
    """
    rc = RC.NO_ERR

    if use_sn:
        # need to init the sequence number?
        if self.seq_num == 0:
            self.seq_num = 1
        sn = "%02d " % self.seq_num
        self.seq_num += 1
    else:
        sn = ""

    if use_ts:
        ts = TimeUtils.getTS() + " "
    else:
        ts = ""

    hdr = sn + ts
```

```
        # if self.file_ref is None then a file has not yet been
        # opened for this instance
        if self.file_ref == None:
            rc = RC.NO_FILE

        # do not proceed if errors encountered
        if rc == RC.NO_ERR:
            try:
                dstr = " %f" % float(dataval)
            except Exception, e:
                rc = RC.INV_DATA
                print "%s" % str(e)

            if rc == RC.NO_ERR:
                outstr = hdr + dstr + "\n"

                try:
                    self.file_ref.write(outstr)
                except Exception, e:
                    rc = RC.WRITE_ERR
                    print "%s" % str(e)

        return rc


class ASCIIDataRead:
    """ Defines an object for reading ASCII data records from a
        standard text file. Each object is unique, and more than
        one object may be in use at any one time.
    """
    def __init__(self):
        self.file_ref  = None


    def openInput(self, path, file_name):
        """ Opens a file for ASCII data input.

            If path is not specified (an empty string is given as
            the path), the function will attempt to open the
            named file in the current execution directory.
        """
        rc = RC.NO_ERR

        # create the fully qualified path name
        file_path = os.path.join(path, file_name)

        try:
            self.file_ref = open(file_path, "r")
        except Exception, e:
            rc = RC.OPEN_ERR
            self.file_ref = None

        return rc
```

```python
def closeInput(self):
    """ Closes an already opened input file.

        If file is not already open, an error is returned.

        Calls the module function closeFile() to do the actual
        close.
    """
    rc = RC.NO_ERR

    if self.file_ref and self.file_ref != None:
        rc = closeFile(self.file_ref)
    else:
        rc = RC.NO_FILE

    return rc


def readDataRecord(self):
    """ Reads a complete record string and returns it as-is.

        Reads one record at a time and returns the entire record
        string as-is from the file. An EOF returns an empty
        record string.

        Returns a 2-tuple consisting of a return code and the
        record string.
    """
    rc = RC.NO_ERR

    # verify that there is a valid file to read from
    if self.file_ref != None:
        # fetch a line from the file
        try:
            record = self.file_ref.readline()
        except Exception, e:
            record = ""
            rc = RC.READ_ERR
    else:
        record = ""
        rc = RC.NO_FILE

    return rc, record


def readDataFields(self):
    """ Reads fields from a record in an ASCII data file.

        Reads one record at a time, and returns each record
        as a list object with one list element per field. An
        EOF returns an empty list.

        The data for each field is converted from strings to
        the appropriate data type based on the number of fields
```

```
            in the record.

            Returns a 2-tuple consisting of a return code and the
            field's list object.
        """
        rc = RC.NO_ERR
        readflds = []
        retflds = []

        # fetch record string from file
        rc, recstr = self.readDataRecord()

        # split record into component elements
        if rc == RC.NO_ERR:
            if len(recstr) > 0:
                readflds = recstr.split()

                # Use a try-catch in case data is an invalid type
                # for given conversion to int or float.
                try:
                    if len(readflds) == 4:
                        retflds.append(int(readflds[0]))
                        retflds.append(int(readflds[1]))
                        retflds.append(readflds[2])
                        retflds.append(float(readflds[3]))
                    elif len(readflds) == 3:
                        retflds.append(int(readflds[0]))
                        retflds.append(readflds[1])
                        retflds.append(float(readflds[2]))
                    elif len(readflds) == 2:
                        retflds.append(int(readflds[0]))
                        retflds.append(float(readflds[1]))
                    elif len(readflds) == 1:
                        retflds.append(float(readflds[0]))
                    else:
                        rc = RC.INV_FORMAT
                except Exception, e:
                    print str(e)
                    retflds = []
                    rc = RC.INV_DATA
            else:
                rc = RC.NO_DATA

        return rc, retflds


    def getData(self):
        """ Returns just the data portion of a record.

            Returns a 2-tuple consisting of the return code and the
            data value.

            A record should always have a data field. This method
            returns just the data field, and nothing else, as a
            floating point value. If the data field does not exist
```

```
                    or if an error occurs retrieving a record, then it will
                    return None.
        """
        retdata = None

        rc, infields = self.readDataFields()
        if rc == RC.NO_ERR:
            # assume that readDataFields() has done its job correctly
            # and we have a valid number of fields to work with.
            if len(infields) == 4:
                retdata = float(infields[3])
            elif len(infields) == 3:
                retdata = float(infields[2])
            elif len(infields) == 2:
                retdata = float(infields[1])
            elif len(infields) == 1:
                retdata = float(infields[0])
        return rc, retdata


# Module functions

def closeFile(file_id):
    """ Close an already opened input or output file.

        file_id is a reference to a Python file object.
    """
    rc = RC.NO_ERR

    try:
        file_id.close()
    except Exception, e:
        rc = RC.INV_FILE
        print "%s" % str(e)

    return rc


if __name__ == "__main__":
    fout = ASCIIDataWrite()

    fin  = ASCIIDataRead()

    fout.openOutput(".\\", "futest.dat")

    fout.writeData(2.5, use_ts=True)
    fout.writeData(2.6, use_ts=True)
    fout.writeData(2.7, use_ts=True)
    fout.writeData(2.8, use_ts=True)
    fout.writeData(2.9, use_ts=True)
    fout.writeData(3.0, use_ts=True)

    fout.closeOutput()

    fin.openInput(".\\","futest.dat")
```

```
print "Read Records"
print "%d %s" % fin.readDataRecord(),
print "%d %s" % fin.readDataRecord(),
print "%d %s" % fin.readDataRecord(),
print "%d %s" % fin.readDataRecord(),
print "%d %s" % fin.readDataRecord(),
print "%d %s" % fin.readDataRecord(),

fin.closeInput()

fin.openInput(".\\","futest.dat")

print "Read Fields"
print "%d %s" % fin.readDataFields()
print "%d %s" % fin.readDataFields()
print "%d %s" % fin.readDataFields()
print "%d %s" % fin.readDataFields()
print "%d %s" % fin.readDataFields()
print "%d %s" % fin.readDataFields()

fin.closeInput()
```

When FileUtils.py is executed from the shell command line, you will see the following output:

```
$ python FileUtils.py
Read Records
0 100906 17:06:21  2.500000
0 100906 17:06:21  2.600000
0 100906 17:06:21  2.700000
0 100906 17:06:21  2.800000
0 100906 17:06:21  2.900000
0 100906 17:06:21  3.000000
Read Fields
0 [100906, '17:06:21', 2.5]
0 [100906, '17:06:21', 2.6000000000000001]
0 [100906, '17:06:21', 2.7000000000000002]
0 [100906, '17:06:21', 2.7999999999999998]
0 [100906, '17:06:21', 2.8999999999999999]
0 [100906, '17:06:21', 3.0]
```

Some functionality that would be nice to have (but not absolutely essential) would be the ability to "rewind" an input file instead of closing and then reopening it in order to access the first record at the start of the file. It might also be handy to be able to pull out a particular record, perhaps by position (the *n*th record), by sequence number, or by time or date range. Well, there's something interesting to do if you feel so inclined.

Binary Data Files

A binary file is typically much more compact than an ASCII file for raw data storage. The reason is simply that an unsigned 16-bit value in ASCII might look like 48373, which takes up five characters, but in binary it requires only two bytes of storage, which in hexadecimal would be written as BC F5. A file with 16K (2^{14} entries) worth of unique data values in ASCII could end up being 81,920 (82K) bytes in size (assuming each value is five characters), but in binary form it will always be 32K (two bytes per value).

The downside to binary files is that they really must be read via software intended for that purpose. A binary file can be opened in a binary file editor, but editing one is both tedious and error-prone. It's much better to read it with software that inherently "knows" the structure of the file and can efficiently extract the data from it.

Binary data files are the preferred format for things like image data, large numeric arrays, and structured data that might contain either pure binary values or a mix of binary and ASCII. A compressed data file is an example of a binary file that is composed of structured binary data.

Flat Binary Data Files

Just like a flat ASCII file, a flat binary file consists of one or more records. Each record may be fixed-length, or, with a little extra work, they can be variable-length.

For example, what if you wanted to pass data to another program using a binary file, and that program expects records with an internal structure in the file that will map directly to a C or C++ structure data type? In order to get this into a transportable binary form you will need to take the values from a Python program, load them into one or more structures, and then write the structures out to a file.

Here's a simple C structure:

```
typedef struct {
    int     seq_num;
    int     chan;
    int     mode;
    double  data_val;
    char    stat_codes[3];
    } input_data;
```

In a C application the most intuitive way to store data in binary format would be to write out structures like this directly to a file, with each structure a unique record. Typically one would also want some kind of header data in the file that, at the very least, contains the total number of structures present. Figure 12-5 shows how the data might be organized in a file that uses the structure we've just defined.

Don't worry too much about what the header fields in Figure 12-5 mean; the important thing to take away here is that there is a header section (or block, as it is sometimes called), and it contains a count of the number of data structures we can expect to find in the file. Each subsequent block following the header contains a complete data structure in binary form.

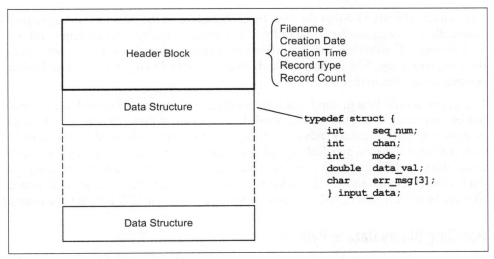

Figure 12-5. Example binary data file structure

This brings us to the subject of padding. Computers have a preferred memory data size, which is based on the size of the internal registers and how the memory addressing is handled. For example, a 32-bit CPU will most likely have a preferred memory data size of 32 bits, which means that moving data to and from memory in 32-bit chunks is the most efficient way to get data into and out of the CPU. Many 32-bit CPUs can also handle 16-bit words without much extra effort, but if the data is 8 bits, the CPU will need to do some extra work to accommodate it. In the interests of efficiency, it is a good idea to pad out a structure so that things line up evenly on 32- or 16-bit boundaries.

In Figure 12-6 we can see how the structure shown in Figure 12-5 maps into memory space. Notice that two pads (the shaded areas) are employed; the first pads out the last of the three of the 16-bit integer variables to produce an even 32-bit space. Although this probably isn't necessary, it does prevent the 8-byte double-precision value that follows from hanging across 32-bit boundaries, which is not a particularly good thing.

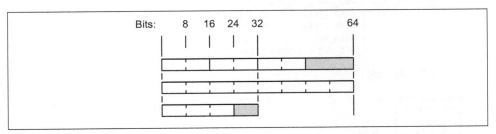

Figure 12-6. Structure padding

Also notice in Figure 12-6 that the three bytes that make up the `stat_codes` array (which is actually a three-character string in Python) have an extra byte of padding to fill out a 32-bit word. Fortunately, most compilers are capable of applying the necessary padding automatically. The Python methods that deal with binary data can also handle padding issues internally.

Lastly, you should bear in mind that a binary data file that uses structured records may not be very flexible. In other words, what data types are stored in it and how the data is organized is determined in advance by the structure definitions used for the records. This is especially true when dealing with applications compiled from C or C++ source code. With an ASCII data file, on the other hand, so long as whatever is reading the data is clever enough to work out what is in the file, you can store just about anything that can be represented in ASCII (this is an advantage of using CSV for data exchange).

Handling Binary Data in Python

The Python library includes a few handy modules for dealing with binary data in the form of C structures. One of these is `ctypes`, and another is the `struct` module. First we'll take a look at what `ctypes` can do, and then we'll focus on the `struct` library module.

Using the ctypes module to handle structured binary data

As we saw in Chapter 5, the `ctypes` library module is typically used to access functions in foreign library modules without the need to resort to writing an extension module in C or using something like SWIG (in Chapter 14, we'll see a real-life example in the Python interface for the LabJack data acquisition device). However, it can also be used to create and manipulate binary data objects from within a Python program.

Here is an example, called `ctypes_struct.py`, that shows how to use the various types defined in the `ctypes` module to create a binary structure object and assign values to it:

```
# ctypes_struct.py

import ctypes

class DataRecord(ctypes.Structure):
    _fields_ = [ ('seq_num', ctypes.c_short),
                 ('chan', ctypes.c_short),
                 ('mode', ctypes.c_short),
                 ('data_val', ctypes.c_double),
                 ('err_msg', ctypes.c_char * 3) ]

drec = DataRecord()

drec.seq_num = 1
drec.chan = 4
drec.mode = 0
drec.data_val = 2.355
drec.err_msg = '030'
```

```
print "seq_num : %d" % drec.seq_num
print "chan    : %d" % drec.chan
print "mode    : %d" % drec.mode
print "data_val: %f" % drec.data_val
print "err_msg : %s" % drec.err_msg
```

DataRecord inherits the ctypes class Structure. Objects of type Structure (and Union, too) must define an attribute called _fields_, which is a list of 2-tuples, each containing a field name and a field type. For the err_msg field I used the "* 3" notation to indicate three contiguous instances of the character type to hold the string (we'll see why this matters shortly). Also notice that I opted to instantiate the drec object without initializing it, which is OK. The values for the fields were assigned later using explicit field names. You could, however, do it all in one swoop where drec is instantiated by passing the data values to the constructor method, like this:

```
# ctypes_struct2.py

import ctypes

class DataRecord(ctypes.Structure):
    _fields_ = [ ('seq_num', ctypes.c_short),
                 ('chan', ctypes.c_short),
                 ('mode', ctypes.c_short),
                 ('data_val', ctypes.c_double),
                 ('err_msg', ctypes.c_char * 3) ]

drec = DataRecord(1, 4, 0, 2.355, '030')

print "seq_num : %d" % drec.seq_num
print "chan    : %d" % drec.chan
print "mode    : %d" % drec.mode
print "data_val: %f" % drec.data_val
print "err_msg : %s" % drec.err_msg
```

The output will be exactly the same for both versions. I prefer the explicit version myself, because it allows for less chance of erroneously assigning the wrong value to a structure element, and to me it's more readable. If you elect to use the constructor initialization approach, just be careful to ensure that the data values appear in the same order as the fields where they are supposed to be assigned.

Now, let's see how it works. You can execute ctypes_struct.py or ctypes_struct2.py by typing:

python ctypes_struct.py

or:

python ctypes_struct2.py

You should see the following response from Python:

```
seq_num : 1
chan    : 4
mode    : 0
```

```
data_val: 2.355000
err_msg : 000
```

But wait, there's more. As you may recall, Python has no native structure type. That's true, with "native" being the operative term here. With the `ctypes Structure` class, you can create and manipulate structure objects in Python just as you would in C or C++. Why would you want to do this? Well, if you're using Python as a prototyping language, with the eventual goal being conversion to production C or C++ code, then working with structure-like objects from the outset can help make the transition a little easier. Also, if you are creating code that needs to be very robust, then avoiding the use of dictionary objects (which can be modified on the fly within the software) in favor of structure objects (which are fixed once defined) might be worth considering. Lastly, we can create a structure object and write it to a binary file for some other application to read. We could also send the structure object via a network socket connection. By the same token, we can read structure objects from a binary file or network socket and extract their internal data elements.

The example script `ctypes_struct_file.py`, shown next, will write the contents of a binary structure to a file and read it back to prove that it worked:

```python
# ctypes_struct_file.py

import ctypes

class DataRecord(ctypes.Structure):
    _fields_ = [ ('seq_num', ctypes.c_short),
                 ('chan', ctypes.c_short),
                 ('mode', ctypes.c_short),
                 ('data_val', ctypes.c_double),
                 ('err_msg', ctypes.c_char * 3) ]

drec = DataRecord()

drec.seq_num = 1
drec.chan = 4
drec.mode = 0
drec.data_val = 2.355
drec.err_msg = '000'

print "Written to structure:"
print "seq_num : %d" % drec.seq_num
print "chan    : %d" % drec.chan
print "mode    : %d" % drec.mode
print "data_val: %f" % drec.data_val
print "err_msg : %s" % drec.err_msg
print "\n"

# write out binary data
fout = open('bindata.dat', 'wb')
fout.write(drec)
fout.close()

# now read it back into a new instance of DataRecord
```

```
fin = open('bindata.dat', 'rb')

drec2 = DataRecord()
fin.readinto(drec2)
fin.close()

print "Read from structure:"
print "seq_num : %d" % drec2.seq_num
print "chan    : %d" % drec2.chan
print "mode    : %d" % drec2.mode
print "data_val: %f" % drec2.data_val
print "err_msg : %s" % drec2.err_msg
```

Note the way in which the three-character string, err_msg, is defined in these examples. ctypes has both a character (byte) type and a string pointer type (ctypes.c_char_p). If you use the pointer type there is an implicit use of a buffer to hold the string data, and the resulting structure will contain an address, not a series of character byte values. It is *not* portable between program execution sessions when stored in a file.

ctypes_struct_file.py uses a method that has been a source of some controversy in the Python community in the past, namely, the readinto() file object method. If you query Python for help on it, you'll get this back (with Python version 2.6.5):

```
>>> help(file.readinto)
Help on method_descriptor:

readinto(...)
    readinto() -> Undocumented.  Don't use this; it may go away.
```

However, in the documentation for version 2.7 you will find the following:

readinto(b)

Read up to len(b) bytes into bytearray b and return the number of bytes read.

Like read(), multiple reads may be issued to the underlying raw stream, unless the latter is 'interactive'.

A BlockingIOError is raised if the underlying raw stream is in non blocking-mode, and has no data available at the moment.

(from the Python Standard Library document, I/O Base Classes)

This same description also appears in the documentation for Python version 3.x, so I'm going to assume that it's finally been accepted and won't go away any time soon. In any case, if the version of Python you're using works fine for what you're trying to accomplish, then there may not be a good reason to upgrade just because the revision level changes. Depending on what changed, there is also the risk of things suddenly not working like they once did. Like the old adage states: "If it ain't broke, don't fix it."

Now let's look at how we can write a series of structures to a file and read them back again as an array. The example script ctypes_struct_file2.py shows one way to do this:

```python
# ctypes_struct_file2.py

import ctypes

class DataRecord(ctypes.Structure):
    _fields_ = [ ('seq_num', ctypes.c_short),
                 ('chan', ctypes.c_short),
                 ('mode', ctypes.c_short),
                 ('data_val', ctypes.c_double),
                 ('err_msg', ctypes.c_char * 3) ]

drec = DataRecord()

fout = open('bindata.dat', 'wb')

# write 10 instances of the drec structure object to a file
# increment structure member values to show it's working
for i in range(0, 10):
    drec.seq_num = i
    drec.chan = (i + 2)
    drec.mode = 0
    drec.data_val = (2.0 + (i/10.0))
    drec.err_msg = '000'

    # write out binary data
    fout.write(drec)

fout.close()

print "Read from file:"

# create an array of structures
# q is a dummy counter variable
drec2 = [DataRecord() for q in range(0,10)]

# now read it back into a new instance of DataRecord
fin = open('bindata.dat', 'rb')

for i in range(0, 10):
    try:
        rc = fin.readinto(drec2[i])
    except:
        pass
    else:
        if rc > 0:
            print "rec num : %d" % i
            print "rec size: %d" % rc
            print "seq_num : %d" % drec2[i].seq_num
            print "chan    : %d" % drec2[i].chan
            print "mode    : %d" % drec2[i].mode
            print "data_val: %f" % drec2[i].data_val
            print "err_msg : %s" % drec2[i].err_msg

fin.close()
```

The first part of the script generates ten instances of the structure object drec and writes them to a file. It then closes the file and reopens it for reading. A loop pulls out each structure instance using the readinto() method, and loads the data into an array of structure objects. The read loop terminates when the loop count reaches the limit, an exception occurs, or the return value (rc) is zero. An exception is handled silently, although the readinto() method does have some associated exception methods (if you're curious, refer to the Python library documentation for details).

Using struct to handle structured binary data

This being Python we're discussing, then we should expect that there is another way to do what we just saw with ctypes. There is, of course, and it's the struct module.

Like ctypes, struct is handy for dealing with binary data structures without resorting to creating a custom extension for the job. You can find the detailed description in section 7 of the Python Standard Library document (String Services). Unlike ctypes, struct works by dealing with binary data as strings of binary values (which is probably why its description resides in the String Services part of the library documentation).

The struct module provides five functions, listed in Table 12-4.

Table 12-4. struct functions

Function	Description
pack(fmt, v1, v2, ...)	Returns a string of binary values packed according to the specified format (the fmt parameter).
pack_into(fmt, buffer, offset, v1, v2, ...)	Packs the data values according to the specified format and then writes the data into a buffer starting at a specific offset.
unpack(fmt, string)	Unpacks the data values from a packed string according to the specified format and returns an *n*-tuple containing the data values.
unpack_from(fmt, buffer[, offset=0])	Unpacks the contents of a buffer according to the specified format beginning at a given offset into the buffer.
calcsize(fmt)	Returns the size of the structure (i.e., the packed binary string) according to the specified format. In other words, calcsize() translates the format specification into the expected structure size.

In addition to the functions listed in Table 12-4, there is also a Struct class, which provides a set of methods identical to the functions, and also includes two additional object attributes: format and size. The Struct class methods do not take a format parameter. Instead, the structure format is set when the class object is instantiated. All of the methods will use this initial format definition for a particular instantiation of a Struct object. The size attribute contains the size of the packed data according to the format specification, which is contained in the format attribute. Requesting help on the Struct object from the Python prompt results in the following output (I've reformatted the text slightly to fit in the page margins):

```
class Struct(object)
 |  Compiled struct object
 |
 |  Methods defined here:
 |
 |  __delattr__(...)
 |      x.__delattr__('name') <==> del x.name
 |
 |  __getattribute__(...)
 |      x.__getattribute__('name') <==> x.name
 |
 |  __init__(...)
 |      x.__init__(...) initializes x; see x.__class__.__doc__
 |      for signature
 |
 |  __setattr__(...)
 |      x.__setattr__('name', value) <==> x.name = value
 |
 |  pack(...)
 |      S.pack(v1, v2, ...) -> string
 |
 |      Return a string containing values v1, v2, ... packed according
 |      to this Struct's format. See struct.__doc__ for more on format
 |      strings.
 |
 |  pack_into(...)
 |      S.pack_into(buffer, offset, v1, v2, ...)
 |
 |      Pack the values v1, v2, ... according to this Struct's format,
 |      write the packed bytes into the writable buffer buf starting
 |      at offset.  Note that the offset is not an optional argument.
 |      See struct.__doc__ for more on format strings.
 |
 |  unpack(...)
 |      S.unpack(str) -> (v1, v2, ...)
 |
 |      Return tuple containing values unpacked according to this
 |      Struct's format. Requires len(str) == self.size. See
 |      struct.__doc__ for more on format strings.
 |
 |  unpack_from(...)
 |      S.unpack_from(buffer[, offset]) -> (v1, v2, ...)
 |
 |      Return tuple containing values unpacked according to this
 |      Struct's format. Unlike unpack, unpack_from can unpack values
 |      from any object supporting the buffer API, not just str.
 |      Requires len(buffer[offset:]) >= self.size. See struct.__doc__
 |      for more on format strings.
 |
 |  ----------------------------------------------------------------------
 |  Data descriptors defined here:
 |
 |  format
 |      struct format string
 |
```

```
|     size
|         struct size in bytes
|
|     ----------------------------------------------------------------
|     Data and other attributes defined here:
|
|     __new__ = <built-in method __new__ of type object>
|         T.__new__(S, ...) -> a new object with type S, a subtype of T
```

Whereas the **ctypes** module defined data object types, the **struct** module uses format codes. These are listed in Table 12-5.

Table 12-5. struct data type format codes

Format code	C type	Python type	Packed size
x	pad byte	no value	1
c	char	string of length 1	1
b	signed char	integer	1
B	unsigned char	integer	1
?	_Bool	bool	1
h	short	integer	2
H	unsigned short	integer	2
i	int	integer	4
I	unsigned int	integer	4
l	long	integer	4
L	unsigned long	integer	4
q	long long	integer	8
Q	unsigned long long	integer	8
f	float	float	4
d	double	float	8
s	char[]	string	Variable
p	char[]	string	Variable
P	void *	integer	OS dependent

For a detailed discussion of the format codes refer to the Python Standard Library document.

Now, let's create a packed binary string using the same structure definition we saw earlier in the **ctypes** example:

```
# pack_struct.py

import struct
import binascii
import ctypes
```

```
# original ctypes structure definition
# _fields_ = [ ('seq_num', ctypes.c_short),
#              ('chan', ctypes.c_short),
#              ('mode', ctypes.c_short),
#              ('data_val', ctypes.c_double),
#              ('err_msg', ctypes.c_char * 3) ]
#
# Equivalent struct format string:
# 'hhhd3s'

seq_num = 1
chan = 4
mode = 0
data_val = 2.355
err_msg = '030'

srec = struct.pack('hhhd3s', seq_num, chan, mode, data_val, err_msg)

# use binascii.hexlify so we can see what's in the binary string
print binascii.hexlify(srec)
```

When pack_struct.py is run, you should see the following output:

python pack_struct.py

```
0100040000000000d7a3703d0ad70240303330
```

Most of the struct format codes will accept a numeric count or size prefix. In pack_struct.py the 3s in the format string indicates that a three-element string is expected. In the case of a nonstring format code specifying something like 3h is the same as using 'hhh'. The format string could have been written as '3hd3s' instead of 'hhhd3s', but with complex format strings it might be clever to do so, but it may not be easily readable.

If you prefer to use the Struct class then note that the Struct constructor takes the format string as its only parameter when the object is instantiated. The format string is subsequently available in the format attribute. The script pack_struct_obj.py uses the Struct class to achieve the same result as pack_struct.py:

```
# pack_struct_obj.py

import struct
import binascii

# original ctypes structure definition
# _fields_ = [ ('seq_num', ctypes.c_short),
#              ('chan', ctypes.c_short),
#              ('mode', ctypes.c_short),
#              ('data_val', ctypes.c_double),
#              ('err_msg', ctypes.c_char * 3) ]
#
# Equivalent struct format string:
# 'hhhd3s'
```

```
seq_num = 1
chan = 4
mode = 0
data_val = 2.355
err_msg = '030'

datavals = (seq_num, chan, mode, data_val, err_msg)
sobj = struct.Struct('hhhd3s')
srec = sobj.pack(*datavals)

print binascii.hexlify(srec)
```

For our last example before we move on, let's verify that **struct** and **ctypes** can play nicely with one another using the example script in **pack_struct_file.py**:

```
# pack_struct_file.py

import struct
import binascii
import ctypes

# original ctypes structure definition
# _fields_ = [ ('seq_num', ctypes.c_short),
#              ('chan', ctypes.c_short),
#              ('mode', ctypes.c_short),
#              ('data_val', ctypes.c_double),
#              ('err_msg', ctypes.c_char * 3) ]
#
# Equivalent struct format string:
# 'hhhd3s'

seq_num = 1
chan = 4
mode = 0
data_val = 2.355
err_msg = '030'

srec = struct.pack('hhhd3s', seq_num, chan, mode, data_val, err_msg)

print binascii.hexlify(srec)

fout = open('bindata.dat','wb')
fout.write(srec)
fout.close()

# now read it back into a new instance of DataRecord
class DataRecord(ctypes.Structure):
    _fields_ = [ ('seq_num', ctypes.c_short),
                 ('chan', ctypes.c_short),
                 ('mode', ctypes.c_short),
                 ('data_val', ctypes.c_double),
                 ('err_msg', ctypes.c_char * 3) ]

fin = open('bindata.dat', 'rb')

drec = DataRecord()
```

```
fin.readinto(drec)
fin.close()

print "Read from structure:"
print "seq_num : %d" % drec.seq_num
print "chan    : %d" % drec.chan
print "mode    : %d" % drec.mode
print "data_val: %f" % drec.data_val
print "err_msg : %s" % drec.err_msg
```

In the first part of the example I've used struct's pack function to create a packed binary string and then write it to a file. The second part reopens the file and reads the data into a ctypes structure definition. When you run pack_struct_file.py you should see the following:

```
python pack_struct_file.py
0100040000000000d7a3703d0ad70240303330
Read from structure:
seq_num : 1
chan    : 4
mode    : 0
data_val: 2.355000
err_msg : 030
```

Well, that was fun, and you now have two new binary data tools for your Python toolbox. Which technique you use depends on what you're trying to do and, to some extent, on your own sense of programming aesthetics.

Image Data

I would now like to examine another commonly encountered form of binary data: images. A 2D array consisting of data representing the amount of light energy across something like a CCD (charge-coupled device) sensor (as found in a common CCD camera) is sometimes called (correctly) a "luminance map." You may also encounter the term "intensity map," and while it could be used to refer to image data, it's a more generic term that refers to an array of data representing the intensity of something across the array space. Intensity maps are found in many data representation applications, such as a plot of smog density across a city, or temperatures across a grid of points on a printed circuit board, or the intensity levels from the detector array in an X-ray machine at the hospital. None of these are "images" in the conventional sense, but once the intensities are converted into a grayscale image format (or even color, depending on the application and the type of data) they can be viewed and interpreted by a human being.

Then there is what is called the "geometry" of an image. An image is a 2D array with width and height defined in terms of pixels, with a total size, in pixels, that is the product of the width and height. There is also a third dimension, so to speak, which is the size of data, in bits, used to represent the luminance (or intensity) at each x, y pixel position in the array. Some grayscale images utilize 8-bit data, and some use 16 bits per pixel.

You will sometimes see the pixel data size expressed as "8bpp" or "16bpp." These are just shorthand ways to say *n* bits per pixel, where *n* can be 8, 16 or whatever (some color image formats use 24 or 32bpp to hold the color data for each pixel). Together the width, height, and pixel size parameters define the basic geometry of an image.

In instrumentation and control systems there usually isn't a lot of need for image data, but when data is treated as an intensity map things can get interesting. For instance, if the application involves monitoring the internal temperatures of a stack of beehives, say five wide by five high, then the data could be mapped into an intensity map in real time to show the hottest and coolest hive boxes in the array and perhaps provide some indication of heat flow through the stack. Bees generate heat, and on a warm day you can see some of them sitting just outside the entrance to the hive beating their wings to move cool air inside—a living air conditioning system. Each hive box might be represented by a square block of pixels 50 wide by 50 high, and assigned a luminance intensity proportional to the data value for each location. The result would be an "image" 250 by 250 pixels in size, as shown in Figure 12-7.

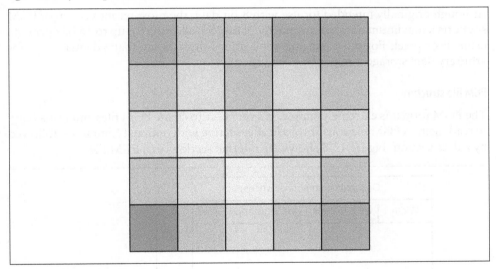

Figure 12-7. Data displayed as an image

If the application generates a series of these images, perhaps 24 a day, then they can be accumulated into a movie of sorts to show patterns of change in the temperatures that would otherwise be difficult to see just by looking at static data or tables of numbers.

PGM

There are numerous image formats in use, some of which we use every day when we browse the Web (PNG, JPEG, and GIF images are an integral part of web pages). Other formats may not be quite as common, but they are useful for specific applications. One of these is the Netpbm family of image formats.

One of the formats in the Netpbm suite is PGM (or, Portable Grayscale Map). PGM is one of the simplest image data formats around. The documentation for the PGM format states: "The PGM format is a lowest common denominator grayscale file format. It is designed to be extremely easy to learn and write programs for. (It's so simple that most people will simply reverse engineer it because it's easier than reading this specification)." You can find the PGM format specification here: *http://netpbm.sourceforge.net/ doc/pgm.html*.

One of the main attractions of PGM is the utility afforded by its simplicity. It can, of course, be used to store grayscale (luminance map) image data, but it can also be used to store just about any other kind of 8- or 16-bit data as well. The data doesn't even have to be a 2D array. Also, as the format specification points out, it can be used to create "synthetic images" from data that was not originally intended to be an image. The Netpbm tools can then convert that data into something readily viewable, such as a JPEG image. There are some interesting data visualization tricks lurking there, such as the beehive example presented earlier.

Although originally intended for use with 8-bit data, the most recent version of PGM supports a maximum data size parameter of 65,535, allowing for up to 16 bits per data element or pixel. For most imaging applications this is more than adequate, but for arbitrary data storage it might be a limitation.

PGM file structure

The PGM format is extremely simple. It's very easy to create PGM files and just as easy to read them. A PGM file consists of a header section with optional comments, followed by a data section. Figure 12-8 shows the internal sections in a PGM file.

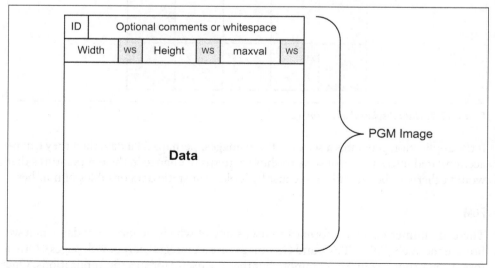

Figure 12-8. PGM file structure

One of the things I like about the PGM format is that everything in the header section is in printable ASCII. On one of my past projects, PGM was used to capture raw image data from remote imaging instruments. When the data was written to a file (one image per file) the comments were autogenerated and used to hold things like a timestamp value, the full image name, the name of the instrument, and the values of various settings (exposure time, filters used, and the camera's X and Y pointing orientation, to name just a few). This allowed us to scan through a directory of images and pull out all the lines beginning with the # comment marker. A simple script was then used to create a nicely formatted catalog of images.

pgmtest.py is an example of a simple script that will create a 256 × 256-pixel PGM image containing random data:

```
# pgmtst.py
# generates an 8bpp "image" of random pixel values

import random as rnd

# print ID string (P5)
# print comments (if any)
# print width
# print height
# print size
# print data

#rnd = random
rnd.seed()

width  = 256
height = 256
pxsize = 255

# create the PGM header
hdrstr = "P5\n%d\n%d\n%d\n" % (width, height, pxsize)

pixels = []
for i in range(0,width):
    for j in range(0,height):
        # generate random values
        pixval = int(255 * rnd.random())
        # some values will be 256, so fix them
        if pixval > pxsize:
            pixval = pxsize
        #endif
        pixels.append(pixval)
    #endfor
#endfor

# convert array to character values
outpix = "".join(map(chr, pixels))

# append the "image" to the header
outstr = hdrstr + outpix
```

```
# and write it out to the disk
fimg = open("pgmtest.pgm","w")
fimg.write(outstr)
fimg.close()
```

When this script is executed, the result will be the file *pgmtest.pgm*. You can use a tool such as ImageJ (available from *http://rsbweb.nih.gov/ij/*) to view it. When you open the file you should see an image like the one in Figure 12-9.

Figure 12-9. Example 8bpp PGM image

Well, I must admit, Figure 12-9 isn't very exciting (unless you happen to like watching the "snow" on an old-fashioned analog TV set). But with some modification to the code, it can become a lot more interesting. This is why I like the PGM format for quick-and-dirty visualization chores—it's trivial to create a PGM image file.

The nested for loops in pgmtest.py are where the actual image generation occurs. Once the 2D matrix is built, it is appended to the image data list object using Python's join() and map() methods:

```
outpix = "".join(map(chr,pixels))
```

This statement iterates through the array pixels, mapping each integer value to a character (byte) value and then joining the resulting one-character string to the list outpix. The Python documentation describes the built-in map() method like this (from the Python Standard Library document, Section 2, "Built-In Functions"):

map(*function*, *iterable*, ...)

Apply *function* to every item of *iterable* and return a list of the results. If additional *iterable* arguments are passed, *function* must take that many arguments and is applied to the items from all iterables in parallel. If one iterable is shorter than another it is assumed to be extended with None items. If *function* is None, the identity function is assumed; if there are multiple arguments, map() returns a list consisting of tuples containing the corresponding items from all iterables (a kind of transpose operation). The *iterable* arguments may be a sequence or any iterable object; the result is always a list.

You might notice that there is a limitation with this approach. Since the result of map(chr, pixels) is a one-character string, it can only deal with 8-bit values in the range of 0 to 255. So how do we work with 16-bit data?

The solution is to use struct to build the 16-bit data. The next example is a complete PGM image output utility function. It takes a list of data elements in either 8- or 16-bit form and creates a simple PGM image:

```
# PGMWrite image generator utility function
import struct

def PGMWrite(imgsrc, imgname, filename, width, height, bitdepth=8):
    """ Generates an 8bpp or 16bpp PGM image from arbitrary data.

    Parameters:

        imgsrc:    source of image data (a list of integer values)
        imgname:   image name string written into image file header
        filename:  output file name for image data
        width:     width of image
        height:    height of image
    """

    # verify source data type (must be a list)
    if type(imgsrc) != list:
        print "Input data must be a list of integer values"
        return

    # verify pixel bit depth
    sizemult = 0
    if bitdepth == 8:
        sizemult  = 1
        img_depth = 255
    elif bitdepth >= 9:
        sizemult  = 2
        img_depth = 65535
    else:
        print "Invalid pixel depth"
        return
```

```
# generate image parameters
img_height = height
img_width  = width
img_size   = img_height * img_width
data_size  = img_size * sizemult

# initalize the image output array
pixels = []

# generate the image array from input data
i = 0   # input index
# load data into the image array
for y in range(0, img_height):
    for x in range(0, img_width):
        inval = imgsrc[i]

        if (bitdepth == 8) and (inval > 255):
            pixval = 255
        elif inval > 65535:
            pixval = 65535
        else:
            pixval = inval

        i += 1
        pixels.append(pixval)

if bitdepth == 8:
    pix_data = "".join(map(chr,pixels))
else:
    pix_data = pixels

# load the header data variables and get string lengths
img_type_str   = "P5\n"
img_name_str   = "#%s\n" % imgname   # comment in image header
img_width_str  = "%d\n"  % img_height
img_height_str = "%d\n"  % img_width
img_depth_str  = "%d\n"  % img_depth

img_name_len   = len(img_name_str)
img_width_len  = len(img_width_str)
img_height_len = len(img_height_str)
img_depth_len  = len(img_depth_str)

# create the image header structure
hdrvals  = (img_type_str, img_name_str, img_width_str,
            img_height_str, img_depth_str)

hdrobj = struct.Struct('3s %ds %ds %ds %ds'% (img_name_len,
                                              img_width_len,
                                              img_height_len,
                                              img_depth_len))
# create the pixel data
if sizemult == 1:
    pixobj = struct.Struct('%dc'% (img_size))
```

```python
    else:
        pixobj = struct.Struct('%dH'% (img_size))

    # pack the data into the structures
    img_hdr_data = hdrobj.pack(*hdrvals)
    img_pix_data = pixobj.pack(*pix_data)
    img_data = img_hdr_data + img_pix_data

    # now write it all out to the file
    fimg = open(filename,"wb")
    fimg.write(img_data)
    fimg.close()


if __name__ == "__main__":
    # generate 8bpp image
    datavals = []
    for i in range(0, 65536):
        datavals.append(i/256)

    PGMWrite(datavals,
             "incshade8",
             "incshade8.pgm",
             256, 256,
             bitdepth=8)

    # generate 16bpp image
    datavals = []
    for i in range(0, 65536):
        datavals.append(i/256)

    PGMWrite(datavals,
             "incshade16",
             "incshade16.pgm",
             256, 256,
             bitdepth=16)
```

Figure 12-10 shows what the 16bpp output looks like with an input divisor of 256 (we'll talk about this shortly).

There are many things about this function that deserve some discussion. I'll start with the code at the bottom of the module that calls PGMWrite() when invoked as a standalone script.

Two images are generated, one with 8-bit pixel size and the second with 16-bit pixel size. In both cases an array (list) is built with a series of incrementing values. Notice that the values obtained from the for loop index are divided by 256 before they are written into the array. This "scales" the data into the image geometry. You should try changing the value to something like, say, 128 or 16 and see what happens. It might not be what you expect, and it would be worthwhile to take some time and try to understand the behavior. You could also use other types of array data as the input to generate a grid pattern, imaging targets, compression performance grids, the variation in temperature or humidity in a room over the course of a year, and so on.

Figure 12-10. 16bpp example image

Now let's look at PGMWrite() itself. The function starts off by checking the input array for the correct type and verifying that the bit size parameter is either 8 or some value greater than 8. In a production application this function might be used to handle zero-padded 10- or 12-bit data from a camera or other image data source, so it's just more convenient to assume that anything with a bit size greater than 8 will be treated as 16-bit data.

Next up are the image parameters that will be used to read the data from the input array and write it into the output array. The output array itself is created using a pair of nested for loops. This isn't strictly necessary, but it leaves the door open if you want to modify the loops to support things like subsampling or contrast scaling.

Within the innermost loop (the *x*-axis) there is a check to ensure that pixel values don't exceed the allowable range for the selected image type. Any value that exceeds this range is simply set to the allowable maximum. What this means is that if you feed this function an input array containing values greater than the allowable maximum, those pixels will simply show up as white when the image is viewed. Basically, it's a defensive programming technique.

After the image data array is generated, the function creates the strings for the image header and computes the length for each one. When the format string for the header data struct object is created, these values will be used to tailor the size of the fields.

Next up is the image data itself, which is pure binary. There is only one struct definition for the header, but two for the image: one for an 8bpp image and one for a 16bpp image.

The header data structure string is then concatenated with the image data string. This works because these are packed strings, so Python will happily concatenate them into a single string object.

Finally, PGMWrite() opens the specified file and writes out the structure. The result is a complete PGM image file with the same internal layout that we saw in Figure 12-8.

Although you may never have a need to work with images, this function contains a good selection of many of the topics we've discussed up to this point. Remember that the PGM format can be used to store binary data for things other than images, and there's no reason why you need to stick with the *x*, *y* image array loading scheme; you could just as easily use a 1D array.

I will leave it as an exercise for the reader to write a function to read the data from a PGM file, but I will say that it's actually rather easy. We've already seen how to deal with header data and extract a packed structure. That's really about all there is to it. Your read function only needs to treat a PGM as a file with a set of leading strings followed by binary data. Hint: remember that if you're reading PGM files where the amount of header data is unknown, you'll need to read each line and examine it to determine if it's an embedded comment or parametric data, and remember that in the PGM header there are exactly three parameter fields (width, height, and bit depth) before the start of the binary data array.

Summary

In this chapter we've looked at ASCII and binary data, along with some applications for dealing with each type. We've also seen how Python's built-in and library methods are used when we need to convert from one form to another, and how to mix both in the same script to create complex data objects such as images. Finally, we examined a working example of a binary image data generator function and saw how many of the topics introduced earlier come into play to create the function.

Suggested Reading

The following articles and books are a good place to start if you're looking for more information on reading and writing data files:

RFC20, "*ASCII Format for Network Interchange.*" *Vint Cerf, 1969.*
    This early RFC document is available online at *http://www.faqs.org/rfcs/rfc20.html.*

RFC 4810, "Common Format and MIME Type for Comma-Separated Values (CSV) Files." Y. Shafranovich, Network Working Group, The Internet Society, 2005.

> RFC 4810 defines the format used for the "text/csv" MIME type for CSV files. It is available at *http://tools.ietf.org/html/rfc4180.*

PEP 305, "CSV File API." K. Altis et al., python.org, 2008.

> PEP 305 defines the API for Python's standard CSV module. It is a helpful supplement to the documentation for the Python standard library. PEP 305 is available at *http://www.python.org/dev/peps/pep-0305/.*

Beautiful Data: The Stories Behind Elegant Data Solutions. T. Segaran and J. Hammerbacher (eds.), O'Reilly Media, 2009.

> A fascinating collection of essays and technical papers covering a wide range of topics in data acquisition, processing, and visualization. A great book to browse for ideas when you need to find a way to present data sets in a comprehensible form.

Python Essential Reference, 4th ed. David M. Beazley, Addison-Wesley, 2009.

> Although not a book I'd recommend to someone just starting out with Python, this is an excellent reference work that covers the core Python language and libraries, including Python's advanced features, such as generators, coroutines, closures, metaclasses, and decorators. Includes descriptions of low-level methods and options not fully covered in the standard Python documentation.

Lastly, Wikipedia has an informative write-up on configuration files (including some interesting historical trivia) at *http://en.wikipedia.org/wiki/Configuration_file.* There is also more information available at *http://en.wikipedia.org/wiki/INI_file.*

## CHAPTER 13

User Interfaces

*The Principle of Least Astonishment: Make a user
interface as consistent and as predictable as possible.*

—Anonymous

Unless an application is deeply embedded, or specifically designed to run as a background process, it will probably need some type of user interface. In this chapter we will explore different ways to communicate with a user. We'll start by examining what you can do with just the command line. Next we'll look at how to use an ANSI-capable terminal emulator program to display data and accept input, and then the curses screen control package for Python. After this we'll move to the realm of bright colors, fancy graphs, images, and dialogs, with a look at the TkInter GUI toolkit provided with the standard Python distribution. We'll also take a quick tour of the wxPython GUI package.

Text-Based Interfaces

Text-based interfaces are the foundation of all display-based computer user interfaces. I say display-based because technically, the first interfaces were panels full of lights and switches. Printing terminals came next, but it wasn't until the advent of CRT terminals that human-machine interface (HMI) devices began to come into their own.

The Console

The most straightforward way to interact with any program, Python or otherwise, is through the console interface. Under Windows this is the so-called "DOS box," or the "cmd prompt" as it's currently known (the Windows shell application is called *cmd.exe*). On a Unix or Linux system it is the shell prompt for *sh, bash, ksh, tsch*, or whatever else you may happen to be using for a shell interface. If no window manager is active, the whole screen is the console, but it behaves just like the windowed form.

Sending data to the shell, in the form of strings, is easy—that's what the print statement does. Getting input back from a user is not as intuitively obvious, mainly because Python does not have cross-platform equivalents of getch() or getche() (get character and get character with echo, respectively). It does, however, have the raw_input() built-in method, which can handle most of the common user input chores, and it works on all the platforms that Python supports. Shortly I'll show you how to use *ctypes* and the C runtime library for both Linux and Windows, but first let's see how much we can do with just the console interface.

Example console display

While you could always just use occasional print statements to output data to the console, it might be difficult for a user to tell what's happening as the data scrolls by on the screen. Establishing a template for the data display and using a fixed format makes the data easier to read and greatly reduces user frustration (and that user might be you).

If you want to use a fixed format for data output to the console, you'll need at least two things: some way to clear the screen, and a template to contain your data. We'll look at the template first.

Unless we resort to ANSI terminal control strings (discussed in the next section), a program doesn't have any way to position the cursor in the console window. Each line in the display needs to take care of its own positioning and data display formatting. The listing for console1.py shows how this is done:

```
#! /usr/bin/python
# console1.py
#
# Demonstrates console output using the built-in print method.
#
# Source code from the book "Real World Instrumentation with Python"
# By J. M. Hughes, published by O'Reilly.

import time

ainstat   = ['OFF','OFF','OFF','OFF']
aindata   = [0.0, 0.0, 0.0, 0.0]
discstate = ['OFF','OFF','OFF','OFF','OFF','OFF','OFF','OFF']
discin    = [0,0,0,0,0,0,0,0]

print '\n' * 50
print ""
print "System Status"
print ""
print "Analog Input 0  : %10s  %f" % (ainstat[0], aindata[0])
print "Analog Input 1  : %10s  %f" % (ainstat[1], aindata[1])
print "Analog Input 2  : %10s  %f" % (ainstat[2], aindata[2])
print "Analog Input 3  : %10s  %f" % (ainstat[3], aindata[3])
print ""
print "Discrete Input 0: %3s  %d" % (discstate[0], discin[0])
```

```
print "Discrete Input 1: %3s  %d" % (discstate[1], discin[1])
print "Discrete Input 2: %3s  %d" % (discstate[2], discin[2])
print "Discrete Input 3: %3s  %d" % (discstate[3], discin[3])
print "Discrete Input 4: %3s  %d" % (discstate[4], discin[4])
print "Discrete Input 5: %3s  %d" % (discstate[5], discin[5])
print "Discrete Input 6: %3s  %d" % (discstate[6], discin[6])
print "Discrete Input 7: %3s  %d" % (discstate[7], discin[7])
print ""

time.sleep(2)
```

Vertical positioning is based on the order in which the lines are printed out to the console, and horizontal positioning is determined by how each line is formatted. The line of code immediately following the four variable initialization lines, `print "\n" * 50`, simulates a "clear screen" by generating 50 blank lines. I used 50 because I have large command-line windows, but generating more blank lines than the window supports does not hurt anything. The result looks like this:

```
System Status

Analog Input 0  :      ACTIVE  0.000000
Analog Input 1  :         OFF  0.000000
Analog Input 2  :      ACTIVE  0.000000
Analog Input 3  :         OFF  0.000000

Discrete Input 0: OFF  0
Discrete Input 1: OFF  1
Discrete Input 2: OFF  0
Discrete Input 3: OFF  0
Discrete Input 4: OFF  0
Discrete Input 5: OFF  0
Discrete Input 6: OFF  0
Discrete Input 7: OFF  0
```

Since the raw console I/O doesn't have a generic clear screen function, a series of print statements with empty strings can be used to scroll off anything currently on the display in order to make room for new data. Note that if the window is larger than the number of lines in the template, the template text will end up at the bottom of the window (the last line printed will be just above the prompt).

However, there is another way. We can find out what type of OS the code is running under and then use the appropriate method to issue a screen clear command, like this:

```
def clrDisp(numlines=50):
    if os.name == "posix":
        os.system('clear')
    elif os.name in ("nt", "dos", "ce"):
        os.system('CLS')
    else:
        print '\n' * numlines
```

Here is an example of this technique:

```
#! /usr/bin/python
# console2.py
```

```
#
# Demonstrates console output using the built-in print method and
# an OS-specific screen clear technique.
#
# Source code from the book "Real World Instrumentation with Python"
# By J. M. Hughes, published by O'Reilly.

import time
import os

ainstat   = ['OFF','OFF','OFF','OFF']
aindata   = [0.0, 0.0, 0.0, 0.0]
discstate = ['OFF','OFF','OFF','OFF','OFF','OFF','OFF','OFF']
discin    = [0,0,0,0,0,0,0,0]

def clrDisp(numlines=50):
    if os.name == "posix":
        os.system('clear')
    elif os.name in ("nt", "dos", "ce"):
        os.system('CLS')
    else:
        print '\n' * numlines

def drawData():
    print ""
    print "System Status"
    print ""
    print "Analog Input 0  : %10s  %f" % (ainstat[0], aindata[0])
    print "Analog Input 1  : %10s  %f" % (ainstat[1], aindata[1])
    print "Analog Input 2  : %10s  %f" % (ainstat[2], aindata[2])
    print "Analog Input 3  : %10s  %f" % (ainstat[3], aindata[3])
    print ""
    print "Discrete Input 0: %3s  %d" % (discstate[0], discin[0])
    print "Discrete Input 1: %3s  %d" % (discstate[1], discin[1])
    print "Discrete Input 2: %3s  %d" % (discstate[2], discin[2])
    print "Discrete Input 3: %3s  %d" % (discstate[3], discin[3])
    print "Discrete Input 4: %3s  %d" % (discstate[4], discin[4])
    print "Discrete Input 5: %3s  %d" % (discstate[5], discin[5])
    print "Discrete Input 6: %3s  %d" % (discstate[6], discin[6])
    print "Discrete Input 7: %3s  %d" % (discstate[7], discin[7])
    print ""

ainstat[1] = "ACTIVE"
ainstat[3] = "ACTIVE"
aindata[1] = 5.2
aindata[3] = 8.9
discstate[0] = "ON"
discin[0] = 1
clrDisp()
drawData()
time.sleep(1.0)

ainstat[1] = "OFF"
ainstat[3] = "OFF"
aindata[1] = 0.0
```

```
aindata[3] = 0.0
ainstat[0] = "ACTIVE"
ainstat[2] = "ACTIVE"
aindata[0] = 5.2
aindata[2] = 8.9
discstate[0] = "OFF"
discin[0] = 0
discstate[1] = "ON"
discin[1] = 1
clrDisp()
drawData()
time.sleep(1.0)
```

Now we have the foundation for a usable text-based display. To update the display, the screen is first cleared using the appropriate command, and then the lines from the template are written using the print method. This results in quicker screen regeneration than the multiple-lines method, and it looks nicer, too. If the OS cannot be determined, the function defaults to the blank-line method to clear the display. Figure 13-1 shows the flow chart for a text-based console data display based on what we've seen so far.

Reading user input

Now we have a means to display data, but there's still one thing missing: user input. Fortunately, Python does have a one-size-fits-all input method to read input from the console. The raw_input() method reads a line of input from the console and returns it as a string. A line, in this case, is defined as zero or more characters terminated with an EOL. The EOL will not be appended to the string returned by raw_input().

The raw_input() method can also display a prompt string, and if the readline module is installed it will use that to support input line editing and provide input history. Here is the third iteration of the console example with raw_input() incorporated into the code:

```
#! /usr/bin/python
# console3.py
#
# Demonstrates console output using the built-in print method and the
# raw_input() method.
#
# Source code from the book "Real World Instrumentation with Python"
# By J. M. Hughes, published by O'Reilly.

import time
import os

ainstat    = ['OFF','OFF','OFF','OFF']
aindata    = [0.0, 0.0, 0.0, 0.0]
discstate = ['OFF','OFF','OFF','OFF','OFF','OFF','OFF','OFF']
discin     = [0,0,0,0,0,0,0,0]
x = 0

def initData():
```

```
        global ainstat, aindata, discstate, discin

        ainstat   = ['OFF','OFF','OFF','OFF']
        aindata   = [0.0, 0.0, 0.0, 0.0]
        discstate = ['OFF','OFF','OFF','OFF','OFF','OFF','OFF','OFF']
        discin    = [0,0,0,0,0,0,0,0]

    def readData():
        global ainstat, aindata, discstate, discin, x

        initData()
        discstate[x] = 'ON'
        discin[x] = 1
        x += 1
        if x > (len(discin) - 1):
            x = 0

    def clrDisp(numlines=50):
        if os.name == "posix":
            os.system('clear')
        elif os.name in ("nt", "dos", "ce"):
            os.system('CLS')
        else:
            print '\n' * numlines

    def drawData():
        print ""
        print "System Status"
        print ""
        print "Analog Input 0  : %10s  %f" % (ainstat[0], aindata[0])
        print "Analog Input 1  : %10s  %f" % (ainstat[1], aindata[1])
        print "Analog Input 2  : %10s  %f" % (ainstat[2], aindata[2])
        print "Analog Input 3  : %10s  %f" % (ainstat[3], aindata[3])
        print ""
        print "Discrete Input 0: %3s  %d" % (discstate[0], discin[0])
        print "Discrete Input 1: %3s  %d" % (discstate[1], discin[1])
        print "Discrete Input 2: %3s  %d" % (discstate[2], discin[2])
        print "Discrete Input 3: %3s  %d" % (discstate[3], discin[3])
        print "Discrete Input 4: %3s  %d" % (discstate[4], discin[4])
        print "Discrete Input 5: %3s  %d" % (discstate[5], discin[5])
        print "Discrete Input 6: %3s  %d" % (discstate[6], discin[6])
        print "Discrete Input 7: %3s  %d" % (discstate[7], discin[7])
        print ""

while True:
    readData()
    clrDisp()
    drawData()
    instr = raw_input("Command: ")
    if instr.upper() == 'X':
        break
```

console3.py will step through the discrete input lines one at a time each time the Enter key is pressed. If an x (or X) character is entered, it will terminate.

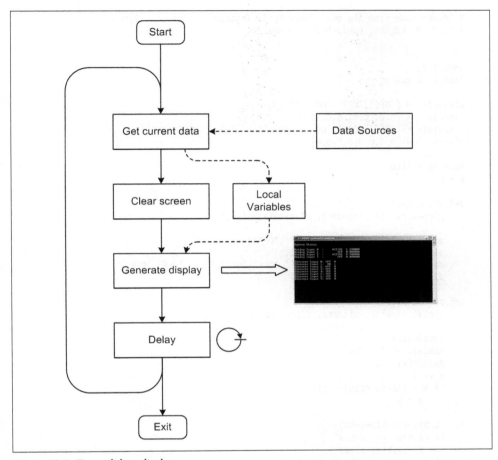

Figure 13-1. Textual data display

There is a downside here, however. The `raw_input()` method only works in a blocking mode. In other words, it will block until the user enters something. This means that the display cannot automatically update itself based on a timer so long as the `raw_input()` is in the main display loop. It won't fetch new data and update the display until the user presses any key other than X.

It turns out that there is a solution, though: this is a perfect place for a thread. We can let a thread fetch the input from the user, and a flag can be used to notify the main loop that it's time to terminate. The code for this is shown here as `console4.py`:

```
#! /usr/bin/python
# console4.py
#
# Demonstrates console output using the built-in print method and the
# raw_input() method in a separate thread.
#
```

```
# Source code from the book "Real World Instrumentation with Python"
# By J. M. Hughes, published by O'Reilly.

import time
import os
import threading

ainstat   = ['OFF','OFF','OFF','OFF']
aindata   = [0.0, 0.0, 0.0, 0.0]
discstate = ['OFF','OFF','OFF','OFF','OFF','OFF','OFF','OFF']
discin    = [0,0,0,0,0,0,0,0]

running = True
x = 0

def initData():
    global ainstat, aindata, discstate, discin

    ainstat   = ['OFF','OFF','OFF','OFF']
    aindata   = [0.0, 0.0, 0.0, 0.0]
    discstate = ['OFF','OFF','OFF','OFF','OFF','OFF','OFF','OFF']
    discin    = [0,0,0,0,0,0,0,0]

def readData():
    global ainstat, aindata, discstate, discin, x

    initData()
    discstate[x] = 'ON'
    discin[x] = 1
    x += 1
    if x > (len(discin) - 1):
        x = 0

def clrDisp(numlines=50):
    if os.name == "posix":
        os.system('clear')
    elif os.name in ("nt", "dos", "ce"):
        os.system('CLS')
    else:
        print '\n' * numlines

def drawData():
    print ""
    print "System Status"
    print ""
    print "Analog Input 0  : %10s  %f" % (ainstat[0], aindata[0])
    print "Analog Input 1  : %10s  %f" % (ainstat[1], aindata[1])
    print "Analog Input 2  : %10s  %f" % (ainstat[2], aindata[2])
    print "Analog Input 3  : %10s  %f" % (ainstat[3], aindata[3])
    print ""
    print "Discrete Input 0: %3s  %d" % (discstate[0], discin[0])
    print "Discrete Input 1: %3s  %d" % (discstate[1], discin[1])
    print "Discrete Input 2: %3s  %d" % (discstate[2], discin[2])
    print "Discrete Input 3: %3s  %d" % (discstate[3], discin[3])
    print "Discrete Input 4: %3s  %d" % (discstate[4], discin[4])
```

```
        print "Discrete Input 5: %3s  %d" % (discstate[5], discin[5])
        print "Discrete Input 6: %3s  %d" % (discstate[6], discin[6])
        print "Discrete Input 7: %3s  %d" % (discstate[7], discin[7])
        print ""
        print "Enter X to terminate"

def getCommand():
    global running

    while True:
        instr = raw_input()
        if instr.upper() == 'X':
            running = False
            break

#-------------------------------------------------------------------
# launch the raw_input() handler thread
getinput = threading.Thread(target=getCommand)
getinput.start()

while running:
    readData()
    clrDisp()
    drawData()
    time.sleep(1.0)
```

Now we really do have a generic framework that can be used to create a console data display that can also accept basic commands, and it does it all using nothing more than the print and raw_input() built-in methods.

Just in case you might be thinking that a console-based text-only display isn't particularly useful, Figure 13-2 shows a screenshot of a set of text display windows used to test some of the instruments used for a space mission.

Each of the six windows uses only ASCII text. There's no ANSI positioning or anything else fancy going on here (we will get to ANSI display control shortly). The displays show the command interface to the spacecraft's CPU, the responses sent back via the telemetry channels, and the status of the telemetry processing functions. There's even a window for command inputs, although this system was typically driven with another tool (not shown) that sent sequences of commands in the format expected by the flight software.

OS-specific console I/O

One of the advantages (perhaps the biggest advantage) of using text-based displays like those we've just seen is that they are largely platform-independent. The print and raw_input() methods are not platform-sensitive, and only the screen clear methods require some knowledge of the underlying OS. There are limitations, however, to what you can do with just print and raw_input(), and situations may arise where you need to have more control over the display and the I/O with the user.

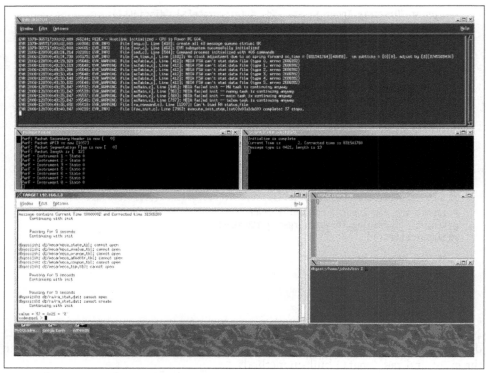

Figure 13-2. Text-based test system data displays

Both Linux and Windows provide a basic set of functions for dealing with low-level console I/O. With Linux, console I/O utility functions such as getch() and ungetch() are found in the curses library; they are not part of the standard I/O functions library. Windows provides these and other functions as part of the msvcrt DLL module. Python includes the library module msvcrt for accessing functions in the Microsoft *msvcrt* DLL, and the curses library module for Unix/Linux environments. In the next section we'll see how to put these and other low-level console I/O functions to work to create structured text-based interfaces using the ANSI terminal control sequences and the curses screen display package. But, before we delve into ANSI and curses, let's look at how these basic functions can be used with text-based displays.

Linux and Windows text display differences

We have now reached the point where Linux and Windows start to go their separate ways. Once we leave the domain of simple print statements and raw_input(), we begin to encounter some significant differences arising from the underlying philosophies of these two operating systems.

The ability to control a display using ANSI control sequences has long been a part of Unix, and later Linux. Unix evolved in a multitasking time-sharing environment based on minicomputers and mainframes, with terminals for user interfaces, and Linux has inherited that paradigm. Windows, on the other hand, evolved from DOS, with no multitasking support and a single screen for one user. It wasn't until Microsoft released the `ANSI.sys` driver module that PCs could interpret ANSI sequences to control cursor positioning and directly manipulate a text-based display. Nowadays Windows support for ANSI screen controls is almost nonexistent. With its emphasis on a GUI for user interaction, Windows doesn't appear to have much need for the old way of doing things.

However, the lack of multitasking and threads (at least initially, with DOS) forced some innovation, and as a result one useful function that appears in DOS and Windows environments is `kbhit()`. It's so useful, in fact, that it's a standard part of the Microsoft Visual C Run-Time library (the `msvcrt` DLL module), and has been for a long time. There is no direct equivalent in Linux.

`kbhit()` is a nonblocking function that will return `True` if there is a character waiting in the console input buffer. This allows a program running in a single-task, nonthreaded environment to check for input in a main loop without blocking the loop (recall the blocking behavior of the `console3.py` example from earlier). In the `console4.py` example, a thread is used to achieve functionality something like that of `kbhit()`. There is, of course, another way to do this under Linux that involves the use of the `select()` function, but I won't get into that here. I do, however, encourage you to explore it on your own; it's an interesting journey.

Under Windows the `getche()` function does essentially what Python's `raw_input()` method does when getting a single character from the user. To read a string of characters, one approach is to put `getche()` inside a loop that executes until an EOF is detected. This works, but it's not very elegant. Python's `raw_input()` method is considerably more powerful, and it's easier to use.

Using Python's msvcrt library module

For Windows environments, Python includes a handy module that allows a program to access some of the low-level functionality provided by the Microsoft runtime library `msvcrt`. Note that this does not apply to Linux platforms. We will see what can be done with Linux in the next section, when we look into `curses` and ANSI control sequences. Table 13-1 lists the functions available through Python's `msvcrt` library module.

Table 13-1. Python's msvcrt module functions

msvcrt function	Description
kbhit()	Returns `True` if a keypress occurred and a character is waiting to be read from the input buffer.
getch()	Blocking call; waits for a keypress and then returns the character in the input buffer. Does not echo the input character to the console, and does not wait for an EOL before returning.
getwch()	The "wide char" version of `getch()`; returns a Unicode value.

msvcrt function	Description
getche()	Identical to getch() except that the incoming character will be echoed to the console if it is a printable character.
getwche()	The "wide char" version of getche(); returns a Unicode value.
putch(*char*)	Prints a character directly to the console without buffering.
putwch(*unicode_char*)	The "wide char" version of putch() that accepts a Unicode character value for output.
ungetch(*char*)	Performs a "push-back" of the given character into the console buffer so that it will be the next character read by getch() or getche().
ungetwch(*unicode_char*)	The "wide char" version of ungetch() that accepts a Unicode character value to push back.

The listing for example program console5.py, shown next, illustrates how kbhit() can be used to replace the thread and raw_input() technique we saw in console4.py:

```
#! /usr/bin/python
# console5.py
#
# Demonstrates console output using the built-in print method and the
# use of the kbhit() function from msvcrt.
#
# Windows only! Will not work under Linux.
#
# Source code from the book "Real World Instrumentation with Python"
# By J. M. Hughes, published by O'Reilly.

import time
import os
import msvcrt

ainstat   = ['OFF','OFF','OFF','OFF']
aindata   = [0.0, 0.0, 0.0, 0.0]
discstate = ['OFF','OFF','OFF','OFF','OFF','OFF','OFF','OFF']
discin    = [0,0,0,0,0,0,0,0,0]

running = True
x = 0

def initData():
    global ainstat, aindata, discstate, discin

    ainstat   = ['OFF','OFF','OFF','OFF']
    aindata   = [0.0, 0.0, 0.0, 0.0]
    discstate = ['OFF','OFF','OFF','OFF','OFF','OFF','OFF','OFF']
    discin    = [0,0,0,0,0,0,0,0,0]

def readData():
    global ainstat, aindata, discstate, discin, x

    initData()
    discstate[x] = 'ON'
```

```
        discin[x] = 1
        x += 1
        if x > (len(discin) - 1):
            x = 0

def clrDisp(numlines=50):
    if os.name == "posix":
        os.system('clear')
    elif os.name in ("nt", "dos", "ce"):
        os.system('CLS')
    else:
        print '\n' * numlines

def drawData():
    print ""
    print "System Status"
    print ""
    print "Analog Input 0  : %10s  %f" % (ainstat[0], aindata[0])
    print "Analog Input 1  : %10s  %f" % (ainstat[1], aindata[1])
    print "Analog Input 2  : %10s  %f" % (ainstat[2], aindata[2])
    print "Analog Input 3  : %10s  %f" % (ainstat[3], aindata[3])
    print ""
    print "Discrete Input 0: %3s  %d" % (discstate[0], discin[0])
    print "Discrete Input 1: %3s  %d" % (discstate[1], discin[1])
    print "Discrete Input 2: %3s  %d" % (discstate[2], discin[2])
    print "Discrete Input 3: %3s  %d" % (discstate[3], discin[3])
    print "Discrete Input 4: %3s  %d" % (discstate[4], discin[4])
    print "Discrete Input 5: %3s  %d" % (discstate[5], discin[5])
    print "Discrete Input 6: %3s  %d" % (discstate[6], discin[6])
    print "Discrete Input 7: %3s  %d" % (discstate[7], discin[7])
    print ""
    print "Enter X to terminate"

def getCommand():
    global running

    if msvcrt.kbhit():
        inchar = msvcrt.getch()
        if inchar.upper() == 'X':
            running = False

#----------------------------------------------------------------------
while running:
    readData()
    clrDisp()
    drawData()
    getCommand()
    if running == True:
        time.sleep(1.0)
```

One major difference between console4.py and console5.py is in how the function getCommand() is implemented. In console5.py it's no longer a thread, and raw_input() has been replaced with kbhit(). Just entering an X is now sufficient, instead of X followed by the Enter key as in console4.py. However, the primary difference between `console4.py` and `console5.py` is that `console5.py` will *not* run under Linux, even though the behavior of both is virtually identical. Using the `msvcrt` module has rendered `console5.py` OS-specific and confined it to the Windows environment.

ANSI Display Control Techniques

The mid-1970s saw the advent of the Video Display Terminal (VDT) as a successor to the keypunch and teletype machines that were prevalent at the time. The success of the VDT was due partly to how it was interfaced with the computer system, and partly to its ability to support flexible and dynamic displays. A simple serial interface (typically RS-232) was all that was needed to connect a terminal to the mainframe and, with the appropriate time-sharing OS, the system could now support multiple users at the same time. This was possible because the chores of screen management and keyboard input were offloaded onto the terminal, so all the mainframe had to do was send data and commands to the terminal, and get the input from the user when it became available. In a sense, it was an early application of distributed processing.

Things evolved quite rapidly, and it soon became apparent that it would be nice to have the ability to position the cursor anywhere on the screen to support data entry into preformatted display templates, or forms. The ability to control the cursor position was also necessary to implement full-screen text editors such as *vi* (Unix) and *edt* (used on DEC's VMS OS). Incidentally, people also discovered that screen control was useful for games, and if you've ever played with Rogue, Nethack, or Empire you've seen the direct descendants of those early games. Some of them were quite impressive, given that they used only the ASCII character set.

Initially, terminal manufacturers went about devising their own unique schemes for doing the screen control, as manufacturers are wont to do. This quickly became a problem, because if you wanted to add more terminals to a system, there was a risk that the new terminals wouldn't work with the existing software. In most schemes the idea is to send a nonprintable character (or set of characters) to alert the logic in the terminal to receive a sequence of characters for display control, or to alter the behavior of the terminal itself. So long as terminal brand X recognizes the same sequences as terminal brand Y, all is well. But that wasn't always the case. Unix systems dealt with this by implementing "termcap," the terminal capabilities translation scheme, which could select the appropriate control sequence for a given function based on the terminal model. On Linux systems you can still find the *termcap* database file in the */etc* directory, although it has since been superseded by *terminfo*.

An initial standard for ANSI escape sequences came into existence in 1976 as ECMA-48. It later evolved into ISO/IEC 6429. The ANSI identification was adopted around 1981, when it was formalized as ANSI X3.64, and this is still the most common way to refer to the standardized terminal control sequences. Throughout the rest of this chapter, when I use "ANSI" you can assume that I'm referring to ECMA-48/ANSI X3.64.

Even though VDTs are now largely extinct, the ANSI control sequences live on, and probably will for as long as there are textual displays of one sort or another. For example, the Xterm utility on Linux (and Unix) systems supports the DEC VT100 VDT set of control sequences, which is arguably the most common implementation of the ANSI standard. Xterm can also support color, and even has a Tektronix 4014 emulation mode for (simulated) vector graphics. See the URL in "Suggested Reading" on page 544 for more information about Xterm's ANSI capabilities.

ANSI and Windows

Windows itself does not directly support ANSI console screen control, and I do not recommend the use of the 16-bit *ANSI.sys* driver. An open source replacement for *ANSI.sys* is Jason Hood's *ansicon* package, which contains ANSI drivers for both 32-bit and 64-bit Windows. After installation of either *ANSI32.dll* or *ANSI64.dll*, the *cmd.exe* window will be able to handle a useful subset of the ANSI control sequences, but it won't work with the full set of ANSI sequences. You will need to be judicious about what you throw at it. The source code is also included. You can download it from *http://adoxa.110mb.com/ansicon/index.html*.

There are some ANSI-aware console shell replacements and terminal emulators available for Windows. Some are better than others; some are free, and some cost money. We have already seen the Tera Term terminal emulator and looked at the com0com virtual serial port utility and some of its uses in Chapters 7 and 10. Here's another use for this handy little software gadget. With com0com you can write your Python application such that its I/O is routed through a serial port, connect to one of com0com's virtual ports, and then use Tera Term with its VT100 terminal emulation to connect to the other port, and all on the same machine.

Basic ANSI control sequences

Let's see what the ANSI control sequences look like. Table 13-2 is a partial listing of the ANSI control sequences set, consisting of what I consider the most immediately useful sequences for our purposes, namely, the cursor positioning and some display management sequences. I've left out things like the display attributes controls (bright, dim, color, and so on), because at this point they only add complexity to a subject I'd like to keep simple. However, if you really need bright blue blinking characters on an orange field, by all means feel free to use them.

Note that <ESC> represents the ASCII "escape" character, which can be written as a Python string in the form \x1b. Variable names in italics represent modifiable decimal parameters; e.g., *row* would be replaced by a row number. For some of the sequences, two command forms are shown. The second form is the default form, where you can omit the numeric parameters if the default behavior is acceptable. Finally, some of the sequences have just an <ESC> character at the start, while others use a two-character sequence consisting of <ESC>[(that's an escape character, \x1b, followed by a left-bracket, [).

Table 13-2. Basic ANSI control sequences

Sequence	Function	Description
`<ESC>[`*row*;*col* H `<ESC>[H`	Cursor Move or Home	Sets the cursor position where subsequent text will begin. If no row/column parameters are provided (i.e., `<ESC>[H`), the cursor will move to the home position at the upper-left corner of the screen.
`<ESC>[`*count* A `<ESC>[A`	Cursor Up	Moves the cursor up by *count* rows; the default count is 1.
`<ESC>[`*count* B `<ESC>[B`	Cursor Down	Moves the cursor down by *count* rows; the default count is 1.
`<ESC>[`*count* C `<ESC>[C`	Cursor Forward	Moves the cursor forward by *count* columns; the default count is 1.
`<ESC>[`*count* D `<ESC>[D`	Cursor Backward	Moves the cursor backward by *count* columns; the default count is 1.
`<ESC>E`	Next Line	Moves to start of next line.
`<ESC>[s`	Save Cursor	Saves current cursor position.
`<ESC>[u`	Unsave Cursor	Restores cursor position after a Save Cursor.
`<ESC>D`	Move Down (Index)	Moves the cursor down one line in the same column.
`<ESC>M`	Move Up (Rev Index)	Moves the cursor up one line in the same column.
`<ESC>[0K`	Erase to End of Line	Erases from the current cursor position to the end of the current line.
`<ESC>[2K`	Erase Line	Erases the entire current line.
`<ESC>[2J`	Erase Screen	Erases the screen with the background color and moves the cursor to home.

The next example, `bgansi.py`, is an example of a bar-graph–type display using the control sequences from Table 13-2:

```
#!/usr/bin/python
# bgansi.py
#
# Demonstrates basic ANSI screen control. Also demonstrates how to use
# stdout from the sys library module.
#
# Source code from the book "Real World Instrumentation with Python"
# By J. M. Hughes, published by O'Reilly.

import random
import time
from sys import stdout

MAXEXT  = 30
ROWSTRT = 7     # first row at 8th screen row
COLSTRT = 9     # column start offset
VALPOS  = 45    # column for value

ran = random.random
```

```python
output   = stdout.write
outflush = stdout.flush

def generateBars():
    # clear the screen
    output("\x1b[2J")

    # put eight ID strings and markers on the screen in the leftmost
    # column starting at the 8th row from the top (row 7)
    i = 1
    for row in range(ROWSTRT,15):
        # set cursor position
        output("\x1b[%d;%dH" % (row, 0))
        # write marker character
        output("Chan %d |" % i)
        i += 1


# bars are numbered 0 through 7
def updateBar(barnum, extent):
    # adjust to match actual position of bar
    row = barnum + ROWSTRT

    # limit extent to keep from hitting right edge of display
    if extent > MAXEXT:
        extent = MAXEXT
    # make sure something always gets printed
    if extent < 1:
        extent = 1

    # clear the line first (lets graph line shrink)
    output("\x1b[%d;%dH" % (row, COLSTRT))
    # erase to end of line
    output("\x1b[0K")

    # walk through all positions up to extent
    for col in range(0, extent):
        # set position
        output("\x1b[%d;%dH" % (row, COLSTRT+col))
        # use an equals sign to fill the bar
        output("=")
        # write the actual value used
        output("\x1b[%d;%dH" % (row, VALPOS))
        output("%d" % extent)
        outflush()


def runTest():
    generateBars()

    for x in range(0, 100):
        for barnum in range(0, 8):
            # the random number function returns a float value
            # between 0 and 1 use it to scale MAXEXT
            val = int(ran() * MAXEXT)
```

```
            updateBar(barnum, val)
            # sleep briefly
            time.sleep(0.1)

    output("\x1b[%d;%dH" % (20, 0))
    outflush()
    print ""

if __name__ == '__main__':
    runTest()
```

The output of `bgansi.py` is shown in Figure 13-3. This is just a single snapshot of the screen; when running, it is rather active.

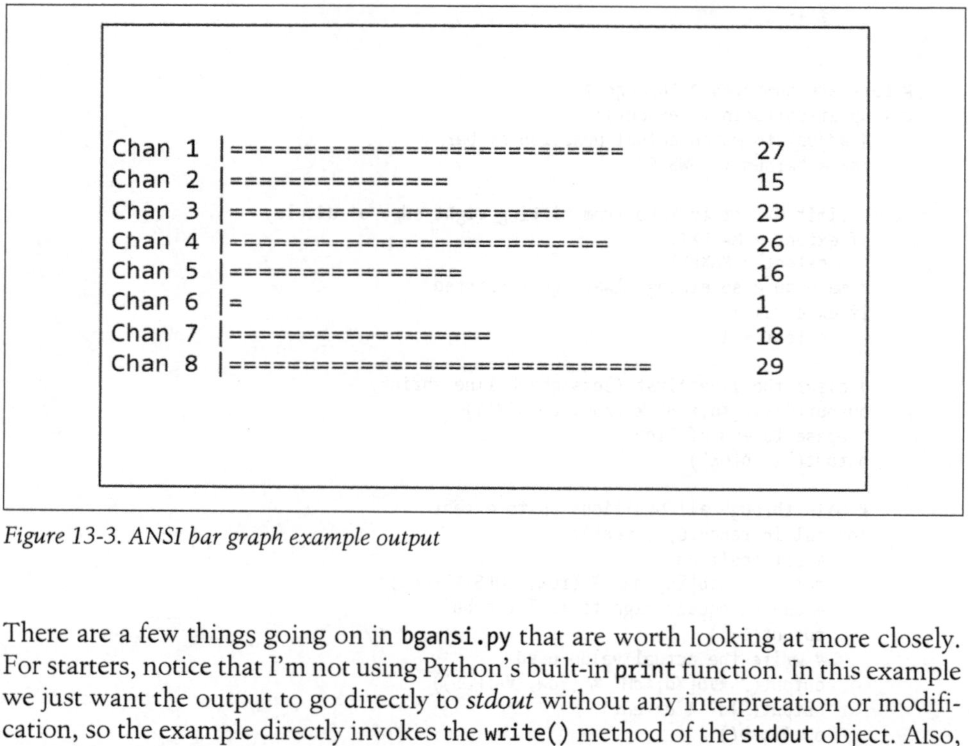

```
        Chan  1 |============================         27
        Chan  2 |=================                    15
        Chan  3 |=========================            23
        Chan  4 |===========================          26
        Chan  5 |================                     16
        Chan  6 |=                                    1
        Chan  7 |===================                  18
        Chan  8 |=============================        29
```

Figure 13-3. ANSI bar graph example output

There are a few things going on in `bgansi.py` that are worth looking at more closely. For starters, notice that I'm not using Python's built-in `print` function. In this example we just want the output to go directly to *stdout* without any interpretation or modification, so the example directly invokes the `write()` method of the `stdout` object. Also, since *stdout* is buffered internally, the `flush()` method is used to make sure all the output really does make it out when intended.

One significant thing to notice in `bgansi.py` is that the `\x1b[` sequence keeps showing up, and that the ANSI control strings that use it are not very intuitive. Writing code that uses the ANSI control codes in this fashion definitely qualifies as doing things the hard way. One could hide a lot of this by using pseudo-macro assignments, like this:

```
CSI = "\x1b["
CLR = "2J"
```

But that's not really the best solution. A better solution is a library of methods that do more than just sweep the details under the rug. In the next section we'll see such a library, which not only eliminates the need to look up the sequences but also handles I/O redirection. After that we will examine Python's interface to the curses library.

The SimpleANSI library

Not all applications need all the capabilities of the complete ANSI control sequence set. Sometimes just being able to move the cursor around and accept user input from specific locations is sufficient. But, truth be told, the sequences do tend to be somewhat clumsy to work with and cryptic to read, so having a nice, clean wrapper API of some type can help quite a bit.

Let's assume that we have a screen layout that looks like Figure 13-4.

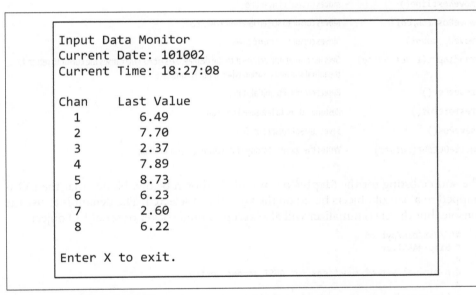

```
Input Data Monitor
Current Date: 101002
Current Time: 18:27:08

Chan      Last Value
  1          6.49
  2          7.70
  3          2.37
  4          7.89
  5          8.73
  6          6.23
  7          2.60
  8          6.22

Enter X to exit.
```

Figure 13-4. ANSI data display

Now let's take look at SimpleANSI, a library module that provides basic screen control functions via the ANSITerm class, and see how it can be used with Figure 13-4. The ANSITerm class supports the control sequences listed in Table 13-2 and includes a couple of modifications to allow for optional control of the initial cursor position for the *Erase to End of Line* and *Erase Line* sequences (the ANSITerm methods clrEOL() and clrLine(), respectively).

The ANSITerm class provides 17 public methods for ANSI screen control, listed in Table 13-3. It also handles socket, serial, and console I/O modes.

Table 13-3. ANSITerm class methods

Method	Description
clrEOL(*row*, *col*)	Clears line from position at *row*, *col* to EOL.
clrLine(*row*)	Clears entire line (*row*) in display.
clrScreen()	Clears entire screen.
indexDown()	Moves/scrolls down one line.
indexUp()	Moves/scrolls up one line.
moveBack(*count*)	Moves cursor left *count* columns.
moveDown(*count*)	Moves cursor down *count* rows.
moveForward(*count*)	Moves cursor right *count* columns.
moveHome()	Moves cursor to upper-left corner.
moveNextline()	Moves to start of next line.
movePos(*row*, *col*)	Moves cursor to screen location *row*, *col*.
moveUp(*count*)	Moves cursor up *count* rows.
readInput(*reset=False*)	Gets user input and echoes it to the display. *reset=True* causes the cursor to return to the initial starting position when input is complete.
resetDev()	Resets terminal to initial state.
restorePos()	Restores cursor to last saved position.
savePos()	Saves current cursor position.
writeOutput(*outstr*)	Writes the specified string at the current cursor position.

The source listing for the SimpleANSI module is shown below. Notice that the I/O is mapped to a pair of objects based on the type of I/O selected. The default is to use the console, but the class initializer will also accept a valid socket or serial I/O object:

```
#! /usr/bin/python
# SimpleANSI.py
#
# A minimal set of functions for ANSI screen control.
#
# Source code from the book "Real World Instrumentation with Python"
# By J. M. Hughes, published by O'Reilly.

""" Simple VT100/Xterm ANSI terminal functions for Python.

    This module is based on C code originally written for use with
    VxWorks running on embedded controllers. It is used to control
    the display of an ANSI-capable terminal or terminal emulator.
    It will work with Xterm on Unix and Linux systems, CygWin under
    Windows, and also with Tera Term under Windows.

    The ANSITerm class supports I/O via an ANSI-capable console,
    a serial connection, or a network socket.
```

This is not a replacement for curses, and was never intended
to be. It is a quick and simple way to put formatted data on
a display; nothing more. It is useful for diagnostics, status
displays, and simple command interfaces.

The pseudo-macro CSI is the ANSI "Command Sequence Introducer."

NOTE: This code has not been tested in all possible environments
for all possible (or feasible) use cases. It may contain errors,
omissions, or other unpleasant things.
"""

```python
from sys import import stdout
import time

ESC = "\x1b"
CSI = ESC+"["

CON = 0
SKT = 1
SIO = 2

class ANSITerm:
    """ Simple ANSI terminal control.

        Supports I/O using the console, a network socket, or a serial
        port.

        When communicating via a network socket, it is assumed that
        the physical port is a socket with send and receive methods,
        and that it has already been opened elsewhere.

        When using a serial port, the port must already be open. In
        this case ioport must reference a valid pySerial object.

        The default I/O mode is to use the console, which must support
        ANSI control sequences (otherwise the ANSI sequences will just
        be printed, not interpreted). Also note that all user input
        via the console requires that the Enter key be pressed when
        input is complete. This is an artifact of Python's raw_input()
        function, since it has no native getch()-type function.

        Screen coordinates are specified as (row, col), or in other
        words, as (y, x). This is the same as how curses does it.
    """
    def __init__(self, ioport=None, porttype=CON):
        """ Initialize the ANSITerm object.

            If porttype is anything other than CON, ioport must
            reference a valid I/O port object.

            If porttype is CON, self.port is assigned the value of
            None.

            The defualt I/O method is the console.
```

```
        """
        self.pktsize = 1024      # just a default value for SKT mode
        self.port    = ioport    # SKT and SIO port object
        self.portOK  = False     # valid port indicator

        # map to the appropriate I/O handlers
        if porttype == SKT:
            if self.port:
                self.portOK   = True
                self.outfunc  = self.__sktOutput
                self.inpfunc  = self.__sktInput
        elif porttype == SIO:
            if self.port:
                self.portOK   = True
                self.outfunc  = self.__sioOutput
                self.inpfunc  = self.__sioInput
        else:
            self.port     = None
            self.portOK   = True
            self.outfunc  = self.__conOutput
            self.outflush = self.__conFlush
            self.inpfunc  = self.__conInput

    #------------------------------------------------------------------
    # I/O handlers
    #------------------------------------------------------------------
    # Although this could have been done without the use of a set of
    # one-line methods, this approach leaves the door open to easily
    # expand this scheme in the future: the inclusion of some type of
    # error handling, for example, or perhaps the ability to capture
    # and log data I/O.
    #
    # Note that the socket and serial I/O methods assume that a
    # standard Python socket object or a pySerial port object will
    # be used. Another type of I/O object may require different
    # methods for reading and writing.
    #------------------------------------------------------------------
    def __sktOutput(self, outstr):
        self.port.send(outstr)

    def __sioOutput(self, outstr):
        self.port.write(outstr)

    def __conOutput(self, outstr):
        stdout.write(outstr)

    def __conFlush(self):
        stdout.flush()

    def __sktInput(self):
        return self.port.recv(self.pktsize)

    def __sioInput(self):
        return self.port.readline()
```

```python
    def __conInput(self):
        return raw_input()       # no prompt is specified for raw_input

    #----------------------------------------------------------------
    # Cursor positioning
    #----------------------------------------------------------------
    def moveHome(self):
        """ Move cursor to upper-left corner.
        """
        if self.portOK:
            self.outfunc("%sH" % CSI)

    def moveNextline(self):
        """ Move to start of next line.
        """
        if self.portOK:
            self.outfunc("%sE" % ESC)

    def movePos(self, row, col):
        """ Move cursor to screen location row, col.
        """
        if self.portOK:
            self.outfunc("%s%d;%dH" % (CSI, row, col))

    def moveUp(self, count):
        """ Move cursor up count rows.
        """
        if self.portOK:
            self.outfunc("%s%dA" % (CSI, count))

    def moveDown(self, count):
        """ Move cursor down count rows.
        """
        if self.portOK:
            self.outfunc("%s%dB" % (CSI, count))

    def moveFoward(self, count):
        """ Move cursor right count columns.
        """
        if self.portOK:
            self.outfunc("%s%dC" % (CSI, count))

    def moveBack(self, count):
        """ Move cursor left count columns.
        """
        if self.portOK:
            self.outfunc("%s%dD" % (CSI, count))

    def indexUp(self):
        """ Move/scroll up one line.
        """
        if self.portOK:
            self.outfunc("%D" % ESC)

    def indexDown(self):
```

```python
    """Move/scroll down one line.
    """
    if self.portOK:
        self.outfunc("%M" % ESC)

def savePos(self):
    """ Save current cursor position.
    """
    if self.portOK:
        self.outfunc("%ss" % CSI);

def restorePos(self):
    """ Restore cursor to last saved position.
    """
    if self.portOK:
        self.outfunc("%su" % CSI);

#-------------------------------------------------------------------
# Display control
#-------------------------------------------------------------------
def clrScreen(self):
    if self.portOK:
        self.outfunc("%s2J" % CSI);

def clrEOL(self, row=None, col=None):
    """ Clear line from given or current position.

        If row and col are None, the current position is used.
    """
    if self.portOK:
        if row and col:
            self.movePos(row,col);
        self.outfunc("%s0K" % CSI)

def clrLine(self, row=None):
    """ Clear entire line (row) in display.

        If row is None, the current position is used.
    """
    if self.portOK:
        if row:
            self.movePos(row, 1)
        self.outfunc("%s2K" % CSI)

def resetDev(self):
    """ Reset terminal to initial state.
    """
    if self.portOK:
        self.outfunc("%sc" % ESC)

#-------------------------------------------------------------------
# Input
#-------------------------------------------------------------------
def readInput(self, reset=False):
    """ Get user input and echo it to the display.
```

If a prompt is required it must be generated at the
appropriate location before this method is called.

If reset is True, when the input handler returns the
cursor will be repositioned to the starting location prior
to user input. This capability is provided mainly to
compensate for the use of Python's raw_input() function
when interacting with a console, as the user will need to
press the Enter key to complete an input.
```python
        """
        instr = ""
        if self.portOK:
            if reset: self.savePos()
            instr = self.inpfunc()
            if reset: self.restorePos()
            return instr

    #-------------------------------------------------------------------
    # Output
    #-------------------------------------------------------------------
    def writeOutput(self, outstr):
        """ Writes an arbitrary string at the current cursor position.
        """
        if self.portOK:
            self.outfunc(outstr)
            self.outflush()


# self-test
if __name__ == "__main__":
    term = ANSITerm(None, 0)

    term.clrScreen()

    # number the rows on the display from 1 to 24
    for i in range(1,21):
        term.movePos(i,0)
        term.writeOutput("%0d" % i)

    # write some text to the display
    term.movePos(14,4)
    term.writeOutput("* This is line 14, column 4")
    time.sleep(1)
    term.movePos(15,4)
    term.writeOutput("* This is line 15, column 4")
    time.sleep(1)

    # create a diagonal series of characters
    for i in range(2,12):
        term.movePos(i,i+4)
        term.writeOutput("X")
        time.sleep(0.1)

    for i in range(2,12):
```

```
        term.movePos(i,i+4)
        term.writeOutput(" ")
        time.sleep(0.1)

    for i in range(2,12):
        term.movePos(i,i+4)
        term.writeOutput("X")
        time.sleep(0.1)

    # do some blinking the hard way
    for i in range(0,10):
        term.movePos(17,10)
        term.writeOutput("blick blink")
        time.sleep(0.5)
        term.clrEOL(17,10)
        time.sleep(0.5)

    term.movePos(18,4)
    term.writeOutput("Did it blink? (y/n): ")
    instr = term.readInput()
    term.movePos(19,4)
    term.writeOutput("You answered %s, thank you for playing." % instr)

    term.movePos(22,1)
    # and that's it
```

Using SimpleANSI

Referring back to Figure 13-4, the first thing to notice is that it is a fixed-format display. One way to create this type of display is to use a predefined template to generate the base screen display and continually redraw it with new data. This is how the console4.py example did it. This works, but it's much more efficient if you can just draw the static portions of the display once and only change the data fields as necessary. console6.py incorporates the ANSITerm class to handle variable data display and accept user input. It only generates the main display screen once, and all subsequent changes occur at specific locations in the main display area. Here is the source listing for console6.py:

```
#!/usr/bin/python
# console6.py
#
# Demonstrates the use of the SimpleANSI module.
#
# Source code from the book "Real World Instrumentation with Python"
# By J. M. Hughes, published by O'Reilly.

import random
import time
import datetime
import threading
import SimpleANSI

data_vals = [0.0, 0.0, 0.0, 0.0, 0.0, 0.0, 0.0, 0.0]
```

```
    currdate = ""
    currtime = ""
    updt_cnt1 = 0
    updt_cnt2 = 0

    ran = random.random

    def getDate():
        global currdate

        t = datetime.datetime.now()
        currdatetime = t.timetuple()

        yr = str(currdatetime[0])
        currdate = "%02d"%int(yr[2:]) + "%02d"%currdatetime[1] +\
            "%02d"%currdatetime[2]

    def getTime():
        global currtime

        t = datetime.datetime.now()
        currdatetime = t.timetuple()

        currtime = "%02d:"%currdatetime[3] + "%02d:"%currdatetime[4] +\
            "%02d"%currdatetime[5]

    # write data and time to display
    def writeDateTime():
        getDate()
        getTime()

        term.clrEOL(2,15)
        term.movePos(2,15)
        term.writeOutput("%s" % currdate)
        term.clrEOL(3,15)
        term.movePos(3,15)
        term.writeOutput("%s" % currtime)

    # get simulated data input values
    def getDataVals():
        global data_vals, updt_cnt1, updt_cnt2

        data_vals[0] = ran() * 10.0
        data_vals[1] = ran() * 10.0

        if updt_cnt1 >= 4:
            for i in range(2,5):
                data_vals[i] = ran() * 10.0
            updt_cnt1 = 0
        else:
            updt_cnt1 += 1

        if updt_cnt2 >= 10:
            for i in range(4,8):
                data_vals[i] = ran() * 10.0
```

```
            updt_cnt2 = 0
        else:
            updt_cnt2 += 1

    # write channel data values
    def writeDataVals():
        idx = 0
        for i in range(6,14):
            term.movePos(i,10)
            term.writeOutput("%6.2f" % data_vals[idx])
            idx += 1
        # put cursor below display text when update is done
        term.movePos(16,1)

    # generate the main display
    def mainScreen():
        term.clrScreen()

        term.movePos(1,1)
        term.writeOutput("Input Data Monitor")

        term.movePos(2,1)
        term.writeOutput("Current Date:")
        term.movePos(3,1)
        term.writeOutput("Current Time:")
        writeDateTime()

        term.movePos(5,1)
        term.writeOutput("Chan    Last Value")

        rownum = 1
        for row in range(6,14):
            term.movePos(row,1)
            term.writeOutput("  %d" % rownum)
            rownum += 1

        writeDataVals()

        term.movePos(15,1)
        term.writeOutput("Enter X to exit.")

    # raw_input() handler thread
    def getCommand():
        global exit_loop

        while True:
            instr = raw_input()
            if instr.upper() == 'X':
                exit_loop = True
                break
            time.sleep(0.1)

    #-----------------------------------------------------------------
    # Main loop
    #-----------------------------------------------------------------
```

```
term = SimpleANSI.ANSITerm(None, 0)

exit_loop = False

# launch the raw_input() handler thread
getinput = threading.Thread(target=getCommand)
getinput.start()

mainScreen()

while exit_loop == False:
    writeDateTime()
    getDataVals()
    writeDataVals()
    time.sleep(0.2)
```

console6.py is actually a slightly more realistic version of the console4.py example. I've reused the thread trick to prevent Python's raw_input() method from suspending the main loop while waiting for user input. Python's date and time methods are also put to use. The primary objective here is to show how ANSI control sequences, via the SimpleANSI module, can be used to generate a dynamic ASCII display based on a static template.

Python and curses

 This discussion of curses and Python's curses implementation is intended mainly for Python on Unix/Linux systems. Python will not import the curses library module on a Windows system (the Windows version of Python does not have the curses module). Although there are some possible workarounds, Windows applications should probably just use something like the SimpleANSI module with the *ANSI32.dll* driver.

This section isn't about programming frustration, although I have no doubt that software development has led to some very creative cursing. No, this section is about the curses library for manipulating characters on a terminal display using ANSI control sequences.

We've just seen some of what you can do using only a handful of simple ANSI control sequences, and if you've ever used the *vi*, *Emacs*, or *edt* editors, you've seen examples of what can be done with the full set of ANSI sequences. Although the subset of the ANSI control sequences we've used so far will take us a long way, realizing the full capabilities of the ANSI sequences would require some significant programming. Fortunately, it's already been done for us with the curses library.

The curses library can be used to do things like manipulate specific areas of a display while leaving other areas undisturbed (i.e., curses does windows), change text styles and colors, scroll text, and other neat tricks. You can also create drop-down menus, checkboxes, and other useful user-input aids.

curses background

curses originated on BSD Unix systems in the early 1980s and was later adopted and extended for ATT's System V Release 4.0 (SVr4). On Linux systems ANSI screen control is provided by the ncurses library (ncurses stands for "new curses," an open source replacement for the SVr4 curses library). From now on, when I refer to curses you should take it as meaning ncurses.

It is important to note that curses is a Unix/Linux thing, and there is no native port of the curses library available for Windows. Attempting to import curses into a Python program running under Windows will result in an error, because the curses library module isn't supplied with the Windows version of Python. While there have been some attempts at creating curses-compatible displays for Windows, I've not tried any of them and I can't comment on them.

Python's curses library module

Python's curses library module is simply a wrapper around some of the standard ncurses library functions. It is not a complete wrapper, but it does implement a fairly large number of the most commonly used functions. I won't try to cover all of the Python curses library module here; I recommend that you take a look at the Python documentation to get more details. We will look at the basic concepts behind curses, and see how it can be used to manage an ASCII screen display in an Xterm window.

Any Python program that uses curses must first initialize the curses library and instantiate a curses window object to manage the entire display area. To end a curses session and release control of the display screen, the endwin() function is called. This is shown in the following example, which does nothing but start up curses and then shut it down again:

```
import curses
stdscr = curses.initscr()

# curses statements go here

curses.endwin()
```

In curses the primary logical object is the window, and the various windows in a display are arranged as a hierarchy, with the first window (stdscr, the entire display area) as the parent. Figure 13-5 is a pseudo-3D illustration of this arrangement.

Writing a curses-based application is basically a matter of defining the windows to be used, implementing whatever dynamic control they may need (drop-down menus need to appear at the appropriate places, the cursor may need to respond to the Tab key, and so on), and then populating them with the necessary text and data input fields. Internally, curses keeps track of where things are relative to each window, such as cursor position. Sounds simple enough, so let's try it out.

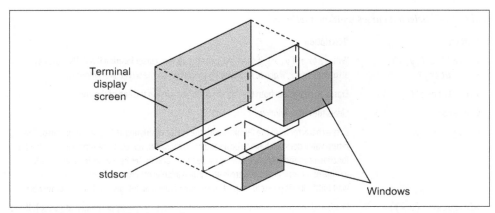

Figure 13-5. curses window hierarchy

A simple data display using curses

First off, let's translate the `console6.py` example into `curses`. This will allow us to see how the basic ANSI control sequences we've already used fit into the `curses` scheme of things. Note that although the output will look the same, it will no longer work with MS Windows, for the reasons already stated.

`curses` functions and methods come in two forms: module-level functions that pertain to the behavior of the entire `curses` module, and window-specific methods that operate on a window object. We don't need all of the functionality from `curses` for this project, only a subset. Table 13-4 lists the definitions for the `curses` library functions we'll be using initially, and Table 13-5 defines the window object methods we'll need. Square brackets indicate optional parameters.

Table 13-4. Selected curses library functions

Function	Description
`cbreak()`	Enables cbreak mode. In this mode normal line buffering is disabled, and input characters may be read one by one from the input. Special key characters, such as Control-C, will still have the expected effect.
`nocbreak()`	Exits from cbreak mode and returns to the normal buffered input mode of operation.
`echo()`	Enables echo mode, wherein each character input is echoed to the display as the user enters it.
`noecho()`	Disables echo mode, so characters entered by the user are not echoed to the display.
`initscr()`	Initializes the `curses` module. The object returned (a `WindowObject`) represents the whole display screen. This is the top-level window.
`endwin()`	Shuts down `curses` and returns the terminal to its normal state.
`curs_set(`*`visibility`*`)`	Controls the visibility of the cursor. The *`visibility`* parameter can be one of 0, 1, or 2, with the effect being invisible, noticeable, or very visible, respectively. Exactly what "very visible" means depends on the terminal (or terminal emulator) in use.
`ungetch(`*`ch`*`)`	Pushes *`ch`* back into the input stream so that the next call to `getch()` will return it.

Table 13-5. Selected curses window methods

Method	Description
win.addstr([y, x], str[, attr])	Writes str at [y, x], if specified, or at the current cursor location if not. Uses display attributes attr, if given. Any existing characters on the screen are overwritten.
win.clrtoeol()	Erases all characters from the current cursor location to the end of the line.
win.erase()	Clears the entire window.
win.getch([y, x])	Gets a character from the terminal with the cursor positioned at [y, x], if specified. The return value does not have to be a valid ASCII character, but could be some value > 255 for function keys and such. In no-delay mode (nonblocking, set by the nodelay() method), a value of −1 is returned if there is no input available; otherwise getch() will block and wait until a key is pressed. Suspect the return of being an integer until proven otherwise.
win.getstr([y, x])	Reads and returns a string from the user with the cursor initially positioned at [y, x], if specified. Provides limited line-editing capability.
win.move(new_y, new_x)	Moves the cursor to position (new_y, new_x) in the window.
win.nodelay(yes)	Controls the blocking behavior of getch(). If yes is 1, getch() will be a nonblocking call.
win.subwin([nlines, ncols], begin_y, begin_x)	Returns a subwindow object. The upper-left corner is defined by (begin_y, begin_x), and the width and height are defined by ncols and nlines, respectively. If ncols and nlines are omitted, the new window will extend to the lower-right corner of the display area.

It's interesting to observe that ANSITerm actually provides more low-level functionality than curses. In other words, the curses library encapsulates many of the low-level ANSI control sequences in its methods, whereas ANSITerm exposes them. This shouldn't be too surprising, since ANSITerm is really nothing more than a fancy wrapper around the ANSI sequences and does not provide any support for window management or other high-level functions.

The first example, curses1.py, doesn't do anything fancy. It just creates a continuously updated display like the one that console6.py generates:

```
#!/usr/bin/python
# curses1.py
#
# Demonstrates the use of Python's curses module.
#
# Translated from the console6.py example.
#
# Source code from the book "Real World Instrumentation with Python"
# By J. M. Hughes, published by O'Reilly.

import random
import time
import datetime
import curses
import traceback

data_vals = [0.0, 0.0, 0.0, 0.0, 0.0, 0.0, 0.0, 0.0]
```

```
currdate = ""
currtime = ""
updt_cnt1 = 0
updt_cnt2 = 0


ran = random.random

def getDate():
    global currdate

    t = datetime.datetime.now()
    currdatetime = t.timetuple()
    yr = str(currdatetime[0])
    currdate = "%02d"%int(yr[2:]) + "%02d"%currdatetime[1] +\
        "%02d"%currdatetime[2]

def getTime():
    global currtime

    t = datetime.datetime.now()
    currdatetime = t.timetuple()
    currtime = "%02d:"%currdatetime[3] + "%02d:"%currdatetime[4] +\
        "%02d"%currdatetime[5]

# write data and time to display
def writeDateTime(win):
    getDate()
    getTime()

    win.move(2,15)
    win.clrtoeol()
    win.addstr("%s" % currdate)
    win.move(3,15)
    win.clrtoeol()
    win.addstr("%s" % currtime)
    win.refresh()

# get simulated data input values
def getDataVals():
    global data_vals, updt_cnt1, updt_cnt2

    data_vals[0] = ran() * 10.0
    data_vals[1] = ran() * 10.0

    if updt_cnt1 >= 4:
        for i in range(2,5):
            data_vals[i] = ran() * 10.0
        updt_cnt1 = 0
    else:
        updt_cnt1 += 1

    if updt_cnt2 >= 10:
        for i in range(4,8):
            data_vals[i] = ran() * 10.0
        updt_cnt2 = 0
```

```
        else:
            updt_cnt2 += 1

    # write channel data values
    def writeDataVals(win):
        idx = 0
        for i in range(6,14):
            win.move(i,10)
            win.clrtoeol()
            win.addstr("%6.2f" % data_vals[idx])
            idx += 1

        win.refresh()
        # put cursor below display text when update is done
        win.move(16,1)

    # generate the main display
    def mainScreen(win):
        win.erase()

        win.move(1,1)
        win.addstr("Input Data Monitor")
        win.refresh()

        win.move(2,1)
        win.addstr("Current Date:")
        win.move(3,1)
        win.addstr("Current Time:")
        win.refresh()

        writeDateTime(win)

        win.move(5,1)
        win.addstr("Chan     Last Value")
        win.refresh()

        rownum = 1
        for row in range(6,14):
            win.move(row, 1)
            win.addstr("  %d" % rownum)
            rownum += 1
        win.refresh()

        writeDataVals(win)

        win.move(15,1)
        win.addstr("Enter X to exit.")
        win.refresh()

    def mainloop(win):
        win.nodelay(1)  # disable getch() blocking
        # draw the main display template
        mainScreen(win)

        # run until the user wants to quit
```

```
    while 1:
        # check for keyboard input
        inch = win.getch()
        # getch() will return -1 if no character is available
        if inch != -1:
            # see if inch is really the exit character
            instr = hr(inch)
            if instr.upper() == 'X':
                break
        writeDateTime(win)
        getDataVals()
        writeDataVals(win)
        time.sleep(0.2)

def startup():
    # Borrowed the idea of using a try-except wrapper around the
    # initialization from David Mertz
    try:
        # Initialize curses
        stdscr = curses.initscr()

        # Turn off echoing of keys and enter cbreak mode,
        # where no buffering is performed on keyboard input
        curses.noecho()
        curses.cbreak()

        mainloop(stdscr)                # Enter the main loop

        # Set everything back to normal
        curses.echo()
        curses.nocbreak()

        curses.endwin()                 # Terminate curses
    except:
        # In event of error, restore terminal to sane state
        curses.echo()
        curses.nocbreak()
        curses.endwin()
        traceback.print_exc()           # Print the exception

if __name__=='__main__':
    startup()
```

In curses the screen coordinates are specified in (y, x) order—i.e., (row, column)—
which is also how the ANSITerm class does it. After the main window object (stdscr) is
created, the calls to the curses functions noecho() and cbreak() disable local echo and
input buffering. Finally, notice that mainloop() is called with stdscr as its sole parameter. All subsequent window methods used are methods of this object.

Because of the way that curses manages window objects internally, it won't automatically send output to the screen; you have to tell it when to update the display. Part of
the reason for this lies in how a complex curses-driven display might be used. Rather
than have individual lines flickering on the screen as data is updated, the refresh()

method can be used to update the display so that changes occur over a set of display items, or individual windows, and all at once. The other part of the reason for using `refresh()` (and the other related methods) is that when a method like `addstr()` is called it changes the data in the internal representation of the display for a particular window, but it doesn't automatically pass that change to the display. You have to tell it when to do so.

Adding a subwindow

Let's assume that you want to have a subwindow that pops up in response to some user input. The first step is to define the window. In `curses2.py` I've encapsulated the sub-window object in its own function, `openSubWindow()`, which resides in the code just prior to `mainloop()`:

```
def openSubWindow(win):
    # create a subwindow and keep it open until user presses the X
    # key
    subwin = win.subwin(10, 30, 10, 10)
    subwin.nodelay(1)  # disable getch() blocking
    subwin.erase()
    subwin.bkgdset(' ')
    subwin.refresh()
    subwin.addstr(3, 0, "Enter X to exit subwindow")
    subwin.refresh()
    while 1:
        inch = subwin.getch()
        if inch != -1:
            instr = chr(inch)
            if instr.upper() == 'X':
                break
        time.sleep(0.2)
```

This new function is called from within the `mainloop()` function by adding a W command to the input command set, like so:

```
def mainloop(win):
    win.nodelay(1)  # disable getch() blocking
    # draw the main display template
    mainScreen(win)

    # run until the user wants to quit
    while 1:
        # check for keyboard input
        inch = win.getch()
        # getch() will return -1 if no character is available
        if inch != -1:
            # see if inch is really the exit character
            instr = chr(inch)
            if instr.upper() == 'X':
                break
            if instr.upper() == 'W':
                openSubWindow(win)
                # simple way to restore underlying main screen
```

```
        mainScreen(win)
    writeDateTime(win)
    getDataVals()
    writeDataVals(win)
    time.sleep(0.2)
```

When the user presses the w (or W) key, he will see a clear 10×30-character region of the display appear with the single line "Enter X to exit subwindow." When the subwindow function exits, the `mainloop()` function redraws the display to cover up the hole left by the subwindow.

There are, of course, more elegant ways to handle creating and deleting subwindows, but I chose this approach to keep things simple. The `curses2.py` example also does not do things like draw a border around the subwindow or fill in the background with a solid shade or color. How these features and others in the `curses` library will behave is largely dependent on how the display handles ANSI command sequences, which in turn depends on the system's `terminfo` definitions. If you plan to use `curses` for your applications, I would encourage you to spend some time with Python's `curses` module and the `terminfo` manpage. Also, be sure to check out the section "Suggested Reading" on page 544.

To Curse or Not to Curse, Is That the Question?

If you don't need the advanced functionality found in `curses`, and you want your application to be portable without resorting to a full-on GUI, you may want to consider just using something like `SimpleANSI` and be done with it. Most instrumentation applications don't really need a lot of fancy screen controls anyway, and we've already seen how to create data display screens with real-time update capabilities.

However, that being said, `curses` offers some capabilities that one would be hard-pressed to duplicate with a simple ANSI control library, at least not without some serious coding. Since `curses` is already written, and very mature, it makes more sense to use that if you need subwindows, menus, mouse control, and dialogs in your application, and you don't need it to run on Windows.

While `curses` is not a cross-platform solution, it is a cross-display interface. Any system with the ability to display ASCII characters and interpret ANSI control sequences can probably handle a `curses`-driven display. This includes terminal emulators running under Windows with VT100 emulation capability, Xterm windows on Linux systems, and yes, even a dumb terminal like a VT100 (if you happen to have one handy, that is). In an instrumentation system, using an ANSI/ASCII terminal or terminal emulator connected to a remote host system via a serial port or network connection is not as daft as it might sound at first. Servers in large installations often use `curses` for system status display and control interfaces, allowing the operator access to the OS even when no main console (and hence, no GUI) is available.

In an instrumentation system you may want to be able to monitor or control a remote system using a simple communications protocol over a thin cable, rather than trying to snake a hefty cable bundle between the controller PC and the various sensors and actuators. Or it just might not be feasible to be co-located with the host machine, for whatever reasons (explosion hazard, noise, radiation, heat, and cryogenic conditions are a few that spring to mind). The ANSI control sequences offer a quick and relatively easy way to get a readable, and perhaps even elegant, control and data display up and running quickly.

(My apologies to W. Shakespeare.)

Graphical User Interfaces

All modern general-purpose operating systems incorporate some type of graphical user interface (GUI) into their design. Only those operating systems intended for deeply embedded applications don't come with some kind of GUI, since they don't need one anyway (they usually don't have any kind of user interface display, actually).

The GUI is a layer of functionality on top of the core operating system, and in some cases it may even be optional. In a Unix or Linux system, the GUI is started after the operating system loads as a discrete step in the boot sequence, and a Linux system will run just fine without the GUI. In other cases, such as with Windows, the GUI is tightly integrated into the OS, and while still technically a layer of functionality, it is not designed to be easily disabled.

In this section we'll see how to use a GUI with Python. I won't go into detailed code examples, mainly because anything beyond a simple "Hello World" GUI can get rather involved. What we will do is look at where the whole GUI concept originated, and why you might want to use one, rather than simple command-line or ANSI solutions like the ones we're already seen in this chapter. We will wrap up with a look at some simple data display GUIs to give you a sense of what is involved in creating a GUI.

Some GUI Background and Concepts

Before undertaking a quick survey of a couple of GUI toolkits for Python, I'd like to take a look at the history of the GUI as we know it today. Many people still believe that Apple invented the GUI, but this is not true. The first really usable GUI was invented at Xerox's Palo Alto Research Center (PARC) in the early 1970s and ran on Xerox's Alto computer system. Steve Jobs saw it during a tour of the PARC facility in 1979 and the Apple Lisa, and later the Mac, came into existence shortly thereafter. When Microsoft got wind of what Apple was up to, the decision was made to embark on the development of Windows, which would eventually render the DOS command line obsolete. The X Window System, found initially on Unix systems and later on Linux, was another response to the push to create a graphical interface experience for the user.

Xerox itself was unable to get an affordable system to market in time to capitalize on its own invention.

There are multiple levels of abstraction in a modern computer system's graphical interface. The GUI is responsible for managing the placement of application-driven windows on the primary display device, keeping track of the so-called z-order (how the windows overlap and stack on top of one another), and making sure that windows get update notices when they need to redraw portions of their display area. Each application window has its own mechanisms for handling user input, data output, and redraw or refresh activities. In some types of window displays, such as the multiple document interface (MDI), the application's window is a "parent" window that may contain one or more "child" windows, each of which might have a menu bar, buttons, dialogs, image displays, and other components (known as *widgets*). Each level has its own set of display-management functions and can communicate with other windows within the context of the parent window, or the overall top-level system GUI.

A graphical user interface is not only prettier than a command-line or text-based interface, it can also be more intuitive and easier to comprehend. However, as you may have gathered from the previous paragraph, this ease of use does not come without a price.

A GUI is much more complicated than a functionally equivalent text-based interface. A GUI is also more than just an added bit of functionality for an application—in most cases it *is* the application. In other words, if you want to add an ASCII text–type interface to a program, it's basically just a matter of using ANSI terminal control sequences to manipulate a display using conventional I/O calls. There's nothing really special about it. In a GUI, the window manager not only handles the management of the graphical components in the display, but also encapsulates the functionality of the application within its framework. If you want to have "outboard" functionality with a GUI, you will need to start thinking about external processes, named pipes, sockets, and other forms of interprocess communication (IPC) to implement your scheme. Life with a GUI can get very complicated very fast.

So, why would you want to use a GUI? The two main reasons are fidelity and functionality. With a GUI, you can display data much more accurately than you can with an ASCII display. Graphs are a good example of this. A GUI is also capable of displaying images and allowing the user to interact with the images as control inputs. Many high-end industrial control systems use interfaces like this, where a diagram of a plant's process components are displayed with real-time data and the user can select a component and change its operating parameters by clicking on its image in the diagram.

With a GUI you can also present a 3D graph, or even a solid model that the user can rotate to view it from different angles, pan around, and zoom in or out, with the display continuously updated. Some laser interferometer systems use displays like this to show the minute features on an optical surface while continuously acquiring new measurements.

While these are all very impressive features, I'm going to stick to GUI displays that are easy to implement. If you have the desire to learn more, see the section "Suggested Reading" on page 544. You can also get the source code for some of the GUI applications you like (if they're open source, that is) and see how they are implemented.

Using a GUI with Python

In this section I will present two common GUI toolkits for Python: TkInter and wxPython. Although the end result of both is essentially the same, the basic differences between how the toolkits are used and what can be done with them are things you should be aware of when deciding on which one to use. We'll also look at some of the tools available to help with display design and layout.

Before moving on, we need some terminology. But first, I'd like to point out that many of these terms are used interchangeably, sometimes incorrectly so. I will try to be consistent in this chapter and hopefully reduce the potential for confusion.

There are basically two types of objects in a GUI: *containers* and *controls*. A container is used to group other containers and controls and to maintain the functional relationships between the GUI objects within it. Containers include windows, frames, dialogs, and modal windows. A distinguishing characteristic of a window-like object is that it can exist on its own as the top-level object in a hierarchy of display objects.

Controls are those GUI objects that provide an interaction point for a user. They are also known as "widgets," which is how we'll refer to them. A widget might be a button, a scroll bar, or a canvas for drawing. The term can also refer to a text entry field or a complex, composite object composed of other, simpler widgets. In some toolkits there are also special container widgets that aren't really windows, but can be used to logically group a set of functionally related widgets. The panel widget is one such object. Members of the set of objects called controls exist in the context of a window object.

Naturally, there are exceptions and special cases, and things aren't always so neatly and clearly delineated. For example, some window objects, such as frames, can be both a top-level object and a subordinate to another window. In other cases, a widget might be able to act as a container, even though it cannot stand alone without a parent window. It might help to keep in mind that GUI components in Python are objects in the true sense of the word, and it is possible, and quite common, to create new objects by inheriting from existing class definitions. Once you get a sense of how a GUI works and what goes into making one, the gray areas will tend to become less bothersome.

In the meantime, you can generally assume that a window object is where widgets and other windows are located, and that windows don't have control inputs unless they also have widgets.

There are basically three ways to look at a GUI: as OO-based software with child classes derived from parent class definitions, as a structure of hierarchically organized objects sharing a display space but not necessarily related to one another in an OO inheritance sense, and functionally as an event-driven software application. We'll start with the OO view.

GUI objects

In toolkits that employ an object-oriented approach, each window or widget is defined as a class, and each class provides a set of methods and attributes. wxPython is one of these, and the underlying wxWidgets is very much an OO design. Initially the Tk toolkit wasn't a true OO implementation (tcl isn't an OO language), but with TkInter it too has acquired the trappings of classes, objects, and methods. Taking an OO approach also means that you can create a new widget class by inheriting from an existing one, and perhaps override existing methods or add some new ones.

In most cases a widget will be subclassed from a window or widget that itself is derived from a parent class. Thus, a frame object could be subclassed from a window object, and a button widget object might be subclassed from a control object (see Figure 13-6).

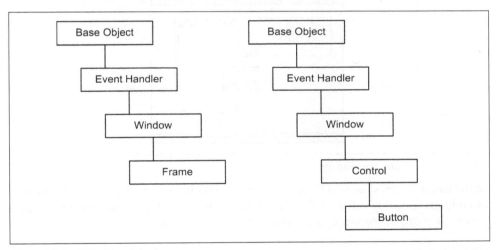

Figure 13-6. GUI object inheritances

Not all GUI implementations follow this particular scheme, which in this case is based on wxPython, but the main distinctions between a window object and a control object will generally apply to both of the toolkits we will be using in this section.

Basic GUI display structure

Structurally, a GUI is typically organized as a hierarchy of graphical components. There is a parent, or base object, which is typically a frame of some type (see Figure 13-6). This object is used as the anchor or parent for subsequent GUI objects, which themselves may be parents, and so on, as shown in Figure 13-7. This is not an inheritance situation, but rather a hierarchy of functional relationships.

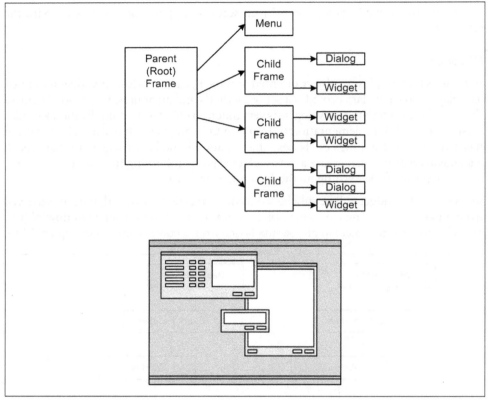

Figure 13-7. GUI object hierarchy

In the tree diagram shown in Figure 13-7, each child has one parent and some number of children (possibly zero) itself. When widgets are bound to a window object like a frame, they can be managed as a group by the parent object.

GUI functionality

Functionally, a GUI is based on a stimulus and response paradigm. A stimulus is referred to as an *event*, and events may come from a user, from an internal process, or from the world outside of the software. When a user inputs a command, perhaps using a mouse to click on a button or pressing a key, an event is generated and the GUI responds in some fashion. While waiting for a command a GUI might be receiving external events and updating data displays, or even generating internal events via timers or other methods. This is what is known as *event-driven programming*, and it is the prevailing model used in modern GUIs.

Events are processed by *event handlers* assigned to *event sources*. This assignment is called *binding*, and an event handler is said to be *bound* to a particular event. An event handler may be self-contained, or it may call other functions or methods to perform

---

some specific processing. Some event handlers are built into the GUI framework. These include notifications of changes to the display, such as when the user moves one window on top of another, or when all open windows are closed at once.

But for the most part, the events that we will be concerned with are those that are generated by the various widgets in a Python GUI. Each button, text field, slider bar, and so on, must have an event handler associated with it. In TkInter these are often referred to as "callbacks" and in wxPython they are known as "event handlers," but the net effect is the same.

Because a GUI is event-driven, the display may suspend until an event of some sort is received. Consider a situation where we might want a GUI to display data from an instrument every second or so. Unless there is some way to generate an event that will call the function to query the instrument for new data and then update the display, the display will sit idle until the user clicks on an "Update" button to specifically request new data. This may sound obvious, but many neophyte GUI programmers have been seen sitting and staring at their pretty creations, wondering how to avoid having to repeatedly click a button to see things change. The solution is to use some kind of internal timer that can generate an event to obtain new data from an external source such as an instrument.

wxPython includes timer functions as part of its design, and these are relatively straight-forward to use. TkInter uses a different approach wherein a widget itself generates an event and invokes a callback after some amount of time has elapsed. This isn't quite as intuitive, but it works fine when used appropriately.

The GUI main loop

In a GUI the execution is driven by a main loop, as shown in Figure 13-8, which is similar to what we saw in the ANSI text-based interfaces earlier. The main loop is responsible for starting the interface, handling events and messages, and then shutting it all down when it's time to leave, among other things.

The `mainloop()` method is a fundamental and necessary part of both TkInter and wxPython GUI applications. How these two toolkits implement the main loop differs in the details, but the net effect is the same. Once the main loop starts it will not return until the GUI shuts down and exits.

TkInter

Python comes with the TkInter GUI toolkit as part of the standard distribution. TkInter refers to the Tk part of the tcl/Tk language (tcl and Tk are usually referred to as one thing). The Tk widget set is relatively easy to use, and it's very mature, having been around now for the better part of 20 years.

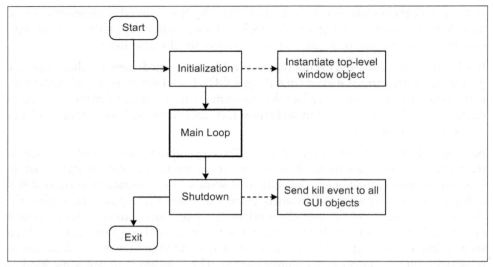

Figure 13-8. GUI main loop

Planning your GUI

Before embarking on a GUI project, one of the first steps is to decide what the interface will look like. Implementing a GUI involves making decisions about things such as what widgets to use, how the positioning of the widgets will be managed, the required functionality (what will happen when the user interacts with a widget), and the use of internal event generators, if necessary. Any GUI with even a modest amount of complexity isn't something one can just throw together and expect to work right off the bat. It pays to take the time to think it through before starting.

When planning a GUI layout, I like to create a drawing of what I think the GUI will look like and then use that as a template to work from. You may have a different technique, but at the very least just jotting down your GUI layout ideas on a piece of paper can be invaluable when you start to actually define the widgets and write the code.

Geometry management

TkInter provides three forms of widget placement control, also known as *geometry management*. These are the pack, grid, and place techniques. Of these, the *pack* method is the simplest and probably the most commonly used. With pack, widgets are added from the outside edges of the window toward the center, in effect packing them as close toward the center of the window space as possible.

When a widget is packed, it will be positioned on the screen so that it is packed next to either a window border or another widget, with additional widgets set next to it, and so on. The pack geometry manager will attempt to arrange the widgets so as to occupy the smallest amount of space in a window. The biggest drawback with pack is that it doesn't give you a lot of direct control over where the widgets will end up, although you can push them around by inserting "padding widgets" (i.e., empty panels and such). If the top-level frame is resized, things can sometimes get scrambled.

The *place* geometry manager uses absolute *x* and *y* pixel coordinates to place widgets in a window. With place you can create some very attractive GUIs, but you really need a layout tool to help with the placement unless your window is small and simple.

The placement method I prefer for a TkInter GUI is the *grid* method. The grid geometry manager organizes the base window by overlaying a placement grid. The width and height of each column and row are determined by the sizes of the widgets themselves.

Simple TkInter example

The following is the source code for a simple TkInter GUI, tkdemo1.py. It uses the grid geometry manager to place six widgets in two columns:

```
#!/usr/bin/python
# tkdemo1.py
#
# Demonstration of TkInter and the grid placement method.
#
# Source code from the book "Real World Instrumentation with Python"
# By J. M. Hughes, published by O'Reilly.

from Tkinter import *

class demoGUI(Frame):
    def __init__(self, master=None):
        Frame.__init__(self, master)
        self.grid(sticky=W)
        self.createWidgets()

    def createWidgets(self):
        # get top-level frame reference
        top=self.winfo_toplevel()
        # set the start location in the window manager
        top.wm_geometry('+50+100')

        # set the window title
        self.master.title("Demo 1")

        # configure the global grid behavior
        self.master.rowconfigure( 0, weight = 1 )
        self.master.columnconfigure( 0, weight = 1 )
        self.grid(sticky = W+E+N+S)

        # create string objects for use with label widgets
        self.var1 = StringVar()
        self.var1.set("")
        self.var2 = StringVar()
        self.var2.set("")

        # output state toggle flags
        self.toggle1 = 0
```

```
        self.toggle2 = 0

        # create three buttons and three label widgets, one of which
        # is a dummy placeholder (for now)

        # bind buttons 1 and 2 to event handlers

        # the two active label widgets will display green text on a
        # black background

        self.button1 = Button(self, text="Button 1", width=10)
        self.button1.grid(row=0, column=0)
        self.button1.bind("<Button-1>", self.button1_Click)

        self.text1 = Label(self, text="", width=10, relief=SUNKEN,
                           bg="black", fg="green",
                           textvariable=self.var1)
        self.text1.grid(row=0, column=10)

        self.button2 = Button(self, text="Button 2", width=10)
        self.button2.grid(row=1, column=0)
        self.button2.bind("<Button-1>", self.button2_Click)

        self.text2 = Label(self, text="", width=10, relief=SUNKEN,
                           bg="black", fg="green",
                           textvariable=self.var2)
        self.text2.grid(row=1, column=10)

        self.button3 = Button(self, text="Quit", width=10,
                              command=self.quit)
        self.button3.grid(row=2, column=0)

        # dummy space filler
        # you could modify this to display something
        self.text3 = Label(self, text="", width=10)
        self.text3.grid(row=2, column=10)

    def button1_Click(self, event):
        if self.toggle1 == 0:
            self.var1.set("0000")
            self.toggle1 = 1
        else:
            self.var1.set("1111")
            self.toggle1 = 0

        print "Button 1"

    def button2_Click(self, event):
        if self.toggle2 == 0:
            self.var2.set("0000")
            self.toggle2 = 1
        else:
            self.var2.set("1111")
            self.toggle2 = 0
```

```
        print "Button 2"

app = demoGUI()
app.mainloop()
```

On a Windows system the `tkdemo1.py` example will create a simple dialog like the one shown in Figure 13-9. It looks much the same on a Linux machine, except for the stylistic differences between the window managers.

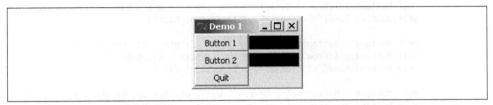

Figure 13-9. TkInter GUI example

In the following example, `tkdemo2.py`, I elected to use the label widgets for text output once again, mainly because it's easy. To be honest, Tk's Text widget is something of a pain to use, so I tend to avoid it. Here's the source code for `tkdemo2.py`:

```python
#!/usr/bin/python
# tkdemo2.py
#
# 2nd Demonstration of TkInter and the grid placement method.
#
# Source code from the book "Real World Instrumentation with Python"
# By J. M. Hughes, published by O'Reilly.
from Tkinter import *
import time

class demoGUI(Frame):
    def __init__(self, master=None):
        Frame.__init__(self, master)
        self.createWidgets()

    def createWidgets(self):
        # get top-level frame reference
        top=self.winfo_toplevel()
        # set the start location in the window manager
        top.wm_geometry('+50+100')

        # set the window title
        self.master.title("Demo 2")

        # create string objects for use with label widgets
        self.var1 = StringVar()
        self.var1.set("")
        self.var2 = StringVar()
        self.var2.set("")

        self.master.rowconfigure(0, weight = 1)
```

```python
        self.master.columnconfigure(0, weight = 1)
        self.grid(sticky = W+E+N+S)

        self.text1 = Label(self, text="", width = 15, height = 4,
                           relief=RAISED, bg="white", fg="black",
                           textvariable=self.var1)
        self.text1.grid(rowspan = 2, sticky = W+E+N+S)

        self.button1 = Button(self, text = "RUN", width = 10, height = 2)
        self.button1.grid(row = 0, column = 1, sticky = W+E+N+S)
        self.button1.bind("<Button-1>", self.button1_Click)

        self.button2 = Button(self, text = "STOP", width = 10, height = 2)
        self.button2.grid(row = 0, column = 2, sticky = W+E+N+S)
        self.button2.bind("<Button-1>", self.button2_Click)

        self.button3 = Button(self, text = "Test", width = 10, height = 2)
        self.button3.grid(row = 1, column = 1,sticky = W+E+N+S)
        self.button3.bind("<Button-1>", self.button3_Click)

        self.button4 = Button(self, text = "Reset", width = 10, height = 2)
        self.button4.grid(row = 1, column = 2, sticky = W+E+N+S)
        self.button4.bind("<Button-1>", self.button4_Click)

        self.entry = Entry(self, relief=RAISED)
        self.entry.grid(row = 2, columnspan = 2, sticky = W+E+N+S)
        self.entry.insert(INSERT, "Command")

        self.text2 = Label(self, text="Stopped", width = 2, height = 2,
                           relief=RAISED, bg="white", fg="black",
                           textvariable=self.var2)
        self.text2.grid(row = 2, column = 2, sticky = W+E+N+S)

        self.rowconfigure(1, weight = 1)
        self.columnconfigure(1, weight = 1)

    def button1_Click(self, event):
        self.var1.set("")
        self.var2.set("Running")

    def button2_Click(self, event):
        self.var1.set("")
        self.var2.set("Stopped")

    def button3_Click(self, event):
        time.sleep(1)
        self.var1.set("Test OK")
        self.var2.set("Stopped")

    def button4_Click(self, event):
        time.sleep(1)
        self.var1.set("Reset OK")
        self.var2.set("Stopped")
```

```
app = demoGUI()
app.mainloop()
```

The output of `tkdemo2.py` is shown in Figure 13-10.

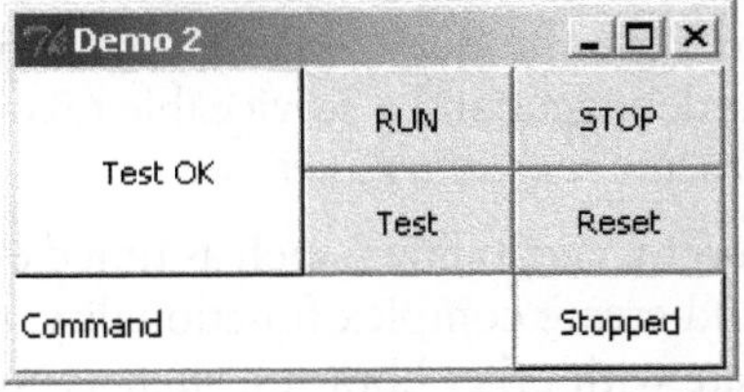

Figure 13-10. tkdemo2 example GUI

There are a few things to note in `tkdemo2.py`. The first is how the grid geometry manager is used to organize widgets of different sizes. The second is how the buttons have an effect on more than just one label widget. Finally, you might have noticed that when either the Test or the Reset button is clicked, the GUI freezes briefly. This is due to the `time.sleep(1)` call in the event handlers for these buttons. It also shows why a GUI should only spend as much time servicing an input event as necessary, and no more.

Tools and resources for TkInter

There are several good layout tools available for TkInter. Google is, of course, one place to start looking. SourceForge (*http://www.sourceforge.net*) is another. Since I tend to build TkInter GUIs by hand, I don't currently have a personal favorite. Nevertheless, here are some links to a couple of TkInter GUI construction tools that you may find useful:

PAGE (http://page.sourceforge.net)
  The PAGE tool is intended to be used to create single windows; it is not a full application construction tool. It's a solid tool that can help alleviate a lot of the tedium of creating complex windows with multiple widgets. Be sure to read the introductory documentation so that you fully understand the intent and limitations of PAGE.

SpecTcl (http://spectcl.sourceforge.net)
  This hasn't been updated in a while, and it may have a few quirks, but the last time I worked with it I liked it. If you're feeling brave, it may be worth a look.

For learning and reference resources for TkInter, be sure to check the section "Suggested Reading" on page 544.

wxPython

wxPython is the new kid on the Python GUI block, but its underlying library has been around for a while. It is actually a wrapper around the wxWidgets toolkit, which is written in C++. One of the primary objectives of wxWidgets is achieving portability while maintaining the look and feel of the host operating system.

Whereas with TkInter I tend to just build a simple GUI by hand using the grid geometry manager, with wxPython I prefer to use a tool and specify exact widget locations using pixel coordinates. For this I use the Boa Constructor wxPython GUI builder, which also incorporates a decent debugger and a serviceable text editor. You can download Boa from *http://boa-constructor.sourceforge.net*.

wxPython has some very useful capabilities, such as timed event generators, the ability to subclass GUI objects and create complex functionality, thread-safe operation, and the ability to easily integrate with other libraries, such as NumPy and PIL (the Python Imaging Library). Granted, TkInter can do many of these things as well, and it has the excellent canvas widget, so I'm not advocating one over the other. But, as with anything else, some things may be easier to accomplish in one venue than in another. It all comes down to picking the right tool for the job at hand.

Designing a wxPython GUI

As I stated earlier for TkInter, it's a good idea to have a plan for your GUI. Although a visual tool like Boa makes it easy to try out different widget arrangements, it's also easy to get lost in the details. Keep it simple.

Once you've decided on the general appearance of your GUI, the next step is to start up Boa (assuming that you have already installed it, of course). After it initializes you'll see three windows, as shown in Figure 13-11.

Building a simple wxPython GUI

Boa has the ability to assist with the creation of the entire GUI, from a top-level `wx.app` object through to the various frames and dialogs it might need. However, it's still up to you to assemble it all into a working application. What we'll look at here is a simple single-frame dialog-type GUI similar to what we've already built using TkInter.

This GUI will have some data display fields, some buttons, and some bitmap status indicators. It's actually a GUI variation on what we saw earlier in this chapter with the ANSI data displays.

With Boa running and ready, the first step is to create a new design. In the top window, select the "New" tab (it should already be selected). Then select the sixth button, `wx.frame`. The main window should now contain some Python code. This is the skeleton on which we'll build our application.

Now comes the fun part. Select the icon with the blue arrow in a box in the toolbar just above the code editor display. You should now see a new window that looks like the one shown in Figure 13-12.

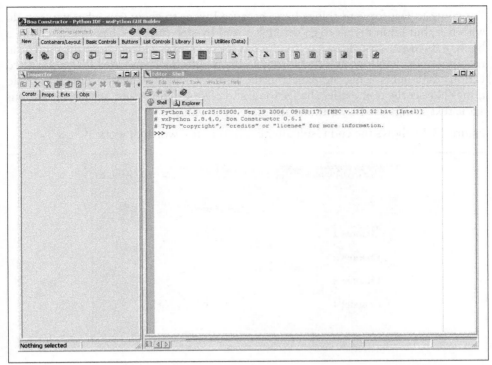

Figure 13-11. Boa Constructor user interface

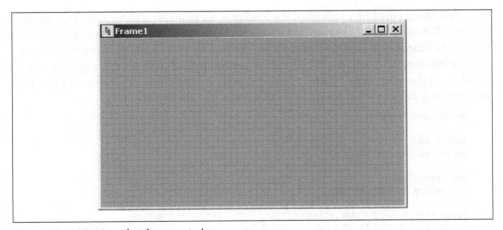

Figure 13-12. Boa's widget layout window

I'm going to fast-forward things here, because I want to show you what you can do with Boa, but I don't want to go through a step-by-step tutorial (that would require a book of its own!). Instead, what I've done is select various widgets from the toolbar in the uppermost window, and then dropped them onto the layout area. I've also edited various data items using the panels in the leftmost window. These allow you to do things like set the frame title, change fonts and colors, define sizes, and set the various static text strings used for buttons and static text widgets.

Figure 13-13 shows the end result after a few minutes' worth of work.

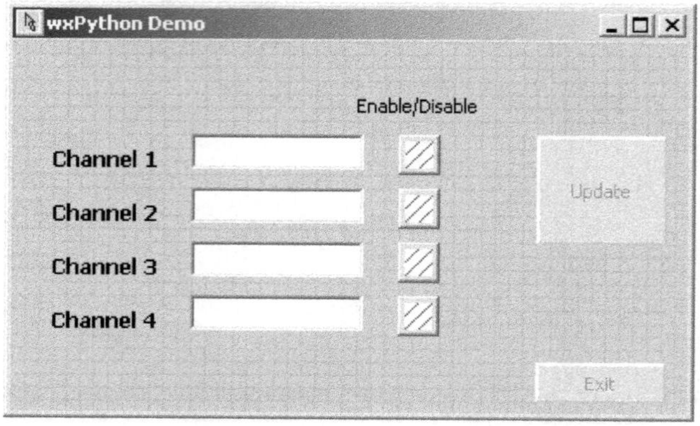

Figure 13-13. Finished layout

To create this frame I first lightened the background color, and then placed the various widgets. I then assigned appropriate names and generated the event handler skeletons for the six buttons. In case you're curious, the four buttons with the diagonal lines are bitmap buttons. In other words, a bitmap can be applied to them dynamically, which I will do in the next step. When I click on the blue checkmark at the top of the editor window Boa converts the design into code, which is shown here:

```
#Boa:Frame:Frame1

import wx
import wx.lib.buttons

def create(parent):
    return Frame1(parent)

[wxID_FRAME1, wxID_FRAME1BITMAPBUTTON1, wxID_FRAME1BITMAPBUTTON2,
 wxID_FRAME1BITMAPBUTTON3, wxID_FRAME1BITMAPBUTTON4, wxID_FRAME1EXITBUTTON,
 wxID_FRAME1STATICTEXT1, wxID_FRAME1STATICTEXT2, wxID_FRAME1STATICTEXT3,
 wxID_FRAME1STATICTEXT4, wxID_FRAME1STATICTEXT5, wxID_FRAME1TEXTCTRL1,
 wxID_FRAME1TEXTCTRL2, wxID_FRAME1TEXTCTRL3, wxID_FRAME1TEXTCTRL4,
 wxID_FRAME1UPDTBUTTON,
] = [wx.NewId() for _init_ctrls in range(16)]
```

```
class Frame1(wx.Frame):
    def _init_ctrls(self, prnt):
        # generated method, don't edit
        wx.Frame.__init__(self, id=wxID_FRAME1, name='', parent=prnt,
              pos=wx.Point(331, 258), size=wx.Size(400, 250),
              style=wx.DEFAULT_FRAME_STYLE, title='wxPython Demo')
        self.SetClientSize(wx.Size(392, 223))
        self.SetBackgroundColour(wx.Colour(187, 187, 187))
        self.SetToolTipString('')

        self.staticText1 = wx.StaticText(id=wxID_FRAME1STATICTEXT1,
              label='Channel 1', name='staticText1', parent=self,
              pos=wx.Point(24, 64), size=wx.Size(61, 14), style=0)
        self.staticText1.SetFont(wx.Font(9, wx.SWISS, wx.NORMAL, wx.BOLD, False,
              'Tahoma'))

        self.staticText2 = wx.StaticText(id=wxID_FRAME1STATICTEXT2,
              label='Channel 2', name='staticText2', parent=self,
              pos=wx.Point(24, 96), size=wx.Size(61, 14), style=0)
        self.staticText2.SetFont(wx.Font(9, wx.SWISS, wx.NORMAL, wx.BOLD, False,
              'Tahoma'))

        self.staticText3 = wx.StaticText(id=wxID_FRAME1STATICTEXT3,
              label='Channel 3', name='staticText3', parent=self,
              pos=wx.Point(24, 128), size=wx.Size(61, 14), style=0)
        self.staticText3.SetFont(wx.Font(9, wx.SWISS, wx.NORMAL, wx.BOLD, False,
              'Tahoma'))

        self.staticText4 = wx.StaticText(id=wxID_FRAME1STATICTEXT4,
              label='Channel 4', name='staticText4', parent=self,
              pos=wx.Point(24, 160), size=wx.Size(61, 14), style=0)
        self.staticText4.SetFont(wx.Font(9, wx.SWISS, wx.NORMAL, wx.BOLD, False,
              'Tahoma'))

        self.textCtrl1 = wx.TextCtrl(id=wxID_FRAME1TEXTCTRL1, name='textCtrl1',
              parent=self, pos=wx.Point(104, 56), size=wx.Size(100, 21),
              style=0, value='')
        self.textCtrl1.SetEditable(False)
        self.textCtrl1.SetToolTipString('')

        self.textCtrl2 = wx.TextCtrl(id=wxID_FRAME1TEXTCTRL2, name='textCtrl2',
              parent=self, pos=wx.Point(104, 88), size=wx.Size(100, 21),
              style=0, value='')
        self.textCtrl2.SetEditable(False)
        self.textCtrl2.SetToolTipString('')

        self.textCtrl3 = wx.TextCtrl(id=wxID_FRAME1TEXTCTRL3, name='textCtrl3',
              parent=self, pos=wx.Point(104, 120), size=wx.Size(100, 21),
              style=0, value='')
        self.textCtrl3.SetEditable(False)
        self.textCtrl3.SetToolTipString('')

        self.textCtrl4 = wx.TextCtrl(id=wxID_FRAME1TEXTCTRL4, name='textCtrl4',
              parent=self, pos=wx.Point(104, 152), size=wx.Size(100, 21),
              style=0, value='')
```

```python
        self.textCtrl4.SetEditable(False)
        self.textCtrl4.SetToolTipString('')

        self.bitmapButton1 = wx.BitmapButton(bitmap=wx.NullBitmap,
              id=wxID_FRAME1BITMAPBUTTON1, name='bitmapButton1', parent=self,
              pos=wx.Point(224, 56), size=wx.Size(24, 24),
              style=wx.BU_AUTODRAW)
        self.bitmapButton1.SetToolTipString('')
        self.bitmapButton1.Bind(wx.EVT_BUTTON, self.OnBitmapButton1Button,
              id=wxID_FRAME1BITMAPBUTTON1)

        self.bitmapButton2 = wx.BitmapButton(bitmap=wx.NullBitmap,
              id=wxID_FRAME1BITMAPBUTTON2, name='bitmapButton2', parent=self,
              pos=wx.Point(224, 88), size=wx.Size(24, 24),
              style=wx.BU_AUTODRAW)
        self.bitmapButton2.SetToolTipString('')
        self.bitmapButton2.Bind(wx.EVT_BUTTON, self.OnBitmapButton2Button,
              id=wxID_FRAME1BITMAPBUTTON2)

        self.bitmapButton3 = wx.BitmapButton(bitmap=wx.NullBitmap,
              id=wxID_FRAME1BITMAPBUTTON3, name='bitmapButton3', parent=self,
              pos=wx.Point(224, 120), size=wx.Size(24, 24),
              style=wx.BU_AUTODRAW)
        self.bitmapButton3.SetToolTipString('')
        self.bitmapButton3.Bind(wx.EVT_BUTTON, self.OnBitmapButton3Button,
              id=wxID_FRAME1BITMAPBUTTON3)

        self.bitmapButton4 = wx.BitmapButton(bitmap=wx.NullBitmap,
              id=wxID_FRAME1BITMAPBUTTON4, name='bitmapButton4', parent=self,
              pos=wx.Point(224, 152), size=wx.Size(24, 24),
              style=wx.BU_AUTODRAW)
        self.bitmapButton4.SetToolTipString('')
        self.bitmapButton4.Bind(wx.EVT_BUTTON, self.OnBitmapButton4Button,
              id=wxID_FRAME1BITMAPBUTTON4)

        self.updtButton = wx.lib.buttons.GenButton(id=wxID_FRAME1UPDTBUTTON,
              label='Update', name='updtButton', parent=self, pos=wx.Point(304,
              56), size=wx.Size(76, 65), style=0)
        self.updtButton.SetToolTipString('Fetch fresh data')
        self.updtButton.Bind(wx.EVT_BUTTON, self.OnUpdtButtonButton,
              id=wxID_FRAME1UPDTBUTTON)

        self.exitButton = wx.lib.buttons.GenButton(id=wxID_FRAME1EXITBUTTON,
              label='Exit', name='exitButton', parent=self, pos=wx.Point(304,
              192), size=wx.Size(76, 25), style=0)
        self.exitButton.Bind(wx.EVT_BUTTON, self.OnExitButtonButton,
              id=wxID_FRAME1EXITBUTTON)

        self.staticText5 = wx.StaticText(id=wxID_FRAME1STATICTEXT5,
              label='Enable/Disable', name='staticText5', parent=self,
              pos=wx.Point(200, 32), size=wx.Size(70, 13), style=0)

    def __init__(self, parent):
        self._init_ctrls(parent)
```

```
def OnBitmapButton1Button(self, event):
    event.Skip()

def OnBitmapButton2Button(self, event):
    event.Skip()

def OnBitmapButton3Button(self, event):
    event.Skip()

def OnBitmapButton4Button(self, event):
    event.Skip()

def OnUpdtButtonButton(self, event):
    event.Skip()

def OnExitButtonButton(self, event):
    event.Skip()
```

Even as just a skeleton, there is still of lot of code there. Fortunately, we won't really have to worry about anything above the __init__() method. What we're interested in now are the six button event handlers.

Since the Exit button doesn't do anything yet, let's add the code so it will actually exit:

```
def OnExitButtonButton(self, event):
    self.Destroy()
```

If your application needs to do some housekeeping before shutting down, this is one place to do it. In our code we'll simply call the Destroy() method and drop it on the floor.

Next up are the four Enable/Disable buttons. For these I'm going to use small bitmap images to indicate the on/off status. The images are swapped out by the event handlers.

A new method, initButtons(), will be used to set the initial state of four tracking variables and assign a red bitmap to each of the buttons:

```
def initButtons(self):
    self.cnt = 1

    self.btn1State = Flase
    self.btn2State = Flase
    self.btn3State = Flase
    self.btn4State = Flase

    self.bitmapButton1.SetBitmapLabel(bitmap=
        wx.Bitmap(u'red24off.bmp',wx.BITMAP_TYPE_BMP))
    self.bitmapButton2.SetBitmapLabel(bitmap=
        wx.Bitmap(u'red24off.bmp',wx.BITMAP_TYPE_BMP))
    self.bitmapButton3.SetBitmapLabel(bitmap=
        wx.Bitmap(u'red24off.bmp',wx.BITMAP_TYPE_BMP))
    self.bitmapButton4.SetBitmapLabel(bitmap=
        wx.Bitmap(u'red24off.bmp',wx.BITMAP_TYPE_BMP))
```

The variable `self.cnt` is used by the Update button. `initButtons()` is called from within `__init__()` after the controls have been initialized:

```
def __init__(self, parent):
    self._init_ctrls(parent)
    self.initButtons()
```

Here is the event handler for the first button:

```
def OnBitmapButton1Button(self, event):
    if self.btn1State == False:
        self.btn1State = True
        self.bitmapButton1.SetBitmapLabel(bitmap=
                wx.Bitmap(u'green24on.bmp', wx.BITMAP_TYPE_BMP))
    else:
        self.btn1State = False
        self.bitmapButton1.SetBitmapLabel(bitmap=
                wx.Bitmap(u'red24off.bmp', wx.BITMAP_TYPE_BMP))
```

Except for name changes, the other three are identical. Finally, the event handler for the Update button will push a string into each of the four text widgets each time the Update button is clicked:

```
def OnUpdtButtonButton(self, event):
    self.textCtrl1.SetValue(str(self.cnt))
    self.textCtrl2.SetValue(str(self.cnt))
    self.textCtrl3.SetValue(str(self.cnt))
    self.textCtrl4.SetValue(str(self.cnt))
    self.cnt += 1
```

To get it going, all we need is this little bit of code at the end of the file:

```
if __name__ == '__main__':
    app = wx.PySimpleApp()
    frame = create(None)
    frame.Show(True)
    app.MainLoop()
```

This uses wxPython's `wx.PySimpleApp()` class to create an app object to provide the main loop. When `wxexample.py` is run, the resulting display looks like Figure 13-14.

There were a lot of details in the creation of `wxexample.py` that I didn't go into. If you want to know more about wxPython or Boa Constructor, I would encourage you to attempt to duplicate this example for yourself. If you want to look at the settings for the widgets, just load the source into Boa and examine the various settings panels.

Tools and resources for wxPython

We've already seen how a tool like Boa Constructor can be used to create a wxPython application, but there are other tools available as well:

wxGlade (http://wxglade.sourceforge.net)
> Modeled on the Glade GUI designer tool for the GTK+/GNOME environment, wxGlade is not a complete application tool like Boa, but it is a capable tool for building individual windows and dialogs, much like the PAGE tool for TkInter.

PythonCard (http://pythoncard.sourceforge.net)
> Intended as a tool for quickly creating simple GUI applications, PythonCard employs templates and a basic selection of widgets. With its focus on new programmers, it may be a good place to start. However, be forewarned that the code hasn't been updated since 2007, and both Python and wxPython have moved along since then. Some features may no longer work.

There is a large amount of information available on the Web, and the section "Suggested Reading" on page 544 lists some essential sources of information.

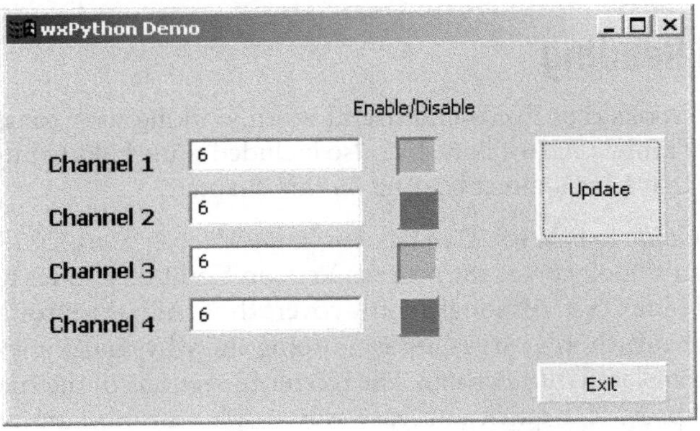

Figure 13-14. wxexample.py

Summary

In this chapter we've looked at both text-based and graphical interfaces. We've seen that while a text-based interface is fine for a lot of applications, there are times when characters alone simply won't provide the level of display fidelity or the interface functionality needed for an application.

One thing you may have noticed about the two styles of interface programming is that they both employ a main loop of some form to handle input, output, and update functions. This is probably one of the oldest patterns in computer programming, and it makes a lot more sense than trying to scatter the screen control functionality around a program and then keep track of it all (I've seen that done, actually, and as you might guess, it wasn't very robust or easy to maintain).

Creating TkInter examples by hand and a wxPython example using a tool allowed me to illustrate both approaches, as well as highlighting the differences in ease of use between TkInter and wxPython that are rooted in their design philosophies. In the case of TkInter, many professional software developers don't even bother with a tool, because they can quickly create functional and aesthetically pleasing interfaces using TkInter's native geometry management capabilities. While it is perfectly feasible to take the same approach with wxPython, I chose to use the Boa Constructor tool to illustrate the steps involved in the process. Most GUI tools for both TkInter and wxPython (and other GUI libraries) will work in similar ways, so this example should be applicable across a variety of tools and situations.

It is my hope that what you've seen here will give you some ideas for your own applications. As I stated several times in this chapter, if you're going to do any serious work with things like curses or a GUI, you owe it to yourself to check out the books and links in the "Suggested Reading" section below.

Suggested Reading

Here are some books that I've found useful when working with curses and with the wxPython and TkInter GUI toolkits. I've also included some links to interesting sources of information that have a direct bearing on this chapter:

Programmer's Guide to ncurses. Dan Gookin, John Wiley & Sons, 2007.
> Dan Gookin's book covers the ncurses Version 5.5 library and is relevant to Unix, Linux, and Mac OS X. Although it only covers the C API, the tutorial material helps to clarify what Python's curses library is doing and why, and many of the examples are easily translated into Python. The reference sections of the book are also very useful and provide a quick and easy way to look up obscure or half-forgotten functions.

wxPython in Action. Noel Rappin and Robin Dunn, Manning Publications, 2006.
> Covers the Python API for the wxWidgets library. Includes numerous examples, but there's a lot to cover here, so some topics get a more in-depth treatment than others. Just be prepared to either dig into the wxPython source or translate from the C++ sources in the wxWidgets code if you have a need for some arcane knowledge on a topic not fully covered in the book. In any case, if you want to work with wxPython you need to have this book on your desk.

Cross-Platform GUI Programming with WxWidgets. Julian Smart, Kevin Hock, and Stefan Csomer, Pearson Education/Prentice Hall, 2005.
> The definitive reference for wxWidgets. This book is thick and full of details, and when wxPython doesn't make sense, this is where you can turn to find out what should be going on. Be forewarned that you will need to be able to read and understand at least the basics of C++ to get the most out of this book.

Python and Tkinter. John E. Grayson, Manning Publications, 2000.
Covers the TkInter GUI toolkit in detail, with numerous examples and descriptions of the available widgets. It does tend to omit some details for the sake of brevity, and the references to the Python Megawidgets (pmw) add-on library are now out of date (which is not surprising, considering that the book is now 10 years old). The BLT module used by pmw, in particular, seems to be woefully out of date, and last time I checked it had issues with Python 2.6. But if you'd rather use TkInter and don't need the functionality in BLT, it shouldn't be a problem.

http://arstechnica.com/old/content/2005/05/gui.ars/4
Jeremy Reimer's article, "A History of the GUI," is a concise walk-through of the notable milestones in the timeline of the GUI, leading up to modern times. While not technical, it does a good job of highlighting the key concepts that are now fundamental and familiar parts of the computer systems we interact with every day.

http://articles.sitepoint.com/print/real-history-gui
Mike Tuck's entertaining article, "The Real History of the GUI," gives an overview of the career paths of some of the main players in the development of the GUI as we know it today, and also lists some links to interesting related articles.

http://invisible-island.net/xterm/ctlseqs/ctlseqs.html
"Xterm Control Sequences" is a list of the command sequences recognized by Xterm. Originally compiled by Edward May of the University of California at Berkeley, it is terse, but chock-full of useful information. If you plan on working primarily in a Linux environment with Xterm windows, you really should have this document handy.

http://www.ecma-international.org/publications/standards/Ecma-048.htm
The ECMA-48 specification is available for download as a PDF file from ECMA International at this URL. It addresses not only ANSI-type control sequences, but also the ASCII character set. At over 100 pages it's not a light read, but the detailed glossary and references to other ECMA standards make it worth the download.

http://www.catb.org/~esr/writings/taouu/taouu.html
The entire text of Eric Raymond's *The Art of Unix Usability* is available online at this URL. Unfortunately, I couldn't locate a PDF version, and I like to read from paper rather than squinting at a screen. Mr. Raymond provides some deep insights peppered with an occasional poke at various companies and operating systems, and explores the history and reasoning behind user interfaces, from early keypunch and teletype machines through to the present day. The section "Rules of Usability" contains some real gems that too often seem to be missing in user interface design. The quote at the start of this chapter is one of the rules, although I don't know if it originated with Mr. Raymond or not.

http://www.joelonsoftware.com/articles/Biculturalism.html
In his blog *Joel on Software*, Joel Spolsky offers an intelligent and insightful review of Eric Raymond's *The Art of UNIX Programming* (the predecessor to *The Art of Unix Usability*). Although oriented toward working software developers, the

review provides some interesting insights into the cultural differences between the worlds of Unix and Windows. Although Python has evolved into a language that manages to straddle both of those worlds and smooth out a lot of the differences in the user experience, it is worthwhile to take the time to understand why, from a user's perspective, Unix (and Linux) is like the cockpit of the space shuttle, and Windows is a comfortable four-door sedan with electric windows, automatic transmission, and more knobs and buttons on the stereo than on the dash. Even if you don't plan on making a career out of software development, you will come away from this essay with a better understanding of why things are the way they are when it comes to modern operating systems and their user interfaces.

http://www.pythonware.com/library/tkinter

A combination of tutorial introduction and reference, this web-based document by Fredrik Lundh presents a solid introduction to TkInter. It also available as a PDF document, although in an odd layout as a two-up landscape document. Unfortunately this renders it basically useless for printing and saving in a common ring binder. But, formatting issues aside, the examples are generally well chosen and easy to follow. If you have no other material on TkInter but this, the NMT reference listed below, and the Python documentation, you should be able to create usable TkInter GUIs without any major difficulties.

http://infohost.nmt.edu/tcc/help/pubs/tkinter/

The online document "Tkinter 8.4 Reference: A GUI for Python" is available from New Mexico Technical University at the above URL. It is also available in PDF format from the same location. Although not exhaustive, this is a substantial reference (120 pages in PDF format) that covers topics such as layout methods, attributes, and the various common Tk widgets, including Tk's rather unique canvas widget.

## CHAPTER 14

Real World Examples

*Beware of computer programmers who
carry screwdrivers.*

—Leonard Brandwein

This chapter is intended to be a summarization of some of what I've presented in this book, so it's not going to contain a lot of in-depth discussions. Rather than a step-by-step analysis and guide, it's intended to be an inspiration for your own problem solving. You should be able to answer most questions that arise regarding the examples in this chapter by referring to the material we've covered in the preceding chapters, and if you need more details than can be found here you can look to the references and links provided in the chapters and the appendixes.

As you have probably surmised by this point, there are basically two main classes of instrumentation interfaces: those that require some type of add-on hardware that plugs into a computer, and those that require only a cable of some type. In this chapter we will wrap up our journey by examining examples of those devices that require only a cable. Drawing from what we've seen so far, we will see how RS-232 serial and USB interfaces can be used to acquire data and control devices in the real world.

We'll start off with a data capture application for a DMM with a serial output (the same one we discussed briefly in Chapter 11), and then look at some other types of serial interface I/O devices that employ a more conventional command-response protocol. Next up is a USB data acquisition and control device, the LabJack U3. We'll spend some time with the U3, mainly because it's a complex device, but also because it's typical of many devices of this type.

Serial Interfaces

When serial interfaces are mentioned, most people will think of RS-232, or perhaps RS-485. But in reality, a serial interface can take on a variety of forms. If, for example, we use a device to convert from USB to GPIB and back via a virtual serial port, we're effectively using a serial interface, even though GPIB itself is a parallel data bus. The adapter and its USB driver perform what is called "serialization" of the data stream, so from the viewpoint of the software controlling or monitoring the device, it's a conventional vanilla serial interface.

Serial interfaces based on RS-232 have the inherent advantage of being easy to work with, at least in terms of sending and receiving commands and data. Another aspect is that almost all instruments or devices with a serial interface use a command-response protocol. It is not that common to find instruments that will send data without being commanded to do so, but they do exist. One such exception is the tpi model 183 DMM, which we will look at next.

Simple DMM Data Capture

The tpi model 183 is an inexpensive DMM (around $130 from multiple distributors) with a variety of functions and reasonably good accuracy. It also provides a serial port in the form of a 3.5 mm jack and can continuously output a stream of ASCII data at 1,200 baud. If you connect the optional interface cable for the meter to a PC, you can capture this data and display it or save it to a logfile. Figure 14-1 shows the 183. The RS-232 interface is located on the righthand side of the case.

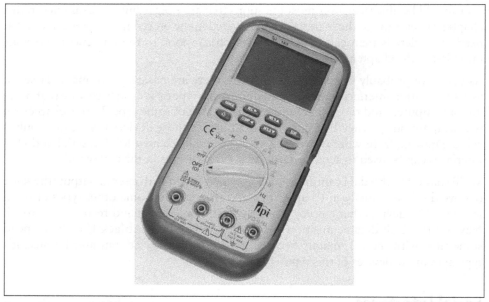

Figure 14-1. tpi model 183 DMM

There is a version of the 183, known as the 183A, that uses a different interface. This discussion is relevant to the original 183, not the 183A.

To start the RS-232 output, you hold down the "COMP" button while turning on the meter by rotating the dial. When the serial output is active the meter's automatic power-off feature is disabled, so it can eat up a battery in short order. There is no provision for an external power source, so it's not a good candidate if you need to leave it running for extended periods of time.

A serial interface kit is available for the 183 that includes some sample software and a special RS-232 cable. The serial interface is optically isolated, so the cable brings in DC power to the optical isolator in the meter by tapping one of the RS-232 control lines on the PC's serial port. The cable for the 183 includes some additional internal components, so a conventional RS-232 cable won't work. If you have a notebook or netbook PC without a true RS-232 serial port you can use an RS-232–to–USB adapter and communicate via a virtual serial port, so long as the USB adapter is able to supply the necessary RS-232 control line voltage.

The 183 uses the format shown in Figure 14-2 to encode the meter function, range mode, range, and data value into an ASCII string.

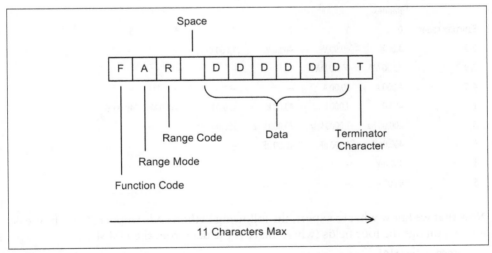

Figure 14-2. tpi model 183 data output format

There are four distinct data items, or fields, and the function code field is actually hexadecimal. There are 11 possible values with one unused code, for a total of 12, so the numbering ranges from 0 to B.

Table 14-1 shows how to interpret the function code, and Table 14-2 shows the encoding used for the range codes.

Table 14-1. 183 DMM function codes

Code	Function
0	AC volts
1	Ohms
2	DC volts
3	DC mV
4	AC amps
5	DC amps
6	Diode measurement
7	DC mA
8	Not assigned
9	AC mA
A	Capacitance
B	Frequency

Table 14-2. 183 DMM range codes

Function codes	Ranges					
	0	1	2	3	4	5
0, 2	4.00 V	40.00 V	400.0 V	1,000 V	–	–
7, 9	40.00 MA	400.0 MA	–	–	–	–
4, 5	4.000 A	10.00 A	–	–	–	–
1	400.0	4.000 k	40.00 k	400.0 k	4.000 M	40.00 M
B	200.00 Hz	2.0000 kHz	20.000 kHz	200.00 kHz	–	–
A	400.0n F	4.000 μF	40.00 μF	–	–	–
3	400 mV	–	–	–	–	–
6	4.000 V	–	–	–	–	–

Now that we know what to expect, the following Python code snippet shows how easy it is to pull out the four fields (where `instr` is the data from the DMM):

```
fcode = instr[0]
mcode = instr[1]
rcode = instr[2]
data = instr[4:len(instr)-1]
```

The first three fields are always one character in length. The last field is taken to be whatever lies between the space (at `instr[3]`) and the end of the string minus 1 (we don't care about the terminator character). The string itself must be longer than nine characters. Any time we get a string from the meter with nine or fewer characters, it should be tossed out.

There are several routes we might take when writing an application to capture data from this meter, and two that come to mind immediately. One is to just wait in a loop for the meter and handle things like writing to a logfile or updating a display in between readings. The other is to employ a thread to get the incoming data and push it into a queue that a main loop can then pull out and write into some type of display (or save to a file). The first approach is the more straightforward to implement. While the second is more flexible, it is also slightly more difficult to implement.

It's important to account for the fact that the strings sent by the meter have no EOL character. Shortly after one string is finished, another is transmitted. In this case the safest way to get the data is to use *pySerial*'s `read()` method and fetch one character at a time while looking for the terminator character. This is where the string length limit I just mentioned comes into play: if the capture application happens to start reading characters in the middle of a string, it could still see the terminator character and attempt to extract data from an incomplete string. There's no way to know what the meter's output will look like when your application starts listening to it, so it will need to synchronize with the meter. Ensuring that at least 10 characters have been read and the terminator is present greatly reduces the odds of getting invalid data.

The code for a simple script to read the data stream from a 183 DMM is shown here as `read183dmm.py`:

```
#!/usr/bin/python
# 183 DMM data capture example
#
# Simple demonstration of data acquistion from a DMM
#
# Source code from the book "Real World Instrumentation with Python"
# By J. M. Hughes, published by O'Reilly.

import serial

sport = serial.Serial()
sport.baudrate = 1200
sport.port = "com17"
sport.setTimeout(2) # give up after 5 seconds
sport.open()

instr = ""
fetch_data = True
short_count = 0
timeout_cnt = 0
maxtries = 5    # timeout = read timeout * maxtries

while fetch_data:
```

```
getstr = True
# input string read loop - get one character at a time from
# the DMM to build up an input string

while getstr:
    inchar = sport.read(1)
    if inchar == "":
        # reading nothing is a sign of a timeout
        print "%s timeout, count: %d" % (inchar, timeout_cnt)
        timeout_cnt += 1
        if timeout_cnt > maxtries:
            getstr = False
    else:
        # see if the terminator character was read, and if so
        # call this input string done
        if inchar == '&':
            getstr = False
        instr += inchar
        timeout_cnt = 0      # reset timeout counter

# if timeout occurred, don't continue
if timeout_cnt == 0:
    if len(instr) > 9:
        # chances of this being a valid string are good, so
        # pull out the data
        fcode = instr[0]
        mcode = instr[1]
        rcode = instr[2]
        data = instr[4:len(instr)-1]

        # actual display and/or logging code goes here
        # the print is just a placeholder for this example
        print "%1s %1s %1s ->  %s" % (fcode, mcode, rcode, data)

        # reset the short read counter
        short_count = 0
    else:
        # if we get repeated consecutive short strings,
        # there's a problem
        short_count += 1
        # if it happens 5 times in a row, terminate the
        # loop and exit the script
        if short_count > 5:
            fetch_data = False
    # in any case, clear the input string
    instr = ""
else:
    # we get to here if a timeout occurred in the input string
    # read loop, so kill the main loop
    fetch_data = False

print "Data acquistion terminated"
```

read183dmm.py has no provision for user input. It will terminate after a read timeout has occurred five times consecutively, so to exit this all you need to do is either turn off the

DMM or pull the interface cable out of the jack. It will also terminate if it receives five consecutive short strings (`len(instr)` < 10), which indicates a communications problem.

You would probably want to replace the `print` following the field extraction statements with something a bit more useful, such as the ability to save the data to a file or get command input from the user. The threaded technique we saw in Chapter 13 would work well here for user input. Also, from what we've already seen in Chapter 13, it would be a straightforward task to extend `read183dmm.py` with a nice display. I'd suggest an ANSI display for this situation, although it wouldn't be that difficult to build a GUI for it if you really wanted to.

Serial Interface Discrete and Analog Data I/O Devices

Writing data capture and control applications for serial interface devices is usually rather straightforward once you know the command-response protocol. The tpi 183 DMM is just one example, albeit an off-nominal one (it only sends data, and has no commands). The D1000 series data transmitters from Omega Engineering are another, more common, example. These devices are fairly typical of data acquisition modules that utilize a conventional serial interface to receive commands from a host controller PC and send back responses via a serial interface. I chose them for this section not because I prefer them over any other device of this class, but rather because they have a rich command set and a lot of functionality stuffed into a small package. They aren't the least expensive serial data acquisition modules available, but like most of Omega's products they are easy to use and ruggedly built, and I've yet to have one fail.

Figure 14-3 shows one member of the Omega D1000 series of digital data transmitters, which in this case happens to be a D1112. The analog input members of the D1000 family return data values from a sensor of some sort, typically a temperature sensor. They also have the ability to establish alarm set-points and scale the data, and some models provide extended discrete digital I/O capabilities.

The D1000 devices utilize a device addressing scheme as part of the command protocol, wherein the commands are prefixed with a device ID number, like so:

    $1RD

The device will respond with something like this (depending on the input and the scaling):

    *+00097.40

The device ID prefix allows multiple D1000 units to share a single RS-232 or RS-485 interface in a "daisy-chain" fashion. This is similar to the scheme described in Chapter 11 for RS-485 motor controllers. Figure 14-4 shows how several D1000-type devices can be used to monitor and control temperatures in a thermal chamber.

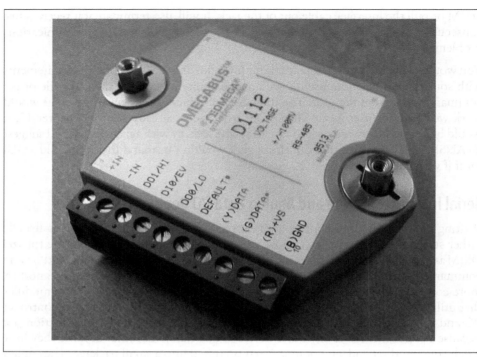

Figure 14-3. Omega D1112 RS-485 data transmitter

The setup shown in Figure 14-4 uses four sensors: two for the test articles in the chamber to prevent thermal damage, one for the chamber temperature, and one for the external ambient temperature. These could be thermocouples, thermistors, or resistive thermal device (RTD)–type sensors, so long as the input to the 1121 does not exceed 1 V (other models have different input voltage ranges). The devices labeled SENSOR 1 and SENSOR 2 are not used as control inputs to regulate chamber temperature, but rather as shutdown inputs should a test article exceed some preset temperature limit. SENSOR 3 would be the primary input to the temperature controller. The controller might use a bang-bang control, or it could use a PID algorithm, depending on how tightly the temperature needs to be regulated and the type of heating (and possibly cooling) system used with the chamber. SENSOR 4 is just an ambient external temperature sensor. Although it has no role to play in the operation of the chamber, data collected from this sensor could be used to determine how well the chamber is able maintain a specific temperature at different external ambient temperate levels. In other words, if the chamber is not well insulated and it is heating, the heating unit will work harder when the external temperature is low as it attempts to overcome heat loss from the chamber. By comparing the data from the external sensor with the internal temperature and the operation of the heating unit, we could work out an estimate of the insulation efficiency of the chamber.

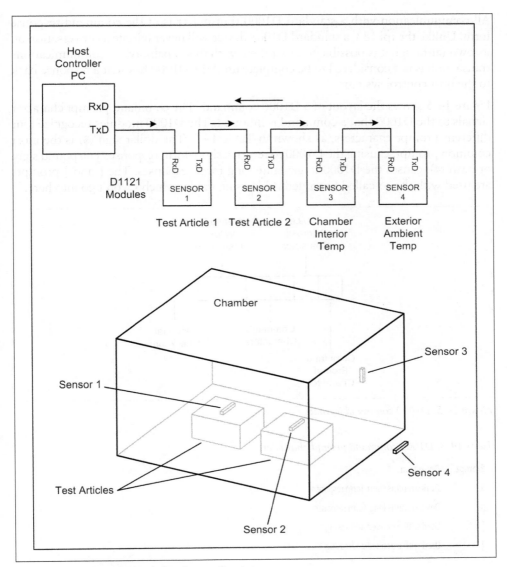

Figure 14-4. D1121 thermal chamber application

For their small size, the D1000 modules pack in a considerable amount of functionality. The devices may be commanded to respond with two different string formats, which Omega calls *short-form* or *long-form*. Each module may also be assigned an identification string. One module might be "HEATER," another might be "COOLER," and so on.

All communication with a standard D1000 transmitter is of the command-response form. Unlike the tpi 183, a standard D1000 device will never initiate a conversation on its own (although it is possible to order them with this capability). A communications transaction is not considered to be complete until the D1000 has sent a response back to the host control system.

Figure 14-5 shows the layout of a D1000 command. The command prompt character signals to the D1000 that a command is inbound. The D1000 modules recognize four different prompt characters, as shown in Table 14-3. The dollar sign ($) is the most common prompt, causing the D1000 to return a short-form response. The pound sign, or hash (#), causes the D1000 to generate long-form responses. The [and] prompts are used with the so-called Extended Addressing mode, which I won't go into here.

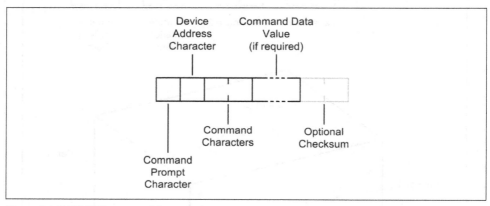

Figure 14-5. D1000 command format

Table 14-3. D1000 command prompt characters

Prompt	Definition
$	Device returns short-form response
#	Device returns long-form response
[	Used with extended addressing
]	Used with extended addressing

Following the prompt is a single device address character. D1000 devices are assigned an address by the user. Any printable ASCII character is acceptable as an address character, but in the interests of keeping things sane it's a good idea to stick with the range 0 to 9, or perhaps 0 to F. Using address characters that don't translate easily from a numeric sequence can make it awkward to use a loop to step through a set of daisy-chained devices.

After the address character come the device command characters, of which there may be two or three. Next is any parametric data the command might require. Some commands, such as query commands, do not require any additional data. Last, the command may use an optional two-character checksum, which is described in the D1000 user manual. Table 14-4 is a summary of the D1000 command set. For more details, including a discussion of each command and its nominal response, refer to the user manual.

Table 14-4. D1000 command set

Mnemonic	Definition	Short-form return
DI	Read Alarms or Digital Inputs	*<data>
DO	Set Digital Outputs	*
ND	New Data	*<float value>
RD	Read Data	*<float value>
RE	Read Event Counter	*<event counter value>
REA	Read Extended Address	*<ext address>
RH	Read High Alarm Value	*<high alarm value><mode char>
RID	Read Identification	*<ID string>
RL	Read Low Alarm Value	*<low alarm value><mode char>
RPT	Read Pulse Transition	*<transition chars>
RS	Read Setup	*<setup values>
RZ	Read Zero	*<float value>
WE	Write Enable	*
CA	Clear Alarms	*
CE	Clear Events	*
CZ	Clear Zero	*
DA	Disable Alarms	*
EA	Enable Alarms	*
EC	Events Read & Clear	*<event counter value>
HI	Set High Alarm Limit	*
ID	Set Module Identification	*
LO	Set Low Alarm Limit	*
PT	Pulse Transition	*
RR	Remote Reset	*
SU	Setup Module	*
SP	Set Setpoint	*
TS	Trim Span	*
TZ	Trim Zero	*
WEA	Write Extended Address	*

A D1000 response to a command begins with a prefix character, followed by data, an error message, or nothing at all. There are two possible response string prefixes: an asterisk (*) and a question mark (?). A third type of response scenario is when the D1000 returns nothing at all, and a timeout condition is declared. The asterisk indicates a no-error return, and a question mark indicates an error condition. With error conditions, the question mark is followed by the module ID, and then an error message. Here is a possible error response to a command with an extra character:

```
$1RDX
?1 SYNTAX ERROR
```

Checking the response involves looking at the first character in the response string. If it's an asterisk, all is well; otherwise, an error has occurred and must be handled. Analog data is returned as a nine-character string consisting of a sign character, five digits, a decimal point, and two digits for the fractional part. For example, the RD command will cause the device to respond with something like this:

```
*+00220.40
```

Conveniently, Python will accept the entire data value part of the string as-is and convert it to a float value, with no extra steps required.

Some commands do not return a data string in short-form mode, but all nonerror responses will return at least an asterisk character. The response for each command type is unique to that command (there's no one-size-fits-all command response), so the software will need to be aware of what to expect from the device.

When dealing with devices like the D1000, especially if you find yourself working with them often, it might be worthwhile to create a class with a set of methods to handle the various functions. This is a lot cleaner and easier than the alternative of sprinkling the commands around in the code. It also allows for changes to be made in a single place (the class definition) and to take effect anywhere the class is used.

The Omega D1000 series devices are just one example of the kinds of products available for data I/O with a serial interface. There are many devices available for thermocouple inputs, RTD sensors, discrete digital I/O, and a mix of both analog and digital I/O. Entering the search strings "digital I/O RS-232" or "digital I/O RS-485" into Google will return hits for numerous vendors selling everything from kits to high-end devices for industrial applications. I would suggest that when shopping for serial interface I/O devices you make sure you're not ordering a device intended for use with a DIN rail in an industrial setting. While there's nothing wrong with these devices, the physical mounting requirements may prove more troublesome than something with just some plain mounting holes, and they tend to be more costly.

Serial Interfaces and Speed Considerations

RS-232–based serial interfaces are typically rather slow, as RS-232 is limited to about 20 kbps, and that value starts to drop as cable length increases. RS-485 is much faster, with a maximum speed of 35 Mbps, and USB 2.0 can move data at a theoretical maximum of 480 Mbps. But the speed of the interface isn't the whole story; there's also the issue of how fast the software controlling the interface can send and receive the data.

For the types of applications described in this book a cyclic acquisition time of 10 ms (100 Hz) would be considered fast, and 100 Hz is well within the capability of Python running on a modern PC. However, update rates of 20 Hz are usually more than sufficient for many common data acquisition and control applications. Also remember that as the acquisition speed increases, so does the cost of the hardware and the complexity of the software.

The bottom line here is that there is absolutely nothing wrong with a device that uses a slow RS-232 serial interface for data acquisition or control, so long as it's fast enough for the intended application. Here's how we can do the math to see if a serial interface is fast enough.

Let's say that we have a device with a 9,600-baud RS-232 interface. Each command is 8 bytes in length, and responses are a maximum of 10 bytes. There is a maximum 1 ms latency in the acquisition device between command and response (the latency is partly determined by the conversion time of the internal ADC in the device, and partly by the time required for any command or data processing between acquisition events).

At 9600 baud it will require about 8.3 ms to send a command from the host to the device, about 10.4 ms for the response to come back, and some time for the Python application to do something with it. If we add up all the times we might get about 21 ms for a complete command-convert-response-process transaction cycle. That works out to about 48 Hz. From this we can see that the serial interface transfer time dominates the acquisition rate of the device, which is typical for devices with slow serial interfaces. As the interface speed goes up, the time required for the command-response transaction becomes less of a limiting factor.

Although 48 Hz is usually more than fast enough for applications like thermal control, environmental monitoring, or stellar photometry, it may not be fast enough to acquire events such as pulses or other transient phenomena that might occur between the data acquisition events. Since the total cycle time of the control system is mostly the time involved in communicating with an external device or system, increasing the baud rate or switching to RS-485 are two ways to increase the speed and shorten the overall cycle time.

There is another way, however, and that is USB. In the next section we'll see how to use a USB data acquisition and control device, which offers higher speeds and multifunction operation, albeit with slightly higher software complexity.

USB Example: The LabJack U3

Technological advancements in USB devices have continued to drive the cost of I/O devices with a USB interface ever lower. Just five years ago devices with the capabilities of this new breed of I/O modules would have cost many hundreds or even thousands of dollars. Prices today range from around $100 and up, depending on factors such as speed, conversion resolution, and the type and quantity of I/O channels.

One low-cost device is the LabJack U3, which is shown in Figure 14-6. This data acquisition device provides discrete digital I/O, analog I/O, and counter/timer I/O. It uses a USB interface for all command and data response transactions.

Figure 14-6. LabJack U3 USB DAQ device

The U3 is powered from the USB interface. There is no provision for an external power supply, which is common for devices of this type. So even though there is +5 V DC available at some of the terminal positions, care should be taken not to draw too much current and cause the USB channel to go into shutdown.

LabJack Connections

Figure 14-7 shows a diagram of the U3's connections. Many of the terminal points on the U3 can be configured for different modes of operation, and the configuration can be saved to ensure that the unit starts in the correct state at power-up. In addition to the terminal block connections, there is also a DB-15 connector that brings out 12 additional signal lines.

You can connect more than one LabJack at a time to a PC by using USB hubs, but keep in mind that the increase in data traffic can result in slower response times for all connected devices.

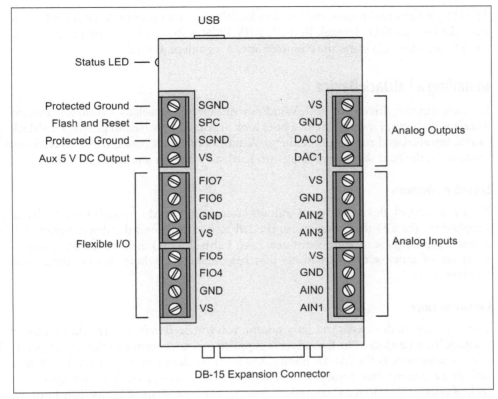

Figure 14-7. LabJack U3-HV connections

The LabJack U3 provides eight FIO (Flexible I/O) ports on the terminal blocks, and eight EIO (Extended I/O) ports and four CIO (Control I/O) ports on the DB-15 connector. In addition, there are two DAC outputs, six VS (+5 V DC) terminals, five common ground terminals, and two protected ground terminals. Notice that the terminals labeled AIN0 through AIN3 are actually FIO ports FIO0 through FIO3. These are configured as analog inputs by default, but you can change their function by modifying the LabJack's configuration. You can use the LJControlPanel tool for Windows (supplied with each LabJack) for this purpose, or you can set the device configuration using the interface driver commands.

With the exception of the U3-HV model, each FIO and EIO port may be configured as a digital input, a digital output, or an analog input. On the HV version of the U3 the lines FIO0 through FIO3 are set as analog inputs and cannot be reconfigured. The four CIO lines on the DB-15 connector are dedicated digital lines.

The two DAC outputs operate in either 8-bit or 16-bit mode with a range of between about 0.04 and 4.95 volts. Using the 8-bit mode may result in a more stable output with less noise.

The U3 contains two timers and two clocks. Whenever a timer or clock is enabled, it will take over an FIO channel. In the U3-HV FIO4 is first, followed by FIO5, and so on. The standard U3 starts the counter/timer assignment at FIO0.

Installing a LabJack Device

LabJack supplies drivers for both Windows and Linux, as well as a complete Python interface wrapper. First we'll take a brief look at what is involved in getting a LabJack device installed and running on either a Windows or Linux machine—it's very easy, actually. In the next section we'll dig into LabJack's Python interface.

LabJack on Windows

To use a LabJack device with a Windows system, you need to install the UD driver supplied on the CD that comes with the LabJack unit. Install the driver before you connect the LabJack to your computer. Each LabJack DAQ device includes a single-sheet set of quick-start instructions that help make the whole process quick and painless.

LabJack on Linux

To use a LabJack device with a Linux system, you will need to first install the Exodriver package from LabJack. The Exodriver is supplied in source form and the only dependency requirement is the *libUSB* library. On most modern Linux systems this should already be present, but if not it can be easily installed using a package manager. You will, of course, also need a C compiler (since *gcc* comes with most Linux distributions, this should not be an issue).

Building the driver should just be a matter of typing make and, if it's successful, make install. You'll need to be *root* (or use *sudo*) to do the install step. The LabJack website contains detailed directions at *http://labjack.com/support/linux-and-mac-os-x-drivers*.

LabJack and Python

The Python interface for LabJack devices, called LabJackPython, is a wrapper for the UD and Exodriver low-level interfaces. It allows access to the driver functions, and it supports both Modbus register-based commands and the low-level functions in the LabJack drivers.

Installing and testing LabJackPython

Once you have a LabJack device installed and running, you can download the Python wrapper and install it. You can get more information about the Python binding at *http://labjack.com/support/labjackpython*, including installation instructions.

In summary, all that you really need to do is download the latest LabJack Python file (in my case it was *LabJackPython-7-20-2010.zip*), unpack it, change into the *src* directory, and type in:

```
python setup.py install
```

That's it. You should then be able to start Python and import the LabJack module, like so (if you have a U6, import that instead):

```
>>> import u3
```

Next we need to create a new object of the U3 class, which will be used for subsequent commands to the device:

```
>>> u3d = u3.U3()
```

Provided that your LabJack is plugged in and ready, you should see nothing returned from this statement, and you'll be ready to start entering commands and reading data.

LabJack driver structure

We're now well out of the land of serial interface devices and deep into API territory, which means we will need to understand how the LabJack driver API is structured in order to use it effectively. Dealing with a device like the LabJack is very much like working with a bus-based device and its low-level drivers. There is a lot of functionality there, but it's not quite as easy to get at as it is with something like the serial devices we saw earlier.

Before getting too deep into things, you should take a moment to at least glance through the LabJack user's guide. You should also have the source files `LabJackPython.py` and `u3.py` (or `u6.py`, as the case may be) close at hand, because you will need to refer to them from time to time.

The driver API for LabJack is organized as a series of layers, starting with the Exodriver or UD driver and eventually culminating in functionality tailored to a specific model of LabJack device. This is illustrated in Figure 14-8, which also shows the u12 interface, which is a standalone API that uses its own hardware driver, *liblabjackusb.so*, but doesn't use the `LabJackPython` interface module. The u12 is included in Figure 14-8 for completeness only; in this section we will focus mainly on the u3.

Our primary areas of interest are the `LabJackPython.py` module and the `u3.py` module. The u3 module contains the U3 class definition, which is a derived class based on the `Device` class found in `LabJackPython`. Figure 14-9 shows the inheritance relationship between the `Device` and U3 classes.

In addition to the `Device` and U3 classes, there are also functions in the `LabJackPython` and u3 modules that are very useful, but you need to make sure that a particular function isn't OS-specific. For example, the ePut() and eGet() functions in `LabJackPython.py` are Windows-specific. If you do elect to use these functions, bear in mind that your program will no longer be portable.

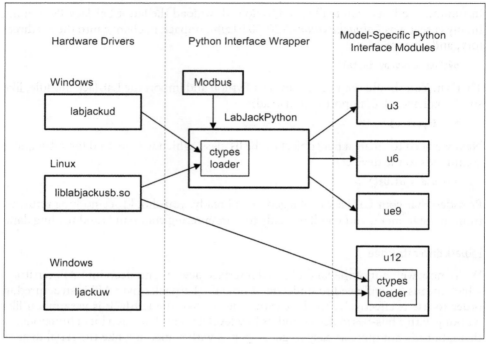

Figure 14-8. LabJack software interface components

In addition to the U3 class, there are functions and classes available in the LabJack Python modules that may be accessed without using the U3 class. For example, to get a listing of U3-type devices connected to the system you can use the listAll() function, like this:

```
>>> import u3
>>> u3.listAll(3)
```

The parameter value of 3 indicates that you want a list of U3 devices. For U6 devices you would use a 6. In my case I get a dictionary object in response that shows a single U3:

```
{320037071: {'devType': 3,
'serialNumber': 320037071,
'ipAddress': '0.0.0.0',
'localId': 1}}
```

If you have Epydoc installed (see Chapter 8), I would suggest using it to create a set of HTML pages as online documentation for the various Python components. You'll get nicely formatted documentation that is a lot easier to read than using Python's help() command or reading through the source code. When used on the modules LabJackPython.py, Modbus.py, and u3.py, the output of Epydoc looks like the screen capture in Figure 14-10.

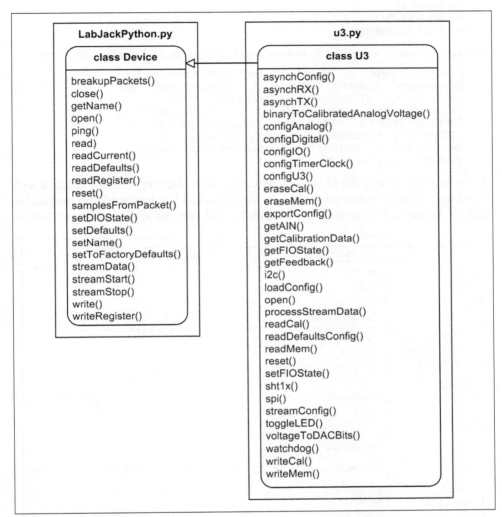

LabJackPython.py	u3.py
class Device	**class U3**
breakupPackets()	asynchConfig()
close()	asynchRX()
getName()	asynchTX()
open()	binaryToCalibratedAnalogVoltage()
ping()	configAnalog()
read)	configDigital()
readCurrent()	configIO()
readDefaults()	configTimerClock()
readRegister()	configU3()
reset()	eraseCal()
samplesFromPacket()	eraseMem()
setDIOState()	exportConfig()
setDefaults()	getAIN()
setName()	getCalibrationData()
setToFactoryDefaults()	getFIOState()
streamData()	getFeedback()
streamStart()	i2c()
streamStop()	loadConfig()
write()	open()
writeRegister()	processStreamData()
	readCal()
	readDefaultsConfig()
	readMem()
	reset()
	setFIOState()
	sht1x()
	spi()
	streamConfig()
	toggleLED()
	voltageToDACBits()
	watchdog()
	writeCal()
	writeMem()

Figure 14-9. U3 interface class derivation

U3 configuration

It is important to manage the configuration of a U3 device so that the port definitions will be as expected for a particular application when the device is powered on. The U3 class provides the methods configIO(), configAnalog(), configDigital(), config TimerClock(), and configU3() for this purpose. The sections "Python API Types and Functions" on page 171, "The Method Table" on page 172, and "Method Flags" on page 172 of the LabJack documentation describe the configuration management methods. Here's how to use configU3():

```
>>> import u3
>>> u3d = u3.U3()
>>> print u3d.configU3()
```

This returns a dictionary object. In my case the output looked like the following:

```
{'TimerClockConfig': 2, 'TimerClockDivisor': 256, 'LocalID': 1,
'SerialNumber': 320037071, 'CIOState': 0, 'TimerCounterMask': 64,
'DAC1Enable': 1, 'EIODirection': 0, 'DeviceName': 'U3-HV',
'FIODirection': 48, 'FirmwareVersion': '1.24', 'CIODirection': 0,
'DAC0': 0, 'DAC1': 0, 'EIOAnalog': 0, 'CompatibilityOptions': 0,
'EIOState': 0, 'HardwareVersion': '1.30', 'FIOAnalog': 15,
'VersionInfo': 18, 'FIOState': 0, 'BootloaderVersion': '0.27',
'ProductID': 3}
```

If you have access to a Windows machine, or you're planning to use a LabJack with Windows, I would suggest using the LJControlPanel tool, at least until you get familiar with the configuration management methods and functions in the interface modules.

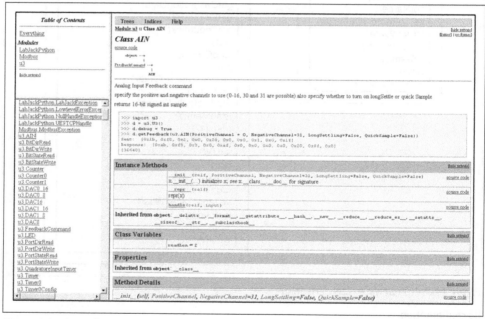

Figure 14-10. Epydoc output for LabJackPython

Using the Python interface with the getFeedback() method

If you've taken a peek at the u3.py module, you may have noticed that there are a number of little class definitions in addition to the U3 class, each of which is derived from the FeedbackCommand() class. (If you haven't done so yet, now would be a good time to take a look at this module.) They are used to perform various operations in the context of the getFeedback() method in the U3 class.

Here is the definition for the getFeedback() method from the U3 class:

getFeedback(*self, *commandlist*)
> The parameter *commandlist* is a list of FeedbackCommand-type objects. The method getFeedback() forms the list into a packet and sends it to the U3.
>
> Returns a list with zero or more entries, one entry per object in the input list.

Here's a simple example for controlling the status LED on the side of the U3:

```
>>> import u3
>>> u3d = u3.U3()
>>> u3d.getFeedback(u3.LED(0))
[None]
>>> u3d.getFeedback(u3.LED(1))
[None]
```

To set the DAC output levels, you could do the following:

```
>>> u3d.getFeedback(u3.DAC16(Dac=0, Value = 0x7fff))
[None]
>>> u3d.getFeedback(u3.DAC16(Dac=1, Value = 0xffff))
[None]
>>> u3d.getFeedback(u3.DAC16(Dac=0, Value = 0x0))
[None]
>>> u3d.getFeedback(u3.DAC16(Dac=1, Value = 0x0))
[None]
```

After entering the first two DAC commands, you should be able to measure an output level of around 2.5 volts on DAC0's output terminal, and about 4.95 volts for DAC1 (0x7fff is half of 0xffff). The last two commands set the DAC outputs back to zero. The getFeedback() method uses the u3.DAC16() function to send the value to the DAC. Notice that the return value is None.

The following is a list of the FeedbackCommand derived class commands in the u3.py module. For readability, I've listed each class with the parameters passed to its __init__() method as if it was a function or method:

- AIN(*PositiveChannel, NegativeChannel=31, LongSettling=False, QuickSample=False*)
- WaitShort(*Time*)
- WaitLong(*Time*)
- LED(*State*)
- BitStateRead(*IONumber*)
- BitStateWrite(*IONumber, State*)
- BitDirRead(*IONumber*)
- BitDirWrite(*IONumber, Direction*)
- PortStateRead()
- PortStateWrite(*State, WriteMask=[0xff, 0xff, 0xff]*)
- PortDirRead()

- PortDirWrite(*Direction, WriteMask=[0xff, 0xff, 0xff]*)

- DAC8(*Dac, Value*)

- DAC0_8(*Value*)

- DAC1_8(*Value*)

- DAC16(*Dac, Value*)

- DAC0_16(*Value*)

- DAC1_16(*Value*)

- Timer(*timer, UpdateReset=False, Value=0, Mode=None*)

- Timer0(*UpdateReset=False, Value=0, Mode=None*)

- Timer1(*UpdateReset=False, Value=0, Mode=None*)

- QuadratureInputTimer(*UpdateReset=False, Value=0*)

- TimerStopInput1(*UpdateReset=False, Value=0*)

- TimerConfig(*timer, TimerMode, Value=0*)

- Timer0Config(*TimerMode, Value=0*)

- Timer1Config(*TimerMode, Value=0*)

- Counter(*counter, Reset=False*)

- Counter0(*Reset=False*)

- Counter1(*Reset=False*)

Although these will look like functions when used in your code, they are actually class
definitions that instantiate objects. It is these objects that are invoked by the u3d.get
Feedback() method to perform a particular action or set of actions. Refer to the u3.py
source code for descriptions (or the Epydoc output, if you've already generated it). Also,
after importing the u3 module you can use Python's built-in help() facility, like so:

```
>>> import u3
>>> help(u3.WaitLong)
```

Now that we've seen what the getFeedback() method can do, let's put it to work.
u3ledblink.py is a simple script that will blink the status LED until the input voltage
at the AIN0 terminal exceeds some preset limit:

```
#!/usr/bin/python
# LabJack demonstration
#
# Blink the U3's status LED until the AIN0 input exceeds a limit value.
#
# Source code from the book "Real World Instrumentation with Python"
# By J. M. Hughes, published by O'Reilly.

import u3
import time

u3d = u3.U3()
```

```
LEDoff  = u3.LED(0)
LEDon   = u3.LED(1)
AINcmd  = u3.AIN(0, 31, False, False)

toggle = 0

while True:
    # blink the LED while looping
    if toggle == 0:
        u3d.getFeedback(LEDon)
        toggle = 1
    else:
        u3d.getFeedback(LEDoff)
        toggle = 0

    # getFeedback returns a list with a single element
    inval = u3d.getFeedback(AINcmd)[0]
    print inval
    if inval > 40000:
        break
    time.sleep(1)

u3d.getFeedback(LEDon)
print "Done."
```

Any voltage source with a range between 0 and 5 V DC will work as the input to AIN0. Touching a jumper wire between the AIN0 terminal and any of the VS terminals will also do the trick.

getFeedback() isn't limited to just one command at a time. You can stack up multiple commands. Here's an example where FIO4 (which is configured as a digital output in my setup) is rapidly toggled on and off. It's fast, and you'll need an oscilloscope if you want to see this activity:

```
>>> biton = u3.BitStateWrite(4,1)
>>> bitoff = u3.BitStateWrite(4,0)
>>> u3d.getFeedback(bitoff, biton, bitoff, biton, bitoff)
```

When using getFeedback() you should bear in mind that some commands may take too long to respond with the default timeout setting, and you'll get an exception from the driver. The WaitLong() class command may look appealing, but it's safer to just use Python's sleep() method instead of embedding a delay in the middle of a command object list. Just remember to keep things short and don't pile too many command objects into getFeedback().

You now have enough information to start doing useful things with a LabJack. We've only skimmed the tops of the waves, however, as there is much more that the device can do. The user's guide and the LabJackPython source code contain the information you will need to be able to use the more advanced features.

Summary

The examples in this chapter are just a small sample of what is available in terms of instrumentation hardware, and of what can be done with Python to acquire data and control external devices. We didn't discuss specific examples of GPIB or bus-based I/O, although these types of devices are used extensively in instrumentation systems. However, if you look back at Chapters 2, 7, and 11, these topics are covered there at length.

The devices discussed in this chapter were selected specifically to illustrate some shared concepts in the world of instrumentation hardware, such as the ubiquitous command-response paradigm. From this perspective a serial data acquisition device is similar in many ways to a GPIB device, and some lab instruments have the ability to communicate via a serial port while still using the SCPI model. The LabJack data acquisition devices employ a driver API and a Python interface layer that is very similar to what you might expect to find with a multifunction I/O card for the PCI bus. Once you understand the basic concepts behind the various interfaces, you'll be well on your way to being able to deal with just about any kind of instrumentation device.

With a modest outlay you can convert almost any PC into a data acquisition and control system, and with Python you can program it to do what you want it to do and take advantage of the powerful and extensible Python development environment. Your programs can be as simple or as complex as you need them to be, and because it's your software, you can modify it when you need to in order to keep up with changes in the requirements and the instrumentation environment.

If you're comfortable with electronics you can even build your own I/O hardware, such as the parallel port interface we discussed in Chapter 11. You can also extend the capabilities of your system by incorporating networking and distributed control.

We've only just scratched the surface of what is possible. As you work with instrumentation devices and systems, more possibilities will begin to become apparent. Worthy candidates for some degree of automation are all around us in our labs and workshops, out on the production floor, in our vehicles, and in our offices and homes. With some practice, a little patience, and your creativity, you can apply the information in this book to design and build robust and elegant data acquisition and control systems to suit your specific needs.

Suggested Reading

The topics covered in this book are intended to provide you with the information you need to use the devices presented in this chapter. The primary sources of information for installing and programming devices such as data transmitters and DAQ units are, of course, the manuals supplied by the manufacturers. You should carefully read the documentation for a new device, as not all devices are intuitive or simple to use (very few are, actually). To that end, I've assembled a few links to online documents and other sources of information for the devices covered in this chapter:

http://www.omega.com/DAS/pdf/D1000.pdf
An overview of the D1000 family of data transmitter products from Omega.

http://www.omega.com/Manuals/manualpdf/M0662.pdf
The Omega D1000 series user's manual.

http://labjack.com
The source for the U3 and U6 LabJack devices, as well as the Python interface. The website contains application notes, a blog, and many other items of interest to LabJack users.

Free and Open Source Software Resources

This appendix is a listing of the various tools and library add-on modules mentioned in this book, but it is by no means an exhaustive listing. There are many excellent open source software packages available for working with Python on both Linux and Windows systems, and I would encourage you to explore websites like SourceForge and Berlios for other alternatives. The main site for Python, *python.org*, also has links to other Python-specific packages that may be of interest to you.

Python 2.6.5 sources

http://www.python.org
> The official Python distribution website.

http://www.activestate.com
> The website for ActiveState, a Windows-centric distribution of Python. Includes some tools unique to ActiveState's distribution.

Integrated development environments

Boa Constructor
> A basic IDE for Python that also includes a full-featured GUI designer.

> *http://boa-constructor.sourceforge.net*

Eclipse
> A powerful Java-based IDE that uses a plug-in (*PyDev*) for Python support.

> *http://www.eclipse.org*

Idle
> A multiwindow IDE supplied with the Python distribution packages from *python.org*.

PythonWin

A Windows-specific Python IDE supplied with the ActiveState distribution. Also available as a separate package from SourceForge. Roughly equivalent to Idle.

http://sourceforge.net/projects/pywin32/

Add-on libraries

pySerial

A cross-platform interface library with support for RS-232 standard serial interfaces. *pySerial* provides a file-like API with methods such as `read()` and `write()`, and provides binary data transmission (no EOL translation or byte stripping).

http://pyserial.sourceforge.net

pyParallel

A parallel port interface library that supports access to a standard parallel port on both Windows and Linux platforms.

http://pyserial.sourceforge.net/pyparallel.html

pyUSB

A Python library for accessing USB devices on either Linux or Windows via low-level drivers and Python's `ctypes` library.

http://sourceforge.net/apps/mediawiki/pyusb/index.php?title=Main_Page

PyVISA

A cross-platform Python API for the commercial *visa32.dll* and similar DLL modules from various instrument vendors. VISA support for Linux is provided by the `libvisa.so.7` library object, available from National Instruments.

http://pyvisa.sourceforge.net

NumPy

The Numeric Python package, with support for *n*-dimensional array objects and array masking, and functions for linear algebra, Fourier transforms, and random number generation.

http://numpy.scipy.org

SciPy

An extensive library of tools that provides functions for mathematics, science, and engineering.

http://www.scipy.org

PyUniversalLibrary

An interface wrapper for Measurement Computing's Universal Library driver and interface suite. Works only on Windows systems.

https://code.astraw.com/projects/PyUniversalLibrary/

GUI libraries and development tools

Boa Constructor (wxPython)

A wxPython GUI designer that also includes an editor and a debugger.

http://boa-constructor.sourceforge.net

PAGE (Tkinter)

A drag-and-drop GUI builder written in tcl/Tk that generates a Python module using the TkInter library.

http://page.sourceforge.net

PythonCard (wxPython)

A template-based GUI designer for wxPython.

http://pythoncard.sourceforge.net

pmw (Tkinter)

The Python megawidgets add-on for TkInter. Contains additional widgets and functionality not found in the base distribution of TkInter.

http://pmw.sourceforge.net

SpecTcl (Tkinter)

Another TkInter GUI window design tool. Originally developed by Sun Microsystems, it is open source with a Sun license.

http://spectcl.sourceforge.net

wxGlade (wxPython)

A wxPython GUI designer modeled on the Glade designer tool.

http://wxglade.sourceforge.net

wxPython

The wxPython library package for Python, which is itself a wrapper for the wxWidgets library. wxWidgets is not required to use wxPython.

http://wxpython.org

Plotting tools

gnuplot

A powerful plotting package for both Linux and Windows. Supports both 2D and 3D plots and has an extensive collection of built-in math functions.

http://gnuplot.sourceforge.net

gnuplot.py

An interface layer and command translation helper for using *gnuplot* with Python.

http://gnuplot-py.sourceforge.net

System tools and utilities

ansicon

A replacement for the Windows *ANSI.dll* driver that supports newer 32- and 64-bit versions of Windows.

http://adoxa.110mb.com/ansicon/index.html

com0com

A kernel-mode driver for creating pairs of null-modem-connected virtual serial ports under Windows.

http://com0com.sourceforge.net

Cygwin and Xcygwin

Provides an emulation of a Linux environment under Windows. The Xcygwin package includes an X server and various X applications (Xterm, Xclock, Xfig, etc.).

http://www.cygwin.com

Tera Term

An old but still very useful terminal emulator with a well-done scripting language.

http://hp.vector.co.jp/authors/VA002416/teraterm.html

tty0tty

This is the Linux equivalent to com0com that allows two tty devices to cross-connect in null-modem fashion.

http://tty0tty.sourceforge.net

Image data tools and libraries

ImageJ

A flexible and highly configurable image viewer and image processing tool from the National Institutes of Health.

http://rsbweb.nih.gov/ij/

Netpbm

The Netpbm library of image conversion and processing tools.

http://netpbm.sourceforge.net/doc/pgm.html

Data acquisition device driver packages for Linux

Comedi

A collection of low-level drivers to allow a Linux system to communicate with various types of data acquisition and digital interface cards. Includes SWIG scripts to create Python wrappers for the drivers.

http://www.comedi.org

Measurement Computing Linux Drivers

Warren Jasper from NCSU has written a suite of Linux drivers for many of Measurement Computing's products. Note that these are just the Linux drivers; no Python API is provided. You need to be prepared to create your own Python wrappers.

ftp://lx10.tx.ncsu.edu/pub/Linux/drivers/

There can be no doubt that I have missed a package or two (or more) that might be relevant to this book, but the oversight is not intentional. Some searching on Google or SourceForge with phrases like "Python control systems" or "Python data acquisition" will most likely turn up some more interesting packages.

A list of Python packages is also available at *http://pypi.python.org/pypi/*. I can't attest to how current it is, but it is rather long. Also, if you're using Linux, be sure to check your package manager to see what might be available for Python; it's a lot easier than doing the installation manually (which includes resolving any package dependencies).

Lastly, I'd like to point out that you should be aware that if you're using an open source package it might not be as polished as a commercial product, and it may have some bugs or be incomplete. But also bear in mind that it has cost you nothing, and that the people who wrote it are working on their own time, mainly just for the love of software development and a desire to share their work with others.

Instrument Sources

This appendix contains a listing of test equipment and data acquisition instrument manufacturers and used equipment outlets. It is provided as a convenient reference for you to use when looking for equipment; it is not an endorsement of any of them.

Bear in mind that capabilities and cost will vary considerably, and the two aren't always correlated. It pays to do some research before paying out hundreds (or even thousands) of dollars for a piece of hardware, only to discover that it doesn't quite do what you need it to do.

Another reason for this appendix is to help you locate technical documentation for older instruments. There are many older DMMs, controllers, switches, and data acquisition units available that are still perfectly functional, provided you have the user documentation to go with them. You may even have a few such items languishing on a shelf in your lab, or tucked away in a storage closet.

Manufacturers

The following is a short list of instrument and test equipment manufacturers. The list of product types for each manufacturer is only representative, and in some cases it's a small fraction of what they produce.

Agilent
>   Oscilloscopes, logic analyzers, digital meters, signal generators, spectrum analyzers, power supplies, data acquisition units, etc.
>
>   *http://www.agilent.com*

AMETEK
>   Power supplies and electronic loads
>
>   *http://www.programmablepower.com*

Anritsu

RF, microwave, optical, and data communications test equipment

http://www.us.anritsu.com

Bitscope

USB oscilloscopes, signal generators, and logic analyzers

http://www.bitscope.com

B&K Precision

Oscilloscopes, digital meters, signal generators, spectrum analyzers, power supplies, etc.

http://www.bkprecision.com

Elan Digital Systems

Miniature USB oscilloscopes, function generators, pulse generators, and counters

http://www.elandigitalsystems.com/measurement/index.php

Fluke

Handheld and bench meters, signal sources, analyzers, and oscilloscopes

http://www.fluke.com

Keithley

Data acquisition systems, function generators, digital meters, and power supplies

http://www.keithley.com

LeCroy

Oscilloscopes, logic analyzers, and protocol analyzers

http://www.lecroy.com

Saleae

Low-cost USB logic analyzers

http://www.saleae.com

Stanford Research Systems

Scientific data acquisition and control instruments, plus test and measurement equipment

http://www.thinksrs.com

Tektronix

Oscilloscopes, logic analyzers, digital meters, signal generators, spectrum analyzers, power supplies, data acquisition units, etc.

http://www.tek.com

Used Test Equipment Sources

The following is a small sample of companies offering used and refurbished test equipment. Although it is possible to get some great deals on equipment from eBay or your local surplus outlet, when you buy from a company that specializes in used test equipment it is usually calibrated (or it can be, if you ask) and usually carries a 90-day warranty against failure. Typically you will also get all the necessary probes, cables, and leads, instead of dealing with the frustration of someone on eBay pulling them off beforehand in the hopes of selling them separately. In some cases a user manual is also included at no extra charge.

AccuSource Electronics
 http://www.accusrc.com

Metric Test
 http://www.metrictest.com

Test Equipment Depot
 http://www.testequipmentdepot.com

Test Equity
 http://www.testequity.com

Tucker Electronics
 http://www.tucker.com

Manuals

Sometimes a manual for an older piece of equipment just can't easily be found, either because the manufacturer no longer exists or because it's just not available for download. If you find yourself in such a situation, you might want to check out the following websites. In many cases they have the original manuals available, rather than just a PDF file, but be prepared to pay between $20 and $50, and sometimes more if the manual is large or rare. Sometimes the electronic document versions are free for download.

eServiceInfo
 http://www.eserviceinfo.com

Manuals Plus
 http://www.manualsplus.com

Technical Specialists
 http://schematics4you.com

Your Manual Source
 http://www.yourmanualsource.com

Index

Symbols

16bpp image, 483
8bpp PGM image, 480
>> (chevron operator), 114
>>> (Python command-line prompt), 62
{ } (curly brackets), 127
(hash character)
    preprocessor directives and, 128
    Python, 85
+ (plus) operator (Python), 72
?: (ternary conditional), 130

A

AC (alternating current), 19, 30
AC circuits, 30–39
AC power controller simulator, 371–380
    (see also SPC)
    simulator block diagram, 373
activity diagrams, 267
ADCs (analog-to-digital converters), 4, 44, 45
aliased cyclic function readout, 371
ALL command (SPC), 375
Allen wrenches, 197
alternating current (AC), 19, 30
amperes (A or amp), 20
amplitude, 31
AN/ARC-220 mobile radio, 213
analog data, 2, 3
analog data sampling, 45
analog I/O, 44
analog-to-digital converters (ADCs) (see ADCs)
AND gate logic, 24
AND operator (C language), 139
ANSI bar graph example output, 504

ANSI escape sequence standards, 500
ANSI X3.64, 500
ansicon package, 501
ANSITerm class, 505
arithmetic operators (C language), 134
arithmetic operators (Python), 78
arrays (C language), 150
ASCII character encoding standard, 439
ASCII data files, 438–463
    configuration files, 449–451
    flat files, 442
    I/O utilities for, 454–463
    Microsoft Excel and, 443
    Python handling of ASCII characters, 439
    reading, 445
    string conversion with AutoConvert.py,
        451
    writing, 444
ASCIIData formats, 454
ASCIIDataWrite and ASCIIDataRead classes
    (Python), 454–463
assert statement (Python), 86
assertEqual( ) and assertNotEqual( ) methods,
    291
assignment operators (C language), 136
assignment operators (Python), 81
assignment statement (Python), 86
asynchronous serial data communication, 52
AT bus, 397
atom organization, 16
attributes, 60
augmented assignment operators (C language),
    137
augmented assignment statements (Python),
    86

We'd like to hear your suggestions for improving our indexes. Send email to *index@oreilly.com*.

583

NewID( ) function (Python), 116
noise (in simulations), 371
noisy data, 434
nonblocking function calls, 421
None (Python object type), 187
nonlinear control systems, 306
nonlinear pulse control, 307
nonprintable characters, risks of using, 439
null-modem cable, 224
numeric data objects (Python), 66
nut drivers, 197

O

object files (C language), 160
object types (Python), 64
object-oriented programming, 60
octal notation, 66
ohms, 20
Ohm's law, 25
oledll interface class, 184
Omega D1112 RS-485 data transmitter, 553
Omega Engineering, 553
on-off controllers, 326
open( ) method, 113
open-collector output, 43
open-loop control systems, 5, 319
operators (C language), 134–140
    operator precedence, 140–142
operators (Python), 78–83
    operator precedence, 83
OR operator (C language), 139
orbital shells, 16
ord( ) function (Python), 440
oscilloscopes, 198
    bandwidth, 199
overstuffed toolkit, 190

P

packages (Python), 101
pack_struct_file.py, 475
padding, 465
panel-mount connectors, 209
parallel interfaces, 54
pass statement (Python), 87
PC bus interface hardware, 241–244
PCB-mount terminal block, 214
PCBs (printed circuit boards), 208

PCI (Peripheral Component Interconnect) bus, 242
PCI DAQ (Data Acquisition) cards, 244
PCI Express bus, 242
PCI GPIB interface cards, 244
PDevAPI.c, 179
PEP-257, Docstring Conventions, 281
PEP-8 coding style, 117
PEP-8, Style Guide for Python Code, 281
performance requirements, 257
PGM (Portable Grayscale Map) image format, 478
    file structure, 478
pgmtest.pgm, 480
pgmtest.py, 479
PGMWrite( ) function (Python), 484
physical interfaces, 207
    older interfaces, 245
PID (proportional-integral-derivative) controllers, 334–339
    Python, implementation in, 342–346
PID control block diagram, 335
pins, 40
pipes, 383
pixel data size, 477
place geometry manager, 531
planning, 249
    project objectives, 253
    projects, defining, 250
    requirements, 253–265
        capturing requirements, 264
        characteristics of well-formed requirements, 256
        requirement types, 257
        software requirements in development flow, 257
        traceability, 261
        use cases, 258
    requirements-driven design, 251
    statement of need, 252
plant, 2, 319
PLC (programmable logic controller), 332
plug-in circuit boards, 396
pointers (C language), 151–153
popen( ) method (Python), 386
ports, 40
POW command (SPC), 375
power, 20
preprocessor directives, 127, 128–132

print statement (Python), 87, 114, 445
procedural programming, 60
process, 361
process control, 13
programmable logic controller (PLC), 332
proportional control term, 337
proportional controller droop, 338
proportional term control response, 337
pseudocode, 270
pull-up and pull-down resistors, 43
pulse-width modulation (PWM), 50
PWM (pulse-width modulation), 50
PyArg_Parse( ) method, 174
PyArg_ParseTuple type codes, 174
PyArg_ParseTuple( ) method, 173, 174
PyArg_ParseTupleAndKeywords( ) method,
    173, 174
PyArg_UnpackTuple( ) method, 174
PyArg_VaParse( ) method, 174
.pyd extension, 168
pyParallel package, 410
pySerial package, 406–409
PySims package, 357
Python extensions, 167
    (see also C programming language)
    C extension API, 169–184
        API types and functions, 171
        extension source module organization,
            169
        generic discrete I/O API, 175–177
        generic wrapper example, 178–181
        method flags, 172–174
        method table, 172
        passing data, 174
    calling extensions, 181–184
        error checking, 182
    creating, 168
    ctypes library (see ctypes library)
    hierarchy, 168
Python manpage, 63
Python programming language, xv, 59
    command line, 61
    curses library (see curses library)
    data types, 65
        ctypes data types, compared to, 186
    input and output, 110–114
        command-line parameters, 112
        console output using print, 114
        files, 113

redirecting print output, 114
installing, 60
interface support packages, 406–412
loading and running programs, 108
objects, 64
Python extensions (see Python extensions)
simulators, creating in (see Python
    simulators)
text editors and IDEs, 117
unittest facility, 289
Python simulators, 356–380
    AC power controller simulator, 371–380
    data I/O simulator, 357–371
    packages and modules, 356
PythonCard, 543
PyUniversalLibrary, 412
PyVISA package, 411
Py_BuildValue( ) method, 174

Q

quantization and quantization error, 45
quoting of string literals (Python), 91

R

range( ) function (Python), 89
rapidly changing average data, 434
raw_input( ) function (Python), 110
RDD (requirements-driven design), 251
read-modify-write, 183
read183dmm.py, 551
readData( ) method, 368
readinto( ) file object method, 469
records, 442
reference input, 311
regression testing, 278
relay driver circuit, 43
replace( ) method (Python), 73
requirement and test case relationship, 274
requirements traceability matrix, 263
requirements-driven design (RDD), 251
reserved keywords in Python, 85
reset, 339
resistance, 20, 25
resistors, 27
resolution of data, 45
RetCodes module, 356
return statement (Python), 87
rjust( ) method (Python), 73

wxGlade, 543

About the Author

John M. Hughes is an embedded systems engineer with over 30 years of experience in electronics, embedded systems and software, aerospace systems, and scientific applications programming. He was responsible for the surface imaging software on the Phoenix Mars Lander, and has worked on digital engine control systems for commercial and military aircraft, automated test systems, radio telescope data acquisition, and realtime adaptive optics controls for astronomy. Hughes has been using Python for many years in a variety of applications, including the software for a multiwavelength laser interferometer system for verifying the alignment of telescope mirror segments on the James Webb Space Telescope. He is currently using Python for imaging systems simulation and analysis at the University of Arizona.

Colophon

The animal on the cover of *Real World Instrumentation with Python* is a hooded crow (*Corvus cornix*). Known also as a Scotch crow, a Danish crow, a Grey crow, and a Corbie, the bird enjoys a wide distribution across Europe and the Middle East. Because the hooded crow is so similar to the common carrion crow, the two were previously considered to be of the same species. As of 2002, however, Brân Lwyd (as it is known in Welsh) has enjoyed full species status, and has four recognized subspecies.

The hooded crow's plumage is mostly ash gray, though it sports glossy black feathers on its wings, tail, and especially on its head and throat, giving the appearance of the hood for which the animal is named. When full grown, the birds average a wingspan of 98 cm, and can measure from 48 to 52 cm in length. Like the carrion crow with which it is closely associated, the hooded crow is an omnivorous scavenger. It is known for stealing eggs from the nests of other bird species, and in costal regions will drop mollusks and crabs from a height in order to break them open.

The image of a hooded crow holds special significance in traditional Celtic folklore, and it is associated with fairies in the Scottish highlands and in Ireland. During the 18th century, Scottish shepherds were known to make offerings to the animals to prevent them from attacking their sheep. Elsewhere, a maiden on the Faroe Islands of Denmark would watch the flight of the hooded crow on the morning of Candlemas to determine the provenance of her future husband.

The cover image is from *Johnson's Natural History*. The cover font is Adobe ITC Garamond. The text font is Linotype Birka; the heading font is Adobe Myriad Condensed; and the code font is LucasFont's TheSansMonoCondensed.

Have it your way.

O'Reilly eBooks

- Lifetime access to the book when you buy through oreilly.com
- Provided in up to four, DRM-free file formats, for use on the devices of your choice: PDF, .epub, Kindle-compatible .mobi, and Android .apk
- Fully searchable, with copy-and-paste, and print functionality
- We also alert you when we've updated the files with corrections and additions.

oreilly.com/ebooks/

Safari Books Online

- Access the contents and quickly search over 7000 books on technology, business, and certification guides
- Learn from expert video tutorials, and explore thousands of hours of video on technology and design topics
- Download whole books or chapters in PDF format, at no extra cost, to print or read on the go
- Early access to books as they're being written
- Interact directly with authors of upcoming books
- Save up to 35% on O'Reilly print books

See the complete Safari Library at safaribooksonline.com

©2014 O'Reilly Media, Inc. O'Reilly logo is a registered trademark of O'Reilly Media, Inc. 14373

Get even more for your money.

Join the O'Reilly Community, and register the O'Reilly books you own. It's free, and you'll get:

- $4.99 ebook upgrade offer
- 40% upgrade offer on O'Reilly print books
- Membership discounts on books and events
- Free lifetime updates to ebooks and videos
- Multiple ebook formats, DRM FREE
- Participation in the O'Reilly community
- Newsletters
- Account management
- 100% Satisfaction Guarantee

Signing up is easy:

1. Go to: oreilly.com/go/register
2. Create an O'Reilly login.
3. Provide your address.
4. Register your books.

Note: English-language books only

To order books online:
oreilly.com/store

For questions about products or an order:
orders@oreilly.com

To sign up to get topic-specific email announcements and/or news about upcoming books, conferences, special offers, and new technologies:
elists@oreilly.com

For technical questions about book content:
booktech@oreilly.com

To submit new book proposals to our editors:
proposals@oreilly.com

O'Reilly books are available in multiple DRM-free ebook formats. For more information:
oreilly.com/ebooks

©2014 O'Reilly Media, Inc. O'Reilly logo is a registered trademark of O'Reilly Media, Inc. 14373